Strategy in the Contemporary World

Strategy in the Contemporary World

An Introduction to Strategic Studies

Edited by John Baylis, James J. Wirtz, Colin S. Gray, and Eliot Cohen

Second Edition

OXFORD

UNIVERSITY PRESS

OXFORD
UNIVERSITY PRESS

Great Clarendon Street, Oxford OX2 6DP

Oxford University Press is a department of the University of Oxford.
It furthers the University's objective of excellence in research, scholarship,
and education by publishing worldwide in

Oxford New York

Auckland Cape Town Dar es Salaam Hong Kong Karachi
Kuala Lumpur Madrid Melbourne Mexico City Nairobi
New Delhi Shanghai Taipei Toronto

With offices in

Argentina Austria Brazil Chile Czech Republic France Greece
Guatemala Hungary Italy Japan Poland Portugal Singapore
South Korea Switzerland Thailand Turkey Ukraine Vietnam

Oxford is a registered trade mark of Oxford University Press
in the UK and in certain other countries

Published in the United States
by Oxford University Press Inc., New York

British Library Cataloguing in Publication Data

Data available

Library of Congress Cataloging in Publication Data

Strategy in the contemporary world : an introduction to strategic
studies / edited by John Baylis, [et al.].—2nd ed.
       p. cm.
  ISBN-13: 978–0–19–928978–3
  1. Strategy. 2. Military policy. 3. National security.   4. Security,
International.   5. World politics—21st century.   I. Baylis, John, 1946–
   U162.S85252 2006
    355′.03—dc22   2006033143

Typeset by Newgen Imaging Systems (P) Ltd., Chennai, India
Printed in Great Britain
on acid-free paper by
Ashford Colour Press Ltd, Gosport, Hants

ISBN 978–0–19–928978–3

10 9 8 7 6 5 4

Brief Contents

Detailed Contents

Introduction   1

John Baylis and James J. Wirtz

Part I Enduring Issues of Strategy   17

1 The Causes of War and the Conditions of Peace   19

John Garnett

2 The Evolution of Modern Warfare   42

Michael Sheehan

DETAILED CONTENTS

Guided Tour of Learning Features

This text is enriched with a range of learning tools to help you navigate the text material and reinforce your knowledge of Strategic Studies. This guided tour shows you how to get the most out of your textbook package and do better in your studies.

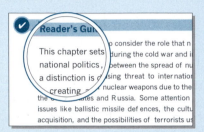

Reader's Guides

Reader's Guides at the beginning of every chapter set the scene for upcoming themes and issues to be discussed, and indicate the scope of coverage within each chapter topic.

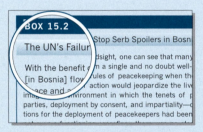

Boxes

A number of topics benefit from further explanation or exploration in a manner that does not disrupt the flow of the main text. Throughout the book, boxes provide you with extra information on particular topics that complement your understanding of the main chapter text.

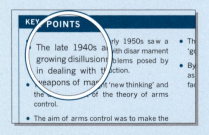

Key Points

Each main chapter section ends with a set of Key Points that summarize the most important arguments developed within each chapter topic.

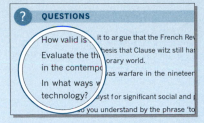

Questions

A set of carefully devised questions has been provided to help you assess your comprehension of core themes, and may also be used as the basis of seminar discussion and coursework.

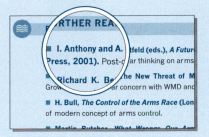

Further Reading

To take your learning further, reading lists have been provided as a guide to find out more about the issues raised within each chapter topic and to help you locate the key academic literature in the field.

Web Links

At the end of every chapter you will find an annotated summary of useful web sites that are central to Strategic Studies and that will be instrumental in further research.

Guided Tour of the Online Resource Centre

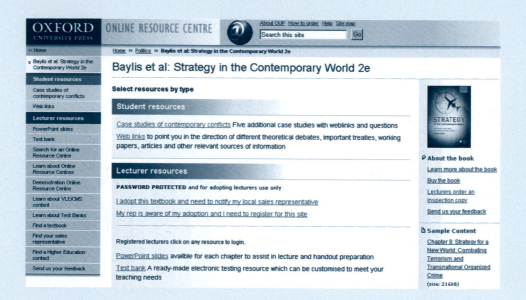

 www.oxfordtextbooks.co.uk/orc/baylis_strategy2e/

The Online Resource Centre that accompanies this book provides students and instructors with ready-to-use teaching and learning materials. These resources are free of charge and designed to maximise the learning experience.

For students

Case studies

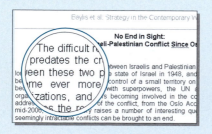

Five additional case studies with web links and questions on the following conflicts:

The US-Coalition invasion and occupation of Iraq

The civil war in the Congo

The Russian war in Chechnya

The Israel-Palestinian struggle from the Oslo Accords to the present day

The Iran-Iraq war of the 1980s

Web links

Two series of annotated web links, one organized by chapter and one organized by issue area, have been provided to point you in the direction of different theoretical debates, important treaties, working papers, articles and other relevant sources of information.

For instructors

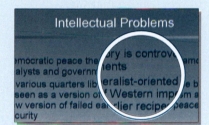

PowerPoint slides

These complement each chapter of the book and are a useful resource for preparing lectures and handouts. They allow you to guide students through the key concepts and can be fully customized to meet the needs of the course.

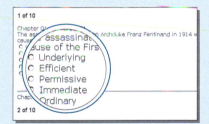

Test bank

A fully customizable resource containing ready-made assessments with which to test your students. Downloadable into Questionmark Perception; via Respondus into Blackboard and WebCT; and most other Virtual Learning Environments. Also available in print format.

Acknowledgements

We would like to thank those who participated in the annual Monterey Strategy Seminar held at the Naval Postgraduate School in September 2005. In particular the editors are grateful to the sponsors of the conference—David Hamon and Kerry Kartchner of the US Advanced Systems Concepts Office, Defense Threat Reduction Agency and Dave Saylor and Bob Vince at the US Navy Treaty Implementation Program—for providing us with a venue to discuss contemporary strategic issues. We would also like to thank Bryn Willcock from Swansea University who ably assisted with the production of the book in its final stages.

List of Contributors

JOHN BAYLIS is Professor of Politics and International Relations and Pro-Vice-Chancellor at Swansea University. His Ph.D. and D.Litt. are from the University of Wales. His most recent books include *The Globalization of World Politics* (3rd edn. with Steve Smith, Oxford University Press, 2005) and *The United States and Europe: Beyond the Neo-Conservative Era* (ed. with Jon Roper, Routledge, 2006).

STEPHEN BIDDLE is a Senior Fellow at the Council on Foreign Relations. He holds Ph.D. (1992, Public Policy), MPP (1985), and AB (1981) degrees from Harvard University. He is the author of *Military Power: Explaining Victory and Defeat in Modern Battle* (Princeton University Press, 2004).

ELIOT A. COHEN is Robert E. Osgood Professor and Director of the Philip Merrill Center for Strategic Studies at Johns Hopkins University's School of Advanced International Studies. He earned his degree in political science from Harvard (Ph.D. 1982). He is the author, among other works, of *Supreme Command: Soldiers, Statesmen, and Leadership in Wartime* (Free Press, 2002).

RUDOLPH DARKEN is the Director of the Defense Modeling and Simulation Institute at the Naval Postgraduate School in Monterey, California. He received his Ph.D. (1995) in Computer Science from The George Washington University. His research is in the area of game-based simulations for training, measuring human performance, and spatial cognition.

THEO FARRELL is Professor of War in the Modern World at King's College London. He is Associate Editor of *Security Studies*. His latest books include *The Norms of War* (Lynne Rienner, 2005) and, as co-editor, *Force and Legitimacy in World Politics* (Cambridge University Press, 2006).

JOHN FERRIS is a Professor of History at The University of Calgary. He received a Ph.D. in War Studies from King's College, London (1986). He recently published *Intelligence and Strategy, Selected Essays* (Routledge, 2005).

LAWRENCE FREEDMAN is Professor of War Studies and Vice Principal (Research) at King's College London. He was educated at Manchester, York and Oxford Universities. His most recent books include *Deterrence* (Polity, 2004), the two-volume *Official History of the Falklands Campaign* (Routledge, 2004) and *The Transformation of Strategic Affairs* (Taylor & Francis for IISS, 2006).

JOHN GARNETT was formerly Woodrow Wilson Professor of International Politics at the University of Wales, Aberystwyth and is currently Chairman of the Centre for Defence Studies at King's College, London. He was educated at the London School of Economics where he obtained a first class honours degree and Masters in International Relations. His most recent publication is *British Foreign Policy: Constraints and Choices for the 21st Century* (Royal Institute of International Affairs) with Sir Lawrence Martin.

COLIN S. GRAY is Professor of International Politics and Strategic Studies at the University of Reading. His D.Phil is from Oxford. His most recent books are *Another Bloody Century: Future Warfare* (Weidenfeld & Nicolson, 2005), and *Strategy and History: Essays on Theory and Practice* (Routledge, 2006).

DARRYL HOWLETT obtained his Masters degree from Lancaster University and his Ph.D. from the University of Southampton. He currently teaches courses on international security at the University of Southampton. His most recent publications include, `Nuclear Proliferation', in John Baylis and Steve Smith (eds.), *The Globalization of World Politics. An Introduction to International Relations* (Oxford: Oxford University Press, 2005); and 'The Emergence of Stability: Deterrence-in-Motion and Deterrence Reconstructed', in Ian R. Kenyon and John Simpson (eds.), *Deterrence and the Changing Security Environment* (London: Routledge, 2006).

JAMES D. KIRAS is an Assistant Professor of Comparative Military Studies at the School of Advanced Air and Space Studies, Maxwell Air Force Base, Alabama. He received his Ph.D. in politics and international studies from the University of Reading in the United Kingdom in 2004. Dr Kiras is the author of *Special Operations and Strategy: From World War II to the War on Terrorism* (London: Routledge, 2006).

JEFFREY S. LANTIS is Chair of the Department of Political Science and Associate Professor of Political Science/International Relations at the College of Wooster, US. He is author of *Strategic Dilemmas and the Evolution of German Foreign Policy since Unification* (2002) and numerous articles and book chapters on strategic culture, transatlantic relations, and foreign policy decision-making. Lantis received a J. William Fulbright Senior Scholar Award for research in Australia as a Visiting Fellow at the University of New South Wales in 2006–7. He received his Ph.D. in Political Science from Ohio State University.

THOMAS G. MAHNKEN is a Professor of Strategy at the US Naval War College, Newport, RI, and a Visiting Fellow at the Philip Merrill Center for Strategic Studies at Johns Hopkins University's Paul H. Nitze School of Advanced International Studies. He earned his degrees in international affairs from Johns Hopkins (MA 1989, Ph.D. 1997). He is the co-editor of the *Journal of Strategic Studies*.

DANIEL MORAN is Professor of International and Military History in the Department of National Security Affairs at the Naval Postgraduate School in Monterey, Calif, and visiting Professor of History at Stanford University. His most recent books are *Wars of National Liberation* (Smithsonian, rev. edn 2006), and *The People in Arms: Military Myth and National Mobilization since the French Revolution* (Cambridge University Press, 2003).

JUSTIN MORRIS is Senior Lecturer in the Department of Politics and International Studies and Deputy Dean of the Faculty of Arts and Social Sciences at the University of Hull, UK, where he also undertook his postgraduate studies (MA 1991). With Professor Nigel White and Dr Richard Burchill he recently edited *International Conflict and Security Law: Essays in Honour of Hilaire McCoubrey* (Cambridge University Press, 2005).

JACOB N. SHAPIRO is a Homeland Security Fellow at the Center for International Security and Cooperation, Stanford University. He is a doctoral candidate in political science at Stanford University. His recent work includes 'The Greedy Terrorist: A Rational-Choice Perspective on Terrorist Organizations' Inefficiencies and Vulnerabilities', in *Terrorist Financing in Comparative Perspective* (Stanford University Press, 2006).

MICHAEL SHEEHAN is a Professor of International Relations at Swansea University and Director of the Callaghan Centre for the Study of Conflict. He is a graduate of Aberystwyth University (B.Sc. in International Politics 1976, Ph.D. 1985). His most recent book is *International Security: An Analytical Survey* (Lynne Rienner, 2005).

MARK SMITH is a Research Fellow in the Department of Politics and International Relations, Swansea University. He obtained his Ph.D. from the University of Wales, Aberystwyth. He is the author of *NATO Enlargement during the Cold War: Strategy and System in the Western Alliance* and co-author with Lorna Arnold of *Britain, Australia and the Bomb: The Nuclear Tests and their Aftermath*.

C. DALE WALTON is an Assistant Professor of Defense and Strategic Studies at Missouri State University in Fairfax, Va., and the Managing Editor of the journal *Comparative Strategy*. He received his Ph.D. in Politics from the University of Hull, UK, in 1999. He is the author of *The Myth of Inevitable US Defeat in Vietnam* (London: Frank Cass, 2002).

PHIL WILLIAMS is Professor of International Security in the Graduate School of Public and International Affairs, University of Pittsburgh. He has a BA in politics and history from University of Wales, Swansea (1969), an M.Sc. (Econ.) in strategic studies, University College Aberystwyth (1971) and a Ph.D in political science from the University of Southampton (1988). Professor Williams is co-editor of *Combating Transnational Crime* (Cass 2001).

JAMES J. WIRTZ is a Professor of National Security Affairs at the Naval Postgraduate School, Monterey, California. He earned his degrees in political science from Columbia University (M.Phil. 1987, Ph.D. 1989). Professor Wirtz recently edited *Nuclear Transformation: The New U.S. Nuclear Doctrine* (Palgrave Macmillan, 2005).

Preface to the Second Edition

The first edition of *Strategy in the Contemporary World* reflected the notion that too much emphasis in security studies literature had been given to non-military security issues. This situation reflected the euphoria that followed the relatively peaceful end of the cold war, a mood that cast the first Gulf War, the conflicts associated with the disintegration of Yugoslavia, and tribal wars in Africa as aberrations that highlighted the positive trends in world politics. The argument contained in the book was that, useful as this new literature was, there was still room for writing and scholarship that focused on the sad, but continuing, reality that military power remained a significant feature of the world in which we live. What the book attempted to do was to take many of the theories, which had been developed during the cold war (during what had been called 'the golden age of strategic studies') and see how far they were relevant to the new post-cold war environment. The aim was to try to show what insights from this era remained relevant, which ones needed to be redefined, and what new ideas might be incorporated into strategic studies.

Just as this first volume went to print, it became clear that ideas of 'perpetual peace' were not going to be realized anytime soon. The attacks on the World Trade Center and the Pentagon in September 2001 occurred as the first edition was published. In the aftermath of the attacks, the relevance and significance of the first edition changed. There was now an increased need to address issues of war and peace which were of immediate concern, especially terrorism, irregular warfare, the spread of weapons of mass destruction, and the revolution in military affairs. Strategy had returned.

Our second edition contains a more mature set of reflections on the role of military power in the contemporary world. This involves analyses of the recent conflicts from Afghanistan to the Iraq war and the ongoing debates about the lessons that can be learnt from these wars. In particular, attention is given to the debates about whether there has been a revolution in military affairs and the future of warfare given the phenomenal pace of innovation in electronics and computer systems. Attention is also given to the strategic implications of the changing structure of global politics and the role of American military power in a unipolar world. At a broader conceptual level, this edition goes further than the first volume by analysing the continuing relevance of the various theories of peace and security in a world that is vastly different from the cold war era when these concepts were central to most thinking about strategic studies. There is also considerably more emphasis in this edition on the implications of 9/11 and the war on terrorism, as well as on the prospects for further proliferation of weapons of mass destruction, not only by states but also by non-state actors.

As a result of this new focus, while some of the chapters from the first edition have stood the test of time and have been simply modified to take account of new ideas and events, others have been dropped and new chapters have been written. In particular, we have added chapters on the 'Evolution of Modern Warfare', 'Culture and National Security Policy', 'Geography and Warfare', 'Homeland Security', 'Conventional Power and

Contemporary Warfare'. Given the contemporary importance of terrorism we have also added a new chapter focusing on the link between terrorism and organized crime.

We would like to thank the participants at the annual Monterey Strategy Seminar held at the Naval Postgraduate School in September 2005. As part of the proceedings, many of our contributors presented their views to an international group of scholars, policy-makers, and military strategists, producing a lively exchange of ideas. We are especially grateful to the sponsors of the conference—David Hamon and Kerry Kartchner at the Advanced Systems Concepts Office, Defense Threat Reduction Agency, and Dave Saylor and Bob Vince at the Navy Treaty Implementation Program—for providing us with a venue to discuss contemporary strategic issues.

Introduction

JOHN BAYLIS AND JAMES J. WIRTZ

Chapter Contents

- What is Strategic Studies?
- Strategic Studies and the Classical Realist Tradition
- What Criticisms are made of Strategic Studies?
- What is the Relationship between Strategic Studies and Security Studies?

Books often reflect a specific historical context, shaped by the hopes, fears, and problems that preoccupy authors and policy-makers alike. This is especially true of books on strategy, security studies, and public policy because contemporary issues are of paramount importance to authors in these fields. Our efforts also reflect contemporary threats and opportunities. When we gathered in September 2000 to present chapters for the first edition of this volume, we wanted to create a textbook that demonstrated the continued relevance of strategy and strategic studies and to interpret contemporary issues using insights gained from the classic works on strategy. Little did we know that less than a year later the 'New World Order' would be shattered by the Al-Qaeda attacks on the Pentagon and the World Trade Center. The wars in Afghanistan and Iraq, the terrorist bombings in Madrid in 2004 and London in 2005, and the possible proliferation of nuclear weapons to North Korea and Iran, have erased any lingering doubts about the relevance of strategy to today's students and practitioners of foreign and defence policy. When we gathered again to discuss our contributions to this volume in September 2005, it was with the realization that we face real and immediate threats to national and international security; these threats demand the return of strategy.

It is clear to us now that interest in strategic studies is cyclical and reflects the times. Strategic studies emerged during the early years of the cold war when political leaders, government officials, and academics interested in security issues wrestled with the problems of how to survive and prosper in the nuclear age, when Armageddon might be just minutes away. Given the experiences of the 1930s, when appeasement and 'utopian' ideas of collective security had largely failed to ensure peace, the prevailing mindset during the cold war was one of 'realism'. It was believed that, in a world characterized by anarchy and unending competition, states inevitably exercised power to secure their national interests. For nuclear age realists, however, power had to be exercised in a way that promoted the interests of the state, while at the same time avoiding a conflict which would lead to the destruction not only of the states involved but of civilization as a whole. This predicament gave rise to theories of deterrence, limited war and arms control that dominated the literature of strategic studies (and indeed international relations) during the period from the 1950s to the 1980s. Writings by Herman Kahn, Bernard Brodie, Henry Kissinger, Albert Wohlsteller, and Thomas Schelling became classics in the field.

Did the key assumptions inherent in the strategic studies literature lead to the adoption of particular security policies or did policy itself drive the writing on the subject? The answer to these questions remains a matter of debate. Some believed that the literature reflected existing realities, others believed that the writings themselves helped to generate a particular way of looking at the world and legitimized the use of military power. An iterative process was probably at work, however, as theory and practice modified and reinforced each other.

The great strength of the literature on strategic studies was that it reflected the harsh realities of a world in which military power was (regardless of 'utopian' ideals) an instrument of state policy. One of its weaknesses, however, was the inherent conservatism in realist thinking that implied that the contemporary world was the best of all possible worlds. For good theoretical and practical reasons, realists hoped that the cold war, with its magisterial confrontation between the United States and the Soviet Union, would continue into the indefinite future. Significant change, because it raised the spectre of nuclear

Armageddon, was a prospect that was nearly too horrific to contemplate and too risky to act upon.

With the relatively peaceful collapse of the Soviet Union, realism came under suspicion and the ideas and policies of disarmament advocates and utopian thinkers began to hold greater sway in policy circles. The 1990s was the decade of the 'peace dividend' and 'dot.com' mania as the information revolution entered consumer and business culture. The preoccupation of strategists with the state, and its use of military power, was viewed by a new generation of 'utopian' scholars as part of the problem of international security itself. Strategists were often seen as 'dinosaurs'. Preoccupied with 'old think', they appeared unwilling to come to terms with the fact that force was apparently fading as a factor in world politics. The traditional emphasis on the military aspects of security was challenged by scholars who believed that the concept should be broadened and deepened. According to this view, there were political, economic, societal, and environmental aspects of security which had been ignored. Some scholars asserted that 'security' as a concept had been used by political elites to push issues to the top of the political agenda or to secure additional resources for particular policies and government organizations and military programmes. In the view of some critics, official policy was pushed along by armies of military contractors and manufacturers, government workers, and members of the military themselves had a vested interest in 'keeping war alive' to preserve their careers and livelihoods.

By the mid-1990s, these criticisms of traditional realist thinking were transformed into mainstream scholarship. Security studies emerged as an area of intellectual enquiry which increasingly eclipsed strategic studies. Researchers came to focus on the nature of security itself and how greater security might be achieved at the individual, societal and even global levels, compared with the cold war preoccupation with state security, defined only in military terms. Although security studies reflected a wider range of theoretical positions than had characterized strategic studies in the past, there was a strong normative (realists would say 'utopian') dimension to much of the writing, especially from those of a post-positivist persuasion. The end of the cold war fundamentally challenged the conservative tendency in realism (and the strategic studies literature). Peaceful change was now a reality and military power was no longer seen by many as the predominant prerequisite for security. The balance of terror between East and West had not simply been mitigated (in line with the theories proposed in the strategic studies literature) but had now been transcended, opening up the prospects for a new more peaceful world.

The post-cold war euphoria and the literature that followed in its wake was very much a product of its time, but there were warning signs in the years leading up to the millennium that the emergence of peace, or as Francis Fukuyama put it 'an end of history' (meaning an end of major conflicts), might have been premature. The first Gulf War, the conflicts associated with the disintegration of Yugoslavia, and tribal wars in Africa demonstrated all too clearly that military force remained a ubiquitous feature of the contemporary world. It was at this point, just as the attacks on the Twin Towers and the Pentagon took place in September 2001, that the first edition of this book was published. The book reflected a growing feeling that perhaps too much emphasis in security studies literature had been given to non-military security. The argument contained in the book was that, useful as this new literature was, there was still room for writing and scholarship that focused on the sad, but continuing, reality that military power remained a significant feature of world politics.

The book was very much a product of its time, and things changed on the morning of 11 September 2001.

Although the first edition had much to say about our present circumstances, this second edition reflects a more mature set of reflections on the role of military power in the contemporary world and the changes that have occurred over the last decade. This new volume reflects analyses of the recent conflicts from Afghanistan to the Iraq war and the ongoing debates about the lessons that can be learnt from these wars. We also explore the debates about whether there has been a revolution in military affairs and the future of warfare given the phenomenal pace of innovation in electronics and computer systems. Attention is also given to the strategic implications of the changing structure of global politics and the role of American military power in a unipolar world. At a broader conceptual level this edition goes further that the first volume by analysing the continuing relevance of the various theories of peace and security in a world that is vastly different from the cold war era when these concepts were central to most thinking about strategic studies. There is also considerably more emphasis in this edition on the implications of 9/11 and the war on terrorism, as well as on the prospects for further proliferation of weapons of mass destruction, not only by states but also by non-state actors.

To set the scene for the chapters that follow, this introduction answers three questions: (1) What are strategic studies? (2) What criticisms are made of strategic studies? and (3) What is the relationship of strategic studies to security studies?

What is Strategic Studies?

The definitions of 'strategy' contained in Box 1 display some common features but also significant differences. The definitions by Carl von Clausewitz, [Field Marshal] Count H. Von Moltke, B. H. Liddell Hart, and Andre Beaufre all focus on a fairly narrow definition which relates military force to the objectives of war. This reflects the origins of the word 'strategy' which is derived from the ancient Greek term for 'generalship'. The definitions from Gregory Foster and Robert Osgood, however, draw attention to the broader focus on 'power', while Williamson Murray and Mark Grimslay highlight the dynamic quality of 'process' inherent in the formulation of strategy. Recently, writers have emphasized that strategy (particularly in the nuclear age) has a peacetime as well as a war time application. Strategy embodies more than just the study of wars and military campaigns. Strategy is the application of military power to achieve political objectives, or more specifically 'the theory and practice of the use, and threat of use, of organized force for political purposes' (Gray 1999). Broader still is the concept of *Grand Strategy* which involves the coordination and direction of 'all the resources of a nation, a band of nations, towards the attainment of the political objectives' sought (Liddell Hart 1967).

Because strategy provides the bridge between military means and political goals, students of strategy require knowledge of *both* politics and military operations. Strategy deals with the difficult problems of national policy, the areas where political, economic, psychological, and military factors overlap. There is no such thing as purely military

BOX 1

Definitions of Strategy

Strategy (is) the use of engagements for the object of war.

Carl von Clausewitz

Strategy is the practical adaptation of the means placed at a general's disposal to the attainment of the object in War.

Von Moltke

Strategy is the art of distributing and applying military means to fulfill the ends of policy.

Liddell Hart

Strategy is . . . the art of the dialectic of force or, more precisely, the art of the dialectic of two opposing wills using force to resolve their dispute.

Andre Beaufre

Strategy is ultimately about effectively exercising power.

Gregory D. Foster

Strategy is a plan of action designed in order to achieve some end; a purpose together with a system of measures for its accomplishment.

J. C. Wylie

Strategy is a process, a constant adaptation to the shifting conditions and circumstances in a world where chance, uncertaintity, and ambiquity dominate.

Murray and Grimslay

Strategy must now be understood as nothing less than the overall plan for utilizing the capacity for armed coercion—in conjuction with economic, diplomatic, and psychological instruments of power—to support foreign policy most effectively by overt, covert and tacit means.

Robert Osgood

advice when it comes to issues of strategy. This point also has been made in a different way by Henry Kissinger who stated that 'the separation of strategy and policy can only be achieved to the detriment of both. It causes military power to become identified with the most absolute application of power and it tempts diplomacy into an over-concern with finesse' (1957).

Strategy is best studied from an interdisciplinary perspective. To understand the dimensions of strategy, it is necessary to know something about politics, economics, psychology, sociology, and geography, as well as technology, force structure, and tactics. Strategy also is essentially a pragmatic and practical activity. This is summed up in Bernard Brodie's comment that 'Strategic theory is a theory of action'. It is a 'how to do it' study, a guide to accomplishing objectives and attaining them efficiently. As in many other branches of politics, the question that matters in strategy is: will the idea work? As such, in some ways strategic studies are 'policy relevant'. They can be an intellectual aid to official performance. At the same time, however, they also can be pursued as 'an idle academic pursuit for its own sake' (Brodie 1973).

Strategic studies, however, cannot be regarded as a discipline in their own right. They form a subject with a sharp focus—the role of military power—but no clear parameters, and rely upon arts, sciences, and social science subjects for ideas and concepts. Scholars who have contributed to the literature on the subject have come from very different fields. Herman Kahn was a physicist, Thomas Schelling was an economist, Albert Wholstetter was a mathematician, Henry Kissinger was a historian, and Bernard Brodie was a political scientist.

Given the different academic backgrounds of strategic thinkers, it is not surprising that strategic studies has witnessed an ongoing debate about methodology (i.e. how to study the subject). Bernard Brodie, who more than anyone else helped to establish strategic studies as a subject in the aftermath of the Second World War, initially argued that strategy should be studied 'scientifically'. He was concerned that strategy was 'not receiving the scientific treatment it deserves either in the armed services or, certainly, outside them'. In his 1949 article entitled 'Strategy as Science', Brodie called for a methodological approach to the study of strategy similar to the one adopted by economics. Strategy, he argued, should be seen as 'an instrumental science for solving practical problems'. What he wanted was a more rigorous, systematic form of analysis of strategic issues compared with the rather narrow approach to security problems adopted by the military, who were preoccupied with tactics and technology.

As Brodie himself was later to recognize, however, the enthusiasm for science, which he had helped to promote, meant that strategic studies in the 1950s 'developed a scientistic strain and overreached itself'. By the 1960s, Brodie was calling for a 'mid-course correction'. The conceptualization of strategy using economic models and theories had been taken further than he had expected. Brodie was concerned about the 'astonishing lack of political sense' and the 'ignorance of diplomatic and military history' that seemed to be evident among those writing about strategy. Brodie's worries were heeded. From the 1970s onwards, more comparative historical analysis was introduced into strategic studies.

The academic approach to the study of strategy also raised concerns about the neglect of operational military issues. For Brodie (echoing Clemenceau) strategy was too serious a business to be left to the generals. As strategic studies developed in the late 1940s, civilian analysts came to dominate the field. By the 1980s, however, there was a growing feeling that many of the civilian strategists in their university departments and academic 'think tanks' were ignoring the capabilities and limitations of military units and operations in their analyses and theorizing. For a new breed of strategists, the reality of operational issues had to be brought back into their studies. Military science had become the 'missing discipline'. Writing in 1996, Richard K. Betts suggested that: 'if strategy is to integrate policy and operations, it must be devised not just by politically sensitive soldiers but by military sensitive civilians'. Just as Brodie had been concerned about the overly narrow approach of the military in 1949, so Betts was concerned that the pendulum had swung too far in the opposite direction. Although as Stephen Biddle has demonstrated in his recent volume entitled *Military Power*, in the end it was left to a civilian strategist to make headway in understanding the changes unfolding on the modern battlefield (Biddle 2005).

This concern with operational issues helped to revive an interest among strategists with the different 'elements' or 'dimensions' of strategy. In his study *On War*, Clausewitz argued that 'everything in strategy is very simple, but that does not mean that everything is very easy'. Reflecting this sentiment, Clausewitz pointed out that strategy consisted of moral, physical, mathematical, geographical and statistical elements. Michael Howard, in a similar vein, refers to the social, logistical, operational, and technological dimensions of strategy. This notion of strategy consisting of a broad, complex, pervasive, and interpenetrating set of dimensions also is explored in Colin Gray's recent study, entitled *Modern Strategy*. Gray identifies three main categories ('People and Politics'; 'Preparation for War'; and 'War Proper') and seventeen dimensions of strategy. Under the 'People and Politics' heading he focuses on people, society, culture, politics, and ethics. 'Preparations for War' includes economics and logistics, organization, military administration, information and intelligence, strategic theory and doctrine, and technology. The dimensions of 'War Proper' consists of military operations, command, geography, friction, the adversary, and time. Echoing Clausewitz, Gray argues that the study of strategy is incomplete if it is considered in the absence of any one of these (interrelated) dimensions.

Strategic Studies and the Classical Realist Tradition

What are the philosophical underpinnings or assumptions of the scholars, soldiers, and policy-makers who write about strategy? Most contemporary strategists in the Western world belong to the same intellectual tradition. They share a set of assumptions about the nature of international political life, and the kind of reasoning that can best handle political-military problems. This set of assumptions is often referred to by the term 'Realism'.

Although there are differences between 'Realists', there are certain views and assumptions that most would agree upon. These can be best illustrated under the headings of human nature; anarchy and power; and international law, morality, and institutions.

Human Nature

Most realists are pessimistic about human nature. Reflecting the views of philosophers like Thomas Hobbes, people are seen as 'inherently destructive, selfish, competitive and aggressive'. Hobbes accepted that human beings are capable of generosity, kindness and cooperation but the pride and egoism inherent in human nature mean that humankind also is prone to conflict, violence, and great evil. For realist writers, one of the great tragedies of the human condition is that these destructive traits can never be eradicated. Reflecting this view, Herbert Butterfield argued that 'behind the great conflicts of mankind is a terrible human predicament which lies at the heart of the story' (in Butterfield and Wight 1966). Thus, realism is not a normative theory in the sense that it purports to offer a way to eliminate violence from the world. Instead, it offers a way to cope with the ever present threat of conflict by the use of strategy to minimize the likelihood and severity of international violence. Realists tend to stress what they see as the harsh realities of world politics and are somewhat contemptuous of Kantian approaches that highlight the possibility of 'permanent peace'. As Gordon Harland has argued: 'Realism is a clear recognition of the limits of reason in politics: the acceptance of the fact that political realities are power realities and that power must be countered with power; that self-interest is the primary datum in the action of all groups and nations' (in Herzog, 1963). In an anarchical system, power is the only currency of value when security is threatened.

Anarchy and Power

Given this rather dark view of the human condition, realists tend to view international relations in similarly pessimistic terms. Conflict and war are seen as endemic in world politics and the future is likely to be much like the past. States (upon which realists focus their attention) are engaged in a relentless competitive struggle. In contrast to the way in which conflicts are dealt with in domestic society, however, the clash between states is more difficult to resolve because there is no authoritative government to create justice and the rule of law. In the absence of world government, realists note that states have adopted a 'self-help' approach to their interests and especially their security. In other words, they reserve the right to use lethal force to achieve their objectives, a right that individuals living in civil society have given up to the state. Who wins in international relations does not depend on who is right according to some moral or legal ruling. As Thycidides demonstrated in his account of *The Pelopponesian Wars*, power determines who gets their way. In international relations, *might* makes *right*.

International Law, Morality, and Institutions

Realists see a limited role for 'reason', law, morality, and institutions in world politics. In a domestic context, law can be an effective way for societies to deal with competing selfish interests. In an international system without effective government, states will agree to laws when it suits them, but will disregard them when their interests are threatened. When states want to break the rules, there is very little to stop them from doing it apart from countervailing force.

Similarly, realists do not believe that moral considerations can significantly constrain the behaviour of states. Some realists believe that very little attention should be given to moralizing about the state of world politics. They point to the absence of a universal moral code and to the disregard of constraining moral principles by policy-makers, especially when they believe their vital interests are threatened. This is not to argue that realists are wholly insensitive to moral questions. Great realist thinkers, including Rheinhold Niebuhr and Hans Morgenthau, agonized about the human condition. Most realist writers, however, attempt to explain the way the world is, rather than how it ought to be. Realists view international institutions (e.g. the United Nations or the Nuclear Nonproliferation Treaty) in much the same light as they view law and morality. Just as law and morality are unable to constraint state behaviour significantly when important state interests are threatened, international institutions also can only play a limited role in preventing conflict. Realists do not dismiss the opportunities created by institutions for greater cooperation. They see these institutions, however, not as truly independent actors but as agents set up by states to serve their national interests. As long as they do this, the member states will support the institution, but when support for the institution threatens national interests, nations tend to abandon or ignore them. Realists point to the inability of the League of Nations in the inter-war period to stop aggression, or the way the United Nations became a hostage to the cold war as evidence of the limited utility of these organizations. When it really mattered, international institutions could not act against the interests of their member states.

What Criticisms are made of Strategic Studies?

Although the shared philosophical underpinnings of strategists have helped to give the subject intellectual coherence, many realist assumptions have been subjected to fierce criticism. This critique has been discussed in detail elsewhere (Gray 1982), but our purpose here is to give a flavour of the concern expressed by critics of strategic studies. Strategists are said to be:

- obsessed with conflict and force;
- insufficiently concerned with ethical issues;
- not scholarly in their approach;
- part of the problem, not the solution;
- state-centric.

Many critics argue that, because strategists focus on the role of military power, they tend to be preoccupied by violence and war. Because their view of the world is conflict-oriented they tend to ignore the more cooperative, peaceful aspects of world politics. This leads critics to claim that strategists have a distorted, rather than realistic, view of the world. Some critics even suggest that strategists are fascinated by violence, and even take grim satisfaction in describing the darker side of the human condition.

For their part, strategists accept that they are interested in violence and conflict. In their own defence, however, they point out that, just as a doctor of heart disease does not claim to deal with all aspects of health, so they do not claim to be studying every aspect of international relations. They reject the view that they have a distorted view of the world, and that they are fascinated in an 'unhealthy' sense by violence.

The claim to moral neutrality, sometimes made by strategists, is another shortcoming identified by critics. Strategists are depicted as clinical, cool, and unemotional in the way they approach the study of war, despite the fact that, in the nuclear age, millions of lives are at risk in the calculations that take place about strategic policies. Emphasizing the moral outrage felt by some, J. R. Newman described Herman Kahn's book, *On Thermonuclear War*, as 'a moral tract on mass murder, how to comment on it, how to get away with it, how to justify it' (1961: 197). Philip Green, in his study of *Deadly Logic*, also accused strategists who wrote about nuclear deterrence as being 'egregiously guilty of avoiding the moral issue altogether, or misrepresenting it' (1966: 250).

Although many strategists have justified the moral neutrality of their approach in terms of scholarly detachment, some have been sensitive to this criticism. As a result, a number of studies of ethical issues have been written. These include Joseph Nye's book on *Nuclear Ethics*, Michael Walzer's *Just and Unjust Wars*, and Steven P. Lee's study of *Morality,*

Prudence and Nuclear Weapons. These books (together with the moral critical studies by writers like Green) now form an important part of the literature on strategic studies.

Another important criticism levelled against strategic studies is that it represents 'a fundamental challenge to the values of liberal, humane scholarship, that define a University'. The implication is that it is not a scholarly subject and should not be taught at a university. This criticism has a number of related parts. First, according to Philip Green, it is pseudo-scientific, using apparent scientific method to give it a spurious air of legitimacy. Second, because strategists often advise governments on a paid basis, they are operating 'in a manner incompatible with the integrity of scholarship'. E. P. Thornton described the cosy relationship between strategists and government officials as 'suspect, corrupt and at enmity with the universal principles of humane scholarship'. Third, critics charge that strategists not only provide advice to governments, but they also are involved in policy advocacy—which is not part of scholarship. Critics claim that strategists are a vestige of government and spend their time either providing advice on how to achieve or justify dubious international objectives.

With a qualification on the issue of policy advocacy, strategists reject the view that their subject should not be found in a university. They would argue that war cannot be made to disappear simply by ignoring it. (Leon Trotsky, a leading figure in the Bolshevik revolution, put it best: 'You might not have an interest in war, but war has an interest in you.') They argue that the study of war and peace are issues of profound importance that can, and should be, studied in a scholarly way. There have been attempts at developing a 'scientific' approach to strategy (and as Brodie recognized, some writers might have taken this too far) but the debate about methodology is not confined to strategic studies. The nature of 'science' in a social science context remains a lively, ongoing debate.

In general, strategists recognize the dangers of developing too cosy a relationship with officials when they advise governments on a paid basis. Like many other experts,

---

BOX 2

Strategic Studies in the Academy

The study of strategy in Universities may be defended on several different, yet complementary, grounds. In strictly academic terms, the subject poses sufficient intellectual challenge as to merit inclusion in, or even as, a course of study fully adequate to stretch mental resources. In, and of itself, that argument is sufficient to justify the inclusion of strategic studies in University curricula, but one can, and should, proceed to argue that the study of strategy is socially useful . . . . Many views are defensible concerning the proper and appropriate duties of a university. This author chooses a liberal, permissive perspective. He sees value in a field of study that seeks truth and may have relevance to contemporary policy and, as a consequence, may contribute to the general well-being.

(C. S. Gray)

In strategic studies the ability to argue logically and to follow a piece of strategic reasoning is very important, but even more important is the elusive, almost indefinable quality of political judgement which enables a man to evaluate a piece of analysis and locate it in a wider political framework.

(J. C. Garnett)

(e.g. economists), however, they see no necessary inconsistency between scholarship and advice. Because it is a practical subject, there are some benefits from analysing strategic issues at close hand, providing that a 'detached' approach is adopted. Policy advocacy, however, is a different matter. Some strategists do drift into the realm of advocating specific policies, but when they do so they slowly but surely lose their credibility. People who make a career out of arguing for the adoption of specific policies or weapons systems gain a reputation for knowing the 'answer' regardless of the question that is posed.

Another forceful criticism of strategic studies is that it is part of the problem, not the solution. What opponents mean by this is that the Clausewitzian perspective of strategists, which sees military power as a legitimate instrument of policy, helps to perpetuate a particular mindset among national leaders and the public that encourages the use of force. It is this realist thinking, critics argue, which lies behind the development of theories of deterrence, limited war, and crisis management which were so dangerous during the cold war. Anatol Rapoport is one writer who charges strategists with a direct responsibility for promoting a framework of thinking about security which is largely hostile to what he regards as the proper solution to global conflict, namely disarmament. In a stinging attack he argues that 'the most formidable obstacles to disarmament are created by the strategists who place their strategic considerations above the needs of humanity as a whole, and who create or help maintain an intellectual climate in which disarmament appears to be unrealistic' (Rapoport 1965). Instead of spending their time thinking about how to better justify and conduct mass murder, critics suggest that strategists should spend their time devising disarmament strategies, cooperative security arrangements, and global campaigns to denounce violence.

Linked to this criticism is the view that, because strategists are so pessimistic about human nature and the chances of significant improvements in the conduct of international politics, they *ignore the opportunities that exist for peaceful change*. It is suggested that to see the past as a history of constant conflict and to suggest that the future will be the same is to help create a fatalistic impression that plans for human progress will always fail. By emphasizing mistrust, self-help, and the importance of military power in an anarchic international system, their advice becomes self-fulfilling. In other words, if policy-makers take strategists' advice to heart, deterrent threats and defence preparations would lead to a spiral of hostility and mistrust as leaders respond to the defence policies of their competitors. Given this 'socially constructed' view of the world, it is not surprising that states will constantly find themselves in conflict with each other.

Once again, strategists vigorously contest these criticisms. They argue that their ideas reflect (rather than create) the 'reality' of world politics. The fact that most policy-makers and elected officials tend to share their 'realist' assumptions is due to an intellectual climate 'socially constructed' not by academic strategists but by the challenges and threats presented to them by international relations. The notion that strategic studies as a subject is 'a monstrous crime committed by self-interested strategists against the general public' is seen as absurd. Of course, throughout history, various observers have championed war as a preferred instrument of statecraft. Often they depict war in romantic or heroic terms; today's romantic image of war is simply a slightly more technologically embellished version of this traditional imagery. Enthusiasts see war as a relatively bloodless contest in which technically adept professionals use their superior skills and equipment to paralyse the opponent's military command, leading to quick and humane victories. Strategic studies, however, stand as a major impediment to those who claim to have found a quick and easy path to guaranteed victory. Because they recognize the true nature of war, most strategists consider armed conflict to be a tragedy, an activity unfit for human beings that must be limited to the greatest extent possible.

On the question of 'peaceful change', strategists do not dismiss the fact there are opportunities for periods of peaceful coexistence. They are, however, very sceptical about the prospects for 'perpetual peace' based on a radical transformation of world politics. They believe that conflict can be mitigated through effective strategy, but it is highly unlikely that it can be transcended completely. In such a context, it is impossible to abolish the need for strategic studies.

The fact that strategists focus on the task of creating effective national strategies or international initiatives creates the basis for another criticism of the enterprise. Strategic studies incorporate a state-centric approach to world politics. According to this critique, strategists are so preoccupied by threats to the interests of states that they ignore security issues within the state or new phenomenon such as transnational terrorist networks. Many observers argue that the state is not the most appropriate referent for studying security. Rather, attention should be focused on the individual whose security is often threatened rather than protected by the state. Other writers who perceive the growing erosion of the state prefer to focus on 'societal security' or even 'global security' issues.

Strategists would argue that, while they have stressed the role of the state, they have not neglected intra-state conflict. Clausewitz himself dealt with peoples war and a considerable part of the strategic studies literature addresses revolutionary warfare. As wars of national disintegration (Bosnia, Kosovo, Chechnya) have become more prevalent, more attention has been given in the literature to the problem of ethnic conflict. The emergence of Al-Qaeda has led to an explosion of research and writing on the origins, objectives, strategies, and tactics of violent non-state actors with an eye towards destroying international terrorist networks and other criminal organizations. Despite the prevalence of intra-state violence or the rise of important non-state actors, strategists continue to argue that, even with all the contemporary challenges to the modern state, it continues to be the major actor in world politics. In fact the importance of the state, with its access to a myriad of resources and instruments of control and surveillance, has only been highlighted by the emergence of 'super-empowered individuals' and transnational terrorism. Strategists offer no apologies for their continuing interest in issues of state security.

What is the Relationship between Strategic Studies and Security Studies?

One of the main challenges to strategic studies since the end of the cold war has come from those who argue that attention should be shifted away from the study of strategy to the study of security. According to this view 'security', defined in terms of 'freedom from threats to core values', is a more appropriate concept for analysis. The problem with strategy, it is argued, is that it is too narrow and increasingly less relevant at a time when major wars are declining and threats to political, economic, social, and environmental security interests are increasing. Because it is defined more broadly, security is depicted as more valuable than strategy as an organizing framework for understanding the complex, multidimensional risks of today.

However, as Richard Betts, noted in his article 'Should Strategic Studies Survive?', those who champion new definitions of security run two risks. First, Betts noted that even though it is appropriate to distinguish between 'strategy' and 'security' studies, security policy requires careful attention to war and strategy. In other words, military power remains a crucial part of security and that those who ignore war to concentrate on non-military threats to security do so at their peril. Second, he argued that 'expansive definitions of security quickly become synonymous with "interest" and "well-being", do not exclude anything in international relations or foreign policy, and this becomes indistinguishable from those fields or other sub-fields'. In other words, by including potentially everything that might negatively effect human affairs, security studies creates the risk of being too broad to be of any practical value.

The contributors to this book recognize the importance of security studies while at the same time sharing these concerns about the coherence of the field. 'Strategy' remains a distinctive and valuable area of academic study. Strategy is part of security studies, just as security studies are part of international relations, which itself is part of political science. This relationship is expressed in the figure below.

Despite all of the changes that have occurred in world politics since the late 1980s there is in many respects an underlying continuity with earlier eras. The euphoria produced by the hope that a fundamental transformation of international relations was underway, has proved to be ill-founded. As we have seen from the first and second Gulf Wars, the Iraqi insurgency, Bosnia, Kosovo, Chechnya, and the terrorist attacks launched by Al-Qaeda and various fellow travellers, force and military power continue to be an important currency in the international system at the beginning of the twenty-first century. Certainly important changes are taking place in world politics, associated with the twin forces of globalization and fragmentation, and wars between the great powers, for the moment at least, have

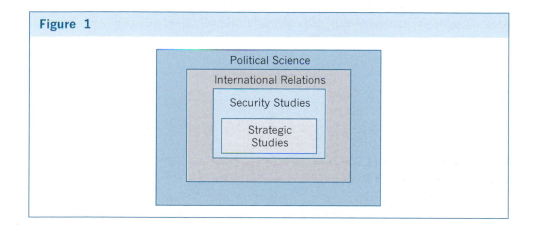

Figure 1

Political Science

International Relations

Security Studies

Strategic Studies

slipped into the background. The sad fact remains, however, that the utilization of military power as an instrument of political purpose and, therefore, strategic studies remain just as relevant today as they have been in the past.

Our exploration of strategy in the contemporary world is divided into four sections. In Part I, our contributors describe the enduring issues that animate the study of strategy and provide a historical and theoretical overview of the topic for our readers. Our study opens with an essay on the causes of war, a complex issue that ultimately shapes approaches to mitigating interstate violence. It then offers two essays of grand historical and theoretical sweep: one on the evolution of warfare since the Napoleonic age; the other a tour d'horizon of strategic thinkers and thinking. The issues of culture, morality, and war also are addressed in this section. Despite popular imagery, cultural, legal, and moral considerations play a role in shaping both the recourse to and the conduct of war. These chapters are important because they illustrate the normative basis for strategy: to help to mitigate both the occurrence and death and destruction produced by war.

Two further chapters focus on two perennial factors that shape warfare. Geography—land, sea, air, space, and now even cyberspace—has shaped the conduct of war and technology itself—the so-called 'revolution in military affairs' or 'transformation'—continues to shape the evolution of warfare and strategies in each of these geographic settings.

In Part II, our contributors explore issues that appear in today's headlines and that animate strategic debate today. Peacekeeping and humanitarian intervention pose unique problems for military forces, especially when treated by policy-makers as an afterthought in the global war on terrorism. Fears about North Korean and Iranian nuclear programmes, and the possibility that terrorists might acquire and use weapons of mass destruction, suggest that it is time for a reappraisal of the threat posed by nuclear, radiological, chemical, and biological weapons. This section also explores emerging issues that are likely to animate debate not only about weapons of mass destruction but also about conventional military power in the decade ahead. Part II also explores emerging issues related to Homeland Defence and the link between domestic counter-terror operations and strategy. Given the contemporary importance of terrorism a new chapter has been added to this edition dealing with the links between terrorism and organized crime.

Part III offers a conclusion to our overview of contemporary strategy not by summarizing the findings of each of our contributors, but by considering new approaches to the study of security that have emerged in recent years and by charting a new way forward for strategic studies after the challenges the subject faced at the end of the cold war.

FURTHER READING

Nature and development of strategic studies

■ J. C. Garnett, 'Strategic Studies and its Assumptions', in John Baylis, Ken Booth, John Garnett, and Phil Williams, *Contemporary Strategy: Theories and Policies* (London: Croom Helm, 1975).

■ John S. Gray, *Strategic Studies: A Critical Assessment* (London: Aldwych Press, 1982).

Historical view of strategy

■ Williamson Murray, Macgregor Knox, and Alvin Bernstein (eds.), *The Making of Strategy: Rulers, States, and War* (Cambridge: Cambridge University Press, 1994).

Other useful studies

■ Andre Beaufre, *An Introduction to Strategy* (London: Faber & Faber, 1965).

—— *Deterrence and Strategy* (London: Faber & Faber 1965).

■ B. Brodie, *War and Politics* (London: Cassell, 1973).

■ C. S. Gray, *Modern Strategy* (Oxford: Oxford University Press, 1999).

■ A. Herzog, *The War-Peace Establishment* (London: Harper & Row, 1963).

■ Michael Howard, *War in European History* (Oxford: Oxford University Press, 1976).

■ H. Kahn, *On Thermonuclear War* (Princeton: Princeton University Press, 1960).

■ H. A. Kissinger, *Nuclear Weapons and Foreign Policy* (New York: Harper & Row, 1957).

■ B. H. Liddell Hart, *Strategy: The Indirect Approach* (London: Faber & Faber, 1967).

■ R. Niebuhr, *Moral Man and Immoral Society* (London: Charles Scribner's Sons, 1932).

■ R. E. Osgood, *NATO: The Entangling Alliance* (Chicago: University of Chicago Press, 1962).

Criticism of strategic studies

■ P. Green, *Deadly Logic* (Ohio: Ohio State University Press, 1966).

■ R. Newman, Review in *Scientific American, 204/3* (1961).

Other useful studies

■ R. K. Betts, 'Should Strategic Studies Survive?', *World Politics*, 50/1 (Oct. 1997).

■ S. Biddle, *Military Power* (Princeton: Princeton University Press, 2005).

■ H. Butterfield and M. Wight, *Diplomatic Investigations* (London: Allen & Unwin, 1966).

■ A. Rapoport, 'The Sources of Anguish', *Bulletin of Atomic Scientists*, 21/10 (Dec 1965).

■ E. P. Thornton, 'A Letter to America', *The Nation*, 232 (24 Jan. 1981).

 Visit the Online Resource Centre that accompanies this book for lots of interesting additional material http://www.oxfordtextbooks.co.uk/orc/baylis_strategy2e/.

PART I

Enduring Issues of Strategy

1

The Causes of War and the Conditions of Peace

JOHN GARNETT

 Chapter Contents

- Introduction
- The Study of War
- Human Nature Explanations of War
- Wars 'Within' and 'Beyond' States
- Conclusion

 Reader's Guide

Scholarship dealing with the causes of war is voluminous and multidisciplinary. This chapter describes and explains theories that have been advanced by biologists, philosophers, political scientists, and sociologists about why wars occur. It groups their ideas into categories and shows how different explanations of war give rise to different requirements or conditions for peace. Distinctions are drawn between 'immediate' and 'underlying' causes of war; between 'permissive' and 'efficient' causes; between 'learned' and 'instinctive' causes; and between 'necessary' and 'sufficient' causes. The chapter pays particular attention to explanations of war based on 'human nature' and 'instinct', but it also considers those psychological theories that emphasize 'misperception' and 'frustration' as causes of aggression. The ideas of those who find the causes of war in human collectives—states, tribes, and ethnic groups, and those who favour 'systemic' rather than 'unit' explanations—also are described.

Introduction

Though 'strategy' these days is as much concerned with the promotion of peace as with the conduct of war, the phenomenon of war remains a central concern. Previous generations might have seen virtues in war, for example, as an instrument of change or as a vehicle for encouraging heroic virtues, but these ideas have been rendered obsolete by the destructiveness of modern warfare. (See Introduction.) In the twentieth century abolishing war became a top priority. The first step in ending war, however, is to identify its causes.

Historians sometimes argue that, since wars are unique events, the causes of war are as numerous as the number of wars and nothing in general can be said about them. This chapter takes a different view. It identifies similarities and patterns between the causes of wars so that we can group causes under such headings as human nature, misperception, the nature of states, and the structure of the international system. Its aim is twofold. First, to relate contemporary scholarship across a range of disciplines—biology, political science, philosophy, and history—to the problem of war causation, and second, to elaborate a number of distinctions which help us to identify different kinds of 'cause' (e.g. 'underlying' and 'immediate' causes, or 'conscious' and 'unconscious' motives). Throughout the chapter these distinctions are used to identify the various causes of war and to discriminate between them.

Since there is little scholarly agreement on what causes war, this chapter is directed towards explaining the debate rather than to answering the question in a decisive way. The arguments are more than academic because, if the cure for war is related to its causes, then different causes will lead to different policy recommendations. If, on the one hand, wars are caused by arms races, then policies of disarmament and arms control are appropriate solutions to the problem of war. (See Chapter 11.) On the other hand, if wars are instigated by despotic or authoritarian states, then the way to peace lies in the spread of democracy. If the basic cause of war is deemed to be the 'international anarchy' which characterizes the current system of states, then attempts to rid the world of war will be geared towards promoting 'system change'—perhaps in the direction of strengthened international law or a system of collective security or world government.

BOX 1.1

Five distinctions which may help clarify our thoughts about the causes of war.

1. 'Instinctive' vs 'learned' behaviour.

2. 'Immediate' vs 'underlying' causes.

3. 'Efficient' vs 'permissive' causes.

4. 'Conscious' vs 'unconscious' motives for war.

5. 'Necessary' vs 'sufficient' causes.

Some explanations for war offer less hope for finding a way to end armed conflict than others. For example, those that locate war in a fundamentally flawed human nature suggest a bleaker future for the human race than those that locate the causes of war in 'learnt' behaviour. If war is learnt rather than instinctive, then there is a possibility that it can be eliminated through social engineering.

Three conclusions emerge from this analysis. First, the search for a single cause appropriate to all wars is futile. Second, because war comes in a variety of forms and has a multiplicity of causes, its elimination will almost certainly require simultaneous domestic and international political action. Third, a worldwide 'just' peace is unattainable.

The Study of War

In the field of international relations no question has attracted more attention than 'Why war?' The reason for this interest is that war is almost universally regarded as a human disaster, a source of misery on a catastrophic scale, and, in the nuclear age, a threat to the entire human race. But war has not always been viewed so negatively. In the nineteenth century, for example, numerous writers identified virtues in war. The philosopher G. W. F. Hegel believed that war preserved the ethical health of nations, and in a similar vein H. von Treitschke regarded war as 'the only remedy for ailing nations' (Gowans 1914: 23). For Treitschke, war was one of the conditions for progress, the cut of the whip that prevents a country from going to sleep, forcing satisfied mediocrity to leave its apathy. This kind of thinking alerts us to the idea that war can be thought of as a purposive, functional thing. E. H. Carr regarded it as 'the midwife of change' (1942: 3): 'Wars . . . Break up and sweep away the half-rotted structures of an old social and political order.' These authors suggested that wars herald rapid technological progress, territorial change, strengthened group consciousness, and economic development. The idea of war as a purposive, functional thing, however, sits uneasily in an age that typically interprets war as an abnormal, pathological condition that threatens us all.

Idle curiosity or an aimless spirit of enquiry has not motivated most investigations into the causes of war. Theorists have studied war to abolish it. They have believed that the first step towards eliminating war is to identify its causes because, in much the same way that the cures for disease are related to the causes of disease, so the cures for war are to be found in its causes. So long as students of war do not allow their enthusiasm for prescription to affect their diagnostic skills, no harm is done. But there is a danger that researchers may be tempted to gloss over the more intractable causes of war in favour of those which suggest the possibility that solutions to human conflict can be readily found.

Many social scientists recoil from the idea that, though particular wars may be avoided, war is endemic in the human condition. The idea that war is inevitable is pretty difficult to swallow, psychologically speaking, and that may explain why pessimistic interpretations of the causes of war meet with resistance. Take, for example, the view that the root cause of war is to be found in human nature, that is, that aggression and violence are genetically

> **BOX 1.2**
>
> ### Jean-Jacques Rousseau's 'Stag Hunt' Analogy
>
> Rousseau imagines a situation in which several solitary and hungry hunters existing in 'a state of nature' where there is neither law, morality, nor government, happen to come together. Each of them recognizes that his hunger could be satisfied by a share of a stag, and so they 'agree' to cooperate to catch one. In Rousseau's words:
>
> If a deer was to be taken, everyone saw that in order to succeed, he must abide faithfully by his post; but if a hare happened to come within reach of any of them, it is not to be doubted that he pursued it without scruple, and, having seized his prey, cared very little if by so doing he caused his companions to miss theirs.
>
> **(Rousseau 1993: 87)**
>
> The point of the story is that in conditions of anarchy, the hunter who grabbed the hare could not feel confident that one of his fellow hunters would not do likewise if presented with the same opportunity, in which case he would go hungry. Given this predicament the sensible thing to do is to behave selfishly and seize the hare.

built into humans and that we do what we do because of what we are. Despite some scientific evidence in support of this idea, there is enormous resistance to it. Why? Because, if human nature is fixed in our genes, we are helpless in the face of ourselves. For many observers, the conclusion that war is built into us is an intolerable counsel of despair even though it is a useful reminder that just because the elimination of war is desirable does not mean that it is therefore possible.

A gloomy interpretation of human nature and an admission of its intractability, however, do not automatically lead to despair of ever being able to rid the world of war. Some would argue that wars are not caused by human *nature*; they are caused by human *behaviour*. And while it may not be possible to change human nature, it is certainly possible to modify human behaviour—by offering rewards, by making threats, by education programmes, or by propaganda. Richard Dawkins has pointed out that 'our genes may instruct us to be selfish but we are not necessarily compelled to obey them all our lives. It may . . . be more difficult to learn altruism than it would be if we were genetically programmed to be altruistic', but we should try 'to *teach* generosity and altruism, because we are born selfish' (1976: 3). Civilized societies spend a great deal of energy on making people behave themselves despite their natures. The law, the police, schools, and churches all play a part in modifying human behaviour in the domestic environment. The possibility of modifying state behaviour also is widely recognized. Diplomacy, force, trade, aid, and propaganda are all instruments used by leaders to affect the behaviour of the states they are dealing with. Deterrent strategists, for example, argue that even if human nature is fatally flawed (and most of them think it is), states can still be deterred from aggression by the threat of unacceptable punishment in much the same way that many potential criminals can be deterred from robbing banks by the threat of imprisonment. (See Chapter 7.)

Unlike those who believe that peace can best be promoted by removing the causes of war, nuclear deterrent strategists hardly care at all about why wars occur. Their policy is simply to make the *consequences* of war so bad that nobody will dare fight even if they want to. In other words, the strategy of nuclear deterrence is unique in that its effectiveness does not depend either on particular interpretations of why wars occur or on treating the underlying pathologies that cause people or states to fight. The only assumption that deterrent theorists make about human beings is the fairly uncontroversial one that on the whole people prefer to be alive rather than dead and hence are likely to be deterred from aggression by the threat of annihilation.

Difficulties in studying war

No clear authoritative answer has emerged, and perhaps one never will, to the question 'Why war?' One of the reasons for this is that the word 'war' is a blanket term used to describe diverse activities. There are total wars and limited wars, regional wars and world wars, conventional wars and nuclear wars, high-technology wars and low-technology wars, interstate wars and civil wars, insurgency wars and ethnic wars. In recent years, wars also have been fought by coalitions on behalf of the international community. It would be very surprising if these widely different activities—linked only by the fact that they involve organized military violence—could be explained in the same way.

Another reason for the absence of an authoritive answer is that the question 'What are the causes of war?' is a complicated, 'cluster' question. Under its umbrella, as Hidemi Suganami has pointed out, we may be asking a number of different questions. We may, for example, be asking 'What are the conditions that must be present for wars to occur?'; or we may be asking 'Under what circumstances have wars occurred most frequently?'; or we may be asking about how a particular war came about (1996: 4). Lumping these questions together inevitably leads to complicated and unsatisfactory answers.

An additional reason for complex answers to the question of war causation is that the concept of 'causation' itself is fraught with philosophical difficulties. One may note that X is often a prelude to Y, but that is not at all the same as proving that X caused Y. Various writers, for example, noting that wars are often preceded by arms races between the belligerents, have claimed that arms races *cause* wars. Arms races sometimes cause war, but an *automatic* connection has not been conclusively demonstrated. Arguably, human beings do not fight because they have weapons; they acquire weapons because they already wish to fight. And it is worth pointing out that not all arms races have led to war. Anglo-French naval competition in the nineteenth century led to the Entente Cordiale, while the cold war arms race between the United States and the Soviet Union led to a deterrent stalemate and one of the most prolonged periods of peace in European history.

Given the difficulties inherent in the problem of causation, some writers (particularly historians) have preferred to talk about the 'origins' of wars rather than 'causes'. They believe that the best way of explaining why wars occur is to describe how they come about in terms of the social context and events from which they spring. Thus, if we are investigating the causes of the Second World War, we need to look at the Treaty of Versailles, the world depression, the rise of Hitler, German rearmament, the foreign policies of Britain and France, etc. When we have done this we are well on the way to understanding the circumstances that led to the Second World War. Those who emphasize the 'origins' of wars hold the view that telling the story of how they come about is as close as we can get to understanding why they come about.

Historians who favour this very specific 'case-study' approach to the identification of the causes of war tend to believe that, since every war is a unique event with unique causes, the causes of war are as numerous as the number of wars. Hence, providing an authoritative answer to the question 'What are the causes of war?' would involve a detailed examination of every war that has ever occurred. The uniqueness of every war means that there is nothing in general to be said about them. For investigations concerned with the causes of individual wars this is a fair point. Nevertheless, while acknowledging the uniqueness of individual wars, most political scientists see merit in shifting the level of analysis from the particular to the general so that we can see patterns and similarities between the causes of one war and another. At this more general level of analysis we may identify some causes which are common to many, if not all, wars.

'Immediate' and 'underlying' causes

One of the most useful distinctions to be drawn between the various causes of war is between 'immediate', proximate causes and 'underlying', more fundamental causes. Immediate causes, the events that trigger wars, may be trivial, even accidental. For example, the spark that ignited the First World War was the assassination of the Austrian Archduke Franz Ferdinand who was visiting Sarajevo and being driven in an open car. The death of the archduke was a tragedy, but it was essentially a trivial event, and no one seriously believes that its occurrence provides an adequate explanation for the momentous events that followed. What is more, it was an 'accident' which might easily not have happened. If the duke's chauffeur had not deviated from the planned route and then stopped the car to rectify his error, the assassin would not have had an opportunity to shoot the archduke and his wife. The assassination was undoubtedly the immediate cause of the First World War, and it is true to say that if it had not happened the war which broke out in 1914 would not have happened. But there is plenty of evidence to suggest that a war would have occurred sooner or later. In 1914 war was in the air: Europe was divided by hostile alliance systems; tensions were rising; mobilization timetables were pressuring decision-makers; and an arms race was under way. In short, the background circumstances were highly inflammable, and if the assassination of Franz Ferdinand had not set the powder keg alight, sooner or later something else probably would have provided the spark. Most commentators believe that a useful examination of the causes of the First World War should pay more attention to those underlying causes than to the immediate triggering events.

Emphasis on underlying causes is a *structural interpretation* in the sense that it emphasizes the importance of international circumstances rather than deliberate state policies in causing wars. It suggests that statesmen are not always in control of events; they sometimes find themselves caught up in a process which, despite their best intentions, pushes them to war. Suganami has pointed out that there are occasions when 'the background conditions appear already so war prone that the particular path through which the actual war broke out seems only to have been one of a number of alternative routes through which a war like that could have been brought about' (1996: 195).

Of course, background conditions are not always a reliable barometer of the danger that war will break out. In some situations the setting seems relatively benign and responsibility for war is more easily allocated to the particular policies followed by the governments involved. Wars often come about as a result of aggressive, reckless, thoughtless, and deliberate acts by statesmen. It would be impossible to discuss the causes of the Second World War, for instance, without drawing attention to the persistently aggressive behaviour of Hitler and the weak, appeasing policies of Chamberlain. Similarly, the actions of Nasser in seizing the Suez Canal and Eden in responding to it with military action were critically important causes of the Suez War. The same point can be made about both the Falklands War and the Gulf War. In the case of the Falklands, the Argentinian decision to invade South Georgia and Margaret Thatcher's decision to resist seem at least as important as any 'structural' causes that might be identified. In the case of the Gulf War, Saddam Hussein's decision to seize territory in Kuwait and the decision of Western governments not to allow him to get away with it were more obvious causes of the Gulf War than any background circumstances.

'Efficient' and 'permissive' causes

Another useful distinction lies between 'efficient' and 'permissive' causes of war. 'Efficient' causes are connected to the particular circumstances surrounding individual wars. War may result because state A has something state B wants. In this situation the 'efficient' cause of the war is the desire of state B. Examples of these causes abound. The efficient cause of the Gulf War between Iraq and Iran was the desire of Saddam Hussein to regain from Iran the Shatt-al-Arab waterway; the efficient cause of the 1990 war between Iraq and the Western coalition was Saddam's desire to acquire Kuwaiti territory and resources. The 'efficient' cause of the 2002 war with Iraq was the decision of the United States and the United Kingdom first to topple Saddam and second to bring democracy to Iraq. If President Bush and Prime Minister Blair had not taken that decision to intervene militarily in Iraq there would have been no war.

Since the rise of the state system there has been a general presumption *against* this kind of intervention in the internal affairs of sovereign states. The traditional view is that states have no business meddling in the internal affairs of other states. Although the idea of non-intervention has become a basic principle of international order, in recent years there has developed a consensus that, in exceptional circumstances and as a last resort, even military intervention may be justified, both legally and morally. When, for example, genocide is being practised, when there are gross violations of human rights, when states are collapsing into chaos, and when there is a serious threat to peace and security—in these extreme situations intervention is deemed permissible, particularly if it enjoys United Nations approval. Few would quarrel with the prevailing consensus on this point, but we have to acknowledge that in an obvious sense it is a cause of war.

In terms of success and failure, the record of military intervention is mixed. The 2002 Iraq War and its messy aftermath provides the most recent example of the difficulty of bringing military intervention to a satisfactory conclusion. As this message sinks in, the current enthusiasm for intervention may fade, and as it does, this particular cause of war may become less common.

'Permissive' causes of war are those features of the international system which, while not actively promoting war, nevertheless allow it to happen. In this context, the fact that we live in a world of independent sovereign states with no authority above them, and no institutions sufficiently powerful to regulate their relations, is a 'permissive' cause of war. Kenneth Waltz is renowned for the emphasis he puts on 'permissive' rather than 'efficient' causes of war (1959). Although the causes of war are bewildering in their variety, notes Waltz, the most persuasive explanation for it is to be found in international anarchy—the fact that in an ungoverned international system there is nothing to prevent conflict from occurring. And because there is nothing to prevent war there is, in international relations, a permanent expectation of violence and a permanent sense of insecurity which pushes states to behave aggressively despite whatever peaceful intentions they may have. Waltz uses Rousseau's famous 'stag hunt' analogy to show that warlike behaviour arises not primarily from any defect in human nature or some inherent flaw in states, but from the predicament in which leaders find themselves (1959: 167–8). In the face of systemic or structural inadequacy, war cannot be avoided forever and is always just around the corner.

Kenneth Thompson has made the same point in a slightly different way (1960: 261–76). He imagines a situation where, during the rush hour, someone waiting for a train on the platform of an underground railway station finds himself being pushed by a surging crowd of fellow travellers towards the electrified line. Our passenger is a good man who means no harm. What should he do? The Christian ethic tells him to turn the other cheek, but if he does he will end up dead on the rail tracks. And so our good man kicks and struggles and fights to stay alive. He behaves in this aggressive way not because he is wicked or violent, but because he finds himself in an environment where he cannot afford to be good. The Sermon on the Mount is not much use if you live in the jungle. And so it is with states: because they exist in a system where others behave badly, doing likewise is the only way to survive.

If the main cause of war is to be found in the anarchic international system in which sovereign states pursue their interests without the constraint of world government, then an essential condition of peace is the transformation of that system from one of competing states to a unified world ruled by a single authority sufficiently powerful to compel peaceful behaviour. The trouble with this recommendation is that there is no practical way of implementing it. We did not *choose* to live in the world of independent states which emerged from the Peace of Westphalia in 1648 and we cannot now choose not to live in it. Though the international system is constantly changing, for all practical purposes it is a *given*, something we have to accept as a fact of life. We are where we are, and whatever conditions of peace we may recommend must take that into account. Another reason for scepticism that 'world government' will solve the problem of war is that even if we achieved it we might not like it. World government might turn out to be world dictatorship and inter-state wars might simply become civil wars.

Those who regard the ungoverned international system as the root cause of war often compare it with Hobbesian anarchy; but in reality the society of states bears little resemblance to Hobbes's 'state of nature'. Although it is not an integrated society comparable to domestic society, it is neither chaotic nor wholly unpredictable. States do not live in conditions of permanent terror. International society is a regulated, rule-governed environment in which states can build upon their common interests, and in which international organizations, customs, habits, mores, and laws built up over hundreds of years moderate and order their behaviour. Of course, no one would claim that the world of sovereign states is the best of all worlds; it may not even be the best of all possible worlds. But it is better than some imaginable alternatives—even better, perhaps, than world government—and we ought not to try to jettison it without being very sure that what succeeds it will be an improvement.

'Necessary' and 'sufficient' causes of war

Various writers have found it useful to distinguish between 'necessary' and 'sufficient' causes of war.[1] A 'necessary' condition for war is one that *must be present* if war is to occur. In other words, if war cannot break out without that condition existing, then it is a necessary condition. The existence of armaments is a necessary condition of war because without them no war could be fought. For wars to occur it also is necessary for human beings to be organized in discrete collectives—states, tribes, ethnic groups, nations, or factions. Additionally, it is a necessary condition of war that there be no effective mechanism for preventing it. An effective *world* government, for example, would make it impossible for interstate wars to occur, and an all-powerful *state* government would make it impossible for civil wars to occur. Thus, the absence of these mechanisms is a necessary condition of war.

There is an element of tautology in the above analysis in the sense that if we define war as organized violence between groups, then it is obvious that wars cannot occur if human beings are not organized in groups that have the capacity for organized violence. It is equally obvious that wars cannot occur if there is a mechanism that prevents them. More controversially, it has been suggested that one of the necessary conditions of war is that at least one of the parties to it must have a non-democratic government.

A 'sufficient' cause of war is one that, if present, *guarantees* the occurrence of war. A is a sufficient cause of B if B always occurs whenever A exists. If two states hate each other so much that neither can tolerate the independent existence of the other, then that is a sufficient cause of war which makes war between them inevitable. But it is not a *necessary* condition of war since many wars occur between states which do not share that degree of hatred and are perfectly content with each other's continued existence as independent states in international society. Clearly, a cause of war can be sufficient without being necessary, and the converse of this also is true—a cause can be necessary without being sufficient. For example, the existence of weapons is a necessary condition of war, but it is not a sufficient cause of war since even the existence of high levels of armaments does not always lead to war.

The categories 'necessary' and 'sufficient' do not cover all the possible causes of war. We must not fall into the trap of thinking that the causes of war must be *either* necessary *or* sufficient because there are many causes which are *neither* necessary *nor* sufficient. For example, the desire of statesmen to annex territory belonging to neighbouring states is a common cause of war but it is neither a necessary nor a sufficient cause. It is not a necessary cause because many wars are fought for reasons which have nothing to do with territory, and it is not a sufficient cause because the desire to annex territory may not be acted upon—perhaps because of deterrence.

Human Nature Explanations of War

There is widespread agreement that one of the things that distinguishes human beings from animals is that most of their behaviour is *learnt* rather than *instinctive*. No one knows what the relative percentages are and there is an ongoing debate about the relative importance of 'nature' versus 'nurture' (heredity versus environment) as a determinant of human behaviour. Inevitably this debate has raised the question of whether war is an example of 'innate' or 'learnt' behaviour. If it is innate then we must accept it, since in any reasonable timescale biological evolution is too slow to modify it. If it is learnt, however, then it can be unlearnt and there is hope for us all. Liberal thinkers prefer to emphasize the importance of 'nurture' and are naturally attracted to the idea that aggression and war can be tamed. Conservative thinkers tend to throw their weight behind 'nature' and are therefore sceptical about the possibilities of ridding the world of war.

Though they are disposed to minimize its significance, even committed liberals admit that there is a genetic, instinctive element in human behaviour. We do not start with clean slates on which life's experiences are written to make us what we are. We come with genetic baggage, biologically programmed, with built-in drives and instincts, one of which, it is argued, is a predilection for aggression and violence. In a celebrated exchange of letters in 1932 both Albert Einstein and Sigmund Freud agreed that the roots of war were to be found in an elemental instinct for aggression and destruction. Einstein thought that 'man has in him an active instinct for hatred and destruction', and Freud believed he had identified a 'death instinct' which manifested itself in homicide and suicide (Freud 1932). In the 1960s, ethological and socio-biological research brought new life to 'instinct' theories of aggression. Konrad Lorenz argued, largely on the basis of his observations of the behaviour of birds and fish, that an aggressive instinct is embedded in the genetic make-up of all animals (including man), and that this instinct has been a prerequisite for survival (1976). Robert Ardrey, in *The Territorial Imperative*, reached a similar conclusion and suggested a 'territorial' instinct to run alongside Lorenz's four instincts—hunger, fear, sex, and

BOX 1.3

The Causes of War

If one seeks in political philosophy the major causes of war the answers are bewildering in their variety and in their contradictory qualities. To make this variety manageable, the answers can be ordered under three headings: within humanity, within the structure of separate states, within the state system.

Within humanity

There is deceit and cunning and from these wars arise.

(Waltz 1959)

Whatever can be said in favour of a balance of power can be said only because we are wicked.

(Confucius)

Within the structure of separate states

A steadfast concert for peace can never be maintained except by a partnership of democratic nations. No autocratic government could be trusted to keep faith within it or observe its covenants . . . Only free peoples can hold their purpose and their honor steady to a common end and prefer the interests of mankind to any narrow interests of their own.

(Jonathan Dymond)

Within the state system

It is quite true that it would be much better for all men to remain always at peace. But so long as there is no security for this, everyone having no guarantee that he can avoid war, is anxious to begin it at the moment which suits his own interest and so forestall a neighbour, who would not fail to forestall the attack in his turn at any moment favourable to himself.

(Woodrow Wilson)

Force is a means of achieving the external ends of states because there exists no consistent, reliable process of reconciling the conflicts of interest that inevitably arise among similar units in a condition of anarchy.

(Jean-Jacques Rousseau)

aggression (1966). Edward Wilson in *On Human Nature* noted that human beings are disposed to react with unreasoning hatred to perceived threats to their safety and possessions, and he argued that 'we tend to fear deeply the actions of strangers and to solve conflict by aggression' (1978: 119).

Although Richard Dawkins in his book *The Selfish Gene* has shifted the level of analysis from the individual to the genes that help make him what he is, he too is under no illusions about human nature. His argument is that 'a predominant quality to be expected in a successful gene is ruthless selfishness. This gene selfishness will usually give rise to selfishness in individual behaviour' (1976: 2). 'Much as we might wish to believe otherwise, universal love and welfare of the species as a whole are concepts which simply do not make evolutionary sense' (1976: 2–3). This analysis leads Dawkins to the bleak conclusion that 'if you wish . . . to build a society in which individuals cooperate generously and unselfishly towards a common good, you can expect little help from biological nature' (1976: 3).

The 'human nature' explanation of war is a persuasive one, but at least two qualifications need to be made about it. First, we need to ask whether the evidence produced by the study of animals is really relevant to the behaviour of human beings. The animal behaviourists say it is, because man is simply a higher animal, connected to the rest of the animal kingdom by evolution. To deny that human beings have instincts in the same way that animals do is to deny the almost universally accepted principle of evolution, which links all life on the planet. Even so, we cannot help wondering whether the kind of 'cross-species' generalization engaged in by biologists is valid. After all, human beings are very different from animals. They are more intelligent. They have a moral sense. They reflect about what they do; they plan ahead. Some would claim that these differences are so important that for all intents and purposes they lift man out of the animal world and reduce his instincts to no more than vestigial significance. Waltz notes that arguing that human nature causes war is not very helpful since if human nature causes war then, logically, it also causes everything else that human beings do. In his words, 'human nature may in some sense have been the cause of war in 1914, but by the same token it was the cause of peace in 1910' (1959: 28). In other words, human nature is a constant and cannot explain the wide variety of activities that humans exhibit.

'Frustration' explanations of war

Social psychologists, while still locating war in 'man', offer explanations for its occurrence which rely less on instinct and more on *socially programmed human behaviour*. Typically, they argue that aggression is a result of frustration. When individuals find themselves thwarted in the achievement of their desires, goals, and objectives, they experience frustration which causes pent-up resentment that needs to find an outlet—and this frequently takes the form of aggressive behaviour which, in turn, has a cathartic effect of releasing tension and making those who engage in it feel better. Usually aggression is levelled at those who cause the frustration, but sometimes it is vented against innocents who become scapegoats. This psychological process of transferring aggression to a secondary group is called 'displacement'. Sometimes individuals project their frustrated desires and ambitions on to the group or collective, be it tribe or state, to which they belong. In the words of Reinhold Niebuhr, 'the man in the street, with his lust for power and prestige thwarted by his own limitations and the necessities of social life, projects his ego upon his nation and indulges his anarchic lusts vicariously' (1932: 93).

There is a sense in which the '*Frustration/Aggression*' hypothesis, which emphasizes the connection between violence and the failure of human beings to achieve their objectives, is somewhat more optimistic than 'instinct' theories of aggression. Although frustration in life is unavoidable, it may be possible either to channel aggression into harmless activities like sport (psychologists call this sublimation) or to organize society in ways which minimize frustrations (sociologists call this social engineering).

'Misperception' explanations of war

Accepting that wars cannot occur unless statesmen decide to wage them, many believe that decisions to go to war are often the result of misperception, misunderstanding, miscalculation, and errors of judgement. Essentially, those who think in this way regard wars as *mistakes*, the tragic consequences of failing to appreciate things as they are. This being the case, they are caused more by human frailty or fallibility than malice. Robert Jervis (1976), building on the ideas of Kenneth Boulding (1956), has contributed enormously to our understanding of these *psychological causes of war*. He makes the point that in order to make sense of the world around us, we develop images of reality through which we filter the welter of information that bombards our senses. These 'images' of reality are more important than reality itself when it comes to determining our behaviour; they act as a distorting lens which inhibits our ability to see reality as it is and predispose us to judge the world in ways that confirm our pre-existing concepts.

Critically important misperceptions likely to lead to war include mistaken estimates of both enemy intentions and capabilities, inaccurate assessments of the military balance between adversaries, and failures to judge the risks and consequences of war properly. Quite frequently these kinds of misperceptions are made by both sides involved in a conflict. For example, Greg Cashman has argued that in the Gulf War, Saddam Hussein may have perceived a threat from Kuwait's reluctance to allow Iraq to cancel its debts and its unwillingness to pump less oil. He may even have perceived a joint American–Israeli–British conspiracy to deny Iraq sophisticated weaponry. On the other hand, leaders in virtually all of the Middle East capitals underestimated the degree of threat posed by Iraq and were taken by surprise when Kuwait was invaded. Thus, while Iraqi leaders overestimated the degree of threat to their interests, their opponents underestimated the hostility of Iraq (Cashman 1993: 63). But perhaps the most critical misperception of all was Saddam Hussein's failure to anticipate Western resolve and the creation of a powerful military coalition against him. There were at least as many misperceptions surrounding the 2002 Iraq war. Despite the unambiguous warnings he had received Saddam was convinced that the United States and Britain would not invade. For their part the Americans and the British believed that Saddam possessed weapons of mass destruction and was well on the way to acquiring nuclear capability. They also believed that invasion would be universally welcomed, that Iraq was a haven for terrorists, and that democracy could be created with relative ease. None of these beliefs were true, but for the participants they formed the psychological reality against which they made their decisions.

Before the Second World War, Hitler mistakenly believed that Britain would not fight and Chamberlain mistakenly believed that Germany could be appeased by concessions. Other delusions and misconceptions that contributed to the outbreak of war in 1939 have been identified by A. J. P. Taylor. Mussolini was deluded about the strength of Italy; the French believed that France was impregnable. Churchill believed that Britain could remain a great power despite the war, and Hitler 'supposed that Germany would contend with Soviet Russia and the United States for mastery of the world' (Nelson and Olin 1979: 153–4). In Britain hardly anyone expected that German blitzkrieg tactics would bring France down in a matter of weeks, and throughout Europe people grossly overestimated the power of strategic bombing. Given this plethora of misunderstandings, misjudgements, and misperceptions, it is easy to argue that statesmen stumbled into the Second World War because they were out of touch with reality.

Much the same point can be made about the Falklands War. Misperceptions abounded. Britain seriously misinterpreted Argentine intentions with respect to invasion, and Argentina badly misjudged Britain's determination to resist. For years the two governments had been involved in intermittent negotiations about a possible transfer of sovereignty, and, though little progress had been made, the Conservative government could not believe that the Argentine Junta would seize South Georgia before the possibilities of negotiation had been exhausted. What the British government failed to appreciate was the significance of the Malvinas in the Argentine psyche and the domestic pressures to act that this put on President Galtieri and Dr Costa Mendez. For its part, the government of Argentina could not believe that, at the end of the twentieth century, a Eurocentric, post-colonial Britain was prepared to spill blood for the sake of a barren relic of empire 10,000 miles away.

There is a sense in which the misconceptions prevalent both in Germany before the Second World War and in Argentina before the Falklands War are understandable. The signals transmitted by the policy of appeasement may have suggested to Hitler that, since he had got away with swallowing the Rhineland in 1936, and Austria and the Sudetenland in 1938, he could probably get away with aggression against Poland in 1939. In the case of the Falklands, the casual pace of British diplomacy and the absence of any serious military capability in the area may have suggested to the Argentines that Britain was not much interested in the fate of the Falkland Islands and was unlikely to defend them. Perhaps, in both of these cases, it was not so much that signals were *misread* but that *the wrong signals were sent*. Either way Britain's enemies made serious miscalculations of her intentions and war resulted.

If wars are caused by misperceptions and misunderstandings created by cognitive biases, then conditions of peace include more clear thinking, better communications between countries, and education. This thought lies behind the UNESCO motto 'Peace Through Understanding', various 'education for peace' proposals, and the attempts that are frequently made to get potential adversaries around the conference table so that they can better understand each other. The basic idea is that if enemies can be brought to appreciate each other's perspectives, then the disputes that divide them will dissolve because they will be seen to be either illusory or not sufficiently serious to justify war. Perhaps we can detect in this approach relics of the idea of a natural 'harmony of interests' which would prevail if only misunderstandings were cleared up.

Before we are persuaded by this idea that wars can be prevented by removing misperceptions and misunderstandings, a word of warning is appropriate. It may not be possible to eradicate misperception from human affairs given the inherent cognitive weaknesses of the human mind. The need to simplify, the inability to empathize, the tendency to ethnocentrism, the reluctance to relinquish or recognize prejudices—all familiar human weaknesses—may make some degree of misperception inevitable. Herbert Butterfield recognized this point when he identified an 'irreducible dilemma' lying in the very geometry of human conflict. Butterfield imagined a situation in which two potential enemies, both armed, face each other. Neither harbours any hostile intent but neither can be sure of the intentions of the other. 'You cannot enter into the other man's counter fear' and 'it is never possible for you to realize or remember properly that since he cannot see the inside of your mind, he can never have the same assurance of your intentions that you have' (1952: 21). Butterfield makes the point that the greatest war in history could be caused by statesmen who desperately want peace but whose cognitive limitations lead them to misinterpret each other's intentions (1952: 19). (Discerning students will realize that Butterfield's 'ultimate predicament' has, in recent years, surfaced in the literature of strategic studies as 'The Security Dilemma'.)

Additionally, not all wars are caused by misperceptions and misunderstandings even though they may be surrounded by them. Some wars—perhaps most—are rooted in genuine disagreement and conflicting interests, and in these cases discussions between enemies simply promote a better understanding of the disputes which divide them. Indeed, in some situations improved understanding may actually exacerbate the divisions between adversaries. When it was suggested to him that international hatred and suspicion could be reduced by getting nations to understand one another better, Sir Evelyn Baring, British governor in Egypt between 1883 and 1907, replied that 'the more they understand one another the more they will hate one another' (Waltz 1959: 50). Perhaps it can be argued that for most of the 1930s Britain was at peace with Germany precisely because the British did not understand Hitler. When, in September 1939, the penny finally dropped, Britain declared war on Germany.

Conscious and unconscious motives for war

The trouble with all these explanations that locate the causes of war within 'man' is that those leaders and statesmen who actually declare wars would almost certainly offer quite different explanations for their decisions. Hitler, if he had been asked why he attacked Poland on 1 September 1939, is unlikely to have replied that he was acting instinctively, or that he was frustrated or a victim of misperception. He would almost certainly have offered rational, practical reasons to do with the plight of Germans in Danzig and the Polish corridor, and the iniquitous way in which the politicians at Versailles had redrawn the map of Europe to Germany's disadvantage. This discrepancy between the explanations of war offered by practitioners and those put forward by philosophers and scientists suggests that it may be useful to distinguish between *conscious* and *unconscious* motives for war.

National leaders have a Clausewitzian, *'instrumental' view of war*. They regard it as a rational tool for the implementation of policy, a technique that is available for practitioners to use in appropriate circumstances for the pursuit of national interests. In other words, officials generally believe that war results from a calculated, purposive, *conscious* decision. But philosophers and scientists trying to look behind a leader's goal-orientated acts often suggest that war results from *unconscious* drives and weaknesses in the human psyche of which practitioners may be unaware but which nevertheless push them towards war.

Those who regard war simply as an instrument of policy, a consequence of rational decisions taken in the national interest, underestimate the pressures and constraints—from public opinion, nationalist sentiment, alliance commitments, and the momentum of events—that may push politicians towards war. They also may make the mistake of thinking that once the costs and consequences of war have been made clear to politicians they will refrain from it. Norman Angell spent much of his life pointing out, quite rightly, that 'wars do not pay', that they are not in the national interest, and that even the victors are usually losers (1914). He thought that once this basic fact had been grasped wars would cease. Sir Norman, however, failed to appreciate two things. First, he did not consider that wars are not always a matter of rational calculation or cost–benefit analysis. Sometimes wars are a kind of madness, explosions of violence far removed from rational policy.

Herman Rauschning, for example, argued that the National Socialist Movement in Germany during the 1930s was impelled towards a war of destruction by its own inherent madness (1939). The second weakness of Angell's analysis is that, although he was right to highlight the disastrous economic consequences of war, he was probably wrong to conclude that waging war was therefore irrational and not in the national interest. Victors may be losers as a result of the wars they fight, but refusing to fight may make them even bigger losers in the long run. Britain, a victor in the Second World War, emerged from it permanently weakened, but if Hitler had not been stopped Britain probably would have ended up in an even worse position. Waging war against Germany certainly 'did not pay', but it was still the rational choice of the less disastrous of two costly outcomes.

'Group' explanations of war

Though embarked upon by individual human beings, war, by definition, is a *group activity*. It is waged by human collectives—factions, tribes, nations, states, and even perhaps by 'civilizations'. This has led some to shift the responsibility for war from human beings to the group within which they live and to which they owe varying degrees of allegiance. Those who argue in this way believe that there is nothing much wrong with human beings *per se*, but they are corrupted by the social structures in which they live. In the words of Friedrich Nietzsche, 'Madness is the exception in individuals but the rule in groups'. Essentially, the argument is that there is something about human collectives which encourages violence.

Perhaps the trouble starts with the sense of difference that we all feel between 'us' and 'them'. Any time people can make a distinction between those who belong to their own collective grouping—be it tribe, state, or nation—and other groups with which they cannot identify easily, they have laid the foundation for conflict. It is all too easy for a group to slide from recognizing that it is different from other groups to believing that it is superior to them. Hence, this sense of differentiation—what Suganami calls 'discriminatory sociability' (1996: 55)—readily leads to group selfishness, intergroup conflict, and ultimately war. As Neibuhr once observed, 'altruistic passion is sluiced into the reservoirs of nationalism with great ease, and made to flow beyond them with great difficulty' (1932: 91).

G. Le Bon was one of the earliest social psychologists to notice that the behaviour of social groups is different from—and usually worse than—the behaviour of the individuals comprising them. He developed the idea of 'crowd psychology', that in a 'crowd' a new entity or collective mind comes into being. He believed that while in groups, individuals lose their normal restraints, become more suggestible, more emotional, and less rational. What is more, groups have reduced feelings of responsibility, because the more responsibility is diffused in 'crowds', the less heavily it weighs on each individual. Since responsibility is everywhere (and therefore nowhere), blame cannot be allocated specifically, and this frees human collectives from normal moral restraints (1897: 41). This thought was neatly captured in the title of Niebuhr's classic *Moral Man and Immoral Society*. Eric Hoffer, in discussing the appeal of mass movements, makes the same point very graphically, 'When we lose our individual independence in the corporateness of a mass movement, we find a new freedom—freedom to hate, bully, lie, torture, murder and betray without shame or remorse' (1952: 118).

Human beings always have lived in differentiated groups and it is unlikely that this will change in the foreseeable future. The interesting question is whether some groups are more war prone than others. In the context of interstate wars, for example, are capitalist states more warlike than socialist states or vice versa? There is no clear answer to that question. Can we argue that democratic states are more peaceloving than authoritarian states? Again there is no clear answer. The historical evidence suggests that 'democracies fight as often as do other types of states' (Kegley and Wittkopf 1997: 358). In the late 1990s, as wars in the Gulf and the former Yugoslavia have shown, democratic states also have demonstrated some enthusiasm for wars of intervention in support of human rights. This current fashion for waging wars in support of liberal values does not augur well for a peaceful world.

Various observers have noted, however, that democracies seldom, if ever, *fight each other.* Michael Doyle, for example, has argued (1983, 1986) that liberal states are more peacefully inclined towards each other because their governments are more constrained by democratic institutions, and because they share the same democratic values. Commercial interdependence between liberal states also gives them a vested interest in peace. If Doyle and those who share his views are right, one of the conditions of peace is the spread of democracy—a trend that has gathered pace particularly since the end of the cold war. For the first time ever, almost half of the world's governments are now democratic. The thesis that the spread of democracy will promote peace is no more than plausible, however, and it would be unwise to accept it uncritically.

KEY POINTS

- Some believe that human beings are genetically programmed towards violence, but there is an ongoing debate about whether war is an example of 'innate' or 'learnt' behaviour.

- Social psychologists have argued that aggression is the result of frustration. Some believe feelings of aggression can be channelled into harmless activities like sport.

- Wars that result from misperceptions, misunderstandings, and miscalculations by statesmen might be prevented by better communications and more accurate information.

- Psychologists, trying to look behind statesmen's decisions, tend to see war as a result of unconscious drives and weaknesses in the human psyche. Practitioners are unlikely to agree.

- Some believe that there is something about human collectives that encourages violence.

- There is some evidence, however, that though democratic states fight as frequently as other states, they do not fight each other.

Wars 'Within' and 'Beyond' States

Whether its decline is connected to the spread of democracy or not, *interstate* violence now seems to be less of a problem than it did just a few years ago. Indeed, it has been calculated that since 1970 less than 10 percent of armed conflicts have been interstate wars fought for traditional objectives. Sometimes, of course, wars straddle both the 'internal' and 'interstate' categories. The Indo-China War, for example is a case in point. What started as a colonial war developed into a civil war which became an interstate war with the intervention of the United States and its allies in Vietnam.

One reason why interstate wars may be going out of fashion is that in a globalized world the expected value of conquest has diminished and its costs—both economic and political—have escalated. States bent on improving their standards of living are better advised to spend their money on education, research, and technology than on conquering other countries and trying to hold down hostile populations. The contemporary moral climate makes aggressive wars difficult to justify, and the media revolution makes it difficult to avoid the opprobrium attached to waging them.

General Sir Rupert Smith is one of the most recent in a long line of commentators who echo this fashionable perception that old-fashioned wars are old hat. Violence exists, he says, but 'wars in the future will not be waged between states. Instead we will fight among the people'. The general may be right, but a little reflection suggests that both he and those who think like him may be premature in their judgement. It is possible to envisage a scenario—perhaps not far into the future—when there is a desperate scramble for scarce resources by capitalist countries that find it increasingly difficult to sustain their profligate lifestyles as vital minerals, particularly fossil fuels, start to run out.

If that should happen, advanced industrial countries might face the stark choice between going under or waging interstate war to secure supplies of essential materials. Take oil, for example. To deny a modern industrial state oil is to deny it the means of survival. Since no state has ever committed suicide, who can doubt that faced with the destruction of their way of life, states will do whatever is necessary to secure adequate supplies of oil—including waging interstate war. In short, interstate war is not yet off the agenda, even for civilized states that pride themselves on their peaceful intentions.

The current decline of interstate war does not explain the rising incidence of internal war, except, of course, in percentage terms. There are a number of reasons why civil wars have become common, but perhaps the most basic is that in many parts of the world sovereign states—which are usually defined in terms of the monopoly of military power which they wield within their territory—have lost that monopoly to a variety of bodies, be they tribes, ethnic groups, terrorists, warlords, splinter groups or armed gangs. When governments lose their monopoly of military force they can no longer control their territory or their people. The domestic environment begins to resemble the ungoverned international system which, as we have seen, is a structural, 'permissive' cause of war. In Hobbesian anarchy ancient tensions and hatreds which were previously contained burst to the surface. We have seen the consequences of this in Bosnia, Kosovo, Chechynia, Afghanistan, Sierra Leone, Somalia, East Timor, Haiti.

What is particularly horrifying about ethnic wars is that people are brutalized and killed not because of anything they have done, not even because of their politics, but simply because of who they are. That is what is so terrible about the persecution of the Tutsis in Rwanda, the Tamils in Sri Lanka, the Kurds in Iraq, the Muslims in Bosnia, and the Albanians in Kosovo. Ethnic wars are quite different from Clausewitzian politically motivated conflicts where the belligerents disagree about something and seek to resolve their disagreement by interstate war—an activity conducted according to moral and legal rules.

BOX 1.4

Some 'Facts' about War

War is difficult to define. Although there is agreement that war involves organized military violence, it is not clear how much violence there has to be before the term 'war' is justified.

Because of this definitional problem, estimates of the number of wars under way at any given time vary—sometimes significantly. The Stockholm International Peace Research Institute (SIPRI) listed 31 major conflicts in 26 different locations during 1998. The International Institute of Strategic Studies (IISS) counted 35 major conflicts for the year 1998–9. The Center for Defense Information in Washington counted 38 major conflicts in 1999, and listed 14 conflicts 'in suspension' that had the potential to restart quickly.

Since 1945 UNESCO has counted over 150 conflicts throughout the world, and has calculated that the number of deaths caused by war in the post-war period is around 20 million (among 60 million total casualties) of whom most are civilians.

It may be going too far to describe run-of-the-mill interstate wars as rational and civilized, but there is a grain of sense in the thought. Ethnic wars are quite different. They are not about the pursuit of interests as normally understood. They are about malevolence and they are unrestrained by any legal or moral rules. 'Ethnic cleansing', like 'the final solution', is surely one of the most sinister phrases to enter the political vocabulary of the twentieth century.[2]

It is ironic that authoritarian governments, so frequently blamed for interstate wars, were instrumental in preventing civil wars in countries like Yugoslavia and the Soviet Union. Hobbes's Leviathian may have its attractions if the alternative is genocidal violence. If the thousands of ethnic groups that exist in the world can no longer be contained within nation states, then we face the break-up of international society into a myriad of micro-groups. The consequences of 'Balkanization' on this scale are unlikely to lead to a more peaceful world.

Wars between states and wars between nations and tribes within states are depressingly familiar, but the idea that future conflicts in global politics will occur between civilizations is a new one. In a provocative and influential article in *Foreign Affairs*, Huntington predicted that the fundamental source of future conflict will be *cultural*. 'The fault lines between civilizations would be the battle lines of the future' (1993*a*: 22). In Europe, for example, as the ideological divisions of the cold war disappeared, the age-old cultural divisions between Western Christendom on the one hand and Orthodox Christianity and Islam on the other reappeared. As W. Wallace has suggested, 'the most significant dividing line in Europe may well be the eastern boundary of Western Christianity in the year 1500'.[3] This cultural fault weaves its way from the Baltic to the Mediterranean and conflict along it is to be expected.

Huntington argues that a civilization is 'the highest cultural grouping of people and the broadest level of cultural identity people have' (1993*a*: 24). He has distinguished eight civilizations—Western, Japanese, African, Latin American, Confucian, Hindu, Islamic, and Slavic Orthodox—that differ from each other in terms of their attitudes towards democracy, free markets, liberalism, church–state relations, and international intervention. The differences between civilizations on these issues is deeper than those between states or ideologies. As a result, international consensus and agreement will become increasingly difficult to achieve. Among the reasons for thinking inter-civilizational conflict is likely is that in many parts of the world 'Western' values are being challenged. There is a resurgence of religion and fundamentalism that has widened the gulf between peoples. The 'communications revolution' also has served to make people more aware of the differences that divide them.

KEY POINTS

- As interstate war has waned, intra-state conflict has become more frequent.

- Ethnic conflicts do not easily fit the Clausewitzian model. They are particularly violent and people are often killed because

- of who they are rather than because of their behaviour and politics.

- In the future, some writers suggest, wars may be between 'civilizations' rather than between states or ethnic groups.

Conclusion

There is no shortage of 'cures' for the 'disease' of war. Some are bizarre. For example, Linus Pauling once suggested that wars are caused by a vitamin deficiency and that we could eat our way out of aggression by swallowing the appropriate tablets. Others—like calls to change human nature, to reconstruct the state system, to redistribute equitably the world's wealth, to abolish armaments, or to 're-educate' mankind—follow with faultless logic from the various causes of war which scholars have identified. But since there is no prospect of implementing them in the foreseeable future, in a sense they are not solutions at all. Henry IV's reputed comment on an equally impractical proposal for peace is still appropriate: 'It is perfect', the king said, 'Perfect. I see no single flaw in it save one, namely, that no earthly prince would ever agree to it.' Hedley Bull has rightly condemned such solutions as 'a corruption of thinking about international relations and a distraction from its proper concerns' (1961: 26–7).

We have to begin by recognizing the limits of what is possible. Maybe we can then edge our way forward by improving our techniques of diplomacy, communication, crisis avoidance, and crisis management; by developing a concept of enlightened self-interest which is sensitive to the interests of others; by extending the scope of international law and building on existing moral constraints; by learning how to manage military power through responsible civil–military relations and sophisticated measures of arms control; and by strengthening cooperation through international organizations and world trade. These are not spectacular, radical, or foolproof solutions to the problem of war. That is why practical foreign policy-making is more akin to weeding than landscape gardening. But they are practical steps that offer the possibility at least of reducing its frequency, and perhaps also of limiting its destructiveness. Even if war could be abolished, we need to remember that peace is not a panacea in which all human antagonisms are resolved. Peace is simply the absence of war, not the absence of conflict. As the cold war demonstrated, it is just as possible to wage peace as it is to wage war. Though 'peace' and 'war' are usually regarded as opposites, there is a sense in which both are aspects of the conflict that is endemic in all social life. War is simply a special kind of conflict that differs from peace only by its violent nature. The fact that peace is not a panacea explains why, when confronted with the stark choice of peace or war, leaders sometimes choose war. Some kinds of peace—under dictatorships, for example—may be worse than some kinds of war. In other words, although almost everyone wants peace, almost no one (apart from strict pacifists) wants only peace or peace at any price. If it were otherwise, the problem of war would disappear since as a last resort states can always avoid war by surrendering. Capitulation might bring peace, but it would almost certainly entail the loss of some of those other things that states want—like independence, justice, prosperity, and freedom. When it comes to the crunch, leaders may think that some fundamental values or goals are worth fighting for.

Ideally, of course, what people want is a worldwide just peace. Unfortunately, this is an unattainable dream. It would require agreement on whose justice is to prevail. It would require a redistribution of the world's wealth from the haves to the have-nots. Just peace would require religious and political movements—Muslims, Christians, Jews, Hindus, communists, capitalists—to tolerate each other. It also would require an end to cultural imperialism and an agreement that differing cultural values are equally valid. It would probably require the disappearance of borders and differentiated societies with their 'them' and 'us' mentalities. In short, it would require human beings to behave in ways in which they have never behaved. It would, to quote one scholar,[4] 'require an animal that is not what human beings are'.

Since 'justice' and 'peace' do not go together, statesmen will have to continue choosing between them. The pursuit of justice may require them to wage war, and the pursuit of peace may require them to put up with injustice. During the cold war years, Western politicians, by abandoning Eastern Europe to its fate under Communism, thought, probably rightly, that peace was more important than justice. Since the end of the cold war, they have tended to put justice before peace—witness the upsurge of violence caused by wars of intervention in support of human rights and democratic values. The critical question now is whether, in juggling the priorities of peace and justice, we have got the balance right, or whether our current enthusiasm for Western values and human rights implies an ever so slightly casual attitude to the problem of war. Perhaps, in the interests of peace, there is something to be said for the Realist policy of fighting 'necessary' rather than 'just' wars.

? QUESTIONS

1. Which of the distinctions in the earlier Box 1.1 do you think is most useful for analysing the causes of war?
2. Do you think the spread of democracy will solve the problem of war?
3. To which would you allocate priority: the pursuit of peace or the pursuit of justice?
4. Is aggressive behaviour instinctive or learnt?
5. How convincing is the argument that wars are a result of misjudgement and misperceptions?

6. Is war inevitable?

7. Is war an instrument of policy or an outburst of irrationality?

8. Are interstate wars going out of fashion?

9. If international order rests on the principle of 'non-intervention' how can military intervention in the internal affairs of sovereign states be justified?

10. Can the problem of war be solved through education?

FURTHER READING

One of the best studies of the causes of war is contained in K. Waltz, *Man, the State and War* (New York: Columbia University Press, 1959). R. Ardrey, *The Territorial Imperative* (New York: Atheneum, 1966) is one of the early studies of animal behaviour. See also K. Lorenz, *On Aggression* (New York: Bantam, 1976). For a socio-biological analysis see R. Dawkins, *The Selfish Gene* (Oxford: Oxford University Press, 1976). K. Boulding, *The Image* (Ann Arbor: University of Michigan Press, 1956) is a very useful account of the role of perception in conflict. See also the following:

■ **N. Angell, *The Great Illusion* (London: Heinemann, 1914).**

■ **H. Butterfield, *History and Human Relations* (London: Collins, 1952).**

■ **E. H. Carr, *Conditions of Peace* (London: Macmillan & Co., 1942).**

■ **R. Jervis, *Perception and Misperception in International Politics* (Princeton: Princeton University Press, 1976).**

■ **W. C. Olson, D. S. Mclellan, and F. A. Sondermann, *The Theory and Practice of International Relations*, 6th edn (Englewood Cliffs, NJ.: Prentice Hall, 1983).**

■ **H. Rauschning, *Germany's Revolution of Destruction*, tr. E. W. Dickes (London: Heinemann, 1939).**

■ **E. O. Wilson, *On Human Nature* (Cambridge, Mass.: Harvard University Press, 1978).**

More general studies of the causes of war

■ **G. Cashman, *What Causes War? An Introduction to Conflict* (New York: Lexington Books, 1993).**

■ **S. Freud, 'Why War?' in L. Bramson and G. W. Geothals, *War: Studies from Psychology Sociology Anthropology* (New York and London: Basic Books, 1968);**

■ **E. Hoffer, *The True Believer: Thoughts on the Nature of Mass Movements* (London: Secker & Warburg, 1952).**

■ **C. W. Kegley and E. R. Wittkopf, *World Politics: Trends and Transformation* (New York: St Martins Press, 1997).**

■ **G. Le Bon, *The Crowd: A Study of the Popular Mind*, 2nd edn (London: Fisher Unwin, 1897).**

■ **K. L. Nelson and S. C. Olin, Jr., *Why War: Ideology, Theory, and History* (Berkeley and Los Angeles: University of California Press, 1979).**

■ **H. Suganami, *On the Causes of War* (Oxford: Clarendon Press, 1996).**

Studies of democracy and peace or ethics and conflict

■ H. Bull, *The Control of the Arms Race* (London: Weidenfeld & Nicolson, 1961).

■ M. W. Doyle, 'Kant Liberal Legacies and Foreign Affairs', *Philosophy and Public Affairs*, 12 (1983).

—— 'Liberalism and World Politics', *American Political Science Review*, 80 (1986).

■ A. L. Gowans, *Selections from Treitschke's Lectures on Politics* (London and Glasgow: Gowans & Gray, 1914).

—— 'Response: If not Civilizations, What? Paradigms of the Post-Cold War World', *Foreign Affairs*, 72/5 (1993*b*).

■ R. Neibuhr, *Moral Man and Immoral Society: A Study in Ethics and Politics* (New York and London: Charles Scribner's Sons, 1932).

■ K. Thompson 'Moral Purpose in Foreign Policy: Realities and Illusions', *Social Research*, 27/3 (1960).

 Visit the Online Resource Centre that accompanies this book for lots of interesting additional material http://www.oxfordtextbooks.co.uk/orc/baylis_strategy2e/.

2

The Evolution of Modern Warfare

MICHAEL SHEEHAN

Chapter Contents

- The Napoleonic Legacy
- The Industrialization of War
- Naval Warfare
- Total War
- Nuclear Weapons and Revolutionary Warfare
- Postmodern War

Reader's Guide

This chapter looks at the way that the theory and practice of war has changed over the past two hundred years. It examines the ways in which the development of modern states have changed the way that wars are fought and looks at the impact of the industrial revolution on the planning for, and conduct of war. It also looks at the influence of some of the key thinkers on war in the past two centuries. War is a social practice, and the conduct of war is influenced by changes in military theory, in the development of new technologies, and crucially, by the evolution of society itself.

The Napoleonic Legacy

War has been a perennial feature of human history. Yet its nature is paradoxical. It is condemned as a base activity in which human beings show the darker side of their nature by using violence and killing to achieve their ends. Yet at the same time war is a peculiarly *social* activity, demanding high levels of organization, and depending upon bonds of loyalty, obedience, and solidarity for its effective prosecution. It is a phenomenon condemned by governments as a menace to stability, order, and progress, yet embraced in self-defence or to pursue political objectives. War can be 'the father of all things' and it can threaten total annihilation.

In the modern period, war between developed states assumed a particular form, characterized by a symbiotic relationship with increasingly well-organized states, the *industrialization of warfare*, and a growing totality in the manner in which it was conducted. In many ways this 'modern' era of warfare was historically unusual. In much of recorded history, wars were typically fought by much smaller armies, for more limited objectives, and absorbed a smaller overall proportion of the states resources than was typical in the modern period. By the end of the twentieth century however, there was some evidence that this era of 'modern' industrial warfare might be ending and a new one beginning.

What do we mean by 'modern' warfare? The answer is simultaneously obvious and controversial. It is the forms of warfare shaped by and reflecting the 'modern' era of human history. But modernity and modern war mean much more than simply technological progress and wars fought with increasingly sophisticated and mass-produced weaponry. The nineteenth-century military theorist Carl von Clausewitz said that the prevailing form of war always reflects the era in which it occurs, and this is certainly the case with modern warfare. It should be noted however, that in any era there is more than just one characteristic *form* of war. The nature of the combatants, and the social and geographical context, means that war shows many faces, apart from that typical of conflicts between the great powers of the day.

The development of modern warfare is the story of modernity playing itself out in the military sphere, as a result of the transformational impact it had on intellectual, political, social, and economic life. Modern warfare developed in terms of a number of broad themes that were increasingly characteristic of society as a whole, such as the growing power of the state through processes of centralization, bureaucratization, and to some extent, democratization. It was influenced by the rise of powerful ideologies, such as nationalism. Other important developments were the rapid development of technological progress and industrialization driven by the scientific method, an associated rapid rise in national populations and a growing insistence that in return for the benefits brought by living in an advanced state, the citizen owed a duty to defend the state and to promote its international well-being through compulsory service in the armed forces in time of conflict.

These forces materialized during the course of the nineteenth and early twentieth centuries in terms of a military revolution focused on mass conscript armies, of ideologically motivated citizens, armed with mass-produced, long-range weapons of incredible killing power, and logistically sustained by industrialized economies that could maintain armies on distant fronts almost indefinitely. These processes produced a form of war where the absolute defeat of the enemy was the objective, and the entire population of the opposing state became potential targets. It was an evolution towards 'total war', which saw its apotheosis in the Second World War (1939–45).

The second half of the eighteenth century in Europe had been characterized by comparatively 'limited' warfare. A number of factors contributed to this development. The spread of the rationalist values of the Enlightenment, and the lingering memory of the horrors of the religious wars of the seventeenth century were influential. Socio-economic factors were also important. The dynastic states of the period had limited tax and recruiting bases. In some states, such as Britain and the Dutch Republic, there were constitutional limitations on the size of the army and the ways in which it could be used.

All states faced major difficulties in both recruiting and retaining soldiers. Military service was not popular and most armies relied upon a combination of long-service professionals and foreign mercenaries. Such professionals were expensive to recruit and train, and governments encouraged their generals not to risk such expensive assets in pitched battles.

Military factors also tended towards limitation. The linear warfare of the age required the soldiers to have great training and discipline, and such trained troops were too valuable to be lightly thrown away. Fighting in line or square meant that infantry could only move very slowly, making it difficult to take opposing armies by surprise or to pursue them to the point of destruction, no matter how keen they were to do so. The ferocious discipline of armies encouraged desertion, making generals reluctant to release their troops for the unrelenting pursuit that might bring absolute victory.

The shadow of the horrors of the previous century also meant that commanders were reluctant to allow their soldiers to pillage. This meant that armies had to carry all their supplies with them, or else amass huge stockpiles of supplies at depots in advance, to which they were subsequently tied. Supply limitations and poorly developed road networks also restricted the size of the armies that states could put into the field.

The eighteenth century saw a number of revolutions. Some of these proved of enduring importance in the development of modern warfare, notably the Industrial Revolution and the French Revolution. Both of these transformations significantly reshaped the relationship between warfare and the societies from which it sprang.

Many of the transformative ideas that characterized the military results of the French revolution had in fact appeared in earlier decades. Eighteenth-century standing armies were as efficient as was possible within the limitations of the political and social structures of the age, but for a variety of reasons, drew on only a limited proportion of the national manpower. French thinkers such as Montesquieu and Rousseau had promoted the idea that in a democracy, a citizen should have an obligation to defend his country and that the army should essentially be the people in arms. Nor was such thinking confined to the *Philosophes*. Military thinkers such as Guibert also advocated the recruiting of a citizen army. Guibert also called for the abandonment of the depot system, and a return to pillage and 'living off the land'.

In a conservative monarchy such as France, such ideas were dangerously radical, and unlikely to be implemented. The basis for change occurred in 1792, with the flight, arrest, and subsequent execution of King Louis XVI, and the creation of the French Republic.

To defend itself against its many enemies the revolutionary regime embraced a radical new approach to the conduct of war, including the creation of a citizen army raised by conscription, the beginnings of economic regimentation and large-scale war production, as well as ideological warfare and indoctrination. These were features typical of modern warfare, rather than the limited 'cabinet wars' of the eighteenth century.

The introduction of conscription in 1793 led to a vast increase in the size of the French armies. The scale of warfare was also affected by other developments, which changed the nature of war. These included the idea of the nation in arms, the impact of ideology and nationalist fervour, and the meritocratic promotions that altered the class basis of the officer corps.

Unlike the limited war of the eighteenth century, the purpose of ideological war became the complete overthrow of the enemy. Rather than minor territorial gains, the objective of war became massive gains or even outright annexation, often involving the overthrow of the existing conservative order. In the Revolutionary and Napoleonic period the French army deliberately sought out battle, and the army's ability to manoeuvre quickly compelled the enemy to fight or retreat.

The huge French army produced by conscription was more than just a larger version of a typical eighteenth-century army. The circumstances of its creation made it different in kind as well as in size. It represented the nation in arms, and a nation marked by ideological and patriotic fervour. This contributed crucially to the changing nature of war.

The French Revolution allowed France to raise mass armies, and these proved decisive in the early years of Napoleon's empire. Only the difficulties of supplying such huge numbers in the age before railways and mass production held back the growth in the size of armies. One of France's greatest generals from the Age of Reason, Maurice de Saxe, had argued that 50,000 men was the maximum practical size for an army. But by 1812, Napoleon invaded Russia with an army of nearly 600,000.

The huge armies raised new issues for generals and strategists. They were too large to be easily moved along a single road, but to spread them along several parallel roads left them vulnerable to being defeated in detail. The creation of the corps system overcame this danger, since each corps was essentially a small army, with its own infantry, cavalry, and artillery, powerful enough to defend against the enemy army until the rest of the French army could be concentrated, yet small enough to advance rapidly. Prior to the French Revolution, the largest unit in an army was the brigade, composed of several battalions of infantry, or regiments of cavalry. The revolution introduced the division, a grouping of several brigades into a larger formation. Napoleon then combined several divisions into *army corps*, effectively small armies of up to 50,000 men, comprising infantry, artillery, and cavalry units. Mobile infantry divisions could be accompanied by field artillery which was lighter and more mobile and capable of being mass produced. Powerful artillery bombardment would now become a feature of battle, and casualties would reflect this. This development had been advocated before the revolution by Du Teil, who emphasized the advantage of concentrating artillery at the point of attack, rather than spreading it along the line of battle.

The new massive armies posed another problem: they were difficult to feed and supply. The traditional supply depots used by eighteenth century armies were soon left behind by the rapidly moving corps, yet the supplies required were so great that they would dramatically slow the army if it had to transport them with it. The solution was a reversion to pre-eighteenth-century practice, a practice condemned as barbaric during the Age of Reason. This was for the army to 'live off the land', to forage ruthlessly in the territories through which it marched.

This in turn meant that war necessarily had to be offensive war. Such foraging could not be practised in one's own country without producing economic and political disaster, so it must be carried abroad where the war could be made to pay for itself. But in doing so, it encouraged an attitude of callous indifference towards the sufferings of those in the lands so pillaged, and triggered a resort to guerrilla war against the French from the peasants who had suffered at their hands. Indeed the Spanish word *guerrilla* comes from the 'little war' practised by the Spanish insurgents against their French occupiers.

With huge numbers of soldiers at their disposal, generals such as Napoleon Bonaparte felt able to squander the lives of their soldiers on a lavish scale in pursuit of military and political ambition. As revolutionary fervour faded, and casualty lists grew, the huge French armies had increasingly to be maintained through the use of the totalitarian powers which the new modern state possessed, which were far greater than the old monarchical regime had at its disposal. Napoleon's empire ultimately conscripted more than three million men and he boasted that he had an 'income' of 200,000 men a year.

In the eighteenth century military thinkers placed little emphasis on numbers. Wars were characterized by manœuvres and sieges and the genius of the commanding general was felt to count for far more than relative numbers. The French successes in the Napoleonic period undermined this view, and in turn eventually encouraged the equally erroneous assumption that *only* numbers were decisive.

The most striking feature of Napoleon's campaigns is the frequency of battle. Unlike his eighteenth-century predecessors, Napoleon commanded armies that could move rapidly enough to *force* their opponents to give battle. He exploited this capacity to the full, deliberately seeking battle in order to defeat the enemy's army, and then to destroy them with an unrelenting pursuit. Destroying a country's army in this way would then allow him to occupy and control the enemy's resources and leave them helpless to resist any political demands that France chose to make (Jones 1987: 350). A classic example of such warfare

---

BOX 2.1

Napoleonic Warfare

At its apogee, the Napoleonic way of war threw armies of unprecedented size on country-smashing campaigns of conquest through decisive manoeuvre and, usually battle. The forces employed to accomplish such heroic tasks were an assemblage of professional soldiers, fairly patriotic French conscripts, and sundry (but increasingly reluctant foreign) mercenaries. The soldiery was articulated into autonomous *corps d'armee* and led with a variable operational artistry by the Zeus of modern war, the Corsican mastermind himself, variously aided and frequently abetted by his Imperial Headquarters (*very* approximate general staff) and, after 1804, his Marshalate. In its prime, which is to say in 1805–07, the Napoleonic style at least appeared to restore the power of swift decision to war as an instrument of foreign policy.

(Gray 2003: 140)

was the 1806 campaign against Prussia. The Prussian army was shattered at the twin battles of Jena–Auerstadt, and then destroyed by a vigorous and continuous pursuit, which over-ran much of Prussia and saw the surrender of most of its soldiers.

KEY POINTS

- The Napoleonic period saw the emer-gence of mass armies produced by con-scription.

- Napoleonic warfare focused on seeking decisive battle in order to destroy the opponent's army and his capacity to resist.

- Ideology and nationalism helped to pro-duce a more ruthless form of warfare and generated resistance by guerrilla war in many countries.

Clausewitz

Carl von Clausewitz (1780–1831) was a Prussian career soldier, with extensive experience of the conduct of war at all levels. His thought was influenced by the German nationalism of Schiller and Goethe and by numerous military writers, such as Berenhorst, who had argued that 'war is a natural social phenomenon, susceptible to analysis' and Von Bulow, who declared that 'victory is not the fruit of theory, but of the proper mobilization of all the resources of the state'. Much of his later career was spent as the Director of the Prussian Military Academy, where he developed the ideas expounded in his classic book, *On War*.

Clausewitz's ideas on war marked a break from the social and political optimism of the eighteenth century. Though he saw war as a political instrument, guided by rational decision-making, he emphasized that it depended on the willingness to inflict violence and to suffer casualties. The purpose of war was to seek battle and to impose one's will on the opponent through violence.

Clausewitz emphasized that victory would come when the opponent's centre of gravity, the focal point of his power, was captured or destroyed. The destruction of the adversary's armed forces was the key to political victory, but this destruction was moral, not *necessarily* physical. It was the destruction of his capacity to resist, though for Clausewitz decisive battle was the surest way to achieve this outcome, and the heart of the enemy army was normally the decisive centre of gravity. Though tactics and strategies could be pursued that were designed to create a decisive advantage on the battlefield, for Clausewitz, numbers were ultimately decisive, all other things being equal. For many, this logic would be deci-sively demonstrated in the Prussian victories over Austria in 1866 and France in 1870.

Clausewitz's view that war represented a continuation of politics, rather than its break-down, also marked a change from Enlightenment thinking. In time his ideas would become decisively influential, though many of his disciples failed to note the caveats in some of his arguments, and underplayed his emphasis on the power of the defensive in war. Although reflecting the lessons of Napoleonic warfare, Clausewitz's thinking was sub-tle and imaginative enough to remain of relevance throughout the period of industrialized mass warfare, and into the age of nuclear weapons and limited war.

BOX 2.2

Clausewitz: Key Ideas

- War is a normal part of politics, differing only in its means.
- War is an act of violence designed to achieve otherwise unattainable goals.
- Each age creates its own form of war.
- War is something in which the entire nation must take part.
- Since war involves people, it is inherently unpredictable.
- Victory is of no value unless it is a means to achieve a political objective.
- Other things being equal, numbers are ultimately decisive.

The Industrialization of War

During the nineteenth century warfare became industrialized in two important senses. Modern technology was applied to the production of more sophisticated weaponry, but in addition a wide variety of developments in essentially civilian technologies proved immensely important for the future conduct of war. Weaponry, ammunition, and all the other material of war could now be mass produced. Armies of much greater size could now be sustained on campaign. Small developments such as the ability to store tinned food made it easier to provide food supplies for campaigning even in harsher winter months. Supplies could be moved quickly to the front in great quantities using the new railways. The first rail journey was made in 1825, and by 1846 Prussia was able to move an army corps, with all its equipment, 250 miles in two days, rather than the two weeks a march would have required. (Preston and Wise 244).

The use of railways meant not only that soldiers could be moved quickly, but that they remained relatively fit and untired at the end of their journey, an important consideration with armies largely composed of reservists. The railway could be used to move wounded troops to rear area hospitals, improving their chances of survival.

This was beneficial for maintaining army strength and for the morale effect on the troops. Railways could also bring replacements and reinforcements on a more regular basis. This meant that states could produce and maintain the mass armies required of Napoleonic warfare. The difficulty of supplying such huge forces, which had limited the size of eighteenth-century armies, no longer applied. In 1870, Prussia invaded France with an army twice the size of the one Napoleon had led into Russia sixty years earlier. The much smaller French army, which had not been able to mobilize quickly enough, was simply overwhelmed. By 1914 the forces employed had doubled again and Germany attacked France with nearly three and a half million men, and her enemies were deploying armies of comparable sizes.

The strategic value of railways was quickly realized. France moved 120,000 men to Italy during its 1859 war with Austria, but failed to move their associated supplies, limiting the army's effectiveness. Two years later, however, the utility of railways for strategic advantage was clearly demonstrated in the opening campaign of the American Civil War. In July 1861, the movement of Johnson's Valley Army to Manassas enabled the Confederacy to achieve numerical parity and to win the Battle of First Manassas, when a defeat might have led to an almost immediate end to the Civil War. The United States subsequently organized a Military Railway Department which played an important role in the ultimate Federal victory in the war, but not before the Confederacy had used the railway system to achieve important strategic advantages in the Kentucky campaign of 1862 and Chickamauga campaign of 1863, while the United States countered the Chickamauga setback with a massive rail movement of reinforcements to relieve besieged Chattanooga. During the Franco-Prussian War of 1870, the superior Prussian use of railways enabled it to heavily outnumber the opposing French armies and overwhelm them.

Another civilian technology of immediate military importance was the telegraph, which allowed political leaderships and theatre commanders to maintain communications with army leaders over distances that would previously have meant delays of days or weeks in communicating orders.

The impact of industrialization also showed itself directly in the weaponry and equipment of the armies themselves. Eighteenth-century strategy and tactics had been built around the restrictions imposed by the smooth bore musket, an inaccurate weapon with an effective range of less than one hundred yards. To achieve real effect, such weapons had to be massed, with infantry forming long, wide firing lines, which were difficult to manoeuvre and that could not advance rapidly.

During the course of the nineteenth century, however, a series of crucial developments in weapons technology transformed both strategy and tactics. Infantry weapons were revolutionized by the introduction of rifled gun barrels, smokeless cartridges, breachloading, and eventually magazine weapons. Rifled weapons were far more accurate, and infantry could now hit their targets at ranges of several hundred yards, without necessarily exposing themselves to counterfire. Rifled weapons rapidly proved their superiority in the early stages of the American Civil War and breachloaders became standard in European armies after the Prussian success using them in the 1866 Austro-Prussian War. In 1884 Prussia introduced the eight-shot magazine rifle. Repeating weapons had been introduced prior to this with mixed success. US cavalry armed with repeating carbines achieved a decisive superiority over their Confederate opponents in the closing stages of the American Civil War. However, the machine gun, which the French army possessed in 1870, was so poorly understood and unintelligently deployed that it initially had no impact whatsoever. By 1884 the development of the Maxim machine gun produced an effective weapon which would revolutionize tactics.

During the 1860s rifled artillery also became the norm, and even muzzle loading examples had ranges of two miles. By 1870 Prussia had produced efficient breach loading rifled artillery, which outranged those of their French opponents, giving them a huge tactical advantage. In the 1890s quick-firing technology increased the effectiveness of artillery still further.

The experience of the American Civil War (1861–5) and Franco-Prussian War (1870–71) demonstrated that the new weapons made it extremely difficult for infantry to successfully close with their enemy and suffered very heavy casualties if circumstances forced them to carry such attacks through. Battles such as Malvern Hill, Fredericksburg, and Gettysburg in the American War and Gravelotte in the Franco-Prussian War, were characterized by infantry suffering very heavy casualties against prepared defenders. When manoeuverability was lost and the enemy entrenched, the difficulties for the attacker became even greater, as the final months of the Civil War in the east demonstrated.

However, European strategists largely missed the significance of this lesson between 1871 and 1914, preferring to believe, on the evidence of the Prussian wars of 1866 and 1870, that mass armies, rapidly transported to the military theatre by train, and manoeuvring swiftly thereafter, would guarantee quick victory to the side prepared to take the offensive. Overlooked was the danger posed if the defender also mobilized rapidly and used railways as efficiently to mass defenders in the attacking army's path (Quester 1977: 80). The wars of the mid-nineteenth century had provided mixed lessons. The Crimean War and Franco-Austrian War had seen the early use of rifled weapons and railways, but in many ways had been characteristically Napoleonic conflicts. The Austro-Prussian War of 1866 had seen the use of mass armies and the importance of technological superiority, but had otherwise demonstrated none of the elements of total war, indeed, Prussia's peace demands were strikingly moderate. This was not the case with the Franco-Prussian War, which saw not only the effective use of staffwork, railways, and the telegraph, but also heavy casualties produced by the new long-range rifled weaponry. Ominously the French defeat had also triggered political revolution and regime change in France, guerrilla warfare against the Prussians by the Francs-Tireurs, and often savage reprisals by the occupying German forces.

European observers in addition failed to take regard of the warnings from outside Europe. Colonial warfare was often notably savage but indecisive, and in addition, a number of the large-scale wars fought outside Europe in the second half of the nineteenth century were all too modern in many respects and demonstrated many of the features of twentieth-century total war. The American Civil War was at the same time the last of the old wars and the first of the new. It was an ideological struggle to the death between two

---

BOX 2.3

Colonial Warfare

Although histories of war tend to focus on the collisions between the major powers in the nineteenth century, for many states, notably Britain, France, and Spain, colonial and imperial campaigns against non-European enemies absorbed much of their military energies and attention. Such conflicts were often characterized by extreme brutality. Decisive victories for the European powers were rare and were invariably followed by years of indecisive guerrilla warfare. Colonial commanders frequently resorted to massacres and the deliberate destruction of the local population's homes and food supplies in order to undermine their opponents' guerrilla campaigns. The contemporary military writer C. E. Callwell argued that 'in small wars, one is sometimes forced into committing havoc that the laws of regular warfare do not sanction'. It was a form of war from which European generals derived few lessons for European war, yet it was a precursor of the total war of the first half of the twentieth century, and a style of war that in some ways would be echoed in the so-called 'New Wars' that followed the end of the cold war.

incompatible nationalisms, which saw the use of mass conscription, a wide range of novel technologies, including rifled weapons, steamships, landmines, barbed wire, and observation balloons. Over 20 per cent of the Southern population fought in the war and the Confederacy enlisted nearly 90 per cent of its available military manpower. Casualties were extremely heavy on both sides and Union forces deliberately targeted the southern civilian population in the Atlanta and Shenandoah campaigns of 1864, General Sherman declaring that 'we are not only fighting hostile armies, but a hostile people and must make old and young, rich and poor, feel the hard hand of war'. However, for the most part it was property rather than the lives of civilians that was targeted (O'Connell 1989:201). Even more savage was the Great Paraguayan War between Brazil, Argentina, and Paraguay which saw the death of over half of Paraguay's male population. Similarly, the Second Boer War of 1899–1902 saw heavy military casualties in the face of the new weaponry, the incarceration of Boer civilians in British 'concentration' camps, guerrilla warfare by the Boers, and repressive countermeasures by the British that soured relations between the two communities for the next century. All these lessons were repeated in the Russo-Japanese War, characterized by massive armies, horrendous casualties, battlefronts of enormous length, and battles that went on day and night, for weeks on end.

KEY POINTS

- The nineteenth century saw the industrial revolution dramatically alter the conduct of war.

- Civilian technologies such as railways, steamships, the telegraph, and mass production made it possible to raise, equip, and control huge armies.

- New weapons such as rifled and breech-loading weapons, machine guns, armoured warships, mines, and submarines made their appearance.

- Governments sought to mobilize their populations to support the war effort.

- Because tactics were slow to change, heavy casualties were typical.

Naval Warfare

Naval warfare went through an equally dramatic revolution during the nineteenth century. During the Napoleonic Wars warships were made of wood and powered by the wind, as they had been for centuries. But as the century progressed they were increasingly armoured in metal, equipped with long-range rifled weapons and most importantly, given engines that enabled them to operate independently of the wind. In 1822 General Paixans published *Nouvelle force maritime*, in which he argued that ships armed with explosive shells and protected with armour plate would be able to annihilate the existing wooden, cannon armed warships (McNeil 1982: 226). The European navies began adopting such naval artillery in the 1830s and steam engines were introduced in the 1840s. The application of armour plate soon followed.

It was France which led the way in naval design in the mid-nineteenth century, with Britain being reluctant to encourage developments that might challenge her supremacy at sea. For decades warships combined sail and steam propulsion, but as guns became more powerful, they needed to be based in revolving turrets, for which masts and sails were an obstacle. Britain launched the first battleship without any sails in 1873. So rapid was the pace of technological development in warships in the last quarter of the century that ships were sometimes obsolete before they could be launched (Howarth 1974:331).

Although warship design was undergoing rapid evolution, strategic thinking about naval warfare was slow to evolve. Only towards the end of the century did significant developments take place. In 1890 Alfred Mahan published *The Influence of Seapower on History, 1660–1783*. The book became enormously widely read, partly because the previous decades had seen such rapid change that naval officers were struggling to keep pace with its implications. Mahan argued that naval power had always been crucial in history, that the purpose of a great power's navy was to attain command of the sea, and that the way to achieve this was to concentrate naval capabilities in a powerful battlefleet and to seek out and destroy the major battlefleet or fleets of the enemy. The influence of Clausewitz on his thinking in this regard was obvious.

New schools of naval thought were emerging, which were unsettling to traditional naval commanders. For example, the *Jeune Ecole* in France argued that new systems such as torpedo boats would make commerce raiding the primary form of naval warfare in the future. Proponents of the new technologies argued that the massive battlefleets of countries like Britain would be made obsolete by submarines and torpedo boats.

These ideas alarmed proponents of traditional naval power in Britain, Germany, and Japan. Navalists, such as Colomb in Britain, Von Maltzen in Germany, and Saneyuki in Japan, argued that seapower would continue to dominate the world, because of its inherent advantages of mobility and flexibility. Admiral Columb's *Naval Warfare: Its Ruling Principles and Practices Historically Treated*, appeared at the same time as Mahan's book. Mahan himself dismissed the idea that attacks on commerce should be a navy's primary role in wartime, insisting that battlefleets would dominate the sea, and thereby dominate the world.

Mahan's ideas were in contrast to those contained in the *geopolitics* of Sir Halford Mackinder. Mackinder argued that world domination would go to the *landpower* that controlled the Eurasian landmass in the era of railways. The theory downplayed the importance of naval power in the contemporary world. These ideas alarmed the navalists, who were therefore happy to subscribe to Mahan's theories. Navalist writers argued that national power, security, and prosperity depended on seaborne trade, and that therefore the countries with large merchant fleets and powerful navies would continue to dominate the world, as they always had. Certainly, the pattern of the previous three hundred years had seen the countries that were dominant at sea prove consistently successful against the major landpowers.

The navalists emphasized that movement of goods in bulk by sea had always been easier and cheaper than by land, and that for most commodities this remained the case even in the railway era. Therefore the use and control of the sea lanes was crucial to the successful accumulation of national wealth. And in the final analysis, it was wealth and economic power that made it possible for a state to maintain powerful armed forces. Of whatever kind.

The proponents of naval power envisaged war at sea in terms strongly reminiscent of key features of Napoleonic and Clausewitzian land warfare. Once the main enemy battlefleet had been located and destroyed, command of the sea could then be exploited by the protection of one's own trade, and the destruction of the enemy's trade, and by the projection of military power ashore.

A somewhat more balanced view was offered by the British naval theorist, Sir Julian Corbett. Corbett stressed a different aspect of Clausewitz's thought, arguing that seapower was no more than a means to a political end. It was therefore important for a state to have a maritime strategy that was in tune with its political aspirations. But Corbett was well aware that seapower on its own could not overwhelm a strong and resolute landpower. Seapower had its limits, and a major naval power like Britain had historically always needed continental allies with landpower at their disposal. He also argued that there was far more to maritime strategy than simply the pursuit of decisive battles.

During the First World War most of the new technologies failed to be decisive and simply made the fleet commanders more cautious. Britain imposed a naval blockade on Germany, which ultimately made a major contribution to the Allied victory. Britain also sought to bring the main German fleet to battle, but the encounters at Dogger Bank in 1915 and Jutland in 1916 were not decisive. Jutland was a tactical victory for the German fleet, but a strategic victory for the British, since the German fleet never again challenged the British and was therefore unable to counter the Allied blockade. Nevertheless, British commanders remained frustrated by their inability to force a decisive 'Mahanian' battle of annihilation. In fact Jutland would turn out to be the last fleet action between battleships in history.

Germany turned instead to submarine warfare, and the submarine campaigns would be vital in both world wars. By late 1917 British merchant shipping losses were becoming almost unsustainable, but as would happen in the Second World War, the introduction of the convoy system, along with better tactics and equipment, allowed the Allies to defeat the German submarine challenge. In the end neither the *navalists* nor the *Jeune Ecole* were vindicated by the outcome of the war at sea, which saw the battlefleets prove largely impotent. The torpedo proved a crucial, but not a war-winning weapon.

Nevertheless, seapower was important to the outcome of the First World War. Allied naval superiority allowed them to seize Germany's overseas colonies, and to impose the ultimately devastating blockade. It also allowed the Allies to transport enormous quantities of men and material from outside Europe to the war zone, including one million French soldiers and two million American troops.

KEY POINTS

- The British navy emerged dominant from the Napoleonic Wars, which saw numerous fleet actions, culminating in the Battle of Trafalgar in 1805.

- Naval technology was revolutionized during the nineteenth century.

- Steam power gave navies even greater flexibility and manoeuvrability.

- Heavy guns in revolving turrets, plus armoured warships produced a new generation of all-gun ironclad battleships.

- Mahan argued that fleets of such warships would dominate the seas, while the *Jeune Ecole* insisted that submarines and torpedo boats would be decisive.

Total War

By the beginning of the twentieth century, the major powers had come to accept the Clausewitzian idea that the threat and use of war were appropriate instruments of political purpose in the industrial era, to be resorted to whenever circumstances required. The experience of the European wars of 1864, 1866, and 1870 encouraged the great powers to believe that any future war between the major powers would be both short and decisive.

But by 1914 the political, economic, social, technological, and doctrinal trends of the nineteenth century had coalesced into a recipe for catastrophe. Doctrinally, armies were convinced of the virtues of Napoleonic warfare—mass armies, seeking out the army of the adversary, enveloping it, destroying it, and then pursuing the remnants of the enemy forces until his ability to resist any political demands had been crushed. Conscription and nationalism would provide the mass armies, which would be transported and supplied using the railway networks and the industrialised economies of mass production. Rapid manoeuvre, combined with the killing power of advanced weaponry, would deliver swift victory to the army that could mobilize and manoeuvre most efficiently.

But by 1914 the battlefield in reality had grown in size enormously in comparison to the Napoleonic era, and so had the armies that occupied it. By the winter of 1914, the trench line on the western front stretched from Switzerland to the English Channel. There were no flanks to go round, and no way of 'enveloping' the enemy army, which by this period consisted of over three million men on each side. Nor could the armies move as rapidly as the era of railways and aeroplanes might suggest. In 1914 warfare was still not fully mechanised. The German army advanced into Belgium and France in 1914 with less than 7,000 motor vehicles, but with 726,000 horses and 150,000 wagons (Addington 1994: 104).

Armed with powerful defensive weapons such as machine guns and long-range artillery, protected by trenches and barbed wire, and supplied with all the resources that the railways could deliver from a mobilized industrial economy, defending armies could not be swiftly shattered and dispersed in the Napoleonic fashion. The defending forces enjoyed an unprecedented ratio of force to space, making the stalemate which followed virtually inevitable. Once this stalemate had been created, it became a war not of rapid military offensives, but of 'economic and human endurance' (Quester 1977: 114).

The enemy had to be worn down by brutal frontal assaults that produced enormous casualty figures, while technological advances were sought which might break the battlefield stalemate. Germany attacked with *poison gas* at Ypres in 1915, while the British introduced *tanks* in the closing stage of the Battle of the Somme in 1916.

The conflict also saw war moving into a new dimension as airpower became increasingly important. Aircraft were used for reconnaissance from the beginning of the war, and fighters evolved to destroy the reconnaissance aircraft. As the war continued, aircraft were increasingly used for tactical fire and bombing support to ground forces, and eventually for long-range strategic bombing. In their reconnaissance and raiding roles, the aircraft of the First World War essentially took on the role played by light cavalry in the Napoleonic period, just as tanks took on the role previously played by heavy cavalry.

Increasingly, too, warfare became more total in its scope and application. Because it was so difficult to break through in the main theatre of war, the geographical scope of war expanded as the combatants sought to place additional pressure on the opponent by opening new theatres of operations, such as Italy, the Balkans, and the Middle East.

The expansion of the geographical scope of war was accompanied by a greater willingness to deliberately target non-combatants. In the First World War this was seen in the use of unrestricted submarine warfare, with merchant ships being sunk without the crews being given a chance to take to the lifeboats, as Germany attempted to prevent France and Britain from being supplied by sea. It was seen also in the blockade of Germany, which, though it made a critical contribution to Germany's military collapse in the autumn of 1918, also caused enormous civilian suffering and death. Both Germany and Britain inaugurated the long-range bombing of cities by aircraft.

In the growing savagery of war, governments were often not acting with deliberate brutality, but were carried along by the social, industrial, and scientific tide. Major war increasingly came to involve much of the manpower, material, and moral resources of the state. Any objective whose destruction promised to weaken the war effort of the enemy came to be seen as a legitimate target. Warfare was increasingly directed as much against the civilians and industries that produced the weapons of war, as against the soldiers who actually used them. The idea of illegitimate objectives or targets, of criteria of justness and proportionality, increasingly came to be seen as irrelevant to the conduct of modern war.

Totality in warfare can be assessed in terms of a number of elements, including the type of weaponry employed, the strategy and tactics used, the proportion of a state's resources that are committed, the degree to which every human and material resource of the opponent comes to be seen as a legitimate target, and the extent to which social and cultural pressures towards unrestricted warfare are operating.

The elements of totality in warfare that had become prominent in the First World War came into full flower in the Second. Once again the combatants mobilized their military, economic, and human resources to the maximum extent possible. Conscription was now extended beyond the men called up in the First World War, to embrace also the female population. Women took the place of men in agriculture and industry, but also served in huge numbers in the armed forces in non-combatant roles. In some cases, such as the Soviet Air Force, they also served as combatants. Industry and the merchant navies were taken under government control and subordinated to the war effort. Rationing was introduced to conserve supplies of vital commodities such as food and oil. Germany not only drew on its own population but, by the use of conscript and slave labour, on that of its enemies as well. The social totality of war increased still further with the systematic use of censorship and propaganda, the promotion of nationalism and demonization of the enemy, and the restriction or imprisonment of groups deemed to have suspect loyalties, such as conscientious objectors or citizens of foreign descent.

At the strategic and tactical level, the Second World War saw the implementation of military doctrines designed to restore the manœuvre and offensive capacity that had been so conspicuously absent for most of the First. Germany scored dramatic successes with its blitzkrieg tactics from 1939–41, in which combined arms tactics involving tanks, infantry, and dive-bombers sought to bypass and disrupt enemy resistance, rather than to destroy it through frontal battles of attrition.

The effectiveness of blitzkrieg owed much to the inferior doctrine of the opposing British and French armies. The Allies outnumbered the Germans in tanks in the campaign

BOX 2.4

Total War

The phrase 'total war', predates the nuclear age. In the long history of warfare, it is natural that some wars will be less limited than others. The causes, the objectives of the belligerents, their cultures and the history of their previous interactions, the beliefs and values of the era, the prospects for victory, the possibility of outside intervention—these and many other factors influence the manner and means of waging war.

Totality in war is a relative rather than an absolute concept. Total war in the absolute sense would mean fighting without any restrictions, as Ludendorf advocated in the 1920's. After the experience of Germany's defeat in the First World War, the former Commander in Chief, Erich Ludendorf was unconvinced by those in the inter-war period who argued that a particular technology such as tanks, aircraft or poison gas would bring swift victory in a future war. Nor did he believe that a tactical or strategic doctrine, such as blitzkrieg could do so.

For Ludendorf, the key to victory in war between industrialised nations, was to follow to its brutally logical conclusion, the social, economic and technological trends that had characterized warfare over the previous century. War should therefore be characterized by total mobilisation of all the military, economic and human resources of the state. The enemy's civilian population would be deliberately targeted, and one's own civilians would suffer similar assault. Mobilization of the population should therefore embrace ideological features to sustain the war effort, and a political dictatorship to focus all the states energy on winning the war.

In reality, war in the modern age saw a movement towards steadily greater totality, without ever quite reaching it.

In total war, governments are as demanding of their own citizens as they are ruthless towards their enemies. States draw on every natural resource that they can successfully mobilize, and treat virtually every element of the adversary's society as a legitimate target, using all the weapons that are available to them. The citizens of the state are obliged to serve in the armed forces or participate in the production of war-material, civil and political rights are constrained, the economy is subordinated to the war effort, every weapon, no matter how indiscriminate or terrible, is utilised, and the armed forces, industrial capacity, and the unarmed citizens of the opponent are deemed legitimate targets, because they all contribute to the enemy war effort in either tangible or psychological ways. This logic reached its height with the systematic area bombing of civilians in the Second World War, and in the cold war plans to inflict genocidal 'assured destruction' in a retaliatory nuclear strike.

In practice wars invariably fall short of totality in one or more dimensions, such as geographical scope, weaponry employed, mobilization of national resources and population, attitude towards neutrals, targeting strategies, and so on.

of 1940 and their tanks were superior in quality. However, the French viewed the tank as an infantry support weapon, as they had in 1918, while the Germans concentrated them in armoured divisions, with a view to rapid mechanized offensives. Germany also integrated its airpower to support its ground offensives. The Luftwaffe was designed for tactical support of the army, a feature that would disadvantage it in the strategic bombing campaign against Britain in 1940–1, but which made it highly effective in the blitzkrieg campaigns of 1939–41.

BOX 2.5

Blitzkreig

Blitzkreig, or 'lightning war', was the term used to describe the successful German tactics for armoured offensives in the opening phase of the Second World War. It was an attempt to overcome the defensive dominance and static warfare characteristic of most of the First World War. Like Napoleonic warfare, it was a triumph based on superior doctrine rather than technological advantage. The theory was propounded by Basil Liddell Hart, Charles de Gaulle and Heinz Guderian during the inter-war years.

Available tanks were concentrated in a limited number of Panzer (armour) divisions, along with plenty of anti-tank and anti-aircraft guns, armoured cars for reconnaissance and infantry support. The emphasis was on rapid advances designed to dislocate the enemy by breaking into the rear and throwing them off-balance. The objective was deep penetration on a narrow front. Certain supporting technologies were important, for example radios in tanks for communication and coordination. Because the speed of the advance made it difficult for heavy artillery support to keep up, tactical airpower was used as a form of artillery to help the breakthrough. The Ju-87 Stuka dive-bomber attacked defenders' positions and also attacked rear-area command and supply positions, reinforcements and even refugee columns in order to create confusion and panic ahead of the advancing Panzer divisions.

The combined arms blitzkrieg doctrine was also employed to great effect by Israel during its 1956 and 1967 wars against Egypt, and was a central feature of the concept of Operational Manœuvre Groups designed to exploit breakthroughs in late cold war Soviet armoured offensive doctrine. A crucial requirement for successful blitzkrieg is that the attacker must achieve air-superiority over the battlefield.

Nevertheless, despite the initial success of blitzkrieg, the technique did not produce ultimate German victory, and by subsequently declaring war on both the Soviet Union and the United States, Hitler condemned Germany to a war against overwhelming odds in which attrition and economic power would once more be ultimately decisive, particularly on the critical eastern front.

As with the First World War, technological advances prior to and during the war were crucial in a way that had not been typical in earlier wars. Radar helped the RAF win the Battle of Britain in 1940, while Asdic and *aircraft carriers* were crucial in the anti-submarine war in the Battle of the Atlantic. Nuclear weapons played a key role in bringing about the unconditional surrender of Japan. German technological breakthroughs, such as the ME262 jet fighter, V-1 cruise missile, and V-2 ballistic missile, became operational too late in the war to affect its outcome. In the European war it was once again mass and industrial power that proved ultimately decisive, along with Germany's strategic problem of fighting a two-front war against the American and Soviet superpowers.

Far more than the First, the Second World War was a conflict between ideologies, and the Allied demand for *unconditional surrender* in order to implement fundamental regime change ensured that the war would be fought to its bitter conclusion in both the European and Pacific theatres. The terrible casualty levels involved in a war of attrition made it effectively impossible to adopt more limited war-aims. Instead, 'the goals to be gained expanded to meet the costs borne' (Weltman 1995:135).

Whereas in the First World War the bombing of civilians had been a secondary tactic in support of the conventional ground war, in the Second it became one of the primary war-fighting strategies. The opponent's cities and populations were deliberately targeted in an attempt to break the will of the enemy to resist by laying waste to his economy and slaughtering his population. By destroying the enemy's productive capacity, such attacks would undermine the ability of his armed forces to operate effectively. This logic reached its peak with the nuclear attacks on Japan in August 1945, when civilian targets were deliberately annihilated in order to compel the Japanese government to bring to an end further resistance in the Pacific theatre.

For much of the war, strategic bombing failed to produce the dramatic results that pre-war advocates such as Douhet had predicted. Losses among the attacking aircrew were extremely heavy, forcing both the Germans and British to carry out their attacks at night, making precision bombing virtually impossible. In the closing months of the European war, as German air defences became increasingly suppressed, the Allies shifted their attacks to key production 'bottlenecks', such as oil refineries. Such attacks proved far more effective in undermining Germany's war-fighting capacity than the earlier assaults on its overall economic capability had been.

The Second World War was global in scope, and naval power was more crucial to the outcome than it had been in the First World War. As island nations, both Britain and Japan depended on resources imported by sea. In the Battle of the Atlantic, Germany sought to strangle the Anglo-American war effort by destroying the merchant shipping bringing supplies, weapons, and soldiers across the Atlantic and into the Mediterranean. Although ultimately unsuccessful, the German u-boat campaign came close to success. In the Pacific, a similar American submarine campaign had brought the Japanese war effort to its knees by the summer of 1945.

Germany succeeded in the early part of the war because land-based airpower compensated for its naval weakness. British naval losses to German air attack in the Crete campaign were equivalent to a major fleet action. Similar losses featured in the early Pacific war, with Britain losing the battleships *Prince of Wales* and *Repulse* to Japanese bombers in early 1942. However, once allied fleets had acquired effective anti-aircraft weapons and carrier-based fighter protection, navies were able to resume their offensive role once more. The early phases of the Second World War demonstrated that, both on land and at sea, obtaining air superiority, or at the very least, denying it to the enemy, had become an essential prerequisite to successful military operations. Airpower on its own could not guarantee victory, but its absence guaranteed defeat. By the end of the war, all major states had come to recognize that 'combined arms' or 'joint' warfare was the key to success in modern industrial war.

Amphibious operations were a minor feature of the First World War and the largest such operation, the landings at Gallipolli in 1915, were a tactical and strategic failure. In the Second World War in contrast, amphibious operations were crucial to the final outcome in both the European and Pacific theatres. The landings in North Africa, Sicily, Italy, and France saw major amphibious landings allow the allies to seize the strategic initiative, while the American 'island-hopping' campaign in the Pacific strategically outflanked and overcame Japanese power in the region, while ultimately moving American forces close enough to Japan to launch devastating conventional and nuclear attacks on the Japanese home islands.

In both the anti-submarine and amphibious offensive campaigns, the role of the aircraft carrier was of decisive importance. The aircraft carrier had replaced the battleship as the primary naval weapons platform, and the Second World War saw five major aircraft carrier battles in the Pacific war, as well as twenty-two other major naval engagements. The Atlantic and Mediterranean campaigns also saw major naval surface actions. In the European war, seapower was a crucial, but not a sufficient cause of the Allied victory, the Soviet land-offensives being decisive. In the Pacific however, seapower was decisive in the ultimate Allied victory.

The Second World War also saw large-scale parachute offensives. These operations were crucial in the German capture of Crete in 1941 and the Allied invasion of Normandy in 1944, as well as the Rhine crossings in 1945. The failure of the Arnhem operation in 1944 however, was a demonstration of the limitations of such forces. Unless reached by substantial heavy reinforcements quickly, parachute forces were too lightly armed to hold against armoured forces, and large-scale parachute operations did not become a feature of the post-1945 environment, though they were employed in the 1956 Anglo-French Suez war against Egypt.

KEY POINTS

- The First World War was a conflict between mass armies, which technology made difficult to decisively defeat.

- New technologies such as chemical weapons and tanks were used in an attempt to regain manœuvre and decision.

- Airpower emerged, but was not yet a decisive weapon.

- Societies were fully mobilized for the war effort.

- All of a state's economic and human resources came to be seen as legitimate targets.

- By the Second World War, airpower had become crucial as a battlefield support and as the means to launch strategic attacks against the opposing homeland. Aircraft carriers emerged as the decisive naval weapon.

- Technology, amphibious landings, and parachute operations sought to avoid the deadlock characteristic of the First World War.

Nuclear Weapons and Revolutionary Warfare

Total war reached a peak with the Second World War. The ultimate example was the destruction of the Japanese cities of Hiroshima and Nagasaki in 1945. Yet paradoxically, the unleashing of the nuclear weapon ushered in an era of limited warfare. During the

1950s, as the United States and Soviet Union acquired larger and larger stockpiles of increasingly accurate and destructive nuclear weapons, it became clear that a full-scale war between the two countries would be mutually suicidal.

As a result, both states saw it as essential to avoid a full-scale war at all costs. They therefore sought to exercise restraint in their relations with each other and to avoid taking military actions that risked escalating to a full-scale conflict which might go nuclear. For the same reason, they sought to restrain the policies and war strategies of their allies and other states over which they had influence, in order to avoid being dragged into conflicts originating elsewhere.

The so-called 'cold war' was therefore characterized not by the total war seen between 1914 and 1945, but by limited war, wars limited in terms of objectives sought, means employed, and geographical area affected. A full scale nuclear war would involve mutual assured destruction, a simultaneous genocide that bore no relation to the idea of war as a political act in the terms in which Clausewitz and his successors understood it.

However, while it was understood that strategic nuclear weapons could not perform a meaningful war-fighting role, their possession in large numbers was seen as necessary in order to deny a unilateral military and political advantage to the other side. They became central to the strategic doctrine of deterrence, while remaining outside the scope of practical war-fighting.

Tactical and to some extent theatre nuclear weapons, however, were seen as retaining a function in war. With more limited nuclear yields, and assuming they were not employed in overwhelming numbers, it was believed that they could play a role in great power war, so long as a final escalation to a full-scale strategic nuclear exchange could be avoided. The dangers involved in such an ambiguous strategy were obvious, and the evidence from wargames manœuvres conducted throughout the cold war suggested that once the nuclear threshold was crossed, escalation to full-scale strategic conflict would be virtually impossible to prevent.

Conflicts during the cold war were therefore characterized by restraint shown by the nuclear superpowers in terms of the kinds of wars they fought. In Korea and Vietnam, for example, the United States limited its war effort in terms of the weaponry used, the geographical scope of the war, and the objectives pursued, all restraints characteristic of limited, rather than total war. Similar restraint was encouraged in others. During the 1973 Arab-Israeli War, the United States and Soviet Union pressured their allies to end the fighting, because they were concerned that it might escalate and draw them into the conflict on opposing sides.

The reluctance of the most powerful states to employ the techniques of total war created an opportunity for their opponents to successfully employ asymmetric tactics and strategies against them. In the Korean War, comparative American restraint meant that the vastly less well-equipped Chinese forces were able to achieve a military stalemate and preserve the independence of communist North Korea. In the Vietnam War, despite an even more dramatic disparity in military resources between North Vietnam and the United States, the North was able to deny the USA victory and, once it had forced the US to withdraw from South Vietnam, it achieved its objective of the unification of Vietnam under a communist government. The Soviet Union encountered similar problems in its war in Afghanistan. The success of North Vietnam showed that war itself had not become an unusable instrument of policy, as some critics contended. However, the war demonstrated that in the nuclear, post-colonial age, the *form* of war was reflecting the characteristics of the age, as Clausewitz had argued would always be the case.

The cold war period was therefore characterized by smaller scale conventional wars and by campaigns of insurgency and counter-insurgency. Conventional wars tended to be limited in their outcomes and duration, and profoundly influenced by the geopolitical context of the cold war environment. The wars between Israel and its neighbours, India and Pakistan, and Ethiopia and Somalia were typical of this pattern. These wars were unusual in one respect, however, in that they were interstate conflicts. More typical was the prevalence of civil rather than international war. Most wars in the second half of the twentieth century were civil wars and insurgencies, most notably in Africa and South-East Asia. Many of these conflicts were anti-colonial conflicts, or conflicts generated by the arbitrary boundaries that colonialism left in its wake. While a 'Third World War' was successfully avoided, a 'Third World' war was not.

KEY POINTS

- Nuclear weapons ended the era of total war.

- Major powers subsequently engaged only in limited war.

- Superpower pressure deterred the escalation of other conventional conflicts.

- Insurgency and counter-insurgency were more typical forms of war.

- The 'Third World' became the arena for such conflicts.

Postmodern War

The end of the cold war also ended the classic period of nuclear deterrence and was followed by a number of wars in Eastern Europe and Africa characterized by the employment of relatively low-tech weaponry, but with very heavy death tolls. Some of these conflicts were also characterized by great savagery, leading some commentators to suggest that these conflicts were a novel form of war and that such wars would be characteristic of the post-cold war, postmodern world, and that the era of industrialized great power war had passed.

The reality is more complex than this. Some of the features identified with postmodern conflict have been present for half a century or longer and their novelty should not be exaggerated. At the same time, there are many features of the previous era that are either still recognizably present, or are evolving along trajectories that place them at odds with other aspects of postmodernity.

It can be argued that global society is in the midst of a transition from modernity to postmodernity. The architecture of world order is changing as part of a long-term process and with it will change the associated institution of war, as happened in the earlier transition to modernity in the seventeenth century. The distinctively 'modern' state is evolving in the face of globalization, and shedding some of its responsibilities to private actors.

This transition to postmodernity can be expected to influence war as a politico-cultural institution. Certain superficial aspects of conflict in the current century seem to suggest this. 'Modern' war was conducted by the state. The postmodern era has seen a dispersal of control over organized violence to many forms of non-state actors. Modern wars were fought by formally organized, hierarchically structured, specialized armed forces of the state. Postmodern wars are fought by a disparate array of fighting forces, many of which are informal or private (i.e. non-state). These include guerrilla armies, criminal gangs, foreign mercenaries, kin/clan-based irregular forces, paramilitary groups raised by local warlords, international peacekeepers, national armies, and deterritorialized terrorist networks. The war objectives of such groups are usually as political as are those of states themselves, so that war has not lost its 'Clausewitzian' character.

However, such conflicts were also characteristic of the cold war era, most of whose conflicts were internal, sub-conventional, and occurred in the Third World. The civil wars in Nigeria, Angola, and Afghanistan were typical in this respect. In many ways they also resemble earlier colonial warfare, such as the conflicts between France and indigenous North African forces in the late nineteenth and early twentieth centuries. At the same time as the shift downwards towards more low-tech wars, the so-called Revolution in Military Affairs has seen the United States at the leading edge of a technology based enhancement of conventional military capability.

The purposes and objectives of armed conflict are also changing. Modern wars originated in the pursuit of perceived national interests. Wars tended to be driven by geopolitical assumptions, such as those fought in defence of the balance of power. Postmodern wars are often focused on 'identity politics'. Power is pursued on the basis of a particular identity. These wars may break out in an effort to pursue ethnic cleansing or religiously inspired holy war. Such conflicts are often particularly ferocious. They are, however, no less political. They are conducted with strategic objectives, such as the acquisition of control over valuable resources or of the determination of state policy.

BOX 2.6

Revolution in Military Affairs

The nature and frequency of such revolutions is a matter of dispute.

Andrew Marshall emphasizes technology, declaring: 'A Revolution in Military Affairs, (RMA), is a major change in the nature of warfare brought about by the innovative application of new technologies which, combined with dramatic changes in military doctrine and operational and organisational concepts, fundamentally alters the character and conduct of military operations.'

Kapil Dak in contrast argues that the 'historical record appears to suggest that technological change represents a relatively small part of the equation, the crucial element in most RMAs being conceptual in nature'.

Broader in concept than an RMA is the idea of a *military revolution*. Whereas many RMAs can be identified in history, true military revolutions are rare. Military revolutions are dynamically interactive social processes which, according to Williamson Murray, 'recast the nature of society and the state as well as of military organisations'.

The political economy of war-making is also being transformed. During the modern era, military forces were maintained by state-based production and financing systems, preferably organized on a national basis. Postmodern non-state institutions of violence tend to draw material sustenance not from such formal and centralized national economies and defence industries, but from private production and finance networks organized either locally or on a global scale. Such sources may include plunder and theft, hostage-taking for ransom, extortion, drug trafficking, arms trafficking, money laundering, remittances and material support from relevant diaspora communities, foreign assistance, and the diversion of humanitarian aid.

Postmodernity is perhaps continuing to loosen the grip that 'modern' war has had for the past two centuries. The emergence of nuclear weapons had already initiated this process by neutralizing the most powerful weapons possessed by the leading military powers, and encouraging a particular security policy restraint. Postmodernity may be reinforcing this process. Just as feudalism and modernity each produced their own distinctive forms of war, so the transition to postmodernity is producing its own unique politico-cultural form of organized violence, even while the *nature* of war remains constant.

War remains a purposeful instrument of political violence in many parts of the world. In all ages, older forms of war and violence do not entirely disappear even as new forms gradually supplant them.

KEY POINTS

- The modern era of industrialized warfare may be over.

- Some developed states can use the revolution in military affairs to maintain military superiority.

- In conflicts outside the major powers' interests, low-tech, self-financed irregular warfare is becoming more prevalent.

- Such conflicts are no less 'Clausewitzian' than modern warfare.

? QUESTIONS

1. How valid is it to argue that the French Revolution unleashed an era of unlimited warfare?

2. Evaluate the thesis that Clausewitz still has something worthwhile to teach students of war in the contemporary world.

3. In what ways was warfare in the nineteenth century significantly affected by advances in technology?

4. Is war a catalyst for significant social and political change, or a reflection of it?

5. What do you understand by the phrase 'total war'? Does modern history provide examples of such a conflict?

6. How would you define 'limited war'? Is limited nuclear war a contradiction in terms?

7. What do you understand by the concept of *either* 'Seapower' or 'Airpower'?

8. Is industrialized war between major powers becoming obsolete in the post-cold war world?

SHEEHAN

9. How useful is the distinction between 'revolutions in military affairs' and 'military revolutions' in understanding the evolution of modern war?

10. In what ways, if any, do the so-called 'new wars' of the post-cold war period differ from earlier forms of war?

FURTHER READING

■ **Geoffrey Best, *War and Society in Revolutionary Europe, 1770–1870*, (London, 1982).** Effectively captures the interrelationship between politics, technology and warfare during this turbulent and formative period in European history.

■ **Jeremy Black, *War* (London, Continuum, 2001).** An interesting, and like most of Black's writings, provocative, exploration of the nature of war in the contemporary age and its likely evolution in the next few decades. Black is sceptical of the wilder claims made by the proponents of the Revolution in Military Affairs thesis.

■ **Carl von Clausewitz, *On War*. tr. and ed. by Michael Howard and Peter Paret (Princeton: Princeton University Press, 1976).** The words of the Master, ably and sensitively translated by two experts in the field. While secondary sources are always useful, there is no substitute for reading the original and Clausewitz is by no means as opaque as is sometimes suggested. His work remains essential reading for any serious student of war.

■ **L. Freedman, *The Evolution of Nuclear Strategy* (New York: St Martin's Press, 1981).** An excellent study of the nature of the strategic nuclear deterrent relationship and the restraints on politico-military thinking that it inevitably encouraged.

■ **A. Gat, *Clausewitz and the Enlightenment: The Origins of Modern Military Thought* (Oxford: Oxford University Press, 1988).** A good book for exploring the intellectual origins of the revolutionary military thinking of the nineteenth century. It helps to bring out both the legacy that the eighteenth century provided for Napoleon, but also the distinctive contribution made by his synthesis of effective practice, and the equally impressive intellectual synthesis of Clausewitz.

■ **A. Gat, *The Development of Military Thought: The Nineteenth Century* (Oxford: Oxford University Press, 1992).** A very useful study of the development of military thought during a crucial period in its evolution.

■ **Archer Jones, *The Art of War in the Western World* (Chicago: University of Illinois Press, 1987).** A very good single volume treatment of the development and evolution of the military art over the centuries. The decisive changes in weaponry, strategy, tactics and social environments are brought out with skill and style, and the influence of leadership is illuminated in each age. One can disagree with some of the interpretations, but this is a lively *tour d'horizon* of the history of the practice of war.

■ **Charles Messenger, *The Art of Blitzkreig* (London: Ian Allen Ltd, 1976).** A very readable analysis of the effectiveness of superior doctrine over numbers and technology and a useful case study of the impact of military evolution (or possibly revolution).

■ **Douglas Porch, *Wars of Empire* (London: Cassell, 2000).** A very accessible and readable study of the 'little wars' of the nineteenth century, written by an acknowledged expert on colonial warfare and the French military experience in particular. Brings out both the fact that many European armies spent much of their energies engaged in this form of warfare and not just industrial war with other great powers, and the fact that the 'new wars' of post-1990 are in many ways not so new after all.

■ **Michael Waltzer, *Just and Unjust Wars* (London, 1978).** Waltzer's book is a study in ethics, but is extremely useful in understanding traditional and contemporary approaches to the question of morality and warfare, and provides a useful basis for analysing the scale of the evolution towards total war between 1800 and 1950.

■ **Gordon Wright, *The Ordeal of Total War 1939–1945* (New York: Harper & Row, 1968).** A book that brings out the scope and totality of the Second World War and the impact it had on civilians as well as the military.

 ## WEB LINKS

● **http://sunsite.utk.edu/civil-war/warweb.html** Excellent resource for the American Civil War.

● **http://www.clausewitz.com/CWZHOME/CWZBASE.htm** Excellent site for Clausewitz studies.

● **http://www.fortunecity.com/victorian/riley/787/Napoleon/** A useful site for the Napoleonic wars.

● **http://members.fortunecity.com/mikaelxii/** A good site for the First World War.

● **http://www.army.mil/cmh-pg/** US Army Centre for Military History. Very good on American military history.

● **http://vlib.iue.it/history/mil/** Excellent military history resource.

 Visit the Online Resource Centre that accompanies this book for lots of interesting additional material http://www.oxfordtextbooks.co.uk/orc/baylis_strategy2e/.

3

Strategic Theory

THOMAS G. MAHNKEN

 Chapter Contents

- Introduction
- The Logic of Strategy
- Clausewitz's *On War*
- Sun Tzu's *Art of War*
- The Enduring Relevance of Strategy
- Conclusion

 Reader's Guide

This chapter discusses strategic theory, which provides a conceptual understanding of the nature of war. It argues that the logic of war is universal. Although strategy is an art, it is one that can be studied systematically. The chapter begins by exploring the logic of strategy. It then discusses some of the most valuable concepts in strategic theory as contained in Carl von Clausewitz's *On War*. It briefly compares and contrasts these with the concepts contained in Sun Tzu's *Art of War* before considering and rebutting the main arguments about the obsolescence of classical strategic theory.

Introduction

The logic of war and strategy is universal; it is valid at all times and in all places. This is primarily because human nature has remained unchanged in the face of material progress. The same passions that motivated those who lived millennia ago continue to drive us today. Although such strategic theorists as the nineteenth-century Prussian officer and philosopher Carl von Clausewitz and the ancient Chinese author Sun Tzu wrote from different historical and cultural experiences and thus viewed strategy from unique perspectives, the phenomenon they described—war—is the same. Arguing that there are uniquely 'Western' and 'Eastern,' 'European' or 'Asian', strategic theories is akin to arguing that there are different sets of physical laws, each of which applies only in a given geographical or cultural setting.

Strategic theory provides the conceptual foundation of an understanding of war. In a world in which so much about the character and conduct of war appears to be changing, an understanding of the theory of war reminds us that the nature of war does not change. Theory offers the student of strategy a toolkit that can be used to analyse strategic problems. An understanding of theory equips the student with a set of questions to guide further study. As Clausewitz wrote, the purpose of theory is not to uncover fixed laws or principles, but rather to educate the mind. As he put it:

> [Theory] is an analytical investigation leading to a close *acquaintance* with the subject; applied to experience—in our case, to military history—it leads to a thorough *familiarity* with it . . . Theory will have fulfilled its main task when it is used to analyze the constituent elements of war, to distinguish precisely what at first sight seems fused, to explain in full the properties of the means employed and to show their probable effects, to define clearly the nature of the ends in view, and to illuminate all phases of warfare in a thorough critical inquiry. Theory then becomes a guide to anyone who wants to learn about war from books; it will light his way, ease his progress, train his judgment, and help him to avoid pitfalls . . . It is meant to educate the mind of the future commander, or, more accurately, to guide him in his self-education, not to accompany him to the battlefield; just as a wise teacher guides and stimulates a young man's intellectual development, but is careful not to lead him by the hand for the rest of his life.

(Clausewitz 1989: 141)

In other words, we study strategic theory to learn how to think strategically.

Because the stakes in war are so high, strategy is a supremely practical endeavour. The most elegant theory is useless if it lacks practical application. Strategic theory thus succeeds or fails in direct proportion to its ability to help decision makers formulate sound strategy. As the twentieth-century American strategist Bernard Brodie put it, 'Strategy is a field where truth is sought in the pursuit of viable solutions' (1973: 452–3).

The Logic of Strategy

Strategy is about how to win wars. Any discussion of strategy must therefore begin with an understanding of war. Clausewitz famously defined war as 'an act of force to compel our enemy to do our will' (1989: 75). Two aspects of this definition are important. First, the fact that war involves force separates it from other types of political, economic, and military competition. Second, the fact that war is not senseless slaughter, but rather an instrument that is used to achieve a political purpose differentiates it from other types of violence.

It is the political context of war, and not the identity of those who wage it, that is its key characteristic (see Box 3.1). Empires, city-states, confederations, and subnational groups have all used war to preserve or aggrandize themselves. The fact that United Nations forces in Somalia in 1993 fought Mohammed Farah Aideed's Habr Gidr clan rather than a recognized state matters less than the fact that both sides were strategic actors possessing political objectives and that each sought to use force to compel the other to bend to their will. Similarly, the Global War on Terrorism fits the classical definition of a war, in that both sides have political aims and are using military means to achieve them. It is, to be sure, a strange war, one waged by irregular forces that use unconventional means. However, the fact that it is a violent clash of wills means that it is amenable to strategic analysis.

The field of strategy is about translating military effects into political results. If tactics is about employing troops in battle and operational art is concerned with conducting campaigns, then strategy deals with using military instruments to fulfil the ends of policy. It is the essential link between political objectives and military force, between ends and means.

Strategy is, or rather should be, a rational process. As Clausewitz wrote, 'No one starts a war—or rather, no one in his senses ought to do so—without first being clear in his mind what he intends to achieve by that war and how he intends to conduct it' (1989: 579). In other words, success in war requires a clear articulation of political aims and the development of an adequate strategy to achieve them. Clausewitz's formulation acknowledges, however, that states sometimes go to war without clear or achievable aims or a strategy to achieve them. As Germany's defeat in two world wars demonstrated, mastery of tactics and operations counts for little without a coherent or feasible strategy.

Strategy is more an art than a science. The tremendous complexity of war makes a positive theory of strategy impossible. Wars contain too many variables and do not repeat themselves with enough regularity to permit reliable prediction. Rather, each military problem has many potentially correct solutions rather than one optimal one. The reciprocal action of the belligerents introduces further complications. Moreover, war is rife with passion, inaccurate information, misperception, and chance. As Clausewitz wrote:

> Efforts were . . . made to equip the conduct of war with principles, rules or even systems. This did present a positive goal, but people failed to take adequate account of the endless complexities involved. As we have seen, the conduct of war branches out in almost all directions and has no definite limits; while any system, any model, has the finite nature of a synthesis. An irreconcilable conflict exists between this type of theory and actual practice.

(1989: 134)

Or, as Sun Tzu put it more succinctly, 'In the art of war there are no fixed rules' (1963: 93).

The fact that strategy is more an art than a science does not mean that it cannot be studied systematically. Rather, the theory of strategy consists of concepts and considerations instead of fixed laws.

Successful strategy is based upon clearly identifying political goals, assessing one's comparative advantage relative to the enemy, calculating costs and benefits carefully, and examining the risks and rewards of alternative strategies. The purpose of strategy is ultimately to convince the enemy that they cannot achieve their aims. As Admiral J. C. Wylie wrote,

> The primary aim of the strategist in the conduct of war is some selected degree of control of the enemy for the strategist's own purpose; this is achieved by control of the pattern of war; and this control of the pattern of war is had by manipulation of the centre of gravity of war to the disadvantage of the opponent.

(1989: 77)

Military success by itself is insufficient to achieve victory. History contains numerous examples of armies that won all the battles and yet lost the war due to a flawed strategy. In the Vietnam War, for example, the US military defeated the Viet Cong and North Vietnamese Army in every major engagement they fought. The United States nonetheless lost the war because civilian and military leaders never understood the complex nature of the conflict they were waging. Conversely, the United States achieved its independence from Britain despite the fact that the Continental Army won only a handful of battles.

It is axiomatic that policy drives strategy. Policy-makers and senior officers nonetheless frequently misunderstand this relationship. During the 1999 Kosovo War, for example Secretary of State Madeline Albright was wrong in arguing that 'Up until the start of the conflict, the military served to back up our diplomacy. Now, our diplomacy serves to back up our military' (Isaacson 1999). Similarly, Lieutenant General Charles A. Horner, at the time the commander of US Air Force units in Saudi Arabia, was wrong when he said that war 'should not be dragged out in an effort to achieve some political objective' (Gordon 1990: 1).

It is worth emphasizing that the primacy of politics applies not only to states, but also to other strategic actors. As Ayman al-Zawahiri, Al Qaeda's chief theoretician, wrote in his book *Knights under the Prophet's Banner* (2001):

> If the successful operations against Islam's enemies and the severe damage inflicted on them do not serve the ultimate goal of establishing the Muslim nation in the heart of the Islamic world, they will be nothing more than disturbing acts, regardless of their magnitude, that could be absorbed and endured, even if after some time and with some losses.

Clausewitz would doubtless approve of Zawahiri's understanding of strategy, if not his goals.

The political context of warfare can in some cases extend to tactical actions, particularly when they hold the potential to change the character of a war. During the North Atlantic Treaty Organization war over Kosovo in 1999, for example, a US B-2 bomber accidentally dropped three precision-guided munitions on the Chinese embassy in Belgrade, killing four. The incident was a tactical error with strategic consequences, triggering a diplomatic crisis between Washington and Beijing, disrupting moves to negotiate an end to the war, and prompting a halt to the bombing of targets in Belgrade for the next two weeks.

Although policy drives strategy, the capabilities and limitations of the military instrument also shape policy. As Clausewitz wrote, the political aim 'must adapt itself to its chosen means, a process which can radically change it' (1989: 87). To choose a ridiculous example to illustrate the point, it was one thing for Saddam Hussein to order his military to occupy Kuwait in 1990; it would have been quite another for Kuwait's army to try to occupy Iraq.

BOX 3.1

War as a Political Instrument

War is a matter of vital importance to the State.
(Sun Tzu 63)

It is clear, consequently, that war is not a mere act of policy, but a true political instrument, a continuation of political activity by other means.
(Clausewitz 1989: I/1. 24. 87)

War is only a branch of political activity; it is in no sense autonomous.
(Clausewitz 1989: VIII/6B. 606)

No major proposal required for war can be worked out of ignorance of political factors; and when people talk, as they often do, about harmful political influence on the management of war, they are not really saying what they mean. Their quarrel should be with policy itself not with its influence.
(Clausewitz 1989: VIII/6B. 608)

The object of war is a better state of peace.
(Liddell Hart 1967: 351)

Just as it would be wrong to view war as nothing more than slaughter, it would be misleading to believe that force can be used in highly calibrated increments to achieve finely tuned effects. War has its own dynamics that makes it an unwieldy instrument, more a bludgeon than a rapier. Interaction with the adversary makes it difficult to achieve even the simplest objective. As Clausewitz reminds us, 'War is not the act of a living force upon a lifeless mass but always the collision of two living forces' (1989: 4). Just as we seek to use force to compel our adversary to do our will, so too will he attempt to use force to coerce us. Effectiveness in war thus depends not only on what we do, but also on what an opponent does. This interaction limits significantly the ability to control the use of military force.

KEY POINTS

- War is an act of force to compel your enemy to do your will.

- Strategy is about how to win wars. It is the essential link between political objectives and military force, between ends and means.

- Strategy is—or should be—a rational process.

- Strategy is more an art than a science.

- Interaction with the adversary makes it difficult to achieve even the simplest objective.

Clausewitz's *On War*

Carl von Clausewitz's masterpiece, *On War*, forms the cornerstone of any understanding of strategic theory. Unfortunately, the book is all too often misunderstood. *On War* is an unfinished work, left incomplete due to the author's death from cholera in 1831. Book 1, chapter 1, was the only part of the book that Clausewitz considered complete. Like the Bible, *On War* is more frequently quoted than read, and more frequently perused than comprehended. It is not a book that can be understood fully after a single reading, but rather demands careful study and reflection, raising as many questions as it answers and forcing serious readers to grapple with the author's concepts.

Clausewitz's methodology, which distinguishes between war in theory or 'absolute war' and war in reality, has led many mistakenly to identify him as an apostle of total war. In fact, he uses the approach of defining war in its ideal or pure form as a way of identifying the many considerations that shape war in reality. It is akin to a physicist examining mechanics in a frictionless environment or an economist describing an ideal market. In each case the observer is portraying the theoretical, not the real. In fact, Clausewitz argues that war can be fought for limited or unlimited aims with partial or total means.

As Hugh Smith has written, Clausewitz views war in four different contexts (Smith 2005: chs. 7–10) First and foremost, in his view war is ultimately about killing and dying. He is dismissive of the notion that war can be waged without bloodshed. As he put it:

> Kind-hearted people might of course think that there was some ingenious way to disarm or defeat an enemy without too much bloodshed, and might imagine that this is the true goal of the art of war. Pleasant as it sounds, it is a fallacy that must be exposed: war is such a dangerous business that the mistakes which come from kindness are the very worst.

(Clausewitz 1989: 75)

Second, war is a contest between armies, generals, and states. Clausewitz invokes the metaphor of wrestling to describe war as a physical and mental competition, with each side trying to pin the other while simultaneously trying to avoid being pinned.

Third, war is an instrument of policy. It is not to be pursued for its own sake, but rather to serve the ends of the state.

Finally, he argues that war is a social activity. As someone who had lived through the French Revolution and fought in the Napoleonic Wars, he was acutely aware of the fact that social conditions have an impact on the character and conduct of war.

A number of the concepts that Clausewitz introduces in *On War* are central to the study of strategy. These include the trinity, the need to understand the nature of a war, the difference between limited and unlimited wars, the rational calculus of war, and friction.

The trinity

Clausewitz's description of war is one of his most enduring legacies. He views war as a 'paradoxical trinity—composed of violence, hatred, and enmity . . . the play of chance and probability . . . and of its element of subordination'. He wrote that each of these three tendencies generally (but not always) corresponds to one of three groups in society: the people, the military, and the government (1989: 89). Passion is most often associated with the people, whose animosities move states to fight. Probability and chance are the realm of the military. Indeed, soldiers most constantly deal with uncertainty and friction. Reason is generally a characteristic of the government, which determines the aims of war and the means for waging it.

Clausewitz argued that the relative intensity of and relationships among these tendencies change according to the circumstances of the war.

> Three different codes of law, deep-rooted in their subject and yet variable in their relationship to one another. A theory that ignores any one of them or seeks to fix an arbitrary relationship between them would conflict with reality to such an extent that for this reason alone it would be totally useless. Our task therefore is to develop a theory that maintains a balance between these three tendencies, like an object suspended between three magnets.

(1989: 89)

The interaction of these three tendencies thus determines the character of a war.

Understanding the nature of a war

Clausewitz argues that understanding the nature of a war is a necessary preconception to developing an effective strategy. As he put it

> The first, the supreme, the most far-reaching act of judgment that the statesman and commander have to make is to establish by that test the kind of war on which they are embarking, neither mistaking it for, nor trying to turn it into, something that is alien to its nature. This is the first of all strategic questions and the most comprehensive.

(1989: 88–89)

Understanding the nature of a war is both necessary and difficult. In August 1914, for example, the political and military leaders of the European great powers all believed that the war upon which they were embarking would be short, limited in scope, and end in triumph for their side. If they had known the character of the war that was about to unfold—a protracted, attritional conflict that would devastate the victor as well as the vanquished—it is doubtful that they would have gone to war in the first place.

Similarly, during the Vietnam War soldiers and statesmen disagreed as to whether the conflict was an international communist war against South Vietnam, a civil war between North and South Vietnam, an insurgency in the South supported by the North, or all of the above. Such judgements had profound implications for US strategy in the war.

In Clausewitz's view, the nature of a war is the result of the interaction of the objectives of the two sides; the people, government, and militaries of the belligerents; and the attitudes of allies and neutrals: 'To assess these things in all their ramifications and diversity is plainly a colossal task. Rapid and correct appraisal of them clearly calls for the intuition of a genius; to master all this complex mass by sheer methodological examination is obviously impossible' (Clausewitz 1989: 585–6). The fact that strategy is more an art than a science is reflected by the difficulty inherent in accurately assessing the nature of a specific conflict.

Because the nature of a war is the product of the interaction of the belligerents, every war is unique. The nature of a war is dynamic because a change in any of its elements can alter the nature of the conflict. A change in the aims of one or more of the participants, for example, can shift the nature of a war. So too can the entry of new participants. China's entry into the Korean War, for example, markedly changed its complexion.

Inherent in understanding the nature of a war is gaining an appreciation of one's comparative advantage. This, in turn, forms the basis of sound strategy. The key to doing so, in Clausewitz's view, is understanding the enemy's centre of gravity. As he put it, 'One must keep the dominant characteristics of both belligerents in mind. Out of these characteristics a certain centre of gravity develops, the hub of all power and movement, on which everything depends. That is the point against which all our energies should be directed' (1989: 595–6).

In Clausewitz's view, a state achieves victory by seeking out and attacking the enemy's centre of gravity. He wrote that the centre of gravity was most likely the enemy's army, capital city, principal ally, leader, and public opinion, in descending order. In practice, however, it can often be difficult to determine the adversary's centre of gravity. In the 1991 Gulf War, for example, US officials viewed Iraq's military—particularly its Republican Guard—as the centre of gravity, when in fact the 'hub of all power' was Saddam Hussein's government.

Limited versus unlimited wars

Wars can be fought for a wide range of objectives, from a quest for land and resources to the utter destruction of the enemy. In a note for the revision of *On War*, however, Clausewitz drew a distinction between wars fought for limited aims and those fought for unlimited aims.

> War can be of two kinds, in the sense that either the objective is to *overthrow the enemy*—to render him politically helpless or militarily impotent, thus forcing him to sign whatever peace we please; or *merely to occupy some of his frontier districts* so that we can annex them or use them for bargaining at the peace negotiations. Transitions from one type to the other will of course recur in my treatment; but the fact that the aims of the two types are quite different must be clear at all times, and their points of irreconcilability brought out.

(Clausewitz 1989: 69)

This distinction affects the way that wars are fought and how they end. In wars for limited aims, soldiers and statesmen must translate battlefield success into political leverage over the adversary. As a result, they must continually reassess how far to go militarily and what to demand politically. Such wars end through formal or tacit negotiation and agreement between the warring parties. Wars for unlimited aims are fought to overthrow the adversary's regime or achieve unconditional surrender. They end in a peace settlement that is imposed rather than negotiated.

The 1991 Gulf War and 2003 Iraq War illustrate the difference between the two types of wars. In 1991, the US-led coalition fought to liberate Kuwait from Iraqi occupation, restore Kuwait's government to power, ensure the safety of US citizens in the region, and ensure the security and stability of the Gulf region. In 2003, the United States and its allies fought to overthrow Saddam Hussein's Ba'athist regime.

The end of limited wars can lead to dissatisfaction on the part of one or more of the parties as well as a prolonged military commitment. A strong case can be made, for example, that the US-led coalition ended the 1991 Gulf War prematurely, before Saddam Hussein had been forced to admit defeat. As a result, the United States acquired a prolonged commitment to the Gulf region, one that led to the stationing of US forces in Saudi Arabia and fostered resentment among Muslims in the region and across the globe. The aftermath of a war for unlimited aims leads to a protracted commitment of another sort, as the victors must install or support a new government. In the wake of the 2003 Iraq War, the United States and its partners faced the tremendous task of rebuilding Iraq in the face of an insurgency.

The rational calculus of war

Another concept that flows from Clausewitz's work is the notion that there should be a correlation between the value a state attaches to its ends and the means it uses to achieve them.

> **❝** Since war is not an act of senseless passion but is controlled by its political object, the value of this object must determine the sacrifices to be made for it in *magnitude* and also in *duration*. Once the expenditure of effort exceeds the value of the political object, the object must be renounced and peace must follow. **❞**

(Clausewitz 1989: 92)

States should thus be willing to fight longer and harder to secure or defend vital interests than peripheral ones. This observation helps to explain, for example, why the US government chose to withdraw from Somalia after the death of eighteen soldiers but remained in Korea despite suffering 33,000 deaths.

The notion of a rational calculus of war would appear to be one area in which strategy most resembles a science. Although the notion makes sense in theory, it is problematic in practice. It is often impossible, for example, for soldiers and statesmen to determine the costs and benefits of military action beforehand. Moreover, estimates of the political, social, and economic costs change as war unfolds. As Clausewitz notes, 'The original political objects can greatly alter during the course of the war and many finally change entirely since they are influenced by events and their probable consequence' (1989: 92). States may continue fighting beyond the 'rational' point of surrender when their leaders' prestige becomes invested in the war or the passions of the people become aroused.

Friction

Another concept with enduring value is that of friction, which Clausewitz defined as 'the only concept that more or less corresponds to the factors that distinguish real war from war on paper' (1989: 119). Clausewtiz derived the name and the concept from physics. As he wrote in *The Principles of War*, 'The conduct of war resembles the workings of an intricate machine with enormous friction, so that combinations which are easily planned on paper can be executed only with great effort' (quoted in Smith 2005: 77). The sources of friction include the danger posed by the enemy, the effort requires of one's own forces, the difficulties presented by the physical environment, and the problem of knowing what is occurring.

Examples of friction abound in recent wars. For example, the largest Iraqi counterattack of the 2003 Iraq War, which occurred early on 3 April near a key Euphrates River bridge south-west of Baghdad, surprised US forces. US sensors failed to detect the approach of three Iraqi brigades composed of 8,000 soldiers backed by seventy tanks and armoured personnel carriers (*Technology Review* 2004; Grant 2005).

KEY POINTS

- Clausewitz viewed war as fighting, a contest between armies, an instrument of policy, and a social activity.

- He views war as a paradoxical trinity composed of passion, probability, and reason. These tendencies generally correspond to the people, the military, and the government.

- Understanding the nature of a war is a necessary but difficult preconception to developing an effective strategy.

- In war it is important to identify and attack the enemy's centre of gravity. In Clausewitz's view, this was most likely the enemy's army, capital, ally, leader, or public opinion.

- Clausewitz distinguished between wars fought for limited and unlimited aims. The former are fought over territory; the latter are fought to overthrow the enemy's regime or achieve unconditional surrender.

- Clausewitz argues that there should be a correlation between the value a state attaches to its ends and the means it uses to achieve them. In practice, however, this is often difficult to determine.

- The concept of friction describes that which makes the simplest of activities in war difficult.

Sun Tzu's *Art of War*

There is a seemingly wide gulf between Clausewitz and Sun Tzu. The former wrote from the perspective of early nineteenth-century Europe, the latter from the perspective of someone who lived in ancient China. The books they wrote also are strikingly different. Whereas *On War* is often a thicket of prose, much of *The Art of War* is made up of deceptively simple aphorisms. Whereas *On War* is close to 600 pages, *The Art of War* totals less than 40 pages in English and 6,600 characters in Chinese. Yet as the British strategist Basil Liddell Hart observed, Clausewitz's *On War* does not differ much from Sun Tzu's *Art of War* as it would appear to do on the surface (Handel 2001: 20).

Sun Tzu does, however, provide contrasting perspectives on several aspects of strategy. For example, the two authors exhibit different strategic preferences and offer contrasting views of **intelligence** and **deception**.

Strategic preferences

Sun Tzu's strategic preferences are significantly different from those of Clausewitz. Sun Tzu extols victory without bloodshed as the ideal, writing that 'to subdue the enemy without fighting is the acme of skill' (Sun Tzu 1963: 77). Clausewitz, by contrast, is sceptical of such an approach to combat, arguing that a reluctance to shed blood may play into an opponent's hands.

Sun Tzu sees war as a search for comparative advantage. He believes that success in war is less a matter of destroying the adversary's army and more one of shattering his will to fight. In his view, the most successful strategies are those that emphasize psychology and deception.

To Sun Tzu, information represents a key to success in war. 'Know the enemy and know yourself; in a hundred battles you will never be in peril' (Sun Tzu 1963: 84). Typically, however, such pithy injunctions conceal the many challenges that make it difficult to understand one's self and one's adversary, including imperfect information, ethnocentrism, and mirror-imaging.

Whereas Clausewitz writes that destroying the enemy's army is most often the key to victory in war, Sun Tzu recommends that the best alternative is to attack the enemy's strategy. The next best alternative is to attack the opponent's alliances. Destroying the enemy's army ranks third on his list of preferred strategies.

Intelligence

Another contrast involves the two authors' views of intelligence. Sun Tzu is an optimist regarding intelligence, claiming that the outcome of a war can be known in advance if the leader makes a complete estimate of the situation.

> **“** To gauge the outcome of war we must compare the two sides by assessing their relative strengths. This is to ask the following questions: Which ruler has the way? Which commander has the greater ability? Which side has the advantage of climate and terrain? Which army follows regulations and obeys orders more strictly? Which army has superior strength? Which officers and men are better trained? Which side is more strict and impartial in meting out rewards and punishments? On the basis of this comparison I know who will win and who will lose. **”**

(Sun Tzu 1993: 103–4)

Two aspects of this passage are noteworthy. First, he emphasizes 'relative strengths', not absolute capabilities. In other words, one's capabilities only matter when considered in relation to those of the adversary. Second, most of the factors that Sun Tzu identifies as being important are qualitative, not quantitative, considerations in war.

Clausewitz, by contrast, is sceptical of intelligence:

> **“** Many intelligence reports in war are contradictory; even more are false, and most are uncertain . . . One report tallies with another, confirms it, magnifies it, lends it color, till he has to make a quick decision—which is soon recognized to be mistaken, just as the reports turn out to be lies, exaggerations, and so on. In short, most intelligence is false, and the effect of fear is to multiply lies and inaccuracies. **”**

(Clausewitz 1989: 117)

The failure of the US intelligence community—indeed, of all major intelligence services—to determine that Iraq did not possess nuclear, biological, or chemical weapons prior to the 2003 Iraq War is evidence of the fact that, despite the development of highly sophisticated intelligence collection means, intelligence continues to be an uncertain business.

Sun Tzu is also a proponent of deception. Sun Tzu repeatedly discusses how the successful general can surprise and deceive an opponent and how he should gather good intelligence and weaken the morale of the enemy. Yet he seldom alludes to the fact that an enemy may be able to do the same.

KEY POINTS

- Sun Tzu argues that success in war comes from shattering the adversary's will to fight rather than destroying his army.

- He recommends that the best alternative is to attack the enemy's strategy.

- He claims that the outcome of a war can be known in advance if the leader makes a complete estimate of the situation.

The Enduring Relevance of Strategy

In recent years, both scholars and practitioners have questioned the utility of classical strategic theory. Some have argued that the advent of the information age has invalidated traditional theories of warfare. They claim that technology either has or will soon overcome much of the friction that has historically characterized combat. As Admiral William A. Owens wrote several years ago:

> Military theorists from Sun Tzu to Clausewitz have pointed out the value of understanding one's enemies and the geographical-political-social-context in which they operate. What is different, however, is that some technologies—available either now or soon—will give the United States an edge that approaches omniscience, at least relative to any potential opponent.

(Owens 1995: 133)

Those who take this view argue that the advent of the information age demands a new body of strategic theory, one drawing its inspiration from business theory, economics, or the so-called new physical sciences. Vice Admiral Arthur K. Cebrowski and John J. Garstka, for example, have written that 'there is *as yet* no equivalent to Carl von Clausewitz's *On War*' for the information age (emphasis added). The implicit assumption, of course, is that such a work is needed (Cebrowski and Garstka 1998: 29).

A second group agrees that the classical approach to strategy is anachronistic, but for a much different reason. These critics allege that the utility of classical strategic theory is limited to wars between armies and states, whereas war today more often involves trans- or subnational groups. In John Keegan's characterization, Clausewitzian thought makes 'no allowances for . . . war without beginning or end, the endemic warfare of non-state, even pre-state peoples' (1993: 5). Implicit in this critique is the assumption that such conflicts obey logic distinct from those involving states.

Finally, some have argued that strategy itself is an illusion. In this view, strategic concepts are misleading, even harmful. The military historian Russell Weigley has written that 'War in the twentieth century is no longer the extension of politics by other means. It is doubtful whether the aphorism affirming that war is such an extension of politics was ever true enough to warrant the frequency with which it has been repeated' (1988: 341).

Although each of these arguments has its adherents, each is flawed. Those who criticize Clausewitz have at best a limited understanding of his strategic thought. First, although the growth and spread of stealth, precision, and information technology has had a dramatic influence on recent conflicts and portends even greater changes, there is as yet no evidence that it has altered the fundamental nature of war. Recent conflicts have demonstrated the enduring value of such concepts as friction. If anything, the increasing complexity of modern war may actually multiply sources of friction.

Proponents of new theories of war drawn from business literature and science frequently confuse novelty with utility. As Richard K. Betts has correctly noted, 'Critics would have to demonstrate that more recent and numerous theories in other fields are *better* theories—more useful to understanding the world—than the fewer and older ones of strategy. Theories may endure because each new one proves wanting. One Clausewitz is still worth a busload of most other theorists' (1997: 29).

Second, it is unclear that war involving non-state actors is any different from that between states. The strategic questions most relevant to the Global War on Terrorism differ little from those in previous wars. Although Al-Qaeda looks and operates much differently than a conventional state adversary, it is nonetheless a strategic actor. Indeed, Al-Qaeda supporters have been known to look to strategic theorists such as Sun Tzu for guidance on how best to wage war (Qurashi 2002).

Third, those who argue that strategy is an illusion confuse the difficulty of executing strategy with the existence of an underlying strategic logic. It may be difficult to develop strategy to achieve vague or opaque political goals. In addition, some strategic concepts may be of limited utility in practice. For example, leaders may be unable to estimate the value of an objective before the fact. But each of these concepts is nonetheless important for strategists to take into account.

That critiques of the classical approach are unconvincing is not to say that existing theories of war hold all the answers. Clausewitz has little to say about the impact of technology on war, for example. Yet those who reject the classical approach to strategy have nothing to offer in its place. Indeed, by rejecting strategic thought one must also discard the notion of the use of force as an instrument of policy.

KEY POINTS

- Some argue that classical strategic theory is obsolete because technology either has or will soon overcome much of the friction that has historically characterized combat. The evidence that this is occurring is, however, weak.

- Others argue that classical strategic theory does not explain conflict involving trans- or subnational groups. In fact, however, both states and terrorist groups may be strategic actors.

- Still others argue that strategy itself is an illusion. They confuse the difficulty of executing strategy with the existence of strategic logic.

Conclusion

Strategic theory reminds us that, despite significant changes to the character and conduct of war brought on by the development of new technology, the nature of war is constant. War remains the use of force to achieve political aims, regardless of whether the group seeking those aims is a state or terrorist network. Similarly, interaction with the adversary remains one of the key dynamics that prevents strategy from becoming a science.

Concepts found in Clausewitz's *On War* and Sun Tzu's *The Art of War* have similarly enduring value. Clausewitz's discussion of the remarkable trinity, the need to understand the nature of a war, the differences between limited and unlimited wars, the rational calculus of war, and friction remain as useful as the day they were written. Sun Tzu, for his part, reminds us that victory does not always require the physical destruction of an adversary. He also highlights the importance of intelligence. Together, these concepts can help us better understand contemporary conflicts.

? QUESTIONS

1. Why is it important to study strategic theory?
2. In what ways is strategy an art? A science?
3. What are the main differences between Clausewitz and Sun Tzu's views of strategy?
4. What considerations should decision makers keep in mind as they contemplate using force?
5. What differentiates war from other forms of violence?
6. What are the main contributions of Clausewitz to strategic theory?
7. What are the main contributions of Sun Tzu to strategic theory?
8. Does Clausewitz or Sun Tzu have a more realistic view of intelligence?
9. Which elements of strategic theory are most relevant to the world of the early twenty-first century? Which are least relevant?

FURTHER READING

■ Carl von Clausewitz, *On War*, ed. and tr. Michael Howard and Peter Paret (Princeton: Princeton University Press, 1989). Deserves to be read in its entirety.

■ Richard K. Betts, 'Is Strategy an Illusion?', *International Security*, 25/2 (Fall 2000). Evaluates and rebuts the main arguments against the classical approach to strategy.

■ J. F. C. Fuller, *Armament and History* (New York: Scribner's, 1945). Offers the most articulate consideration of the role of technology in warfare.

■ Colin S. Gray, *Modern Strategy* (Oxford: Oxford University Press, 1999). Argues for the unity of all strategic experience because nothing vital to the nature of warfare changes. Also persuades the Clausewitz stands head and shoulders above other theorists.

■ **Michael I. Handel, *Masters of War*, 3rd edn (London: Frank Cass, 2001).** Makes a convincing case that Clausewitz, Sun Tzu, Mao Tse-tung, and other theorists employ a common strategic logic. Apparent divergences and contradictions are often upon closer examination differences of methodology, definition, or perspective.

■ **B. H. Liddell Hart, *Strategy* (New York: Praeger, 1967).** Argues that decisive victories usually involve prior psychological dislocation of an adversary. Rather than concentrating one's troops, the commander should force his enemy to disperse his forces. Despite the author's overly narrow interpretation of Clausewitz and selective use of history, this is nonetheless an important work.

■ **Edward Luttwak, *Strategy: The Logic of War and Peace*, revised and enlarged edn (Cambridge, Mass.: Belknap Press, 2001).** Explores the paradoxical nature of strategy. Classic treatment of paradox in strategy.

■ **Peter Paret (ed.), *Makers of Modern Strategy: From Machiavelli to the Nuclear Age* (Princeton: Princeton University Press, 1986).** Offers an intellectual history of strategic thought from Machiavelli to modern times. It includes not only chapters on Machiavelli, Clausewitz, Jomini, and Mahan, but also essays on the practice of strategy.

■ **Hugh Smith, *On Clausewitz: A Study of Military and Political Ideas* (New York: Palgrave Macmillan, 2005).** Provides an insightful analysis of Clausewitz's strategic thought.

■ **Sun Tzu, *The Art of War.*** The serious student should read several translations. The best are by Samuel B. Griffith **(Oxford: Oxford University Press, 1963)** and Roger Ames **(New York: Ballentine Books, 1993).**

■ **Barry D. Watts, *Clausewitzian Friction and Future War* (Washington, DC: National Defence University Press, 2004).** Offers a thoughtful consideration of the concept of friction in modern warfare.

■ **J. C. Wylie, *Military Strategy: A General Theory of Power Control* (Annapolis, Md.: Naval Institute Press, 1989).** A valuable work on strategy.

 WEB LINKS

● The Clausewitz homepage, at **http://www.clausewitz.com/CWZHOME/CWZBASE.htm,** contains a variety of useful research resources, including indices and bibliographies.

● The Sun Tzu *Art of War* site, **http://www.sonshi.com/** contains a translation of *The Art of War*, reviews of the other major translations, and other works of strategy online.

 Visit the Online Resource Centre that accompanies this book for lots of interesting additional material http://www.oxfordtextbooks.co.uk/orc/baylis_strategy2e/.

4

Strategic Culture

JEFFREY S. LANTIS AND DARRYL HOWLETT

 Chapter Contents

- Introduction
- Thinking about Culture and Security
- Political Culture
- Strategic Culture and Nuclear Deterrence
- Sources of Strategic Culture
- Construction and Strategic Culture
- Continuing Issues and Future Questions
- Conclusion

Reader's Guide

This chapter discusses the ways that strategic culture may influence security policy in the international realm. Such a study is salient because of the number of conflicts which seem to exhibit cultural dimensions. To facilitate this analysis the chapter is divided into three sections. First, there is an overview both of those approaches to the relationship between culture, strategy, and security policy that emerged during the cold war, and of the various sources of 'strategic culture' identified in the literature. Second, there is a discussion of questions related to strategic culture raised by new constructivist approaches to security studies. Finally, the third section of this chapter examines whether a broader understanding of strategic culture is appropriate in an era of globalization.

Introduction

Many consider that culture has a profound impact on strategic outcomes and recent events have renewed scholarly interest in exploring its role in international security. Scholars and practitioners have begun to interpret challenges like democratic consolidation in post-war Iraq, US-China relations, and the war on terror through the lens of identity and culture. This chapter therefore seeks to consider these aspects by focusing on 'strategic culture' as both a conceptual tool and a basis for policy-making. To accomplish this, several 'generations' of scholarly work on strategic culture are considered, including more recent constructivist approaches. The chapter also devotes attention to the question of 'ownership' of strategic culture and whether non-state, state, and multi-state actors may possess distinctive strategic cultures in the twenty-first century.

Thinking about Culture and Security

There are three main approaches to the study of culture in international security. The first views culture as a value-added explanation of state behaviour. In this sense, culture is used to 'fill in the gaps' of explanation by supplementing theories centred on national interest and the distribution of power. Culture is thus considered a variable that may influence behaviour but is secondary to international systemic pressures. The second approach

---

BOX 4.1

Perspectives on Culture and Politics

Culture is comprised of 'interpretive codes' including language, values, and even substantive beliefs like support for democracy or the futility of war
(Parsons 1951).

Culture is 'an historically transmitted pattern of meanings embodied in symbols, a system of inherited conceptions expressed in symbolic form by means of which men communicate, perpetuate, and develop their knowledge about and attitudes towards life'
(Geertz 1973).

Culture is 'the dynamic vessel that holds and revitalizes the collective memories of a people by giving emotional life to traditions'
(Pye 1985).

Political culture is 'that subset of beliefs and values of a society that relate to the political system'
(Almond and Verba 1965).

views culture as a theoretical model that can explain some, if not all, strategic behaviour. This approach draws on other areas of knowledge such as political psychology in order to create a theory of culture that is falsifiable and also contributes to a cumulative research programme. Culture in this sense is an independent variable that explains security policy as well or better than neorealism or neoliberal institutionalism. The third approach embraces those writers who believe that aspects of human conduct can be understood only by becoming immersed within a culture and, consequently, the search for falsifiable theories is unachievable. Some anthropologists and sociologists consider that culture consists of a combination of discursive (what is said) and non-discursive expressions (what is unsaid). Culture is incredibly powerful, they argue, but impossible to measure as an influence on policy.

Political Culture

The idea that culture could influence strategic outcomes was first captured in classic works, including the writings of Thucydides and Sun Tzu. In the nineteenth century, Prussian military strategist Carl von Clausewitz developed this idea by identifying war and war-fighting strategy as 'a test of moral and physical forces'. The goal of strategy, he argued, was more than defeat of the enemy on the battlefield—it was the elimination of the enemy's morale. Clausewitz stressed that leaders should not forget the potential of a mobilized society to carry out aggression, as he had witnessed first-hand in defeats by Napoleonic armies marching for the glory of the empire (Howard 1991).

The Second World War prompted a new wave of research on the distinctive 'national character' of countries, which were rooted in language, religion, customs, and the interpretation of common memories. Scholars became curious about how a country's national character could lead them to fight wars differently. For example, some sought to understand how Japanese culture fomented a spirit of self-sacrifice, such as in the *kamikaze* attacks against US warships and battles to the death over remote South Pacific islands (Benedict 1946). While this work was criticized for reifying the culture and promoting stereotypes, some sociologists and anthropologists including Margaret Mead and Claude Lévi-Strauss continued to refine this work. In the 1980s, sociologist Ann Swidler proposed a more complex model of the connection between culture and state behaviour by emphasizing the mediating role of what she termed cultural 'strategies of action'. Swidler defined culture quite broadly as consisting of 'symbolic vehicles of meaning, including beliefs, ritual practices, art forms, and ceremonies, as well as informal cultural practices such as language, gossip, stories, and rituals of daily life' (1986: 273). Building on the arguments of Max Weber and Talcott Parsons, she contended that interest-driven strategies were an important mediating condition on state behaviour.

Earlier, political scientists Gabriel Almond and Sidney Verba had generated interest in political culture, which they defined as the 'subset of beliefs and values of a society that relate to the political system' (1965: 11). For Almond and Verba political culture included a commitment to values like democratic principles and institutions, ideas about morality and the use of force, the rights of individuals or collectivities, and predispositions toward the role of a country in the world. This political culture, they argued, was manifest on at least three levels: 'the cognitive, which includes empirical and causal beliefs; the evaluative, which consists of values, norms and moral judgments, and the expressive or affective, which encompasses emotional attachments, patterns of identity and loyalty, and feelings of affinity, aversion, or indifference' (Duffield 1999: 23).

Although sociological models of culture became increasingly complex, subsequent studies of political culture were considered to have yielded little theoretical refinement during this period. Critics argued that the approach was subjective and that the explanatory power of political culture was more limited than its proponents claimed. Cultural interpretive arguments fell out of favour with the behavioural revolution in the social sciences. Conceptual interest remained alive in area studies, but it garnered less attention in mainstream international relations scholarship.

KEY POINTS

- Early studies linking culture and security policy focused on 'national character' as a product of language, religion, customs, socialization, and the interpretation of common historical experiences.

- Almond and Verba integrated cultural approaches into the discipline of political science. Political culture, they argued, included a commitment to values like democratic principles and institutions, ideas about morality and the use of force, the rights of individuals or collectivities, and predispositions towards the role of a country in the world.

- Cultural interpretive arguments fell out of favour with the behavioural revolution in the social sciences.

Strategic Culture and Nuclear Deterrence

In 1977, Jack Snyder brought culture into modern security studies by developing a theory of strategic culture to interpret Soviet nuclear doctrine. Snyder suggested that elites articulate a unique strategic culture related to security-military affairs that is a wider manifestation of public opinion, socialized into a distinctive mode of strategic thinking. Thus, he contended that 'a set of general beliefs, attitudes, and behavior patterns with regard to nuclear strategy has achieved a state of semi-permanence that places them on the level of "cultural" rather than mere policy' (Snyder 1977: 8; see also Booth 1981). Snyder applied his strategic cultural framework to interpret the development of the nuclear doctrines of the Soviet Union and the United States as a function of different organizational, historical, and political contexts, as well as technological constraints. He concluded that the Soviet military exhibited a preference for the pre-emptive, offensive use of force and the origins for this could be found in a Russian history of insecurity and authoritarian control.

BOX 4.2

Definitions of Strategic Culture

Strategic culture is 'a set of general beliefs, attitudes, and behavior patterns with regard to nuclear strategy that has achieved a state of semi-permanence that places them on the level of "cultural" rather than mere policy'
(Snyder 1977).

Strategic culture is the 'ideational milieu that limits behavioral choices', from which 'one could derive specific predictions about strategic choice'
(Johnston 1995).

Strategic culture is comprised of 'beliefs and assumptions that frame . . . choices about international military behavior, particularly those concerning decisions to go to war, preferences for offensive, expansionist or defensive modes of warfare, and levels of wartime casualties that would be acceptable'
(Rosen 1995).

Snyder's approach to strategic culture sought to develop a richer account of the international environment than the one derived from neorealism. Subsequent work on strategic culture, such as Ken Booth's *Strategy and Ethnocentrism* (1979), continued to explore the ideational foundations of nuclear strategy and superpower relations. Colin Gray (1981) also suggested that distinctive national styles, with 'deep roots within a particular stream of historical experience', characterize strategic development in countries like the United States and the Soviet Union. Nuclear strategy could thus be linked to historical political orientations. Gray defined strategic culture as 'modes of thought and action with respect to force, which derives from perception of the national historical experience, from aspirations for responsible behavior in national terms' and even from 'the civic culture and way of life'. Thus, strategic culture 'provides the milieu within which strategy is debated' and serves as an independent determinant of strategic policy patterns. Like Snyder, Gray considered that strategic culture would be a semi-permanent influence on security policy (1981: 35–7).

Sources of Strategic Culture

Several sources of strategic culture, encompassing both material and ideational factors, are identified in the literature. Geography, climate, and resources have been key elements in strategic thinking throughout the millennia and remain important sources of strategic culture today. For many, geographical circumstance is the key to understanding why some countries adopt particular strategic policies rather than others. For example, proximity to great powers has been viewed as an important factor, as the cases of Norway and Finland exemplified during the cold war (Graeger and Leira 2005; Heikka 2005). Additionally, while most territorial borders are settled by negotiation others have been forged through conflict and remain contested. Some states have multiple borders and may be confronted by different strategic factors at each point of contact with neighbouring states: that is, they could have to respond to multiple security dilemmas. Such factors appear to have shaped the strategic orientations of countries like Israel and could explain its motivation for acquiring a nuclear capability. Equally, ensuring access to vital resources is deemed critical to strategy. Geographic factors in the context of a changing global territorial and resource landscape consequently continue to exert influence on strategists in the twenty-first century.

History and experience are important considerations in the birth and evolution of states, and the strategic cultural identities that comprise them. International relations theory has identified several kinds of states ranging from weak to strong, colonial to post-colonial, and pre-modern, modern, and postmodern. This raises the prospect that different kinds of states may confront different strategic problems and with varying material and ideational resources, apply unique responses. [1] For newly formed states the difficulties of nation-building can compound insecurities and help shape strategic cultural identities. Conversely, for those states of ancient standing, the longevity of their existence may prompt consideration of factors that contribute to the rise and fall of great powers or civilizations and shape their policies to suit.

Another source of strategic culture is the nature of a country's political structure and defence organizations. Some countries adopt a broadly Western liberal democratic style of government while others do not. Some are considered mature democracies while others are undergoing democratic transformation and are in various stages of consolidation. Where the latter are concerned there may be cultural variables such as tribal, religious, or ethnic allegiances that operate within and across territorial boundaries, which determine the pace and depth of consolidation. Similarly, many regard defence organizations as being critical to strategic cultures but differ over the precise impact these have. Studies of the Nordic region suggest that issues such as whether the forces are professional or conscript and their experiences in conflict are significant. Military doctrines, civil–military relations, and procurement practices also may affect strategic culture (Neumann and Heikka 2005). Similarly, where civil–military relations are concerned, it is argued the debate is not so much about military doctrines, 'but the preconditions for the deployment and the kind of rationality that is at stake in those deployments' (ibid).

Myths and symbols are considered to be part of all cultural groupings. Both can act as a stabilizing or destabilizing factor in the evolution of strategic cultural identities. The notion of myth can have meaning different from the traditional understanding 'as something unfounded or false'. John Calvert (2004) writes that it can also refer to

> **"** a body of beliefs that express the fundamental, largely unconscious or assumed political values of a society—in short, as a dramatic expression of ideology. The details narrated in a political myth may be true or false; most often they meld truth and fiction in ways that are difficult to distinguish . . . To be effective, political myth must engage not reason, but belief and faith. **"**

Work on symbols has also suggested that these act as 'socially recognized objects of more or less common understanding' and which provide a cultural community with stable points of reference for strategic thought and action (Charles Elder and Roger Cobb, quoted in Poore 2004: 63).

Many analysts regard key texts as an important factor that informs actors of appropriate strategic thought and action. Traditional analyses of peace and conflict have long pointed to the influence of such texts throughout history and in different cultural settings. These may follow a historical trajectory—from Sun Tzu, who was considered to have written the *Art of War* during the time of the warring states in ancient China, through the writings of Kautilya in ancient India, and into Western understanding as a result of Thucydides' commentary on the Peloponnesian Wars and Clausewitz's writings on the nature of war as a result of observations of the Napoleonic period. At the same time, there may be competition between texts for influence on society. In a study of Greek strategic culture, for example, the oscillating influence of two distinct strategic traditions was identified. On the one hand, there are the 'traditionalists', who derive their intellectual sustenance from the exploits of Achilles, hero of the *Iliad*, and who view the world as an anarchic arena where power is the ultimate guarantee of security. On the other hand, there are the 'modernists', followers of Odysseus, the hero of the *Odyssey*, who although viewing the world as an anarchic environment consider that Greece's best strategy is to adopt a multilateral cooperative approach to peace and security (Ladis 2003). This is a dualism in strategic culture that reflects the influence of long held myths and legends, which continue to find resonance in the modern era.

Finally, transnational norms, generational change and technology are also regarded as important sources of strategic culture. Norms are understood as 'intersubjective beliefs about the social and natural world that define actors, their situations, and the possibilities of action' (Wendt 1995). Theo Farrell and Terry Terriff consider that norms can define 'the purpose and possibilities of military change' and provide guidance concerning the use of force (2001: 7). Elsewhere Farrell has studied how transnational norms of military professionalism have influenced national policies and the process by which this occurs. Farrell considers that transnational norms can be transplanted into a country's cultural context either through a process involving pressure on a target community to accept the new norms (termed 'political mobilization'), or by a process of voluntary adoption (termed

---

BOX 4.3

Potential Sources of Strategic Culture

Physical	**Political**	**Social/Cultural**
Geography	Historical Experience	Myths and Symbols
Climate	Political System	Defining Texts
Natural Resources	Elite Beliefs	
Generational Change	Military Organizations	
Technology		

←———————— **{Transnational Normative Pressures}** ————————→

'social learning'). Norm transplantation, as Farrell refers to it, can thus occur via a process of incremental adoption over time eventually achieving a cultural match between the transnational and national norms (Farrell 2001).

Finally, both generational change and technology, particularly information and communications technology, can have important ramifications for issues of empowerment and strategic reach. The arrival of the internet is a relatively recent phenomenon, yet there are now generations who have grown up with this medium of information and communication. This is also a world of individual and group empowerment that is both global in scope and potentially unique in its implications as a dual-use technology. While information and communications technology has transformed societies, it has also allowed individuals or groups to communicate in novel ways and cause disruption at a distance.

KEY POINTS

- Snyder brought the political cultural argument into the realm of modern security studies by developing a theory of strategic culture to interpret Soviet military strategy.

- Scholars have argued that national styles, with 'deep roots within a particular stream of historical experience', characterized nuclear strategy-making in countries like the United States and the Soviet Union during the cold war.

- The sources of strategic culture are considered to be: geography, climate and resources, history and experience, political structure, the nature of organizations involved in defence, myths and symbols, key texts that inform actors of appropriate strategic action, and transnational norms, generational change, and the role of technology.

- Strategic cultures may be influenced by international norms.

Constructivism and Strategic Culture

In the 1990s, the influence of constructivism prompted renewed interest (or what has been referred to as a 'third generation' of research), in developing further the theoretical work on strategic culture. Some writers have also sought to produce a theoretical framework that will supplant neorealism.

The constructivist research programme devotes particular attention to identity formation resulting from organizational processes, history, tradition, and culture. Constructivists focus on social structures at the international systems level and the role of norms in international security. According to Alexander Wendt, constructivism sees state identities and interests as 'socially constructed by knowledgeable practice' (1992: 392). For Valerie Hudson, constructivism 'views culture as an evolving system of shared meaning that governs perceptions, communications, and actions' (1997: 28–9). Consequently, Hudson considers that at 'the moment of action, culture provides the elements of grammar that define the situation, that reveal motives, and that set forth a strategy for success' (ibid.).

Alastair Iain Johnston's *Cultural Realism: Strategic Culture and Grand Strategy in Chinese History* (1995) is a quintessential third-generation work on strategic culture. The study sets out to investigate the existence and character of Chinese strategic culture, and whether this has causal linkages to the use of military force against external threats. Johnston considers that strategic culture is an 'ideational milieu that limits behavioral choices', from which 'one could derive specific predictions about strategic choice'. He chooses the period of the Ming dynasty (1368–1644) as the focus for his theoretical test and from which he derives specific observations. One is that he considers China 'has exhibited a tendency for the controlled, politically driven defensive and minimalist use of force that is deeply rooted in the statecraft of ancient strategists and a worldview of relatively complacent superiority'. He also suggests there have been two Chinese strategic cultures in action: 'one a symbolic or idealized set of assumptions and ranked preferences, and one an operational set that had a nontrivial effect on strategic choices in the Ming period' (Johnston 1995: 1). Johnston's conclusion is that while China does have characteristics of unique strategic cultures, in practice these cultures exhibit elements of classic realpolitik.

Studies of strategic culture in relation to Germany and Japan have directed attention to the significance of their 'antimilitarist political-military cultures' in shaping foreign policy behaviour. Thomas Berger notes that while Japan's economic and technological power placed it in a position to become an economic and perhaps even military superpower at the end of the cold war, the persistent post-war culture of antimilitarism was the defining element of Japan's security policy in the 1990s. In this sense, he considered that 'cultures enjoy a certain degree of autonomy and are not merely subjective reflections of concrete "objective" reality' (Berger 1998: 1). Thomas Banchoff develops a consciously constructivist, 'path-dependent' model of German policy whereby he argues that decisions taken at critical historical junctures have shaped the development of foreign policy over time (1999: 2). John Duffield concludes that, from setting off in adventurous new directions, 'Germany has exercised considerable restraint and circumspection in its external relations since 1990 . . . notwithstanding initial fears to the contrary' (1999: 2). For Duffield:

    " the overall effect of national security culture is to predispose societies in general and political elites in particular toward certain actions and policies over others. Some options will simply not be imagined . . . some are more likely to be rejected as inappropriate or ineffective than others. **"**

(1999: 771)

Another strand of this scholarship focuses on military organizational cultures. For example, Elizabeth Kier (1995) describes the significance of organizational culture in the development of French military doctrine. Steven Rosen provides an account of the ways that the military and organizational cultures in India have shaped strategy over time. Nina Tannenwald's studies (1999, 2005) of the nuclear taboo and the norm of non-proliferation, and Jeffrey Legro's work on military restraint during the Second World War are also examples of this type of contemporary work. Additionally, Roland Ebel, Raymond Taras, and James Cochrane (1991) argue that the cultures of Latin American countries are distinctive, identifiable, and influential in the development of domestic and foreign policies. According to these studies, organizational culture can be interpreted as an independent or intervening variable that directly influences strategic choice.

Case Studies of Strategic Culture

People's Republic of China

Culture plays a particularly strong role in shaping strategic behaviour in China. Scholars have identified two dominant strands of Chinese strategic culture today—the *parabellum* focused on realpolitik and the *Confucian-Mencian* strand, a philosophical orientation used mainly for idealized discourse. Scobell contends that these two strands are sometimes intertwined to shape a 'Chinese cult of defense'. Chinese civilian and military leaders repeatedly stress China's commitment to the Confucian saying 'peace is precious' (*he wei gui*), and they assert that China has never been an aggressive or expansionist state. Alastair Iain Johnston (1995) identifies this as a 'worldview of relatively complacent superiority'. The rationale for this claim that China pursues a purely defensive strategic culture has been under assault given contemporary security dynamics, however. Scobell (2002) concludes that Chinese leaders assume that any war that they fight is just and any military action defensive, 'even when it is offensive in nature'.

United States of America

Several core principles defined US strategic culture during the cold war, including American leadership of the Western Alliance, with a preference for multilateral action, nuclear deterrence, and a shared belief in the utility of military force to achieve security objectives. The 11 September 2001 terrorist attacks on the United States and the Bush administration's declaration of a war on terrorism represented a fundamental conversion in strategic culture, however. New strategic cultural orientations include a positive reaffirmation of American dominance in international security affairs, with priority consideration of homeland security, a new doctrine of pre-emption that includes a willingness to use military force to achieve security objectives, and a preference for unilateral action to reduce external constraints

on American behaviour. In spite of dramatic transformation, these new strategic cultural orientations have been packaged rhetorically as a demonstration of continuity in American support for democracy and freedom (Lantis 2005).

Japan

Throughout the cold war, Japan fostered an 'antimilitarist political-military culture' that was characterized by pacifism and dependence on security alliance with the United States. The Yoshida Doctrine stressed that Japan focus on its own economic and technological development while establishing military security through alliance with the United States. For Thomas Berger, Japan's antimilitarist sentiments became deeply institutionalized through a long historical process that included legitimated compromises. However, in wake of the 11 September attacks, Japan faces important questions of remilitarization in response to security threats. The government has provided logistical support to US and multinational coalition forces fighting in Afghanistan and Iraq, and it has pursued significant defence modernization. Japan has also bolstered its contribution to United Nations peacekeeping operations around the world (Berger 1998; Hughes 2004).

The Nordic Region: Denmark, Finland, Sweden, and Norway

The strategic cultures of Denmark, Finland, Norway and Sweden have been shaped by their proximity to great powers during the cold war (and in previous eras). Analyses of Sweden and Denmark have also revealed two forms of strategic culture. In the case of Sweden the first form emphasizes professional and technologically advanced military forces, while the second revolves around notions of a people's army based on conscription and the democratic involvement of citizens of the state. Where Denmark is concerned the two forms have been labeled cosmopolitanism and defencism. Cosmopolitanism stresses neutrality, alternative non-military means of conflict resolution and the importance of international institutions such as the former League of Nations and the United Nations. In contrast, defencism emphasizes the importance of military preparedness encapsulated in the dictum 'if you want peace, you must prepare for war' and the importance of regional military organizations, such as NATO, in defence and deterrence (Graeger, Leira 2005; Heikka, 2005).

Federal Republic of Germany

German strategic culture is a product of both geopolitical circumstances and historical memory. A deep-seated historical narrative in West Germany combined strands of

pacifistic, antimilitaristic attitudes with a sense of war guilt. These values became embedded in political institutions as well as elite discourse throughout the cold war. It was only with the fall of the Berlin Wall, German unification, and the collapse of the Soviet Union that leaders began to question their reluctance to consider the use of military force. Scholarly debate centred on the implications of 'normalization' of German foreign and security policy in the 1990s, while political discourse gradually shifted emphasis from constitutional constraints to *responsibilities* for action. Today, Germany remains a 'civilian power' willing to consider the use of force in multilateral operations endorsed by the international community (Lantis 2002).

Continuing Issues and Future Questions

Generations of scholarship have sought to produce greater understanding of the relationship between culture and state behaviour. Strategic cultural studies have consequently provided rich descriptions of specific cultures and identities, and researchers have acknowledged important links between different determinants of strategic policy. Studies have also been informed by material derived from other disciplines such as anthropology, history, sociology, and psychology. Additionally, influenced by constructivism, scholars have begun exploring the ways that strategic culture is shaped and may evolve over time. As a result, even those sceptical of this kind of analysis acknowledge that contemporary works on culture offer more than an 'explanation of last resort'.

Nevertheless, it is acknowledged there is room for refinement of the research programme. Areas for further attention include: the development of a common definition of strategic culture to build theoretically progressive models; delineation of the ways that strategic culture is created, maintained, and passed on to new generations; the question of the universality of strategic culture; and refinement of the linkages between the various sources of strategic policy. While some scholars suggest that adoption of cultural approaches represents a rejection of structure, contemporary research suggests it is possible to develop more comprehensive frameworks of strategic behaviour short of falsification of the neorealist programme. Many cultural scholars also recognize the need for a defined ontology as well as falsifiable, middle-range theory. Several important areas therefore remain for the refinement of strategic cultural analysis in a comparative perspective.

The search for a common definition

Given decades of scholarship on cultural determinants, it might be assumed that strategic culture has become an accepted *independent* variable in analyses of state behaviour: it has not. Snyder's definition of strategic culture, as 'a set of semi-permanent elite beliefs, attitudes, and behavior patterns socialized into a distinctive mode of thought', set the tone for decades of research. Today, scholars seem to agree that distinct strategic cultures exist but definitions still blur the line between preference formation, values, and state behaviours. Constructivism may have energized work on strategic culture, but the search for a common definition remains elusive.

Although not without its criticisms, Johnston's work has offered one means for developing a progressive research programme on strategic culture by characterizing it as 'an ideational milieu which limits behavior choices'. He frames strategic culture as 'shared assumptions and decision rules that impose a degree of order on individual and group conceptions of their relationship to their social, organizational or political environment'. While he noted that strategic subcultures could exist he also considered, 'there is a generally dominant culture whose holders are interested in preserving the status quo'. This approach to strategic culture as a set of shared assumptions and decision rules allows for the separation between strands of culture from dependent variable outcomes like strategic choice. Additionally, Johnston's conceptual approach to strategic culture was designed to be falsifiable, 'or at least distinguishable from non-strategic culture variables . . . [that would] provide decision-makers with a uniquely ordered set of strategic choices from which we can derive predictions about behavior' (Ebel *et al.* 1991: 246). This work is informed by studies in political psychology as well as contemporary sociological analyses of the complex connections between culture and state behaviour.

In summary, there is potential in the latest generation of work on strategic culture, which has tended to be more focused in its conceptualization of independent variables such as strategic cultural principles and dependent variables in specific security policy decisions.

Who are the 'keepers' of strategic culture?

Identifying strategic culture as a set of shared assumptions and decision rules prompts the question of how they are maintained and by whom? Most scholars prefer descriptions of political and strategic cultures as the 'property of collectivities rather than simply of the individuals that constitute them' (Duffield 1999: 23). If political culture is manifest in cognitive, evaluative, and expressive dimensions, it is conceivable that actors who carry those values might be identified. But various political leaders and institutions are engaged in historical interpretation and development of the foreign policy path. This, in turn, prompts coalition- and consensus-building efforts by specific political players. For Duffield, 'institutional sources of national predispositions are likely to reside in the central governmental organs charged with the formulation and execution of policy'. They may shape policy by constraining the information presented to policy-makers. Berger suggests that political culture can only be understood as a combination of norms and political institutions, which 'exist in an interdependent relationship'.

Elites are often the purveyors of the common historical narrative (see e.g. Banerjee 1997). Most scholars agree that elites are instrumental in defining foreign policy goals as well as the scope and direction of policy restructuring in the face of new challenges. Similarly, there is a view that elites are cognitively predisposed to maintain the status quo. But Berger's work on policy discourse suggests that strategic culture is best characterized as a 'negotiated reality' among elites. Leaders pay respect to deeply held convictions such as multilateralism and historical responsibility, but the record of past behaviour for many countries also shows that leaders chose when and where to stake claims of strategic cultural traditions; they decided when and where to consciously move beyond previous boundaries of acceptability in strategic behaviour. Ultimately, contemporary scholarship contends, elite behaviour may be more consistent with the assertion that leaders are strategic 'users of culture' who 'redefine the limits of the possible' in key foreign and security policy discourses.[2]

Political institutions—including parties and domestic coalitions—also have an impact on foreign policy behaviour. In this respect, the organizational culture literature indicates that state behaviour is a function of specific institutional orientations. Studies of Japan's and Germany's foreign policy decisions in the 1990s, for example, identified enduring institutional manifestations of strategic culture. But the keepers of the culture are not necessarily *military* bureaucracies. In Germany, the Foreign Ministry has control over foreign and security policy. In Japan, political institutions from the Diet to the Liberal Democratic Party to the Japan Self-Defence Forces share commitments to a foreign policy of restraint. Lynn Eden argues that 'organizational frames' are developed by institutions to identify problems and find solutions. These frames include 'what counts as a problem, how problems are represented, the strategies used to solve those problems, and the constraints and requirements placed on possible solutions' (Eden 2004: 51).

KEY POINTS

- There remain differences in defining strategic culture.

- Identifying strategic culture as a set of shared assumptions and decision rules prompts the question of how they are maintained and by whom. Elites are often the purveyors of the common historical narrative. Political institutions including parties and domestic coalitions can have an impact on state foreign policy behaviour.

Continuity or change?

The focus of most studies of strategic culture is on continuity or at least semi-permanence in state behaviour. Harry Eckstein (1998) suggested that the socialization of values and beliefs occurs over time. Past learning becomes sedimented in the collective consciousness and is relatively resilient to change. Lessons of the past serve as a filter for any future learning that might occur. In contrast, one dimension of the latest generation of cultural studies informed by constructivism is the recognition of the possibility of change over time.

If historical memory, political institutions, and multilateral commitments shape strategic culture, then, recent studies observe, it would seem plausible to accept that foreign policies around the globe are undergoing 'enduring transformations'. This contribution to the strategic culture literature is informed both by studies of foreign policy restructuring and constructivist ideas on foreign policy as discourse. Essentially, this work seeks to challenge 'the distinction between behaviour and culture' by considering 'culture as practice' (Rassmussen 2005: 71). It also represents a response to the criticism of prior generations of cultural approaches as static and unresponsive to international systemic pressures (see e.g. Lockhart 1999).

Under what conditions can strategic culture change? When might foreign policy decisions transcend the traditional bounds of strategic culture? Jeffrey Lantis (2002) contends that at least two conditions can cause strategic cultural dilemmas and produce changes in security policy. First, external shocks may fundamentally challenge existing beliefs and undermine past historical narratives. For German leaders in the 1990s, the scale of the humanitarian tragedies in the Balkans served as a catalyst for consideration of policy options outside the traditional bounds of German strategic culture. The recognition that groups were being systematically targeted for genocide and ethnic cleansing created a moral imperative for German action. Thus, the intensity of external shocks prompted a re-examination on all sides of the proper response. Some writers have even suggested that ethnic cleansing in Bosnia eroded the moral legitimacy of pacifism on the German political left and led to an atmosphere more permissive of the use of force to stop such violence (Lantis 2002).

Many scholars also consider that any process of change would not be easy. Potential catalysts for change, Berger argued, might be 'dramatic events or traumatic experiences [such as revolutions, wars, and economic catastrophes]' that would 'discredit thoroughly core beliefs and values' (Duffield 1999: 23). Such change would be accompanied by extreme psychological stress and require a resocialization process, involving participation by various groups in the crafting of a compromise on a new political cultural orientation.

Second, foreign policy behaviour may break the traditional bounds of strategic cultural orientations when primary tenets of strategic thought come into direct conflict with one another. In other words, a country with interpretive codes of support for democracy and an aversion to the use of military force faces a strategic cultural dilemma when confronted by a challenge to democracy that necessitates a military response. Japan's government confronted this question in relation to the struggle for self-determination in East Timor. The same type of dilemma may arise from a conflict between commitments to multilateralism and unilateral convictions that norms are being violated. Michael Thompson, Richard Ellis, and Aaron Wildavsky argue that cultures remain vital only if their core principles continue to generate solutions that satisfy human needs and make sense of the world (1990: 69–70). Products of this strategic cultural *dissonance* include occasional state defections from multilateral arrangements, the development of alternative diplomatic initiatives, or stipulations for policy cooperation.

Thus, strategic cultural dilemmas define new directions for foreign policy and demand the reconstruction of historical narratives. Changes—including abrupt and fairly dramatic reorientations of security policy behaviour—are possible and strategic cultural analysis must be more reflective of the conditions that draw out such changes. Swidler recognizes that the relationship between state behaviour and strategic culture becomes especially apparent 'in unsettled cultural periods . . . when explicit ideologies govern action [and] structural opportunities for action determine which among competing ideologies survive in the long run' (1986: 273). As NATO leaders implement a new strategic concept, China pursues liberalized trade policies, Iraq struggles for democratic consolidation, and the United States leads a global war on terrorism in the twenty-first century, research on strategic culture must also adapt for long-term relevance.

Perhaps Berger is correct that strategic culture is best understood as a 'negotiated reality' among foreign policy elites. While leaders pay respect to deeply held convictions associated with strategic culture, the story of foreign policy development may best be understood as the pursuit of legitimation for preferred policy courses that may, or may not, conform to traditional cultural boundaries. Cruz contended that elites have more latitude than scholars generally allow. They may 'recast a particular agenda as most appropriate to a given collective reality or . . . recast reality itself by establishing a (new) credible balance between the known and the unknown'. In short, Cruz argued, they 'redefine the limits of the possible, both descriptively and prescriptively'. (She acknowledged that this raises a critical dichotomy between culture as a system of meaning and culture as practice: 2000: 278.)

The universality of strategic culture?

The events of 11 September 2001 and the war on terrorism have prompted renewed attention to the role of culture in shaping state (and non-state) behaviour. One of the more complex questions carried over through several generations of scholarship relates to what types of actor are likely to have defined strategic cultures and what is the context in which these emerge? For example, Snyder's proposition that the Soviet state had a distinctive strategic culture and this influenced its nuclear policy was framed within the broader parameters of the East–West cold war. The context was significant but did it also imply that authoritarian political systems are more likely to have defined strategic cultures than democratic ones? Conversely, are authoritarian political systems less likely to have definable strategic subcultures? Can non-state actors have strategic cultures? Can regional organizations or meta-cultural groups have some form of strategic culture?

The latter question is important for the future of the European Union (EU). The EU formalized a common European Security Strategy (ESS) for the first time in its history in December 2003. Some hailed the achievement as marking a common European strategic culture, but others question whether the regional organization will be capable of forging a bond of common threat perceptions and interests. Optimists such as Paul Cornish and Geoffrey Edwards (2001), contend that 'there are signs that a European strategic culture is already developing through a socialisation process'. They define EU strategic culture as simply 'the institutional confidence and processes to manage and deploy military force as part of the accepted range of legitimate and effective policy instruments' (2001: 587; see also Longhurst and Zaborowski 2005). Similarly, for Christoph Meyer (2004), the European Council vote on ESS in December 2003 provided a necessary 'strategic concept' around which to focus attention and resources. In contrast, Julian Lindley-French (2002) considers that Europe lacks both the capabilities and will to establish a common foreign and security policy in the foreseeable future. He characterizes the Europe of today as 'not so much an architecture as a decaying arcade of stately structures of varying designs reflective of a bygone era' (2002: 789).

Samuel Huntington's 'civilizational thesis' contends that states are part of broader civilizations that share strong bonds of culture, societal values, religion, and ideologies (1993a, 1993b, 1996). The most important of these bonds, he argued, is religion, and 'the major civilizations in human history have been closely identified with the world's great religions' (1996: 47). Meta-cultural ties, taken to the broadest level of categorization, are civilizational identities that shapes change in the world. The crux of the civilizational thesis is Huntington's argument that conflict is more likely to occur between states of different civilizations in the post-cold war era. Ultimately, Huntington insisted, decision-makers would be 'much more likely to see threats coming from states whose societies have different cultures and hence which they do not understand and feel they cannot trust' (1993a: 34).

Finally, can the strategic culture approach apply to non-state actors operating across territorial boundaries where identities may be formed in the realms of both physical and cyber space? The advent of the cyber revolution has generated several issues concerning our understanding of conflict and security (Rattray 2002: 221–45; Schwartzstein 1996, 1998). Emily Goldman writes that threats in cyberspace 'range from the systematic and persistent, to the decentralized and dispersed, to the accidental and non-malevolent' (2003: 1). Additionally, while acknowledging that the technologies associated with globalization have enabled terrorist groups to conduct operations that 'are deadlier, more distributed, and more difficult to combat than those of their predecessors', James Kiras argues that these same technologies 'can be harnessed to defeat terrorism by those governments with the will and resources to combat it' (2005: 479). According to Victor Cha's globalization-security spectrum, 'The most far-reaching security effect of global-ization is its complication of the basic concept of "threat" in international relations' (2000, see also Arquilla and Ronfeldt 2001: 1). Technology enhances 'the salience of substate extremist groups or fundamentalist groups because their ability to organize transnationally, meet virtually, and utilize terrorist tactics has been substantially enhanced by the globalization of technology and information' (Cha 2000: 392; see also Cronin 2002/3).

Do these developments imply that transnational non-state terrorist actors can have a strategic culture? This could depend on the approach to strategic culture adopted. If the approach considers that strategic cultures apply to actors that have a material basis, especially a defined territory, then only states could be included in the framework. Conversely, if ideational factors such as myths and symbols are deemed important and that these gain significance transnationally and via new communication modes such as cyberspace, then this approach could encompass such actors.

KEY POINTS

- The focus of most studies of strategic culture is on continuity of state behaviour. However, one dimension of the latest generation of cultural studies is the possibility of change over time.

- At least two key factors may cause strategic cultural change: external shocks and strategic cultural dissonance.

- One of the more complex questions that carries over through generations relates to what types of actors are most likely to have defined strategic cultures: states, regional organizations, civilizations, and even non-state groups such as terrorist networks?

- Globalization and revolutions in information technology suggest that future threats will be more diffuse, more dispersed, and more multidimensional.

Conclusion

Recent events have renewed scholarly and policymaking interest in strategic culture. Events, challenges and new developments like the democratic consolidation in post-war Iraq, US–China relations, the war on terror, and the advent of new technologies have generated a requirement to think innovatively about the relationship between culture and strategic policy outcomes. This chapter has identified a number of conceptual and empirical issues associated with the development of the literature in this area. To accomplish this, several generations of scholarly work on strategic culture have been considered, including more recent constructivist approaches. The chapter has also considered the question of 'ownership' of strategic culture and whether non-state, state, and multi-state actors may possess distinctive strategic cultures in the twenty-first century.

One overarching conclusion from this survey of strategic culture is that research still needs to be done to provide detailed studies of strategic cultures for the purposes of comparative perspective. At the same time, culturalists remind us of a key caveat in these pursuits: in seeking to identify causal relations there is a risk of over-simplifying the social world and consequently categories from one case may be applied inappropriately to others. An inadequate knowledge of a given strategic culture may lead to misinterpretation of attributes such as pride, honour, duty, and also security and stability. Considering strategic culture as 'a dynamic interplay between discourse and practice' may offer one means for accommodating the issue of the mutable nature of strategic culture. Similarly, it could illuminate both how strategic culture evolves from generation to generation and is transformed by competing groups through negotiation and debate (Howlett and Glenn 2005: 129).

Finally, whether strategic cultural research can illuminate the actions of transnational non-state terrorist actors is also crucial to this research endeavour. Much has been accomplished already in responding to the challenges the post-9/11 world has engendered. This should not be overlooked, but the world does not stand still and neither do strategic cultures. In a globalized and technologically dynamic environment where material and ideational forces are at work this could be the key to developing future policies. Further research could therefore seek to integrate the knowledge gleaned into threat assessments. And analyses of trends in strategic cultures of all types could seek to identify changes occurring over time, providing some warning when new challenges emerge and be as well prepared as pragmatically feasible to respond when the time comes.

? QUESTIONS

1. What are the different definitions of culture and what implications do these differences have for the study of security policy?

2. Why is there no universally accepted definition of culture?

3. What are some specific examples of strategic cultures (or historical narratives) in countries around the world?

4. What are the sources of these strategic cultures? In your opinion, which are the most important and why?

5. What should be the historical 'starting point' for research on strategic culture?

6. How valuable are cultural explanations of security policy? Can state behaviour be explained without reference to culture or national style?

7. What conditions might cause strategic cultural change?

8. Identify what are the primary themes that define a country's strategic culture. Can you imagine scenarios in which these themes might come into conflict with one another? And what would government leaders do in such situations?

9. Can a strategic cultural framework be applied to a non-state actor such as a terrorist organization? Can it be used to understand regional security policies?

10. What are the implications of globalization for our understanding of strategic culture?

WEB LINKS

● **http://mofa.go.jp** This is the official website of the Japanese Ministry of Foreign Affairs, where you can learn more about Japan's foreign and security policy posture.

● **http://sipri.se/projects/Milex/Introduction.html** The Stockholm International Peace Research Institute (SIPRI) monitors trends in military expenditures and policies throughout the world.

● **http://sunsite.nus.edu.sg/noframe.html** Sun SITE Singapore is an information base for on-line resources related to countries and security policies in southeast Asia.

● **http://europa.eu.int/institutions/cfsp/index_en.htm** This is the main website of the European Union, which includes valuable archival materials as well as descriptions of contemporary EU foreign and security policy institutions and initiatives.

● **http://www.ccc.nps.navy.mil/si/2005/Oct/khan2Oct05.asp** The October 2005 special issue of the online journal, *Strategic Insights*, examines the theme of comparative strategic culture. The journal is sponsored by the Center for Contemporary Conflict at the Naval Postgraduate School in Monterey, California.

 Visit the Online Resource Centre that accompanies this book for lots of interesting additional material http://www.oxfordtextbooks.co.uk/orc/baylis_strategy2e/.

5

Law, Politics, and the Use of Force

JUSTIN MORRIS

Chapter Contents

Reader's Guide

This chapter discusses the role of international law in international politics, focusing specifically upon the efficacy of legal constraint of the use of force by states. It is not intended that the chapter will provide a detailed examination of the substantive legal provision relating to the use of force, though the basic proscriptions will be outlined and commented upon. Rather the intention is to focus upon the manner in which legal regulation influences the behaviour of sovereign states and in particular the political and strategic decisions that they take. It will be argued that international law exerts a significant, though by no means always decisive, influence on the behaviour of states, and that this is the case even when states are dealing with issues which are perceived to be of great national interest and where the use of force is at issue.

The Efficacy of International Law

There is a commonly held view that international law has little effect upon the behaviour of states. According to this view international law is simply a tool in the diplomatic kitbag that can be utilized to justify politically motivated actions. Ken Matthews captures this sentiment:

" The common view seems to be that international law is honoured more in its breach than in its observance and that since it seems to be broken so much it can hardly be said to exist at all. Moreover . . . there is little evidence that international law restrains states from pursuing their interests in the international system. "

(1996: 126)

This assessment of international law is reflected in the dominant approach to international politics known as realism. Realists portray the world as being dominated by states that act only in pursuit of their national interests. These states interact in a world that is anarchic, in the sense that sovereign states recognize no higher authority. In such a world, interaction is regulated through the exercise of power (and ultimately through the utilisation of military power). For realists there is little scope for effective international legal regulation.

This view of world and international law's role within it is challenged by scholars such as Louis Henkin. Henkin observed that 'it is probably the case that almost all nations observe almost all principles of international law and almost all of their obligation almost all of the time' (1968: 47). So why does the common perception of international law not reflect this? The answer lies in what one might call a perception/reality gap. This operates at a number of levels. The low regard in which international law is commonly held is partially a consequence of inappropriate parallels drawn between domestic and international law, often leading to the unwarranted conclusion that international law lacks the status of true 'law'. Even amongst those immersed in international law such doubts sometimes appear, as Sir Hersch Lauterpacht famously commented, 'international law is the vanishing point of law' (1952: 381). The common assumption is that at the international level the norm in response to legal edicts is breach, whereas domestically the norm is compliance.

BOX 5.1

Symptoms of the Perception/Reality Gap

Perception	Reality
International law is regularly flouted	International law is usually obeyed
Military conflict is the norm	Military conflict is the exception
International law regulates the use of force	International law regulates almost all aspects of inter-state activity
Law is prohibitive	Law is facilitative

In reality the norm in both cases is compliance, though this may be less so at the international level than at the domestic.

The common failure to recognize this is the consequence of another misleading idea, namely that to operate effectively it is essential that a system of law possesses the 'legal trinity' of a legislature, an effective and centralized police force, and judiciary. At the international level this is all but absent; notwithstanding the contributions of United Nations organs such as the Security Council, General Assembly, and the International Court of Justice, and other bodies such as the International Criminal Court, the international system lacks these facilities. But the argument is misleading because it is predicated on the notion that domestic law is synonymous with criminal law, resulting in a preoccupation with issues of apprehension and enforcement, and hence the legal trinity. As the late Hilaire McCoubrey noted: 'Enforcement—specifically processes of criminal enforcement—tends to be emphasised in external observation of the operation of law and legal systems . . . but it can be argued that this is a seriously misplaced emphasis' (1998: 271).

It is of course true that, in theory if to a lesser extent in practice, domestic criminal law is obligatory, policed by the state and enforced through the imposition of judicially passed sanctions—though sadly it does not follow from this that it is always effective. But it should also be remembered that other forms of legal regulation function effectively without such characteristics. Contract law, for example, impinges only upon the lives of those who choose to enter into contracts, its enforcement is dependent upon the parties resorting to self-help, and in many systems it does not provide a punitive response to breaches. The fact that international law does not conform to familiar models of criminal law does not deprive it of its status as law nor, necessarily, of its efficacy.

Another reason for the perception–reality gap is the way in which we learn about international law and the ways it influences the behaviour of states. Academic writing on international relations tends to concentrate on conflict rather than cooperation. This focus has two main implications: first, that international law is often broken, and secondly, that its main function is to regulate the use of force. Neither is true; interstate military conflict is the exception, and for the most part international law provides for orderly and predictable intercourse between states at a mundane, 'everyday' level that has nothing to do with military conflict. The media's coverage of world events shares academia's preoccupation with conflict, and while in the commercial world of journalism the need to generate attention-grabbing headlines and stories is readily understandable, the breadth of the audience makes its impact all the more deleterious.

KEY POINTS

- Most states obey most of the law most of the time.
- International law has a significant, though not necessarily decisive, influence upon the policies that states adopt.
- Concerns regarding enforcement of the law tend to be over-emphasized.
- Parallels drawn between international and domestic law, particularly where the focus is upon criminal law, are often inappropriate, ill-informed, and misleading.

Why States Obey the Law

The observation that states generally obey the law should come as no great surprise. International law, and indeed law more generally, is designed not to prohibit those actions which states (or individuals in the domestic setting) would normally choose to undertake, but rather to codify accepted modes of behaviour; good law is facilitative, not prohibitive. International law comprises behavioural regulations that states wish others to obey and which they are prepared to obey themselves. Law reflects and strengthens social order and values, it does not seek to impose them and were this not the case it would be both ineffective and short-lived. The law should not be viewed as an end in itself, but rather as a means to an end. It is a mechanism through which societies seek to achieve political objectives, though once these objectives have become enshrined in law, the law in turn serves to condition acceptable political activity (Reus-Smit 2004).

This observation raises a further difficult question: *which* social values and objectives are to be legally codified. For realists, it will always be those that secure and perpetuate the privileged position of the satisfied powers, but this is an over-simplification of the complexities involved in the development of normative frameworks (Morris 2005). Nevertheless, even advocates of international law acknowledge the difficulties inherent in codification:

> Since law is generally a conservative force, it is more likely to be observed by those more content with their lot. Nations that believe that they have a particular stake in world order will themselves attend to law, and their compliance will establish a comfortable position from which to insist that others do the same.

(Henkin 1968: 53)

The challenge, therefore, is to establish an order premised upon the codification of behavioural norms in which a sufficiently large proportion of states believe themselves to have an interest. 'Even the rich and the mighty . . . cannot commonly obtain what they want by force and dictation and must be prepared to pay the price of reciprocal or compensating obligation. Even they, moreover, seek legitimacy and acceptance for their policies' (1968: 31).

The compromise required is to preserve international order while accommodating the interests of both the privileged 'haves' and the struggling 'have nots'. In other words, the international order must be, and must be seen to be, just. Order and justice are in this sense symbiotic, though the balance between them is likely to be a source of perpetual disagreement. Such tensions notwithstanding, it follows that in a reasonably just international order states will obey international law because they deem it to be in their interests to do so.

The suggestion that states obey the law because they deem it to be in their interests is not to reaffirm the realist position that law is simply a diplomatic tool to be employed to justify politically motivated actions. Ian Hurd's work provides a particularly lucid explanation of this point. Hurd (1999) explains how states are induced to accept rules through coercion, calculations of self-interest, and/or legitimization. Coercion involves an asymmetric power relationship in which one actor is, through the exercise of power, forced to comply with a rule. Where compliance results from calculations of self-interest, it is self-restraint motivated by the likelihood of a beneficial outcome that induces compliance. In both cases compliance results from prudential calculation. In neither are the content of the rule or its associated institution(s) valued or relevant. What distinguishes the two scenarios is that in cases of coercion states obey the law for fear of punishment but find themselves, in contrast to cases of self-interest, ultimately disadvantaged by doing so. Systems which depend on coercion in order to ensure compliance are difficult to sustain because the resource costs required to ensure compliance are high. Systems that depend on self-interest to ensure observance are less costly, but they tend to be unpredictable and unstable because of their reliance on *ad hoc* cost—benefit calculations. For these reasons it can be concluded that legal systems which depend primarily on coercion and/or self-interest for their observance are likely to be ineffective and short-lived. Sustainable and effective legal regulation depends, therefore, on a widespread shared perception of legitimacy. In such cases compliance is motivated neither by fear of punitive sanction nor by self-interest (as defined above) but rather by the belief that the law is, in some sense, of intrinsic value. In such circumstances its observance and general standing form a constituent element of states' interests and identities. Interest is defined in relation to the law itself rather than by consideration of the beneficial or detrimental consequences of compliance. While states are 'interested' in the sense that they pursue goals, they do so within behavioural parameters that are internally driven and hence non-compliance is the exception to the rule.

Whether in any particular case it is fear of coercion, calculations of self-interest, or perceptions of legitimacy that lead to observance of the law is likely to be unclear and any claims on the matter non-falsifiable. In keeping with the generally low esteem in which international law is held there tends to be an assumption that prudential calculations are the primary motivating factor. However, as Hurd notes: '[i]t is unreasonable to use the difficulty of proving any one motivation to justify the retreat to the default position that privileges another, without requiring similar proof. . . . We have no better reason to assume coercion [or self-interest] than to assume legitimacy' (1999: 392). In fact, given its nature, in the case of international law coercion is unlikely to be the most significant motivation.

BOX 5.2

Why do States Obey International Law?

Coercion. Involves an asymmetric power relationship in which one actor is, through the exercise of power, forced to comply with a rule.

Self-interest. Involves an ad hoc calculation of whether compliance with a rule will result in a beneficial or detrimental outcome.

Legitimacy. Compliance results from the belief that a rule is of value. Rule compliance is an integral part of an actor's identity.

Considerations of self-interest and legitimacy provide more plausible explanations, though determining the relative importance of these motivational factors is a complex process. Consider, for example, the reputational benefits that states derive from observance of legal obligations. States seek to avoid the stigma of being branded a 'law-breaker'—or in current parlance a 'rogue state'. They expect that having a trustworthy reputation will be advantageous because others will reciprocate in future dealings with them, not simply with regard to the specific rule or agreement in question, but with regard to legal commitments more generally. This could, therefore, be said to be a prudential calculation, that is, observation is motivated by self-interest. Against this, however, there is ample evidence that policy leaders, and particularly those who operate within systems long immersed in liberal-democratic traditions, do not want to be branded law-breakers because they attach significant value to the notion of the rule of law. They consider rule observance to be of value in itself.

A second reason for abiding by the law is the perception that it is of substantive value, that is to say that the modes of behaviour enshrined within particular rules warrant respect. Legal rules are a means by which societies pursue collective goals. The greater the extent to which states share these aspirations, and that a specific rule assists in their attainment, the more likely it is that the rule will be accepted and obeyed by states (Franck 1990). A third reason why state officials observe international legal obligations is that they perceive international law to be of functional value. While the importance of a particular law may be questioned, leaders recognize the contribution that legal regulation as a whole makes to international society. Since the authority of the law will be undermined if states pick and choose the rules by which they abide, all rules must be followed. In both these cases prudential and legitimacy concerns again come into play. Consider, for example, rules pertaining to non-use of force, territorial integrity, and the inviolability of borders. These clearly serve to protect states at an individual level and so it can be argued that states obey them out of self-interest. But there is ample evidence to suggest that states value order as a social good and since the collapse of colonialism there is a general and growing acceptance that states have the right to political independence and freedom, and so to determine their own futures.

A final factor that gives rise to the general acceptance of legal regulation and conformity to the law is inertia: states become habituated into formulating and adopting policies which

---

BOX 5.3

Understanding Breaches of the Law

- The fact that a state breaches a rule of international law does not in itself demonstrate the inefficacy of the rule or of international law more generally.
- Breaches of the law invariably occur against a background of general conformity to both the specific rule and the law in general.
- Widespread censure following a breach reinforces the rule.
- Breach is invariably accompanied by an explanation based on recourse to legal argument.

accord with legal rules. This may be because under monist constitutional arrangements international legal obligations become incorporated into the body of domestic law (Brownlie 1990: 32). Where this occurs government policies that violate international legal obligations may give rise to action in the domestic courts. There is, however, a less tangible way in which states become habituated into following the law: individuals who comprise governing elites and bureaucracies become socialized into behaving in certain prescribed ways. Moreover, to the extent that those charged with formulating policy are subject to public, media, and legislative scrutiny, policies which violate legal obligations may be perceived as non-viable.

Although states generally act in accordance with the law, they do not *always* obey it. What do breaches of international law tell us about its role and status in international politics? While perhaps counter-intuitive, law-breaking often serves to demonstrate the strength of the law, at least in so far as it remains the exception. (See Box 5.3) Because states normally obey the law, any breach is likely to occur against a background of general conformity to both the body of international law in general and to the specific rule in question. Where the breaking of a rule attracts widespread international censure, this demonstrates the efficacy, rather than inefficacy, of the rule. Iraq's 1990 invasion of Kuwait was such a clear breach of international law and was so overwhelmingly criticized that its effect was to bolster, rather than undermine, the legal prohibition of the use of force in international relations. In less clear-cut cases where there exists legal ambiguity, 'breach' may result from a genuine disagreement over the legality of an act and may, therefore, in fact embody some element of conformity. The general prohibition of the use of force, for instance, is subject to numerous alternative interpretations regarding the extent of the prohibition and the permissibility of exceptions to it (e.g. pre-emptive strike and human-itarian intervention) Finally in this regard it should be noted that violations of the law are invariably accompanied by an assertion that, while the rule in question is perceived by the offending state to be ordinarily valid and applicable, exceptional circumstances or the existence of a competing principle necessitate breach. Particularly in the latter case a degree of caution is necessary; history is replete with claims of this sort which are clearly disingenuous, but it is clear that, from invulnerable superpowers to the most delinquent of rogues, when states opt to break the law they seek to justify their actions in terms of the law. Hollow, cynical, and hypocritical as these invocations of the law may be, the very fact that they are made is instructive.

KEY POINTS

- States are motivated to obey the law by a complex combination of factors (fear of coercion, self-interest, and perceptions of legitimacy).

- Breaches of the law often serve to demon-strate its strength and not its weakness.

- Where states break the law they very rarely seek to repudiate the validity of international law completely and invari-ably attempt to justify their actions in terms of the law.

International Law and the Use of Force

The two broad functions of the laws of armed conflict are performed respectively by the *jus ad bellum* and the *jus in bello*. The *jus ad bellum* (lit. the law towards war) governs and seeks to avert or limit resort to armed force in the conduct of international relations. The *jus in bello* (lit. the law in war) governs and seeks to moderate the actual conduct of hostilities. It should be made clear from the outset that that these sectors are distinct in both purpose and implication. The applicability of the *jus in bello* is not affected by the legitimacy or otherwise of the initial resort to armed force by either of the belligerents; if it were otherwise the door would be opened to a return to the worst excesses not of premodern 'just war' concepts as such, but to its systematic historic abuses. If, despite the legal restraints of the *jus ad bellum*, armed conflict breaks out, the *jus in bello* becomes operative and equally applicable irrespective of which party initially transgressed the law. These are pragmatic objectives rooted in the practical experience of warfare. Yet the idea of legal constraint upon the waging of war, though ancient in origin, seems profoundly paradoxical. Two distinct lines of argument underpin this apparent paradox, each corresponding to the two areas into which the laws of armed conflict (see Box 5.4) are divided.

The *jus as bellum* seeks to control the circumstances in which states use force in their international relations. When the logic of 'power politics' appears at its most intense, however, factors mitigating in favour of legal observance may be most compromised. To quote more fully Sir Hersch Lauterpacht: 'If international law is . . . the vanishing point of law, the law of war is even more conspicuously the vanishing point on international law' (1952: 381).

That states do not consider the use of force as a viable or acceptable part of day-to-day international relations is clear. Yet it is equally apparent that it is considered as a policy of last resort. In such circumstances the normal rules of international intercourse are most strained. As the German Chancellor Theobald von Bethmann-Hollweg stated in his infamous *Reichstag* speech at the outset of the First World War: 'We are now in a state of necessity, and necessity knows no law. . . . He who is menaced as we are, and is fighting for his highest possession, can only consider how he is to hack his way through' (Wilson 1928: 305). The German Chancellor's statement is of interest, however, not only because of the relationship which it suggests between necessity and law, but also because it indicates that the

---

BOX 5.4

The Laws of Armed Conflict

Jus ad bellum (the law towards war)

Governs and seeks to limit resort to armed force in the conduct of international relations

Major source: Article 2(4) and Chapter VII of the UN Charter

Jus in bello (the law in war)

Governs and seeks to moderate the actual conduct of hostilities

Major source: the four 1949 Geneva Conventions and the Hague Conventions of 1899 and 1907

decision to invade two neutral states was taken not in *disregard* for the law, but rather in *conscious* breach of it. The lawfulness of the action being contemplated was clearly a pertinent issue in the decision-making process.

This is not to suggest that legal questions are at the forefront of policy-makers' minds when they contemplate the use of force. The uppermost questions will be ones relating to whether policy objectives can be achieved through the use of force at a reasonable cost. What constitutes a 'reasonable' cost will depend, of course, upon the perceived importance of the objective in question. In a fight for ultimate survival almost any cost may appear reasonable, whereas in one fought for political aggrandizement or to secure the welfare of non-nationals, the threshold of acceptability may be much lower. We may conceive of the notion of 'cost' in several ways. There are the direct costs of conflict, of lives and assets, both military and civilian, lost in the fray. Given the destructive power of modern weaponry these may be almost without limit; in such situations legal niceties may seem at best a tangential consideration. There are political costs: what will be the response, both domestically and internationally, to a policy involving the use of force? Much may here depend upon the outcome of the conflict, but even victory cannot guarantee acclaim. If the action is perceived to be in violation of the accepted norms of international behaviour enshrined within international law even political allies may disapprove. Despite the improbability of effective direct sanction, legal considerations are here paramount, for international law provides the medium of political exchange upon the basis of which states will formulate, articulate, and justify their response.

Normative costs also must be considered. What will be the likely long-term impact of a breach of the cardinal rule prohibiting the use of force upon international order? Repeated violations can only undermine an order in which both the powerful and the weak have a vested interest. For the former the incentive in preserving the existing order and its rules is readily apparent, though the rules themselves may militate against great powers adopting policies which are blatantly self-interested. For the weaker members of international society the legal framework's prohibition of the use of force is also beneficial. Many states are militarily incapable of defending themselves and their survival is therefore dependent upon the general observance of these rules. As Robert Jackson observes: 'Ramshackle states today are not open invitations for unsolicited external intervention. They are not allowed to disappear juridically . . . They cannot be deprived of sovereignty as a result of war, conquest, partition, or colonialism such as frequently happened in the past' (1993: 23–4). This may have as much to do with the utility of territorial possession in contemporary international politics as with more enlightened post-1945 political outlooks, but nevertheless, for a significant number of the world's states, sovereign independence is primarily legally enshrined rather than militarily ensured.

According to this argument international law plays a crucial role in preserving international order. Conflicts do, however, still occur. What role can international law play *once hostilities have commenced*? War, as an ultimate collapse of 'normal' international relations, appears to be a situation in which the most ruthless use of force must prevail and in which the acceptance of legal constraint can serve only as a potentially fatal self-inflicted impediment to effective action. If it was indeed the purpose of legal norms to obstruct and diminish the combat efficacy of fighting forces, such strictures would be fully justified and norms so conceived could not long endure. That, however, is neither their purpose nor their effect. The real foundation of legal constraint upon warfare can be found clearly stated in a much misrepresented passage in Carl von Clausewitz's classic work *On War*. The great Prussian strategist wrote that,

> **"** He who uses force unsparingly, without reference to the bloodshed involved, must obtain a superiority if his adversary uses less vigour in its application . . . From the social condition both of States in themselves and in their relations to each other . . . War arises, and by it War is . . . controlled and modified. But these things do not belong to War itself, they are only given conditions; and to introduce into the philosophy of War itself a principle of moderation would be an absurdity. **"**
>
> **(Clausewitz 1982: 102)**

If war is analysed as a phenomenon in isolation, a logic of illimitable force might indeed seem to be suggested. However, as Clausewitz indicates, wars and armed conflicts do not arise in isolation, but occur in the real context of international relations, which imports expectations that not only condition reactions to armed conflict but themselves have real political and military effect.

In the first place, needless barbarity renders both the conduct and the ultimate resolution of conflict more difficult than it otherwise might be. As Colonel Klaus Kuhn commented: 'the quickest way of achieving and maintaining a lasting peace is to conduct hostilities humanely . . . It is evident that humanitarian considerations cannot be dissociated from the strategic concept of military leaders' (1987: 1). The proscription of unnecessary barbarity is counselled not only by ethical and humanitarian considerations but also by reference to the response of other states to a belligerent power and the likelihood that conflict will be prolonged when fear of probable mistreatment renders a cornered enemy desperate. The idea is not new, it was asserted in the fifth century BC by the Chinese philosopher Sun Tzu in advising commanders, 'Do not press a desperate foe too hard'. There is ample historical evidence to support the contention. In 1945 the forces of the Third Reich sought to resist the advancing Soviet army, whose fury was at least in part occasioned by prior German conduct, long after it was clear that all hope of success was gone and even as vast numbers hastened to surrender to the Allies in the west. All wars must eventually end, if only through the economic exhaustion of the belligerents. Peaceful relations must be resumed. This process is, *ex hypothesi*, never easy and the more brutal the conflict the more difficult post-war reconstruction will be.

A second criticism levelled at the *jus in bello* is that, to the extent that it humanizes war, it also encourages it. This argument, however, has a major flaw: the inherent cruelty of war does not prevent its occurrence. If the argument were correct, it is difficult to imagine how war could have been contemplated after the carnage of Verdun, the Somme, and Passchendaele. That war continues to occur is a reflection of the fact that rarely do those who start wars have to fight in them or otherwise become their victims. To deny humanitarian mitigation to those who do find themselves engaged in combat would be a cruel logic indeed.

There are powerful ethical and practical arguments for norms of constraint in armed conflict. However, norms governing the conduct of war, in distinction from those governing resort to armed force, are by their nature no more than mitigatory in effect. If it were to be pretended that either ethics or law could render war as such humane, the 'absurdity' to which Clausewitz referred would rapidly become all too evident.

KEY POINTS

- Even in the most extreme of circumstances, such as those involving contemplation of the use of force, legal factors continue to influence the decisions that officials make.

- War is a social phenomenon and hence the notion of legal regulation of warfare remains pertinent.

- Norms governing the conduct of war are no more than mitigatory in effect.

Jus ad Bellum

The *jus ad bellum* is now founded primarily upon Article 2(3)(4) and Chapter VII (Articles 39–51) of the UN Charter. Article 2(3)(4) of the UN Charter provides that:

> (3) All Members shall settle their international disputes by peaceful means in such a manner that international peace and security, and justice, are not endangered.
>
> (4) All Members shall refrain in their international relations from the threat or use of force against the territorial integrity or political independence of any State, or in any other manner inconsistent with the Purposes of the United Nations

The basic proscription set out by Article 2(4) is recognized as having the character of *jus cogens* and as such is, under Article 53 of the Vienna Convention on the Law of Treaties 1969: 'a peremptory norm of general international law . . . accepted and recognised by the international community of States as a whole as a norm from which no derogation is permitted . . .' The Article 2(4) prohibition is qualified by two essential exceptions: (1) the inherent right of individual and collective self-defence in the face of armed attack, preserved by Article 51; and (2) action for the maintenance or restoration of international peace and security authorized by the UN Security Council under Article 42.

Article 51 of the UN Charter states: 'Nothing in the present Charter shall impair the inherent right of individual or collective self-defence if an armed attack occurs against a Member of the United Nations, until the Security Council has taken the measures necessary to maintain international peace and security.' Taken in conjunction with the wording of Article 2(4), Article 51 raises a number of issues. In the case of Article 2(4) what, for example, constitutes 'the threat or use of force' and is such a threat or use which is not 'against the territorial integrity or political independence' of a state permissible? What, under the terms of Article 51, constitutes the 'inherent right of individual or collective self-defence' and at what point can the Security Council be deemed to have 'taken the measures necessary to maintain international peace and security'? These questions have emerged in debates regarding the legality of practices such as anticipatory self-defence, action taken in response to terrorism, military intervention to protect nationals abroad, and humanitarian intervention.

The terrorist attacks of 11 September 2001 and the subsequent pursuit of the 'War on Terror' have brought such debates into even sharper focus. Those who argue in favour of a relaxation of the rules prohibiting the use of force maintain that the presence of global terrorist networks which reject all aspects on international regulation, combined with their potential use of nuclear, chemical, and biological weapons, necessitates a reinterpretation of the law so that states can legally undertake preventive military action against such networks and the states which harbour or otherwise assist them. This argument goes well beyond that put by states such as Israel that Articles 2(4) and 51 of the UN Charter must be understood to allow for acts of anticipatory self-defence. This argument was premised upon the idea that 'inherent right' of self-defence included the pre-Charter right to carry out a pre-emptive strike. Such a strike, it was recognized, must be proportionate, and could be undertaken only against a threat that was imminent and not preventable by peaceful means (Arend and Beck 1993: 71–9). Reformulated to take account of recent events, many advocates of anticipatory self-defence now argue for the right to make preventive strikes, discarding the requirement that the threat of attack posed must be imminent. Security strategies issued by both the United States (2002: 15) and the European Union (2003: 7) allude to such a right and it was a key issue in the debates over the legality of the 2003 Iraq War. The fact the member states of the EU, despite their 2003 declaration on the matter, were bitterly divided over the conflict is evidence of how controversial the issue of self-defence has become and is likely to remain.

Notwithstanding the legal, moral, or political merits of arguments in favour of a more flexible application of the rules regulating the use of force, their propensity to emanate from the more powerful members of the international community is a reason for caution. Consider, for example, the conclusion of Franck and Rodley in relation to humanitarian intervention, that while the saving of lives was meritorious: 'A study of interventions in practice . . . [however] reveals that most have occurred in situations where the humanitarian motive is at best balanced, if not outweighed, by a desire to . . . reinforce socio-political and economic instruments of the *status quo*'. (1973: 278).

A proliferation of exceptions to Article 2(4) would leave little of the basic prohibition of the use of force. In an international environment consisting of sovereign states that admit of no higher authority, order is sufficiently vulnerable. At the same time, the destructive capacity of modern warfare heightens the need to limit the use of force. That states will, when they see no other means by which to achieve vital national goals, resort to force is an inevitable condition of international politics. To loosen the bonds of legal control when such strictures clearly serve to limit conflict, however, would run counter to the ultimate goals of international society. State practice, in its general renunciation of those that do resort to force, provides support for this position; exceptions to the prohibition of the use of force, it may be concluded, should be interpreted in an extremely restrictive manner.

One more issue regarding the *jus ad bellum* requires consideration, namely the relationship between the prohibition of the use of force enshrined in Article 2(4) and the collective security provisions of the United Nations Charter. The drafters of the UN Charter envisaged not only the establishment of a legal structure which would prohibit the use of force (other than in the case of self-defence) but also the creation of a collective security mechanism which would operate to ensure the security of states. In accordance with Article 39 of the Charter, 'The Security Council shall determine the existence of any threat to the peace, breach of the peace, or act of aggression and shall make recommendations, or decide what measures shall be taken in accordance with Articles 41 and 42, to maintain or restore international peace and security'. In the case of a positive determination, the Security Council may, under Article 40, decide upon 'provisional measures' for the aversion of any escalation of the crisis and, where necessary, may impose non-military (primarily economic) sanctions under Article 41 or military measures under Article 42. Article 42 provides that: 'Should the Security Council consider that the measures provided for in Article 41 would prove inadequate or have proved to be inadequate, it may take such action by air, sea, or land forces as may be necessary to maintain or restore international peace and security . . .'

Articles 41 and 42 should not be understood as being mandatorily sequential. It is entirely lawful in appropriate cases to proceed straight from Article 39 to Article 42, as is made clear by the provision of Article 42 that it may be applied if the Council considers that Article 41 sanctions 'would prove inadequate'. The assumption that economic measures are necessarily the more humane approach has been severely undermined by evidence that economic sanctions fall disproportionately on the population rather than the leadership. As technology allows ever more precise military targeting, economic sanctions may come to be seen as the indiscriminate option, especially when leaders of target states are less interested in the welfare of their citizens than in the political capital which can be generated by images of suffering appearing in the world's media. The prospect of increasingly 'clean' military conflicts with minimal 'collateral damage' that modern technology appears to offer is, of course, to be welcomed. It should be noted, however, that to the extent that 'acceptable', and ultimately legal, war comes to be equated with 'clean' war, it has very significant political implications. 'Smart' weaponry is currently the preserve of the powerful few and is likely to so remain for many years. If the use of force becomes the exclusive legal preserve of the powerful then the implications for the *jus ad bellum* are considerable.

The Chapter VII mechanism gives rise to a number of grey areas, not least of which is what constitutes a 'threat to the peace, breach of the peace, or act of aggression'? The Charter provides no guidance as to what constitutes such situations and it is clear from the *travaux préparatoires* that those responsible for the Charter intended that the Security Council should have a wide discretion in reaching such a determination. Proposals to include a definition of aggression were rejected because states were reluctance to shackle the Council's activities. The decision also reflected the fact that the Council was intended to act as a political rather than a judicial body and legalistic definitions were therefore deemed inappropriate. The Council's remit was restricted, dealing with matters that were *international*, that is, interstate, but this relatively restrictive interpretation has, through practice, been eroded over time. More recent UN practice suggests that some internal use of force might fall within this category, at least where it threatens regional stability. N. D. White suggests that the term 'threat to the peace' should be understood to denote:

> situations [that] have at their core the use of armed force, either internal or international. The integrity of the concept has been maintained by many of the recent uses of the term by the

Security Council, covering issues such as threats of force (provocative action directed by Iraq against Kuwait), widespread violations of international humanitarian law (including 'ethnic cleansing' in Bosnia), massive humanitarian crises (caused by the genocide in Rwanda in 1994 which led to related problems in Burundi and Zaire in 1996), and breach of a Security Council arms embargo (relating to Rwanda). 🗯

(1997: 45)

In addition to the—now much depleted—restriction that the Security Council can only act with regard to international uses of force, a further restriction was imposed upon the Chapter VII mechanism; the activities of the Security Council's five permanent members (China, France, UK, USA, and USSR) would, as a result of the veto power granted to them under Article 27(3), be exempt from UN sanction. In this way the organization's architects sought to resolve a major dilemma: the five permanent members were the most powerful states of the day and it could be argued that they were, therefore, the states whose behaviour was most likely to need policing. Yet any attempt to so police the behaviour of the 'P5' would almost inevitably lead to major conflict and the destruction of the UN. A veto-induced stalemate was deemed to be the preferable alternative, a view that was widely held by delegates at the UN's founding conference. As the Indian delegate to the San Francisco Conference stated: 'The veto power . . . is . . . an implicit guarantee to all members that they will not be asked to wage a war, in the name of the United Nations, against any of the big powers.' (Claude 1962: 161).

Hence the drafters of the Charter proceeded not upon the basis that consensus would be maintained and the veto would not be called upon, but upon the understanding that disagreements might occur and that where this was the case the Security Council would be incapacitated. As Inis Claude remarks:

🗯 The conclusion is inescapable that a conscious decision was made at San Francisco to avoid any attempt or pretence at subjecting the major powers to collective coercion . . . The security scheme of the Charter . . . was conceived as an arrangement for collective action against relatively minor disturbers of the peace, in cases where the great powers were united in the desire to permit or take action. 🗯

(1962: 161)

In this light, criticisms premised on the notion that the UN is an idealistic organization seem somewhat ill-founded, though the unanticipated extent to which the US–Soviet confrontation would incapacitate the organization does raise issues about the practicality of the UN system.

That the UN collective security system never developed as initially anticipated is now a matter of historical record. The onset of the cold war prevented the conclusion of agreements earmarking national armed contingents for UN operations as envisaged under Article 43. A Military Staffs Committee—intended, in accordance with Article 47, to provide strategic, though not tactical, guidance on the use of such forces—was established, but as a general staff without an army to command it stands as a monument to the UN's failings. Even more destructive than these deficiencies was the decision-making paralysis which afflicted the Security Council as a result of the ideological schism that characterized post-1945 international politics. As a consequence the UN was unable, save perhaps for its operation in Korea and the limited contributions it was able to make through peacekeeping operations, to fulfil the role of security guarantor ascribed to it.

The shortcomings of the UN's security apparatus raise one final question; should Article 2(4) be viewed as being *contingent* upon the effective operation of Chapter VII? In the absence of an effective collective security mechanism, the apposition of the Article 2(4) prohibition appears far less sound. Despite the absence of an effective collective security mechanism for almost sixty years no state directly refuted the validity of Article 2(4) or, indeed, its standing as a norm with the status of *jus cogens*. The opening years of the twenty-first century have, however, seen this central facet of the UN system challenged in two ways. The first of these is grounded in the arguments in favour of a more expansive right of self-defence discussed earlier. The second challenge comes in the assertion that, where the Security Council fails to authorize through the passing of a resolution action to maintain or restore international peace and security, states may nevertheless act in order to do so. In insisting that they were acting to enforce legally binding obligations imposed by the Security Council in 1991, the US and its allies made this argument the central legal point of their justification for action against Iraq in 2003 (Kritsiotis 2004). This represents a fundamental departure from previous state practice and one which the response to the 2003 Iraq War suggests is far from being accepted by the majority of states.

KEY POINTS

- The *jus ad bellum* governs and seeks to limit resort to armed force in the conduct of international relations.

- Recourse to force is prohibited other than in cases of individual or collective self-defence and where action is taken to restore international peace and security as mandated by the UN Security Council.

- Exceptions to the prohibition of the use of force should be interpreted restrictively.

- The prohibition of the use of force is not viewed by most states as being contingent upon the successful operation of the UN collective security mechanism. The 2003 Iraq conflict challenged this view.

- No state has openly repudiated the general prohibition of the use of force.

Jus in Bello

The *jus in bello* has two principal subdivisions, which have conventionally been categorized as 'Geneva' and 'Hague' law, in recognition of the principal treaty series upon which each is founded. Modern 'Geneva' law is specifically concerned with the protection of the victims of armed conflict. 'Hague' law is concerned with methods and means of warfare, including controls on weapons types and usage, and on tactics and the general conduct of

BOX 5.5

Jus in bello

'Geneva' law	**'Hague' law**
Concerned with protection of victims of armed conflict	Concerned with methods and means of warfare
Based primarily on the four 1949 Geneva Conventions	Based primarily on the 1899 and 1907 Hague Conventions

hostilities. It should be noted that the 'Geneva/Hague' distinction is today artificial; both are premised upon a humanitarian concern for the moderation and mitigation of warfare and for this reason there is a considerable degree of overlap between them. In modern usage the term 'international humanitarian law'—historically used to refer specifically to 'Geneva' law—is taken to comprise the whole *jus in bello* in both its 'Geneva' and 'Hague' dimensions.

Both sets of norms rest ultimately upon a fundamental principle of proscription concerning the infliction of militarily 'unnecessary suffering'. This principle was stated expressly in the 1868 Declaration of St Petersburg:

> The only legitimate objective which States should endeavour to accomplish during war is to weaken the military forces of the enemy . . . this objective would be exceeded by the employment of arms which uselessly aggravate the suffering of disabled men . . . [and] the employment of such arms would therefore be contrary to the laws of humanity.

The modern foundations of the 'Hague' sector are primarily to be found in the Hague Conventions of 1899 and 1907 and the 1977 Additional Protocol I to the Geneva Conventions which makes provision for methods and means of warfare and discrimination in bombardment. Modern 'Geneva' law is based on the four 1949 Geneva Conventions, dealing respectively with: (I) Wounded and Sick on Land; (II) Wounded, Sick, and Shipwrecked at Sea; (III) Prisoners of War; and (IV) Civilians. On the basis of this treaty and customary provision the basic rules of the *jus in bello* are, it may be said, well settled. Equally, it must be conceded, they are applied neither consistently nor unproblematically.

International humanitarian law is closely related to the general law of human rights, and this creates a powerful argument that the obligations created by it are essentially unilateral and non-reciprocal in nature. Common Article 1 of the four 1949 Geneva Conventions provides that: 'The High Contracting Parties undertake to respect and ensure respect for the present Convention *in all circumstances*' (emphasis added). On this basis Jean Pictet noted: '[The Convention] is not an engagement concluded on a basis of reciprocity, binding each party to the content only in so far as the other party observes its obligations. It is rather a series of unilateral engagements solemnly contacted before the world as represented by the other Contracting Parties' (Pictet 1985: 90).

This argument of general non-reciprocity relates ultimately back to the so-called Martens clause, named after the Russian statesman Frederick de Martens, which was adopted at the Hague Peace Conferences and which states:

> " The High Contracting Parties deem it expedient to declare that in cases not included in the Regulations adopted by them, the inhabitants and the belligerents remain under the protection and the rules of the principles of the law of nations as they result from the usages established amongst civilised people, from the laws of humanity and the dictates of public conscience. "

Although found only in a Preamble, and therefore in a sense only advisory, the Martens clause was approvingly cited at the Nuremberg Tribunals. It confers a very particular status upon some fundamental provisions of international humanitarian law. Three levels of obligation emerge in connection with international humanitarian legal norms: first, those rules and principles which form part of customary international law or *jus cogens* (including the bulk of the Geneva Conventions and much of the established 'Hague' law) and are therefore binding on all states irrespective of reciprocity; those principles that otherwise fall within the scope of the Martens clause and are not subject to a requirement of reciprocity; and other provisions which are either innovatory and not yet established as customary, or non-customary and not fundamental in nature, and that remain subject to the principle of reciprocity (see Box 5.6). Accordingly, a compelling case may be made that at least the fundamental humanitarian principles of the *jus in bello* have the quality of *jus cogens* and are rules from which there may be no derogation and from which reservation is not permitted. To this extent, the international community has established a universally applicable system of legal regulation in keeping with the principle of unnecessary suffering expressed in the Declaration of St Petersburg well over a century ago.

The more cooperative post-cold war environment proved conducive to further significant developments in international humanitarian law. A growing public awareness resulting from twenty four-hour real-time TV-coverage, advances in global communications, and the campaigning work of non-governmental organizations such as Amnesty International and Human Rights Watch has also been important in this regard. The high profile now enjoyed by humanitarian issues places considerable political pressure on governments and was a significant factor, for example, in the successful adoption of the Convention on the

BOX 5.6

Jus in bello: Levels of Obligation

Three levels of obligation can be suggested to arise in connection with the *jus in bello:*

- rules and principles which form part of customary international law or *jus cogens* (including the bulk of the Geneva Conventions and much of the established 'Hague' law) and are binding on all states irrespective of reciprocity
- fundamental principles which otherwise fall within the scope of the Martens clause and which are, therefore, also not subject to a requirement of reciprocity
- provisions which are either innovatory and not yet established as customary or non-customary and not fundamental in nature which remain subject to the principle of reciprocity.

Prohibition of Anti-Personnel Landmines which came into force on 1 March 1999. Another huge advance in humanitarian law was the establishment of the International Criminal Court. The court is competent to prosecute cases of genocide, crimes against humanity, war crimes, and potentially at some future date the crime of aggression. Its jurisdiction extends over nationals of states parties and crimes committed on their territory where such states are either unable or unwilling to prosecute themselves (Schabas 2004). The court is not without its detractors, most notably the United States, but while it is yet to prove itself in action its very existence is a development which few can realistically have even dreamt of only fifteen years ago.

Not all recent developments are so positive. Inter-ethnic conflicts such as those in Rwanda and the former Yugoslavia were horrifically barbarous in nature, with combatants routinely failing to conform to the—perhaps idealized—traditional expectations of regular military forces. The trend in conflict patterns toward a greater incidence of intra-, rather than interstate conflict does not bode well in this regard, but it must also be acknowledged that even regular military forces, including those of the most developed states, are not devoid of such practices. The United States, and to a lesser extent, the United Kingdom, both stand accused of violating humanitarian law in their treatment of prisoners taken during the war in Iraq. The US treatment of those detained in the wider theatre of the War on Terror and held at the US base in Guantanamo Bay is also cause for particular concern. Such concern arises in part from the actual conditions in which the detainees are held, but also from the US assertion, made in the face of overwhelming legal opinion to the contrary, that those held are not entitled to the protection offered by the Geneva Conventions.

The extent to which the *jus in bello* is able to realize the objectives which it enshrines is contingent upon the degree to which the modes of behaviour so prescribed become embedded within practice. Once again, excessive concern with punishment, in this case of war crimes, misses the point that the primary function of international humanitarian law is not to punish those who violate its edicts but rather to protect the victims of armed conflict by preventing war crimes in the first instance. Indeed, before any question of punishing war crimes or other enforcement action can arise, failure in this primary endeavour must be presupposed and in this sense issues of enforcement must be viewed as secondary to the imperatives of effective dissemination and training. That in many states the latter is now a foundational element of military training bodes well, though such practice is far from ubiquitous and deficiencies in this regard are often exacerbated through shortcomings in discipline and command and control.

KEY POINTS

- The *jus in bello*, often split into the subdivisions of 'Geneva' and 'Hague' law, governs and seeks to moderate the actual conduct of hostilities.

- 'Geneva' law is concerned with the protection of victims of armed conflict. 'Hague' law is concerned with methods and means of warfare.

- The bulk of 'Geneva' and 'Hague' law have the status of *jus cogens*.

- The primary function of the *jus in bello* is to protect the victims of armed conflict through preventing war crimes. Such objectives should, therefore, be pursued primarily through education and training rather than through post-violation prosecution.

Conclusion

The low regard in which international law is customarily held is the consequence of several factors. It is a result of our perception of the world of international politics and the extent to which we tend to see this as an environment characterized by conflict. In such a world, the notion of states forming a society appears inappropriate and it follows that law seems equally out of place. This perception is profoundly misleading. Rather than wringing our hands over the extent of military conflict in the world we might, without forgetting the devastation and suffering inherent in conflicts when they do arise, marvel at the degree to which an increasing number of states manage to coexist in a cooperative and often mutually beneficial manner. It would be folly to suggest that this is the consequence of some great legalistic enterprise, but equally it would be foolhardy to suggest that international law had no role to play in influencing the manner in which states behave. To borrow a phrase from Robert Keohane, international law 'prescribes behavioural roles, constrains activity, and shapes expectations' (1989: 3).

At times, of course, international law, like all law, is broken. This, however, is the exception rather than the rule. Moreover, in cases where international law is broken one would be hard pressed to find a transgressor who does not at least attempt to provide a legally couched justification for their behaviour, and the more prominent and significant the breach, the greater the efforts become. Nowhere are breaches of international law more significant or prominent than with regard to the laws of armed conflict. Nowhere are the stakes higher or the pressures greater. It is, therefore, all the more noteworthy that even here the law prevails.

? **QUESTIONS**

1. Why is international law held in such low regard? Is this a deserved reputation?

2. Does international law really influence the behaviour of states? If so, how and why?

3. Can you cite examples involving the use of force, in which states have breached international law and not attempted to justify their actions in terms of the law?

4. Are exceptions to the prohibition of the use of force—such as anticipatory self-defence, action to protect nationals abroad, action to punish state-sponsored terrorism and humanitarian intervention—justifiable?

5. Should the prohibition of the use of force be contingent upon the existence of an effective mechanism by means of which the security of states can be assured?

6. What role does the UN play in international law? Is it an effective role?

7. Are limitations upon the means by which war is waged practicable?

8. Assess the potential of the International Criminal Court.

9. Have recent conflicts increased or decreased the force of international law?

10. What does the behaviour of states pursuant to the 'War on Terror' tell us about humanitarian law?

FURTHER READING

In addition to the texts referred to throughout the chapter, the following texts are recommended:

■ I. Brownlie, *International Law and the Use of Force by States* (Oxford: Clarendon Press, 1963). On the laws of armed conflict relating to the *jus ad bellum*.

■ H. McCoubrey, International Humanitarian Law, 2nd edn (Aldershot: Dartmouth, 1998). On the *jus in bello*.

■ McGoldrick, Rowe, and Donnelly (eds.), *The Permanent International Court: Legal and Policy Issues* (Oxford: Hart Publishing, 2004). On the International Criminal Court.

International relations theory in general

■ J. Baylis and S. Smith, *The Globalization of World Politics: An Introduction to International Relations*, 3rd edn (Oxford: Oxford University Press, 2005).

■ S. Burchill *et al., Theories of International Relations,* 3rd edn (London: Macmillan, 2005).

Normative regulation in international politics

■ H. Bull, *The Anarchical Society: A Study of Order in World Politics* (London: Macmillan, 1977).

■ R. O. Keohane, *International Institutions and State Power: Essays in International Relations Theory* (San Francisco: Westview Press, 1989).

■ A. Wendt, *Social Theory of International Politics* (Cambridge: Cambridge University Press, 1999).

Politics of international law

■ M. Byers, *The Role of Law in International Politics: Essays in International Relations and International Law* (Oxford: Oxford University Press, 2000).

■ L. Henkin, *How Nations Behave: Law and Foreign Policy* (New York: Columbia University Press, 1968).

Legal developments relating to the 'War on Terror' and/or the 2003 Iraq War

■ M. Byers, (2004), 'Agreeing to Disagree: Security Council Resolution 1441 and International Ambiguity', *Global Governance*, 10/2: 165–86.

■ L. Feinstein, and A.-M. Slaughter (2004) 'A Duty to Prevent', *Foreign Affairs*, 83/1: 136–50.

■ T. Franck (2001). 'Terrorism and the Right to Self-Defense', *American Journal of International Law*, 95/4: 839–43.

■ C. Gray (2002) 'From Unity to Polarization: International Law and the Use of Force against Iraq', *European Journal of International Law*, 13/1: 1–19.

■ M. E. O'Connell (2002). 'The Myth of Preemptive Self-Defense', *American Society of International Law* http://www.asil.org/taskforce/oconnell.pdf.

WEB LINKS

- United Nations **http://www.un.org**

- International Court of Justice **http://www.icj-cij.org**

- International Criminal Court **http://www.icc-cpi.int/home.html**

- Amnesty International **http://www.amnesty.org**

- Human Rights Watch **http://www.hrw.org**

 Visit the Online Resource Centre that accompanies this book for lots of interesting additional material http://www.oxfordtextbooks.co.uk/orc/baylis_strategy2e/.

LAW, POLITICS, AND THE USE OF FORCE

6

Geography and Strategy

DANIEL MORAN

 Chapter Contents

- Introduction: The Lay of the Land
- Land Warfare: The Quest for Victory
- Maritime Strategy
- Airpower
- The Final Frontier: Space War
- War by Other Means: Cyberspace

 Reader's Guide

This chapter explores the diverging strategic possibilities that are presented by war-fare in different physical environments. It identifies the particular strengths and weaknesses of forces that fight on land and sea and in the air. It also considers the strategic potential of warfare in space, and of new information technologies that may some day be employed as weapons.

Introduction: The Lay of the Land

Strategic theory is concerned with the use of force—that is, of violence—by political communities for their collective purposes in relation to each other. The psychological effects that violence engenders among those who employ it, and suffer it, do not vary in any predictable way with respect to the means by which harm is inflicted. A blow delivered from the sea is much the same as one from the land, and it will inspire the same desire to defend oneself, to strike back, or to give in, regardless of where or how the attack originated. Carl von Clausewitz, the Prussian theorist whose work *On War* (1832) remains at the foundation of strategic studies to this day, wrote exclusively about war on land. But the distinctive characteristics of war as he conceived it—the overwhelming effects of fear, chance, and uncertainty on the conduct of those who fight; the escalatory dynamic that drives adversaries to ever more extreme measures; the superior strength of the defensive; the difficulty of sustaining military action over long periods; the need for constant adaptation to the unexpected moves of the enemy—all these are no less familiar to those who have fought on the sea or in the air. The contest of wills that is at the heart of every strategic encounter will play itself out in roughly the same fashion, irrespective of the physical environment in which it occurs.

As a practical matter, however, the conduct of war is overwhelmingly shaped by its geographical setting. It is on this basis that armed forces are most naturally characterized. The armies of the world resemble each other far more than they do the navies and air forces that fight under the same flags. A modern army, for that matter, resembles an ancient one more than it does a modern navy, since its most basic problems have not changed at all from one millennium to the next. The same is true for the other major military branches. Before any armed force can come to grips with its opponent, it must first master the immediate challenges of its physical environment. Ships must float. Aircraft must (however improbably) remain suspended in the air. Armies must propel themselves as best they can across an unyielding landscape rich with obstacles large and small. Warfare, the *making* of war, is first of all about making the most of one's chances within the constraints imposed by Mother Nature. Only after that has been accomplished can the enemy be given the attention he deserves.

Physical geography defines the tactical identities of armed forces. It may also shape, limit, or amplify their strategic effects. An explosive shell delivered from a warship, an aircraft, or a long-range artillery piece will feel very much the same to those on the receiving end. But that does not alter the fact that armies, navies, and air forces possess distinctive strengths and weaknesses at the strategic level, which is to say, the level at which military effort gets translated into political results. A political community that fights chiefly with land forces will be confronted with different strategic possibilities from those available to one that fights mainly on the sea or in the air. The aim of this chapter is to highlight those distinct possibilities: to consider the conduct of war in different geographical environments, with a view to identifying the characteristic strategic risks and opportunities that each affords.

It must be admitted that under modern conditions, and specifically since the invention of the airplane, the discussion that follows is a somewhat artificial exercise: a thought experiment rather than a description of reality. The best armies and navies today never operate without seeking to control the skies over their heads. The major weapons systems of a carrier-based navy like that of the United States are aerial weapons in any case, tactically indistinguishable from those of a modern air force. An air force in turn depends on a ground-based infrastructure whose establishment and defence will generally be the work of an army. These kinds of synergies are at the heart of 'joint' military operations, in which land, sea, and air forces seek to cooperate to their best collective advantage. The superiority of joint operations over those conducted by a single service is now so apparent that under most circumstances it is simply taken for granted by military planners. Left to their own devices, armies, navies, and air forces each present a limited and one-dimensional set of strategic capabilities. However profound their individual strengths, they are offset by equally distinctive weaknesses. Joint warfare is now the norm or, more properly the ideal, because it allows military organizations to exploit the strengths and mask the weaknesses of their component parts.

Yet the strengths and weaknesses remain, and they are worth contemplating as a way of understanding the choices that political leaders face when called upon to use force as an instrument of policy. The focus in what follows is thus on the distinctive strategic considerations that surround the conduct of war in different physical environments: on land and sea, in the air, in space, and finally in 'cyberspace', a metaphorical realm whose strategic possibilities, although scarcely yet realized in practice, have lately attracted sufficient attention to merit independent discussion.

Land Warfare: The Quest for Victory

Land armies are the pre-eminent form of military power almost everywhere. This is owing to their role in the creation and sustainment of political communities, whose independent existence depends on their ability to defend themselves against other similar groups. Only land armies can secure territorial frontiers, and it is by virtue of their ability to exercise continuous control over defined territory that sovereign states are most readily distinguished from other competing political forms. Political entities that are not states can make war. But unless they can field an army of the requisite size and skill they cannot control territory, and absent such control they will never be able to take their place among the sovereign nations of the world. In historical terms, armies and states create each other. While some states today are so fortunately situated as to require only vestigial land forces to defend themselves, none is able to dispense with them entirely.

In strategic terms the outstanding advantage of armies is their defensive strength. Land warfare is the only kind of fighting that is intended to seize and hold, and not merely to destroy, its objectives. That armies seek to destroy each other is also true, as it is for navies and air forces. But death and destruction in war are always a means to an end, and if the end is to gain control of a human population, then only an army will do. Navies and air forces cannot occupy territory after they have killed or run off whatever enemy forces may have been there. Only armies can do that, and once they have done it the difficulty of dislodging them is considerable. 'Regime change', as the conquest of another country is now called, is inherently an army mission, and cannot be contemplated by any state that is not prepared to commit its land forces to the fight.

Such a commitment is now widely perceived to be an especially weighty one. For a country like the United States, which is able to inflict massive damage and suffering by means of naval and air forces, the decision to employ its army is often more politically perilous than the decision to use force in the first place. Any military operation involving ground forces will have a heightened significance for public opinion in a democratic society, if only because of the additional risk of friendly casualties that such a commitment involves. Such a step is normally considered only after some form of strategic bombardment has been tried and found wanting. The major American interventions in Korea, Vietnam, and Iraq (in 1990–1) were all incremental processes, in which an initial decision to employ air and naval forces was followed by a separate, independently considered one to send in the army. The fact that no such step-wise process occurred in connection with the invasion of Iraq in 2003 is a reflection of the fact that in that instance the total overthrow and occupation of the enemy state was the objective right from the start.

Apart from the increased likelihood of friendly casualties that land warfare involves, the additional political scrutiny that attaches to it is owed chiefly to the fact that such a commitment has a kind of finality about it that does not apply to naval and air operations. If the outstanding advantage of armies is their defensive strength, their outstanding disadvantage is that they are cumbrous and difficult to move around. Bringing them to bear against an enemy requires enormous determination. One reason to do so is precisely to communicate such determination to the opponent. Once the commitment has been made, however, it is appallingly difficult to undo. Land forces engaged with an undefeated adversary cannot easily disengage without incurring some kind of tactical risk, quite apart from presenting a spectacle of failure and retreat for all the world to see. Ships and airplanes may come and go. An army comes and stays. That is its nature and purpose, both tactically and strategically.

The defensive resilience of land armies is a double-edged sword, since it renders the delivery of a successful attack extremely difficult. Land warfare at all times is a grinding, wearisome business. The 'art of war' at any given moment is devoted to figuring out how to make it less so. The goal of land warfare, as the sixteenth-century Austrian field marshal Raimondo de Montecucolli said, is 'victory', an unexceptionable observation in itself, but one that stood out at the time it was made because it cast aside a wide range of other objectives—honour, glory, plunder, prestige—which the aristocratic elites of that era were inclined to rate more highly than the political interests of the state. In strategic terms 'victory' is a political, and not merely a military, concept. This is why Montecucolli's modern successors tend to add the word 'decisive', meaning victory that goes beyond the accomplishment of some local tactical goal and achieves results of sufficient magnitude to alter the political conditions that brought the war about in the first place. Victory of this kind cannot be gained by pushing the enemy around, or even by pushing him away. It requires that his powers of resistance be broken and disorganized, so that he is forced to confront the possibility that, at some point in the future, he may become entirely defenceless.

In modern times military theorists have identified three general paths to this kind of success. The first, whose basic characteristics emerge in the strategic literature of the eighteenth century, is to manœuvre against the flanks and rear of the opposing army. The fighting elements of land armies represent only a fraction of their total manpower. The rest are devoted to the maintenance of the complex supply system that is required to keep the army moving, eating, and fighting. Attacks directed against that system came to be recognized as having disproportionate destructive effects, and they remain to this day the most desirable form of offensive military operation. Precisely because this critical vulnerability is so widely recognized, however, it usually proves difficult to exploit. Armies take good care to protect their communications and logistics if they can. Nor is it easy to engage in bold manœuvre against the enemy's rear areas while also protecting one's own against similar assault. Modern armies have striven mightily to outmanœuvre each other, and when they have succeeded, as in the German offensives against France in 1870 and 1940, the results have been impressive. But such outcomes are also historically rare, for the simple reason that armies of similar size, fighting with similar methods, whose basic tactical objectives are readily anticipated on the basis of well-understood strategic principles,

---

BOX 6.1

Manœuvre versus Attrition

Writing on land warfare routinely distinguish between 'manœuvre warfare' and 'attrition'. The distinction, needless to say, is not hard and fast: all armies manœuvre in the sense that they try to put themselves in an advantageous position from which to engage their opponents. At the same time, opportunities for manœuvre may only arise as a result of preparatory, systematic destruction of enemy forces, which is what one normally means by 'attrition'. Nevertheless, the difference between the two approaches is sufficiently clear to bear thinking about.

Attrition emphasizes cumulative destructiveness, achieved by the systematic application of superior firepower. It is often the natural choice of the side with greater material resources, which does not feel that it needs to do anything fancy to win. Tactical decisions focus on choices among different sets of targets or objectives, which are prioritized according to some doctrinally codified scheme. Because the methods of attritional warfare tend to be generic and repetitive, it is also a natural choice for a country that is uncertain who its future adversaries may be, so that it must emphasize methods that are thought to work pretty well in general, rather then being optimized for use against a particular opponent.

The idea of manœuvre, on the other hand, only has meaning in relation to a particular opponent. It seeks to capitalize on an adversary's specific vulnerabilities—the fact that his forces move slowly, for instance, or are poorly supplied with bridging equipment, or have bad morale—in order to achieve disproportionate effects. Although most people associate 'manœuvre' with rapid movement, it is really a more general concept, which tries to gain exceptional leverage from the control of relatively small amounts of space and time: the provision of local security to isolated villages by small detachments of American forces during the Vietnam War is an example of manœuvre warfare, because the aim was not the systematic destruction of enemy forces, but rather to thwart the enemy's intentions by controlling relatively small but critical bits of territory—the bits where people actually lived.

In all cases, however, manœuvre warfare is intended to achieve some kind of disproportionate effect: to accomplish a great deal while committing relatively limited forces, because the forces are used in a way that exploits some perceived, critical vulnerability. It is for this reason that bold and aggressive manœuvre has often been the recourse of the weaker side in war, because it is the weaker side that must make up its inherent deficiencies by recourse to some remarkable, highly leveraged method of fighting. Yet because the aim of manœuvre warfare is not systematic destruction, but the *systemic disruption* of the enemy's capacity to resist, it also has great appeal to a strong country like the United States, whose political goals, at least in recent years, have caused it to try to limit, as far as possible, the general destructiveness of its military actions.

have little chance of manœuvring against each other so swiftly and unexpectedly as to knock their opponent entirely off-balance. When such efforts fail, as in the German offensive against France in 1914, the grim realities of attrition swiftly reassert themselves.

An obvious solution is to have an army that is not of similar size, but is instead much larger than that of your opponent. Modern states possess means of mobilizing their populations for war, either by persuading them to fight or, more commonly, by coercing them to do so, that are far superior to those of traditional societies. Until the turn of the nineteenth century, however, governments were reluctant to call upon the mass of their subjects to bear arms, because they could not afford to equip the huge armies that would have resulted, but also because doing so entailed political risks: people mobilized for war might well expect political concessions in return. The fact that they had just been trained and equipped for fighting was also thought to heighten the possibility that they might simply seize those concessions for themselves. It is thus not surprising that universal military conscription was first attempted by a revolutionary government, that of France in 1793, as a way of defending the nascent regime from attack, and of mobilizing the population in support of the Revolution itself. The resulting army dwarfed those of France's adversaries, and could only be defeated once Europe's other great powers had accepted the risk of adopting similar methods.

Over the course of the nineteenth century major land armies grew dramatically in size. The consequences of this development were amplified by modern weaponry, whose range and lethality far exceeded all previous experience. As soldiers pondered this new reality, they recognized that it cut strongly against the possibility that they might somehow outmanœuvre their opponents. Armies, as has already been noted, are inherently slow and awkward on the move. Forces numbering in the millions could scarcely be manœuvred in any meaningful sense, and once they got within weapons' range of each other, no outcome seemed possible except massacre on an epic scale.

If there was a way out, the best observers concluded, it could only be found at the very outset of hostilities, when it might still be possible to catch the enemy unprepared, with his forces not yet mobilized and ready for action. The best chance for decisive victory, it seemed, lay with the side that could strike hardest right at the start. Here was a third path to victory, one whose temptations have so far survived the considerable record of disappointment that has accumulated around it. A large share of the major wars of the twentieth century have begun with massive attacks designed to achieved such swift and stunning success as to render pre-war calculations of the relative strengths of the opponents irrelevant. Consider, for instance, the Japanese offensive against Russia in 1904, and against America and Great Britain in 1941; the German offensive of 1914, and the so-called blitzkrieg campaigns of 1939–41; the North Korean invasion of South Korea in 1950; the Iraqi offensives against Iran in 1980, and Kuwait in 1990; the pre-emptive attacks by Israeli against Egypt and Syria in 1967, and by Egypt and Syria the rejoinders in 1973. This list could be expanded without difficulty, but the basic impression would not change, which is that on the whole the advantages of attacking first have not proven sufficiently decisive as to outweigh more fundamental sources of military strength. Land armies at all times are voracious consumers of men and materiel. On balance, victory on land has gone to belligerents with sufficient political determination, social resilience, and economic productivity to sustain military effort over the long haul.

Most thoughtful soldiers nevertheless remain convinced that it is their duty to win quickly if they can. Not all, however. Revolutionary insurgency is also a form of land warfare, one that embraces protraction as a source of strategic leverage, by which an opponent may eventually be worn down. Insurgents take advantage of a terrain feature that conventional ground forces prefer to avoid: the civil population, within which the insurgent seeks to conceal himself, and which he holds hostage as a means of delegitimizing the authorities. Such methods are as timeless as war itself. Whenever the weak have fought the strong they have relied on ambushes, traps, terrorism, hit and run attacks, and so on, in the hope that, just by staying alive and engaged, victory may come to them.

If revolutionary and unconventional warfare have loomed large in recent years, it is partly because of the relative decline of conventional land warfare as a feature of the international system. Since the end of the Second World War advanced societies have assiduously avoided fighting each other, with the result that major wars have only been waged by or against second-rate powers. It is also true that the insurgents' chances have improved owing to better technology, above all in the area of communications. A few radios connecting otherwise isolated rebel bands or terrorist cells can make an enormous difference at the tactical level, while the ability to communicate with the civil population via the public media, on something like an equal footing with the government, has gone some distance towards evening the odds in a contest whose basic terms are always defined ideologically.

Particularly when considered in isolation from the long-range aerial strike systems that are now required to lubricate the tactical movement of large ground forces, counter-insurgency can reasonably be considered the principal and most distinctive mission of contemporary land armies. This is a reality that only a minority of today's soldiers are prepared to embrace, if for no other reason than because doing so threatens to relegate ground forces to the role of 'exploiting' victory, rather than achieving it. The swift overthrow of the organized forces of the enemy remains the acme of professional military achievement at the turn of the twenty-first century. Setting this traditional standard aside will require a re-examination of the basic assumptions on which land warfare has been conducted for the last three hundred years.

KEY POINTS

- Land armies are distinguished from other military branches by their ability to seize and hold, rather than simply to destroy, their objectives.

- Land warfare in the industrial era has shown a strong tendency toward stalemate and attrition.

- The aim of manœuvre warfare is to strike the enemy at times and places that achieve disproportionate destructive or disruptive effects; most commonly his logistical and communications systems.

- Modern wars often begin with massive initial offensives designed to win before the other side is fully mobilized; an expedient that has generally failed strategically, however striking its tactical success.

- Revolutionary insurgency is an unusual form of land warfare in that it does not seek to win quickly, but rather by slowly eroding the moral and political resolve of the enemy.

Maritime Strategy

Seventy per cent of the earth's surface is comprised of water. This fact is sufficient to explain the centrality of war on the sea. Human populations have always been concentrated near the world's oceans, or along the navigable stretches of the rivers that lead to them. The advent of aircraft and missiles has now placed most of mankind within range of naval weapons systems. A modern navy is capable of inflicting very considerable damage quite far inland. Historically, however, bombarding the shore has been the least significant of naval missions. The distinctive strategic contribution of navies has instead turned upon their activity on the sea itself, always keeping in mind that nothing that happens there can matter unless it impacts the thinking and actions of those living on the land.

From ancient times until roughly the sixteenth century, the main military role of navies was simply to transport soldiers to an enemy shore. Given the perennial difficulty of military movement on land the ability to do this conferred important advantages, above all the freedom to chose the time and place of an attack. Such navies were tactical adjuncts to armies, with no distinctive strategic role. Naval warfare existed, in the sense that when warships met on the sea they tried to fight each other. But such episodes were rare and inconsequential. What mattered were the armies that the navies carried. It was their combat that decided the war.

The development of sailing warships capable of traversing the world's oceans altered this once-familiar picture in ways whose long-term consequences can scarcely be exaggerated. Sailing navies were the principal instruments by which European overseas empires were created, from which has arisen the highly integrated, rapidly globalizing world economy that we know today. The role of navies in this process was twofold: to transport soldiers, merchants, missionaries, and settlers to the far corners of the world; and to protect, or to prey upon, the rapidly expanding network of seaborne trade that resulted.

Maritime strategy as traditionally understood sought to gain leverage from the financial advantages that access to these trading networks afforded. The inelastic agrarian economies of continental states could offer nothing to compare to the wealth generated by long-distance trade, which sailing navies existed to foster and protect. They functioned as instruments of economic warfare, and their strategic effects were achieved by virtue of their impact on international trade. When the American navalist Alfred Thayer Mahan coined the term 'sea power' at the end of the nineteenth century, it was this remarkable interaction between naval power, commerce, and colonial expansion that he had in mind. From Mahan's perspective, states whose navies could 'command' the sea—that is, employ it for their own military and commercial purposes, while denying such use to others—were destined to dominate those who could not.

By the time Mahan wrote, however, the seemingly organic relationship between naval power and maritime trade was already beginning to break down. This was owed partly to the industrial revolution, which allowed continental states to match the economic productivity afforded by overseas commerce; and also, paradoxically enough, to the increasingly intricate economic dependencies that such trade created. On its face, the strategic significance of sea power would seem to increase in proportion to the value of the goods that moved across the world's oceans. This is certainly what Mahan and his contemporaries assumed would happen. Over the course of the nineteenth century however, and most certainly during the twentieth, the world economy simply became too large and complex to be coerced by direct military means.

One can see this easily enough by considering the operations of the Royal Navy against Napoleonic France at the start of the nineteenth century, and in its equally desperate struggle against Germany at the start of the twentieth. Naval warfare in the first of these contests centred on a close blockade of the enemy's coast. British warships, too powerful and numerous to be driven off by their French counterparts, could simply lurk in the maritime approaches to the major French ports, cutting them off entirely from seaborne trade. In addition, British ships on the high seas could stop, search, and seize any commercial vessel, on suspicion that it was trading with the enemy. Neutral powers had no choice but to accept this interference in their rightful affairs, since their own navies were no match for the British either, while Britain itself lived chiefly off of trade with its own colonies. In time businessmen throughout Europe and even in the Americas preferred to transport their goods in British ships, because such vessels were immune to interference by the Royal Navy. Naval superiority also allowed Britain to seize France's overseas colonies, whose trade also shifted to the British side of the ledger. None of this could prevent Napoleon's armies from running roughshod over his opponents in the short run. But over the longer term the financial leverage that accrued to Britain and her allies proved so overwhelming that it could not be matched even by the most remarkable military conquests the world had yet seen. The final campaigns that brought Napoleon down were not conducted by British armies, but they were mostly paid for by the British treasury, grown fat from the proceeds of maritime strategy in its classic form.

Nothing remotely similar was possible a century later. Close blockade had by then been rendered impracticable by the new weaponry of the industrial age—long-range coastal guns, underwater mines, torpedoes, and so on—which made it too dangerous for warships to patrol directly off an enemy's coast. Britain was obliged instead to attempt a 'distant' blockade of the entire European continent, an effort that, apart from stretching its naval resources to their limit, constituted a grave affront to the rights of neutral states, who were no longer willing to sit still for this sort of thing as they once had. Britain's ability to wage war was no less critically dependent on access to world markets than Germany's—more so, in fact—and the prospect that Britain's trading partners might unilaterally refuse to do business with Britain, or even enter the war on the other side, set strict and debilitating limits on how British seapower could be exercised.

Against Napoleon, the British had grown rich by cornering the market on overseas trade. Against Germany they grew poor borrowing money from the United States, in order to finance their own war effort, and also to pay off neutral trading states for the cost of being cut off from their traditional customers. The task of depriving a great industrial nation of the means to carry on war proved far beyond the power of the Royal Navy; to which was added the defensive burdens of Germany's retaliatory submarine campaign, by which Britain's own overseas trade was now seriously threatened for the first time. Britain's relations to the globalized world economy that it helped to create had thus ceased to be a source of strategic leverage, and became instead a strategic vulnerability, one that is now shared to some degree by every advanced society.

Economic warfare is no longer an important naval mission less because it is infeasible in tactical terms—though it certainly poses problems in that regard—than because the political and economic consequences of employing it on a large scale have grown unmanageable. In its absence the strategic advantages afforded by seapower have diminished, and become less distinctive than they once were; though it goes without saying that any nation separated from potential adversaries by the world's oceans will require a navy if it wishes to get across. At present, however, there is only one nation on earth that is in that situation—the United States—which explains why it possesses the only remaining navy of independent strategic significance.

That significance rests less upon its ability to 'command the sea' than to project power from sea to shore almost anywhere on earth. In this role it functions rather like a specialized sort of air force, which compensates for the relatively short range of its weapons by the ability to move its bases around as it likes. The advantages of being able to do this should not be underestimated. Land-based air forces require a massive fixed infrastructure, whose

---

BOX 6.2

Gunboat Diplomacy

'Gunboat diplomacy' is a derisive phrase from the heyday of European imperialism. It referred to the fact that colonial powers were sometimes in the habit of conveying their wishes to those less powerful than themselves by dispatching a warship in lieu of an ambassador; so that a few rounds of gunfire might substitute, as needed, for the customary diplomatic note. Such practices have gone out of a fashion, and the phrase with it; but the underlying reality to which it refers is nevertheless important to an understanding of the strategic leverage that naval forces afford.

A powerful navy like that of the United States today, or of Great Britain in the nineteenth century, always has a significant proportion of its ships at sea even in peacetime. Armies and air forces are garrison troops. They are only configured and deployed for combat when danger looms, and the possibility of violence has become apparent to all. Naval forces operating on the high seas in peacetime have the same capabilities as they would in time of war. They are armed and ready for action, and can appear wherever they can find water under their keels.

A nation that maintains such 'forward-deployed' naval forces acquires significant strategic options. Naval forces can convey a threat to an opponent (or reassurance to a friend) without engaging in any warlike act whatsoever. Because they are already 'out there' where trouble may arise, they are almost always the first to respond in a crisis; and indeed the speed with which warships already on station can respond to trouble may help to deter certain kinds of bad behaviour in the first place. While it is certainly true that long-range land-based aircraft can go anywhere, including many places where warships cannot, the military options they afford when they arrive are pretty much limited to blowing something up, and returning home. Naval forces provide a much more diverse array of choices, ranging from simple observation through the delivery of an implied or explicit threat, to the conduct of air strikes and the mounting of an amphibious assault.

The ability to do such things has never been the primary reason to have a navy; but it is an important extra benefit if you have one anyway. Like any military action, the practice of 'gunboat diplomacy', even its most benevolent forms, entails some risk, in particular that of providing adversaries with isolated targets of opportunity—a peril well illustrated by the surprise attack on the USS *Cole* during a port visit to Yemen in October 2000. Nevertheless, forward-deployed naval forces are especially well suited to a security environment characterized by diffuse threats and rapidly emerging crises, including natural catastrophes like the Indian Ocean tsunami of 2004, in which the first effective humanitarian relief was delivered by warships already at sea.

location may well limit how those forces can be used. Aircraft operating from bases sufficiently remote as to be safe from enemy attack may be required to fly through neutral air space to reach their targets, for which permission can simply be denied (and in moments of crisis and danger often will be). Forward bases constructed to obviate this requirement need time and resources to build, and are no more readily defensible than any other fixed asset that is within range of enemy weapons. If such bases are built on enemy territory, then the territory must first be seized. If they are built on neutral or allied territory, then operations again become subject to political requirements that may prove difficult to control. Warships do not suffer from any of these liabilities, but can generally approach their targets directly from international waters. Once on the scene, moreover, they can sustain operations almost indefinitely, being continuously replenished and resupplied at sea.

There can be no guarantee that such advantages will last forever. The strategic utility of a navy like that of the United States is ultimately hostage to the continuing evolution of long-range strike systems and other weapons of 'access denial'—naval mines, submarines, and so on—which are designed to hold an approaching navy so far off shore that it cannot employ its own weapons effectively. Such weapons are easy enough to envision, but they are far from being realized in practice. In the mean time, naval forces offer a unique combination of striking power, speed, and flexibility that is well suited to a security environment in which threats cannot be anticipated and prepared for long in advance. If naval forces can no longer be expected to decide the outcome of a major war, as they once were, their ability to perform the kind of constabulary function required in a world of brushfire conflicts and rapidly emerging crises remains undiminished.

KEY POINTS

- Navies in the Age of Sail achieved their strategic influence mainly by virtue of their impact on international trade.

- The strategic leverage afforded by navies as instruments of economic warfare has declined in the industrial era, as continental economies have become more robust, and as the complexity and connectivity of the global economy has increased.

- The ability of warships to operate freely in international waters can sometimes afford a dominant navy direct strategic access to an opponent, which may be available in no other way.

- At the turn of the twenty-first century, the traditional goal of naval warfare—to 'command the sea'—has been largely displaced by the challenges of projecting effective military power from sea to shore.

Airpower

Few human inventions have been as widely or eagerly anticipated as the 'flying machine', images of which can be found in the art and literature of the West since the Renaissance. What such a device might look like was of course anyone's guess; but few doubted that, whatever its ultimate form, it would find many remarkable applications as an instrument of war. The history of air warfare has accordingly been shaped to an unusual degree by exaggerated theoretical expectations of one kind or another, compared to which the real-life capabilities of air forces have often seemed to fall short.

The tens of thousands of military aircraft that fought each other in the skies over the Western Front in the First World War did so for no better purpose than to perform reconnaissance, in the vain hope of getting the vast armies beneath them moving again. They possessed nothing like the striking power envisioned by H. G. Wells a few years before in his celebrated novel *Wings* (1908), in which a vast air armada, launched from Germany, devastates New York City. Technological advances over the next twenty years increased the ability of aircraft to lift high explosives off the ground, and so to drop them back down on it. By the end of the Second World War British and American air forces were wreaking havoc on a scale resembling the apocalyptic fantasies of airpower enthusiasts like Julio Douhet, whose book *Command of the Air* (1923) held out the hope that aerial bombardment would be so terrible as to bring any war to a swift conclusion, sparing everyone the need to endure stalemate and attrition on the ground.

This prediction had failed to come true, however, and afterwards many wondered whether the bombing campaigns by which the cities of German and Japan had been devastated had not merely amplified the horrors of modern war, spreading them haphazardly among civil populations that might as well have been spared. The grim prophecy of British Prime Minister Stanley Baldwin, looking at the other side of the coin, had proven equally faulty. He had told an alarmed House of Commons in 1934 that 'the bomber will always get through'. They most certainly had not. By 1945 the Royal Air Force had suffered more casualties than the Royal Navy, testimony to something that real airmen had always understood: that war in the air is difficult, dangerous, and disappointing, just like war everywhere else.

There can be no question that the integration of aerial weapons into the conduct of war was the central military problem of the twentieth century. Looking backward from the early years of the twenty-first, it is apparent that a great deal was accomplished, so that a surprisingly clear and convincing picture has emerged. The frustrations of the world wars were owed partly to immature technologies, partly to the tendency of institutional interests to compromise objective analysis. The strongest advocates of airpower were invariably convinced that only independent air services, co-equal with armies and navies, could master this new method of fighting. Their desire for institutional independence led to exaggerated claims that airpower alone, and specifically the long-range bombardment of economic and civil infrastructure, could directly decide the outcome of war—which claims in turn inspired equally exaggerated scepticism that airpower was all it was cracked up to be. The resolution of these bureaucratic quarrels (invariably in favour of independent air forces), combined with the continued progress of technology, have given rise to a more stable and convincing picture, in which airpower is featured not so much as the universal solvent of modern war, but as the all-purpose glue that makes modern combined arms operations possible.

If airpower retains an independent strategic role, it is at the extreme ends of the conflict spectrum. Nuclear weapons, should they ever be employed by an organized government, will be delivered by aircraft or missiles, and it is easy enough to believe that the effect of

BOX 6.3

Command of the Air

Air forces have always struggled to live up the expectations of their most avid enthusiasts. This was especially true during the period between the world wars, when rapid improvements in the speed and power of military aircraft gave rise to claims that their actions might render the clash of armies and navies unnecessary. One of the most influential proponents of this view was Guilio Douhet, an Italian officer who conceived of the air as an environment analogous to that of the world's oceans. Like the sea, he thought the air could be 'commanded' by a superior air force in a way that would deny its use to the enemy; and also that the ability to accomplish this would, for all practical purposes, decide future wars. The passage that follows illustrates his efforts to work out the strategic implications of this vision.

To have command of the air means to be in a position to prevent the enemy from flying while retaining the ability to fly oneself. . . . An aerial fleet capable of dumping hundreds of tons of bombs can easily be organized; therefore, the striking force and magnitude of aerial offensives, considered from the standpoint of either material or moral significance, is far more effective than those of any other offensive yet known. A nation which had command of the air is in a position to protect its own territory from enemy aerial attack and even to put a halt to the enemy's auxiliary actions in support of his land and sea operations, leaving him powerless to do much of anything. Such offensive actions can not only cut off an opponent's army and navy from their bases of operations, but can also bomb the interior of the enemy's country so devastatingly that the physical and moral resistance of the people would also collapse . . .

To conquer the command of the air means victory; to be beaten in the air means defeat and acceptance of whatever terms the enemy may be pleased to impose . . .

From this axiom we come immediately to this first corollary: In order to assure an adequate national defense, it is necessary—and sufficient—to be in a position in case of war to conquer the command of the air. And from that we arrive at this second corollary: All that a nation does to assure her own defense should have as its aim procuring for herself those means which, in case of war, are most effective for the conquest of the command of the air . . .

Any diversion from this primary purpose is an error. In order to conquer the air, it is necessary to deprive the enemy of all means of flying, by striking at him in the air, at his bases of operation, or at his production centers—in short, wherever those means are to be found. This kind of destruction can be accomplished only by aerial means, to the exclusion of army and navy weapons . . .

Victory smiles upon those who anticipate the changes in the character of war, not upon those who wait to adapt themselves after the changes occur. In this period of rapid transition from one form to another, those who daringly take to the new road first will enjoy the incalculable advantages of the new means of war over the old. This new character of war, emphasizing the advantages of the offensive, will surely make for swift, crushing decisions on the battlefield. . . . Those who are ready first not only will win quickly, but will win with the fewest sacrifices and the minimum expenditure of means.

(Douhet 1984: 24–30)

their detonations, if sufficiently numerous, will render the activities of armies and navies of little consequence to whatever comes next. More interesting, and certainly more unexpected from the point of view of traditional airpower theory, is the role of air weapons in lesser conflicts, in which the stakes are low, so that only limited force is justified. Airpower has become the main tool by which strong countries seek to coerce weak ones, at least in matters that do not entail complete capitulation, for two general reasons. The first is that for all practical purposes Stanley Baldwin's prophecy has now come true. Bombers almost always do get through, owing to doctrinal and technological developments that allow the best air forces to completely suppress all but the very best air defence systems. Although any pilot flying a combat mission is undoubtedly risking his or her life, the risk is small compared to that entailed by any other comparably destructive act of war. And of course it is even further reduced if the blow is delivered by ballistic or cruise missiles. Once through, moreover, bombers and missiles can be counted on to strike their targets with a consistency that was scarcely imaginable in earlier times. In the era of the world wars aerial weapons were synonymous with indiscriminate destruction. Today they are synonymous with stealth and precision, which between them helped reduce the risks traditionally associated with their use.

Whether this is an altogether good thing depends on how one views the gap between peace and war, which has appreciably narrowed in recent years, by virtue of the ease and safety with which aerial strike operations can be mounted. The use of air strikes to punctuate a diplomatic demand or enforce a sanctions regime may pose little risk to the personnel immediately involved, but the possibility that such activities will inspire some kind of unexpected retaliatory response on the other side cannot be discounted. The aim of violence in war is always to break the enemy's will. Yet its immediate effect may be to harden his heart, stiffen his spine, and stimulate his imagination instead.

The mobilization of society for war is a delicate business. Peacetime disputes and desires must be set aside in order to redirect psychological and material resources toward the war effort. Private life becomes smaller, the public sphere larger and more intrusive. Successful mobilization instills civil society with the emotional energy required to inflict pain, and to bear it. Moral distinctions between combatants and non-combatants become blurred. In its ideal form, a society mobilized for war becomes a single, unified entity, whose members are envisioned as interchangeable parts in an integrated engine of belligerency.

Strategic bombing, as originally conceived, depended on just such a holistic view of the enemy, in which damage inflicted anywhere was presumed to be felt everywhere. Thus an army might be disabled by demolishing the factories that made its weapons, or the homes and bodies of those who worked in the factories. Casualties at the front would react upon civilian morale. Civilian deaths would demoralize or delegitimize the government. Enemy governments in turn were seen as a direct and authentic expression of their societies. This view provided both a moral justification and a tactical rational for the far-reaching destruction that aerial bombardment entailed.

Liberal democracies in particular are now inclined to think of their adversaries rather differently. They no longer take the psychological unity of armed forces, state, and society for granted. On the contrary, these are now seen as being artificially stitched together by political convenience, brute force, or some other similarly fragile thread. The resulting seams have become the principal targets of strategic bombardment in its current form. The aim of an air campaign conducted with precision weapons is to inflict suffering differentially against the government and the armed forces, in order to detach them from their social base while leaving the latter intact. This sort of approach has the undoubted advantage of sparing human life, and of making the reconstruction and rehabilitation of a defeated society easier. But whether its psychological foundations are more reliable than those that prevailed in the past is necessarily an open question. The currently prevailing understanding of how airpower works politically has been refined in campaigns against internationally isolated, despotic regimes, none of which possessed 'the consent of the governed'. Yet this is a quality that democratic countries may be too quick to deny their opponents. Totalitarian and criminal regimes, particularly those arising in the wake of revolutionary upheaval, may be quite thoroughly rooted in their surrounding societies, and correspondingly difficult to coerce without inspiring the kind of escalatory reactions that may lead to general war.

KEY POINTS

- The integration of aerial weapons into the conduct of war was the dominant operational problem confronting the armed forces of advanced societies in the twentieth century.

- Expectations about what air forces can achieve in theory have often run far ahead of what has been possible in practice.

- Modern air campaigns are no longer oriented towards the infliction of mass destruction, but are intended instead to disable an enemy government and its armed forces, while inflicting the least damage possible to the surrounding society.

- The combination of precision weaponry and a relatively low risk of friendly casualties has made aerial bombardment the weapon of choice in the conduct of war that is intended simply to coerce a concession from the enemy, rather than to force his complete capitulation.

The Final Frontier: Space War

The outstanding attribute of war in the air is undoubtedly the speed and precision with which blows can be struck by weapons that operate there. In most respects these advantages have reached their culminating point as far as their strategic utility is concerned. Doubling the speed of an airplane or cruise missile may make some marginal difference to its tactical application, but it isn't going to matter in strategic terms, because the time required to reach the political decision to use it takes just as long as it ever did. Further improvements in precision likewise promise diminishing returns at best. A weapon that blows a fifty foot hole in something, and strikes reliably within five feet of its target, is going to work pretty much the same if it can be made to strike within three feet. Compared to the land or the sea, the air has proven to be a remarkably permissive arena of war, at least for those who can operate there unopposed.

Yet its characteristics can still be improved upon. Beyond the earth's atmosphere lies, well, nothing. That is what space is: a perfectly transparent, friction-free environment, which has never yet been employed for any warlike purpose other than to observe the goings-on of the planet's surface below. In this regard it has already acquired very considerable importance. Space may be nothing, but it is not empty. Hundreds (if not thousands) of military satellites are already there, performing all manner of communicative and reconnaissance functions, as well as providing the terminal guidance that is making the accuracy of all major weapons systems increasingly independent of their range. If the land, sea, and air forces of the United States were somehow deprived of their ability to communicate with the space-based systems orbiting over their heads, the effect would be fully comparable to the most catastrophic battlefield defeat. To that extent, space war already exists.

Whether space holds strategic possibilities independent of the contribution that space-based systems already make to the conduct of war is a matter of speculation. The military use of space is currently governed by two international legal norms. The first holds that claims of national sovereignty do not apply beyond the earth's atmosphere; the second that actual weapons cannot be deployed there. Like most such agreements, these are not so much barriers to action as reflections of a prevailing political consensus. The first has undoubtedly contributed to the exploitation of space for reconnaissance and communications. Under its terms any country capable of launching a satellite is free to peer down on its neighbours without let or hindrance. This arrangement is widely regarded as having contributed to the stability of strategic deterrence during the later years of the cold war, since it afforded both the United States and the Soviet Union a high degree of confidence that each knew what the other was up to.

The prohibition of the 'weaponization' of space is less a matter of perceived mutual advantage than of apparent futility. The transparency that makes space such an ideal environment for reconnaissance and communications makes it a poor place for weapons. These would be highly vulnerable to detection and destruction, without affording any special tactical capabilities compared to those already operating on the planet's surface. One possible exception would be orbital systems designed to disable nearby communications satellites. This could be accomplished, for instance, by detonating one or more nuclear warhead outside the earth's atmosphere. But a country capable of doing such a thing would undoubtedly have a large stake in space-based communications itself, and these would be no less crippled than those of its enemy. In any case, such a disabling attack could be launched just as easily, and far more cheaply, from the earth's surface.

For now, the strategic applications of space appear likely to remain confined to the collection and distribution of information, activities for which it affords compelling advantages. If anything, the challenges in this area lie less in collecting data than in employing it effectively. For an advanced society, it is easier to launch satellites capable of recording every cell phone conversation in, say, Afghanistan, or of photographing every flatbed truck on the streets of Shanghai, than it is to field the army of Pastun speakers and photo-analysts required to interpret the results. Throughout history, those who have gone to war have always hungered for more information. In some respects that hunger is now on the verge of satiation. Yet the results may prove less digestible than our ancestors might have imagined.

KEY POINTS

- Space systems are already vital to the conduct of war on land, sea, and in the air. Most of the sophisticated information systems on which the armed forces of advanced societies depend have space-based components, whose destruction would severely degrade military performance.

- So far as is publicly known, there are no weapons currently based in space, because the tactical advantages of doing so are unclear.

War by Other Means: Cyberspace

In the final analysis, modern war has been all about people hurling pieces of metal at each other. Its historical development has been marked by a steady increase in the size, velocity, range, and variety of the pieces, and by the introduction of ever more powerful chemical explosives to propel them along and amplify their lethal effects once they reach their destinations. Nuclear weapons represent a modest departure from this pattern, since their destructiveness is achieved by somewhat different means. Yet they too are products and expressions of a massive industrial-age infrastructure, and impose huge economic, logistical, and organizational burdens on those who wish to employ them.

What if it were otherwise? What if war could be fought without the need to store up and discharge massive amounts of kinetic energy? What would that be like? No one has the faintest idea. But the extraordinary flourishing of information technology over the last twenty years has at least made the question sufficiently plausible as to remove it from the realm of fantasy. Whether 'cyberspace' really deserves to be treated as an independent realm of war may of course be disputed. It is, after all, a wholly imaginary place, whose functioning is dependent on physical systems that are no less subject to direct attack than any other military or civilian object. The increasing centrality of those systems to the conduct of war in all forms has already been alluded to, and to that extent 'cyberwar', like 'space war', already exists. Indeed, the two are closely related, since a large share of critical information systems depend to one degree or another on space-based infrastructure.

One reason information warfare has lately come in for so much scrutiny is the uneasy realization that complex information systems, on which the conduct of even the most mundane military operations now depend, are unusually vulnerable to attack compared to other major military assets. This is a grave problem, but it remains a tactical one, and should not be confused with the direct use of information as a strategic weapon. The latter is also readily distinguishable from 'propaganda', in the so-called 'the war of ideas'. Strategy is not about persuasion, at least not primarily. It is about the *forcible* imposition of one's will upon one's adversary.

Whether this sort of result can be accomplished by information alone is difficult to say. A computer virus that disabled a national stock exchange would arguably have consequences comparable to those of a major military attack. If such a blow were delivered in the course of a 'shooting' war it would require no special explanation or analysis, and would merely be one more means by which one belligerent sought to injure the other. On its own, however, a cyber-attack of this kind would appear to be difficult to exploit for strategic purposes, if only because, once its source and purpose were revealed, it might well invite a 'kinetic' response by way of rejoinder. The risk of indiscriminate collateral damage would also be immense. Such a virus, once set loose on the world, might well end up anywhere. In this respect information war suffers from some of the same limitations as biological warfare, which loomed ominously on the strategic horizon for most of the twentieth century without ever having been realized in practice, precisely because its fratricidal risks appear to outweigh its prospective benefits.

In most respects, then, the strategic geography of cyberspace remains *terra incognita*. It is to all appearances a realm where it is very cheap to operate, and perhaps also to fight undetected. This suggests that its greatest appeal may be to terrorists and others who lack the means to fight elsewhere; who do not mind if they are not given credit for their deeds; and who are not themselves especially dependent on information technology. Which is to say that, from the point of view of advanced societies, information warfare appears to be mainly a defensive problem, with little to offer in the way of positive strategic leverage. In any event, it would be naïve to suppose that the expansion of war into this new and nebulous realm, should it occur, will have any sort of moderating effect on its destructiveness. However and wherever war is waged, it will remain the brutal business it has always been, in which victory will go to those with the material and emotional resources required to stand the strain.

KEY POINTS

- As modern weapons have become increasingly reliant upon precision sensors and advanced communications systems for their effectiveness, the question whether information itself may somehow become a weapon has gained increasing attention.

- The sophisticated information technologies on which the best armed forces, and all modern societies, now rely pose an attractive target to potential adversaries, above all those that are not especially dependent upon similar technologies.

? QUESTIONS

1. The commitment of ground forces in war appears to require a higher level of political commitment than the commitment of air and naval forces. Does this have the effect of eroding, or strengthening, the psychological barrier that separates peace and war?

2. If having a large and powerful navy is a good idea, why is the United States the only country on earth that has one?

3. Are there any circumstances under which we can expect this US commitment to a large navy to change?

4. In peacetime, strategic decision-making often translates into decisions about where and how to spend money on defence. Where, between its army, navy, and air force, should an advanced society be investing its marginal defence dollars today?

5. Would the answer to the relative balance of forces be different for a developing society in Africa or Eurasia? How about for a country like Iran or North Korea, which feels itself threatened by the United States?

6. Given that further advances in the precision guidance of weapons are now entering a zone of diminishing returns (after several decades of rapid advance), where should air, sea, and land forces be looking in their search for new technologies to improve their combat effectiveness?

7. If you could invent a new weapon for a modern navy, army, or air force, what would it do?

8. Do you expect the current international consensus against the 'weaponization' of space to continue indefinitely?

9. What kinds of developments would you expect to undermine this consensus?

10. Do you agree that information warfare is largely a defensive problem?

 FURTHER READING

■ **J. B. A. Bailey, *Field Artillery and Firepower* (Annapolis, MD: Naval Institute Press, rev. edn. 2004),** Supplements Bellamy's work (below). The title does not convey the scope and interest of its contents.

■ **Christopher Bellamy, *The Evolution of Modern Land Warfare: Theory and Practice* (London and New York: Routledge, 1990).** Slightly out of date with respect to recent developments, but it remains the outstanding survey of its subject.

■ **Peter L. Hays, James M. Smith, Alan R. Van Tassel, and Guy M. Walsh, eds., *Spacepower for a New Millennium: Space and U.S. National Security* (New York: McGraw-Hill, 2000.** On the strategic exploitation of space.

■ **Benjamin S. Lambeth, *The Transformation of American Air Power* (Ithaca, NY: Cornell University Press, 2000).**

■ **Gregory J. Rattray, *Strategic Warfare in Cyberspace* (Cambridge, MA: MIT Press, 2001).** Compares innovation in information warfare to the tortuous but ultimately triumphant progress of airpower in the twentieth century.

■ **Geoffrey Till, *Seapower: A Guide for the Twenty-First Century* (London: Frank Cass, 2004).**

Visit the Online Resource Centre that accompanies this book for lots of interesting additional material http://www.oxfordtextbooks.co.uk/orc/baylis_strategy2e/.

7

Technology and Warfare

ELIOT COHEN

Chapter Contents

- Technophiles and Technophobes
- Some Ways of Thinking about Military Technology
- Mapping Military Technology
- The Revolution in Military Affairs Debate
- Challenges of the New Technology
- The Future of Military Technology

Reader's Guide

Although the development and integration of technology into military forces and strategy is often depicted as a simple matter, the role of technology in war is controversial. Debate exists about the relative importance of technology when compared to other factors such as training or morale, in achieving victory in battle. Scholars also offer competing explanations about how and why certain technologies are integrated into military organizations while others are ignored. The pace of technological change also is not uniform: some technology and procedures become fixtures in militaries while others become obsolete quickly and are discarded. To complicate matters further, some observers today believe that the world is witnessing a revolution in military affairs, a relatively rare event when technologies are combined to produce a fundamental transformation in the way war is fought. This chapter explores these issues and describes some changes that the revolution in military affairs is producing in military organizations. It also offers some observations about the emerging technological trends that are likely to transform future warfare.

Technophiles and Technophobes

Military historians—and sometimes soldiers themselves—cannot make up their minds about how to view military technology. Some technical experts and enthusiasts are fascinated by the nuances of the various models of the German Panzerkampfwagen Model IV; much contemporary policy debate centres on technical decisions—how many aircraft to buy, what type, over what period of time, and so on. The public at large tends to ascribe remarkable—sometimes even magical—properties to modern military technology.

By contrast, many military historians and soldiers deprecate the importance of technology. They believed that the skill and organizational effectiveness, not pieces of hardware, determine the outcome of battle. Although technical enthusiasts and sceptics sometimes clash in their assessment of a particular contest, rarely does the debate occur at a conceptual level. Only one major figure in the last century—Major General J. F. C. Fuller, a British war planner, pioneer of armoured warfare, and prolific military historian—attempted to write theoretically about the role of technology in strategic studies (1945, 1932, 1926, 1942). This chapter therefore introduces some concepts about military technology, and then discusses the key technological issues and trends of our time.

Some Ways of Thinking about Military Technology

Consider as a point of departure the question: 'Where does military technology come from?' We often think of technology as something predetermined. In this common view, scientists develop technology in war much like people walking down a corridor lined with closed rooms containing treasure chests. Progress consists of walking along the hallway, unlocking the doors, and picking up the chests. The fruits of technology, in other words, lie available to those who have the keys to the doors and the strength to carry away the treasure chests.

In fact, however, historians of technology and engineering usually reject this view. A variety of forces shapes technology, whose final form is far from being predetermined (MacKenzie 1990). The most common view along these lines is that 'form follows function': military technology evolves to meet particular military needs. There are, however, other possibilities. One author, Henry Petroski, talks about 'form following failure', a concept first applied to his study of the history of bridge building, but applicable to military technology as well (1982). In this view, new technology emerges as a response to some perceived failure or fault in existing technology. Other theories of technological invention include the suggestion that technologies emerge from aesthetic or other non-rational considerations, such as custom or organizational convenience (Creveld 1989). These different theories offer varying explanations of how innovation occurs or fails to occur. Why, for example, did it take more than thirty years for the United States, which successfully deployed unmanned aerial vehicles (UAVs) in Vietnam, to introduce them into the armed forces? The technology may have been immature (the corridor-and-doors theory); there may have been no mission crying out for UAVs (form follows function); there may have been no visible failure in the existing technology (form follows failure); or, finally, the technology may have been thwarted by pilots hostile to the notion of aircraft without pilots (non-rational explanations).

No one of these theories is completely satisfying. Their very range, however, should prompt us to look more closely at how and why military technologies come into existence. There are distinctive national styles, for example, in military technology: the Israeli Merkava tank differs subtly from American M1 Abrams. These changes reflect differences in design philosophy stemming from where the two countries believe they will fight (the slow Israeli tank is designed for the rocky Golan Heights; the much faster Abrams tank can exploit its high speed best in desert warfare). The Israelis have given exceptionally high value to crew safety. They accepted mechanical inefficiency by placing the engine in front of the crew space rather than (as is normal) behind it. In armoured warfare, most hits occur on the frontal armour of the tank, and the engine can thus absorb the impact of a hit. The Americans, by purchasing a fuel-hungry high-powered turbine engine, assumed that they could readily resupply their tanks with fuel in vast quantities on the battlefield.

National styles in technology may reflect political assumptions about war at the time that a design was frozen. In 2006, for example, the United States was poised to buy large numbers of the Joint Strike Fighter (JSF), a short-ranged fighter bomber. This decision reflects a political assumption, namely, that the United States would fight its wars within a few hundred miles of its opponents, and, presumably, with extensive access to secure fixed bases.[1]

BOX 7.1

The M1A2 vs the merkava

	M1A2	Merkava (Mk3)
Weight (fully armed) (tons)	69.54	62.9
Length (gun forward) (metres)	9.8	8.8
Height (metres)	2.9	2.8
Width	3.7	3.7
Range (miles)	265	311
Crew	4	4
Road speed (km/hour)	90+	55
Main armament	120 mm	120 mm
Engine	Gas turbine	Diesel

Although similar in some respects, the Merkava is very different from the M1 in others. It is much slower (perhaps half as fast): the Israelis value absolute speed much less than the ability to manœuvre under fire, particularly over the lava-strewn Golan Heights. They also lack the super-fast infantry fighting vehicles to keep up with the tanks. There is a rear hatch on the Merkava that allows the evacuation of wounded or resupply of ammunition without exposing the crew—again, requirements derived from the peculiar problems of keeping a firing line on the Golan Heights. Finally, the Israeli engine is at the front of the tank, where it can absorb an incoming round—a sacrifice of mechanical efficiency for crew protection. The M1 gets a similar effect by unusually good (and expensive) armour.

Sources: http://.army-technology.com/projects/merkava/specs.html; http://www.army-technology.com/projects/abrams/index.html specs. Note: the stated speed for the M1A2 is considerably too slow.

One way to penetrate the essence of national design style is to ask what kind of trade-offs designers accepted. All engineers make choices among desired features of hardware; all pieces of military technology reflect those choices. A tank has three fundamental characteristics: protection, firepower, and mobility. Increase the amount of armour and one sacrifices the tank's ability to move quickly; put a small-bore, low-recoil cannon on it and one gains a great deal of mobility for a penalty in firepower; increase horsepower and pay a penalty in terms of the size of the tank (and hence protection) or how far it can go (and hence mobility).

Military technology also reflects processes of interaction. Tanks did not grow to be today's 60-ton monsters because of the growth of their power plants or guns. Developments in armour were to blame. Tank armour once consisted of rolled homogeneous steel. Today, it may consist of a variety of substances—exotic metals such as depleted uranium, composites that include alternating layers of metal and ceramics, and sandwiches of metal and high explosive. These changes reflect the development of ever more powerful antitank weapons—depleted uranium rods and so-called shaped charges (explosives configured to create a jet of hot metal that burns its way through armour). Even in peacetime, measure and countermeasure rule the choices designers make. These interactions create a kind of evolutionary process, by which a weapon system settles into its own 'ecological' niche. Birds and lizards evolve an amazing variety of counters to their predators, who in turn come up with a range of adaptations that enable them to find and devour their prey. So too with weapon systems. As in nature, interaction may yield odd outcomes, where one kind of highly sophisticated adaptation to a particular environment makes a platform utterly unsuited to a different battlefield. The first two generations of stealth aircraft, for example, evolved to avoid detection through the use of adroitly shaped surfaces that would disperse or absorb radar energy: they were difficult (not impossible) to detect using the radar technology of the time. Their odd shaping, however, made them slower and less manœuvrable than other aircraft; they have therefore become night-time-only systems that would be vulnerable to optical detection during the day.

In assessing military technology one should look at invisible technology as well. What gave the German tanks an edge over their French counterparts in the Second World War, for example, was not superior armour, guns, or engines, so much as a piece of technology barely noticed by outside observers—the radio (Stolfi 1970). Often, the most important elements of a military system are not the ones most evident to the casual observer, yet mastery of such technologies may weigh most in battle. American forces in the south-west Pacific in the Second World War struggled not only with the Japanese, but also with disease. The insecticide DDT, as much as any bomber or battleship, won the fight for New Guinea.

One should consider the role of systems technology and not just its parts. A novelist described a Second World War warship this way:

> One way of thinking of the ship was as of some huge marine animal. Here on the bridge was the animal's brain, and radiating from it ran the nerves—the telephones and voice tubes—which carried the brain's decisions to the parts which were to execute them. The engine-room formed the muscles which actuated the tail—the propellers; and the guns were the teeth and claws of the animal. Up in the crow's nest above, and all round the bridge where the lookouts sat

raking sea and sky with their binoculars, were the animal's eyes, seeking everywhere for enemies or prey, while the signal flags and wireless transmitter were the animal's voice, with which it could cry a warning to its fellows or scream for help. **"**

(Forester 1943: 22–3)

As the war progressed, the brain of the ship vanished into its bowels, so to speak—becoming the combat information centre of modern vessels. But Forester's point was that the effectiveness of the ship rested not simply on the working of all the different technologies individually, but rather on their effectiveness as a whole. The very use of the term weapon *system* implies that the art of putting technologies together is more important than their individual excellence. In war, more than in most other activities, the whole can be far greater than the sum of its parts.

Our last concept is that of the technological edge. It is not always decisive, but it is almost always important. J. F. C. Fuller (1945: 18) once suggested that Napoleon himself would have succumbed to the semi-competent British general in the Crimea, Lord Raglan, simply because the latter's army had rifles, while the former had smoothbore muskets. It is only recently that the advanced powers have assumed that they would go to war with a decided technological edge over their opponents, and that this advantage would prove decisive. Technological superiority does not necessarily extend across the board. In the Persian Gulf War of 1991, for example, some Iraqi artillery pieces (their South African made G-5 howitzers) outranged Western counterparts such as the American Paladin system, by 6 kilometres or more (30 vs 24 km, to be precise)—much as Russian-made 122 mm guns outranged their American 155 mm counterparts in Vietnam.[2] The poorer, smaller, or weaker side may have some niche competencies that will surprise a richer and more powerful opponent. The technological edge may be dramatic (the quintessential case being the Dervish armies of the Khalifa crumpling under the fire of Lord Kitchener's Anglo-Egyptian infantry using the Henry-Martini rifle), or quite subtle—a matter of a few seconds' difference in the flight time of an air-to-air missile, or a few hundred yards in the effective range of a tank gun. The technological edge may have a psychological dimension that vanishes over time, as with Second World War-era German dive bombers with their unearthly wailing sirens, or American heliborne infantry in Vietnam appearing from the skies in remote jungles; or it may reflect fleeting disparities in commercial technology (e.g. commercial Global Positioning System navigation receivers purchased by Americans, but not Iraqis, in the Gulf War).

KEY POINTS

- There are a range of different theories about how military technology develops.

- Military technologies often reflect different national styles.

- Different national styles are determined by a variety of things, such as political assumptions, trade-offs between various features of hardware, processes of interaction, invisible technologies, systems technology, and the search for technological edge.

Mapping Military Technology

It can be difficult enough to understand military technology when it remains static: the authors of novels about the Napoleonic era war at sea, such as Patrick O'Brian or C. S. Forester, have a considerable challenge (which those two meet wonderfully well) in describing the complex technology of early nineteenth-century naval warfare. But the problem of under-standing military technology is more difficult because it changes continuously. Indeed, since the middle of the nineteenth century, change in military technology has become a constant, through what Martin van Creveld has called 'the invention of invention'. The traditional picture of soldiers suspiciously rejecting new technology in favour of old standbys was always overdone: before the First World War, for example, the armies of Europe embraced the machine gun and the aeroplane. Their difficulty lay, and lies today, in recognizing what broader changes new technology may entail. For powerful institu-tional reasons, military organizations tend to fit new technologies into old intellectual and operational frameworks.

One question to ask in assessing technological change is whether what one is witnessing is a change in quantity or a change in quality. It is a more complicated question than it might appear. Marginal increases in speed, protection, mobility, or payload, to take just a few design parameters, are quantitative: they may have cumulative effects, but in and of themselves should not bring about radical changes in war. Sometimes, however, a seem-ingly quantitative change is, in fact, qualitative. Early firearms, for example, delivered rather less effective lethality than a good long bow; oil-fired ship engines offered moderate increases in speed over their coal-powered counterparts; and the first generation air-to-air missiles provided only marginal improvements over a well-aimed burst of cannon fire. All of these changes, however, foreshadowed tremendous upheavals in the conduct of war. Mastery of the long bow could take a lifetime. Mastery of the musket took a few months of drill, and its incidental qualities—the noise, smoke, and flash, none of which had direct effects on the enemy—made it a more fearful, that is, psychologically effective, weapon. Oil propulsion reduced the size of crews, increased the speed of ships, and, perhaps most importantly, made the world's oil fields prime strategic real estate. Air-to-air missiles improved far beyond the capability of mature aircraft cannon, to the point of engaging targets well beyond visual range.

Contemporary observers will often get it wrong. Military organizations (the US Navy in particular) had experimented with satellite-based navigation systems since the early 1960s (Friedman 2000). It took the experience of the Gulf War in 1991, however, to make average sailors, pilots, and soldiers realize that the Global Positioning System could transform all aspects of navigation from art to science, or rather mere technique. By contrast, the advent of nuclear weapons in the late 1940s and 1950s convinced some professionals that all military organizations would have to be radically restructured to accommodate the new weapons. As it turned out, however, only selected military organizations needed to adapt their tactics and structures to the new devices (Bacevich 1986). Military organizations and platforms do not change at a uniform rate. Some aspects of military technology change very little over the decades. Visit an aircraft carrier's deck, and one is struck by how little many procedures have changed in half a century. Steam catapults—themselves solid pieces of mid-twentieth-century engineering—loft jet aircraft off angled decks devised shortly after the Second World War. The crews, in multicoloured jerseys, each of which identifies their function, work pretty much as their fathers did during the Korean war. Inside, the Air Boss and his (or her) staff track the movement of aircraft using model aeroplanes on a large flat table; below decks illuminated glass grids show the status of all aircraft. There are important changes—more accurate and powerful bombs, far better intelligence flowing in, better aircraft—but the structure is remarkably durable. The same might be said of a battalion of paratroopers ready to drop on an airfield and seize it. Their aircraft, C-130s designed in the early 1950s and first fielded in 1956, are crammed with men carrying parachutes whose fundamental design goes back to the Second World War.[3] The process of training, loading, and deploying those men remains, in its essentials, the same.

Some military processes change to a considerably greater extent. A large desert armoured battle, for example, bears some resemblance to the clashes of the Second World War: masses of ponderous armoured beasts manœuvring over open ground, generating vast clouds of smoke and dust, swirling in a mêlée where the advantage goes to the quicker shot and calmer head. But much has changed, too. Today's armoured battle might take place at night, using thermal imaging devices that are in many ways better than optical sights even on a clear day. This is a far cry even from the night battles of the 1973 Yom Kippur war, in which Syrian tanks using crude infrared projectors attacked after daylight; for the modern armoured force, there is no important difference in visibility between day and night. The armour, gun power, and speed of the tanks today are much greater than during the Second World War, as is tank size. Those are important quantitative changes, but the biggest shift is in the accuracy of their weapons. A well-calibrated gun, with even a moderately competent crew (aided by laser range finders and ballistic computers) can score a first-round hit at a distance of several kilometres—a significant change in the way tank battles are fought.

Sometimes there are changes that fundamentally alter war fighting. The first night of an air operation, for example, is now completely different from what occurred during the Second World War, Korea, and Vietnam. In one or two nights a competent air force can shut down an enemy's air defence system, rather than wearing it out by a process of attritional struggle with defending fighter aircraft. Precision weapons—now ubiquitous in the arsenals of developed countries—mean that an initial attack can, in theory at least, prove paralysing. It is not the case that airpower can do more efficiently that which it did in the past—it can do things that it never could have done before. Thus, for example, with adequate intelligence and planning, a well-conducted air strike can cripple a nation's telecommunications system, in part by attacking targets (relay towers or switching centres) that previously were not susceptible to mass attack.

KEY POINTS

- One of the problems of understanding the role of military technologies is the constant process of change that takes place.

- One difficult issue concerns the relationship between qualitative and quantitative change.

- Another difficulty is that some technology is slow to have an effect, while some is much more immediate and radical in its impact.

The Revolution in Military Affairs Debate

When a set of changes comes together, the result (some soldiers and historians would argue) is a revolution. Normally, military technology merely evolves, at greater or lesser speeds, and unevenly. Occasionally, however, several developments will come together and yield a broader transformation. Thus, in the middle of the nineteenth century the combination of the telegraph (which allowed real-time links between civilian authority and military commanders, and between commanders in large military organizations), the railway (which permitted mass movements of troops and their sustenance during winter or while conducting sieges), and the rifle (which made infantry engagements lethal at greater ranges than ever before) transformed war. The mass conflicts of the wars of German unification and the American Civil War involved industrialized masses, and spelt the end of battles conducted in compressed periods of time and narrowly defined locations. They foreshadowed the slaughter of the First World War, as a few prescient observers noted.

Since the late 1970s, a number of observers have suggested that a revolution in military affairs is under way. Soviet writers—senior military officers, including the then Chief of the Soviet General Staff, Nikolai Ogarkov—suggested that modern conventional weapons would soon have the effectiveness of tactical nuclear weapons. Long-range sensors, including powerful radars mounted on aircraft, combined with precision weapons, would allow the detection and destruction of armoured units long before they ever approached the battlefield. Soviet military leaders believed that the United States, with its superior technological base, would drive these developments, and that their consequence would fall very much to the disadvantage of the Soviet Union, reliant as it was on waves of armoured forces that could move into Europe from their mobilization areas in the western USSR.

In the West, a number of technologists had similar, if less well-articulated, aspirations for weapon systems that would combine accuracy, range, and above all 'intelligence'—the ability to home in on, or even select, their own targets. It took the 1991 Gulf War to convince a broad spectrum of officers that very large changes in the conduct of war had occurred. The lopsidedness of that war, the undeniable effectiveness of precision weapons, and the emergence of a host of supporting military technologies (stealth, for example, which is actually a cluster of technologies) convinced many observers that warfare had changed fundamentally. The developments first noted in the Gulf War continued in a decade of smaller scale military engagements thereafter, including repeated American and British strikes against Iraqi targets, and NATO operations against Yugoslavia as a result of the wars in Bosnia in 1995 (Operation Deliberate Force) and in Kosovo in 1999 (Operation Allied Force). Attacking both by night and by day, and using primarily guided weapons, the United States and (to a lesser extent) its allies conducted operations with extraordinary accuracy and negligible combat losses. Similarly, the combination of special operations forces, unmanned aerial vehicles, and aircraft delivering precision weapons (and unguided ones for that matter) had a devastating effect on admittedly ragtag Taliban troops in Afghanistan in 2001. These and American regular ground and air forces occupied Iraq, and crushed the regime of Saddam Hussein, and its admittedly fragile and obsolescent military, in less than three weeks in 2003.

An adequate conceptual description of these changes, however, remained elusive. The Vice-Chairman of the American Joint Chiefs of Staff, Admiral William Owens, described what he termed 'the system of systems' as the ultimate potential of the new technologies, if not their actual achievement (Owens and Offley 2000). By integrating long-range, precision weapons with extensive intelligence, surveillance, and reconnaissance, and vastly improved capabilities for processing information and distributing it, he believed the United States could hope to detect and destroy any enemy target over swathes of the earth's surface as large as two hundred by two hundred miles. Some in the military scoffed at this as a technologist's fantasy, pointing to the persistence of what Carl von Clausewitz termed 'the fog of war' even in seemingly immaculate military operations against feeble opponents—the limited success of NATO aircraft in knocking out Serb tanks in 1999 being a case in point. Owens himself declared that enormous bureaucratic impediments—the persistence of individual service cultures, in particular—stood in the way of his dream being achieved.

In truth, the revolution in military affairs debate remains unsatisfying. Clearly, large changes are at work, but a mere recitation of new technologies does not describe the kinds of changes emerging in warfare. The military tests that have occurred thus far involved the wildly disproportionate forces of the United States and its allies against far smaller opponents. In 1999, for example, Yugoslavia's gross national product was barely a fifteenth the size of the American defence budget. The outcome of such ill-matched encounters could serve as indicators, perhaps, but not proof of a large change. It is possible that a revolution in military affairs has occurred, but it will require evidence gathered in a much larger conflict to become manifest. It is more likely that it would require the pressure of major great power competition in the arena of conventional armament to press modern armed forces to realize such changes to their fullest. At the moment, such competition does not exist, although in theory the rise of China in opposition to American dominance in the Pacific could provide the occasion for a real revolution to make itself known. One can, however, discern at least three broad features of the new technological era in warfare: the rise of quality over quantity, the speciation of military hardware, and the centrality of commercial military technology.

The rise of quality over quantity

Historians will describe the period extending from the French Revolution to at least the middle of the twentieth century as the era of mass warfare (e.g. already Howard 1975: 75 ff). During this time, the dominant form of military power was the mass army, recruited (in wartime, at least) by conscription, and uniformly equipped with the products of heavy industry. Those countries that could mobilize men and military production most effectively could generate the most military power—and this was true of the largest powers (like the Soviet Union) and the smallest (like Israel). Broadly speaking, the bigger the force the better—a far cry from the days of the eighteenth century when military authorities believed that armies could not operate beyond a certain optimal size, and when the way of war and contemporary economics dictated the protection of civil society from widespread compulsory military service.

The age of the mass army is over (see Moskos *et al.* 2000). The near-annihilation in 1991 of the Iraqi army, the world's fourth largest, marked the appearance of a world in which modestly obsolescent technology had become merely targets for more sophisticated weapons. Around the world, states abandoned compulsory military service and shrank the size of their armed forces, even in those countries (China and Turkey, for example) where they actually increased their defence expenditures substantially. Several converging developments produced these changes: the growing incompatibility between civil and military culture, the increased expense of military training and technology, and the vulnerabilities created by large forces. But nothing mattered more than the emerging importance of the technological edge in combat.

A simple *gedanken* experiment confirms this. Ask any group of field grade army officers which side they would prefer to command: an American armoured battalion task force of 54 M-1 tanks plus small numbers of infantry and other supporting arms, or an Iraqi Republican Guards division of over 300 moderate-quality T-72 tanks, with the full panoply of divisional artillery and support. They will choose, unanimously, the American armoured task force.[4] The combination of superior technology and better trained and led soldiers means that, in certain kinds of combat, force ratios hitherto thought utterly unacceptable—1 to 3, or even worse—could nonetheless yield victory to the seemingly hopelessly outnumbered side. To be sure, this observation may not apply equally to all forms of combat, or might not hold true in particular situations, but the broad truth remains: to a degree far greater than, say, during the Second World War, quality now trumps quantity. That quality, moreover, lies in the combination of manpower and technology. Superbly trained troops in mediocre tanks and aircraft might do well against mediocre troops in correspondingly magnificent weapon systems, but in the real world such match-ups rarely occur. The old systems of estimating military power no longer apply, be they the crude tabular comparisons of forces that appear in the newspapers or weekly news-magazines, or the seemingly scientific calculations of attrition-driven Pentagon models. The emergence of quality as the dominant feature in military power has rendered obsolete, if not absurd, today's systems of calculating relative military power.

The speciation of weapons

In the nineteenth century, and for most of the twentieth, the armed forces of the world shared similar weaponry. There have always been minor differences: even an early twentieth-century Mauser differed from a Lee Enfield or Lebel rifle. More important differences began to emerge in the First World War when, for example, the Allied states invested heavily in tanks, where the Germans did not; and certainly by the Second World War, when the United States and Great Britain developed heavy bombers that were imitated by neither their enemies nor their chief ally, the Soviet Union. The British, moreover, concentrated on aircraft optimized for night bombing, with heavy payloads and sophisticated night navigation, but little defensive ability, where the Americans concentrated on daylight bombing of industrial targets. Still, during the Second World War, and even during much of the cold war, basic weapon systems were similar. By the end of the twentieth century, however, weapons had evolved much like a sophisticated ecological system. This development had

BOX 7.2

Second World War Fighter Aircraft

	Spitfire	P-51	Bf-109	Zero
Date entered service	July 1938	April 1942	Sept. 1939	July 1940
Weight (fully loaded, lbs)	5,800	8,800	5,523	5,313
Range (miles)	395	950+	412	1,160
Speed (mph)	364	387	354	331
Armament	8 × 303 in. machine guns	4 × 20 mm cannon	2 × 7.92 mm machine guns 2 × 20 mm cannon	2 × 7.7 mm machine guns 2 × 20 mm cannon
Engine horsepower	1,030	1,150/1,590	1,100	940

Many aspects go into the performance of an aircraft: the statistics here are but a few of the key indicators of effectiveness—others include climb and turn rates, for example. But some anomalies here are suggestive. The Japanese extracted tremendous range out of the Zero, which they needed for operations in the Pacific region. They got that by good design—and by stripping out armour. The result was a highly manœuvrable but vulnerable aircraft that when hit was often destroyed. The P-51 was a hulking brute of an airplane; once the powerful Merlin engine was installed—a power plant with 50 per cent more capacity than its competitors—the Allies had a long-range fighter that could escort bombers to the heart of Germany or deliver bombs as well as cannon fire. More subtle differences (for example, the American and British preference for standardized weapons, as opposed to the mix of armaments on the Bf-109 and Zero) speak to national styles of weapons design, to include a strong priority on aerial firepower.

three parts: the evolution of the actual implements of destruction, the emergence of unique platforms, and the creation of larger systems of military technology.

An example of the first development is the British runway-attack munition JP-233. This system discharged 30 penetrating rockets and over 200 scattered mines from a low-flying Tornado fighter bomber. The Royal Air Force developed tactics and practised skills suited to its capabilities; when put to the test in the Gulf War, however, it proved nearly useless and indeed dangerous for pilots who had to fly low and straight over Iraqi runways. JP-233, an extremely expensive munition was, in truth, designed for a single scenario, that is, conventional conflict in Europe. Its purpose was to slow down a surge of Soviet fighter planes early in an East–West war by temporarily disabling Warsaw Pact airbases, allowing outnumbered NATO forces to gain air superiority over time. In Iraq, however, the numerical (not to mention the qualitative) balance was on the other side; Iraqi airbases were far larger than their Warsaw Pact counterparts, meaning that RAF pilots had to make longer (and hence more dangerous) runs over defended perimeters. Iraqi bases also had numerous runways and taxiways (unlike their Warsaw Pact counterparts) and could still service fighter aircraft—which, however, being outnumbered and outclassed, had very little inclination to take off!

The day of the simple high-explosive bomb is, if not over, close to it. Antitank missiles may carry not one but several warheads specifically designed to detonate layers of reactive armour and then to penetrate the sophisticated composite armour of tanks. A guided bomb may have a sophisticated nose that will not merely penetrate several layers of concrete and dirt, but actually count the number of floors it has penetrated before detonating (presumably) at the right one.

Military technology has diversified in another way. Whereas in the past all powers of the first rank had similar kinds of weapons systems, that is no longer the case. Only one country, the United States, can afford a large, stealthy, long-range bomber like the B-2. Relatively few countries can afford large sophisticated surface warships. Most countries, by contrast, can afford surface-to-surface ballistic missiles. This does not guarantee success to one side or the other, but it means that to the extent they still occur, arms races are more likely to be asymmetric. Thus Syria, which once hoped to achieve conventional parity with Israel in the late 1970s and early 1980s, has stopped trying to match the Israeli Air Force in the air. It relies, instead, on sophisticated Russian-made air defences and thousands of surface-to-surface missiles and rockets of varying types and quality.

A third form of military evolution has to do with the development not of weapons systems *per se*, but of meta-systems of extraordinary complexity. Networked sensors and command and control, such as the air operations centres that managed Allied air forces in the Gulf and Yugoslav Wars, are one example, but others will surely emerge. The US Navy's Cooperative Engagement Capability, which allows all the ships in a task force to share a common picture based on the sum of all data in the system, is a prototypical example. So too are the space command and control systems that allow military staffs to track most objects in close orbit, and to coordinate the movements of spacecraft. Increasingly, these systems reflect less a traditional system of military command and control—in which information flows up and decisions down—but a far less hierarchical sharing of information and with it a certain dilution of authority as traditionally understood.

Engineers use the term 'systems integration' to describe the art of putting together a complex of technologies to achieve a purpose. Not all countries excel at it: the United States and several European states have, as the triumph of their aerospace industries indicates. Japan has found it more difficult, while China and Russia have mixed records (Hughes 1998). Conventional military power rests, increasingly, on the ability of states to put together combinations of sensors and weapons and to make them function together in a fluid environment. Other forms of military power (terror or low-intensity warfare at one level, weapons of mass destruction at the other) do not demand these qualities.

The rise of commercial technology

Some percentage of military technology has always derived from the civilian sector. The famous Higgins boat of the Second World War, for example, which landed hundreds of thousands of Allied soldiers on beaches around the world, was a modification of a small craft originally designed for work in the Everglades swamps of Florida.[5] More broadly, civilian technologies have, from time to time, had an enormous effect on the conduct of war. The telegraph and the railway were, of course, both civilian technologies. Following the Second World War, however, to an unprecedented degree the armed forces of the developed world created vast research establishments operating on the cutting edge of technology; military inventions tended to spill over into the civilian realm more than the other way around. The transistor and modern jet engines, to take two radically different-sized technologies, emerged from military research and development. This held true at the beginning of the information age as well. The Internet originated in the United States

Department of Defense's ARPANET—a system developed by the Advanced Research Projects Agency to enable the transmission of messages in the event of nuclear war. Similarly, space-based sensing emerged out of Western and Soviet efforts to exploit space for military purposes.

The information age is fundamentally different in this respect. Civilian technology, particularly in the area of software, leads military applications. The shift from supercomputers (once a prerogative chiefly of security institutions such as the National Security Agency, responsible for breaking the ciphers of foreign nations) to massive parallel processing, which used the linked power of many smaller computers to take on tasks hitherto reserved for much larger machines, is one example of a broader trend. Even when civilian technology does not yet lead military technology (in space-based sensing, for example) it is not very far behind: civilian satellites today can achieve resolutions (one metre or less) barely imaginable for their military counterparts only a decade or two ago.[6] Tourists looking for maps, satellite imagery, and GPS co-ordinates, as well as automated directions, can obtain them all—for free—with a tap on the keyboard of any computer connected to the internet. These trends will continue as vast sums of money for research and development—and with it talented scientists—turn to the civilian and away from the military sector. Information has no value without military technology to act on it, to be sure, but information, and the ability to process it, is the heart of modern conventional warfare.

These three trends—the rise of quality, the speciation of weapons, and the increased role of commercial technology—generally work to the benefit of developed open societies. They require a sophisticated industrial base for their manufacture, a skilled workforce for their maintenance, and, above all, flexible organizations for their intelligent use. These are qualities most likely to be found in democracies. As recently as a few decades ago, many thoughtful observers believed that democratic states stood at a near-ineradicable disadvantage *vis-à-vis* authoritarian or totalitarian counterparts, and indeed many of those weaknesses persist: the potential for indecision and volatility, indiscipline, and more recently, a pervasive sensitivity to casualties. Outweighing these and other weaknesses, however, are liberal democracies' strengths: their wealth (which makes military hardware affordable), their citizens' relative comfort with technological change, and fluid, egalitarian social relationships that breed a willingness to share rather than hoard information. For the moment, at any rate, the rise of the information technologies seem to ensure the conventional dominance of liberal democracies.

KEY POINTS

- On occasions in history several developments have come together to create a revolution in military affairs (RMA).

- Following the Gulf War in 1991, changes in accuracy, range, and intelligence led many to believe a new RMA was taking place.

- Recent conflicts between unequal adversaries make it difficult to discern if a real RMA has occurred.

- There are three main features of the new era in warfare; the importance of quality over quantity; the speciation of military hardware; and the increased role of the commercial technologies.

Asymmetric challenges

There is an apparent strategic paradox in the increasing technological edge of advanced, conventional powers who find themselves baffled or even defeated by irregular opponents. Israel's unsuccessful decade-long war (from 1991 to 2000, although preceded by skirmishes beforehand) with Hizbollah guerrillas in southern Lebanon is a dismaying example of how a vastly superior force, armed with high tech weapons, can find itself defeated by an adroit opponent who knows how to play on the sensitivity of a democracy to its own casualties, and on world concern for civilians caught in a crossfire. American forces in Iraq following the overthrow of the Saddam Hussein regime in 2003 were bedevilled by a robust insurgency that, through the use of IEDs (improvised explosive devices), suffered far heavier casualties than it did during the swift, violent, and overwhelming march to Baghdad. These experiences, like those of Russia in Chechnya in the preceding decade, have caused some to suggest that guerrilla or irregular warfare can reduce or eliminate the importance of technological advantage on the modern battlefield.

This is not quite true. Modern guerrillas and terrorists make use of cell phones, electronic triggering devices, and extremely sophisticated explosives for their bombs; those countering them use even more sophisticated forms of electronic sweeping and neutralization, unmanned aerial vehicles looking for those who plant IEDs, and precision guided missiles to destroy specific vehicles or rooms in a building. In the hard urban fight for Falluja in November 2004, US Army and Marine forces took casualties in the scores, not the hundreds that would have been characteristic of city fighting even during Vietnam. The Israelis experienced similarly low losses in their operations in the urban environment of the West Bank and Gaza in years preceding. Technology remains critical even in low-intensity conflict, and technological competitions—between bomb-maker and bomb-seeker, between guerrilla in ambush and convoy ready to fight its way through, between those protecting voting places and those seeking to prevent elections—persist.

The same might be said of another asymmetric strategy for technologically inferior powers—the resort to missile forces equipped with weapons of mass destruction, which offer non-democratic states the possibility of counterbalancing some, if not all, of the conventional predominance of their richer and more sophisticated opponents. Even the best missile defenses (and these have been deployed, and are being developed further) cannot guarantee a state's safety against such threats. And yet on the other hand, in the competition between advanced and less developed states, a real nuclear edge, if such a thing exists, will go to the more developed state. In the ensuing stand-off, low-intensity conflict will flourish.

It is true, no doubt, that irregular warfare evens the playing field somewhat, but more in terms of strategy than operations. Guerrilla or terrorist strategies work when public opinion and political resolve are vulnerable to attrition of will. It is not clear that prosperous liberal democracies can always cope well with these threats. Democracy can wage conventional warfare and remain true to itself; it is far more difficult for it to battle terror and insurgency without resorting to strategies—to include extensive surveillance of its own citizens, population control, and even assassination—that are, in the long run, corrosive to its values. No society of this type, moreover, has yet had to absorb sudden, massive levels of casualties comparable to those suffered by the inhabitants of Tokyo, Dresden, or Hiroshima at the end of the Second World War. How resilient rich, free countries will be in the face of such suffering remains to be seen.

On the other hand, thus far it turns out that advanced liberal states can use modern technology—from biometrics to robotics—to fight irregular opponents, and succeed. Israel's success in containing the second Palestinian intifada, reducing its own casualties, and inflicting crippling losses on the middle and senior levels of leadership of extremist organizations, speaks to the effectiveness of high technology, and the kind of will that can be evoked in the face of what society agrees is a serious threat. Similarly, the United States public has displayed remarkable persistence in a counter-insurgency operation in Iraq that has inflicted substantial casualties (more than 2,000 deaths as of 2006, and nearly seven times as many wounded), and that was, arguably, badly mismanaged in its early phases. In both cases, high technology played a role in limiting losses and achieving some successes.

KEY POINTS

- Superior conventional technology can be counterbalanced, to some extent, by asymmetric responses, such as irregular warfare and the threat of weapons of mass destruction.

- High technology, however, continues to play a role in conflicts fought out in this sphere.

- A critical question, in both cases, concerns societal willingness to persist in such conflicts.

Challenges of the New Technology

The asymmetric threat to the dominance of the new military technologies may take some time to make itself fully felt. Meanwhile, it is difficult enough for modern militaries to cope with the challenges posed by the information revolution. One difficulty has to do with personnel issues. Industrial age militaries could compete fairly easily with private enterprise because, at some level, they resembled it. A caste system resting on soldiers, noncommissioned officers, and officers mirrored a civilian stratification of workers, foremen, and managers. Compensation and deference structures were similar, although room could be made in the military, as in the civilian world, for more highly paid technical experts.

In the information age, the similarities between military and civilian organizations have broken down. Military organizations remain more hierarchical than many of their civilian counterparts, but more importantly, they find it increasingly difficult to obtain the human resources they need. A software engineer in the civilian sector is a highly paid, fairly autonomous employee, working with relatively little supervision. It has become acutely difficult for armed forces to recruit (and more importantly, retain) skilled men and women in these fields. Similarly, talented and aggressive young officers are far more aware than ever before of the possibilities open to them outside the military. Retaining their services in an age of economic opportunity is difficult not merely because of compensation inequities—those have always existed—but because the civilian sector can often offer far more opportunity for change, autonomy, and unfettered responsibility.

The information technologies have other, perhaps more subtle effects on the conduct of war. As a general rule, the greater the flow of information, the more possibility for centralized control. During the Second World War, for example, the Royal Navy and then the United States centralized anti-submarine warfare in shore-based organizations that exploited reliable long-range radio communications and critically important advances in intelligence gathering. Such a development was very much the exception, however. Today, videoconferencing and the electronic transmission of data mean that generals in national capitals can exercise close supervision over their subordinates. This effect exists throughout the military hierarchy: the challenge for mid-level and senior leaders has become one of controlling the instinctive desire to take charge of a more junior officer's problems. That impulse has become all the greater the more politically visible military action has become: when the result of a botched operation shows up immediately on CNN and a hundred websites, the inclination of higher authority to exercise the control that technology makes possible becomes all the greater.

Warfare often now occurs under the watchful eyes of the video camera and satellite uplink. In the Somalia intervention of the early 1990s, for example, American naval commandos (SEALs) slipped ashore (on 8 December 1992) in advance of a larger force, only to find a reception party of journalists awaiting them, brilliant lights blinding the wary sailors. There are exceptions: the Russians excluded the press from much of the second Chechen war, and the Rwanda massacres occurred before journalists could cover them adequately. The Arab–Israeli conflict, however, which resumed in 2000 with a Palestinian insurrection, may prove to be more the norm: rock throwing and shooting watched by (indeed, often staged for) journalists. Propaganda, always an adjunct of war, became a central element in the Arab–Israeli struggle, and both sides found themselves structuring military action with reference not only to the traditional considerations of geography and tactics, but also to the consideration of publicity. Adults manœuvred Palestinian stone-throwing children into positions for optimal camera shots of 14-year-olds with rocks up against 19-year-olds with rifles. Meanwhile, after some abysmal failures (helicopter gunships blowing up empty houses), the Israelis reverted to sniper work and night-time kidnappings and assassinations precisely to avoid teams of journalists. Both sides created their own, and wrecked their opponents', websites as the conflict extended into cyberspace. The real and the virtual battlefields had become a complex and inextricable whole. This development persisted in the Iraq War, which took a much grislier turn. Insurgent strategy included kidnappings and gruesome beheadings, which were the stuff not only of broadcasts on Arab-language television, but of film clips on jihadi websites, seeking to intimidate opponents, discourage foreign development aid, and enlist new supporters. To some extent, moreover, it worked.

The Future of Military Technology

Military technology has contributed to a far more complicated environment for war than that of previous centuries. To the extent one can generalize about its effects, one would have to say that where the dominant forms of war in the past were few, today they are many. The challenges for armed forces are correspondingly immense.

Nor have the changes wrought by the new technologies come to an end. The increasingly easy access by countries to space, and their reliance on space for routine communications, navigation, and information gathering, seems almost certain to propel war into the heavens. For the moment, no country seems to have placed, or at least used, weapons in space that can disable or destroy either other satellites or targets on earth. Similarly, countries have experimented with, but not yet used, technologies on earth capable of affecting space-based systems. Technology, however, clearly permits this, in the form of lasers that can blind satellites, or mere lumps of metal that can hurtle from space to earth delivering enormous amounts of kinetic energy against their targets hundreds of miles below. The opening of space to full-fledged warfare would be as large a change as the opening of the air was during the First World War. New organizations, new operational conditions, new incentives to strike first, new ways of war, will blossom overnight.

Warfare also appears to be moving to cyberspace. Thus far, despite persistent stories about mischievous teenagers, clever criminals, or nefarious agents creating havoc with computer systems, there does not seem to be evidence of really large-scale damage done by cyber-attack—no massive loss of life or even money attributable to cyber-attack alone. It remains a theoretical possibility, however. As with the opening up of space, the realization of the potential for war in cyberspace would elicit an efflorescence of organizations, concepts, and patterns of conflict parallel to, but very different from, those of conventional warfare.

A third sort of change already under way consists of advances in manufacturing, particularly in what are known as the nanotechnologies, robotics, and artificial intelligence. While it is highly unlikely that human beings will ever leave the battlefield (if only because the battlefield will surely come to them), more of the dangerous work may devolve upon small autonomous, intelligent machines that creep or fly, or merely sit and wait, classifying and attacking opponents. Animated, superintelligent minefields transposed on land might make movement or manœuvre by conventional forces extremely difficult. More importantly, the creation of such machines will mean that humans have gradually begun to cede much of their ability to make decisions to silicon chips. It is a process already well under way in some areas—modern aircraft, for example, are so intrinsically unstable that an automatic system, rather than a human being, must adjust their trim.

In all these cases, the most interesting and important consequences of technological change will probably flow from its effect on how human beings think about and conduct war: how they conceive of military action, how they assign responsibility, how they calculate military effects, how they attempt to harmonize means and ends. But a fourth set of changes, perhaps the most profound of all, looms larger yet. The biological sciences increasingly make it possible to change the nature of human beings themselves (Fukuyama 1999). The intriguing theoretical possibility of Greek philosophers has become, in our age, the challenge of scientific researchers. One can scarcely doubt that an Adolf Hitler, or for that matter a Saddam Hussein, would have availed himself of the resources of biotechnology to breed new kinds of human beings—super-soldiers, for one thing, insensitive to fear and truly loyal to the death—who could serve his purposes. Our common understanding of war rests on some of its deeply human features, which have not changed since the days of Homer or Thucydides.[7] This is so, however, only because the same species, *homo sapiens*, has continued to wage it. If—when?—humans are replaced by a variety of creatures, some subhuman, and others, in some respects, superhuman, war itself will have become an activity as different from traditional human conflict as are the murderous struggles between competing anthills or the stalking of herds of deer by packs of wolves.

? QUESTIONS

1. Take a representative military technology such as the tank. Using several examples, how would you characterize the national style embedded in the design of these armoured vehicles?

2. What is stealth technology? Does the concept of interaction apply to it?

3. In what cases does military technology require high levels of technical expertise and education, and in what cases does it actually reduce or even eliminate such a requirement?

4. What are some of the military technologies that only the United States has available to it? Other great powers? Smaller states? Non-state actors?

5. What are some examples of 'the technological edge'? How fragile are such leads by one state or another?

6. Is cyberwarfare really 'warfare'? Are there other metaphors that might explain it better?

7. What implications are there if warfare extends to space—will it impact more on commercial or military technology?

8. What are some of the technologies most useful to the conduct of Irregular warfare, to include guerrilla and terror operations?

9. Are democracies better placed than authoritarian/totalitarian regimes to adapt to the changing nature and problems of technological warfare?

■ **John D. Bergen, *Military Communications: A Test for Technology* (Washington, DC: Center of Military History, 1986), chs. 16–17, pp. 367–408.** Describes an interesting competition in communication technology and electronic warfare between an extremely sophisticated state (the USA) and a considerably more backward one (North Vietnam) in which the more developed society did not necessarily do well.

■ **Alan Beyerchen, 'From Radio to Radar: Interwar Military Adaptation to Technological Change in Germany, the United Kingdom, and the United States', in Williamson Murray and Allan R. Millett (eds.), *Military Innovation in the Interwar Period* (Cambridge: Cambridge University Press, 1996).** A good example of how national style appears even in the electronic realm.

■ **Winston Churchill, *The World Crisis, 1911–1914* (New York: Charles Scribner's Sons, 1926), ch. 6, 'The Romance of Design', pp. 125–49.** Brilliantly describes some of these challenges from the point of view of a decision-maker.

■ **Arthur C. Clarke, 'Superiority', in *Expedition to Earth* (New York: Harcourt, Brace & World, 1970), pp. 92–104.** A science fiction story with a whimsical but wise warning on the dangers of becoming too sophisticated.

■ **Martin van Creveld, *Technology and War from 2000 B.C. to the Present* (New York: Free Press, 1989).** Considerably more up to date than Fuller 1945.

■ **J. F. C. Fuller, *Armament and History; A Study of the Influence of Armament on History from the Dawn of Classical Warfare to the Second World War* (New York: Charles Scribner's Sons, 1945).** Remains an excellent short treatment of the relationship between technology, tactics, organization, and strategy.

■ **Wayne Hughes, *Fleet Tactics: Theory and Practice* (Annapolis, MD.: Naval Institute Press, 1986).** A thoughtful treatment of the role of technology in warfare.

■ **Henry Petroski, *To Engineer is Human: The Role of Failure in Successful Design* (New York: Random House, 1982).**

■ ——— ***The Evolution of Useful Things* (New York: Vintage Books, 1992).**

■ **George Raudzens, 'War-Winning Weapons: The Measurement of Technological Determinism in Military History', *Journal of Military History*, Vol. 54 (Oct. 1990), 403–33.** A sceptical view of technology's importance.

 Visit the Online Resource Centre that accompanies this book for lots of interesting additional material http://www.oxfordtextbooks.co.uk/orc/baylis_strategy2e/.

PART II

Contemporary Problems

8

Irregular Warfare: Terrorism and Insurgency

JAMES D. KIRAS

 Chapter Contents

- Introduction
- Definitions
- Subverting the System
- Protecting the System
- Bringing the System Down or Thriving on its Margins?
- Technology
- Conclusion

Reader's Guide

Western democracies have had considerable difficulty conceptualizing responses to and understanding the phenomenon of global violent extremist terrorism. Does such violence constitute a new reality and are previous lessons learnt against terrorists and insurgents irrelevant? Or has the context for such violence merely changed? Two recurrent themes run through the long history of irregular warfare. The first theme is that all forms of irregular warfare, including terrorism and insurgency, are appealing to those who seek change in the status quo against a more powerful adversary. But how important is the significance of politics and political factors to those willing to kill themselves and many others in order to achieve rewards in the afterlife? For reasons that will become clear in this chapter, global violent extremists share much in common with their historical antecedents. The second theme is that conducting irregular warfare successfully to achieve change is a very challenging undertaking. Historically the balance sheet favours those who fight against terrorist and insurgent groups. For dissatisfied groups and individuals, however, irregular warfare will continue to appeal as it offers the potential to change a variety of injustices and imbalances, perceived or otherwise. This is because irregular forms of violence are often the only practical method by which a weaker party can diminish and overrun an intractable foe to gain political power.

Introduction

At the height of the period in irregular warfare known as the 'wars of national liberation' (1962–5), journalist Robert Taber, who had spent time in Cuba during the revolution there, stated that 'the guerrilla fighter's war is political and social, his means are at least as political as they are military, his purpose almost entirely so. Thus we may paraphrase Clausewitz: *Guerrilla war is the extension of politics by means of armed conflict*' (emphasis in original; Taber 1970: 26). Although postmodern and critical theorists challenged this interpretation, and offered that what was required was a better understanding of the identity and contextual circumstances behind substate violence (Munck 2000), the terrorist attacks on 11 September 2001 suggested that religiously inspired terrorism now overshadows both politics and culture. In other words, terrorism and insurgency are no longer forms of 'political violence' but rather religious violence for its own sake.

The aim of this chapter is to demonstrate that the spirit of Clausewitz is still very much relevant to current and future terrorist and irregular campaigns. Historical experience cannot be summarily dismissed. Religious, social, cultural, and economic factors do play a substantial role in defining the character and conduct of irregular conflicts. Terrorists and insurgents (and those who fight against them), however, ultimately seek to achieve a *political* result from their use of force. These political results in turn serve goals defined by states fighting insurgencies or those aspiring to change the system through armed conflict.

Such motives are discernible even in the case of Al-Qaeda and the insurgency in Iraq. The primary impediment in understanding the current trend in terrorist and insurgent violence lies in the nature of fundamentalist Islam itself. As Johannes Jansen points out 'Islamic fundamentalism is both fully politics and fully religion' (1997: 1). In other words, unlike the Western political tradition that distinguishes between the affairs of the church and those of the state, within fundamentalist Islam the two are inseparable. Indeed, according to the worldview of fundamentalist Islam, adherence to religious tenets becomes a form of governance itself. Yet despite the primacy placed on religion, militant leaders such as Ayman al-Zawahiri stress the requirement to achieve political power and control: 'victory of Islam will never take place until a Muslim state is established in the manner of the Prophet in the heart of the Islamic world, specifically in the Levant, Egypt, and the neighboring states of the Peninsula and Iraq' (al-Zawahiri 2005: 2). From this established political base, the revolution can continue to spread and transform the religious, social, and economic character of the region.

Definitions

The first problem associated with the study of terrorism and irregular warfare relates to the subjective and relative lenses that one applies to the subject. For example, in comparison to the number of annual highway fatalities in any developed state, or the potential casualties resulting from an attack using weapons of mass destruction, terrorism generates fear disproportionate to the damage it causes. Given the number of terrorist attacks on American soil, some critics suggest that the Department of Homeland Security's 2004 budget of $36.4 billion dollars far exceeds the nature and scope of the threat. Much of the confusion associated with terrorism and irregular warfare stems from the use of either value-laden or emotive language. 'Freedom fighters' sound appealing and worthy of support whereas the term 'terrorists' conveys cowardly violence, fear, and intimidation. The term 'guerrilla' still connotes a spirit of adventure and romance to rebellious Western youth, evoked by the memory of Ernesto 'Che' Guevara nearly four decades after his death. There is also little agreement on what to call these types of violence: political violence, terrorism, irregular warfare, military operations other than war (MOOTW), low-intensity conflict (LIC), people's war, revolutionary warfare, war of national liberation, guerrilla war, partisan war, warfare in the enemy's rear, imperial policing, and small wars, among others. Indeed recent attempts by US policy-makers to define the term 'irregular warfare', outlined in the most recent Quadrennial Defense Review, stalled over arguments of what it covered and what it excluded. As if this was not confusing enough, the effectiveness of terrorist and irregular action is often questioned. Terrorist and irregular campaigns are seen as military nuisances that fail to or rarely achieve their stated political aims without the support of conventional forces. In addition, many military officers view terrorism and insurgency as 'dirty war'. The reasons for this perception are that the lines between combatants and non-combatants in counter-terrorism and counter-insurgency are unclear and there is a lack of clearly defined objectives and timelines for victory. In addition, the activities conducted by military forces more closely resemble those of police forces, with all of the dangers of military operations, as well as some problematic ethical choices, but little of the glory. Even worse, critics add, irregular diversions detract from what state-based military organizations are most comfortable with, namely preparing to fight against one another.

In order to grasp the fundamentals of a subject as complicated and contentious as terrorism and irregular warfare, it is necessary to provide working definitions of the key terms. Irregular warfare is the umbrella term used to describe violence used by substate actors and includes different forms, including terrorism and insurgency. For the purposes of this chapter, terrorism is defined as *the sustained use of violence against symbolic or civilian targets by small groups for political purposes, by inspiring fear, drawing widespread attention to a political grievance, and/or provoking a draconian or unsustainable response.*

Terrorism does not result in political change on its own, but is undertaken in order to provoke a response. That response should show the true nature of the state and therefore elevate the consciousness of the people to the realities of their current situation. If irregular warfare is the approach of the weak in order to combat the strong, then terrorism is the approach of the weakest as their message appeals only to a narrow audience. Some debate exists over whether terrorism is a tactic within a broader strategy of insurgency or whether groups can conduct a strategy of terrorism (O'Neill 1990: 24). What separates terrorism from other forms of violence is that the acts committed are legitimized to a degree by their political nature. Hijacking, remote bombing, and assassination are criminal acts but consideration of their legal status can be mitigated if carried out in the name of a political cause that is recognized. The bombings conducted by Anarchists against monarchs in the late nineteenth and early twentieth centuries are considered acts of terrorism given their

---

BOX 8.1

T. E. Lawrence on Irregular Warfare

The influence of the writings of Thomas Edward Lawrence (1888–1937, better known as 'Lawrence of Arabia') to the development of theory on irregular warfare cannot be overstated. Many future practitioners of the trade, from Mao Tse-tung to German special operations expert Otto Skorzeny, acknowledged the debt they owed to Lawrence in the development of their own thoughts. A quixotic character whose historical impact still remains the subject of much controversy, Lawrence nevertheless managed to explain lucidly in less than 250 words the essence of a guerrilla struggle:

It seemed that rebellion must have an unassailable base, something guarded not merely from attack, but from fear of it; such a base as we had in the Red Sea Ports, the desert, or in the minds of men we converted to our creed. It must have a sophisticated alien enemy, in the form of a disciplined army of occupation too small to fulfil the doctrine of acreage: too few to adjust the number to space, in order to dominate the whole area effectively from fortified posts. It must have a friendly population, not actively friendly, but sympathetic to the point of not betraying rebel movements to the enemy. Rebellions can be made by 2 per cent. active in a striking force, and 98 per cent. passively sympathetic. The few active rebels must have the qualities of speed and endurance, ubiquity and independence of arteries of supply. They must have the technical equipment to destroy or paralyse the enemy's organized communications, for irregular warfare is fairly Willisen's definition of strategy, 'the study of communication' in its extreme degree, of attack where the enemy is not. In fifty words: Granted mobility, security (in the form of denying targets to the enemy), time, and doctrine (the idea to convert every subject to friendliness), victory will rest with the insurgents, for the algebraical factors are in the end decisive, and them perfections of means and spirit struggle quite in vain.

(Lawrence 1920:69).

---

stated objective of changing the political environment. The unusual 'pizza bomber' case in Erie, Pennsylvania, in August 2004, in contrast, is considered a criminal act as the primary motivation behind it was financial gain. Problems exist in determining *who* recognizes the cause, beyond the terrorists themselves, as well as difficulties in differentiating between motives that can change over time. Terrorism traditionally has been based on the need to generate domestic and international empathy for a plight that 'drove' the terrorists to arms. Whether or not this remains so is the subject of discussion in the subsection on 'new' terrorism.

Defining insurgency is as problematic as defining terrorism for vastly different reasons. Whereas terrorism is an emotive and subjective issue, many believe that insurgency is perhaps best understood by first considering what it is not. Insurgency is not conventional war or terrorism, for example, but it shares with them the use of force to achieve a political end. The crucial difference is the scope and scale of the violence. Terrorism seeks to bring awareness to a political grievance but rarely, if ever, results in political change on its own. Insurgency, on the other hand, is an attempt to bring about change through force of arms. The principal difference between irregular and conventional war is relatively simple: the latter involves adversaries more or less symmetric in equipment, training, and doctrine. In an insurgency, the adversaries are asymmetric and the weaker, almost always a substate group, attempts to bring about political change by administering and fighting more effectively than its state-based foe through the use of guerrilla tactics. These tactics are characterized by hit-and-run raids and ambushes against the security forces of their adversary. Insurgency is also characterized by the active and/or passive support and mobilization of a significant proportion of the population. In addition, individual insurgencies differ widely in terms of character (social, cultural, and economic aspects) and type (revolutionary, partisan, guerrilla, liberation, or civil war) but ultimately the ability to wield political power is the desired outcome. Coups, however, are not insurgencies as they are revolutions conducted by a small elite against the ruling elite with little or no popular support required. Finally, external physical and moral support for an insurgent cause is a prerequisite for success. The point to remember is that these are attempts at functional definitions for the purpose of this chapter and not the final word on irregular warfare or terrorism.

Definitions act as gateways into the areas of study but rarely convey its complexity in theory or practice. In addition, capricious categorizations can lead to a misleading and seemingly irreconcilable divide between forms of irregular conflict. Terrorism and other forms of irregular warfare are plainly not the same activity. But how does one then classify the so-called 'urban guerrilla' phenomenon and its ideological impact on terrorist groups during the 1960s? In addition, some terrorist groups adopt parallel efforts that are more commonly associated with insurgencies—have they now become insurgents, do they remain terrorists, or have they become something else? The Lebanese organization known as Hizbollah demonstrates the difficulties inherent in assigning a label to a specific group. The group was responsible for spectacular acts of terrorism early in its history, including several high-profile kidnappings and the suicide bombings of the US Marine and French compounds in 1983. Yet members of Hizbollah also fought a protracted guerrilla campaign against Israeli forces that led to the latter's withdrawal from southern Lebanon after eighteen years. Finally, the political arm of Hizbollah manages a substantial number of public service operations largely funded by Syrian backers or monies derived from legitimate and illicit commercial operations. Ultimately, some arbitrary distinctions must be made in order to grasp the business at hand, without losing perspective on the numerous 'grey areas' endemic to this and other areas of strategic studies.

Subverting the System

Those undertaking insurgency and terrorism are trying to find a way to use their strengths such as mobility, organization, and relative anonymity or stealth, against the weaknesses of their more powerful adversary. Bernard Fall reduced this equation even further when he suggested that 'When a country is being subverted, it is being out-administered, not out-fought' (1999: 55). But subversion is a time-consuming and resource-intensive activity that does not guarantee success. In almost every case, the length of terrorist and irregular warfare campaigns is measured in *decades* not years. They achieve success by gaining an advantage over their adversaries in terms of time, space, legitimacy, and/or support.

These dimensions of conflict are not mutually exclusive and excellence in one dimension will not compensate for drastic shortcomings in the others. Regardless of the space and time available, for example, a terrorist or insurgent campaign will almost always fail if it cannot attract substantial internal or international support. Like war and politics, insurgencies or terrorist campaigns are dialectical struggles between competing adversaries; outcomes are determined by the interaction between opponents (Gray 1999a: 23–5). The goal for the irregular leader is to pit the organization's strengths against enemy weaknesses. The value ascribed by different writers to perceived relationships between time, space, legitimacy, and support create substantial variations in the theories of irregular warfare. These theories often reflect the circumstances that are unique to specific conflicts, a fact that has contributed to failed government efforts to stop insurgents or terrorists. The unconsidered application of a theory based on one case history to another conflict can lead to disaster.

Time

Time is the most important element required for the successful conclusion of an insurgent and terrorist campaign as it is a commodity that can be exchanged to make up for other weakness. With sufficient time, an insurgent group can organize, sap the resolve of its adversary, and build a conventional force capable of seizing control of the state. Mao organized time in his writings into three interrelated phases: the strategic defensive, the stalemate, and the strategic offensive.

Each phase, carefully conducted, would lead one step closer to victory no matter how long it eventually takes. Mao once stated, for example (in 1963), that his forces had 'retreated in space but advanced in time'. He understood that the sequence of phases leading to victory was not necessarily linear; unforeseen circumstances could lead to setbacks and perhaps regression to a previous phase of the insurgency. Endless struggle without an obvious victory would eventually lead to the exhaustion, collapse, or withdrawal of the enemy. The dimension of space works with time, providing insurgents with the leeway to manoeuvre and demonstrates their superior legitimacy to the population. Perceived legitimacy in turn will generate internal and external support for the insurgents. With popular support, insurgents will be able to raise a superior army, launch bolder attacks, and achieve victory.

Most irregular campaigns can remain unresolved for a substantial period of time: the insurgency waged by the Liberation Tamil Tigers of Eelam (LTTE) for political autonomy within Sri Lanka remains unresolved after thirty-three years. Occasionally, guerrilla struggles can end quickly. The most famous quick insurgent success is the Cuban revolution (1957–9). Led by Fidel Castro against the regime of Fuguenaldo Batista, this irregular war was concluded in just three years but featured incidents and actors of which revolutionary myths are made. A number of factors contributed to the rapid collapse of the government forces; in the vast majority of cases, however, few states are as corrupt, inept, and fragile as Batista regime in the late 1960s.

Although brittle adversaries that succumb to short irregular campaign are rare, local circumstances can convince insurgents or terrorists to forego a prolonged struggle. Carlos Marighella believed that circumstances in Brazil in the 1960s demanded a response other than careful Maoist first-stage planning. The Brazilian Communist Party discussed plans for insurrection but Marighella argued in favour of immediate action. He thought time

BOX 8.2

Mao Tse-tung, China in the 1930s and the Three-Stage Theory of Insurgency

Mao Tse-tung (1893–1976) received an education, which was a rarity in China at the time. His first job after graduation was as a librarian at Peking University in the year of the October Revolution in Russia (1917). Mao was an avid reader and began his revolutionary career as a peasant agitator, joining the Chinese Communist Party (CCP) in 1921. The CCP was working towards expelling foreigners and 'gentry' landowners. In 1928 the Chinese Nationalist forces (Kuomintang) went on the offensive and scattered the CCP. The few remaining 'comrades' retired to the mountainous Fukien-Kiangsi area to rebuild. In the wake of a disastrous urban revolution in 1930, Mao developed a theory on how best to conduct irregular war in China. Chinese Nationalists resumed the offensive and drove the Communists out of their sanctuary, leading to the famous 'Long March' to Shensi province in 1933.

The situation in China changed drastically in 1937. Not content with the acquisition of Manchuria, Japanese hawks within the Kwantung Army engineered the 'Marco Polo bridge incident' as the pretext for invading China. Mao's best-known works include *Problems of Strategy in China's Revolutionary War* (1936), *Problems of Strategy in Guerrilla War Against Japan* (1938), and *On Protracted War* (1938), from which the following synopsis is derived (Tse-tung 1966: 210–19).

Stage I, Strategic Defensive

This phase is characterized by avoidance at all costs of pitched, set-piece battles. Given limited resources, the adversary needs to conduct a quick military campaign and seize key cities to force a quick end to the war. One key goal of the insurgents is to get the adversary to reach what Clausewitz termed as 'the culminating point of victory': although victories and territory are won, the foe no longer has adequate forces to defend the gains made. Tactical offensives, with local numerical superiority, are carried out to further stretch enemy resources. The moral superiority of the guerrillas is established with the local population, political indoctrination is carried out and new recruits are trained to fight as irregulars in remote, safe bases.

Stage II, Stalemate

This phase begins the prolonged battle to attrit the enemy's physical and moral strength and assume de facto control over a larger segment of the population. Government control, in the form of local officials, is targeted and its representatives killed or forced to leave. The enemy is now on the defensive strategically and the insurgents will use the initiative to force the enemy from the countryside into towns and cities. With government presence in rural areas neutralized, the population can be drawn upon for moral and physical support. The focus of the guerrillas must remain unchanged and peace proposals rejected; the enemy will try and subvert opinion within the guerrilla movement.

Stage III, Strategic Offensive

The end game of the conflict, in which the insurgents begin the battle of manœuvre and use overwhelming force destroy decimated enemy forces in their defensive positions.

was not on the side of the insurgency: the Brazilian state grew stronger every month while the revolutionaries continued to do little. By taking action, Marighella believed that the 'urban guerrillas' would build a critical mass for the guerrilla organization, catch the Brazilian state authorities off-guard, and provoke an extreme response. In other words,

Marighella believed that the state of affairs within Brazil called for reversing the typical relationship between the guerrilla and time.

Space

Space allows irregulars to decide where and when to fight. If their adversary appears in overwhelming numbers, irregulars can make use of space to withdraw and fight when the odds are in their favour. Defenders against sedition cannot be everywhere at once without spreading their forces too thinly and inviting attack from locally superior guerrilla forces.

The exploitation of formidable terrain that limits the manœuvre of government forces is a potent way in which lightly armed and mobile terrorists or insurgents offset their relative weaknesses in technology, organization, and numbers. Insurgents have often used difficult terrain for tactical advantage, often against foes ill equipped to deal with the challenges presented by mountains, jungle, swamps and even deserts. For example, Afghan Mujahaddin guerrillas used mountainous terrain to ambush predominantly road-bound Soviet forces, just as their forefathers did against the British. Triple-canopy jungle limited US and South Vietnamese attempts to apply overwhelming manœuvres and firepower against the Viet Cong and North Vietnamese forces. Urban terrain can also be an arduous obstacle as the Russians found in 1994. Chechen guerrillas used buildings and narrow roads to offset their weakness and isolate and destroy Soviet formations during the battle for Grozny. Iraqi insurgents tried to do the same in Fallujah against US forces a decade later. Terrain difficult for government forces provides insurgent forces with the opportunity to establish safe areas or bases from which to expand the struggle.

Force-to-space ratios also influence the course and duration of insurgencies. If much territory needs to be defended by a government, terrorists or insurgents can compensate for their operational or strategic inferiority by massing forces locally to achieve tactical superiority. Government forces often attempt to defend territory or resources that have political, economic, social, and/or military value. For example, governments under siege often abandon the countryside in favour of more defensible cities and military bases. More often than not, states have the resources to protect many, but not every local target as their resources are stretched. Col. T. E. Lawrence, for instance, used the Arab force-to-space ratio advantage against the Turks to good effect during the Arab Revolt (1916–18). Given the amount of terrain to be covered, Lawrence calculated that the Turks would need 600,000 troops to prevent 'sedition putting up her head' across the entirety of the Transjordan, a figure six times larger than the forces available to the Turks (Lawrence 1920: 60). One of the most persistent criticisms against US and coalition leaders in defeating the ongoing insurgency in Iraq is the lack of enough forces, including competent Iraqi ones, to address the space of that country.

Force-to-space ratio superiority does not require irregulars to operate over huge geographic area in order to be successful. In the case of guerrilla campaign conducted against the British in Cyprus, the nationalist group EOKA was limited to a space little more than 3 per cent of that roamed by Lawrence's forces. EOKA's leader, George Grivas-Dighenis, based his strategy on the assumption that substantial numbers of British troops would attempt to put down the insurgency. EOKA members operated in small groups and conducted ambushes, bombings, and assassinations. These actions convinced the British that the benefits of remaining in Cyprus were not worth the political and military price to be paid.

Support

Few insurgencies or terrorist campaigns succeed without some form of support. Although Iraq and Afghanistan may prove to be the exceptions, in general only so much equipment can be manufactured or captured for use by the insurgents. Regardless of the amount of munitions available, insurgents must also look after casualties and continually replenish their supplies, including food and water. In addition, they must constantly update their intelligence on the whereabouts and activities of government forces as well as train new recruits. Support, however, is interlinked with and inseparable from the legitimacy of the organization. Violence conducted without a comprehensible political purpose will generate little popular support. Without support, insurgents and terrorists will eventually succumb to the efforts of the state. Clausewitz suggested that support, in the form of public opinion, was one of the centres of gravity in a popular uprising (1993: 720).

Insurgents and terrorists can look for support from both domestic (internal) and international (external) sympathizers. Almost all theorists agree that substantial popular support is required to compensate for the resources available to the state. Even Carlos Marighella, who believed initially that urban guerrillas could find and seize the necessary resources in major towns and cities to sustain the struggle, eventually relented and recognized the need to cultivate rural popular support. Domestic support can be forced from the population, using terror and intimidation, but long revolutionary struggles should not rely exclusively on such measures.

Although it is now a cliché, Mao's analogy describing the relationship between the guerrilla and the people is still evocative. The guerrillas were likened to 'fish' that swim in a 'sea' of popular support. Without the sea, the fish will die. A dramatic example of the consequences of failing to have domestic support is the fate of Che Guevara. Guevara believed that conditions in Bolivia in 1967 were ripe for a guerrilla insurrection led by his 'foco'. He overestimated, however, the amount of support he could receive from local Communists and farmers in Bolivia. The Bolivian Communists were hostile to advice on how to run their revolution from outsiders. More importantly, the local peasants were indifferent to the message preached by Guevara given government-sponsored land reform initiatives that addressed some of their grievances. Guevara and his 'foco' lacked popular support; the insurgents were either killed or captured within seven months of the first shots being fired.

Support is also contingent on the circumstances within a specific country. A danger exists in trying to reproduce success elsewhere using a previously effective revolutionary formula without first identifying the specific base of potential popular support. The uprising of the urban proletariat was considered a necessity in Marxist-Leninist revolutionary theory but failed dismally when attempted in China (1930) and Vietnam (1968). The agrarian character of China and Vietnam doomed urban revolts to failure; in both states most of the rural population were peasants. As a result, Mao Zedong and Vietnamese General Vo Nguyen Giap respectively modified their strategies and were eventually successful.

BOX 8.3

Ernesto 'Che' Guevara and the Theory of the 'Foco'

Argentinian-born Ernesto Guevara de la Serna Rosario (1928–1967) was educated as a medical doctor and plagued throughout his life by health problems including asthma. Ernesto spent much of his time after graduation travelling throughout Latin America where he gained an appreciation of the stoicism of the Latin American peasantry. He also became aware of the huge disparity between wealth of the substantial number of American companies in the region and that of the average peasant. After his political awakening he travelled to Mexico where he made the acquaintance of Fidel Castro and assisted Cuban exiles to train for revolutionary struggle. 'Che', as he is popularly known, was a member of the *Granma* expedition that landed in Cuba in November 1956. He served as Castro's political adviser and later as a field commander. His major work, *Guerrilla Warfare*, was published two years after the end of the Fidelista revolution. Che subsequently worked within the Ministry of Industries but disagreed with Castro over the direction Cuban socialism should take. The final acts in Che's life were failed attempts to foment revolution in the Congo (1965) and finally in Bolivia (1966–7).

Che's contribution to irregular warfare theory (and articulated most effectively by Regis Debray) was the idea of *foco* or the centre of gravity of the guerrilla movement. Practically, the *foco* refers to the initial critical mass of the guerrillas, the vanguard of the revolution, from which all else is derived. Philosophically, the *foco* represents the political and military 'heart' of the insurgency and from it Guevara and Debray believed that the *guerrilla movement itself* could generate the conditions for a revolutionary victory (the title of a book by Debray reflects this shift: *The Revolution within the Revolution*). They believed that guerrilla success will eventually 'inspire' local peasants to come to support them, allowing the organization to grow in strength.

External support for irregulars largely depends on both the geography of the country and the political relations maintained by the insurgents or terrorists. Such support can be material, in the form of resources or cross-border sanctuaries, or moral, in the case political recognition and lobbying. Many Marxist terrorist groups during the 1970s, such as the German Rote Armee Faktion, received physical support from Soviet or client states. Tangible support included money, advanced weapons, and training. Insurgent and terrorist leaders in countries ranging from the Dutch East Indies (1950, later becoming Indonesia) and British Palestine (1948, later becoming Israel) received external support, as part of a backlash against colonialism, that tipped the balance in their favour. States harbour or support terrorist groups for reasons of political expediency and to suit policy goals, as opposed to the genuine sympathy for the cause espoused by the terrorists. The ruling authorities in Jordan and Afghanistan made decisions regarding the relative political cost of providing sanctuary for their respective 'guests': the Palestinians in Jordan (1970) and Osama bin Laden and Al-Qaeda under Taliban protection in Afghanistan (2001). In addition, irregulars can serve to fight proxy wars against their patron's rivals. For example, Iran and Iraq sponsored rival terrorist groups designed to conduct attacks below the threshold of conventional war. With the regime of Saddam Hussein deposed, Iran continues to provide support and sanctuary for terrorist groups operating against coalition and Iraqi forces until their specific policy goal, namely a regime amenable to Iranian influence, is met.

Legitimacy

The use of armed force without a moral cause or reasonable justification will not be popular. Strong democracies can experience public discontent over the use of airpower, for instance, but they will survive even if political unrest provokes a change of administration. The same cannot be said in the context of terrorism and irregular warfare, where internal or external support is required to sustain the struggle. Terrorists and insurgent leaders need to convey the reason for their actions or lose sympathy for its cause. They often seek to legitimize their use of violence and translate this into meaningful support for their cause by demonstrating moral superiority over those who represent the state; supplanting the functions of the state at the local level; and spreading a persuasive message.

The moral superiority of the guerrillas is a cornerstone of all irregular and terrorist theory especially those fuelled by religious zeal. Insurgents derive support from the people and they often cultivate their relationship with them. Mao went so far as to outline a 'code of conduct' for the guerrillas, known as 'The Three Rules and Eight Remarks', as a way to demonstrate their moral superiority. The most important job of the guerrilla is to demonstrate this moral superiority in routine contact so that people differentiate the guerrillas from bandits or 'counter-revolutionaries.' Che Guevara insisted that the peasants understand that the guerrillas were as much social reformers as they were protectors of the people.

BOX 8.4

Mao's 'Three Rules and Eight Remarks'

Rules

1. All actions are subject to command.
2. Do not steal from the people.
3. Be neither selfish nor unjust.

Remarks

1. Replace the door when you leave the house.*
2. Roll up the bedding on which you have slept.
3. Be courteous.
4. Be honest in your transactions.
5. Return what you borrow.
6. Replace what you break.
7. Do not bathe in the presence of women.
8. Do not without authority search the pocketbooks of those you arrest.   (Tse-tung 1961: 92)

* The translator to this edition, retired US Marine Corp Brigadier General Samuel B. Griffiths, notes that 'In summer, doors were frequently lifted off and used as beds.'

Peasants who cooperate with the insurgents often face harsh retaliation from the government but frequently this only further legitimizes the revolutionary cause. Abdul Haris Nasution, military leader of the various Indonesian guerrilla actions against the Dutch from 1945 to 1949, described the vulnerability of peasants in a guerrilla war:

> It is common practice that an occupation army takes harsh measures against sabotage. Collective punishment, extensive torturing, even the elimination of whole kampongs [villages] and the machine gunning of the people on a mass basis is common. Therefore, a people at war must be prepared for all the consequences so that the people's spirit will remain unbroken and will allow the guerrilla army to launch even harsher measures against the enemy.

(Nasution 1965: 35)

Disproportionate government responses to suspected collaboration only drives the people further into the arms of the insurgents. Government brutality also allows insurgents to act as the avengers of the people, helping to cement the ties between them. Carlos Marighella, for example, hoped that the actions of the Brazilian authorities would demonstrate conclusively that the 'government is unjust, incapable of solving problems, and that it resorts simply to the physical liquidation of its opponents. The political situation in the country is transformed into a military situation in which the "gorillas" appear more and more to be the ones responsible for violence, while the lives of the people grow worse' (1969).

Of course, the admonitions to behave better than government troops often are applied only to those who actively assist insurgents in their struggle. In a number of irregular conflicts, guerrillas and government forces alike regarded an unwillingness to help as aiding and abetting the enemy. Absolute popular support can never be guaranteed. Populations invariably split into willing assistants, staunch foes, and the undecided majority. To help make up the minds of those undecided, insurgents can demonstrate legitimacy by becoming the de facto government in areas under their control. This can include taking 'positive meadures' such as the establishment of schools and clinics or 'negative measures' such as tax collection. The use of terror as a negative measure to intimidate the population is a matter of debate by irregular warfare practitioners to this day. For Che Guevara, terror tactics were unjustified because they invariably delegitimize the guerrilla's message. Both Mao and Marighella disagree, noting that acts of terror may be necessary to convince the population of the occupational hazards of working for the government, or to provoke a repressive response. In practice, extensive discussion often proceeded and followed rural acts of terror and the Viet Cong often went to great lengths to provide the justification for their actions during the Vietnam War (1960–75). Negative measures backed by proselytizing can be an effective way of legitimizing the insurgent cause by showing conclusively that the government can no longer protect them. Intercepted communications between Al-Qaeda leaders suggest that negative measures in Iraq are counterproductive to their other short- and long-term goals in the country.

The most powerful method of legitimizing a struggle is to link military operations with a justifiable political end. Causes vary, but self-determination has been the most pervasive and successful rallying cry. Given the fundamental rights outlined in the Atlantic Charter (1941) and the United Nations Charter (1945) it was difficult for nations such as Great Britain, France, the Netherlands, and Portugal to maintain possession of overseas colonies

BOX 8.5

Popular Support and Negative Measures in the Jihad in Iraq

The following correspondence, intercepted and translated in October 2005, suggests concern among senior Al-Qaeda leadership about the tactics used by Al-Qaeda in Iraq. In particular, Ayman al-Zawahiri acknowledges the importance of popular support to the insurgents there and suggests that Abu Musab al-Zarqawi focus less on negative measures and more on educating the masses:

And it's very important that you allow me to elaborate a little here on this issue of popular support. Let's say:

(1) If we are in agreement that the victory of Islam and the establishment of a caliphate in the manner of the Prophet will not be achieved except through jihad against the apostate rulers and their removal, then this goal will not be accomplished by the mujahed movement while it is cut off from public support, even if the Jihadist movement pursues the method of sudden overthrow. This is because such an overthrow would not take place without some minimum of popular support and some condition of public discontent which offers the mujahed movement what it needs in terms of capabilities in the quickest fashion. Additionally, if the Jihadist movement were obliged to pursue other methods, such as a popular war of jihad or a popular intifadah, then popular support would be a decisive factor between victory and defeat.

(2) In the absence of this popular support, the Islamic mujahed movement would be crushed in the shadows, far from the masses who are distracted or fearful, and the struggle between the Jihadist elite and the arrogant authorities would be confined to prison dungeons far from the public and the light of day. This is precisely what the secular, apostate forces that are controlling our countries are striving for. These forces don't desire to wipe out the mujahed Islamic movement, rather they are stealthily striving to separate it from the misguided or frightened Muslim masses. Therefore, our planning must strive to involve the Muslim masses in the battle, and to bring the mujahed movement to the masses and not conduct the struggle far from them.

(3) The Muslim masses—for many reasons, and this is not the place to discuss it—do not rally except against an outside occupying enemy, especially if the enemy is firstly Jewish, and secondly American.

This, in my limited opinion, is the reason for the popular support that the mujahedeen enjoy in Iraq, by the grace of God.

As for the sectarian and chauvinistic factor, it is secondary in importance to outside aggression, and is much weaker than it. In my opinion—which is limited and which is what I see far from the scene—the awakening of the Sunni people in Iraq against the Shia would not have had such strength and toughness were it not for the treason of the Shia and their collusion with the Americans, and their agreement with them to permit the Americans to occupy Iraq in exchange for the Shia assuming power.

(4) Therefore, the mujahed movement must avoid any action that the masses do not understand or approve, if there is no contravention of Sharia in such avoidance, and as long as there are other options to resort to, meaning we must not throw the masses—scant in knowledge—into the sea before we teach them to swim, relying for guidance in that on the saying of the Prophet to Umar bin al-Khattab: lest the people should say that Muhammad used to kill his Companions.

(al-Zawahiri 2005)

in the face of native insurgencies claiming the right of self-governance. Leaving aside the ideological dimension of the Rhodesian insurgency (1965–80) and the eventual corruption of the subsequent regime, few could argue at the time against the cause of (black) majority rule. The legitimacy of the East Timorese claim of independence led to internal and external pressure on the Indonesian government to end a twenty-five-year insurgency. Other successful causes blend social, cultural, and economic issues into a powerful political message that the government or an international audience finds difficult to counter or resist.

KEY POINTS

- Terrorism and insurgencies can be examined in terms of time, space, legitimacy, or support, reflecting specific local contexts rather than predetermined goals attributed to a general theory.

- Time is an important element in the success of insurgencies, involving a non-linear progression that includes: the space to manœuvre and to gain legitimacy and/or support, all of which are necessary for eventual victory.

- Terrain is important to offset weaknesses and gain tactical advantages, including

- gaining 'force-to-space' superiority at the time and place of your choosing.

- Support is dependent on legitimacy; it is derived internally from the quality of the interaction with the local populace and externally via resources from allies and sympathizers.

- Moral justification provides the cornerstone to sustain the struggle, usually blending cultural and social causes with political ends.

Protecting the System

The difficulties facing governments besieged by insurgents or terrorists may seem insurmountable at first glance, but numerous works have been written to explain how to quell them. This literature ranges from general theories and practical suggestions, based on hard-won experience, to complicated empirical models purporting to predict outcomes or test practical advice. Commentators have reduced complicated political-military struggles against forceful usurpers to a number of principles or formulas for success. Brigadier General Samuel B. Griffith suggested in his translation of Mao's *Yu Chi Chan* that antiguerrilla operations could be summed up in three words: location, isolation, and eradication (Tse-tung 1961: 32). Griffith's summary is a useful reference point for exploring how to apply the strengths of a state (or group of states) against an irregular threat.

Location

The most important phase of any counter-insurgency or counter-terrorism campaign is recognizing that the threat exists. Counter-insurgency expert Robert Thompson believed it necessary to tackle an insurgency during its subversion and organization phase or at the first signs of a sustained campaign of violence (Thompson 1966: 50). In other words, he believed it necessary to defeat insurgents in both physical space *and* time. The problem is to distinguish between lawful or unlawful forms of discontent. Restricting guaranteed rights and freedoms every time a bomb is detonated will undermine the credibility and intentions of the government. Waiting too long to uphold the rule of law, however, will

BOX 8.6

Principles, Prerequisites, and Laws of Counter-Insurgency and Counter-Terrorism

Material is quoted from specific texts in chronological order.

Charles Callwell. Guiding principle of small wars (1899: 4). 'Over-awing the enemy by bold initiative and by resolute action, whether on the battlefield or as part of the general plan of action.'

Charles W. Gwynn (1934):
- policy remains vested in civil government;
- minimum use of force;
- firm and timely action;
- cooperation between civil and military authorities.

Samuel Griffith. Summary of anti-guerrilla operations (1961):
- location;
- isolation;
- eradication.

Roger Trinquier. Aspects of a successful counter-insurgency (1964):
- extensive *police operation;*
- intensive *propaganda effort;*
- broad *social programme.*

David Galula. Laws of counter-insurgency (1964):
- Support of the population is necessary.
- Support is gained through an active minority.
- Support from population is conditional.
- Intensity of efforts and vastness of means are essential.

Robert Thompson. Principles of counter-insurgency (1966):
- It must have a clear political aim.
- The government must function in accordance with the law.
- The government must have an overall plan.
- The government must give priority to defeating the political subversion, not the guerrillas.
- The government must secure its base areas first (in the guerrilla phase).

John McCuen. Counter-revolutionary strategy forms (1966):
- counter-organization;
- counter-terrorism;
- counter-guerrilla warfare;
- counter-mobile warfare.

Julian Paget. Prerequisites for fighting the insurgents (1967):
- essentials for counter-insurgency operations: civil–military understanding; a joint command and control structure; good intelligence; mobility; and training.

- defeating insurgents: support of the local population; bases; mobility; supplies and information; and the will to win.
- winning hearts and minds.

N. I. Klonis. Counter-guerrilla measures (1972):

- prevention = non-military solutions;
- psychological operations;
- energetic military countermeasures.

Frank Kitson. Framework for an effective counter-insurgency campaign (1977):

- good coordinating machinery (between civil and military agencies);
- establishing the sort of political atmosphere within which the government measures can be introduced with the maximum likelihood of success;
- intelligence (right information 5 sensible policy);
- law (upholding the rule of).

Paul Wilkinson. Prerequisites for a successful counter-terrorist strategy (1986):

- upholding the rule of law without adopting totalitarian methods; all assets under civil control (military and civilian); no concessions/no deals;
- development of high-quality intelligence long before the insurgency surfaces; need to coordinate resources.

Richard Clutterbuck. Countering destabilization and insurgency (1990):

- rule of law (to be preserved);
- intelligence (tactics formed around);
- security (tactics formed around).

Bard O'Neill. Evaluative criteria (1990):

- environment;
- popular support;
- organization and cohesion;
- external support.

G. Davidson Smith. Capabilities and resources required to conduct counter-terrorism operations (1990):

- consistent, clear, and firm policy;
- experience;
- infrastructure (interagency cooperation);
- law enforcement agencies;
- armed forces;
- legislation;
- the media.

US Government. Simultaneous action 'fronts' to combat terrorism (2003):

- *Defeat* terrorist organizations of global reach by attacking their sanctuaries; leadership; command, control, and communications; material support; and finances.

- *Deny* further sponsorship, support, and sanctuary to terrorists by ensuring other states accept their responsibilities to take action against these international threats within their sovereign territory.
- *Diminish* the underlying conditions that terrorist seek to exploit by enlisting the international community to focus its efforts and resources on the areas most at risk.
- *Defend* the United States, our citizens, and our interests at home and abroad by both proactively protecting our homeland and extending our defenses to ensure we identify and neutralize the threat as early as possible.

give the insurgents or terrorists the necessary time to build a robust organizational infrastructure that only the most dedicated efforts might hope to defeat.

Terrorism and insurgency can be staved off with enough early warning, but this implies that an effective intelligence-gathering and assessment organization is operating. Few states possess such resources or foresight. Subversion, therefore, remains an attractive option for those discontented. Those willing and able to destroy the system need to be identified and tracked: this requires the assistance of a supportive populace. The question in pluralist systems is whether or not *potentially* seditious individuals can be taken under surveillance or arrested without violating civil liberties and undermining the rule of law.

Upholding the rule of law is crucial if states are to preserve the legitimacy of their cause and maintain the moral high ground over insurgents or terrorists (Clutterbuck 1990: 10–11; Wilkinson 1986: 127). Methods to counter terrorism, for example, must be effective yet stay within the boundary of the rule of law. This applies to both domestic and international measures. Citizens of democratic states are loath to give up rights and freedoms to combat threats, especially if they intrude upon personal privacy. Managing how and when (and in what measure) to begin counter-insurgency and anti-terrorism efforts, such as imposing curfews and controlling media access while upholding the rule of law, is the primary challenge to any government under siege. In most democratic societies, however, steps to counter terrorists rarely are preventative and almost always are taken *after* horrific acts of violence have been committed, as Washington's response after September 11 and London's failed attempt to pass a more restrictive Anti-Terrorism Bill after the July 2005 underground attacks suggest. Democracies run into greater trouble when their international actions appear to contravene its domestic laws. The issue of Al-Qaeda detainees continues to influence US counter-terrorism measures domestically and abroad adversely for precisely these reasons.

Once an irregular threat has been identified, various civil and military agencies must localize the threat while coordinating their response. They must identify safe houses, group members, and sources of supply. Gathering such information about the terrorists can be daunting, given the desire of most subversives to keep the organization small, stealthy, and secret. For a state providing direct counter-insurgency or counter-terrorism support into a geographically and culturally unfamiliar country, as the United States did in South Vietnam, obtaining even basic information on subversives takes time. This problem is compounded when a state either does not have an effective and efficient security apparatus (Afghanistan) or when the existing one evaporates or is politically unpalatable (Iraq). The time gained is used by insurgents to retain the initiative and develop the organization further.

Isolation

Isolating insurgents and terrorists from their bases of support is probably the most important element of successful campaigns against them. Isolation can take the form of physical separation or political alienation. Physical separation can be achieved by moving villagers into more easily defended compounds, known in Malaya and Vietnam as 'strategic hamlets'. Preventative measures such as curfews, prohibited ('no-go') areas, food rationing, aggressive patrolling, and overt presence also can physically isolate insurgents. As with any form of deterrence, the threat posed by patrolling and presence must be a credible one and not consist simply of half-hearted 'cordon and search' operations. Isolation also means limiting the mobility and range of the insurgents or terrorists, in effect taking away their space and their time. Insurgents and terrorists also can be cut off from their external sources of support by a combination of diplomatic pressure and military measures. The French managed to stop external support from reaching the Armée Liberation Nationale during the Algerian insurgency (1954–62): the border between Algeria and its neighbours Morocco and Tunisia was shut down by a combination of wire barriers, guardhouses, and patrols. Experts suggest that the insurgency in Iraq cannot be dealt with effectively until supply routes from Iran and Syria are cut off.

Segregating insurgents and terrorists from the population involves more than just physically separating them. To impose meaningful isolation, the state must defuse the irregular's most powerful asset: its political message. Widely held grievances that foster a potent source of recruitment and support must be mitigated by the government. Obviously, some messages are more influential than others: self-determination is difficult to counter by an eternal or occupying power, whereas demands for land reform or increased political representation can be more easily satisfied. The words of the government must be accompanied by effective deeds to show that the state can and will respond to what amounts to political extortion. The terrorist or insurgent's 'propaganda of the deed' must be diffused by government displays of a firm, yet lawful response. The displays can range from enforcing a 'no negotiations with terrorists' policy to simple measures like providing basic necessities and local security. The onus is on the representatives of the state to prove that they are *morally superior* to the guerrillas and terrorists and will provide for the needs of their citizens, including responding to the sources of disgruntlement that led to armed insurrection in the first place. Likewise, the terrorist or insurgent cause must be discredited. Leniency also should be extended to those insurgents and terrorists who give up the armed struggle. Above all, citizens must be convinced that the state's fight is their fight. As Iraq demonstrates, getting citizens to respond to the call to action can be extremely difficult after years of totalitarian rule and where some of the basic instruments of government are feeble. Popular support for the terrorists or insurgents must be denied through credible and efficient actions to win what Sir Gerald Templar called 'the hearts and minds' of the population. With little internal or external sustenance flowing to the rebels and a population willing to support the government, it is only a matter of time before the state's forces destroy the irregular threat.

Eradication

Eradication involves the physical destruction of the insurgents or terrorists, although few would go so far as to follow Robert Taber's rhetorical advice: 'There is only one means of

BOX 8.7

'Hearts and Minds'

The phrase 'the battle for hearts and minds' underscores the *political* dimension of irregular warfare. During the early stages of the Vietnam, or Second Indochina War (1965–1975), the South Vietnamese guerrillas, or Viet Cong, made comprehensive and coordinated efforts to win the battle by coercing peasants. Coercion took forms as divergent as public executions and village propaganda sessions. The former would sow fear among those who were thinking of supporting the government whereas repetitive proselytizing played upon the predispositions of the audience, such as the desire for land reform or the need to escape the tedium of village life, in order to persuade villagers to join or assist the Viet Cong. The response of one particular peasant illustrates the pervasiveness and influence of politics in irregular warfare:

'In the beginning I was very hurt and angry with [the Viet Cong] for killing my father . . . they told me that because my father had done wrong, he had to be punished. . . . *They talked to the point where I felt that they were right.* . . . I came to hate my father even though I didn't know [exactly] what he had done'.

(Donnell 1967–97, Italics added)

defeating an insurgent people who will not surrender, and that is extermination. There is only way to control a territory that harbors resistance, and that is to turn it into a desert' (1972: 11). The state has numerous advantages over its opponents given its control over social, fiscal, and military resources. The most important question in democratic states is whether or not the leaders of the state can apply their resources effectively to extinguish the insurgent flame without alienating popular support for their own authority. Cultural context matters when determining a response. Canadians, for example, would not approve of measures like the so-called 'Wrath of God' retribution campaign conducted by the Israelis against those responsible for the massacre at the 1972 Munich Olympic Games. In another example, the leaders of some European countries were hesitant to cast actions against Al-Qaeda after September 2001 as a 'war' for cultural and historical reasons. Indeed, many continued to see the phenomenon of fundamentalist Islamic terrorism exclusively as a domestic law enforcement issue within their sovereign borders, requiring civilian police or paramilitary forces, and not as a *global* problem that might require the use of military forces.

Regardless of whether civilian or military forces are preferred, counter-insurgency theory is rife with active plans that discuss destruction of guerrillas. These plans range from French Marshal Lyautey's innocuous-sounding 'oil patch' method applied in Morocco in the first quarter of the twentieth century (Gottman 1948: 248) to the more sinister-sounding Nazi German 'spider's web' and 'partridge drive' tactics (Dixon and Heilbrunn 1962: 215–16). All theorists agree that eliminating the insurgents' safe havens must be a priority. Numbers also make a difference. The accepted ratio of government forces to guerrillas is often cited as 10:1. Most theorists also assert that specialist units (e.g. special operation forces or SOF) are needed to defeat the irregulars at their own game. Some advocate the use of technologies not available to the insurgents, such as helicopters and remote sensors, to enhance the force-to-space balance between government and irregular forces and to achieve superior mobility.

There are also passive ways in which the state can subvert an insurgency and thereby diminish the number of guerrillas or terrorists. One such method combines psychological warfare techniques, promises of amnesty (e.g. the *Chieu Hoi*, or 'Open Arms' programme used in South Vietnam) and cash incentives (for weapons and information) to convince insurgents and terrorists that their struggle is in vain. More recently, the approach in Yemen has been to challenge religious-inspired terrorists to theological debates. Those who 'lose' the debates are offered amnesty and possible job opportunities. Combined with tougher measures imposed on Islamic *madrassas* in the country, the net effect has been a dramatic reduction in the numbers of terrorist operatives, recruits, and supporters. Political and economic pressure can be placed on states or groups providing safe havens for terrorists and insurgents.

Passive and active techniques are not mutually exclusive and can be used together synergy for combined effect. During irregular wars in the Philippines (1946–55), Kenya (1952–60), and Rhodesia (1965–80, now Zimbabwe), for example, a sizeable number of guerrillas were persuaded not only to give up the armed struggle but also to operate against their former comrades. The 'pseudo guerrillas', as they were called, would dress as insurgents and patrol villages, gathering information on the whereabouts of active guerrilla units. Occasionally, 'pseudo guerrilla' groups would ambush guerrilla units, fomenting mistrust and occasionally provoking pitched battles among 'friendly forces' (Cline 2005). Other passive measures include engaging in political dialogue with, and offering support for, moderates within an irregular organization, convincing them of the need to start talking and stop fighting.

Political will must underlie efforts to counter terrorism and insurgency. The eradication of an irregular movement is a gradual process of attrition that requires a significant and consistent investment in time and resources. Rarely have national leaders been able to sustain the political will necessary to defeat insurgents or terrorists. Equally daunting is the fact that the underlying causes of discontent often resurface and the embers of insurgency are rekindled in a different form. For example, the government of the Philippines conducted a textbook campaign to defeat a communist insurgency during the 1950s with US assistance and inspired leadership. Yet barely a decade later, the Philippine government faced a new challenge from Muslim separatist and hardcore Marxist guerrillas. Today Philippine leaders continue to struggle against groups such as the Abu Sayyaf Group (ASG), which has sustained itself through a lucrative trade in ransoming hostages among other activities. Some commentators have suggested that terrorism and irregular warfare are analogous to the mythical hydra: cut off one head and several more appear in its place.

The effects of terrorism can be limited through a combination of offensive and defensive measures, but ultimately bringing terrorists to justice, especially for crimes beyond state borders, can be accomplished by a combination of determination to bring those guilty to justice, the political will to sustain the struggle and not compromise core societal valves, and maximized use of the full range of response capabilities. The Bush administration signalled its determination, and that of the American people, for the lengthy struggle against terrorism in the wake of the September 2001 attacks. In conjunction with this stated policy, various officials within the administration emphasized that military action is only one tool in the toolbox of possible US responses. Direct military action has a certain utility but it will not stop terrorism alone; US efforts, and those of its allies, have focused on all measures to root out terrorism, including the eradication of training facilities, financial assets, political sponsorship, and even the individuals themselves who belong to or support Al-Qaeda. Bringing individuals to trial for actions below the threshold of 'an act of war' takes even greater reserves of time, patience, resolve, negotiation, and treasure. It took the United States twelve years and considerable third-party support, for example, to bring those allegedly responsible for the Lockerbie bombing to trial. In the end, the side that will prevail will be the one most willing to continue the struggle and make the least damaging choices for the duration.

KEY POINTS

- Methods used by the state in response to local threats are aimed crucially at maintaining a lawful, hence political/moral, legitimacy.

- The strategy of state success is based on isolating the insurgents both physically and politically.

- The eradication of insurgents is often a slow process and will take different forms in different political and cultural contexts.

Bringing the System Down or Thriving on its Margins?

The supposition that terrorism and irregular warfare involve the use of force strictly for political ends recently has been challenged. As stated in the introduction, some suggest that the irregular conflict is no longer about politics. In other words, wars of national liberation, ideological terrorism, and revolution have joined colonial small wars in the museum of 'conflict past'. Instead, some suggest that contemporary and future irregular threats are driven by a mixture of culture, religious fanaticism, and technology.

Culture

Samuel Huntington suggested that future conflict on the macro level will result from differences in culture between incompatible civilizations (Huntington 1996). Others believe that, on a micro level, substate warrior cultures will become the predominant irregular threat. Westerners fight wars according to established norms and modalities. States, which retain the monopoly on the use of force, go to war with one another to achieve political aims. Examples from Chechnya, Somalia, and the Democratic Republic of Congo, as well as in Afghanistan and Iraq, suggest a new form of irregular warfare is emerging. In this 'fourth generation warfare (4GW)', networks of warriors will utilize their social and culture advantages to offset the technological advantages of Western soldiers (Hammes 2004). According to this argument, modern conventional forces of volunteer or conscripted soldiers cannot match warriors forged for fighting by their culture (Peters 1994). Proponents of this view suggest that the availability of modern small arms and disdain for Western rules of warfare give cultural warriors their military superiority. Political aims matter not to Somali clansmen, high on *khat*, driving around Mogadishu in heavily armed civilian vehicles. Warrior culture dictates goals–such as plunder, or killing to prove virility–instead of politics.

Some observes argue that in the future violence will be ethnic or identity based. According to Martin van Creveld (1991), the political basis for war (the Clausewitzian trinity of the people, the state, and the armed forces) is disintegrating. In his view, states will cease to be viable political entities because they will not represent the will of the people. Under stress, these states will collapse into pockets of conflicting ethnic groups. Without a state to sustain the armed forces, the only surviving element of Clausewitz's trinity is the people. The moral resolve of such cultural and social networks is superior precisely because they exist to fight. The conventional armed forces of developed nations will be increasingly irrelevant in the face of such superior will and approaches to warfare that offset technological advantages. Western powers can try and respond with specialized forces to deal with cultural warriors, or outsource their security requirements to private military organizations. In the final analysis, chaos and mayhem among substate groups will replace war between states in world affairs.

Religious fanaticism

Religious beliefs often shape terrorists' and insurgents' causes and are used to obtain support among a community of the faithful. Throughout history, religion has been a powerful stimulus for political violence by Muslims, Christians, Jews, Sikhs, and other faiths as well. In exchange for personal sacrifice, earthly representatives of some faiths promise terrorist martyrs a glorious afterlife for conducting attacks, suicide or otherwise, that kill non-believers. Religion does, however, provide insurgent and terrorist leaders with a number of advantages for their cause. First, leaders such as Osama bin Laden use religion to provide a competing value structure and ideology to rally the deprived and disillusioned behind their cause. What bin Laden and his followers offer is an alternative to the Western, materialist culture and an attempt to recapture previous glories of mythic past. What has surprised Western analysts is the resonance that this vision has across cultural and ethnic lines—in other words, the degree of popular support for his message. Second, religion offers a rationale for action. Much like Che Guevara, Osama bin Laden and his followers see themselves as social reformers. Terrorist attacks serve to raise the consciousness of the global Islamic community (the *ummah*) to the existing struggle as well to demonstrate to others that there is an alternative to their current situation. Religion can also blind the faithful to certain realities as well. Religious-inspired terrorist movements often overestimate the appeal of their message. As with political ideologues, including Mao Zedong, religious ideologues convince themselves that the future is predetermined based on the righteousness of their cause. In addition, particularly heinous or indiscriminate actions over time may lead even the staunchest supporters, much less allies of convenience, to question the legitimacy and viability of religiously sanctioned terrorism. For example, some affiliated insurgent groups and external supporters of Al-Qaeda in Iraq are distancing themselves from attacks that target or have killed large numbers of fellow Muslims as opposed to occupying coalition forces. The inability of Western democracies to influence a fundamentalist segment of Islamic population raises the spectre of an interminable war of annihilation of the type mentioned by Robert Taber above.

Technology

Weapons of mass destruction (WMD)

Graham Allison (2004), Walter Laqueur (1999), and others suggest that the threat to Western democracies is growing acute because certain religiously motivated groups might use WMD: biological, chemical, and even nuclear weapons. The congruence of religion, WMD, and the belief that the end of mankind is at hand (millenarianism) portends a frightful and very real 'apocalypse now.' Brian Jenkins argued in the 1970s that terrorist use of nuclear weapons was unlikely because 'terrorists want a lot of people *watching*, not a lot of people *dead*' (1987: 352). Modern religious fanatics, it is suggested, do not march to a political drum. Millenarians do not embrace political objectives and instead seek to purge non-believers and accelerate or launch 'the end of days'. Those who believe that millenarianism is a threat point to the ease with which chemical and biological agents, or 'poor man's atom bombs', can be manufactured or acquired; the number of groups that are stockpiling lethal agents; the decreasing frequency but increasing lethality of terrorist acts; and the breaking of a so-called WMD taboo by the Japanese millenarian cult Aum Shinrikyo in Tokyo in 1995 (Laqueur 1999) and the unknown mailer of anthrax spores to the US capital in October 2001. Those who track terrorist attempts to acquire WMD suggest that the question is not 'if' such attacks will occur but rather 'when'—and whether Western democracies will be able to manage the consequences.

Information technology

The internet transcends borders, and therefore some observes believe that future irregular wars will be fought in cyberspace. Given the vulnerability of websites and servers to hackers, terrorists inevitably will become cyberterrorists through the World Wide Web. Serbian and Indonesian hacking of opponents' websites, as well as the 'defacing' of Al-Qaeda affiliated websites by groups such as TeAmZ USA, are examples interpreted by some as evidence that cyberwar is a reality. Hacking and defacing provide glimpses into what ambitious cyberterrorists and activists can accomplish. Policy-makers fear that cyberterrorists and infosurgents will conduct electronic raids on vital national systems controlled by computers (e.g. financial services, transportation networks, and power grids). Fear is no longer based on the prospect of violence: information and the ability to control it has become a form of power.

Whether or not terrorist and insurgent campaigns will be entirely 'virtual' is a matter of speculation. A technological reality is that access to the web, satellite communications, and portable computers greatly enhances the capability of aspiring terrorists and insurgents.

Insurgent cell leaders in Iraq, for example, use readily available commercial cell phones, laptops, and Global Positioning Satellite (GPS) receivers to coordinate attacks. In addition, open access websites such as Google Earth provide them with sources of imagery data that were previously the exclusive purview of major powers. Websites, portals, and weblogs allow the quick dissemination of propaganda materials and with basic equipment, such as a laptop and a CD burner, materials can be produced and disseminated clandestinely. With a computer and connection to the internet, an individual can do more damage than armed terrorist cells or small insurgent movements. More importantly, through technology Al-Qaeda appears to be realizing the dream of a functional 'leaderless resistance' (Beam 1992). The net effect, observed in the Philippines, Iraq, and elsewhere, is that individuals or small insurgent cells can obtain training and mission planning materials, share information, and coordinate their activities with little fear of being caught by security forces.

KEY POINTS

- Religion is useful as a rallying point and enabler for terrorism but cannot provide a strategy to achieve the desired objectives.

- Culturally inspired insurgents might change the nature of uprisings form traditional 'trinitarian' wars to chaotic ethnic conflict.

- The replacement by religious fanatics of the political with 'apocalyptic millenarianism'

possibly portends the lethal combination of martyrs with weapons of mass destruction.

- Information technologies and the World Wide Web have provided terrorists with new capabilities to reach across time and space, creating vulnerability in a state-based system where control of information equals power.

Conclusion

States will be plagued by terrorism and irregular warfare as long as individuals are willing to use violence for political purposes. The shocking cultural details of irregular conflicts, such as Al-Qaeda's recorded beheadings of captives and the use of starvation as a weapon in Sudan and Somalia, can obscure the political purpose behind the fighting. Terrorism and irregular warfare have long been used to change political systems and acquire power; more recently, cultural schisms have led to a rise in terrorism carried out for religious and personal reasons.

Current re-evaluations of irregular warfare and terrorism often lack context. They highlight one dimension of irregular conflicts and ignore the overriding political reason for the conflict and the outcomes desired by the combatants. The rescue of British military personnel held hostage by the 'West Side Boys' in Sierra Leone in September 2000 was conducted ostensibly to ensure the safety of British nationals. Whether the 'West Side Boys' are harbingers of the 'new warrior class' or merely well-armed bandits is irrelevant. The rescue mission was intended to convey an unequivocal political message as valid today as it was during the punitive British expedition to Sierra Leone in 1899: an insult to British national pride would be wiped out, a wrong avenged, and an action would be taken to deter other groups from kidnapping British citizens (Callwell 1899: 8).

Religion, culture, ethnicity, and technology remain important elements of irregular warfare. They define how and why individuals take up arms against perceived injustices. But the *ultima ratio* for the use of irregular methods of war is to achieve *political* results. US militia and patriot groups, for instance, hope to provoke a response to redress the *political* imbalance between what they perceive as illegitimate federal authorities and individuals' rights and freedoms established in the Constitution. Terrorist use of a weapon of mass destruction (WMD) is a frightening prospect. Yet Shoko Asahara, the spiritual leader of the Aum Shinrikyo cult, only attempted to use chemical and biological agents *after* his political ambitions were thwarted in 1990. Revenge for his humiliation at the polls was perhaps the most significant reason for launching chemical and biological attacks. Even in the case of Osama bin Laden, the goal of Al-Qaeda and its affiliated organizations is to achieve a type of political power and base, in the form of a theocratic caliphate, in order to spread his unique vision for religious, social, and political revolution.

Government officials have taken the threat of terrorist use of WMDs seriously; several governments have established rudimentary preventative, protective, and crisis response measures to counter perceived threats that terrorists will soon use WMD. For example, most US spending on homeland security and counterproliferation is designed to provide early detection and interdiction when terrorists attempt to acquire and transport WMD, and efficient crisis management and response should those efforts fail.

Warrior cultures may appear to espouse violence for its own sake but at the root of their struggle is the quest for political autonomy, control, or power. The protracted guerrilla war fought by the Chechens against the Russians is little different from the one conducted in 1856: the Chechens' desire is to gain political autonomy from Moscow. Somali warlords seek to gain political power and influence for their clans. Native Americans fought against the US Army in the nineteenth century to maintain autonomy and protect their traditional hunting grounds. Even ancient irregulars, classified as *barbarii* by the Romans, were resisting attempts to have *Pax Romana* imposed upon them.

So is the trinity of Clausewitz no longer relevant? To suggest so misrepresents its foundation and misconstrues the reasons why irregulars fight in the first place. After all, primordial violence (the people) serves no purpose unless it is subordinated ultimately to policy (the government). Violence undertaken for personal gain, be it financial or enhance one's reputation, is nothing more than a criminal act in civil society and should be treated as such.

? QUESTIONS

1. Does the nature or character of irregular warfare change—or do both?

2. Can terrorists and insurgents sacrifice the element of time to achieve political change and if so, under what conditions?

3. To what extent do global violent extremists share much in common with their historical antecedents?

4. Why is conducting irregular warfare successfully such a challenging undertaking?

5. Why is the element of space easy to discuss in theory but difficult to incorporate in practice?

6. Why are irregular warfare theorists divided on the use of terror as a method of compelling support?

7. Why is there no universal theory of irregular warfare?

8. How is the balance struck between force and the rule of law on both sides of an irregular campaign?

9. Has religion, culture, and technology changed the nature of terrorism?

10. 'Religion, culture, ethnicity and technology remain important elements of irregular warfare.' Which do you think is most important?

 FURTHER READING

■ G. Allison, *Nuclear Terrorism: The Ultimate Preventable Catastrophe* (New York: Times Books, 2004). A good companion volume to Laqueur, *The New Terrorism* (below).

■ A. al-Zawahiri, 'Letter from al-Zawahiri to Zarqawi', tr. the Foreign Broadcast Information Service, October 2005. An unusual document that provides insights into the strategy of Al-Qaeda as well as some of its operational problems.

■ L. Beam, *Leaderless Resistance* (1992). This essay provides valuable insights into both the concept of leaderless resistance and the peculiar worldview of US militia members and 'patriots'. Available online at http://www.crusader.net/texts/bt/bt04.html.

■ C. E. Callwell, *Small Wars: Their Principles and Practice* (London: Her Majesty's Stationery Office, 1899). A problematic source for a number of reasons but one that continues to offer insights into the requirements for successful counter-insurgency campaign.

■ C. Clausewitz, *On War*, ed. and tr. M. Howard and P. Paret (London: Everyman's Library, 1993). This is a classic study of the relationship between politics and war.

■ L. Cline, *Psuedo Operations and Counterinsurgency: Lessons from Other Countries* (Carlisle, Penn.: Strategic Studies Institute, 2005) provides a concise summary and analysis on the value of using turned guerrillas against their former compatriots. Available online at http://www.strategicstudiesinstitute.army.mil/pubs/display.cfm?PubID=607.

■ R. Clutterbuck, *Terrorism and Guerrilla Warfare: Forecasts and Remedies* (London: Routledge, 1990). A useful study of the nature of terrorism and guerrilla warfare by a former British officer turned academic.

■ R. Debray, *Revolution in the Revolution? Armed Struggle and Political Struggle in Latin America* (London: Pelican, 1968). This study, by a French philosopher, develops Che Guevara's concept of the *foco* more fully.

■ C. A. Dixon and O. Heilbrunn, *Communist Guerrilla Warfare* (New York: Praeger, 1962). Provides a useful account of Communist guerrilla tactics in the early cold war period.

■ B. B. Fall 'The Theory and Practice of Insurgency and Counter-Insurgency', *Naval War College Review*, 15/1 (1999), 46–57. A good basic introduction to the core concepts of and relationship between insurgency and counter-insurgency.

■ J. Gottman, 'Bugeaud, Gallieni, Lyautey: The Development of French Colonial Warfare', in E. M. Earle (ed.), *Makers of Modern Strategy: Military Thought from Machiavelli to Hitler* (Princeton: Princeton University Press, 1948). As the title suggests, this is a useful account of the French colonial experience with revolutionary warfare.

■ Gray, C. S., *Modern Strategy* (Oxford: Oxford University Press, 1999). An excellent source that contains a useful chapter on 'Small Wars and Other Savage Violence'.

■ C. Guevara, *Guerrilla Warfare*, 3rd edn (Wilmington, DE: Scholarly Resources, 1997). This is an updated version of Che Guevara's manual on guerrilla warfare based on his Cuban experience.

■ T. X. Hammes, *The Sling and the Stone: On War in the Twenty-First Century* (St Paul, MN: Zenith Press, 2004).

■ B. Hoffman, *Inside Terrorism* (New York: Columbia University Press, 1998). A useful analysis of the phenomenon of terrorism.

■ S. Huntington, *The Clash of Civilizations: Remaking of World Order* (New York: Simon & Schuster, 1996).

■ J. Jansen, *The Dual Nature of Islamic Fundamentalism* (Ithaca, NY: Cornell University Press, 1997). A source that offers numerous insights into the evolution of fundamentalist Islamic thought and its practice by the Muslim Brotherhood in Egypt.

■ B. Jenkins, 'Will Terrorists Go Nuclear?', in W. Laqueur and Y. Alexander (eds.), *The Terrorism Reader: A Historical Anthology* (New York: Meridian, 1987). This chapter deals with the dangers of terrorist groups acquiring nuclear devices.

■ E. J. Katzenbach Jr. and G. Z. Hanrahan, 'The Revolutionary Strategy of Mao Tse-Tung', in F. M. Osanka (ed.), *Modern Guerrilla Warfare: Fighting Communist Guerrilla Movements, 1941–1961* (New York: Free Press, 1962). This study provides an unrivalled analysis of the Maoist theory of protracted revolutionary warfare.

■ W. Laqueur, *The New Terrorism: Fanaticism and the Arms of Mass Destruction* (New York: Oxford University Press, 1999). This title is an expansion of the author's article 'Postmodern Terrorism', *Foreign Affairs*, 75/5 (1996), 24–37, and deals with present-day concerns about nuclear terrorism.

■ T. E. Lawrence, 'The Evolution of a Revolt', *The Army Quarterly*, 1/1 (1920), 55–69. The article is a distilled account of the strategy used during the Arab Revolt that was embellished considerably when published as *Seven Pillars of Wisdom: A Triumph* (London: Jonathan Cape, 1935), 188–96.

■ Mao Tse-tung, *Selected Military Writings of Mao Tse-Tung* (Peking: Foreign Languages Press, 1966). A collection of Mao's most important tracts that provides insights into the evolution of his military thought on irregular warfare.

■ Carlos Marighella, *Minimanual of the Urban Guerrilla* (1969). See http://www.baader-meinhof.com/index.htm. Although repetitive and tactical, this work was the handbook for Marxist terrorists in the 1970s and 1980s.

■ R. Munck, 'Deconstructing Terror: Insurgency, Repression and Peace', in R. Munck and P. L. de Silva (eds.), *Postmodern Insurgencies: Political Violence, Identity Formation and Peacemaking in Comparative Perspective* (New York: St Martin's Press, 2000). Provides a postmodern analysis of the role of identity in present-day terrorist activities.

■ **A. H. Nasution, *Fundamentals of Guerrilla Warfare* (New York: Praeger, 1965).** A useful, if highly derivative, account of the practical problems associated with conducting both insurgent and counter-insurgent campaigns—from an author with experience in both.

■ **R. Peters, 'The New Warrior Class', *Parameters*, 24/2 (1994), 16–26.**

■ **M. Sageman, *Understanding Terror Networks* (Philadelphia: University of Pennsylvania Press, 2004).** A social network analysis of Al-Qaeda.

■ **A. P. Schmid, A. J. Jongman, *et al.*, *Political Terrorism: A New Guide to Actors, Authors, Concepts, Data Bases, Theories, and Literature* (New Brunswick, NJ: Transaction Books, 1988).** A very good reference source with a comprehensive definition of terrorism.

■ **R. Taber, *The War of the Flea: Guerrilla Warfare Theory and Practice* (London: Paladin, 1972).** Interesting for a variety of reasons, including demonstrating the dangers associated with getting to close to one's subject matter.

■ **R. Thompson, *Defeating Communist Insurgency: Experiences from Malaya and Vietnam* (London: Chatto & Windus, 1966).** The most influential work of its day as it provided counter-insurgency advice derived from the author's role in the successful Malayan campaign.

■ **R. Trinquier, *Modern Warfare: A French View of Counterinsurgency* (New York: Praeger, 1964).** Remains the ultimate expression of the ends justifying the means. Full text is available online at http://www.cgsc.army.mil/carl/resources/csi/trinquier/trinquier.asp. A less euphemistic and unapologetic companion volume is P. Aussaresses, *The Battle of the Casbah: Terrorism and Counter-Terrorism in Algeria, 1955–1957* (New York: Enigma, 2005).

■ **M. van Creveld, *The Transformation of War* (New York: Free Press, 1991).** Focuses on the contemporary importance of guerrilla warfare.

■ **Wilkinson, P., *Terrorism and the Liberal State* (London: Macmillan, 1986).** Along with the author's subsequent *Terrorism and Democracy: The Liberal State Response* (London: Frank Cass, 2001), standard works on dealing with the threat of terrorism while upholding democratic values and principles.

WEB LINKS

● Terrorism Knowledge Base **http://www.tkb.org/Home.jsp** A premier web portal that offers links to terrorism centres and programmes, as well as information on terrorist groups, profiles, incidents, and other research resources.

● This is Baader-Meinhof **http://www.baader-meinhof.com/index.htm** This site contains excellent information on the Baader-Meinhof group. It has a section for students and researchers as well as links to or the complete text of seminal works such as Carlos Marighella's 'Minimanual of the Urban Guerrilla' **http://www.baader-meinhof.com/students/resources/print/minimanual/manualtext.html**

● US Marine Corps Small Wars Center of Excellence **http://www.smallwars.quantico.usmc.mil/search/resources.asp** This features links to a comprehensive bibliography of works on counterinsurgency, as well as current and historical doctrine manuals and online books and articles.

● The University of New Brunswick Saint John Ward Chipman Library Low Intensity Conflict and Terrorism Subject Bibliography **http://www.unbsj.ca/library/subject/terror.htm** This research guide provides one of the most comprehensive set of links to irregular warfare resources, including legal documents, annual reports, and handbooks, across a range of subjects.

● **http://www.marx2mao.com** Provides the full text of most of Mao's writings on guerrilla warfare as well as those of V. I. Lenin.

● The Counter-terrorism Blog **http://counterterror.typepad.com/** A weblog for those looking for the latest information on terrorist attacks as well as links to opinion pieces, articles, and books from a number of counter-terrorism experts.

 Visit the Online Resource Centre that accompanies this book for lots of interesting additional material http://www.oxfordtextbooks.co.uk/orc/baylis_strategy2e/.

9

Strategy for a New World: Combating Terrorism and Transnational Organized Crime

PHIL WILLIAMS

✔ **Reader's Guide**

The world of the twenty-first century is one in which transnational non-state actors such as criminal organizations and terrorist networks pose new threats to security. This chapter shows that both transnational criminal organizations and global terrorist organizations are very rational in their behaviour and place great reliance on network structures. The chapter also looks at similarities and differences between criminals and terrorists as well as the possibility of closer relationships between the two kinds of groups. It argues that although such synergies could occur they are currently less important than terrorist use of organized crime methods to fund themselves. The chapter also examines the strategies devised by the United States to combat transnational organized crime and terrorism and highlights their fundamental shortcomings. These shortcomings include poor implementation by government hierarchies which are far less flexible and agile than criminal and terrorist networks.

Introduction

States are good at dealing with security threats from other states. This is not surprising. The state system, which has dominated world politics since the Treaty of Westphalia in 1648, has been characterized both by frequent warfare and by the evolution of diplomatic norms and conventions. States have typically made both peace and war with one another. State departments and foreign offices have largely been responsible for developing and implementing cooperative relations; military forces have provided the wherewithal when diplomacy has failed or been deemed inadequate. Great powers have become particularly adept at the use of force, as the United States demonstrated with its military intervention in Iraq and the toppling of Saddam Hussein. As the subsequent insurgency has demonstrated, however, states are less effective when dealing with challenges posed by non-state and transnational actors. The Iraqi insurgency is a mix of indigenous groups sharing only a deep antipathy to foreign occupation and transnational global jihadists who have come to Iraq to fight for the cause. Moreover, although some elements of the insurgency have support from Syria and Iran, others are self-sufficient, using crimes such as kidnapping to fund the struggle (Looney 2005). Whatever the source of funds, though, the continuing insurgency shows that conventional military superiority does not easily translate into the capacity to impose political stability.

In many respects, the difficulties that the United States is having in Iraq are symptomatic of the broader difficulties that states face in dealing with transnational threats to security and stability in the twenty-first century. It is arguable that the world has entered a new era characterized by a transition from the orderly if often extreme violence of the Westphalian system to a disorderly, fragmented, system in which states have lost the monopoly of the use of violence both domestically and internationally. The characteristics of this new world are perhaps most usefully captured in the notion of the 'new middle ages' or neo-medievalism which, as Philip Cerny (2005) has pointed out, is characterized by: 'competing institutions and overlapping jurisdictions of . . . state, non-governmental and private interest groups; fluid territorial boundaries both within and across states; increasing inequality and isolation of marginalized groups, multiple and fragmented loyalties, contested property rights, and the spread of geographical and social "no go areas" where the rule of law . . . no longer extends'. In such a system, security is no longer about the clash of great powers and strategy is no longer simply about the use or threat of military force.

With this in mind, this chapter—starting from Sun Tzu's contention that it is essential to know the enemy—explains why transnational threats from terrorism and organized crime have become so formidable. It then considers the strategies that have been articulated to respond to these threats. In effect, combating terrorism and organized crime requires a multilateral cooperative approach towards both law enforcement and military measures, as well as unilateral defensive measures initiated by governments to protect potential targets and to mitigate damage in the event that protection fails. Yet devising such strategies is far easier than implementing them.

The Evolution and Nature of the Threat

Neither organized crime nor terrorism is new. Italy, Japan, China, and the United States are all countries in which organized crime flourished for much of the twentieth century. Similarly, terrorism has long been a weapon of the weak against the strong and has been employed by anarchists, nationalists, anti-colonialists, and by political and religious extremists. Yet, in the decade after the end of the cold war and fuelled in large part by globalization, both terrorism and organized crime morphed into far more formidable threats than ever before.

Globalization as motivator and facilitator

Globalization has had paradoxical consequences for both transnational organized crime and international terrorism, acting as both motivator and facilitator. This is not entirely surprising. Although globalization has had many beneficial consequences, it has losers as well as winners—and the pain for the losers can be enormous. Indeed, globalization has had a disruptive impact on patterns of employment, on traditional cultures, and on the capacity of states to deal with problems facing citizens within their jurisdictions, as well as problems that span multiple jurisdictions. In some instances, globalization has created massive economic dislocation that has pushed people from the legal economy to the illegal. In other cases, globalization has been seen as merely a cover for Western, and especially the United States', cultural and economic domination—domination that has created enough resentment to help fuel what has become the global jihad movement.

At the same time, globalization has acted as a facilitator for a whole set of illicit activities ranging from drugs and arms trafficking to the use of large-scale violence against innocent civilians. Many observers assumed that in the post-cold war world, democracy, peace, stability and order could easily be exported from the advanced post-industrialized states to areas of conflict and instability (Singer and Wildavsky 1993). In fact the opposite has occurred. Al-Qaeda was able to attack the United States homeland while based in Afghanistan, thereby illustrating what Robert Keohane described as the transformation of geography from a barrier to a connector (2002: 275). Indeed, one of the most important characteristics of a globalized world is that the interconnections among different parts of the world are dense, communication is cheap and easy, and transportation and transmission, whether of disease, crime, or violence, are impossible to stop. Transnational networks link businessmen, families, scientists, and scholars; they also link members of terrorist networks and criminal organizations. In some cases, networks are successfully integrated into the host societies. In other instances, however, migrants find themselves in what Castells called 'zones of social exclusion' (1998: 72). Muslim immigration from North Africa and Pakistan to Western Europe, for example, has resulted in marginalization and alienation that were evident in the widespread riots in France in the late months of 2005 and that have also helped to fuel radical Islamic terrorism in Western Europe. Moreover, for second and third generation immigrants who have limited opportunities in the licit economy, the illegal economy and either petty crime or organized crime can appear as an attractive alternative. Ethnic networks of this kind can provide both cover and recruitment opportunities for transnational criminal and terrorist organizations. In effect, therefore, globalization has acted as a force multiplier for both criminal and terrorist organizations, providing them with new resources and new opportunities.

Criminal and terrorists as rational actors

One reason that criminal and terrorist organizations have been able to exploit these new resources and opportunities so effectively is that they are highly rational in their behaviour. In effect, both organized crime and terrorism can be understood in classic Clausewitzian terms. Organized crime is, in essence, a continuation of business by criminal means, while terrorism is the continuation of politics through the use of indiscriminate violence by non-state actors. Terrorists can be understood as political individuals, groups, and movements demanding change and using violence to bring it about. It is the peculiar combination of means and ends that gives terrorists their very identity and demarcates them from other social and political activists. Ironically, from the perspective of the victims and many observers, terrorist violence is often dismissed as senseless, particularly as it is usually targeted against innocent civilians. In fact, terrorism is a highly instrumental activity. Terrorists are as Clausewitzian in their resort to violence as most states; for them violence is no more and no less than a continuation of politics by other means. Of course, terrorists do not have the sanction of the state to endow their violence with the legitimacy of warfare. Even more important, the deliberate targeting of civilians or non-combatants is something that has always been regarded as outside the laws of warfare—even though these laws have sometimes been honoured in the breach more than the observance. Nevertheless, acts of terror for the terrorist are the equivalent in utilitarian terms of acts of war for the state. The political objectives being sought by the perpetrators can range from efforts to expel an occupying power from one's country, to the ambitious endeavour of Osama Bin Laden to recreate a global caliphate. In this connection, the United States is a major target of Al-Qaeda because it is the 'far enemy' which supports the 'near enemy', the existing regimes in the Arab world.

Although transnational criminal organizations and global terrorists emerged during the same period, are highly rational, and carefully design strategies to achieve certain objectives, the objectives themselves are very different. Terrorists organizations are quintessentially political organizations; even if they are motivated by religious fundamentalism, their actions are designed to bring about political change. And at the core of this effort to bring about change is the choice of targets and weapons. Terrorist attacks, however, are still best understood as the final result of a whole set of activities that includes fund-raising, recruitment, training, the development of special skills, and attack preparation that can take months or even years. In the case of criminal organizations, the objectives centre around profit. In order to obtain these profits, criminal organizations develop what are, in effect, illicit business strategies. In this sense whether they are marketing cocaine and heroin or trafficking in illegal arms or women and children, their business strategies are not that different from the ways in which companies like Coca-Cola and Pepsi market their soft drinks. At the same time, because the products and the activities are illicit, and normal business rules do not apply, steps have to be taken to manage risks—whether from ruthless competitors seeking to take over market share or from governments and law enforcement agencies seeking to put them out of business. This process of risk management operates at several levels and includes risk avoidance or risk prevention strategies, efforts to combat or control risk, and strategies of mitigation. Risk avoidance is often done through what can be termed jurisdictional arbitrage, in which criminal organizations operate from countries where the state is weak and can do little to combat them effectively. Where the state does confront organized crime, criminal risk management strategies include the use of corruption and violence to neutralize the criminal justice system, to circumvent customs and immigration controls, and ultimately to perpetuate the weakness of the state and maintain the territory as a safe haven. At the third level, criminal organizations adopt strategies to mitigate damage and to maximize resilience. One component of this is the adoption of networked structures that are readily compartmentalized and facilitate regeneration in the event that part of the network is destroyed.

Terrorist and criminal use of violence

Terrorist attacks are designed for maximum psychological impact. The old adage, coined by Brian Jenkins, that terrorism is theatre remains valid (Hoffman 1998: 132). Indeed, in an era of globalization and instant communications through global media, terrorism has become global theatre. At the same time, as Hoffmann has noted, terrorism has also become more lethal (1998). Yet killing more people is not inconsistent with the notion of global theatre. The Mumbai bombings of 1993, the Al-Qaeda attack on the World Trade Center, the Chechen assault on the school in Beslan, and the attacks in Madrid and London, were all designed to kill a lot of people and to obtain maximum media coverage. The World Trade Center attack, in particular, was so spectacular that, perhaps more than any other single event, it raised the prospect that Al-Qaeda would try to follow it with the use of weapons of mass destruction (WMD).

Such an attack would not be entirely unprecedented. Chemical weapons were used in 1995 when the cult group, Aum Shinrikyo released sarin gas on the Tokyo underground. Even though the delivery systems consisting of plastic bags and sharpened umbrellas were relatively primitive, the attack resulted in about 5,000 casualties. There was also a very close call in Jordan in 2004 when terrorists were thwarted while implementing the early stages of what would have been a major chemical attack. Had this attack succeeded it is likely that the casualties would have been somewhere in the region of 20,000 to 80,000. Even more serious is the possibility that terrorists will succeed in acquiring a radiological bomb or a small nuclear weapon. The calculation for terrorist organizations such as Al-Qaeda is whether this would create so much revulsion that it would outweigh the political gains as well as the emotional satisfaction that would come from such a major attack on the United States or its allies. To rely on self-restraint on the part of the terrorists, however, would be a huge mistake. The use of WMD by a terrorist organization would be a product of rational calculation—not least because of the difficulties of retaliation in kind. The fact that terrorist organizations are increasingly elusive distributed networks makes it very difficult for governments to carry out massive retaliatory strikes against them—and, therefore, to deter them. The implication is that the trend in terrorist lethality is likely to continue to increase.

In a few instances—most notably Italy in the early 1990s and Colombia in the late 1980s and early 1990s—criminal organizations have also embarked on campaigns of terror against the state and its citizenry. This appropriation of terrorist methods, however, is rare—not least because it tends to galvanize the state into mobilizing all possible resources against the organization. It typically occurs when the state launches a frontal assault on the criminals, as it did in Colombia through the policy of extraditing drug traffickers to the United States. Alternatively, if the political elites fail to provide the protection that the criminals have come to expect through the development of symbiotic relationships, then once again organized crime will resort to a campaign of violence. This occurred in Italy in the early 1990s when the Mafia felt that it had been betrayed by the Christian Democratic Party, with which it had long enjoyed a mutually beneficial relationship. Significantly, in both cases, organized crime paid a high price for a frontal assault. It is not surprising, therefore, that criminal use of terrorist campaigns is relatively rare.

This is not to suggest that criminal organizations are reluctant to resort to violence. Contract killings, in particular, have been a major feature of organized crime throughout the former Soviet Union. Victims have included prominent reformist politicians, investigative journalists, bankers, businessmen, and rival criminals. In the energy sector, and in the aluminum industry in the mid-1990s, struggles for control resulted in a spate of contract killings. Moreover, it is clear that criminal organizations use violence as part of their efforts to protect themselves and to advance their economic and financial interests. In effect, criminal organizations use contract killings to remove threats, whether from politicians, law enforcement personnel, journalists, or rivals. They also use such killings as a means of removing obstacles to their takeover of legitimate businesses—although in some cases only as a last resort after intimidation tactics have failed. For the most part, therefore, the violence is selective rather than random and usually is a matter of 'business'. In some cases, it is bound up with political rivalry. In Odessa in the mid-1990s, for example, the Mayor and the Oblast Governor, in effect, waged war against one another, and both were in league with major criminal organizations. At issue was control of resources, especially oil, moving through Odessa. Sometimes, of course, the conflicts are over control of criminal routes and illicit markets rather than legitimate businesses. In 2004 and 2005 on Mexico's northern border, for example, there was a series of killings—many taking place in Nuevo Laredo—as the Cardenas drug trafficking organization and the group led by Chapo Guzman struggled for dominance. Both employed paramilitary forces and on occasion the violence spilled over into the United States. Questions of status can also create clashes in the criminal world, and internecine warfare among criminal organizations is sometimes sparked by no more than an insult or personal antipathy.

Criminal use of corruption

As well as violence, however, transnational criminal organizations use corruption as a major instrument—and target it is as carefully as they do the use of violence. In essence, there are two main purposes of corruption. Instrumental or operational corruption is designed to facilitate cross-border trafficking activities. The targets are customs and immigration officers charged with the responsibility for protecting the borders. In this sense, corruption payments are simply the cost of doing business. Perhaps even more serious is what Ethan Nadelmann (1993) termed 'systemic corruption' where organized crime seeks to corrupt policy-makers, bureaucrats, law enforcement personnel, and members of the judiciary in order to maintain a low-risk environment from which they can operate with a high level of impunity. In Mexico, for example, during the Presidency of Carlos Salinas, drug traffickers bought the protection of his brother, Raul Salinas, who eventually ended up with over 130 million dollars in Swiss bank accounts. While terrorists can also use corruption, this is less important for them than finding states which have some sympathy for the cause and provide a territorial safe haven or financial support. When Al-Qaeda was based in Sudan in the early 1990s, Bin Laden invested heavily in infrastructure projects for the country. Although it is possible that some politicians also received corrupt pay-offs, the investments were designed primarily to benefit the country as a whole rather than line the pockets of politicians.

Criminal and terrorist use of alliances

If criminal organizations can be understood as highly rational in their use of violence and corruption, they can also be understood as illicit businesses, and—not surprisingly, in a globalized world—have developed in parallel with licit business. Just as licit business has become more global through the use of cooperative alliances, so too has transnational organized crime. Criminal organizations have developed stable supplier relationships with one another as well as tactical and even strategic alliances. Since the fall of the Medellin and Cali drug trafficking organizations, for example, Colombian drug traffickers have truncated the scope of their activities—primarily to avoid direct confrontation with United States law enforcement and intelligence agencies—and have supplied cocaine to Mexican groups which then bring it into the United States. Moreover as some groups have developed specialized capabilities such as money laundering, other groups have turned to them for assistance. There have even been cases in which ethnic antipathy has not prevented cooperation for mutual gain. Serbs and Albanians, for example, have been known to cooperate in the trafficking of women through the Balkans. Some observers have even sounded warnings about criminal 'summit meetings' (Raine and Cilluffo 1994: 120) and it is clear that, on occasion, leaders of major criminal organizations have met with one another to minimize conflict, carve out spheres of influence, and even initiate cooperative ventures. Characterizing such meetings as summits, however, is a misnomer that oversimplifies the criminal world: there is no single leader of Russian, Italian, Albanian, Chinese, or Nigerian organized crime who can speak on behalf of all the criminal organizations in the country. Nevertheless, the impulse towards cooperation is a very real one and meetings among group leaders can be an important facilitator of such cooperation.

The use of cooperation is also an important characteristic of Al-Qaeda and its leadership of the global jihad. Even prior to September 2001—after which Al-Qaeda was forced on the defensive by the United States response to the attacks—Bin Laden had been very successful in cultivating a whole series of affiliate organizations that shared Al-Qaeda's objectives. These included the Abu Sayyaf Group in the Philippines and Jemaah Islamayah in Indonesia as well as the GSPC and the Moroccan Islamic Combatant Group in Western Europe. These groups have a high degree of autonomy but have received financial support and training from Al-Qaeda and clearly embrace the same cause. Indeed, whereas criminal cooperation is predominantly a matter of expediency and mutual advantage, terrorist cooperation has far more to do with shared values and objectives.

Criminal and terrorist reliance on networks

As suggested above, transnational criminal organizations rely heavily on network structures for their operations. This is not to deny the importance of leadership within the organization; nor is it to claim that criminal organizations lack any hierarchy. In some cases the network is directed by a clear leadership node; in others it operates much more through what can be described as a transactional network, in which illicit goods are moved through a series of independent brokers who have at least a degree of trust in one another. In some cases the network is held together by ties of family, kinship, clan loyalties, or common ethnicity; in others the trust within the network, such as it is, comes from knowledge of and experience with other participants. Whether it is a tight directed network or a loose transactional network, however, the network form provides the flexibility, agility, and adaptability that are essential for operating in the licit or illicit global market-place. As Moises Naim has noted,

    networks are simultaneously global and local. Their ability to exploit their international mobility at great speed and their deep entrenchment within local power structures give them a huge advantage over the national or local governments that try to contain them . . . Survival hinges on the networks' ability to recombine, form collaborations, and dissolve them with equal ease, forging new markets and always keeping a step ahead.

(2005: 34)

Many terrorists including the global jihad movement, are also highly reliant on networks. This was evident, although not widely recognized, prior to 11 September 2001. Indeed, one way to understand the training camps in Afghanistan and elsewhere is that they were—and are—exercises not only in the development of terrorist skills and capabilities but also in the development of networks of individuals who could subsequently come together in cells to carry out attacks. Although it has become fashionable to claim that Al-Qaeda has become much more of a network since the United States destroyed its safe haven in Afghanistan and put the leadership on the defensive, Al-Qaeda has always had this network quality. Indeed, a key part of Bin Laden's strategic genius is the way he established himself as a bridge-builder or boundary spanner, infusing groups as different as Jemaah Islamayah in Indonesia and the Salafists for Call and Combat in Western Europe with a common sense of purpose.

In many respects, transnational networks are ideal organizations for criminal and terrorist operations in a globalized world. Networks are distributed and even though they often have a core, the transnational distribution makes it difficult for states to attack their centre of gravity. Moreover, networks are agile and highly adaptable, often making it difficult for bureaucratic governments—which are accountable to comptrollers and lawyers as well as parliaments and publics—to respond in a timely and effective manner. This is not to deny that networks can sometimes exhibit serious vulnerabilities. The Al-Qaeda network in Western Europe, for example, was characterized by dense communication connections between individual cells in France, Britain, Italy, and Spain. Such close coupling was a major vulnerability and meant that the take-down of a cell in one country would often provide information about cells elsewhere. The result was often a series of cascading arrests that until the Madrid and London bombings proved very effective in preventing attacks. As Madrid and London revealed, however, some cells emerge at the local level and, although they tend to be connected to the broader network, they are very difficult for governments and law enforcement agencies to detect prior to an attack. Not surprisingly, the earlier successes of many West European governments in thwarting terrorist attacks were overshadowed by the failures to prevent the bombings in Madrid in March 2004 and in London in July 2005.

In many respects, these attacks highlight one of the major differences between the threat posed by transnational organized crime and that posed by terrorism. The terrorist threat is rather like smallpox—when it erupts it is immediate and devastating in its impact. Transnational organized crime, in contrast, is rather more like AIDS: it breaks down the defences of the body politic, using corruption as a selectively targeted instrument to weaken or neutralize law enforcement, the judiciary, and even the government as a whole. Moreover, transnational criminal activities such as trafficking in arms or smuggling of aliens pose a direct challenge to the ability of states to determine who or what enters their territory. Even though this notion of sovereignty as territorial control has never been absolute, in the era of globalization, it is particularly fragile.

Synergies between organized crime and terrorism?

One major concern has been possible synergies between organized crime and terrorism. The smuggling of nuclear material from the former Soviet Union by amateur and opportunistic criminals, smuggling networks, and, in some cases, sophisticated criminal organizations, has raised the spectre of material sale to terrorists who could then use it to create either a crude nuclear device or a radiological weapon or 'dirty bomb'. Moreover, cooperation is something that could provide powerful benefits for each kind of group in terms of fund-raising and resource generation, combating government agencies, and enhanced reach and effectiveness. Yet, there is little evidence of a nexus of cooperative relations between criminal and terrorist organizations. There is some cooperation to be sure, and it is clear that, on occasion, terrorists turn to what one intelligence analyst described as 'criminal service providers' for such things as false documents and people smuggling capabilities. Supplier relationships involving drugs and weapons have also been developed, although these appear to be driven by mutual convenience and opportunity rather than any convergence of objectives. Yet, the possibility of much closer links between terrorists and criminals cannot be ruled out. One area where such linkages seem likely to develop is prison, which helps to foster bonding mechanisms that can lead to unlikely alliances after prisoners have been released. In some cases, members of criminal organizations will maintain linkages with terrorists and could provide the weapons or logistic support that facilitates a terrorist attack. In other cases, however, the criminals might actually be converted to Islam and embrace the global jihad. In these circumstances, the result is not cooperation so much as integration. A prime example of this—and one that could easily be replicated in the future—occurred in Spain where members of a small but well-established Moroccan drug trafficking organization led by Jamal Ahmidan, became radicalized and were subsequently integrated into the cell that carried out the Madrid bombings. The contribution of the radicalized drug traffickers is difficult to overestimate: they provided the finance, the logistics, the safe houses, and the connections that enabled the cell to acquire the explosives. Indeed, without their resources and expertise, it is unlikely that the attacks on the trains would have taken place, and certainly not on such a destructive scale. This trend towards radicalization of criminals is likely to become stronger in both Western Europe and the United States, and will significantly enhance the capacity of terrorists to carry out attacks with high levels of casualties.

If criminal–terrorist cooperation is a dangerous trend, however, another phenomenon is currently even more evident: the appropriation of organized crime methods by terrorists in order to fund the cause. As the United States and the international community clamped down on Islamic charities that had been used to fund terrorist activities, Al-Qaeda's affiliated networks as well as individual cells were compelled to become more self-reliant for funds. The Abu Sayyaf Group in the Philippines, for example, has obtained considerable funding through kidnapping and extortion as well as through some limited involvement in drug trafficking. In Western Europe, the trend, if anything, is even more pronounced. As one astute observer has noted, 'Along with drug trafficking, fraud of every sort is a growth industry for European jihadists. Popular scams include fake credit cards, cell phone cloning, and identity theft—low level frauds that are lucrative, but seldom attract the concerted attention of authorities' (Kaplan 2005b: 46). In addition, European jihadists are heavily involved in human smuggling, an activity where they appear to have established cooperative linkages with the Neapolitan Camorra. (Kaplan 2005b: 46) Indeed, the more terrorists behave as criminals to raise money for the cause, the more likely they are to come into contact and cooperate with traditional criminal organizations interested in profit not politics.

This increased self-reliance of terrorist networks makes them difficult to detect unless local law enforcement is sensitive to the possibility that certain kinds of criminal activities are likely to be terrorist related. Developing this sensitivity has to be one of the key components of counter-terrorism strategy—although this also requires an ability to transcend bureaucratic obstacles to information-sharing, something that is not easy. Indeed, although the United States has developed explicit strategies to counter both organized crime and terrorism, these strategies still suffer from serious shortcomings, not least at the level of implementation.

KEY POINTS

- Globalization has helped to bring terrorism and organized crime together to form a formidable contemporary threat.

- Both terrorists and criminals can be thought of in Clausewitzian terms as rational actors.

- Terrorist violence is increasing in scale and although criminals use violence selectively it can sometimes take the form of terrorism.

- Apart from violence transnational criminal organizations also use corruption as a major instrument.

- Terrorists and criminals increasingly use alliances and network structures as part of their operations.

- Effective counter-terrorism requires an awareness of the links between terrorists and criminals especially terrorist use of organized crime methods.

Strategies to Combat Organized Crime and Terrorism

Combating transnational organized crime

In 1998, the United States Department of State unveiled its International Crime Control Strategy to combat what it referred to as international organized crime. It identified eight goals: extend the first line of defence beyond US borders; protect the borders by attacking smuggling; deny safe haven to international criminals; counter international financial crime; prevent criminal exploitation of international trade; respond to emerging international crime threats; foster international cooperation and the rule of law; and optimize the full range of US efforts (*Transnational Organized Crime* 1998). Although the strategy articulated specific objectives that had to be attained in order to reach these goals, the strategy seems to have had little impact.

There are several reasons for this. First, in spite of growing international cooperation among national law enforcement agencies, law enforcement remains a national activity confined to a single territorial jurisdiction, while organized crime is transnational in scope. In effect, law enforcement still continues to operate in a bordered world, whereas organized crime operates in a borderless world. Second, although the United States placed a high priority on denying safe haven or sanctuary to international criminals, many states have limited capacity to enforce laws against organized crime. Consequently, transnational criminal organizations are able to operate from safe havens, using a mix of corruption and violence to perpetuate the weakness of the states from which they operate. Nowhere is this more evident than in Mexico, where a war for control of routes and markets on the northern border has led to violence spilling over into the United States. Third, all too often attacking transnational criminal organizations has been subordinated to other goals and objectives. In spite of the emphasis on attacking smuggling and smugglers, for example, this is not something which has been allowed to interfere with global trade. In effect, reaping the benefits of globalization, tacitly at least, has been deemed more important than combating transnational organized crime. Not surprisingly, therefore, as Moises Naim has pointed out, 'there is simply nothing in the cards that points to an imminent reversal of fortune for the myriads of networks active in illicit trade. It is even difficult to find evidence of substantial progress in reversing or even just containing the growth of these illicit markets'(2005: 221). Fourth, both transnational criminal organizations and the illicit markets in which they operate are highly adaptable. Law enforcement success against a particular organization, for example, tends simply to offer opportunities for its rivals to fill the gap. Moreover, the ability of organizations to move from one illicit product to another makes them even more difficult to combat. In recent years, for example, Burmese warlords have moved from opium to methamphetamine production and have become major suppliers to Asian markets for the drug.

Another problem with the United States strategy for combating transnational organized crime was that the Clinton administration failed to allocate resources commensurate with either the scale of the problem or the ambitious strategy for responding to what was clearly a growing phenomenon. A mismatch of this kind between objectives and resources can reduce strategy to little more than slogans. In some respects the situation became even worse after 11 September 2001, as priorities changed and resources were shifted to combating terrorism. In some instances, such as the effort to combat terrorist finances, the reregulation of financial systems made it slightly more difficult for criminals to launder money. In most respects, however, the strategy against transnational organized crime was largely deprived of both attention and resources. This has begun to change partly because of the massive growth in the United States of youth gangs with connections to Central America, and partly because of concerns about terrorist use of criminal activities for funding and terrorist cooperation with criminal organizations. The United States at the end of 2005 was developing a current assessment of the threat to US interests posed by transnational organized crime. Even so it seems likely that combating transnational crime will remain subordinate to the effort to combat global terrorism.

Combating Terrorist Networks

The Bush administration in February 2003 released its National Strategy for Combating Terrorism. Defining the struggle against terrorism as different from any other war in US history, the strategy noted that 'We will not triumph solely or even primarily through military might. We must fight terrorist networks and all those who support their efforts to spread fear around the world using every instrument of national power—diplomatic, economic, law enforcement, financial, information, intelligence, and military' (White House 2003: 1). At the same time, considerable emphasis was placed on direct action to disrupt, degrade and destroy what the report described as 'a flexible transnational network structure, enabled by modern technology and characterized by loose interconnectivity both within and between groups'(p. 8). This strategy, which was encapsulated in 4Ds—defeat, deny, diminish, and defend (p. 15)—incorporated a comprehensive attack on terrorist organizations through targeting not only the networks themselves but also their leadership, sanctuaries, and finances. The strategy also emphasized the need for a multi-lateral approach, noting that denying terrorist organizations sponsorship and sanctuary required working with willing and able states, enabling weak states, persuading reluctant states, and compelling unwilling states (pp. 20–1) Victory was defined in the strategy as the creation of a world in which 'our children can live free from fear and where the threat of terrorist attacks does not define our daily lives' (p. 12). In operational terms this means reducing the scope and capability of terrorist organizations to a point where terrorism is returned to the 'criminal domain' and is, in effect, unorganized, localized, non-sponsored, and rare (p. 14).

Although this strategy was often criticized because of its focus on defeating terrorism—which in itself is really only a tactic—in many respects the articulation was impressive. The strategy was comprehensive and included an effort to translate broad goals into specific objectives. It also emphasized the need for both defensive and offensive components.

The major defensive goals are to prevent attacks on the United States homeland and to prevent terrorists from acquiring WMD. This focus of the strategy is compelling and few would argue with the objective. There are, however, critics who suggest that the administration has done too little in terms of homeland security, simply creating a new massive bureaucratic department that has been given inadequate resources, in large part because of the war in Iraq. There are also those who fear that the effort to stop terrorists acquiring WMD has not been nearly as energetic and focused as it should have been.

Another important deficiency of the strategy—and this was also evident in the earlier strategy to combat international organized crime—was the absence of measures of effectiveness to measure progress. In a memorandum that was sent to a few select colleagues but subsequently leaked, Secretary of Defense Donald Rumsfeld exhibited considerable candour in noting the difficulties of finding appropriate measures of effectiveness for assessing the war on terrorism. As he put it:

> Today, we lack metrics to know if we are winning or losing the global war on terror. Are we capturing, killing or deterring and dissuading more terrorists every day than the madrassas and the radical clerics are recruiting, training and deploying against us? Does the US need to fashion a broad, integrated plan to stop the next generation of terrorists? The US is putting relatively little effort into a long-range plan, but we are putting a great deal of effort into trying to stop terrorists. The cost-benefit ratio is against us! Our cost is billions against the terrorists' costs of millions.

(*USA Today*, 16 Oct 2003)

Although some critics dismissed the leak as simply a political ploy by the Secretary of Defense, in fact the memo raised some very important—and often neglected—questions about the United States' strategy to combat global terrorism. The tone of the memo reflects what appears to be a genuine frustration about not only the absence of appropriate measures of effectiveness but also the difficulty of determining precisely what metrics are important. Earlier in the memo Rumsfeld had referred to United States' successes against the Al-Qaeda leadership, but the passage quoted suggests that he was less confident about the overall impact of these successes than many of the administration's public statements suggested. His concern that short-term successes might not easily translate into long-term gains is also very compelling. In effect, Rumsfeld's memo identified one of the key weaknesses in the strategy to combat Al-Qaeda and its associates.

Nor is this the only problem with the strategy. At the operational level, for example, attacking networks creates dilemmas that are difficult to resolve and requires trade-offs that are difficult to make. One component of a counter-network strategy, for example, is to aim for the targeted and selective removal of critical nodes which are crucial to the functioning of the network. In some instances, however, it might be better to monitor key communication nodes rather than degrade or eliminate them. Much depends on an assessment of the enemy's ability to adapt rapidly and effectively to operating without these nodes. If elimination will have a seriously crippling effect on the network, then this is likely to be the preferred option; if it only creates a short-term inconvenience and the network is able to adapt by reconstituting its communications through substitute nodes, however, then monitoring might be more effective. The key to determining this, however, is to map the network, put it under stress, and assess its adaptive mechanisms. In other words, network damage assessment is crucial to the whole process of devising a counter-network operational strategy. Yet this is also something that is very difficult to do in a comprehensive way when there is incomplete information about the network and its operations.

Another aspect of Rumsfeld's memo concerns the long term. Implicit in his comments is the expectation that the war on terrorism will be protracted. The implication, however, is that the United States needs to consider how to make the environment less conducive to terrorist recruiting. In fact, as David Kaplan has reported, considerable efforts have been expended in this direction. Although the effort was initially bedevilled by bureaucratic confusion and indecision, a lack of expertise on public diplomacy and propaganda, and the sheer difficulty of conceptualizing an appropriate response to Islamic radicalism, the classified edition of the National Strategy for Combating Terrorism reportedly includes an annex dealing with the war of ideas. This was crystallized into a strategy entitled Muslim World Outreach which recognizes that the United States has a vital interest in the future evolution of Islam and should make all efforts possible to strengthen the moderates within Islam and to create a more favourable image of the United States in both the Arab and the Islamic worlds (Kaplan 2005a). These objectives have been undermined by the United States intervention in Iraq, as well as Washington's support for Israel and for authoritarian regimes such as the Karimov government in Uzbekistan and the Saudi Arabian royal family. Even so, it remains essential to encourage moderate Islam, to isolate the radicals, and to undermine the legitimacy of terrorism as a ways of pursuing a radical Islamic agenda.

In this connection, it is clear that a major factor undermining the Bush administration's war on terrorism, has been the military involvement in Iraq. Based on spurious claims about both WMD and the link between Saddam Hussein and 11 September the attack was a profound strategic disaster. Not only did it take away resources from both the campaign in Afghanistan and the Department of Homeland Security, but it also provided what the National Intelligence Council's report described as a new breeding ground for Islamic terrorism (2004: 94). Indeed, the intervention is all too easily portrayed as United States imperialism and quest for domination over energy supplies, and disregard for Islamic societies and values. At the same time, it is very difficult for the United States to withdraw its forces until it has imposed or created a high degree of stability as it cannot readily allow Iraq to become another sanctuary for the global jihad movement.

For all the criticisms of the Bush administration's strategy to combat global terrorism—and these are valid criticisms—the strategy has some clear strengths. The administration has moved towards a holistic response rather than exclusive reliance on the military and law enforcement, has recognized the importance of long-term considerations as well as short-term imperatives, and has enunciated a clear set of goals and objectives. There are those who would put much more emphasis on dealing with the root causes of terrorism. The difficulty with this, however, is that so long as there is poverty and inequality, alienation and marginalization, terrorist organizations will have a ready flow of new recruits. And so long as there are fundamental differences over the shape of the world and the principles on which all or parts of it should be governed there will always be political and religious activists who are willing to resort to violence in an attempt to bring their conceptions to fruition.

Conclusions

In many respects, the threats posed to the United States and more broadly to the international community of states by transnational organized crime and terrorism can be understood as an important manifestation of the new phase in world politics in which some of the key interactions are between the state system and what James Rosenau (1990) termed the 'multi-centric system', composed of 'sovereignty-free actors'. In this connection, it is notable that the first serious challenge to United States hegemony in the post-cold war world came not from another state but from a terrorist network. Moreover, both criminals and terrorists have certain advantages over states: they are agile, distributed, highly dynamic organizations with a capacity to morph or transform themselves when under pressure. States in contrast are slow, clumsy, hierarchical, and bureaucratic and, although they have the capacity to bring lots of resources to bear on a problem, can rarely do this with speed and efficiency. As discussed above, in the United States war on terror, the strategy for the war of ideas was very slow to develop, not least because of inter-agency differences. The same has been true in the effort to combat terrorist finances. As the Government Accountability Office (2005) has noted, 'the U.S. government lacks an integrated strategy to coordinate the delivery of counter-terrorism financing training and technical assistance to countries vulnerable to terrorist financing. Specifically, the effort does not have key stakeholder acceptance of roles and procedures, a strategic alignment of resources with needs, or a process to measure performance'. Differences of perspective and approach between the Departments of State and Treasury have also seriously bedevilled the effort to 'enable weak states', one of the keys to the multilateral component of the administration's strategy to combat terrorism.

Similar problems have been evident in efforts to combat organized crime and drug trafficking. A striking example is the counter-drug intelligence architecture for the United States which has the Crime and Narcotics Center at CIA looking at the international dimension of drug trafficking, the National Drug Intelligence Center responsible for domestic aspects of the problem, the Treasury's Financial Crimes Enforcement Network focusing on money laundering, and the El Paso Intelligence Center responsible for tactical intelligence. Although this architecture provides clear roles and responsibilities, it also creates bureaucratic seams in the effort to understand and assess what is clearly a seamless process of drug trafficking and money laundering across borders. Although good information exchanges can ease this problem, the architecture is far from optimal.

Yet another problem is that governments have many objectives, whereas criminal and terrorist organizations have a much narrower focus. The result is that governments have to make many trade-offs, some of which are highly controversial. The Bush administration, for example, has chosen to emphasize surveillance at the expense of the privacy of its citizens, an approach that has provoked considerable protest from those who emphasize civil liberties, and generated unease even among many who do not. Yet, it is also clear that, prior to 11September 2001, possible indicators of an impending attack were missed because of legal inhibitions on information-sharing and certain kinds of investigation. Getting the balance right between security and privacy is an inherently difficult and controversial task.

The bottom line on all this is that, even though the United States has developed clear strategies for combating both organized crime and terrorism, the implementation of these strategies is clearly hindered by the dominance of governmental structures that were well-suited to the cold war against a slow, bureaucratic, ponderous adversary but are singularly ill-suited to combating agile transnational adversaries. In the final analysis, fighting terrorism and transnational organized crime is not only about strategy, it is also about appropriate organizational structures to implement strategy. And in that respect, terrorists and criminals have the advantage. The result is that the efforts of the United States and the international community to combat both crime and terrorism are unlikely to meet with unqualified success.

 QUESTIONS

1. What is the connection between globalization and the growth of organized crime and terrorism?

2. Can criminal and terrorist organizations truly be described as Clausewitzian?

3. What are the major similarities and differences between criminal and terrorist organizations?

4. Why do criminals and terrorist rely so heavily on network forms of organization?

5. Why was the US approach to the war on terror so slow to develop?

6. To what extent has Al-Qaeda established effective links with organized crime?

7. What are the major weaknesses in the United States' strategies to combat organized crime and terrorism?

8. Can these weaknesses be overcome or are they inherent in the United States' approach to strategy?

9. Can governments develop effective international strategies to combat organized crime and terrorism in a globalized world?

10. To what extent has the link between crime and terrorism brought a new phase in world politics?

FURTHER READING

■ **J. Arquilla and D. Ronfeldt (eds.), *Networks and Netwars* (Santa Monica: RAND, 2001).** An important set of readings on terrorist and criminal networks. The editors emphasize that it takes a network to defeat a network.

■ **D. Benjamin and S. Simon, *The Next Attack* (New York: Times Books, 2005).** This book offers an important critique of the Bush administration's strategy to fight terrorism and a series of recommendations for significantly strengthening the strategy.

■ **M. Berdal and M. Serrano (eds.), *Transnational Organized Crime and International Security* (Boulder, CO: Lynne Rienner, 2002).** This book is one of the few which explicitly discusses organized crime as a challenge to security.

■ **B. Hoffman, *Inside Terrorism* (New York: Columbia University Press, 1998).** This remains one of the most illuminating studies of contemporary trends in terrorism.

■ **M. Naim, *Illicit: How Smugglers, Traffickers, and Copycats are Hijacking the Global Economy* (New York: Doubleday, 2005).** This important study provides a very good overview of organized crime and illicit trade and its impact on the global economy.

■ **J. N. Rosenau, *Turbulence in World Politics* (Princeton: Princeton University Press, 1990).** Although written at the end of the cold war, this book offers an illuminating understanding of the dynamics of contemporary world politics.

 WEB LINKS

● **http://www.state.gov** The United States Department of State provides an annual assessment of global terrorism as well as the annual International Narcotics Control Strategy Report.

● **http://www.yorku.ca/nathanson/default.htm** This website run by the Nathanson Center for the Study of Organized Crime, at York University in Toronto is an excellent resource for studying transnational organized crime.

● **http://www.unodc.org/unodc/index.html** The website of the United Nations Office on Drugs and Crime highlights the efforts of the UN to combat organized crime, terrorism and corruption.

 Visit the Online Resource Centre that accompanies this book for lots of interesting additional material http://www.oxfordtextbooks.co.uk/orc/baylis_strategy2e/.

10

The Second Nuclear Age: Nuclear Weapons in the Twenty-first Century

C. DALE WALTON AND COLIN S. GRAY

Chapter Contents

- Introduction
- The First Nuclear Age
- Risks in the Second Nuclear Age
- Adapting to the Second Nuclear Age
- Conclusion

Reader's Guide

This chapter sets out to consider the role that nuclear weapons have played in international politics, both during the cold war and in the post-cold war era. In particular, a distinction is drawn between the spread of nuclear weapons to more states, which is creating an increasing threat to international security, and the decline in the absolute number of nuclear weapons due to the reductions in the nuclear arsenals of the United States and Russia. Some attention is also given to other contemporary issues like ballistic missile defences, the cultural dimensions of nuclear weapons acquisition, and the possibilities of terrorists using nuclear weapons in the future.

Introduction

Since their invention, nuclear weapons have played an important role in the international system, even though they have not been used in anger since 1945. During the cold war, both the United States and the Soviet Union built large and diverse nuclear arsenals which included a mix of many different types of weapons and delivery vehicles. During this era, academics and policy-makers struggled with many difficult issues related to these weapons, but in the United States and other North Atlantic Treaty Organization (NATO) countries special attention was paid to deterrence, particularly the use of nuclear weapons to deter the Soviet Union from launching an invasion of Western and Central European NATO countries. Thus, one might say that the main 'theme' of Western nuclear debate during the cold war was the use of nuclear weapons to prevent superpower war, either nuclear or conventional.

This First Nuclear Age—which lasted approximately from 1945 to the 1991 fall of the Soviet Union—was dominated by the Soviet and American superpowers, which first tested nuclear weapons in 1945 and 1949, respectively. Three other countries also became declared nuclear powers during the First Nuclear Age (Great Britain, France, and China), while at least three other polities (South Africa, Israel, and India) became undeclared nuclear states, but the arsenals of all of these countries combined were dwarfed by those of either of the two superpowers. As a result, serious thinking about nuclear issues tended to focus on the United States and Soviet Union—the cold war era was a bipolar one, and that fact was reflected in the superpower nuclear arsenals.

Today, Moscow and Washington still possess the world's largest nuclear arsenals, but international political circumstances have changed dramatically in recent years. The United States and Russia currently do not have a particularly antagonistic relationship, and the danger of a massive nuclear conflict in the foreseeable future appears small. However, in other respects, the international environment is more dangerous than it was during the cold war era. The world has transitioned into a Second Nuclear Age, in which these weapons will proliferate horizontally to more states, including very dangerous and unstable regimes. Therefore, the odds of a nuclear war occurring in any given year are much greater than was the case in the First Nuclear Age.

Our objective in this chapter is to explore the strategic role that nuclear weapons play in international politics and study how that role has changed over time. The transition from the First to the Second Nuclear Age receives particular attention, and the chapter demonstrates how horizontal proliferation, the spread of nuclear weapons to more states or other international actors, is creating new threats to the international security environment as an increasing number of states obtain these weapons even as the fears associated with the bipolar cold war stand-off are decreasing. (Vertical proliferation, by contrast, is an increase in the number of nuclear weapons. Thus, a country that has five nuclear weapons has proliferated vertically if it produces a sixth one. Today, however, the absolute number of nuclear weapons worldwide is decreasing because of the shrinking Russian and American nuclear arsenals.) The chapter explains briefly how ballistic missile defences (BMD) can influence the strategic utility of nuclear weapons. The notion of strategic culture also is relevant to this discussion, and the chapter explains how various states have diverse goals and unique strategic cultures which influence their nuclear acquisition and doctrine. Moreover, we will address the possible roles that nuclear weapons may play in the future, including their possible use by terrorists.

The First Nuclear Age

The first nuclear test occurred on 16 July 1945 in New Mexico, and less than one month later, on 6 and 9 August, these weapons were used against two Japanese cities, Hiroshima and Nagasaki. These devices—nicknamed 'Little Boy' and 'Fat Man'—differed in their designs, but both were fission nuclear weapons. These weapons were the fruit of the Manhattan Project, a massive 'crash program' to which the American government— worried that Nazi Germany might be the first country to obtain nuclear weapons— devoted billions of dollars and thousands of scientists, technicians, and other personnel.

For a brief time, the United States, being the only power capable of building nuclear devices, enjoyed an atomic monopoly. This monopoly was, however, very short-lived, partly because Soviet spies were providing data from the American nuclear programme to Moscow even as the (supposedly very secret) Manhattan Project was ongoing. In 1949, the Soviet Union tested its first nuclear weapon.

Within a few years, both Washington and Moscow built fission-fusion nuclear weapons (more commonly referred to as thermonuclear weapons), which were even more powerful than their fission predecessors. Thermonuclear weapons use fissile material as a trigger to compress two lighter elements (generally deuterium and tritium, two isotopes of hydrogen) so that they fuse to form helium. This enables larger yields—in essence, bigger explosions. In theory, there is no limit to the yields possible with thermonuclear weapons. Nuclear yields are measured in kilotons, thousands of tons of TNT (dynamite) equivalent, and megatons, millions of tons of TNT equivalent. A five kiloton weapon, for example, yields an explosion equivalent to 5,000 tons of TNT, while a two megaton warhead's explosion equals 2,000,000 tons of TNT.

BOX 10.1

Fissile Material

The most important fissile materials are uranium 235 (U_{235}) and plutonium 239 (P_{239}). These radioactive isotopes are difficult to acquire. A given quantity of mined uranium contains very little U_{235}; the latter must be separated from non-fissile uranium. Plutonium is not even found in nature—it is a by-product of nuclear processes guided by humans. The control of fissile materials is very important to preventing nuclear proliferation, but the generation of nuclear power requires fissile material. The International Atomic Energy Agency (IAEA) is tasked with ensuring that non-nuclear weapons countries which have nuclear power plants do not divert fissile material and use it to build nuclear weapons.

Almost immediately after the bombing of Hiroshima, a great debate began over the meaning of nuclear weapons for the future of international relations and, indeed, humanity itself. The first major text examining the impact on nuclear weapons on world politics was edited by Bernard Brodie and entitled *The Absolute Weapon*. The book's title is indicative of Brodie's feeling regarding the importance of these devices—like many other observers, he believed that nuclear devices were something other than 'normal' weapons and that their existence, in turn, would have a radical impact on the future course of international politics. Over the next several decades, a huge body of literature developed which addressed a myriad of issues related to the existence of nuclear weapons. For the purposes at hand, however, the most important writings addressed nuclear deterrence. In essence, nuclear deterrence examined how nuclear weapons could be used to prevent an opponent from undertaking an undesirable action.

In the context of the cold war, perhaps the most critical deterrence issue, from the Western perspective, was deterring the Soviet Union from undertaking an invasion of Western Europe. Throughout the cold war, the Soviet Union enjoyed an enormous advantage over NATO in conventional military forces (all forces except for weapons of mass destruction, a category which includes nuclear, chemical, biological, and radiological weapons, are considered conventional). Strategists struggled with how to ensure that Moscow would not attempt to conquer the vulnerable countries of Western Europe, and their answers almost invariably relied on nuclear deterrence.

Nuclear weapons were so devastating, it was generally believed, that Soviet leaders would not attack Western European countries if they were convinced that the United States would retaliate for this action by using nuclear weapons against the Soviet Union. This is known as a countervalue threat—something that Soviet leaders valued, in this case the Soviet homeland itself, was held hostage to their good behaviour. Another sort of deterrence threat is a counterforce threat—the warning that nuclear weapons would be used against the 'sinews' of state power: military forces, leadership targets, targets relevant to military command and control, and so forth. In general, one can say that the United States relied on a mix of countervalue and counterforce threats to deter the Soviet Union.

BOX 10.2

Credibility

Credibility is central to the success of any deterrence threat. If a threat is not credible—if, in short, the state being threatened does not believe that its foe will carry out the threat—it is likely to ignore deterrence warnings and do what it wishes. One might compare this to crime: if a would-be thief believes that it is very improbable that he will be caught when robbing a house, it is unlikely that he will be deterred. If, on the other hand, he believes that it is probable that he would be caught, it is likely that he will conclude that it is in his best interest not to rob the house. This is surety of punishment. A related concept is severity of punishment: the thief is more likely to be deterred if he believes that the punishment he would receive if caught would be heavy than if he assumes it would be light. Generally speaking, a deterrence threat that is both credible and severe is far more likely to deter an opponent than one that falls short in either, much less both, of these dimensions.

During the First Nuclear Age, the two superpowers each built enormous arsenals of tactical nuclear weapons (TNWs) and strategic nuclear weapons. The distinction between the two types of weapons is somewhat artificial but, as a rule of thumb, TNWs are delivered by means such as tactical aircraft, artillery, or short-range ballistic or cruise missiles. TNWs generally are intended for use in battle, against troop concentrations, ships, or similar targets. (The superpowers even developed nuclear depth charges for use against enemy submarines.) Strategic nuclear weapons, by contrast, usually are delivered at very long ranges by intercontinental ballistic missiles (ICBMs), submarine-launched ballistic missiles (SLBMs) of intercontinental range, or long-range heavy bombers. These weapons can strike deep into enemy territory, thousands of miles from the point at which they were launched.

The United States and Soviet Union accumulated tens of thousands of strategic and tactical warheads with an enormous variety of yields that ranged from less than one kiloton to tens of megatons. In many cases, several warheads were placed on a single delivery vehicle—the American MX ICBM, for example, was designed to carry up to ten multiple independently targetable re-entry vehicles (MIRVs). MIRVed warheads were first deployed in the 1970s. (Before this time, there had been missiles with several warheads, but they were not independently targetable, which meant they could not strike different targets.)

BOX 10.3

Terminology

Ballistic missile. A missile with rocket motors flies on a ballistic trajectory. Ballistic missiles carry a payload of conventional or WMD warheads, also known as re-entry vehicles. Early ballistic missiles were inaccurate and could only carry relatively small payloads for short distances, but advanced missiles can be of intercontinental range and carry a number of independently targetable warheads.

Cruise missile. A missile with an air-breathing motor; in essence a small, pilotless aircraft. Current models travel at subsonic speeds. Bombers can be equipped to carry nuclear-tipped cruise missiles.

Decapitation strike. An attack intended to destroy the leadership and command, control, and communications (C^3) network of an enemy nation.

Disarming strike. An attack that attempts to destroy an enemy's nuclear forces. If a disarming strike is successful, the enemy state will not be utterly destroyed, but will be militarily disadvantaged and compelled to negotiate a peace on the disarmer's terms.

Fallout. Radioactive debris resulting from a nuclear explosion. Heavier particles tend to settle in the area of the explosion, while lighter ones often travel great distances. Fallout contamination can result in serious, and even fatal, health effects.

Triad. The combination of SLBMs, ICBMs, and nuclear-armed long-range bombers that together comprise the strategic nuclear forces of the United States and Russia.

Adapted from Payne and Walton 2002: 162.

KEY POINTS

- Nuclear weapons have not been used in warfare since atomic bombs were dropped on Hiroshima and Nagasaki, Japan, in 1945.

- Nuclear weapons are categorized, along with chemical, biological, and radiological devices, as weapons of mass destruction.

- Competition in the building of nuclear weapons was very closely tied to the cold war between the United States and the Soviet Union and the theoretical models relating to deterrence that were built during that time reflect the bipolar competition between the two superpowers.

- Nuclear weapons are divided into a variety of categories, depending on their design, means of delivery, and other factors. Two of the most important distinctions are between fission and thermonuclear weapons and between tactical and strategic weapons.

Risks in the Second Nuclear Age

It would be excessive to claim that nuclear deterrence is either easy or always impossible in the twenty-first century. Deterrence concepts developed during the cold war continue to be useful when discussing today's challenges, but it perhaps is naïve to assume that twenty-first century actors—particularly, but not only, 'rogue' states such as Iran and North Korea—will act in a manner consistent with the assumptions of cold war deterrence theory. The assumptions regarding behaviour that underpin the body of deterrence theory simply are not universally applicable; every political culture is unique (indeed, every leader is unique), and it should not be expected that states always will act in a manner consistent with deterrence theory. Deterrence is not a panacea—threats, whether presently emerging or as-yet-unforeseen, cannot all be addressed successfully by consulting 'the Cold War Deterrence Manual'.

Far too often, observers of international politics simply assume that leaders will not undertake particular actions because it would not be in their best interest to do so—with 'best interest' being defined by the observer. Thus, it is widely assumed that North Korea or Iran would, for example, never provide nuclear devices to terrorists or pre-emptively or preventively attack South Korea or Israel with such weapons. In both of these extreme examples, this assumption likely is correct—certainly, Pyongyang and Tehran are aware that such actions would be extraordinarily risky. However, even a very high probability that an event will not occur is not the same as a certainty that it will not.

There are still a great many continuing controversies concerning the reliability of deterrence during the cold war. To claim that deterrence theory was proven to have worked 'as advertised' because there was no US–Soviet military conflict, much less a nuclear war, is to assume a causal relationship which may or may not have existed. Certainly, the United States attempted to deter Soviet military aggression, but whether American deterrence actually prevented war between the two powers is unknown and, ultimately, unknowable. History, unlike a laboratory experiment, cannot be repeated, and we have no 'control cold war' to compare to the real cold war.

If American strategists had not developed a sophisticated body of deterrence theory, perhaps a nuclear conflict would have occurred—*or perhaps not*. Similarly, perhaps a US–Soviet nuclear conflict would have occurred despite American deterrence if not for historical happenstance. Notably, in recent years, some scholars—taking advantage of access to previously unavailable Soviet archives—have argued that at the time of his death Soviet leader Josef Stalin may have been seriously contemplating a war against the West; perhaps a well-timed stroke (or poisoning) saved the world from nuclear war in the 1950s (Brent and Naumov 2003).

If we are unable to say with certainty that deterrence prevented the cold war from turning hot, we should be all the more cautious when attempting to predict the future behaviour of opponents whose decision-making is opaque and whose values are foreign to those prevailing in the West. To say that 'State X' will not commit a particular act because it would not be in its best interest to do so requires a judgement regarding the interests of that state. However, it is rare for all of a state's key leaders to hold essentially indistinguishable views on their country's well-being; for an outsider to simply assume that his own perspective inevitably will be reflected in that country's policy is perilous indeed.

It is important to recognize that leaders may have very different value hierarchies; what a British Prime Minister most treasures may be radically different from what his North Korean counterpart considers essential, and thus their conceptions of national interest may differ radically. This, in turn, has enormous implications for deterrence. A leader who places a very high value on the lives of his or her countrymen and/or on the national infrastructure is unlikely to undertake a nuclear attack if retaliation in kind can be expected. Cold war deterrence theory fits such cases very well, as the fear of punishment is likely to outweigh the benefits of aggressive behaviour in the leader's mind. However, traditional deterrence theory has little applicability to a leader with very different fears and motivations.

A good example of such a leader is Osama Bin Laden. He appears to place a higher value on his perceived religious duty than on personal comfort, or even survival; after all, if he was focused on material joys, he could have led a happy existence as an enormously wealthy construction executive. If he were able to obtain a nuclear device, it is plausible that he would attempt to use it regardless of the consequences for himself or even for Al-Qaeda as a whole. One might object that, as a non-state actor, Bin Laden is unusual and the attitudes of a state actor would be different, but such a presumption is based on little more than hope. After all, even great powers occasionally have been in the hands of leaders who were extreme risk-takers or placed certain goals above national survival, such as Adolf Hitler or Japanese leaders of the Second World War era who wished to see their country destroyed rather than accept the humiliation of surrendering to the Americans. One should not necessarily assume that the clerics who control Iran or the leaders of North Korea always will act cautiously.

Prudent leaders must factor in the risk of an unlikely event when making decisions; the mere fact that the use of nuclear weapons in a given situation may be imprudent, or even outright foolish, is no guarantee that such weapons will remain unused. This is not good news for the reliability of deterrence. It is especially troubling when one considers that the two states mentioned above are not the only unpredictable countries that now own, or may soon have, nuclear weapons.

BOX 10.4

Unstable Nuclear States: The Pakistani Case

In the Second Nuclear Age, certain unstable states possess or are attempting to acquire nuclear weapons, and it should be remembered how quickly, and radically, the governments of troubled countries can change. Pakistan provides one example. Although the current military government, which is headed by General Pervez Musharraf, seems fairly prudent, it is generally assumed that internal coup, civil war, or other events could lead to regime change in Pakistan. Musharraf may have power today, but tomorrow he could be deposed and the Pakistani nuclear arsenal could be in the hands of Islamist radicals. Today, India and Pakistan appear to have a reasonably stable deterrence relationship—one certainly could argue that mutual deterrence is working tolerably well in South Asia, and even that a common fear of nuclear usage prevented a hot war from breaking out between the two countries in 2002, but if a different government comes to power in Pakistan that stability could disappear. This highlights one of the dangers of horizontal proliferation to unstable countries—even if the government which obtains nuclear weapons is responsible, its successors may not be.

The simple answer to these uncertainties is to deny nuclear arsenals to rogue, or potentially rogue, states. However, there is every reason to believe that it will be impossible to do so consistently. Rather, we should expect the number of nuclear states to increase over time. This is not to say that there will be no nonproliferation victories. Some states seeking nuclear weapons will be dissuaded from acquiring them (as Libya apparently was by the United States), and on rare occasion a nuclear state may even denuclearize (as South Africa did).

It is, however, very unlikely that this means that the spread of nuclear weapons can be reversed overall. Knowledge about any technology can be expected to diffuse over time and nuclear weapons are an old invention—they were first built six decades ago. Unsurprisingly, there are increasing numbers of individuals from (currently) non-nuclear countries who are knowledgeable about nuclear technology. Moreover, given ongoing advances and concerns about the price of fossil fuels, it is quite likely that nuclear power is about to enjoy a worldwide revival in popularity, a development that would in turn make it all the more difficult to control the spread of fissile material. Although well-designed counterproliferation efforts can slow the spread of nuclear weapons, further proliferation should be regarded as being extremely likely. This, in turn, means that there will be more powers that possess the physical means to initiate nuclear war and, consequently, an increasingly complicated deterrence environment worldwide.

The 'Second Nuclear Age' is distinct from the first in a number of key respects, one of the most important of which is the increasing unreliability of deterrence. As nuclear weapons proliferate horizontally, the risk of nuclear war occurring *somewhere* on earth can be expected to increase—especially as many of the proliferating states are not models of good international citizenship. While nuclear weapons have not been used in anger since 1945, we cannot assume that this record necessarily will continue for another sixty years. Moreover, if a truly undeterrable leader ever comes to possess nuclear weapons and is determined to use them, deterrence would be impossible. Leaders ultimately *choose* to be deterred, which is to say that they decide not to accept the consequences that would flow from taking a particular action—in essence, they are frightened away from doing something which they otherwise would do. If, however, they are willing to accept the consequences of an action, they may do as they like.

Every state has a distinct strategic culture, and this has a deep influence on a country's decision-making. Strategic culture is an aspect of overall culture and, as such, is central to all of a country's strategic choices. While one can strive to be aware of how culture has shaped one's views, one cannot actually *escape* culture—an individual is a product of his/her life experiences, and culture plays an enormous influence is shaping those experiences. A strategic culture certainly reflects the general culture of a state's population, but also the specific subcultures of the individuals who make strategy. Therefore, one cannot extrapolate strategic culture simply by looking at the general culture of a country; one also must examine, for example, which classes and regions that state's political and military leaders come from, their education and ethical/religious attitudes (and how those may differ from the general population), and many other factors which shape their specific life experiences.

While it often is assumed, based on the experience of the cold war, that nuclear weapons make countries more cautious and therefore less likely to go to war, there is reason to doubt that this will be true in all cases. We know very little indeed about nuclear weapons decision-making in certain countries, such as North Korea. Moreover, it is impossible to know how a country such as Iran, which apparently does not yet have nuclear weapons, but likely soon will obtain them, will act once it possesses a nuclear arsenal. Also there are many questions about how willing a country such as China might be to risk nuclear war during a future crisis. Finally, cold war experience may not even provide deep insight into how Moscow might act in the future; strategic cultures change over time, and perhaps can change relatively quickly in a polity undergoing traumatic change, such as Russia has experienced since 1991.

In all likelihood, the countries that are most reliably predictable in regard to nuclear strategic decision-making are stable democracies which have a relatively long 'track record' of nuclear possession; states such as Great Britain, France, and United States would fit into this category. It is, however, far more difficult to predict reliably how a country such as North Korea, Iran, Russia, China, or Pakistan will act in the future. In the case of most of these countries, we have little trustworthy information about their nuclear doctrine. Doctrine guides countries in their use of military power, and in the case of nuclear weapons it helps lay out a 'roadmap' as to the circumstances in which these devices might be used. While the cold war superpowers proved very reluctant to use nuclear weapons in combat, there is no guarantee that all states will be similarly reluctant to do so. Indeed, governments which possess relatively weak conventional forces may see nuclear weapons as offering an inexpensive trump card which they may use against better-armed enemies.

Over time, we will have a clearer notion of how various nuclear states will use their arsenals in negotiations and conflict. In any case, however, it is clear that in this Second Nuclear Age deterrence must be carefully tailored to the cultural, political, military, and other characteristics of the state that one is endeavouring to deter. Not all leaders are similar to those individuals who led the USSR; even if deterrence truly 'worked' during the cold war, it should be assumed that deterrence theory as it developed during that period is not infallible and that deterrence failure is entirely possible.

Another difference between the two nuclear ages that likely will be critical relates to the deployment of missile defences. During the First Nuclear Age, the deployment of BMD was a matter of heated debate. BMD opponents warned that such defences would destabilize the nuclear balance between the superpowers and, therefore, encourage both countries to build more warheads so as to overwhelm the other side's BMD. This arms race and the general sense of instability might, it was feared, in turn increase the likelihood of a US–Soviet war. Regardless of whether the claims of BMD foes were accurate, the end of the First Nuclear Age has very much altered the international security environment. It was not unreasonable to believe that a superpower that already possessed thousands of nuclear weapons might build many thousands more. However, many of the small states constructing nuclear arsenals would be financially and technically incapable of building great numbers of missiles and warheads. In such a case, the fact that other states deploy BMD is unlikely to drive vertical proliferation. While some missile defence opponents worry that American construction of ballistic missile defences will 'force' countries with small nuclear arsenals to build many more warheads, in most cases they simply will not have the resources to do so.

In 1971, the United States and Soviet Union agreed to the Anti-Ballistic Missile (ABM) Treaty. This agreement barred both countries from constructing comprehensive national

---

Table 10.1 The Worldwide Growth of Nuclear Powers

Nuclear Weapons States	Date of Acquisition	Date of 1st Test
United States	1945	16 July 1945
USSR/Russia	25 December 1946	29 August 1949
China	1960–3 (exact unknown)	16 October 1964
United Kingdom	3 July 1948	3 October 1952
France	1959	3 December 1960
India	1966–70 (exact unknown)	18 May 1974
Pakistan	(exact unknown)	28 May 1998
North Korea	(exact unknown)	9 October 2006*
Israel	(exact unknown)	2 November 1966
South Africa	August 1977	22 September 1979
Belarus	25 December 1991	N/A
Kazakhstan	25 December 1991	N/A
Ukraine	25 December 1991	N/A

Other states suspected of past or present nuclear programs include: Algeria, Argentina, Brazil, Iran, Iraq, and Libya. Possession of nuclear weapons has never been confirmed for any of these states. While Israel and North Korea have also never confirmed their possession of nuclear weapons, overwhelming evidence indicates that they are NW states.

* This test occured while this book was in press.

missile defences (however, it did not absolutely ban all missile defences, as it allowed each power to maintain a very strictly limited BMD capability). The treaty was representative of a specific vision of deterrence based on mutual assured destruction (MAD), in which it was assumed that both the United States and the Soviet Union would not use nuclear weapons if they believed that, no matter how successful a first strike might be, it would be impossible to eliminate the ability of the other power to execute a devastating retaliatory strike. MAD, in short, envisioned deterrence stability as requiring that any nuclear war be

Table 10.2 Force Levels of Nuclear Weapons Worldwide 1945–2000: Declared Nuclear Powers

Date	Quantity	States Included
1945–1949	6–374	USA, USSR
1950–1960	374–22,069	USA, USSR, UK
1960–1970	22,069–38,153	USA, USSR, UK, France, China
1970–1980	38,153–54,706	USA, USSR, UK, France, China
1980–1990	54,706–55,863	USA, USSR, UK, France, China
1990–2000	55,863–21,851	USA, USSR, UK, France, China

Source: Natural Resources Defense Council

Table 10.3 Estimated Force Levels 1945–2000: Undeclared Nuclear Powers

Date	Quantity	States Included
1945–1950	0	N/A
1950–1960	0	N/A
1960–1970	?	May include Israel and India.
1970–1980	50–200	Includes Israel, India, and South Africa.
1980–1990	200+	Includes Israel, India, South Africa. May include North Korea.
1990–2000	200–5,000	Includes Israel, India, Pakistan, and North Korea. Temporarily included Belarus, Kazakhstan, and Ukraine.

Sources: FAS.org; American Defense Council; Global Security.org; S. Cohen 2002; Perkovich 2004; Nuclear Weapons Archive.org; Cirincione 2002.

utterly devastating to both sides. At present, however, only the United States and Russia have nuclear arsenals sufficient to allow them to practise MAD reliably. Moreover, MAD is largely irrelevant to the current Moscow–Washington relationship, because the contemporary international system differs radically from the cold war environment. Therefore, countries such as the United States can now look beyond MAD and ask how they can best address the potential threats offered by smaller nuclear powers, while the latter countries (as well as would-be new nuclear powers) have to take account of the possibility that the arsenal which they build may be defeated by a foe's missile defense.

KEY POINTS

- With the end of the cold war, the world has entered a Second Nuclear Age in which the number of actors possessing nuclear weapons is progressively increasing even as the absolute number of such weapons is falling.

- Deterrence may prove unreliable in the future. Deterrence theories that were developed in the context of the struggle between the United States and the Soviet Union may prove to be inapplicable to other powers such as North Korea and Iran.

- Strategic culture influences how a country uses its nuclear arsenal for deterrence and/or war fighting.

- Ballistic missile defences will be an important factor in nuclear decision-making in the future, and the existence of BMD perhaps will discourage some countries from attempting to acquire nuclear weapons.

Adapting to the Second Nuclear Age

In many respects, humanity as a whole is far safer today than it was during the cold war. As alluded to above, a US–Soviet nuclear war may have been only narrowly avoided. Such a conflict could well have spelt the end of modern civilization, at least in the northern hemisphere. Today, there appears to be little immediate danger of a civilization-shattering nuclear conflict. It is far more likely that the next nuclear war will involve, at most, a few dozen warheads rather than the tens of thousands that might have been used in a US–Soviet apocalypse. It may be cold comfort when one contemplates the horrors that even a 'small' nuclear war would entail, but the fact there appears to be little danger that the modern world will be wiped out in an afternoon is important nonetheless.

In this Second Nuclear Age, several presumptions, common in the cold war era, may prove to be problematic: that nuclear-armed powers always will be 'reasonable'; ballistic missile defences undermine deterrence; and that arms control and disarmament treaties are the best means to counter proliferation. The potential problems with the first two assumptions already have been addressed, and we now shall address the third one.

Nonproliferation and counterproliferation can involve a variety of measures, including military force. both relate to efforts to prevent the horizontal proliferation of nuclear weapons. While sometimes it is difficult to distinguish between the two activities, as a general rule one could say that the term 'nonproliferation' generally is used in reference to international legal arrangements such as the Non-Proliferation Treaty (NPT). Counterproliferation, a term which has become popular in recent years, is more often used to refer to the *enforcement* of the NPT and other international agreements. Counterproliferation can involve a variety of measures, including military force.

The NPT, which was opened for signature in 1968 and went into force in 1970, is an international agreement that recognizes only five states—China, Great Britain, France, the Soviet Union/Russia, and the United States—as legitimate nuclear powers. All other states which signed the treaty agreed to refrain from obtaining nuclear weapons. With a small number of exceptions (including India, Israel, and Pakistan), all of the world's states are signatories to the NPT.

The overall success of the NPT is debatable. While it is true that the number of nuclear powers has not exploded in the years since the agreement first came into effect, it should be noted that the great majority of countries signing the NPT surely would not, in any case, have obtained nuclear weapons. Most states are too small and/or too poor to afford nuclear arsenals, and many of those which could afford to maintain a nuclear force are inhibited by domestic pressures from obtaining one or simply feel that they do not need such weapons to ensure their security. Most leaders in countries such as Germany, Japan, and South Korea, for example, believe that their countries are well protected by the American 'nuclear umbrella' and therefore think that a national nuclear arsenal is unnecessary.

One major problem with the NPT and similar universal disarmament agreements is that compliance essentially is voluntary; such treaties have very weak provisions regarding inspection of suspect sites and no mechanism for seriously punishing bad actors. (The reason for this, in turn, is that in order to maximize the number of signatories, such treaties generally accept the 'lowest common denominator'—the provisions must be acceptable to as many states as possible, including would-be bad actors which otherwise would refuse to accede to the agreement.)

The case of Iraq before its occupation by the United States illustrates some of the weaknesses in the NPT in particular. As a militarily defeated state (in the 1991 Persian Gulf War), Iraq submitted to far more intrusive International Atomic Energy Agency (IAEA) inspections than are the norm. It was quickly discovered that not only did Baghdad have a nuclear weapons programme, which was generally assumed even before the war, but that Iraq was quite close actually to building such devices. Despite this, the Iraqi government managed to avoid full disclosure of its WMD programmes and capabilities—and, of course, it now appears that most of the world's intelligence agencies grossly overestimated the progress of the Iraqi nuclear programme during the years between 1991 and 2003. If Iraq could mislead outsiders under such conditions, one can readily imagine how easy it would be for other states to do so. Iraq's Ba'ath Party government eventually paid an enormous price for its refusal to cooperate with IAEA inspections, but this was the result of Washington's initiative, not that of the IAEA or the United Nations. Moreover, as the cases of North Korea and Iran currently illustrate, apparent noncompliance with agreements such as the NPT does not necessarily carry a prohibitive price. Indeed, North Korea has profited greatly from its NPT noncompliance, thanks to the largesse of countries such as Japan, South Korea, and the United States, which have agreed to provide that country with fuel oil, food, and other goods in exchange for ending its nuclear weapons programme. North Korea apparently took the 'payoff' and built nuclear weapons nonetheless.

BOX 10.5

Arms Control Treaties and the International Environment

History appears to indicate that arms control treaties, by themselves, do little or nothing to reduce the danger level in the international environment. If they did, there would never have been a Second World War, as the period after the First World War was a 'golden age' of arms control, with war itself essentially being banned by the 1928 Kellogg—Briand Pact. For example, the fact that the number of warheads possessed by Russia and the United States decreased radically after the end of the cold war is instructive. One could argue that the successful negotiation of the bilateral Strategic Arms Reduction Talks (START) I, START II, and Moscow Treaties did not fundamentally alter the overall geostrategic environment, and that these treaties merely reflected the fact that the Russo-American relationship itself had changed radically.

Counterproliferation measures, such as the Proliferation Security Initiative (PSI)—a US-led programme that allows states to cooperate in various ways to prevent the transfer of WMD materials and knowledge—attempt to plug the 'holes' in the NPT. While one cannot expect arms control and disarmament agreements to solve all proliferation problems, they *can* provide useful leverage for countries that are dedicated to stopping WMD proliferation and are willing to actively enforce counterproliferation. Together, nonproliferation and counterproliferation efforts may succeed in slowing considerably the horizontal proliferation of nuclear weapons, although one should not expect that they can stop it altogether.

Having considered the history of nuclear weapons and their continuing horizontal proliferation, it is useful to consider briefly how the political and military roles of these devices will develop as the Second Nuclear Age matures. Will the 'nuclear taboo' grow stronger, with nuclear weapons eventually being banned outright worldwide? Will technological developments render these devices obsolete? Or will nuclear weapons continue to play a role in international politics?

There appears to be little likelihood that nuclear weapons will cease to be an international political tool, either being eliminated altogether or placed in the hands of an international authority such as the IAEA. Indeed, there has been no compelling evidence that movement has been made toward universal nuclear disarmament in recent years. The absolute number of nuclear weapons in the world is steadily decreasing as the United States and Russia continue to adapt to post-cold war conditions by decreasing the overall size of their arsenals, but this is quite different from complete disarmament. Neither these two countries nor any other declared nuclear weapons states have surrendered their nuclear arsenals or indicated a willingness to do so at any time in the near future, even though they have all agreed publicly that universal disarmament is a laudable goal. Moreover, horizontal proliferation is still, of course, continuing.

The question of whether nuclear weapons will become outdated is a rather more complex one. While a few elegantly simple weapons have remained on the battlefield for millennia—the knife being an excellent example—it is usual for a weapon to have a fairly straightforward life cycle, offering great advantages to its possessors when first introduced and then, progressively, growing more outmoded as new weapons are invented until, eventually, it disappears

BOX 10.6

The Difficulties of Assertive Disarmament

Assertive disarmament is the use of military force to destroy a successful proliferator's actual nuclear arsenal or a would-be proliferator's capability to build nuclear weapons. However, assertive disarmament is very difficult and controversial, and for those reasons it has rarely been undertaken in the past. The examples of North Korea and Iran illustrate these difficulties well. Even though many observers, particularly in the United States, believe that these countries present two very worrying proliferation cases, many factors discourage Washington from attempting to disarm either country forcefully.

Even if the United States possessed highly detailed and specific intelligence on the location and character of all the sites relevant to the North Korean and presumed Iranian nuclear programmes (and it is unlikely that it does in fact have such near-perfect intelligence), it is quite possible that Washington would choose not to strike these facilities. In regard to North Korea, it is likely that the United States would fear that a full-scale war on the Korean Peninsula would result. Given that North Korea possesses enormous numbers of artillery tubes and could inflict massive conventional damage on Seoul—and kill tens of thousands of civilians—just in the early hours of a conflict, the risks of escalation strongly discourage a disarming strike.

The Iranian case is not quite so dire, but it is generally assumed that Iranian facilities are widely dispersed and that destroying them would result in large numbers of civilian casualties. Moreover, American policy-makers greatly fear that such a move would set back reform in Iran and turn the Iranian public—which appears to be increasingly pro-Western—against the United States. The American presence in Iraq further complicates matters. Some observers expect an Israeli strike against Iran's facilities, but this is not certain—Israel has its own difficult political questions to struggle with, and it should not simply be assumed that Jerusalem will forcibly disarm Iran because it did something similar to Iraq in the mid-1980s.

North Korea and Iran are, in short, proliferation 'hard cases' that are unlikely to be resolved through the use of military force. Thus, responsible policy-makers and military planners must work under the assumption that these powers will have nuclear weapons.

entirely from military use. In due course, this perhaps will be the fate of nuclear weapons, but this life cycle process likely will require many decades, if not centuries. It is possible that the nuclear weapon will be dethroned from its position as 'the absolute weapon' by an even more devastating new weapon of mass destruction (there has been speculation, for example, on the feasibility of an 'antimatter bomb' that would be enormously powerful), and, certainly, militaries on the technological cutting edge will continue to deploy ever-more-potent conventional weapons. However, for the foreseeable future, nuclear weapons will remain the most powerful engines of destruction possessed by human beings.

Given these factors, it is clear that nuclear weapons will continue to have an international political role. While it is not possible to predict precisely how many states will come to possess these devices over the next few decades, it is very likely indeed that the number of nuclear-armed states will increase, perhaps dramatically. Nuclear proliferation tends not to be an isolated event. Instead, a newly declared nuclear weapons state will provoke a regional rival or rivals to follow suit. So, proliferation is likely to occur in pairs, triads, or even larger grouping. As more states acquire nuclear weapons—and as the nuclear club becomes ever-more diverse ideologically and culturally—we will learn more about how

BOX 10.7

A Nuclear Taboo?

Many observers contend that there is a taboo against the use of nuclear (as well as chemical and biological) weapons. From this perspective, the use of these devices is considered so disreputable and immoral that states are extremely reluctant to use them; the use of such weapons would make the state in question an outcast, despised by its peers, including those who might otherwise be sympathetic to it. Therefore, the taboo is a strong firebreak that helps to prevent the occurrence of nuclear war. Certainly, the use of nuclear weapons is controversial, and the fact that they have not been used in combat since 1945 is strong evidence that states possessing these weapons are reluctant to use them. However, 'taboo' is a very strong word, implying a deep-rooted and long-standing repugnance shared by almost all members of a particular society (most cultures, for example, have a taboo against cannibalism).

One must, however, consider the fact that there have been no truly 'hard cases' in which a nuclear state chose not to use its arsenal; for example, no nuclear-armed country has chosen to allow itself to be destroyed rather than use its arsenal against an invader. Indeed, since 1945 no nuclear-armed state even has fought a war in which it lost as many as 100,000 troops, a small figure compared to the millions of deaths suffered by various major powers in the World Wars (the Soviet Union alone suffered approximately twenty-seven million deaths in the Second World War). Perhaps the closest that any state has come to using nuclear weapons in recent decades was Israel in the early part of the 1973 Yom Kippur War, when it was faced by an invasion by several Arab states. Israel supposedly prepared for the possible use of its arsenal, but eventually the invasion was turned back by conventional means. If the Arab armies instead had achieved a decisive breakthrough and the survival of Israel was thought to be in danger, it is quite possible that the Israeli cabinet would have permitted nuclear use.

In this light, the fact that nuclear weapons have not been used is not particularly impressive, because no nuclear-armed country has faced very intense pressure to do so. The real proof of the existence of a strong nuclear taboo would be if states prove willing to suffer truly terrible consequences rather than use these weapons.

robust deterrence is under a variety of conditions involving different actors. Perhaps we will find that there actually is a strong nuclear taboo which prevents leaders worldwide from 'pushing the button'. It is, however, all too likely instead that we will see the breaking of the long 'nuclear truce'.

KEY POINTS

- Nonproliferation and counterproliferation measures are used to control, and ideally prevent, the horizontal proliferation of nuclear weapons.

- The NPT acknowledges only five nuclear weapons states (China, France, Great Britain, the Soviet Union/Russia, and the United States) and forbids all other signatories from obtaining nuclear weapons. Most of the world's states are signatories, although some (including nuclear-armed countries such as India, Israel, and Pakistan) are not.

- Effective enforcement of universal disarmament agreements such as the NPT has proven difficult, especially as such agreements generally only have very weak enforcement provisions.

- It is very unlikely that nuclear weapons will become obsolescent in the next few decades, or that the world's nuclear powers all will agree to dismantle their arsenals.

Conclusion

Since 1945, nuclear weapons have played a central role in international relations, but over time that role subtly has changed. During the decades immediately following the invention of 'the bomb', nuclear weapons only were possessed by a small number of states, with the two superpowers amassing arsenals far larger than those of all the world's other countries combined. However, as the world has transitioned to the Second Nuclear Age, the 'nuclear club' has become far less exclusive, and even some relatively minor powers, such as Pakistan and, presumably, North Korea, now possess nuclear arsenals and the means to deliver them.

While nonproliferation and counterproliferation efforts may slow the spread of nuclear weapons, it should be expected that the number of nuclear-armed countries will continue to grow. There are several reasons for this, but the military utility and consequent usefulness of these devices for deterrence and coercion, as well as the prestige associated with possessing a nuclear arsenal, are the most important. Quite simply, nuclear devices are the most potent weapons yet devised by mankind. Moreover, they are particularly valuable to states that, in conventional terms, are militarily weak relative to their foes. For example, in a conventional conflict, most states would find the military power of the United States overwhelming, but even a small nuclear arsenal would greatly complicate US war planning and raise the possibility of horrific US and allied casualties. In some cases, it might even be possible to deter Washington from undertaking any military action, making it possible for a country such as North Korea or Iran to 'win' in a crisis with the United States by deterring Washington from using its military power. Even a very small nuclear arsenal could give North Korea or Iran 'escalation dominance'. Nuclear possession also is commonly associated with high status in the international community, since most very powerful states have nuclear arsenals. Although owning nuclear weapons alone does not make a country a great power, there certainly is a unique status associated with nuclear possession, and this surely is one of the reasons why some of the aforementioned lesser powers went to such extraordinary (and expensive) efforts to circumvent international nonproliferation regimes.

While deterrence theories developed during the cold war continue to provide useful guidance, as the group of nuclear-armed states has diversified, the continued validity of these theories has become questionable. As we have seen, every country has a unique strategic culture, and cultural factors can have a significant influence on decisions related to nuclear acquisition, deterrence, and use. We should not expect that the very diverse group of leaders who will wield nuclear weapons in this century all will act as their Soviet and American counterparts did during the cold war.

The simple 'MAD worldview', which assumes that any nuclear war would involve thousands, or even tens of thousands, of nuclear warheads, and be utterly devastating both to the participants and to other countries (which would experience the environmental side effects of the massive nuclear exchange), is obsolete. In the cold war, the greatest fear held by both sides was that the other would be able to disarm it almost entirely in a well-planned first strike. There was relatively little concern that surviving nuclear weapons, especially those mounted on SLBMs and ICBMs, might hit the enemy; so long as the command and control system and a modest percentage of a superpower's arsenal remained intact, it could hit its foe with a devastating counterstrike. Certainly, some warheads would fail to strike their targets for any number of reasons—mechanical failure, simple inaccuracy, or whatnot—but the superpower nuclear arsenals were so large that such failures would not undermine the ability to deliver a devastating blow.

Most of today's nuclear powers possess rather small arsenals and missile defences can complicate nuclear war planning exponentially. When a state with a small nuclear arsenal considers attacking a foe with a missile defence, the attacker cannot be certain how many, if any, of its warheads will break though the defence and strike their targets. It is likely that the proliferation of missile defences in the future will provide many states with a 'shield' which they can use to defend against the nuclear sword wielded by their enemies. Moreover, many states no doubt will, like the United States, seek to have both a nuclear sword and a BMD shield. Thus, the argument, commonly made in the West during the cold war, that building defences against nuclear weapons is a waste of effort because many warheads (presumably) would 'leak through' any defence is irrelevant in regard to most of the countries that are, or will be, nuclear-armed in this century. When a state has only a small number of nuclear weapons, it is conceivable that they could all be intercepted by a well-designed missile defence.

For all of the above reasons, it very likely indeed that the Second Nuclear Age will differ radically from its predecessor. While there are many good reasons to celebrate the end of the First Nuclear Age and the consequent greatly diminished probability of a massive nuclear exchange, it is, regrettably, very easy indeed to imagine that the present Nuclear Age will be marked by one or more relatively small nuclear wars.

? QUESTIONS

1. What were the key characteristics of the First and Second Nuclear Ages? In what key respects do the two Nuclear Ages differ?

2. Why might the cold war model of nuclear deterrence be less relevant in Second Nuclear Age? In what respects might it still be relevant?

3. Does the horizontal proliferation of nuclear weapons make nuclear war more likely? If so, why?

4. How does strategic culture influence decisions related to the acquisition and use of nuclear weapons?

5. What are some historical examples of how strategic culture has guided nuclear decision-making?

6. If many countries acquire ballistic missile defenses, how will this likely affect horizontal proliferation worldwide? How will this likely affect vertical proliferation worldwide?

7. Is it possible to stop the horizontal proliferation of nuclear weapons? If so, how?

8. If it is not possible stop horizontal proliferation, is it at least possible to significantly slow the spread of these devices? If so, how?

9. Has the Non-Proliferation Treaty significantly slowed the horizontal proliferation of nuclear weapons during the last several decades? If so, why? If not, why not?

10. Is there a strong taboo against the use of nuclear weapons?

FURTHER READING

■ **L. Freeman, *Deterrence* (Cambridge: Polity Press, 2004).** This short work introduces key deterrence concepts and explores how deterrence theory has evolved over time.

■ **C. S. Gray, *The Second Nuclear Age* (Boulder, CO: Lynne Rienner, 1999).** This book describes the concept of a Second Nuclear Age in detail.

■ **P. R. Lavoy, S. D. Sagan, and J. J. Wirtz, *Planning the Unthinkable: How New Powers Will Use Nuclear, Biological, and Chemical Weapons* (Ithaca, NY: Cornell University Press, 2000).** This edited volume offers perspectives on a variety of issues related to the horizontal proliferation of WMDs.

■ **D. Miller, *The Cold War: A Military History* (New York: St. Martin's Press, 1998).** This work provides a general discussion of how the US and Soviet nuclear arsenals developed during the Cold War.

■ **P. Morgan, *Deterrence Now* (Cambridge: Cambridge University Press, 2003).** This work considers some of the arguable flaws in deterrence theory and makes recommendations regarded how they may be corrected.

■ **Keith B. Payne, *Deterrence in the Second Nuclear Age* (Lexington, KY: University Press of Kentucky, 1996).** This volume explores in detail why Second Nuclear Age is distinct from its predecessor.

_____ ***The Fallacies of Cold War Deterrence and a New Direction* (Lexington, KY: University Press of Kentucky, 2001).** This work explains some of the arguable flaws in Cold War deterrence theory and why these are significant in the context of the Second Nuclear Age.

 WEB LINKS

● **http://www.fas.org/nuke/guide/index/** This guide is maintained by the anti-nuclear Federation of American Scientists. It contains information about the nuclear arsenals of various countries.

● **http://www.nrdc.org/nuclear/** This site, maintained by the anti-nuclear National Resource Defense Council, includes a variety of information and links.

● **http://www.nuclearfiles.org** The Nuclear Files is maintained by the anti-nuclear Nuclear Age Peace Foundation. It contains a variety of material concerning nuclear weapons and deterrence.

● **http://nuclearweaponarchive.org** This site contains a variety of material related to nuclear weapons, as well as a variety of useful links.

 Visit the Online Resource Centre that accompanies this book for lots of interesting additional material http://www.oxfordtextbooks.co.uk/orc/baylis_strategy2e/.

11 The Control of Weapons of Mass Destruction

JOHN BAYLIS AND MARK SMITH

Chapter Contents

- Introduction
- Arms Control during the Cold War
- Arms Control and the 'Long Peace'
- The Residual Role of Arms Control in the Post-Cold War Era
- Post-Cold War WMD Proliferation: Strategic Responses
- Strategic Response in Operation
- Analysis and Assessment
- Conclusions

Reader's Guide

This chapter charts the shift that took place during the cold war from disarmament to arms control, and the shift in relative importance that has taken place in the post-cold war period from arms control to more forcible means to tackle proliferation. The chapter shows how concerns emerged in the 1980s and 1990s about the continuing utility of arms control as an effective means of dealing with weapons of mass destruction and how new ideas began to take shape, first in the Clinton administration, and then in the Bush administration, about more militarily driven approaches, associated with counterproliferation. The chapter ends with a discussion of counterproliferation and an evaluation of its ability to control weapons of mass destruction today.

Introduction

Establishing controls over weapons or delivery systems is a difficult and painstaking process. Despite this, arms control has a long history, and at least one writer has traced a lineage back to ancient times (Croft 1996). As an academic subject, arms control is a more recent arrival: the post-1945 period saw a new but burgeoning literature that coincided with a configuration of global politics that was doubly anomalous. First, it was bipolar in that it was dominated by two superpowers and therefore reflected a new structure of international power, and, second, the two superpowers were extensively armed with weapons of unprecedented destructive capacity.

A decade or so after the onset of the cold war in 1947, academic analysis and international policy began to converge, as the prospect of using arms control to stabilize the superpower relationship began to find favour. The hair-raising experience of the Cuban Missile Crisis only served to drive home that the relationship could be dangerously unstable and could not be relied upon to run itself. In a wider context, the lesson of the twentieth century seemed to be that warfare would almost always escalate upwards to the most destructive level, and increasingly it was not only the superpowers that possessed the most destructive technology. The spread of weapons of mass destruction (WMD), a term coined and defined by United Nations in 1948, became a key concern.

Consequently, the latter half of the twentieth century saw the establishment of a network of WMD control regimes that survives to this day. This network comprised multilateral, agreements on WMD and a set of bilateral arrangements between the super-powers. The former were *disarmament agreements* while the latter were *arms control agreements*. That is, the multilateral agreements stigmatized weapons entirely, while the superpower arrangements controlled certain *types* of nuclear weapons, especially their associated delivery systems.

As the century drew to a close, the superpower confrontation ended, but the global problem of WMD proliferation remained, and began to grow as so-called 'rogue states' emerged as an important security issue. The increasing salience of this issue was accompanied by an increasing concern that the network of disarmament regimes might be losing their effectiveness. In turn, that concern, accompanied by the slow realization that the end of the cold war offered new possibilities for action as well as new threats, helped produce an interest in how the military force might be used to offset or even eliminate the menace of WMD.

This chapter charts these developments, and aims to help students understand the underlying principles behind superpower arms control and the global WMD regimes, and the criticisms levelled at them. It then examines the major changes that have occurred in the post-cold war era and the new approaches associated with controlling weapons of mass destruction. Particular attention is given to the emergence of strategic responses, in which military force is deployed as a tool against proliferation.

Arms Control during the Cold War

Following the arms races and the slide to war in the late 1930s, disillusionment with disarmament, as a way to achieve peace and security, characterized official attitudes the immediate aftermath of the Second World War. The limited attempts at arms control or disarmament that were made by the two emerging superpowers in the new cold war that developed only helped to reinforce the sceptical judgement of the day. Neither side was prepared to take risks with their own security (as they perceived it), especially when it came to weapons which could be a decisive influence in a future conflict. Far from easing the growing tension between the two superpowers in the late 1940s, the modest international control negotiations that were undertaken only exacerbated mistrust and heightened hostility.

By the mid-1950s, the lack of success in disarmament negotiations and growing awareness of the dangers of nuclear war produced a change in approach to arms control. Efforts to negotiate a comprehensive disarmament treaty were abandoned in favour of what were known as 'partial measures', such as the 1955 'Open Skies' agreement and the test ban negotiations. Arms control was increasingly viewed as dealing with specific problems created by the cold war arms race.

This move towards greater flexibility at the policy level led to what has been described as 'new thinking' within the defence community. Although the ideas that emerged were not as original as the proponents sometimes claimed, a new literature began to appear in the late 1950s developing the theory of arms control. In contrast to the literature on disarmament, the writing on arms control questioned the feasibility of general and comprehensive disarmament and argued that greater international stability could be achieved by managing military competition. Attention was focused on the mutual interest that existed between the superpower adversaries to avoid nuclear conflagration.

These new arms control theorists intended to work within the prevailing system of nuclear deterrence rather than to try to abolish it. Arms control was designed to 'strengthen the operation of the balance of military power against the disruptive effects of the arms dynamic, especially arms competition, arms racing and technological developments that tend to make nuclear and non-nuclear deterrence more difficult' (Buzan and Herring 1998: 212). Its essential aim was to reduce the likelihood and costs of war and to reduce expenditures on both nuclear and conventional arsenals.

The October 1962 Cuban Missile Crisis gave additional impetus to the arms control project. As the superpowers edged back from the nuclear abyss both realized, more than ever before, that they had a mutual interest in effective crisis management. The crises highlighted the dangers of inadvertent escalation and miscalculation during periods of military confrontation and intense political instability. In June 1963, the United States and the Soviet Union signed a 'hot line' agreement to provide a secure, official, and dependable channel of communication between Moscow and Washington.

The Cuban Missile Crisis also highlighted the issue of nuclear testing. Reflecting the less ambitious agenda of the new arms control school, the United States, Britain, and the Soviet Union agreed on a Partial Test Ban Treaty in August 1963. The treaty prohibited all nuclear tests in the atmosphere, but allowed tests to continue underground. There was also an escape clause inserted in the treaty, which allowed testing to be resumed after a period of three

BOX 11.1

Definitions of Arms Control

While the terms 'arms control' and 'disarmament' are sometimes used interchangeably, they reflect very different views about international politics. Hedley Bull, in his book *Control of the Arms Race*, defines disarmament as 'the reduction or abolition of armaments. It may be unilateral or multilateral; general or local; comprehensive or partial; controlled or uncontrolled.' Arms control, on the other hand, according to Bull, involves 'restraint internationally exercised upon armaments policy, whether in respect of the level of armaments, their character, deployment or use'.

John Spanier and Joseph Nogee in their study of *The Politics of Disarmament* provide a similar, although more specific definition of the differences between arms control and disarmament. In their formulation, 'while disarmament refers to the complete abolition or partial reduction of the human and material resources of war, arms control deals with the restraints to be imposed upon the use of nuclear weapons' (Spanier and Nogee 1962: 15).

months' notice. This escape clause was designed to protect signatories who felt threatened by future technological advances or cheating. Significantly, neither French nor Chinese officials (who tested nuclear weapons in 1960 and 1964 respectively) were prepared to accede to the treaty because they believed it benefited more advanced nuclear states.

Limited as the treaty was, it encouraged further arms control initiatives. Between 1963 and 1968, the superpowers focused on their mutual interest in trying to negotiate a wider agreement to prohibit further nuclear proliferation. This culminated in the Non-Proliferation Treaty, which was signed in July 1968. Once again China and France refused to sign, and a number of other states rejected the treaty on the grounds that it froze the nuclear status quo and incorporated only a limited commitment by the nuclear powers to give up their own weapons.

The nuclear explosion by India in 1974, ostensibly for peaceful purposes, highlighted the weaknesses of the treaty. Despite this, the treaty provided some limited, but not unimportant benefits. It became the central plank of the nascent nonproliferation regime, which helped restrain the pace of further nuclear proliferation. It also emphasized the opportunities for cooperation between the super powers, during rocky times in their relationship.

By the mid-1970s, the superpowers also recognized their mutual interest in trying to control the use of pathogens and toxins as weapons of mass destruction. The Biological Weapons Convention (BWC), which entered into force in 1975, banned the development, production, and stockpiling of biological and toxin weapons. It also required states to destroy 'the agents, toxins and weapons equipment and means of delivery in the possession of the parties' to the treaty. The main problem with the convention, however, was that there was no provision for verification of compliance.

Between 1969 and 1972, the superpowers focused for the first time on the difficult task of limiting strategic armaments. In May 1972, the Strategic Arms Limitation Treaty (SALT) I was signed covering a number of different areas, including limitations on ballistic missile defence (the now-defunct Anti-Ballistic Missile Treaty). The aim of SALT I was

BOX 11.2

What are Weapons of Mass Destruction?

In the run-up to the 2002 war in Iraq, the term 'weapons of mass destruction' (WMD) took on a public profile that it had hitherto lacked, and a term that had previously been used largely by specialists (scientists, analysts, government officials, and activists) was now part of political rhetoric. Buzan and Herring (1998) define WMD as 'weapons of which small numbers can destroy life and/or inanimate objects on a vast scale very quickly', but note that this could conceivably be applied to weapons (such as fuel-air explosives) that are normally regarded as 'conventional' weapons.

The term does in fact have an internationally accepted definition, one formulated by the United Nations Commission for Conventional Armaments in 1948. This defined WMD as: 'Atomic explosive weapons, radioactive material weapons, lethal chemical and biological weapons, and any weapons developed in the future which have characteristics comparable in destructive effect to those of the atomic bomb or other weapons mentioned above.'

This definition formed the basis for subsequent international agreements on controlling WMD. Nonetheless, the term should be used with more care than is usually the case in political rhetoric, since by its nature it conflates very different forms of weapon. Today, it can be regarded as a blanket term for nuclear and radiological, chemical, and biological weapons.

Nuclear weapons work by nuclear fission using plutonium or uranium (fission or atom bombs) or by nuclear fusion (thermonuclear or hydrogen bombs). There are seven known nuclear-armed states in the world (Britain, China, France, India, Pakistan, Russia, and the United States). Israel neither acknowledges nor denies it has nuclear weapons but is widely believed to have them. North Korea is believed to possess a small and rudimentary capability, and Iran may be pursuing such a programme.

Radiological weapons are sometimes referred to as 'dirty bombs', and would work by surrounding conventional explosive with radioactive material. They do not involve any nuclear explosion, but rather the large-scale dispersal of radioactive toxic materials, thereby inflicting doses of radiation on nearby victims of the explosion. These weapons are widely associated with terrorists and other non-state actors.

Biological weapons are bacteria, viruses, or biological toxins that are intentionally disseminated in order to infect or poison individuals, such as troops or civilians. Examples of biological substances used in weapons include anthrax, smallpox, and ricin. Similarly, *chemical weapons* use the toxic effects of chemical substances to cause death, permanent harm or incapacity to human beings. Examples include phosgene, mustard gas, and VX.

to 'cap' missile deployments at specific levels to prevent a future unrestricted arms race, which would lead to greater international instability. Despite the unprecedented nature of the agreement, it quickly became the subject of criticism, both within the United States, and in the arms control community itself. According domestic critics of SALT I, it froze the numerical superiority of the Soviet Union while at the same time it allowed the Soviet Union to compete in those qualitative areas where the United States was in the lead. This failure to address the all-important qualitative issues (including missile accuracy and the placement of multiple warheads on ballistic missiles) was particularly disappointing even for many arms control supporters, who were concerned that the arms race had simply been moved from a quantitative to a qualitative arena.

Given the shortcomings in SALT I, it was not long before new negotiations began in Geneva. Progress, however, proved to be slow. The agreement eventually reached (SALT II) followed closely guidelines reached at Vladivostock five years earlier. The ceiling for strategic delivery vehicles were set at 2,400 (to be reduced to 2,250 by 1981), 1,320 for ballistic missiles armed with Multiple Independently Targetable Re-entry Vehicles (MIRV) and strategic bombers, and 1,200 for MIRVed ballistic missiles alone.

Almost immediately, however, the arms control process was derailed by the Soviet invasion of Afghanistan and in January 1980 President Carter asked the Senate to delay the ratification of the treaty. Although the SALT II remained unratified in 1982 both the United States and the Soviet Union continued to abide by the limits of the treaty. Despite this tacit agreement, however, the following three years were characterized by frequent accusations by the Reagan administration that the Soviet Union was in breach of the agreement.

KEY POINTS

- The late 1940s and early 1950s saw a growing disillusionment with disarmament in dealing with the problems posed by weapons of mass destruction.

- The late 1950s brought 'new thinking' and the development of the theory of arms control.

- The aim of arms control was to make the prevailing system work more effectively.

- The Cuban Missile Crisis ushered in a new 'golden age' of arms control agreements.

- By the late 1970s, however, arms control as an approach to peace and security faced increasing problems.

Arms Control and the 'Long Peace'

The question of whether arms control was a significant contributor to the 'Long Peace'[1] during the cold war is a matter of keen debate. For those who think it was, the fact that the cold war did not turn 'hot' is evidence that the arms control agreements reached, especially after the Cuban missile crisis, helped prevent the outbreak of war between the superpowers. The Hot-line agreement, the Partial Test Ban Treaty, the Non-Proliferation Treaty, and the SALT I and SALT II Treaties all contributed to a recognition that the superpowers had a vital mutual interest in avoiding nuclear war. According to this view, constant technological changes and mutual suspicions inherent in a system of international anarchy helped to encourage arms competition which, in turn, posed dangers to international security. By addressing the instabilities of the military balance of power supporters argue that arms control significantly contributed to the absence of great power conflict during the cold war. Even those negotiations that did not succeed, such as the Mutual Balanced Force Reduction (MBFR) Talks, are often seen as important events the contributed to greater understanding between adversaries. Viewed from this perspective, arms control has been the 'high road to peace'.

BOX 11.3

International Regimes on WMD

The three key categories of WMD (nuclear, biological, chemical), plus the missile delivery systems usually associated with them, each have an international regime devoted to their control. They are in various stages of development (some might add disarray) and they have not advanced or progressed at an even pace.

The Treaty on the Non-Proliferation of Nuclear Weapons (NPT) entered into force on 5 March 1970 and currently has 189 member states. Only India, Israel, North Korea, and Pakistan remain outside it. The NPT's signatory states are divided into two categories: nuclear weapon states (NWS) and non-nuclear weapon states (NNWS). Under the terms of the treaty the latter agree to forego nuclear weapons entirely, while the former (the five states—Britain, China, France, Russia and the United States—that possessed nuclear weapons at the signing of the treaty) are committed to 'pursue negotiations in good faith' on nuclear disarmament. This stipulation, set out in Article 6 of the Treaty, has proved recurrently controversial, since none of the five NWS has ever looked likely to seriously move towards such an end.

The other 'devil's bargain' in the NPT is drawn from Article 4, which notes the 'inalienable right' of the NNWS to develop civil nuclear power with the 'fullest possible exchange' of information with the NWS. This exchange of information is subject to various safeguards and inspections conducted by the International Atomic Energy Agency (IAEA see www.iaea.org).

The Chemical Weapons Convention (CWC) is a multilateral treaty banning chemical weapons. It entered into force on 29 April 1997, currently has 164 states parties, and is implemented by the Organisation for the Prohibition of Chemical Weapons (OPCW, see www.opcw.org). The Convention bans development, acquisition, or possession of chemical weapons by signatories; their use or preparation for use; the transfer of chemical weapons or any encouragement of chemical weapons in other states; and the destruction of chemical weapon stockpiles by signatories. The latter is significant: unlike the NPT, the CWC *compels* states parties possessing the banned weapons to dismantle their stocks, and sets out clear timetables and deadlines for this work. In cases of non-compliance, the OPCW can recommend that the states parties take punitive action, and in extreme cases can refer the case to the UN Security Council.

The Biological Weapons Convention (BWC) entered into force on 26 March 1975 and currently has 150 states parties. It bans development, stockpiling, acquisition, retention, and production of biological agents and toxins, and all weapons designed to use them. Unlike the CWC, it does not ban use of such weapons, which is affirmed in the 1925 Geneva Protocol.

The BWC has yet to become a formal institution like the OPCW, and questions of verification and compliance have dogged the Convention almost since its inception. Efforts to negotiate a legally binding protocol took place between 1991 and 2001, but conflicts and disagreements proved impossible to overcome and the BWC still lacks any formal means of verification.

Supporters argue that arms control not only helped prevent war, but also that the agreements contributed to ending the cold war. According to this view, agreements such as the Stockholm Accords in 1986 and the Intermediate Nuclear Force (INF) Treaty in 1987 played an essential part in building confidence between East and West, creating the kind of trust that was crucial in reducing hostility. Viewed in these terms, arms control was itself part of the process that broke the circle of mistrust between the United States and the Soviet Union. The agreements reached were not simply a reflection of the improving climate of East–West relations.

This view, however, is not shared by all of those who have studied the impact of arms control agreements during the cold war. For the critics, arms control played little or no part in keeping the peace during the cold war; the mutual fear associated with deterrence was of much greater significance when it came to keeping the peace. They also argue that arms control was insignificant in helping to end the cold war.

According to critics, the arms control agreements reached during the cold war had little, if any, impact on the prevention of war. Testing continued, despite the Partial Test Ban Treaty; proliferation was not prevented by the Non-Proliferation Treaty; quantitative and qualitative improvements in strategic armaments continued in spite of (and because of) SALT I and II; and MBFR wholly failed to achieve conventional arms limitation. Where agreements were reached, the states involved often just agreed not to do those things they did not wish to do anyway. Critics also argue that arms control negotiations were often used as a source of propaganda and, as such, enhanced distrust between the superpowers.

Colin Gray has stated that arms control is possible when it is unnecessary, and impossible when it is needed. This is referred to as the 'arms control paradox' (Gray 1992). In the context of the end of the cold war and the post-war era, arms control agreements simply reflected the thaw in the political antagonisms between East and West. However, this new political relationship made them largely unnecessary. Critics see the agreements of the 1990s as being of little importance to the process of cooperation which developed between East and West.

Both views are rather stark. A case can be made that during the cold war arms control agreements of various kinds helped to play their part in establishing and maintaining certain norms of state behaviour. The 1968 Non-Proliferation Treaty (NPT), the 1987 Missile Technology Control Regime (MTCR), the 1996 Comprehensive Test Ban Treaty, have all been designed to establish regimes to prevent certain kinds of destabilizing developments. In the case of non-proliferation there are many reasons why states do not develop nuclear weapons and the regime is unlikely to be decisive in its impact on states thinking about developing such weapons. The regime, however, puts up barriers and increases the political price of going nuclear. While it is impossible to quantify its benefits, the fact that so many states have signed the NPT seems to indicate that for them (and for different reasons) it performs a useful and important role.

Similarly, arms control contributed to peaceful change in the late 1980s and early 1990s. While the end of the cold war had many causes, arms control played a limited but significant part. The Graduated Reduction in Tension (GRIT)- type initiatives by Gorbachev between 1985 and 1989, the Stockholm Accords, the INF Agreements, the START negotiations, and progress in conventional arms discussions, all contributed to breaking down the barriers of mutual mistrust between Washington and Moscow (Collins 1998). Initially at least, the effects were largely psychological, but no less important for that. For President Bush Senior conventional and nuclear negotiations during this period were 'part of creating a context of progress in East–West relations'. They were an integral part of the process, not independent from it.

This said, there is certainly something in the argument that arms control becomes much easier when the political climate is benign. Arms control tends to reflect the state of political relations of the time. There has to be some *prior* improvement in international relationships before arms control becomes possible. During the cold war, there were periods of detente when arms control appears to have played a part in helping to enhance confidence between the adversaries, especially by providing a forum for discussion of strategic thinking, the purposes behind force deployments, and concerns about the opponent's force structure and operations. This happened in the aftermath of the Cuban Missile Crisis and in the early 1970s. However, these were short-lived periods and more hostile relations followed. The effects of arms control were clearly limited and temporary. There is very little evidence that arms control helped to improve superpower relations during periods of intense hostility. Indeed, the evidence seems to support the view that differences over arms control more often than not exacerbated the problems which existed.

KEY POINTS

- The end of the cold war brought a major debate about whether arms control did or did not contribute significantly to global peace.

- Supporters viewed it as 'the high road to peace'.

- Opponents argued that it played little part in keeping the peace during the cold war.

- A less stark judgement is that arms control played some part in preventing all-out war but it did not significantly improve relations during the times of intense hostility between East and West.

The Residual Role of Arms Control in the Post-Cold War Era

This somewhat ambivalent view of arms control seems to be confirmed by events since 1989. The ending of the cold war brought a flurry of arms control activity. Following a number of years of detailed negotiation in 1991, a Strategic Arms Reduction Treaty (START I) was finally signed. Instead of imposing limits on increases in weapons, START was designed to halt and reverse the arms race. Under the provisions of the treaty the United States and the Soviet Union agreed to reduce their nuclear arsenals to 1,600 strategic delivery vehicles and 6,000 warheads (of which 4,900 would be ballistic missile warheads, with a ceiling of 1,100 Intercontinental Ballistic Missile (ICBM) warheads. This was followed by a Treaty on Conventional Arms Forces in Europe (CFE) in 1991, finally overcoming the impasses which had led to more than fifteen years of largely fruitless negotiations in the MBFR Talks in Vienna.

With the disintegration of the Soviet Union, President Boris Yeltsin of Russia and President William Clinton continued the momentum of the early post-cold war years by signing a START II Treaty in 1993. The treaty involved two main phases. Phase one was designed to run in parallel with the seven-year timetable for START I, with each side limited to between 3,800 and 4,250 warheads at the end of the period. Phase two aimed to limit both sides to between 3,000 and 3,500 warheads by January 2003 (including the elimination of all ICBMs). As a result of a Protocol to the START I Treaty signed in May 1992, it had been agreed, however, that START II would only enter into force once START I had been ratified by the United States and Russia and entered into force. This also meant ratification by the Ukraine, Kazakhstan, and Belarus (UKB). This was eventually achieved in February 1994. The Russians refused to exchange the instruments of ratification for START I and its Protocol until the UKB acceded to the NPT as non-nuclear weapons states. This was subsequently achieved in December 1994 when the Ukraine finally acceded to the NPT (with the Belarus and Kazakhstan having acceded earlier). Following on from the progress made in these negotiations, in May 1995 the United States and Russia agreed a 'Joint Statement on Transparency and Irreversibility'. As the name implies, this was designed to start a process that would make the reductions that had been agreed irreversible.

After this joint statement, however, progress became more difficult to achieve. While the US Senate approved the ratification of START II in January 1996, the Russian Duma held back. Concern in Moscow centred on three issues: the treaty's costs and strategic effects; the need to resolve a new debate over the ABM treaty before agreeing START II limits; and growing hostility towards North Atlantic Treaty Organization (NATO) expansion plans. Some of these issues were dealt with (at least in part) as a result of subsequent agreements and the decision by NATO in 1997 to limit expansion for the time being to just three former members of the Warsaw Pact. A START II Protocol was agreed in September 1997, which deferred completion of phase one of the reductions from 2001 to 2004 and the second phase of reductions from 2003 to 2007, thereby helping to defer Russian costs of dismantling its weapons. At the same time, the United States agreed to negotiate a START III agreement as soon as START II entered into force. The aim would be to bring the number of warheads down to 2,000–2,500 by 2007. Also in September 1997, 'Demarcation Agreements' were reached which were designed to distinguish between US work on a theatre ballistic missile defence system against 'rogue states' and a strategic system which would alter the balance between Russia and the United States. It was hoped that these missile defence and START-related agreements would persuade the Russian Duma to ratify START II and its Protocol. They failed, however, in the late 1990s to have their desired effects.

The growing difficulty in making progress in arms control negotiations in the late 1990s also was evident in a number of other fields. Despite the indefinite extension of the NPT in 1995, significant disagreements continued between the nuclear and non-nuclear states over the pace of nuclear disarmament (enshrined in Article 6 of the Treaty). At the same time the nuclear tests carried out by India and Pakistan in May 1998 demonstrated the fragility of the whole nonproliferation regime. Similarly, the breakthrough achieved with the Comprehensive Test Ban Treaty (CTBT) in 1996 ground to a halt in late 1999 when the US Senate refused to ratify the treaty.

Attempts to control other weapons of mass destruction also ran into difficulties at about the same time. The Chemical Weapons Convention (CWC), signed in 1993, and which entered into force in April 1997, also suffered from a number of serious weaknesses. The convention was designed to ban the use of chemical weapons, as well as their development, production, transfer, and stockpiling. Stockpiles and production facilities were to be destroyed. Although there was some provision for verification through the Organization for the Prohibition of Chemical Weapons (OPCW) based in the Hague, the widespread industrial and commercial production of chemicals made the convention virtually impossible to police effectively. By 2002, 145 states had ratified both the Biological and Toxins and the Chemical Conventions, but in both cases, there were concerns that a significant number of states were developing weapons covertly.

There also were increasing concerns about the proliferation of nuclear weapons as the new century dawned. Despite the Strategic Offensive Reductions Treaty (SORT) of May 2002, reducing the number of US and Russian warheads to around 2,000 each over the following decade, there appeared to be an increasing incentive for some states and terrorist groups to acquire nuclear weapons and other weapons of mass destruction. With the cold war over and the United States now in the dominant power in the world, those who feared US hegemony or intervention in their internal affairs (like North Korea and possibly Iran) had an interest in developing their own 'ultimate' weapon. Similarly, terrorist groups, like Al-Qaeda, with nothing to lose, have an interest in acquiring such weapons to further their regional and in some cases global ambitions.

What this suggests is that arms control in the post-cold war era has been particularly affected by the changes which have taken place in the international security environment. As A. D. Rotfeld (2001: 5) has argued:

> Security in the past was based on a balance of power, equilibrium of forces and parity. At the beginning of the 21st Century neither balance nor parity exists in Russian–US relations, and the bilateral relationship is no longer the central point of reference for other states in the international system. Moreover, the world has seen the proliferation of nuclear weapons to additional states, and other states are suspected of harbouring ambitions to develop or otherwise acquire them.

As weapons of mass destruction proliferate to weak states and non-state actors, it will be increasingly difficult to bring traditional arms control techniques and principles to bear to address these relatively novel threats.

KEY POINTS

- The post-cold war period saw a flurry of arms control agreements.

- Despite the lessening of hostility between the United States and Russia, however, progress was slow and intermittent.

- Gradually the utility of arms control was perceived to have declined in the changed international environment which emerged, especially after 9/11.

Post-Cold War WMD Proliferation: Strategic Responses

The changed strategic circumstances of the post-cold war (and especially post-9/11) world have led to a search for new ideas about how to control weapons of mass destruction, driven by a perception that arms control has significant flaws and the emergence of so-called 'rogue states'. In particular, the military role in combating and responding to proliferation has taken on an increasing salience: combating proliferation has, in other words, become a strategic issue.

Strategy, according to Liddell Hart, can be defined as 'the art of distributing and applying military means to fulfil the ends of policy'. While the concept of strategy has competing definitions, this essentially Clausewitzian one has clarity and simplicity on its side, and is used for the purposes of this chapter. The acquisition of WMD has always had identifiable strategic motivations, and produces strategic effects on regional security complexes. A strategic *response*, which is to say one that utilises military means, is less easily identified, and in fact the post-cold war period can be viewed as one in which the implications of this lack of clarity became increasingly apparent.

With the cold war over, the possibility of large-scale inter-regional conflict with thermonuclear weapons receded but the chances of *intra*-regional wars remained and perhaps grew. Moreover, there was a heightened possibility that the United States might intervene in such conflicts, now that the prospects of attendant confrontation with the Soviet Union had gone.

The unpleasant surprises of the United Nations and International Atomic Energy Agency inspectors on Iraqi WMD after the 1991 Gulf War, who found that Iraq had made considerably more progress than intelligence assessments had supposed, also suggested that proliferation might be moving more quickly than was apparent. The implications of this were far-reaching. Prior to 1990, US intelligence estimated that twenty states in the world possessed chemical weapons and ten were working on biological ones; it now appeared that either this number might be an underestimate, or that those states might be considerably more advanced than anyone suspected. Concerns about hidden horizontal and vertical proliferation were therefore strengthened by the experience with Iraq, which in turn led to louder calls for more tools to tackle this problem.

Thus it appeared that the end of the cold war had spawned a new set of threats that might be smaller in scale, but more numerous and potentially more acute. In such conflicts, nuclear weapons were regarded as being likely to be deployed to deter, but chemical and biological weapons were potentially more likely to be deployed in order to be *used* (Lavoy *et al.* 2000). The CIA director James Woolsey put this succinctly when he said that 'it was as if we were struggling with a large dragon for 45 years, killed it, and then found ourselves in a jungle full of poisonous snakes'.

The seriousness with which the threat was taken was due to an uncomfortable awareness that WMD might erode the ability of the United States to project military power around the world. Richard Betts alluded to this when he argued that WMD, particularly nuclear weapons, were now 'weapons of the weak—states or groups that are at best second class' (1998: 27). General Sundarji of the Indian Army similarly argued that 'One principal lesson of the Gulf War is that, if a state intends to fight the United States, it should avoid doing so until and unless it possesses nuclear weapons' (quoted in Joseph and Reichart 1995: 4).

Betts and Sundarji were both suggesting that, if Iraq had possessed a nuclear capability in 1991, Operation Desert Storm might never have been possible: the United States and its allies might have been deterred from intervening in Kuwait. Washington's confidence in its ability to resist the deterrent strategies of small hostile states might therefore be significantly eroded once these small states possess nuclear weapons. This also may be true for other NATO members who participated in the coalition, such as Britain, or for important regional allies such as Turkey.

Moreover, this problem was exacerbated by a perception (not one universally shared) that some states, or at least their leaders, are simply not deterrable. This is often raised in the context of the so-called 'rogue states'. Officials and analysts in the United States often claim that these states are not susceptible to deterrent-based strategies because their leaders are either fanatical (i.e. too wedded to ideological or religious fervour), morally bankrupt (i.e. unlikely to recoil from mass casualties on their own soil), or simply crazy or irrational.

These concerns, centring around the possibility that WMD proliferation might either make it difficult for the United States to win a Gulf War-type conflict at an acceptable cost, or deter it from acting at all, are at the heart of the Clinton administration's decision, announced in the Bottom Up Review of 1993, that WMD represented the most direct threat to US security. In December of the same year, US Secretary of Defence Les Aspin unveiled the Defence Counterproliferation Initiative (CPI) in a speech to the National Academy of Sciences.[2]

Aspin noted that the United States and NATO had used nuclear weapons as 'the equalizer' to compensate for Soviet conventional superiority. 'Today,' he continued, 'it is the United States that has unmatched conventional military power, and it is our potential adversaries who may attain nuclear weapons. We're the ones who could wind up being the equalizee.' In Aspin's view, potential US opponents were all at least capable of producing biological and chemical agents and that US commanders now had to assume that US forces were threatened by potential battlefield use of WMD.

The goals of the CPI were subsequently defined as:

1. to deter the acquisition of WMD;

2. to 'reverse WMD programs diplomatically where proliferation has occurred';

3. to ensure that the US had 'the equipment, intelligence capability and strategy to deter the threat or use of WMD'; and

4. to defeat an enemy armed with WMD (Davis 1994: 9).

The goals of 'counterproliferation', however, were considerably better defined than the concept itself, and indeed the term ought to be used carefully, since it means different things to different people. Harald Müller and Mitchell Reiss noted in 1995 that there were at least four different definitions of exactly what constituted counterproliferation. See the Box 11.4 'What's in a Name?' for an explanation of the term and its usage.

Across the Atlantic, a debate also was getting under way in NATO. This was prompted partly by the United States, as is usual with debates in the Alliance, but also by the experience of the Gulf War. Several NATO members, notably Britain and France, had participated in the conflict and were closely involved with the WMD inspections regime, with its sobering implications for covert proliferation. Moreover, NATO was beginning to consider the prospects for an out-of-area role, probably in Eastern Europe but also, perhaps, in other regions where it might come into contact with WMD-armed adversaries.

The increasing salience of the WMD threat across the Alliance should have produced a consensus among NATO allies and a common effort to counteract the effects of WMD proliferation on their power projection capabilities. However, in the Alliance as in Washington, the CPI failed to make significant headway during the late 1990s. Budgetary factors may have slowed the response to the proliferation threat, as well as the fact that most European members prefer to give a stronger priority to an economic or diplomatic response to proliferation (Larsen 1997: 10).

Nonetheless, the Alliance did begin to investigate the threats to its borders and forces, and possible military responses. In June 1994, the North Atlantic Council (NAC) established three committees on proliferation issues, including the Senior Defence Group on Proliferation (DGP), which was set up to 'address the military capabilities needed to discourage WMD proliferation, to deter threats and use of such weapons, and to protect NATO populations, territory and forces'.[3] Jeffrey Larsen notes that 'the DGP effort was

---

BOX 11.4

What's in a Name? The Emergence of Counterproliferation

Counterproliferation is defined by Butcher as 'the military component of non-proliferation, in the same way that military strategy is a component of foreign policy' (2003: 17). This sounds relatively straightforward, but the term is in fact rather slippery and caution should be exercised when using it.

The term was popularized by Les Aspin's Counterproliferation Initiative. A couple of months after his 1993 speech, a National Security Council memo set out a possible definition of counterproliferation: 'the activities of the Department of Defence across the full range of US efforts to combat proliferation, including diplomacy, arms control, export controls and intelligence collection and analysis, with particular responsibility for assuring US forces and interests can be protected should they confront an adversary armed with WMD or missiles' (Davis 1994: 8). This was a less than satisfactory definition, being a bureaucratic division of labour more than a clear statement of policy, and did little more than define counterproliferation as anything involving the Pentagon.

The Bush administration set out its WMD strategy in a companion document published in December 2002 (White House 2002). The term counterproliferation was given a rather clearer definition than it had hitherto possessed, and for the first time it appeared to be privileged over non-proliferation, of which it had hitherto been viewed as a subset. Counterproliferation was defined as having three key elements: interdiction of WMD transfers to 'hostile states and terrorist organisations'; deterrence of use; and defence. Significantly, the document explicitly states that 'US military forces and appropriate civilian agencies must have the capacity to defend against WMD-armed adversaries, including in appropriate cases through pre-emptive measures.' The following year, the US Joint Chiefs of Staff published a statement of its doctrine on countering WMD (Joint Chiefs of Staff 2004). This defined non-proliferation as actions to 'prevent the proliferation of WMD by dissuading or impeding access to, or distribution of, sensitive technologies', and specifically cited arms control and international treaties (especially the regimes and treaties on WMD) in the range of relevant activities. Counterproliferation was defined as military activities taken to defeat the threat or use of WMD, with its objective being to deter, interdict, attack, and defend against the range of WMD acquisition, development, and employment situations. The inclusion of acquisition and development as counterproliferation (that is, military) targets is significant.

essentially the work of five key nations: the United States, France, United Kingdom, Germany and the Netherlands' (1997: 35). This is intriguing, because all of those states would only come into contact with WMD-armed adversaries as a consequence of power projection far from home; the states on NATO's south-eastern flank, which face far more direct threats, do not appear to have become heavily involved.

Despite two high-profile operations in 1998—the cruise missile attacks on a facility wrongly supposed to be producing chemical weapons precursors in Sudan, and the Desert Fox operation in Iraq—the military aspect of combating proliferation in the 1990s failed almost entirely to acquire doctrinal or strategic clarity beyond the protection of forces through theatre missile defence and passive defences. Aspin's initiative failed to resonate with the US military. Despite a 1994 estimate that an extra $400 million *per year* was needed in the defence budget, the military decided that only $80 million was necessary, and the Clinton administration itself settled for a budgetary request of only $165 million. Thomas Mahnken complained in 2001 that 'despite the Counter-proliferation Initiative's efforts to accelerate the acquisition of systems to protect US forces, the US armed services are poorly configured to fight an adversary with nuclear, chemical and biological weapons' (Mahnken 2001: 79).

The decline in interest in counterproliferation is evinced by the Clinton administration's last National Security Strategy document, which had an extensive section given to arms control and nonproliferation but only a single paragraph referring to the CPI (White House 2000). The publication of the Bush administration's National Security Strategy in 2002 appeared to herald a genuine change in this policy. As the administration was attempting to make a case for a pre-emptive/preventive attack on Iraq, its National Security Strategy appeared to generalize from this to make such attacks a part of a wider strategy against proliferation.

Within a very short space of time after publication of the National Security Strategy, the United States had embarked upon the most far-reaching anti-WMD operation ever undertaken. This came with the war against Saddam Hussein's Iraq, undertaken in the face of widespread global suspicion and opposition. The possibilities of a repeat performance in the foreseeable future look remote, to say the least, but pre-emptive and preventive counterproliferation operations do not necessarily mean regime change and pre-emption and preventive war benefits from the element of surprise.

KEY POINTS

- Strategic responses against WMD proliferation are those involving military means. This is sometimes referred to as 'counterproliferation'.

- Post-cold war interest in such responses is driven by a combination of the emergence of smaller but potentially more immediate threats, and a sense that arms control may be of limited use.

- Concern about proliferation of WMD, particularly nuclear weapons, is significantly driven by a concern that they may be used to deter US-led intervention.

- The 1993 Counter-proliferation Initiative was an attempt to develop a coherent strategy to allay those concerns.

- Little progress was made towards achieving the capabilities called for by the CPI.

Strategic Response in Operation

Clausewitz argued that military force has a grammar of its own, but that it is politics that provides the necessary logic, without which grammar is meaningless. The grammar of military responses to proliferation has remained partially developed, principally because they did not always seem to be a definable, separable element of military strategy: rather, they were largely thought of as a set of military operations within a wider plan, such as the attacks on Iraqi chemical weapons facilities during Operation Desert Storm. The surrounding political logic of the concept, therefore, has also remained underdefined.

In the following case-studies, two categories of response are identified: those which are pre-emptive and those which are preventive. The terms pre-emption and prevention are often used interchangeably, but they are in fact quite separate and distinct concepts. However, the two do share a founding assumption, which is that, in Lawrence Freedman's words, 'given the opportunity, an adversary will use force and therefore cannot be afforded the option in the first place'. He contrasts prevention and pre-emption with 'coercive strategies', such as deterrence, which assume that an adversary's decisions *can* be altered or changed (Freedman 2003: 106).

Several recent cases in which the military instrument was deployed against efforts to acquire or stockpile WMD can be identified. In this section we give an overview of each case. The following section uses these case-studies to categorize the different forms of strategic response to WMD proliferation.

Case 1: Osirak, 1981

On 7 June 1981, Israel launched an air attack on the Iraqi nuclear facility at Osirak. The Israeli government had judged that the nuclear reactor, acquired from France, was intended for the production of fissile material. This was a well-founded suspicion, since Iraq had rejected the chance of a more efficient reactor that would *not* produce fissile material, and consequently the decision was taken to bomb the facility before it became operational.

It was therefore a *preventive* operation, designed to snuff out a nascent capability well before it came to fruition. At the time of the attack, and since, Israel stated explicitly that prevention was an intrinsic part of Israeli strategy. The Defence Minister, Ariel Sharon, said: 'The third element in our defence policy for the 1980s is to prevent confrontation states from gaining access to nuclear weapons. Israel cannot afford the introduction of the nuclear weapon . . . We shall therefore have to prevent such a threat at its inception' (Feldman 1982: 122). This national doctrine of preventive action forms the 'political logic' for the Osirak bombing. Iraq was a member of the NPT, and any attempt to circumvent safeguards would have been illegal, but Israel elected not to wait for this to take place.

The attack drew strong condemnation, at least in public, from the United States: 'The United States government condemns the reported Israeli air strike on the Iraqi nuclear facility, the unprecedented character of which cannot but seriously add to the already tense situation in the area', said President Reagan, and the UN Security Council also issued a strongly worded condemnation, describing the attack as a threat to the NPT safeguards regime. As Shai Feldman points out, the raid itself was 'at the very least a vote of no-confidence in IAEA safeguards', although that was, it would seem, borne out by the subsequent covert progress made by Iraq that was not uncovered by the IAEA for another decade.

Case 2: the Gulf War, 1991

Iraq was widely believed to possess chemical and biological weapons prior to the Gulf War, and in fact the US officials repeatedly promised heavy retaliation if these weapons were used. The Iraqis appear to have taken this to mean a nuclear response, although it is far from clear that this was in fact what was meant (White House 1993). The possibility of an attack on troop formations or logistical points using WMD, in particular chemical weapons, was regarded as very real, and the coalition air forces conducted about 970 strikes on Iraqi WMD targets, mostly chemical weapon capabilities.

The attacks proved subsequently to have been limited in effectiveness. Around 150,000 chemical munitions, untouched by the bombings, were found by UNSCOM after the war, and the official survey of the air campaign found that Iraq's nuclear and biological weapons facilities were similarly unaffected. The attacks on known nuclear facilities, as Harald Müller noted, broke new ground that the Osirak operation had not: 'for the first time, nuclear facilities containing irradiated material were purposefully attacked. Previous attacks on nuclear facilities took place when no fuel had been introduced into the reactors' (Müller *et al.* 1994: 131). Iraq's capabilities, which included a workable bomb design but not yet materiel to produce it, were more extensive than had been thought: the air campaign targeted the two known facilities but a further twenty existed unknown to US planners (White House 1993).

WMD are of course useless without a delivery system, and attacks on Iraq's missile capabilities (the famous 'Scud Chase') totalled some 1,500 strikes, but again with limited success. The post-conflict survey found that many targets thought to have been destroyed had in fact been decoys, vehicles, or other objects that generated Scud-like radar signatures. The inspectors subsequently found that Iraq had had the capability to launch chemical and possibly biological weapons on its 950 km-range al-Hussein missile, the system used to attack Israel and Saudi Arabia. This, and the existence of such huge stocks of chemical munitions, strongly indicates that the attacks did little to degrade Iraq's capabilities, and that Saddam was capable of launching attacks throughout the conflict but was, it would seem, deterred from doing so.

This campaign can be viewed as a *mixed case of pre-emption and prevention*. The attacks on chemical weapons and Scuds are clearly pre-emptive, since they were aimed at degrading or destroying an existing capability before it could be used on coalition forces. The surrounding 'political logic' for the operations was, therefore, the same as that of the war itself, grounded in the UN mandate to remove Iraqi forces from Kuwait. The attacks on the nuclear facilities are better described as preventive, like the Israeli attacks on Osirak a decade before. The Iraqi nuclear weapons programme was known to be still in its developmental stages, although intelligence sharply underestimated at which stage of development, and the opportunity to snuff it out in the early stages, à la Osirak, was taken. The 'political logic' surrounding this campaign, therefore, can be found in a longer term strategy of curtailing the emergence of new nuclear powers in the Middle East.

Case 3: Desert Fox, 1998

In the text of Security Council Resolution 687, aptly known as 'the mother of all resolutions', the UN 'decides' (note: not 'insists' or 'demands') that Iraq was to accept unconditionally the destruction of its nuclear, biological, and chemical weapons by UN and IAEA inspectors. This turned out to be rather more extensive than anticipated, however, as the inspectors discovered how much covert progress had been made, and how little the air campaign had degraded the existing capabilities.

A series of recurrent confrontations, accusations, and crises culminated with the US/UK joint air operation Desert Fox, which began in December 1998 and continued for several months afterwards. The mission of Desert Fox was given by the Pentagon as 'to strike military and security targets in Iraq that contribute to Iraq's ability to produce, store, maintain and deliver weapons of mass destruction', and its wider goals as 'to degrade Saddam Hussein's ability to make and to use weapons of mass destruction. To diminish Saddam Hussein's ability to wage war against his neighbours. To demonstrate to Saddam Hussein the consequences of violating international obligations.'

This language is rather circumspect, and with good reason. The main attack included cruise missile and bomber attacks on 100 targets, but none of them were actual weapons facilities. Rather, they were missile production sites and command and control facilities: hence the Pentagon's stated aim of targets that *contribute* to Iraq's ability to produce, store, maintain and deliver' WMD (emphasis added). The US Defense Secretary, William Cohen, stated that the attack on missile and command and control facilities rather than WMD was due to the risk of contamination affecting civilians (Litwak 2003: 77).

The 'political logic' surrounding Desert Fox is murky and often controversial and, like Desert Storm's counterproliferation operations, it can be viewed as a case of *mixed pre-emption and prevention*. Politically it was presented as both an attack on current capabilities and a preventive attack on future development (Weller 2000: 81). The 'political logic' surrounding Desert Fox was linked by US and UK officials to UN Resolutions, but the actual authorization was circuitous, to say the least.

The founding claim was that Iraq was in breach of Resolution 687, and this was never seriously disputed: in early November, as the pre-Desert Fox crisis gathered momentum, the UN Security Council adopted Resolution 1205 condemning Iraq's 'flagrant violation of Resolution 687'. The controversial part was the subsequent US–UK use of force in response to these violations: neither Resolution 1205 nor 687 contained the trigger phrase mandating war, 'all necessary means'. That authorization was, however, contained in the Resolution that mandated the Gulf War in 1990, and the claim was that the 1998 violations constituted 'the authorization to use force given by the Security Council in 1990 may be revived if the Council decides that there has been a sufficiently serious breach of the conditions laid down by the Council for the ceasefire [i.e. Res 687]' (Weller 2000: 86).

This rather roundabout route brings us back to the war in Kuwait as the formal political logic, but with the disarmament obligations of Resolution 687 as the base. The attacks on extant facilities seem to suggest that this was a *pre-emptive* operation, but both US and UK officials stressed that Desert Fox was also a *preventive* operation to curtail Iraqi efforts to reconstitute its WMD programme. If this was the case, General Zinni of the US Central Command acknowledged that any effects would be temporary (Sokolski 2001: 96).

Strategic response withheld? North Korea and Iran

These two states currently represent the foremost nuclear proliferation issues. North Korea was an NPT member state that withdrew membership, suspended withdrawal, and subsequently followed through with formal withdrawal. Despite years of multilateral negotiations with the United States, Russia, China, South Korea and Japan designed to prevent North Korea from acquiring nuclear weapons, the regime conducted its first atomic test in October 2006. Iran remains an NPT member, but the ongoing crisis over its plans for its nuclear power programme shows little sign of resolution. Recent US intelligence estimates, however, suggest that Tehran remains a good ten to fifteen years away from a nuclear capability.

In the case of North Korea, an Osirak-style operation on the Yongbyon facility was, apparently, seriously considered by the Clinton administration (Sokolski 2001: 96). The plans were not taken up, although one member of the Clinton administration wrote in 2003 that 'Washington still has the option' of attacking Yongbyon, and that 'even if US forces struck after the plant goes hot, radioactive contamination would likely remain local' (Samore 2003: 18). No such plans are reported in the Iranian case, but the Bush administration has stated that this option is emphatically 'not ruled out'.

In these cases, the 'red line', noted by Müller, against attacking facilities that contain nuclear fuel, combined with the political consequences of Osirak-style operations, appears to have kept military action off the agenda. Samore goes on to point out that, although the United States could launch a unilateral attack on North Korean nuclear facilities in theory, 'the reaction in Seoul and Tokyo could splinter the alliance' (Samore 2003: 19).

Presumably, similar reasoning can be applied to the Iranian case, and it is noticeable that Washington has maintained its commitment to the six-party talks in north-east Asia, and the EU3 dialogue with Iran, as the preferred way to deal with these proliferation threats. Multilateralism and institutions (the IAEA and the UN) are currently the tools of choice for tackling the Iranian issue, although Washington has repeatedly suggested that this will not continue indefinitely. For example, the American envoy to Iran declared in September 2003 that diplomatic solutions were always possible but would require Tehran to 'change its course and cooperate fully with the IAEA'. The most likely consequence of a breakdown in the EU3 dialogue and the Iran–IAEA relationship, however, would be to refer the issue to the UN Security Council, rather than a unilateral decision to launch an Osirak-style attack.

KEY POINTS

- Preventive strategies are directed at the process of proliferation, and aim to snuff out development or acquisition of WMD.

- Pre-emptive strategies are directed at the deployed weapons and/or facilities, and aim to prevent their use in war.

- Preventive and pre-emptive strategies have been used separately, or combined as in the 1991 Gulf War.

Analysis and Assessment

The case-studies show that there are two ways in which the proliferation of WMD can be met with a strategically driven response. The first of these is *pre-emption*, which is the military response to the *consequences* of proliferation: the weapons themselves and their delivery systems. If non-proliferation efforts fail, then it becomes necessary to find some way to neutralize weapons or delivery systems. This is not as simple as it might sound, given the destructive power of WMD.

Military responses to WMD are, at the minimum, protection for individuals (chemical weapon suits, for example) or collectives (missile defence), but more far-reaching options are available. The latter involve degrading or destroying WMD capabilities. Freedman calls this 'anticipatory self-defence', and most writers concur that it takes place in the existence of an imminent threat (Freedman 2003: 108; Litwak 2003: 54). This may be in the context of an ongoing war, such as attacks on Iraqi missile facilities during the Gulf War, or outside of it, should it be judged that an attack with WMD may be the opening shot in an imminent war.

As a consequence of this, pre-emptive operations have tended to be given their 'political logic' *outside* the context of the WMD regimes. For example, the attacks on Iraqi WMD and missile facilities during Desert Storm were part of the UN-mandated war to eject Iraqi forces from Kuwait; and the attacks on the Sudanese chemical facility was justified as a counter-terrorist response to attacks on American embassies in Dar-es-Salaam and Nairobi.

The second point at which proliferation can be met with a strategically driven response is *prevention*, the response to proliferation *processes*. This refers to the use of military force to interdict, hamper or destroy the process of WMD acquisition. Military tools here may be a range of things from interception of shipping to attack on WMD facilities. Such operations find their 'political logic' in international WMD nonproliferation norms, but not necessarily in the regimes themselves. The most dramatic example of military inter-diction of (supposed) WMD proliferation was of course the invasion of Iraq in 2003, but other examples include the Israeli attack on Iraq's Osirak nuclear reactor in 1981, Iraq's own attacks on the Iranian nuclear plant at Bushehr between 1985 and 1988, and the re-cent Proliferation Security Initiative (PSI).

The PSI is an international interdiction initiative established by the United States in 2003. Its remit is to establish partnerships and agreements that can intercept illegal WMD shipments by plane or cargo ship. It has a set of operating principles which, tellingly, do not refer to the NPT, CWC or the Biological and Toxin Weapons Convention (BTWC). These principles identify 'states and non-state actors of proliferation concern' in the following terms: 'those countries or entities that the PSI participants involved establish should be subject to interdiction activities because they are engaged in proliferation through: (1) efforts to develop or acquire chemical, biological, or nuclear weapons and associated delivery systems; or (2) transfers (either selling, receiving, or facilitating) of WMD, their delivery systems, or related materials'.[4]

There are several problems and dilemmas associated with military responses to prolif-eration. The foremost problem is one of definition: the term 'counterproliferation' can refer to everything from protective clothing for troops to air strikes on nuclear facilities or even regime change. In the latter cases, it requires the surrounding 'political logic' to be more fully developed than is currently the case. Recent documents issued from Washington may suggest an increasing clarity of definitions (see Box 11.4).

One possible place to develop this logic is the international regimes on WMD and the UN. The great unanswered question of these global WMD regimes has always been: what happens in cases of non-compliance? Counterproliferation can be seen as a response to this question that grew from the initial response of 'defend yourself from WMD attack' to more robust ways to use military force. In specific cases (Osirak, etc.) it has proven controversial, and has yet to make the transition in 'political logic' from its origins in national military strategy to an accepted international context. In general cases, such as the PSI, it is undeveloped but potentially more consensual.

Another, more difficult problem is the issue of operations in the face of an 'imminent threat'. This would perhaps get around the difficulties of generating institutional agreement in the UN for military operations, but still faces the prospect of assessing exactly what constitutes an 'imminent' threat (officials on both sides of the Atlantic have, since the invasion of Iraq, gone to extraordinary lengths to deny that they ever presented Iraq as an imminent threat).[5] As the authors of a recent report noted, the United States (and any state, for that matter) has 'the inherent right and a moral obligation' to take pre-emptive action military action in the face of imminent threats, but needs clarification of the standards for 'imminence' (Perkovich *et al.* 2005: 38).

This need to ground counterproliferation operations in a wider political framework is not simply driven by political niceties, but by practical considerations. The United States might again undertake such operations as part of regional interventions, and that inevitably means the operations will be allied ones. Interventions against WMD are likely to be more about negating the impact of such capabilities on regional security complexes, rather than direct threats to the US territory, and as such the operations will need to possess tacit or explicit support from regional allies.

KEY POINTS

- Finding a 'political' logic into which preventive or pre-emptive action can be fitted has not always been easy.

- Pre-emptive operations tend to find their rationale and legitimacy in the context of an ongoing war, such as the 1991 Gulf War operations.

- Preventive operations can find their logic in the international norms surrounding WMD, such as the Proliferation Security Initiative, or in an existing strategic doctrine such as Israel's attack on Osirak.

Conclusions

Cold war lessons suggest that arms control agreements have had a role to play in contributing to international security. The cold war experience also suggests that arms control is rarely of decisive importance and it is not wise to see it as a way of fundamentally resolving the world's problems. Arms control, however, has rarely been seen as decisively important or a solution in its own right. On the contrary, it is a fundamentally conservative policy, aimed solely at introducing some measure of predictability into an adversarial relationship. It cannot *by itself* create stability, much less peace, and to hope otherwise is to saddle it with unreasonable expectations that are bound to go unfulfilled.

Viewed in that more sober and cautious light, arms control as a means to control weapons of mass destruction should be viewed as a means to an end, never as an end in itself, and relies on the assumption that two or more states which are hostile to one another can also see a mutual interest in avoiding outright conflict. The decline in interest in arms control after the cold war was a function of the fact that the confrontation was over, and the role of arms control was no longer to inject some stability or predictability into the conflict itself, but to assist in eliminating what was now surplus military capability. By 2001, it had become clear that consolidation of ageing cold war arsenals no longer required formal, verified treaties. In the context of US–Russian arms control, the informal character of the SORT agreement seems to indicate that formalized, verified treaties are unlikely to be seen again.

Elsewhere, in the context of the global regimes, the BTWC appeared to be in stasis, the OPCW in good shape, and the NPT facing serious challenges: by the time of the next review in 2010, there could be ten nuclear powers (the United States, the United Kingdom, France, Russia, and the People's Republic of China, plus India, Iran, Israel, North Korea, Pakistan) with only the initial five nuclear powers being inside the NPT. This does not imply that the NPT necessarily is in terminal decline. The two outstanding nuclear proliferation issues, the weapons programmes in Iran and North Korea, are both (for the time being at least) being dealt with by diplomatic means.

Militarily driven responses to proliferation took on a renewed prominence partially in response to the growing concerns about the declining efficacy of deterrence and of nonproliferation efforts. The latter appeared to have been fully confirmed by the post-Gulf War inspections regime, but it should be noted that 'counterproliferation' is in fact much older in practice than in name, as the attack on Osirak demonstrates. Aspin's counterproliferation initiative identified a problem that has now evolved to include non-state terrorist syndicates, proliferation entrepreneurs, and super-empowered individuals who might wish to traffic in or employ WMD.

The evolution of strategic responses since the initial counterproliferation initiative has been haphazard and incomplete. This has been due to bureaucratic politics in Washington and the fact that preventive war and pre-emption is now a counterproliferation option. This more activist posture requires some international political legitimacy if it is to succeed. The key requirement here is evidence: it must be possible to point to hard evidence that WMD are a reality or an imminent threat if international support is to be garnered. And the failure to uncover a significant WMD programme in Iraq after the Second Gulf War has greatly called into question the logic of counterproliferation.

Providing evidence ex ante of WMD programmes, which tend to be covert and hidden, is difficult. The record of intelligence on uncovering such developments is not encouraging: the pre-1991 assessments of Iraq's capabilities fell short of the reality, the assessment of the Sudanese alleged chemical weapons facility proved mistaken, and the pre-2002 assessments of Iraq's programme also appears to have been comprehensively wrong. The problem is that strategic responses require reliable and credible intelligence not only to identify targets, but also to justify operations in the first place. Moreover, militarily driven responses have not yet been fully integrated into diplomatic initiatives to produce a coherent strategy. Rather, they remain a set of options when other responses (arms control, sanctions, etc.) have failed. Overcoming this problem, and finding a sound international 'political logic' within which to base the 'grammar' of operations, will be the central challenges for the future of counterproliferation.

? QUESTIONS

1. What are the differences between disarmament and arms control?

2. What role did arms control play in the cold war in preserving strategic stability?

3. What were the key criticisms of arms control by the end of the cold war?

4. How useful has arms control been in helping to preserve peace and security in the post-cold war period?

5. Is arms control compatible with counterproliferation?

6. What is the difference between pre-emptive and preventive military operations against proliferation?

7. Account for the growing interest in strategic military responses to proliferation.

8. What are the advantages and disadvantages of these approaches?

9. Compare and contrast TWO of the following: the Israeli attacks on Osirak, Operation Desert Fox, and the anti-WMD operations in Desert Storm.

10. Why do you think diplomatic methods were preferred when responding to the Iranian and North Korean nuclear challenges?

FURTHER READING

■ I. Anthony and A. D. Rotfeld (eds.), *A Future Arms Control Agenda* (Oxford: Oxford University Press, 2001). Post-cold war thinking on arms control.

■ Richard K. Betts, 'The New Threat of Mass Destruction', *Foreign Affairs*, 77/1 (1998). Growing post-cold war concern with WMD and the so-called 'rogue states'.

■ H. Bull, *The Control of the Arms Race* (London: Weidenfeld & Nicolson, 1961). Development of modern concept of arms control.

■ Martin Butcher, *What Wrongs Our Arms May Do: The Role of Nuclear Weapons in Counterproliferation* (Washington, DC: Physicians for Social Responsibility, 2003), available at http://www.psr.org/documents/psr_doc_0/program_4/PSRwhatwrong03.pdf

■ B. Buzan and E. Herring, *The Arms Dynamic in World Politics* (London: Lynne Rienner, 1998). Discussion of arms control in a domestic context.

■ Ashton Carter and L. Celeste Johnson, 'Beyond the Counterproliferation Initiative', in Henry Sokolski and James Ludes, *Twenty-First Century Weapons Proliferation* (London: Frank Cass, 2001).

■ Joseph Cirincione, Jon B. Wolfsthal, Miriam Rajkumar, *Deadly Arsenals: Nuclear, Biological and Chemical Threats*, 2nd edn (Washington, DC: Carnegie Endowment for International Peace, 2005).

■ A. Collins, 'GRIT, Gorbachev and the End of the Cold War', *Review of International Studies*, 24/2 (Apr. 1998).

■ S. Croft, *Strategies of Arms Control: A History and Typology* (Manchester: Manchester University Press, 1996). Useful history of disarmament and arms control.

■ I. Daalder and T. Terry (eds.), *Rethinking the Unthinkable: New Directions in Nuclear Arms Control* (London: Frank Cass, 1993). Post-cold war thinking on arms control.

■ Zachary S. Davis, 'US Counterproliferation Policy: Issues for Congress', *CRS Report for Congress* (Washington, DC: Congressional Research Service, 1994).

■ Jason Ellis, 'The Best Defence: Counterproliferation and US National Security', *Washington Quarterly*, 26/2 (2003).

■ Shai Feldman, 'The Bombing of Osiraq: Revisited', *International Security*, 7/2 (1982).

■ Lawrence Freedman, 'Prevention, Not Preemption', *Washington Quarterly,* 26/2 (2003).

■ C. S. Gray, *House of Cards: Why Arms Control Must Fail* (Ithaca, NY: Cornell University Press, 1992). Major critique of the futility of arms control.

■ Eric Herring (ed.), *Preventing the Use of Weapons of Mass Destruction* (London: Frank Cass, 2000). The options for preventing use, rather than simply spread, of WMD.

■ Joint Chiefs of Staff, *Joint Doctrine for Combating Weapons of Mass Destruction* (Washington, DC: Dept of Defense, 2004).

■ Jeffrey Larsen, 'NATO Counterproliferation Policy: A Case Study in Alliance Politics', *INSS Occasional Paper 17* (Border, CO: USAF Institute for National Security Studies, 1997). Also available online at www.usafa.af.mil/df/inss/OCP/ocp17.pdf.

■ Peter Lavoy, Scott Sagan, and James Wirtz (eds.), *Planning the Unthinkable: How New Powers Will Use Nuclear, Biological and Chemical Weapons* (Ithaca, NY: Cornell University Press, 2000). Case-by-case analysis of the drivers behind proliferation.

■ Robert Litwak, 'The New Calculus of Pre-emption', *Survival*, 44/4 (2003).

■ Harald Müller and Mitchell Reiss, 'Counterproliferation: Putting Old Wine in New Bottles', *Washington Quarterly* (Spring 1995). Explores the meanings of the term counterproliferation.

■ Harald Müller, David Fisher and Wolfgang Kötter, *Nuclear Non-Proliferation and Global Order* (New York: Oxford University Press, 1994).

■ C. E. Osgood, *An Alternative to War and Surrender* (Chicago: Chicago University Press, 1962). Further analysis of the GRIT theory of arms control.

■ George Perkovich, Jessica Tuchman Matthews, Joseph Cirincione, Rose Gottemoeller, and Jon B. Wolfsthal, *Universal Compliance: A Strategy for Nuclear Security* (Washington, DC: Carnegie Endowment for International Peace, 2005).

■ Gary Samore, 'The Korean Nuclear Crisis', *Survival*, 45/1 (2003).

■ T. Schelling and M. Halperin *Strategy and Arms Control* (Washington, DC: Pergamon-Brassey's, 1985). Development of modern concept of arms control.

■ *SIPRI Yearbook; Armaments, Disarmament and International Security* **(Oxford University Press).** Details of contemporary arms control negotiations.

■ **Henry Sokolski,** *Best of Intentions: America's Campaign Against Strategic Weapons Proliferation* **(London: Praeger, 2001).**

—— **and James Ludes,** *Twenty-First Century Weapons Proliferation* **(London: Frank Cass, 2001).** A number of useful articles, including one on counterproliferation by Thomas Mahnken.

■ **J. W. Spanier and J. L. Nogee,** *The Politics of Disarmament: A Study of Soviet–American Gamesmanship* **(New York: Praeger, 1962).** Useful history of disarmament and arms control.

■ **Marc Weller, 'The US, Iraq, and the Use of Force in a Unipolar World',** *Survival,* **41/4 (2000).**

■ **J. Wheeler-Bennett,** *The Pipe Dream of Peace: The Story of the Collapse of Disarmament* **(New York: Morrow, 1935).** Useful history of disarmament and arms control.

■ **White House (2002)** *National Strategy to Combat Weapons of Mass Destruction* **(Washington, DC: White House).**

 ## WEB LINKS

- The White House **www.whitehouse.gov**
- US Department of Defense **www.defenselink.mil**
- State Department **www.state.gov**
- British Foreign and Commonwealth Office **www.fco.gov.uk**
- International Atomic Energy Agency **www.iaea.org**
- Defense Threat Reduction Agency **www.dtra.mil**
- Organisation for the Prohibition of Chemical Weapons **www.opcw.nl**
- Federation of American Scientists **www.fas.org**
- Carnegie Endowment's Nonproliferation Program **www.carnegieendowment.org/npp/**
- Arms Control Association **www.armscontrol.org**
- Center for Strategic and International Studies **www.csis.org**
- Center for Nonproliferation Studies, Monterey **http://cns.miis.edu/**
- Mountbatten Centre for International Studies, Southampton **www.mcis.soton.ac.uk**
- Nuclear Threat Initiative **www.nti.org**

 Visit the Online Resource Centre that accompanies this book for lots of interesting additional material http://www.oxfordtextbooks.co.uk/orc/baylis_strategy2e/.

Conventional Power and Contemporary Warfare

JOHN FERRIS

 Chapter Contents

- Power and War: A History
- New World Orders: 1945, 1989, 2001
- Power and Hyperpower
- Military Affairs: Revolution and Counter-Revolution
- Arts of War
- Military Balances
- War, What is it Good For?

Reader's Guide

This chapter assesses what conventional power is today. It analyses how, and how far, conventional forces shape the contemporary world, whether by fighting wars or by backing state policy in peace. This chapter also considers trends in their development. It examines how far conventional force has been 'transformed' in recent years, and how it functions in areas ranging from distant strike to urban warfare. This chapter compares the role of conventional power relative to other forms of force, such as WMDs and terrorism. It ends by discussing the conventional strength of states in the world, and trends in its distribution between them, with particular reference to emerging powers.

Power and War: A History

In romance, this is war. States fight, therefore armies enter *decisive battle*. One wins, the other loses, the victor makes great gains, immediately, and both return to their seats. Sometimes war is like a waltz, but mostly not. Often, it is long and destructive, costing both sides more than they gain. Even the victor suffers unintended and undesired damage. Battles are inconclusive, or victories have no value. Enemies will not surrender, or else recover from defeat and force you to battle again. They refuse to fight by your rules, or evade your strength, attack your weaknesses, and force their will on you. In the competition of war, intentions and effects become confused, and paradox rules. Politicians imagine armies are military scalpels for political surgery, but in war, one operates with a battleaxe and without a medical licence on a patient who is trying to amputate one's arm; in the dark.

This chapter examines the present and emerging state of conventional military power, including its nature, distribution, what it can and cannot do, what is changing and what is not. One may understand these trends and their trajectory only by considering the record of conventional war, especially in recent years. Nor can one look just at the states which most often fight such wars, or have the biggest toys. They are not the only players in the game. Second or third rate powers shape conventional war as much as advanced ones. They all do so by their weaknesses as well as their strengths.

When refined, raw power becomes armed forces, which have been remarkably small in size and hard to maintain. Sometimes, states regularly field hundreds of thousands of soldiers (in China between 453 and 221 BCE; the Mediterranean basin between 330 BCE and 380 CE; Europe between 1660 and 1870)—millions in the twentieth century. Yet these periods are unusual, because the maintenance of large armies erodes the wealth of nations and the power of states. In classical Greece, armies usually were less than 15,000 men, rarely more than 50,000; so too Europe from 380 to 1660 CE, most of Asia through most of history, or European empires of the nineteenth century. Since 1989, armies again have slipped in size. The greatest power on earth can send barely 200,000 soldiers on a single expedition beyond its borders. Navies have been even smaller, because they are a rich man's weapon, dependent on industry and wealth. Expensive to build and maintain, fleets vanish without a regular programme of shipbuilding. Few states have maintained a large navy for long; and these have commanded the seas as armies rarely have the land. Seapower is the child of wealth and resolve; so too, airpower. Military power has social roots, many forms, and a competitive nature—your system compared to the enemy's in specific circumstances. The edge of the razor is comparative advantage, your strengths, and your ability to force them on the enemy. Numbers and technology matter, but not enough to win every time. A belligerent able to take heavy losses without surrendering can beat one with high technology and low willpower. Able armies with no material edge can whip larger enemies. Politics and willpower can defeat firepower and technology, or vice versa. Small elite forces can crush large half-trained ones, or not. It all depends on the circumstances.

Until 1945, the most effective form of military power was conventional force. It was the weapon of choice for the strong, yielding particular advantage over the weak. It was commonly used between major states which were adjacent to each other, particularly between 1570 and 1945. It could inflict more precise and powerful damage than irregular

BOX 12.1

The Intricacies of Power

Conventional power is an alloy, formed from the interaction of material factors (geography, demography, and economy) and the administrative capacity and political structure of a state—its ability to command a people and tap their resources. These elements are linked dialectically. The first defines the potential power of a state, the second how much of it can be tapped, and how well. Their relationship converts material power from crude to finished form—from resources to forces. Overwhelming strength in one element may not a great power make, nor weakness in one destroy it. A poor country may remain a great power because of the size and skill of its armed forces, its geopolitical position, the stability of its institutions, or the ability of its statesmen; thus, Prussia, 1740–1866, and Japan, 1900–41. A rich country may not convert its wealth to power, and so matter less in world affairs than possible: namely the Netherlands, 1715–89, Japan, and most Western European states since 1960. Rich states rarely tap their resources systematically for strategic purpose, which bolsters the position of anyone willing to do so, rich or not. In power, resolve matters more than wealth.

Power is a concrete quality; the resources a state taps for strategic purposes, as against those it might do, but does not. It takes different forms in diplomacy, a short campaign between two countries, or a prolonged and total war of attrition involving most members of a state system. Usually, institutions are the main factor in power, because they turn raw into refined strength—a hard task, dominated by marginal superiority. For most of history, a state able to jump from tapping 1 per cent of its potential power to 2 per cent might so double its military capacity. In 1509, Venice fought every other state of Italy, Spain, and Germany, as Britain did in 1782 against half Europe and its American colonists. They were beaten, but the remarkable thing is how little they lost. The relative edge provided by institutions dulled from 1870 because, ironically, they became more effective, numerous, and common. Advanced states adopted many systems (conscript armies, general staffs, central banks, military industrial complexes) which more effectively turned wealth into power. Thus, brute demographic and industrial strength was the key predictor of power in the First and Second World Wars. To tap 1 per cent more of one's power than did a rival offered little advantage when even mediocre states could exploit 20 per cent, though greater differences might exist and did matter. In any case, the value of institutional superiority rose again after 1945, at least so far as developing states were concerned. The secret of Israel's battlefield success has been the fact it possesses techniques like conscription and a quickly mobilized military reserve while its neighbours do not. The same factor underlies the formidable defences of Singapore, where freeways double as emergency landing strips for fighter aircraft.

forces and keep battle from your home, yet it had limits. Sometimes conventional war is unavoidable or an effective way to achieve one's ends. Merely to avoid defeat is good. More is possible if one is strong or smart, or the enemy weak or foolish—preferably both. Yet, as in any competition, the use of conventional force has unpredictable outcomes. Decisive battles are like strikes of lightning—they happen, rarely. Their impact can be dramatic: Prussia unified Germany and dominated Europe through successive victories in 1866 and 1870. The greatest of world powers have emerged through long runs of decisive victories over many enemies—Rome between 250 BCE and 100 CE, Arabs in 632–750, Mongols in 1206–1368, and England between 1690–1919. These circumstances are significant, but not common. The classic example of a decisive battle is Cannae in 217 BCE—yet its victor lost that war. The average outcome of war is attrition, slow and costly to both sides. Conventional war is like gambling. All that is sure is an entry cost, and some combination of risk and gain. Some people love the risk, forget the odds, and think the pay-off certain; others fear to play; skill matters, and the strength of your hand; so does chance.

KEY POINTS

- Conventional power stems from an inter-action between material and institutional factors.

- Conventional forces take many forms, reflecting social and political norms.

- They succeed by exploiting comparative advantages over competitors.

- The outcome of their use is unpredictable. War tends to be attritional.

New World Orders: 1945, 1989, 2001

Between 1815 and 1945, Western military systems proved superior to all others at once. Europeans conquered the earth, creating its first unified political and economic system, and then destroyed each other. From the wreck emerged a new world order, defined by decolonization, the cold war, and nuclear weapons. The industrialized states were divided between two stable alliances, unequal in economics or politics but balanced in destructive capability. They had the deadliest weapons and waged the greatest arms races ever known, with conventional and nuclear, chemical and bacteriological weapons of mass destruction (WMDs). A war between them carried the risk of suicide. This made conventional strength just one part of power, imposed an upper limit on the rationality of force, and reshaped world politics. These alliances spent unparalleled amounts of money on weapons they never used, for fear nuclear bombs would render 'victory' meaningless. Each negated the other's strength. The industrialized states possessed absolutely far more power than in 1939, but in relative terms, their influence in the world declined sharply. Decolonization was the primary political force on earth; the cold war was a local phenom-enon of the industrialized world. No longer did power on one continent determine it everywhere. The European world empires shattered, breaking the world into bits. Power had to be struggled for in each region. Success in one did not determine events in another. The USSR and the United States dominated the industrialized world, but neither picked up the pieces of imperialism. They simply established ties with regional successor states, some of which became stronger than most advanced countries.

Since 1945, the major industrialized states have not fought each other nor, excepting the guerrilla wars which accompanied decolonization, many countries at all. War rarely has been fought by the strong nor practised at the state of the art. The centre of world power was not the centre of world war. That was Asia and Africa, where most states lacked the economic or administrative abilities to fight total wars or win quick and cheap victories.

Most of these conflicts stemmed from the end of imperialism, whether wars of national liberation to overthrow it or of succession between new states, striving to determine their strength, relations, and frontiers against others. They tailed off by 1975. Wars in Africa were prolonged, indecisive, and destructive, because neither side could tap its resources well for military purposes. In Asia, some conventional wars were long and costly, but usually both sides halted long before their resources were exhausted. Three-week wars costing thousands of lives were common, but not three-year ones with hundreds of thousands of dead. Asian regimes pursued limited aims with limited means. Conventional war was an important, but uncommon, aspect of international affairs. In these Third World wars, many states had leading edge weapons but few used them well. They featured military styles ranging from the Space Age to the Stone Age. Some campaigns were slower and costlier than the Somme, others quicker and cheaper than the fall of France. On occasion human wave assaults beat mechanized armies. There was no dominant style of war because no one set of military conditions ruled. The relationship between victory on the battlefield and success at the peace table was complex. Rarely did force achieve great aims, or precise ones—far less so than had been the case in the heyday of Europe over the previous century.

In 1989, with the collapse of the Soviet bloc, the distribution of power in the world altered again, as did its nature. Western states, overwhelmingly superior in military technology, cut their military spending by 25 per cent, and assumed they could master the new world order. They soon were disillusioned. The end of the cold war prompted the collapse of several states and another wave of wars of succession. In most of Asia, strong non-Western states became more powerful, continuing to dominate their regions and acquire WMDs. Most Arab powers, however, slipped in status, because they no longer gained free weapons from superpowers. In the Middle East, the United States used force for *realpolitik*, crippling Iraq and checking Iran. Otherwise, power became decoupled from policy. When Western states actively used their power, they did so in an odd way. Their peoples, reluctant to fight except for vital interests, still sometimes wished one foreign party would cease to bully another and deployed token forces to achieve that end. The results were tragedy and farce. Western states remained uncertain whether to use force and how. They pursued international acts of charity through multilateral military means, driven not by reason of state but by public opinion and humanitarianism, aiming not to defeat a foe but to do good and no bad. Such ends were hard to achieve or even to pursue. Western outrage or troop movements did not make bullies mend their ways. Tiny but ruthless powers defied Western states for years, as in ex-Yugoslavia and Somalia. Regimes in Iraq and Serbia gained political strength by defying the West, which often was divided, as it faced localized but unlimited wars, marked by ethnic cleansing and mass murder. The West found it hard to help the weak, whether in Rwanda or Bosnia. Other states were equally impotent. Israel abandoned much of the West Bank in response to the *intifada*. Russia could not crush insurgents in Chechnya. India failed to end a civil war in Sri Lanka, as did African forces in Sierra Leone, Liberia, and Sudan.

Then, on 11 September 2001, Al-Qaeda launched an act of 'propaganda by the deed', to rally Muslims against the United States. An unconventional terrorist attack inflicted greater damage than almost any conventional one in history, including Pearl Harbor. This tied together every level of force, from terrorism to WMDs, and plugged power back into politics. Rich states, fearing for their security, took their firmest military actions for years. Between 2001 and 2004, their military budgets rose on average by 40 per cent, three times the level of defence-related inflation. The United States ceased to swing between isolationism and internationalism. It undertook massive rearmament, bolstered its conventional power, declared policies of unilateralism and pre-emptive attack against anything it deemed a great threat, and occupied Afghanistan and Iraq. The lonely hyperpower, pillar of the world order, was wounded. It pursued absolute security, which many states saw as a threat to themselves. Its General War on Terror used all types of power to reshape all forms of politics everywhere in the world, at once. This affected the distribution of power, and its use.

KEY POINTS

- Several forms of a unified world political system have existed since 1800. Conventional force played a different role in each one.

- Conventional power was used frequently between 1815 and 1945. Western superiority underwrote European imperialism.

- After 1945, major states rarely used conventional force against each other, but did so more often against weaker states, which fought each other frequently.

- Since 1945, the power of conventional force has been limited by WMDs, and the greater power of guerrilla warfare.

Power and Hyperpower

If riches made strength, Europe would be the greatest power on earth, the United States second, and Japan third, all close together; but the issue is the marriage of will and wealth. One may divide conventional military powers into four groups: the United States, advanced states (industrialized, capitalist, mostly liberal democratic, ranging in size from Singapore to Germany), developing powers (with small to large industrial bases, and mostly authoritarian governments, like Brazil, China, India, Iran, Pakistan, Russia, and Turkey), and weak states (most of those in Africa, and some in Asia). Weak states have little offensive power; their strength is the difficulty of occupation. Any rich country can speedily increase its conventional forces, and so change the distribution of strength in the world or any of its regions, but their will to power varies, judging by declared policies and performance since 1989 and 2001. Most European states, unwilling to change their conscript systems and disinclined to intervene abroad, have large armies at home but little power to project beyond their borders. In functional terms, their conscript systems are ceasing to be military services and becoming social ones. These states are unlikely to be attacked by conventional force or to fight each other. With out of area capabilities small, they are most likely to use force against the weakest of weak states, in humanitarian interventions. Britain and

France, however, can launch sizeable expeditionary forces, second only to the United States. If they complete their declared policies, they may maintain that status for decades, and the ability to shape major events abroad. Australia and Canada retain smaller but notable expeditionary capabilities. Advanced states in Asia, like Singapore, South Korea, and Japan, maintain powerful defensive capabilities to contain immediate threats from neighbours. Conventional power matters more to Israel, and it makes greater sacrifices for that, than any other nation on earth except North Korea. Many developing states tap far more of their resources for forces, and are far stronger in their own regions, or the world, than any rich country except Israel, South Korea, and the United States. Russia and China remain the world's second and third strongest conventional powers, while others have large forces and some offensive capability. All these states, however, are one or many steps behind the state of the art, and have reason to be cautious about using such forces.

Americans have a taste for, and the infrastructure to exercise, power across the world, and a declared policy of pre-empting great threats. Their post-9/11 expansion in military spending has stalled, but at far higher levels than in 2000. No other state in history ever has had the absolute and relative conventional power it possessed in 2005. Overwhelming strength at sea and in air, strike, and, soon perhaps, space, dissuades any head-on challenges in these key areas. The United States has as many aircraft carriers as the rest of the world combined, able to launch ten times as many aircraft. Its air force, the only one with the most advanced equipment, like stealth technology, matches every other on earth together. This capacity underwrites Pax Americana just as seapower did Pax Britannica. It augments nuclear power as a means to deter attack and sustains the United States' loose leadership over all advanced countries, the structure through which it exerts political influence. That, in turn, creates a key phenomenon in contemporary politics, that rich states will not fight each other and often will cooperate. Yet these edges are of limited value in land combat—indeed, the cost needed to develop them may weaken American power in that sphere. Its relative advantage lies in distant strike, compellance, deterrence, and dissuasion, and its weakness in close quarter combat and occupation. The United States could smash the air and naval power of almost any developing country, but could not successfully occupy most medium-sized ones. Threats of force serve Washington more than its use. These are just some of the paradoxes of conventional power in the contemporary world.

KEY POINTS

- Overwhelming conventional power, along with nuclear weapons, makes the United States the world leader. This strength is more useful to support dissuasion and compellance than in war.

- Many rich states have powerful conventional forces at home. Some have great expeditionary capabilities.

- Some developing powers have powerful conventional forces at home. None can project it far from their borders.

- Most states have weak conventional forces.

Military Affairs: Revolution and Counter-Revolution

Since 1989, American military policy has been driven by efforts to ride a revolution in military affairs (RMA). Its major policy statements, Joint Visions 2010 and 2020, advocate forces with 'order of magnitude' improvements in precision, speed and lethality. The aim is comparative advantage: 'frictional imbalance', 'decision superiority', and 'full spectrum dominance—achieved through the interdependent application of dominant maneuver, precision engagement, focused logistics, and full dimensional protection'. The means are a marriage between precision weapons and information technology, the use of 'information superiority as a key enabler and our capacity for innovation'. Advocates of the 'new American way of war' assume this marriage will transform the knowledge available to armed forces, their nature, and that of war. Knowledge will not merely shape the battle—it will be a battlefield. Intelligence and communication, not command and discipline, will be the heart of armed forces. They will act without friction on near perfect knowledge, through the fusion of command, control, communications, intelligence, surveillance, and reconnaissance (C4ISR). They will jettison traditional hierarchies, adopt interconnected and flat structures based on the internet, and conduct netcentric warfare (NCW). Some of these ideas push strategy from the age of Clausewitz to that of the Borg. A commander in one exercise, 'Millennium Challenge 02', noted the aim was 'machine-to-machine talk', so he could 'create an air tasking order with one push of a button. I can see the entire battle in a way that if there's something I don't like, I can fix it'.

The RMA is being applied in many ways. At present, the main American form of operations, 'Command and Control Warfare', turns the 'Air/Land Battle' approach of the 1980s into a form of blitzkrieg, seeking to wreck the enemy's 'information dependent process', so to shatter its ability to perceive and command. War, the next generation, or 'Rapid Decisive Operations', is expected to open with the pursuit of a 'Superior Information Position (Fight First for Information Superiority)' and become 'knowledge-centric'. In both cases, theory says, victory in knowledge destroys enemy command, and then fire kills its body. More radical voices assume these aims can be achieved by the system itself, without command or commanders. They conceptualize war as Nintendo and strategy as shooting, focusing on 'sensors to shooters' systems, in which C4ISR directly links millions of observers and 'one shot one kill' weapons. To be seen is to be shot, to be shot is to be killed, and to be fast is to win. Visionaries imagine a world in which war is started by humans, but terminated by machines. If any of these advocates are right, conventional force has more power as a tool of state and the leading powers greater superiority in it, than since the heyday of European imperialism.

These ideas were tested in three recent conflicts. They failed in Kosovo during 1999, where forces suffering from political interference, overcentralization and confusion between levels of command, engaged an enemy with good strategy, camouflage, and air defence. Airpower did little damage nor did the allies achieve clear victory. In Afghanistan and Iraq during 2001–3, the conversion of military to political success also proved hard. Still, larger forces, better used, unleashed on worse foes, coordinated command

and intelligence with unprecedented skill. This multiplied the strength of all forms of centralized firepower and rapid, precise, and long-distance weapons. Fleeting chances which once would have been lost were exploited—sometimes aircraft hit a ten by ten foot box twenty minutes after its detection by any source. A soldier with a laser range-finder could send the co-ordinates of a target to a command site hundreds of miles away, which fed those co-ordinates onto the bombs of an aircraft in another locale—even changing them in flight. Aircraft received target orders as they reached the edge of Baghdad. These leaps in quality, and in the sheer quantity of aircraft and precision-guided munitions (PGMs), let strike forces matter far more than ever before, equalling armies in land warfare. Iraqi command was shattered, and its forces in open country broken without firing a shot.

Yet victory did not flow straight, or simply, from the RMA. Its keys were air supremacy, vehicle and body armour, the incompetence of Iraqi command, and the psychological effect of the power and invulnerability of coalition artillery and tanks. A Marine colonel noted some of his tanks survived seven RPG rounds, and 'became the unkillable beast and caused them [Iraqis] nightmares'. Even at the peak of success, classic problems of information overload, friction between headquarters, and inexperienced personnel swamped coalition commands. Information dominance existed at higher levels, but never reached forces on the ground. For all the talk of NCW and C4ISR, command and intelligence were no better than in 1944–5. Fortunately, the enemy was worse—the German Army might have smashed an army exhibiting the flaws of 2003. Land and air forces fought separate battles, rather than fusing them. Close air support failed. Distant strike succeeded only when the machine performed without friction. Any friction yielded failure; no system is always perfect. Iraqis did not systematically lure attackers into intense combat in urban centres, but when that happened, the American system collapsed, and its forces had to fight the old-fashioned way. Fortunately, they were better at it than the Iraqis. Thus, on 2 April 2003, Task Force 3–69, the battalion-sized spearhead of the American Army, crossed the Euphrates River into, without knowing it, an enemy 800 per cent stronger, with 8,000 men, and 70 armoured vehicles. It beat them. An enemy which fought by its own rules, however, light infantry willing to die or able silently to steal away, proved greater problems. Close-quarter battle shaped land war as much as distant strike, and mattered far more against guerrillas. The Taliban and Ba'athist enemies were mediocre, by the standards of developing states, in the quality of forces, generals, and political organization. The main lesson from these three campaigns is that Western powers cannot easily defeat any enemy with competent leadership, a decent army, and fair public consent for example, Hezbollah. Nor are Americans the only people who can learn lessons and improve their performance.

These tests show the limits to ideas about transformed forces. Those ideas assume the United States always can play to its strengths, and never will have to defend its weaknesses. They posit a world without strategy, or strategists, a one-dimensional and one-sided struggle. One throws high-technology conventional forces into intense combat against a weak enemy without initiative. It plays to one's strengths. A fine-tuned, high-performance, machine with perfect knowledge and command works perfectly, without any effort being made to hamper its effect. It is convenient when an enemy chooses to be foolish and weak, but that is its choice, not yours. A smart but weak foe may refuse any game where you can apply your strengths, and make you play another one. A tough and able foe might turn the characteristics of your game into a strength of its own, by attacking any precondition for your machine to work and imposing its rules on you. By doing what suits them, they will change their strengths and weaknesses—and yours.

The RMA has value, but has been oversold. It has done many things, but not everything. It has multiplied American strengths but not reduced its weaknesses. The RMA has increased the value of high technology and firepower in conventional war, but for little else; where these things matter, they do more than ever; where they do not, nothing has changed. Its advocates assume that conventional power has grown steadily more powerful, and everything else weaker, that the RMA has universal force across all arms, instead of strength in some and weakness in others. Their arguments are linear, looking at only one development, instead of the reciprocal relationship between several of them. The revolution is getting better; so is the counter-revolution.

Thus, strike weapons enable a new version of gunboat diplomacy, by letting one destroy select targets from a distance, to make a political point, or support coercive diplomacy. They enable conventional forces to hit harder, further, and more accurately than ever before; they have reshaped operations at sea and in the air, and what one can do with them; but that is not all of war, nor is it entirely new. Since 1933, air forces have applied NCW to some aspects of combat—Fighter Command was the world's first netcentric force, before the internet existed!—as have navies since 1955. These command and intelligence systems were sophisticated. They could do far more than was done with them—weapons systems were restrained by limits to weapons, not systems. In 1917, allied intelligence constantly located U-boats, prompting immediate air or surface strikes, which failed because units were slow and their ordnance weak. By 1943, intelligence on U-boats was little better but allied forces far more able to kill. In 1944, Allied air forces could strike any target reported immediately, but not accurately; in 2003, aircraft launched instant, precise, and devastating strikes based on information acquired ten minutes earlier by headquarters 10,000 miles away. The RMA stems less from changes in C4ISR than in weapons. Technology enables transformation; that in 2003 it transformed the power of aircraft far more than that of armies is suggestive. In land warfare, command and intelligence never have worked as they do at sea or air.

Perhaps conventional forces are midway through a decades' long transition from one set of forms—armies, navies, and air forces—to another: close-quarters land forces, navies, strike weapons (whether based on land, sea or air), and space power. If so, some services may not survive as they presently are. If no combat aircraft have pilots, air forces and artillery might merge, and together dominate blue water, where no large surface warships will be able to survive the hostility of the United States, or perhaps several other countries. But this transition is far from over and it will affect armies least of all—perhaps not much. No recent piece of technology except the atom bomb or nerve gas has changed land warfare as greatly as did bayonets, quickfiring artillery, machine guns, tanks, anti-tank guns, or aircraft. In the foreseeable future, land warfare will involve an equal and overlapping combination of close quarters and distant firepower, as it has done since 1940—or 1916.

At one and the same time, the strike capacity of advanced states has risen as has the power of terrorists against them, while nothing has changed in close-quarter combat or guerrilla warfare. Nor can any one master all these domains at once.

KEY POINTS

- Conventional forces take many forms, and their strength is hard to compare.

- High technology forces can strike blows of unprecedented precision and weight, which has transformed seapower, airpower, and all forms of distant strike.

- The power of armies has not been transformed for close-quarter combat, or against guerrillas.

Arts of War

Military power cannot evade economics. To buy one thing is not to buy another. The entry cost for the RMA is high; to pay it will incur opportunity costs at the operational and strategic levels. This situation forces choices on all states, each with a mixture of costs and benefits. The United States will take an unassailable lead in transformed forces, because it cares about them while no one else can keep up in depth and breadth. A head-on competition by anyone simply will make it become stronger against everyone, albeit at cost in other areas. Even a military budget equal to almost every other state on earth has limits, and technology is expensive. So to make anyone else think twice about competition, the United States will keep the entry cost to the RMA high. This will cause problems for its friends as well as its enemies. The transformation of power may unintentionally weaken some advanced states, just as the development of the Dreadnought sank seapowers unwilling to keep up, like France and the Netherlands. Nor is the new American way of war a model for everyone. In transformed power, the United States will be a giant and everyone else a dwarf. Transformation will give no one else quite the same bag for a buck. It will be less cost efficient for weak than for strong states. Its pressure on defence budgets will reinforce the tendencies towards demilitarization in Europe, while complicating life for all other advanced powers. They will transform far less than the United States, but aim to have some component able to work with it and to monitor its activities. This will give them edges over enemies which cannot adopt such innovations, but not revolutionary ones. Israel does not need transformation to master Arab armies. It will not silence North Korean artillery in range of Seoul.

Comparative advantage will take many forms. The United States will own seapower, airpower, and strike, with everything that promises. Even forcing enemies to asymmetry has advantages, as unconventional means often solve problems less well than conventional ones. Thus, between 1914 and 1945 surface fleets let one use the sea, while submarines merely limited one's power to do so. Of course asymmetry can be more successful. Air defence systems cheaply cripple the power of aircraft. Asymmetric means are unlikely to wreck (as against degrade) American strengths in the air or blue water, but the story is different on land. American choices for transformation will leave its enemies with strong cards to play—indeed, it will strengthen some of those they hold. Between 1870 and 1989, the standard form of armies was large conscript forces, able to deliver and absorb heavy punishment. Given their costs in money and skilled personnel, transformed armies will be smaller professional services, with unprecedented reliance on firepower and technology. Like eggshells armed with hammers, they will be able to inflict damage, but not to take it; closer to the model of artillery than infantry. When they are good they will be very good. Every cog of its machine sometimes may work well at the same time, reducing friction to the lowest level possible. They will be better than ever at anything dominated by firepower, but worse at anything else. They cannot take heavy losses; they cannot easily deploy their strengths or shield their weaknesses in close-quarters combat. Once, an army able to defeat an enemy was big enough to occupy it—now, one easily can be powerful enough to crush a foe but too small to hold its territory. Nor do special forces change this situation. These units are useful, but not new, essentially equalling the light infantry or cavalry routinely maintained by many states over past centuries, their mobility multiplied by airpower.

Again, until 1945, nothing limited the upper edge of force except one's ability to get there. If one could annihilate an enemy, one did. No longer is that true, because of the mixture of images, ethics, and opinion aroused by modern media. In Vietnam, doubly so in both Gulf Wars and Kosovo, a desire to minimize the deaths of enemy civilians, even of soldiers, shaped the use of force by Western states. This limits power and confuses its use, as one tries to avoid the upper level of permissable force. Indicatively, legal advisers serve on Western military staffs, so to ensure that international law shapes the selection of targets for strike weapons. Because they are the safest means to navigate near the tolerated limits on force, precision and control are the fundamental gains from transformation. These gloves would come off, however, if any people thought its vital interests at stake— then conventional weapons might wreak mass destruction, to the surprise of the unwary attacker who provoked it. Events in Lebanon during 2006 illustrate all these issues. Meanwhile, terrorists drive their devastation into levels once occupied to conventional forces, precisely because images of ruthlessness and power play to their home demographic.

Developing states will respond to their environment by maintaining large and good forces for close-quarter combat. One lesson from Iraq and Kosovo is the difference a decent army and second-rate kit makes. This is not a new lesson. Over the past century, developing states like Turkey, Vietnam, and Japan developed armies able to inflict heavy punishment while absorbing even more, making willpower a decisive theatre and often beating richer but less resolute enemies. In ground war, defenders will be most strong and attackers least so, home field advantage will matter, and Western armies must deal with cities. Between 1980 and 2000, in Mogadishu, Beirut, and Grozny, Israeli, American and Russian armies larger and better equipped than their foes were caught in costly and inconclusive combat, where battlefield triumph produced political defeat. So too, American forces in Iraq since 2004. Urban combat sucks up time and resources. Compared to battle in the field, it requires more men to conduct and costs more casualties, it divides the value of training, technology, and firepower and multiplies that of morale and the ability to take losses; it creates unpredictable consequences which turn victory to defeat. Civilian casualties, refugees, and relief efforts shape victory or defeat as much as tactics. Official American doctrine on 'Joint Urban Operations' approvingly cites Sun Tzu as saying, 'the worst policy is to attack cities'. It recognizes that urban combat dulls every American edge, while civilian deaths may trump success on the field. In 1968, for example, television coverage helped turn 'the US tactical victory of Hue' into 'part of the strategic defeat of the Tet offensive'. Western forces will not enter urban warfare unless every other military option is exhausted, and the choice is assault or political defeat. These are dicey options. Urban warfare, and the price of occupation, are the functional equivalents of WMDs for weak states. They will deter attack.

Developing countries also will aim to negate high-technology forces through asymmetric strategies. The first step for an able enemy in a war with the United States would be to jam any communications on the electromagnetic spectrum. This would damage American power far more than their own, and perhaps stall its entire machine of war, given its unprecedented reliance on thick and fast communications. That would have happened in 2003 had Iraq been able to jam Geographical Positioning Systems, a central node in C4ISR and an easy target. One also can attack more precise targets, such as the ability to use PGMs. On 6 October 1973, after all, Egypt negated Israeli airpower by guiding through radar systems surface to air missile systems for which the enemy was unready. The effect lasted for only a week, but a week is a long time in the politics of modern war. More broadly, electronic war, cyberwar, psychological warfare, media manipulation, black propaganda, and deception will be central features in postmodern conflicts. The nature of power in these mind games is unclear, but they offer ample room for imaginative asymmetry, and the potential for pay-off. Sooner or later, some state will let slip the bytes of cyberwar, with uncertain effect. It may be Y2K revisited. It may combine terrorism and WMDs—consider the consequences of wrecking the computers controlling a nuclear power plant. A first strike may be so advantageous that it creates an imperative to move first, adding a new twist to deterrence. The United States is the leading power in these areas, but also the most vulnerable.

Above all, the final asymmetric response of enemies to American conventional power will simply be to pick up its pieces and go home—to WMDs or terrorism.

KEY POINTS

- The RMA is not for everyone. It will help the United States more than any other country.

- Transformed fighting services have weaknesses and strengths.

- When they can play to their strengths, they will succeed.

- Rational foes play to their strengths and your weaknesses. Developing countries may trump the RMA through asymmetric strategies, WMDs, urban warfare, guerrilla warfare, terrorism, or good forces with low technology.

Military Balances

Sometimes, conventional power is easy to calculate. Each side fights the same way and has so many archers or armoured fighting vehicles (AFVs); you multiply the quantity by some co-efficient representing assumed quality, and Bob's your uncle. Today, simply to gauge conventional power is problematic, because its forms vary and are changing. Perhaps one can measure power in PGMs for all states, simply by multiplying their quality and quantity by some coefficient representing C4ISR. So too with blue water navies, as they are rare and commentators agree on what makes power for them (that story ends at the brown water mark). Such measurements are harder with armies. Those of developing powers have a strong but short punch, great on their borders but not beyond; perhaps best measured by the number of combat soldiers they could deploy on their frontier. These figures are considerable: North Korea or China could throw millions of soldiers to their main frontiers, India, Pakistan, or Turkey 400,000. Conversely, rich states have armies with longer range but less weight. Their strength is best measured by the combat troops ready for expeditionary service: where Germany, Canada, and Australia might deploy 3,000 soldiers each, France and Britain, 20,000, and the United States, 140,000. World conventional power rests on a combination of a blue water fleet and an expeditionary capability, in which the United States stands alone in its class, Britain and France punch above their weight, while Australia, Canada, and India are the only bantams. To compare these different forms of force is like gauging apples and oranges; the point is precisely where the struggle occurs. In Fukien, the Chinese army would reign supreme; fifty miles off shore, it would drown. France is a great power in Africa, not in Asia. These issues can be illustrated by examining some instances of power.

China and India have much air and maritime equipment of 1970s Soviet vintage. Their conventional power will turn on how far and well they replace it, and to what ends. China has far more old kit than India, some of it creaking: in 2005, 25 per cent of its fighters were MIG 19s, which the Soviets removed from first line service by 1965! India's problem is more easily solved, because no great power blocks its aims. The competition with Pakistan is unlikely to end, but is one-sided. Pakistan strains its resources to remain in the game. Its forces are good, but India has 200 per cent more infantry, 150 per cent more tanks, 300 per cent more guns, and 250 per cent more aircraft, at par. Pakistan can exploit India's greatest weakness, the political fractures of a multinational state, but it really could endanger its rival only with active help from China or the United States. Indian cooperation with Washington trumps that ace. Indian politicians and soldiers distort the danger of Pakistan, because a weak external enemy suits their interests. India, however, does not seek to conquer its neighbours, however much it wishes them subordinate—few things could be more disastrous for India than conquering Pakistan and having to rule its people. Meanwhile, India already can project force far from its shores. It aims to be one of two dominant powers in the Indian Ocean, alongside the United States, and has some means to do so. Its naval bases are good, as is its locale for land-based aviation. Its old carrier and twenty-five decent destroyers and frigates form the equivalent of a carrier battle group, albeit a weak one. This power will rise notably after 2010, as it junks old kit and acquires new, above all purchasing an ex-Soviet carrier, building an Indian one at home, and developing the Indo-Russian BraMos cruise missile. So long as it acts on its declared policies, India has and will keep the world's fourth greatest fleet, if qualitatively below the top three. It cannot sail against American opposition, but then neither can the British or French. So long as India continues its drift towards alignment with the West, and the moderate but sustained investment in new forces of the past generation, it will be a major but regional seapower. That will strengthen its influence throughout the Indian Ocean littoral and Asia, but to what effect remains uncertain. Since 1949, India has found power and strategy hard to deal with. It uses power merely as one means to demonstrate its status, rather than as a tool to pursue specific interests. India, the least of the great powers, punches below its weight. It has more power than it can use.

China has less than it needs. It has a clear sense of power and strategy and great ambitions, which it can achieve only with greater efforts. It aims to absorb Taiwan and regards the American containment of its coasts as a threat. Yet it can do little about that. Over past

---

BOX 12.2

The Future for Power Relations

Future power will turn on the military application of industry. China and India have large sectors in those areas—China's aviation industry alone has 560,000 workers, versus 72,000 for the largest American defence contractor, General Dynamics—government-run, and burdened with the deadweight of failed socialism. Until recently, their quality was low, which leaves problems for the future. In 1998–9, China split its arms industry into smaller pieces, to become more competitive. Time will tell. In India, the production of indigenous aircraft and the acquisition of foreign ones have been delayed for a decade as firms and state tinker with details of contracts, though this happens in rich nations too. The only developing state with an advanced military industrial base is Brazil, which produces large numbers of good aircraft and AFVs—on a continent where conventional power has little positive influence. This capacity will matter more in coming years if Brazil seeks to acquire power to match its wealth. Over the past century, many developing countries have built good armament industries, resting on effective links between businesses and bureaucrats, and built decent kit. They entered the state of the art, learning to copy and then innovate, by forming liaisons with weapons producers in many states, buying large amounts of material and acquiring more through espionage, making some arms under licence and more through reverse engineering, training labour to build munitions and designers to make them. In 1921 all Japanese warships and naval aircraft were versions of British equipment, gained through purchase or joint ventures. Over the next twenty years, it developed good naval and aeronautical industries through hard work and copies of all the kit it could buy. So too, Soviet tanks of 1941 stemmed from development of Western technology purchased a decade earlier, just as its aircraft industry of 1951 relied heavily on American designs acquired by aid and espionage.

Many developing states do the same today aided, as ever, by the hunger of arms firms for profits in a harsh market. Russia leads in the transfer of military technology, but many others follow suit. The United States, conversely, tries to slow the transfer of military technology, which can only damage its interests. India has licences to build or has entered into joint ventures with Russia on much leading edge equipment, like the Sukhoi-30 MKI aircraft and the T-90 tank, while China is acquiring leading Russian aircraft, missiles, destroyers, and submarines. After losing hard-won expertise in military industry between 1979 and 1990 through revolution and Western sanctions, and being forced to rely on espionage and reverse engineering, Iran has built indigenous fighters and tanks, good however derivative in design. These states depend on access to foreign technology; but each tries to work with many partners, through which it builds advanced AFVs, aircraft, and cruise missiles, and to leapfrog past time-consuming stages of technology. Their civil economies have some able elements in high technology. In twenty years, any or all of these states may have established good military industrial complexes, and closed the gap with leading economies, even in the key areas of defence electronics and information technology. Though the edge will remain with the rich, China and India may well then be the world's second and third strongest economies and conventional powers, and growing fast.

decades, Taiwan has had the single-handed maritime and air ability to block Chinese invasion. In 2000, its 450 modern fighters outclassed China's 2,500, including 1800 MIG 19s. China, however, is fast acquiring better aircraft, augmented by rapidly increasing strength in surface to surface missiles (800 in 2005), with cruise missiles under development. By 2020, or earlier, this power will outweigh Taiwan's defences, no matter what technology Washington sells it. Then, the competition will be the United States, precisely on terrain where it is strong and China weak—sea and airpower. Since 1949, China has pursued the maritime strategy of a continental power—to keep rivals far away through land-based force and a brown water navy. In 1985, hundreds of land-based aircraft and submarines created an outer perimeter 200 miles from its shore, within which scores of destroyers and frigates and 1,000 attack boats defended its coast. That was an effective strategy for defence, but cannot easily be retooled for offence. China hopes to push that perimeter towards Japan and Taiwan, but is painfully slow in gathering the means, such as cruise missiles, better aircraft, and bigger ships. Its fleet has shrunk over a generation, as much kit is junked and little acquired. Nor can an Indian-sized investment in seapower achieve Chinese aims. Its efforts are unlikely to bear much fruit before 2020. For decades afterward, the sea and airpower of an American—Taiwanese alignment can easily pin China on its coast, if they wish. Only if and when Taiwan joins China will it break that barrier and, boosted by land-based forces on that island, freely reach blue water; and so become a world power.

These calculations are confused by a further issue. Sino-Japanese relations are unstable. Their interests easily can clash and their leaders evince mutual suspicion. In 2004 Tokyo openly defined China as a possible military threat, while Chinese submarines entered Japanese territorial waters. No major power is more affected by the rise of China than Japan, and none could do more to counter it. Fifteen years ago, Japanese defence industries claimed that, if unleashed from the peace constitution, they could capture half the world's market for tanks, defence electronics, and warships. While this claim is unlikely, Tokyo could easily and immediately become the world's second sea and airpower, so changing the balance of power in east Asia. That region is the crucible for the next new world order.

KEY POINTS

- The distribution of conventional power is changing.

- Western countries are in relative decline.

- Potential new world powers are emerging, especially China and India.

- The impact of these changes will vary with the desire of states to tap economic power for strategic purposes, and the skill of their policies.

War, What is it Good For?

Wars occur from combinations of intention and error. They are unusually likely when the nature and distribution of power are changing rapidly, as states misconstrue their strength while declining ones strive to hold what they have and growing ones to take more. Those circumstances exist today. A classic confrontation is looming between rising and declining powers. Mexican stand-offs rule Asia: between India and Pakistan; North Korea vs South Korea, Japan, and the United States; and Beijing vs Taipei and Washington. North Korea starves itself so to maintain the conventional power to affect regional politics, augmented by strong hints of nuclear capability. Chinese power waxes steadily, but is not yet significant in WMDs or maritime power. Since 1949 China has aimed to maximize its power, and often has provoked high-risk incidents, in the belief that teaching lessons to neighbours is a good thing, while it can control the worst cases— characteristics shared, to lesser degrees, by the United States. Both these countries believe they are on the defensive over Taiwan, and respond to aggression in a tough and self-righteous manner. Meanwhile, as the Soviet collapse reshaped power in east Asia, so would any resurgence of Russia—or Japan.

The Middle East is governed not by stalemate but vacuum. Numerically speaking, several Arab states, particularly Syria and Egypt, match Israel in the main categories of land and air force, while others make some of the largest purchases of advanced weaponry on earth. Excluding the Jordanian army and Hezbollah, however, these forces are poor in quality, while Israeli ones are excellent. The best indicator of the regional military balance is the fact that Israel is reducing its army in size by 25 per cent. Israel is the military master of the Arab world, and will so continue for years to come. It can overawe its neighbours and wreck any threat, yet it cannot directly translate that strength into political power. Israel and America cannot use conventional force to block the biggest dangers to them, such as the rise of a jihadist regime in Saudi Arabia, though that could aid them in containment, as occurred earlier with Iraq and Iraq. Meanwhile, the military weakness of Arab states, the rising turmoil within them, and the war between Americans and jihadists, make that region even less stable than usual—far and away the most chaotic on earth. It is framed by three powers which might use their able conventional forces as threat or tool in cases such as a collapse of Iraq. Iran, aiming to become a great power, certainly becoming a greater one, faces danger and opportunity in two fragmented states on its frontiers occupied by Americans. Turkey and Pakistan stand ready for action in the wings.

In these cases, conventional force is part of power, but not its whole. It does not primarily define the balance between Israel, the United States, and Iran. Its tough neighbourhood may drive Japan to increase its conventional power, but Tokyo has more to gain from nuclear weapons. Expedience may overcome its inhibitions on that issue. China can strengthen its hand against the United States through conventional force to match American strengths, asymmetric force to degrade them, politics, or WMDs. The latter options are its best chances for success. Just as the United States intermittently discusses the idea of integrating conventional and military forces, other states may use nuclear weapons as a quick fix for unavoidable conventional weakness. For most developing states, WMDs offer the simplest military solution to strategic problems—the only possible one for some, like Pakistan, haunted by insecurity and threats to its survival. If China had the assured capability to destroy five American cities, Washington's policy toward Taipei would change, though this also might drive Japan nuclear—and Taiwan. For China in Taiwan, and Iran in Iraq and Afghanistan, political influence is a better tool of policy than armies, just as terrorism is a tool of policy by other means.

Bigger questions loom behind these matters, like the use of WMDs in conventional war. When only one side has chemical weapons, it routinely uses them, but not nuclear weapons. How far can states equipped with WMDs use conventional force against each other? They often have done so, but the rules for these games remain obscure. All major belligerents in Europe during 1939–45 were equipped for gas warfare, but did not use it; so too in the Gulf War of 1991. Nuclear powers have fought each other, most notably India and Pakistan in the isolated region of Kargil during 2000; Soviet pilots shot down many American air intruders over their territory in the 1950s and fought allied airmen in the Korean War, and Israeli ones in the war of attrition during 1970. Again, the single greatest factor in world politics since 1989 has been the relationship between overwhelming American power, and its erratic use. Will Washington continue to follow the Bush doctrine? How will other states respond to a world order created by a wounded hyperpower? Its present search for absolute security will make all its rivals insecure, looking for ways to defend themselves or escape the firing line. Its power and threats have frightened many hostile states into changing their ways, like Syria and Libya, but they will convince any serious rival that it must neutralize that threat, by being able to endanger America. The dominant concept in the public rhetoric of Chinese strategy, opposition to hegemony, once was a code word for resistance to the USSR; today it is the United States. So too, when a leader of the Iranian Revolutionary Guards, General Jafari, claims his forces will work against 'global arrogance'. American success in conventional power will drive any rational enemy to abandon head-on competition, and pursue asymmetry or WMDs; and the latter are easier to build and have a more certain deterrent effect.

Conventional power is a great but limited tool of state. Once it was a sword for the strong against the strong; now, it is most valuable as a weapon against the weak. It remains the main shield for most states, but the sword of choice for few. It is more useful as a negative than a positive tool: to stop others from moving, as against doing so oneself. It is a fundamental means to demonstrate resolve, or support any strategies of dissuasion and compellance, though no more so than nuclear power or diplomatic influence. Any state threatened by conventional force must match it or die. Such forces can save oneself, aid one's friends, destroy one's enemies, and, occasionally, strike like lightning. Still, their relative utility has slipped steadily over the past century, as has the willingness of great states to use them. Conventional force has not been able to achieve specific results predictably or cheaply. The outcome of its use has more uncertain than ever before. Often, it has caused complex collateral damage, or trapped its users in the mire of world war, or guerrilla conflict. Conventional force will be more talked about than used. When deployed, it will face characteristic problems, or victory traps. If one uses cruise missiles for diplomacy, a few civilian deaths will mess your message. No matter the cause—*raison d'etat*, or humanitarian intervention driven by internal opinion and international duty, whether single-handedly, in coalitions of the willing, or under UN control—Western states will use conventional power primarily where the entry cost seems low and chances for success high: that is, against weak or failing ones. This raises immediate questions. Can outsiders end a civil war? Does occupation cause resistance? Will Western publics tolerate the violence necessary for victory except for defence of vital interests? Nor can armies be used on any great issue without raising the issue of WMDs.

Conventional force affects the policies of single actors, and the system as a whole. Many consequences of conventional power lie outside that plane, in what it drives states to do elsewhere. Its impact is most critical in deterring people from using an obvious tool, and in driving them to develop others. In theory, levels of force are divided; in reality, they are intertwined. The pure game of conventional power is played in a narrow field between two limits: WMDs, and terrorism and guerrilla warfare. To be too good in this game is not a blessing. Too much success will drive one's rival off this field to play on others. A rational enemy plays to its strengths, not yours. Conventional power remains a strong card, perhaps the king of trumps in a game where the ace is unplayable, but it cannot take every hand. Perhaps it can take only one out of thirteen. The trick will be learning how to play that card only when it can take the game; and to know when that game is worth the gamble.

? QUESTIONS

1. Did the United States win, or did Iraq lose, the Gulf War of 2003?

2. How does seapower matter today, why, and to whom?

3. What use are airpower and precision weapons to the United States, compared to nuclear power?

4. How does conventional force matter to the countries of western Europe?

5. What is a decisive battle? How common are they? How many of them have happened since 1945?

6. How important is 'information dominance' in conventional war? Compare and contrast its value in distant strike and urban operations.

7. Compare and contrast the conventional military power of Israel, Iran, and India. What good does it do them? What are the limits to its value?

8. How far and how fast can the transfer of military technology help China to further its strategic aims in Asia?

9. How far can states equipped with WMDs engage in conventional war?

10. Is attrition the normal state of conventional war? Is indecisiveness its normal outcome?

11. How, and how easily, can conventional forces defeat terrorists or guerrillas?

12. What can, and cannot, Western states do with expeditionary forces?

〰 FURTHER READING

Good modern accounts of the history of conventional war

■ Christon Archer, John Ferris, Holger Herwig, and Tim Travers, *A World History of Warfare* (University of Nebraska Press, 2002).

■ John Lynn, *Battle: A History of Combat and Culture* (Boulder, CO: Westview 2003).

■ Victor Davis Hanson, *Carnage and Culture: landmark battles in the rise of western power* (New York: Doubleday, 2001).

■ Russell Weigley, *The Age of Battles: The Quest for Decisive Warfare* (Bloomington, IN: Indiana University Press, 1991).

Assessments of the RMA and recent military operations

■ Stephen Biddle, *Military Power: Explaining Victory and Defeat in Modern Battle* (Princeton: Princeton University Press, 2004).

■ Anthony H. Cordesman, *The Lessons of Afghanistan, Warfighting, Intelligence, Force Transformation, Counterproliferation, and Arms Control* (Washington, DC: Center for Strategic and International Studies, 12 Aug. 2002).

——*The 'Instant Lessons' of the Iraq War: Main Report, Seventh Working Draft* (Washington, DC: CSIS, 28 Apr. 2003).

■ John Ferris, 'A New American Way of War? C4ISR, Intelligence and IO in Operation Iraqi Freedom, a Preliminary Assessment', *Intelligence and National Security*, 14/1 (2004*a*).

—— 'Netcentric Warfare and Information Operations: Revolution in the RMA?', *Intelligence and National Security*, 14/3 (2004*b*).

■ Williamson Murray and Robert Scales Jr, *The Iraq War: A Military History* (Cambridge, Mass.: Harvard University Press, 2003).

■ Elinor Sloan, *The Revolution in Military Affairs* (Montreal: McGill-Queen's Press, 2002).

Introductions to military power and strategy

■ Stephen Cohen, *India, Emerging Power* (Washington, DC: Brookings Institution Press, 2002).

■ Michael Handel, 'The Evolution of Israeli Strategy: The Psychology of Insecurity and the Quest for Absolute Security', in Williamson Murray, MacGregor Knox, and Alvin Bernstein (eds.), *The Making of Strategy: Rulers, Wars and States* (Cambridge: Cambridge University Press, 1994).

■ Subrata Kumar Mitra, 'Emerging Major Powers and the International System (An Indian View)', in Alistair Dally and Rosalind Bourke (eds.), *Conflict, the State and Aerospace Power* (Canberra: RAAF Aerospace Centre, 2002), pp. 51–80.

■ Kenneth M. Pollack, *Arabs at War: Military Effectiveness, 1948–1991* (Lincoln, Neb.: University of Nebraska Press, 2002).

■ Andrew Scobell, *China's Use of Military Force: Beyond the Great Wall and the Long March* (Cambridge: Cambridge University Press, Cambridge, 2003).

Authoritative treatments of conventional forces and weapons are included in the International Institute for Strategic Studies, The Military Balance, and the various publications of Janes.

Terry Terrif, Aaron Karp, and Regina Karp (eds.), *The Right War? The Fourth Generation Warfare Debate* (London: Routledge Press, 2006), contains a wide range of comments on the relationship between conventional and guerrilla forces.

 WEB LINKS

● Useful websites on modern military matters include the Air War College Portal to the Internet **http://www.au.af.mil/au/awc/awcgate/awcgate.htm**, which includes copies of many semi-official and official American publications, and links to many other government websites.

The most valuable private websites, including much official and non-official material and useful hot links, are those of the Center for Strategic and International Studies **www.csis.org/**, Global Security **www.globalsecurity.org/**, and the RAND Corporation **www.rand.org/**.

 Visit the Online Resource Centre that accompanies this book for lots of interesting additional material http://www.oxfordtextbooks.co.uk/orc/baylis_strategy2e/.

13 Iraq, Afghanistan, and American Military Transformation

STEPHEN BIDDLE

Reader's Guide

This chapter considers two recent examples of major combat operations (MCO), in Afghanistan in 2001–2, and Iraq from March to April of 2003. Both have proven highly influential for subsequent US defence policy debates, and particularly so for arguments over the need to 'transform' the American military to meet the needs of twenty-first-century warfare. Does the actual experience of combat in these two campaigns support the view that warfare has changed dramatically and now requires a very different kind of military for success? The chapter argues that, in fact, the conduct of both campaigns was more traditional, and less transformational, than widely supposed. In particular, both campaigns involved extensive close combat on the ground against unbroken defenders who survived precision air strikes and fought back when struck by US and allied ground forces. Although there were many new tactics and technologies in both campaigns, there was also a great deal of continuity with prior military experience; to focus only on the change and ignore the continuity is to misunderstand the nature of warfare in the early twenty-first century.

Introduction

The wars in Iraq and Afghanistan continue; events will yet determine whether US war aims in either theatre are met. But some outcomes are already clear: the Taliban no longer govern Afghanistan, and Saddam Hussein no longer rules Iraq. And the military campaigns of 2001–2 and 2003 that did this have already proven highly influential in the American defence planning debate.

In particular, these campaigns gave powerful impetus to a collection of proposals for radical change—or 'transformation'—in the US military. Even before 2001, it was widely believed that a transnational revolution in information processing was transforming the nature of war. The increasing power of networked information, many claimed, was erasing the need for massed conventional ground forces, substituting stand-off precision strike for the close combat of the past and replacing the breakthrough battle with the struggle for information supremacy as the decisive issue for success. The campaigns in Afghanistan and Iraq powerfully reinforced these perceptions: the speed and radically low casualties of the Coalition offensives in Afghanistan and Iraq seemed to offer trenchant empirical evidence to show that the hypothesized changes were in fact real.

This in turn reinforced a series of interconnected proposals for transforming the US military from what has often been described as a heavy, slow-moving, cold war relic into a leaner, faster, higher technology force that exploits the connectivity of networked information to outmanœuvre, outrange, and demoralize enemy forces without requiring their piecemeal destruction in close combat. Some transformation advocates would even bypass the enemy military in the field altogether, using deep strikes from possibly intercontinental distances to destroy key nodes in a hostile economy or political control system in 'effects based' operations (EBO) that prevail by coercive bombing rather than brute force on the battlefield.

These proposals have not gone unchallenged. In particular, critics have long argued that this transformation agenda overlooks the demands of inherently labour-intensive, low-technology missions such as counter-insurgency (COIN) or stability and support operations (SASO). Critics argue that the kind of streamlined, technology-dependent military that transformation advocates want would leave the United States unable to wage sustained counter-insurgencies of the type now ongoing in Iraq and Afghanistan. And the future, they often claim, lies in exactly such low-intensity conflicts (LIC), rather than the high-intensity 'major combat operations' (MCO) around which most high-tech transformation proposals turn.

Yet this critique skirts a more fundamental issue: is the transformation thesis valid even for major combat itself? And in particular, is it a valid interpretation of the reasons for the quick success and low cost of MCO in Afghanistan or Iraq in 2001–2 and 2003? Was the actual conduct of either of these campaigns consistent with the transformation thesis's claims?

In fact the answer is no—the transformation thesis is not consistent with the actual conduct of either campaign. And this suggests that, whatever one thinks of the need for future COIN or SASO, the network-centric, EBO version of American military transformation is ill-advised. What the evidence from MCO in Afghanistan and Iraq actually shows is that speed and stand-off precision will work as claimed only against enemies who lack the skills necessary to evade their effects. Against unskilled enemies such as the Iraqi military or the indigenous Afghan Taliban, a transformed US military would be highly successful—in fact, it is probably the ideal force for such a job. But against enemies with at least the combat skills shown by the Taliban's foreign allies in Afghanistan—and especially Al-Qaeda—traditional close combat capability is needed for success. A transformed military in which close combat capability is traded for increased emphasis on stand-off precision strike could be radically less effective than a traditional military against such enemies. And this suggests that a transformation agenda that trades mass for speed, and close combat for stand-off precision, could be a very risky undertaking in a world where it is uncertain where or against whom the US military may be called to fight.

The chapter presents this case in four steps. First, it discusses the conduct of the 2001–2 campaign in Afghanistan and its consistency with the transformation thesis. Next it does the same for the 2003 major combat phase of the war in Iraq. It then presents an alternative explanation for the low cost and rapid conclusion of these campaigns, and concludes with some implications of the findings for US defence policy.

Afghanistan and the Transformation Thesis

The heart of the transformation school's interpretation of MCO in Afghanistan is that American airpower is held to have used targeting information provided largely by a handful of US special operations forces (SOF) on the ground to destroy the Taliban's military at stand-off ranges, before the Taliban could overrun US commandos or the indigenous allies working with them. In this account, it is the precision munitions that did the real military work; everything else is there to support stand-off firepower delivery. And the precision fires are held to have been sufficient in themselves to destroy the enemy and enable a collection of ostensibly ragtag local militias to advance. This ability to destroy the enemy by stand-off precision is in turn central to this view's implications for the transformation debate: if Afghanistan shows that stand-off precision has made close combat largely unnecessary, then restructuring the military away from close combat and toward stand-off precision makes sense.

And in fact, in its early stages the war did indeed go mostly the way transformation proponents assume. US precision took the Taliban by surprise, and their initial dispositions were poorly chosen for protection against such firepower. Taliban defenders typically deployed on exposed ridgelines with little effort at camouflage or concealment. Entrenchments were haphazard, lacking overhead cover for infantry positions or proper emplacements for combat vehicles. As a result, Taliban positions could be identified from often extraordinary distances. And once located, their poor entrenchment and exposed movement made them easy prey for precision weapons.

The result was slaughter. At Bishqab on 21 October 2001, for example, US SOF pinpointed Taliban targets at ranges of over 8 kilometres. Sceptical Northern Alliance commanders peered through their binoculars at Taliban positions that had stymied them for years and were astounded to see the defences suddenly vaporized by direct hits from 2,000-pound bombs. At Cobaki on 22 October Taliban observation posts were easily spotted at 1,500–2,000 metres and annihilated by precision bombing. At Zard Kammar on 28 October, Taliban defences were wiped out from a mile away. At Ac'capruk on 4 November, exposed Taliban combat vehicles and crew-served weapons on hillsides west of the Balkh river were spotted from SOF observation posts on the Koh-i-Almortak ridge line some 4–5 kilometres distant and obliterated by US air strikes.

The Taliban were not the only ones surprised by this: some allied Afghans initially thought the lasers US SOF used to designate bombing targets were actually death rays, since they apparently caused defences to vanish whenever caught in their cross hairs. Both sides, however, learnt fast.

Within days of the first SOF-directed air strikes, US commandos were already reporting that Taliban vehicles in their sectors had been smeared with mud to camouflage them. By 5 November, the Taliban's Al-Qaeda allies were already making aggressive use of overhead cover and concealment. In the fighting north of Kandahar and along Highway 4 in December, Al-Qaeda defences were well-camouflaged, dispersed, and making use of natural terrain for expedient cover. This pattern continued into Operation Anaconda in March, by which time Al-Qaeda forces were practising systematic communications security, dispersal, camouflage discipline, use of cover and concealment, and exploitation of dummy fighting positions to draw fire and attention from their real dispositions. Indigenous *Afghan* Taliban in the war's early battles were radically exposed, but as the war unfolded the opposition came increasingly to comprise better trained, more adaptive foreign—and especially Al-Qaeda—forces. As these foreign forces adapted their methods they reduced their vulnerability significantly. And as they did, the war changed character.

Finding hidden targets

Among the more important changes was increasing difficulty in finding targets for precision attack. At Bai Beche on 2–5 November, for example, a mostly Al-Qaeda defensive force occupied an old, formerly Soviet system of deliberate entrenchments. With proper cover and concealment, the defenders were able to prevent US commandos from locating the entirety of their individual fighting positions, many of which could not be singled out for precision attack.

By the December fighting along Highway 4 south of Kandahar, even less information was available. In fact, concealed Al-Qaeda defences among a series of culverts and in burnt-out vehicle hulks along the roadside remained wholly undetected until their fire drove back an allied advance. An Al-Qaeda counterattack in the same sector using a system of wadis for cover approached undetected to within 100–200 metres of allied and US SOF positions along the highway before opening fire on friendly forces.

At the village of Sayed Slim Kalay north of Kandahar between 2 and 4 December, concealed Al-Qaeda defenders likewise remained undetected until they fired upon unsuspecting US and allied forces. An Al-Qaeda counterattack using local terrain for cover manœuvred into small arms range of friendly defenders before being driven back.

At Operation Anaconda in March 2002, an intensive pre-battle reconnaissance effort focused every available surveillance and target acquisition system on a tiny, ten-by-ten kilometre battlefield. Yet fewer than 50 per cent of all the Al-Qaeda positions ultimately identified on this battlefield were discovered prior to ground contact. In fact, most fire received by US forces in Anaconda came from initially unseen, unanticipated defenders.

How could such things happen in an era of persistent reconnaissance drones, airborne radars, satellite surveillance, thermal imaging, and hypersensitive electronic eavesdropping equipment? The answer is that the earth's surface remains an extremely complex environment with an abundance of natural and manmade cover available for those militaries capable of exploiting it.

Militarily exploitable cover is commonplace in almost any likely theatre of war. For targets who observe radio listening silence, as Al-Qaeda now does, foliage degrades all current remote sensor technologies; urban areas provide overhead cover, create background clutter, and pose difficult problems of distinguishing military targets from innocent civilians. Each is widely available. More than 26 per cent of Somalia's land area is wooded or urban, as is more than 20 per cent of the Sudan's, 34 per cent of Georgia's, or 46 per cent of the Philippines'. In most countries, the central geostrategic objectives are urban areas; even where the bulk of the national land area is open desert (as in Iraq), the cities are both the key terrain and an ample source of cover (Baghdad alone covers more than 300 square kilometres). The natural complexity of such surfaces offers any adaptive opponent with the necessary training and skills a multitude of opportunities to thwart even modern remote surveillance systems. Against such opponents, remote surveillance will still detect some targets, and remote sensors remain crucial assets, but the only sure means of target acquisition is direct ground contact: a ground force whose advance threatens objectives that the enemy cannot sacrifice and thus must defend compels them to give away their locations by firing on their attackers. Skilled attackers can eventually locate any defensive position by observing the source of the fire directed at them—and this, in fact, is how the majority of the Al-Qaeda positions at Anaconda were found.

Close combat in Afghanistan

As the enemy adapted, their decreasing vulnerability to stand-off attack meant an increasing burden of close combat. Little of this was guerilla warfare. At least until Anaconda in March the Taliban sought to take and hold ground in very orthodox ways—they tried to defend key geographic objectives, not harass their enemies with hit-and-run tactics. These defences, however, were sufficiently covered and concealed to allow important fractions of them to survive American air attack. The resulting ground combat was neither trivial nor wholly one-sided: many battles were close calls, with either initial reverses, serious casualties, or both.

At Bai Beche on 5 November, for example, dug-in Al-Qaeda defenders refused to withdraw after more than two days of heavy US bombing. To dislodge them, Northern Alliance cavalry was ordered to charge the position. The first attempt was driven back. The attached American SOF observed this reverse and began calling renewed airstrikes in anticipation of a second assault. In the process, however, a SOF warning order to the cavalry to prepare for another push was mistaken by the cavalry as a command to launch the assault, with the

BOX 13.1

Key Events in the Afghanistan Campaign, 2001–2002

The Afghan campaign began the night of 7 October 2001, with a programme of air strikes aimed initially at destroying the Taliban's limited air defences and communications infrastructure. Early air attacks produced few results, however, because the country had little fixed infrastructure to destroy. By 15 October, SOF teams designated to make contact with the major Northern Alliance warlords had been inserted. A three-part campaign followed, divided roughly into a northern phase revolving around control of the city of Mazar-i-Sharif, a southern phase centred on the city of Kandahar, and subsequent battles against Taliban and Al-Qaeda forces at Tora Bora and during Operation Anaconda in the Shah-i-Kot Valley.

The fight for Mazar-i-Sharif began when Gen. Abdul Rashid Dostum, supported by US SOF, took the village of Bishqab on the banks of the Dar-ye Suf south of Mazar on 21 October. This was followed by engagements at Cobaki, Chapchall, and Oimetan over the next few days as Dostum fought his way up the river valley. The key battle came when Dostum's troops overran hostile forces occupying old Soviet-built defensive positions at the hamlet of Bai Beche on 5 November. Shortly thereafter, Gen. Muhammed Atta's forces and their accompanying SOF captured Ac'capruk on the Balkh River, and the door swung open for a rapid advance to Mazar, which fell to Atta and Dostum's troops on 10 November. The fall of Mazar unhinged the Taliban position in northern Afghanistan. Kabul fell without a fight on 13 November, and after a twelve-day siege, a force of some 5,000 Taliban and Al-Qaeda survivors encircled in the city of Kunduz surrendered on 26 November.

With the fall of Kabul and Kunduz, attention shifted to the Taliban's stronghold of Kandahar in the south. SOF teams and Hamid Karzai's allied Afghan forces advanced on the city from the north; Gul Agha Shirzai's allied Afghans and supporting SOF advanced from the south. After a series of battles, on the night of 6 December Mullah Muhammad Omar and the rest of the senior Taliban leadership fled the city and went into hiding, ending Taliban rule in Afghanistan.

Allied forces, meanwhile, tracked a group of Al-Qaeda survivors thought to include Osama bin Laden to a series of redoubts in the White Mountains near Tora Bora. These redoubts were taken in a sixteen-day battle ending on December 17, but many Al-Qaeda defenders escaped death or capture and fled across the border into Pakistan.

In March 2002, a second concentration of Al-Qaeda holdouts was finally identified in the Shah-i-Kot Valley east of Gardez. In Operation Anaconda, Western and allied Afghan forces descended on these Al-Qaeda defenders, killing many, dispersing the rest, and bringing to a close the major combat operations in the country to date.

result that the cavalry began its attack much sooner than intended. The surprised Americans watched the Afghan cavalry break cover and begin their advance just as a series of laser-guided bombs had been released from American aircraft in response to the SOF calls for air support. The SOF commander reported that he was convinced they had just caused a friendly fire incident: the bomb release and the cavalry advance were way too close together for official doctrinal limits, and the air strike would never have been ordered if the SOF had known that the cavalry was then jumping off for the second assault. As it happened, the bombs landed just seconds before the cavalry arrived. In fact, the cavalry galloped through the enormous cloud of smoke and dust that was still hanging in the air after the explosions, emerging behind the enemy defences before their garrison knew what was happening. The defenders, seeing Northern Alliance cavalry to their rear, abandoned their positions in an attempt to avoid encirclement.

The result was an important victory—in fact, the victory that turned the tide in the north. But the battle involved serious close combat (cavalry overrunning prepared, actively resisting defences), and the outcome was a very close call. The assault profited from an extremely tight integration of movement with suppressive fire—far tighter, in fact, than either the cavalry or their supporting SOF would ever have dared arrange deliberately. Luck thus played an important role in the outcome. The Northern Alliance might well have carried the position eventually even without the good fortune of an extraordinary integration of fire and movement; this was clearly a crucial battle, and they would presumably have redoubled their efforts if the second attempt had failed. But as fought, the outcome involved an important element of serendipity.

Nor was Bai Beche unique in demanding hard fighting at close quarters. As noted above, Al-Qaeda counterattackers reached small arms range of US and allied forces before being driven back at Sayed Slim Kalay and at Highway 4. At Konduz in late November, Al-Qaeda counterattackers penetrated allied positions deeply enough to compel supporting American SOF teams to withdraw at least three times to avoid being overrun. In Anaconda, allied forces associated with General Mohammed Zia and supported by US SOF were assigned to drive Al-Qaeda defenders from the 'Tri-cities' area (the villages of Shirkankeyl, Babakuhl, and Marzak) in the Shah-i-kot Valley floor; they were instead pinned down under hostile fire from prepared defences in the surrounding mountainsides and eventually withdrew after they proved unable to advance. Only after the Al-Qaeda defenders pulled back under joint, multinational attack by allied airpower, Western infantry, and multinational SOF, were Zia's troops able to enter the Tri-cities and adjoining ridgelines. At Tora Bora, massive American bombing proved insufficient to compensate for allied Afghan unwillingness to close with dug-in Al-Qaeda defenders in the cave complexes of the White Mountains; this ground force hesitancy probably allowed Osama bin Laden and his lieutenants to escape into neighbouring Pakistan.

Among these examples, the fighting along Highway 4 in December is particularly instructive. The US-allied Afghans here were divided among two factions. The first, commanded by Haji Gul Alai, were very capable troops by Afghan standards. They used terrain for cover and concealment, maintained good intervals between elements in the advance, moved by alternate bounds, exploited suppressive fire to cover moving elements' exposure, and were able to exploit the effects of US air strikes by coordinating their movement with the bombing (which many Afghan factions could not). The second faction, by contrast, was much less skilled: the attached SOF commander characterized them as 'an armed mob—just villagers given weapons.' Their tactics consisted of exposed, bunched-up movement in the open, with no attempt to use terrain to reduce their exposure, and little ability to employ supporting or suppressive fires. At the Arghestan Bridge on 5 December, this second faction launched an assault on a dug-in Al-Qaeda position south of the Kandahar airport. Driven back repeatedly, they proved unable to take the position, in spite of US air support. Only after these troops were withdrawn and Haji Gul Alai's forces took over the assault the following day could the Al-Qaeda positions be taken.

Of course, the alliance ultimately ousted the Taliban. And precision US airpower was a necessary precondition for this—together with its SOF spotters it was what turned a stalemated civil war into a dramatic battlefield victory for the United States and its allies. But while precision bombing was *necessary*, it was not *sufficient*. It could annihilate poorly prepared fighting positions, and it could inflict heavy losses on even well-disposed defences. But it could not destroy the entirety of properly prepared positions by itself. And unless such positions are all but annihilated, even a handful of surviving, actively resisting defenders with modern automatic weapons can make great slaughter of unsophisticated indigenous allies whose idea of tactics is to walk forward bunched up in the open. To overcome skilled, resolute defenders who have adopted the standard countermeasures to high-firepower airstrikes still requires close combat by friendly ground forces whose own skills are sufficient to enable them to use local cover and their own suppressive fire to advance against hostile survivors with modern weapons.

By and large, America's main Afghan allies in this war either enjoyed such fundamental skills or profited from accidentally tight coordination of their movement and American fires (as at Bai Beche) or both. The Northern, and later the Southern, Alliances were not uniformly the motley assortment of militiamen they are sometimes said to have been. Enough of them were capable of implementing complex tactics to allow them to exploit the tremendous potential that precision airpower can bring to armies capable of integrating their movement with its firepower.

But not all of America's allies in this war were up to this job. Though the typical combat units on each side were about equally matched (as the stalled pre-intervention battle lines

---

BOX 13.2

The Combatants in Afghanistan

Neither the Taliban nor the Northern Alliance forces allied with the United States comprised homogeneous or uniformly trained armies. The Taliban consisted of at least three militarily very different subcomponents: indigenous Afghan Taliban, mostly with very little training or tactical sophistication; better-trained and better-motivated foreigners fighting on behalf of the Taliban; and the subset of foreign fighters who had been through Osama bin Laden's Al-Qaeda training camps, and who provided the most capable of the Taliban's troops. The Northern Alliance comprised a similarly diverse collection of warlords with forces whose military proficiency varied widely as a function of their past military experience in Afghanistan's civil war. Some had skills comparable to the Al-Qaeda fighters, others were much less adept. Strength estimates for these armies are necessarily inexact. Most accounts, however, credit the Taliban overall with some 40,000–50,000 troops in fall 2001, of whom perhaps 8,000–12,000 were foreign. The Northern Alliance is sometimes credited with 20,000–30,000 troops in fall 2001, though after the campaign began, additional forces were organized from Taliban opponents in the central and southern provinces of Afghanistan in what is sometimes termed the 'Southern Alliance'. Western forces in Afghanistan consisted, initially, of American and multinational SOF, which were later augmented by US regular army infantry (chiefly from the 10th Mountain and 101st Airborne divisions), US Marines from Task Force Rhino, and multinational regular infantry (prominently including a battalion from the Canadian Princess Patricia's Light Infantry Regiment, which played an important role in Operation Anaconda in March 2002). Afghanistan was unique as the first major campaign in which US Special Operations Forces were the 'supported' rather than a 'supporting' command—meaning that their mission was the main effort in the theatre of war.

y), both sides in Afghanistan were actually diverse mixtures of better and worse
ꜟed, more and less motivated troops—and this diversity offers a couple of valuable
ꜟportunities to observe instances of unequally skilled forces in combat. In such unequal
ꜟhts as the first day at Arghestan Bridge and the assault on the Tri-cities in Anaconda, the
ꜟsults suggest that, where the indigenous allies are overmatched tactically, US airpower
ꜟnd SOF support alone may not be enough to turn the tide.

In Afghanistan, America's Afghan allies, eventually combined with the US and
Canadian infantry that fought at Anaconda, together provided significant ground forces
that ultimately shouldered an essential load of old-fashioned close combat against surviving, actively resisting opponents. Even with twenty-first-century firepower, without this
essential close combat capability the outcome in Afghanistan could easily have been very
different.

KEY POINTS

- Early in the Afghan campaign, indigenous Afghan Taliban targets were ill-prepared and exposed. US SOF were able to locate them from great distances and destroy them with stand-off precision air strikes.

- Later, as the indigenous Afghan Taliban were replaced with better trained foreign and Al-Qaeda fighters, exposed targets became less common, stand-off precision

became less effective, and close combat became more frequent.

- Against motivated defenders in properly prepared positions, success required a combination of stand-off precision with ground manœuvre by infantry with the skills needed to reduce their exposure to defensive fire.

Iraq and the Transformation Thesis

The transformation school's interpretation of major combat in Operation Iraqi Freedom
(OIF) focuses on American speed, precision, and situation awareness. These are held to
account for the campaign's quick conclusion and low casualties by leaving the Iraqis
unable to inflict significant losses: in this view, much of Iraq's military refused to fight
against such overwhelming technology, and those who did were destroyed by stand-off
precision strike before they could pose a real threat to Coalition ground forces. Iraqi
threats of scorched earth, moreover, are held to have been pre-empted by the speed of
the Coalition advance: it was widely feared that Saddam would destroy Iraq's economic
infrastructure rather than allow it to fall into Coalition hands, yet Iraqi oilfields, ports,
and bridges were overrun before Saddam's forces could destroy them. Much of the
emphasis on speed, especially in the post-2003 defence planning debate, stems from
this interpretation of its role in Saddam's fall. And the apparent role of stand-off precision
in limiting Coalition losses gave further impetus to the transformation argument
that had already been strengthened by the conventional interpretation of the Afghan
campaign.

But while speed, precision, and situation awareness were surely helpful, they were far from sufficient to explain the low cost of Saddam's ouster. To see why, I will consider in turn the role of close combat, and the absence of scorched earth, in the major combat phase of the war in Iraq.

Close Combat in Iraq

The logic of the transformation account of the Coalition's low MCO casualty rate implies that Coalition losses were averted by avoiding close combat—by reducing the scale of close-quarters fighting against willing combatants on favourable ground to the point where the Iraqis could not inflict heavy casualties. Yet there was actually substantial close combat in Iraq against Iraqi fighters on urban terrain who proved willing to take extra-ordinary risks to kill Americans and Britons—certainly there was far too much close combat to accept explanations that turn on its ostensible infrequency.

The key here is urban warfare. Urban terrain is ordinarily thought highly defence-favourable; defenders in cities should be able to fight at a considerable tactical advantage. The basis for most pre-war fears of heavy Coalition casualties in conventional combat was concern with urban warfare. And in fact there was substantial close combat in Iraqi cities in OIF.

In Baghdad, for example, the US 3rd Infantry Division's 2nd Brigade conducted two successive penetrations (or 'Thunder Runs') into the heart of the city on 5 and 7 April 2003. On both occasions it was met with a fusillade of Iraqi rocket propelled grenade (RPG) and small arms fire, at point blank range, along nearly its entire route. In fact, on 5 April, every single vehicle in the brigade column was hit at least once by Iraqi RPGs, and many took multiple hits. Opposition was especially intense at highway overpasses and key intersections; Iraqi positions there were destroyed but subsequently reoccupied by fighters who infiltrated back behind the moving American columns. The 5 April penetration was a raid, and returned to its origin at the Baghdad International Airport after reaching the city centre, but the 7 April assault established a brigade perimeter at the Tigris River bend to hold the ground. This required a resupply column to be sent forward after nightfall to replenish depleted fuel and ammunition stocks. This resupply convoy, too, had to fight its way through defences that had been reoccupied after having been destroyed in the earlier advance; it lost one ammunition and two fuel trucks in a wild ride through a series of desperate fire fights, suffering two soldiers killed and thirty wounded en route. The next morning, the brigade was counterattacked by waves of paramilitaries hanging over the sides of some 50–100 civilian vehicles and firing small arms and RPGs as they poured over the Tigris River bridges toward the brigade perimeter.

When the division's 3rd Brigade entered Baghdad from the north it, too, fought its way through volleys of massed RPGs fired from practically point blank range. Every armoured vehicle in 3rd Brigade suffered either a hit or a near miss from RPGs while fighting their way into the city.

Similarly, in Nasiriyah Iraqi paramilitaries and elements of the Iraqi 11th Regular Army division waged a week-long urban battle against the US Marine Corps' Task Force Tarawa, a reinforced three-battalion regimental-scale formation. In Samawah, Iraqi paramilitaries fought for a week against the US Army's 3–7 Cavalry, the 3rd Brigade of the 3rd Infantry

Division, and the 2nd Brigade of the 82nd Airborne Division in turn. In Najaf, urban warfare in and around the city centre continued for more than a week, tying down in series multiple brigades of US infantry.

The exact strength of the willing, surviving Iraqi opposition in these and other urban battles cannot be known, but it was clearly enough to produce a major volume of potentially lethal fires at very close quarters. Perhaps 30,000 Iraqi paramilitaries were predeployed in Baghdad, Basra, Najaf, and Nasiriyah before the war began. Another 15,000 Special Republican Guards (SRG) were predeployed in Baghdad and its suburbs. Some 10,000 paramilitary reinforcements were moved south from Baghdad into Nasiriyah and Najaf after it became clear that major battles were under way there for control of the bridges running through these cities. SRG infantry and paramilitaries in mostly civilian clothing were poor targets for Coalition deep strikes, which were aimed chiefly at Iraqi leadership, command, air defence, and heavy weapons targets. While paramilitary losses were heavy in close combat with Coalition forces, there is little evidence to suggest that they suffered much attrition prior to contact with invaders on the ground. And combat motivation, while very weak in Iraqi Regular Army and some Republican Guard units, was stronger elsewhere—and especially among paramilitary fighters in Iraqi cities. In fact, paramilitary combat motivation bordered on the suicidal in 2003. In Nasiriyah, Samawah, Basra, Najaf, Baghdad, and elsewhere, Iraqi paramilitaries executed repeated frontal assaults against US armoured vehicles using civilian sport utility vehicles, pickup trucks, minivans, and even bicycles. In Samawah, Iraqi SUVs rammed American armoured vehicles. Even after initial waves of such kamikaze charges were mowed down, others followed. In Baghdad, Iraqi reinforcements reoccupied devastated positions to resume resistance after US columns drove on. Iraqi defenders of Nasiriyah and Samawah kept fighting long after being bypassed by American spearheads. Basra's garrison held out through a two-week siege until defeated by a British variant on the Baghdad Thunder Runs: multiple British armoured columns drove into the urban centre and broke the resistance by direct fire. This is inconsistent with a model that Iraqi forces were too maldeployed or too demoralized by Coalition speed or precision to offer meaningful resistance.

Of course, none of this is to suggest that Iraqi paramilitaries or SRG infantry were a serious threat to halt the Coalition advance; even at full strength, neither had much chance of holding Iraq's cities against a determined assault. The Thunder Runs in Baghdad and Basra do appear to have broken the defenders' morale once it became clear to them that their best efforts were proving futile. And speed, precision, and situation awareness did leave much of the Iraqi military out of position, unwilling to fight, or destroyed by deep strikes.

But what was left—what the Iraqis did manage to get into close combat with Coalition ground forces on favourable, urban terrain—was in principle more than enough to have caused much heavier Coalition casualties. The Thunder Runs in Baghdad alone received a volume of fire that with historical loss rates might have been expected to have devastated at least two brigades of Coalition forces. Before the war, the US Marines estimated that even with maximum proficiency, their own troops could expect no better than about a 1:1 loss exchange ratio in offensive urban warfare. If the surviving, actively resisting components of the Iraqi paramilitary and Special Republican Guards in Iraq's cities had comprised even 10 per cent of their pre-war totals, an exchange ratio like this could easily have increased Coalition losses by a factor of ten or more. That this did not occur is thus hard to attribute to speed, precision, and situation awareness. While helpful, these capabilities did not in themselves preclude a volume of urban close combat that would normally be expected to yield much heavier casualties.

Scorched Earth in Iraq

Transformation advocates have argued that speed prevented the Iraqis from destroying the Rumaila oilfield, sabotaging the port facilities at Um Qasr, blowing the primary bridges over the Tigris and Euphrates, or flooding the Karbala Gap. Yet there is substantial evidence to suggest that Coalition speed was less important than Iraqi choices for these outcomes. Properly wired bridges, oil wells, pipelines, cranes, or levees can be blown in seconds from safe locations with the pressing of a single button. Secure landline cables connecting switchboxes with explosives would make such commands very difficult to interdict. Predelegated detonation authority could have afforded local commanders the ability to beat invaders to the punch even if unable to communicate with Baghdad. Had the Iraqis taken such precautions, massive damage could have been done in seconds—long before even the fastest invasion could have reached them—and the United States could not have prevented them from doing so if they had otherwise chosen to.

Of course, they did not. Far from it: in fact, the Iraqis did remarkably little to implement Saddam's threat of scorched earth. They neither prepared their infrastructure for destruction on more than a token scale, nor were they in the process of doing so, either before the war or during the fighting. On the contrary, some key facilities were left in their possession for weeks after the fighting actually began, yet were left undamaged and found unprepared for demolition when Coalition forces finally captured them. It is hard to see how the difference between a fast and a slower Coalition advance would have been decisive when even weeks of time could pass without the Iraqis implementing threats that could in principle have been realized in fractions of that time, yet were not. At the margin, speed may have made adequate preparation harder for the Iraqis, but it could not make it impossible, and it does not appear to have been the main reason why the threat was not carried out.

Consider, for example, the issue of oilfield destruction. Of the more than 250 wells in the Rumaila oilfield, only twenty-two had actually been prepared for demolition when the Marines secured the field on 21 March. Of these twenty-two, only nine were actually detonated, causing just seven fires. No gas–oil separation plants (GOSPs), pumping stations, or pipelines were wired for destruction. Nor was there evidence of ongoing efforts at preparing additional wells or other oilfield facilities for destruction in the days before the invasion or the early stages of the invasion itself. Twenty-two wells had been prepared for demolition in advance of the war; the Iraqis then stopped and did not significantly expand their preparations either just before or during the war's initial stages. Even after the war began, and even with a very fast-moving offensive, there were still some forty-eight hours available to the Iraqis between the beginning of hostilities and the time the field was actually secured—they had considerable, but unused, time for setting charges or destroying additional facilities even after they knew the war was on.

In fact, the Kirkuk oilfield in the north remained in Iraqi hands for more than three weeks after the invasion began. Yet at no point in that interval were any oil wells destroyed, or any facilities demolished, or any fires set in the Kirkuk field. No evidence of preparation for demolition was discovered when American troops finally took possession of the field after 7 April; in fact, dirt had been piled around a number of wells to protect them from accidental destruction in the fighting. Even if one were to argue that the Iraqis would have demolished Rumaila if they only had more time, at Kirkuk they had the time—by any standard. Yet they did less demolition at Kirkuk than at Rumaila.

There are many possible explanations for the Iraqis' lack of preparation, ranging from disobedience by oilfield workers to organizational incompetence in the Iraqi military to a lack of intent at the highest levels: perhaps the threat of scorched earth was merely a bluff to deter a Coalition attack. Either way, though, none of these possibilities are consistent with a claim that only a fast-moving advance prevented mass destruction of the Iraqi oil industry. None implies a process which would have yielded significantly wider destruction if the campaign had lasted weeks or even months longer than it did. If time were all the Iraqis needed, then at a minimum, Kirkuk should have been razed. Yet it was not.

Iraqi bridges, port facilities, and inundation follow a similar pattern. The Coalition advance was obviously premised on its ability to use a series of key bridges over the Euphrates River. The towns at these crossings were in fact major battlefields in the war, as the Iraqis apparently understood their importance and sought to contest the bridge sites. Yet few of these bridges were wired for demolition, and even fewer were actually destroyed. At Nasiriyah, the Iraqis fought a week-long battle for a city whose military importance turned on its bridges—yet the Iraqis made no systematic effort to destroy them. Of the five bridges surrounding Basra, only one was wired, and none were actually destroyed. At Objective Peaches south of Baghdad, the key bridge was found wired for demolition, but undestroyed. The key port of Um Qasr, critical to the potential prosperity of post-war Iraq, was undamaged in the war and captured intact by Coalition forces, even though the Iraqis held the port and its facilities for two days prior to its capture and could have done extensive damage had they used this time to do so. American commanders had worried that the Iraqis would flood the Karbala Gap, a key choke point on the road to Baghdad and a potentially promising target for Iraqi WMD (weapons of mass destruction) use against stalled Coalition ground forces. Yet nothing of the kind happened—the closest the Iraqis came to deliberate flooding was some small-scale tactical inundation in the Subiyat Depression near Nasiriyah.

KEY POINTS

- There was substantial close combat against unbroken defenders in Iraq's cities in 2003, in which Coalition forces received heavy fire at often short ranges.

- Saddam Hussein had threatened a scorched earth campaign to destroy Iraq's economic infrastructure if the Coalition attacked, yet few preparations had been made to carry out this threat.

- Neither speed, nor precision, nor situation awareness was sufficient to deny the Iraqis ample opportunities to inflict casualties on Coalition forces in close combat, or to destroy Iraqi oilfields, port facilities, or bridges.

An Alternative View

The transformation school's implications are thus at odds with important elements of the actual conduct of the 2001–2 and 2003 campaigns. In particular, there was too much close combat in either campaign for stand-off precision to have played the role often attributed to it. And Saddam's failure to impose higher costs via scorched earth had little to do with Coalition speed or technology. What, then, was responsible?

Part of the answer lies in idiosyncratic features of Ba'athist Iraq: the Iraqis' failure to destroy oilfields and other economic infrastructure, for example, was ultimately their choice. Either Saddam never meant to carry out this threat, or his people refused to follow his orders, or his organization proved unable to implement his plan. But the failure of scorched earth was caused more by Iraqi than by Coalition actions—even a different or less capable Coalition military might still have averted scorched earth given the Iraqis' apparent unwillingness to carry out their threat, and even a very capable Coalition would have failed if the Iraqis had been able and willing to follow through.

Much of the answer, however, lies in the interaction between Coalition strengths and the enemies' particular weaknesses. Technology's performance depends heavily on its targets' behaviour: armies who present massed, exposed targets against twenty-first century fire-power suffer gravely for their error. But armies who can reduce their exposure and fight effectively from dispersed, concealed positions pose much tougher targets—and espe-cially, targets that are very difficult to destroy through stand-off precision fires alone. The indigenous Afghan Taliban of 2001 and the Iraqi military of 2003 presented precisely the kind of massed, exposed targets against which modern technology can reach proving ground lethality levels. And when weapons' proving ground lethality is as great as today's, the results can be extremely one-sided. An exposed enemy thus enabled US firepower to destroy the Afghan Taliban at stand-off ranges, almost without close combat. And while urban terrain enabled Iraqi paramilitaries and Special Republican Guards to avoid annihilation from stand-off distances, their radically exposed close-combat tactics made it possible for even a small, but well-equipped, Coalition ground force to annihilate them in close combat at very low cost to itself. By contrast, the same precision strike technology that wiped out exposed indigenous Afghan Taliban from stand-off range proved insuffi-cient to do the same against better trained, less-exposed Al-Qaeda opponents in actions such as Bai Beche, Sayed Slim Kalay, Highway 4, or Operation Anaconda. And there is every reason to expect that a more skilled Iraqi opponent in 2003 would have posed much greater challenges than the exposed enemies seen in the actual event.

Iraqi ineptitude in 2003

To see why, it is useful to review some of the more serious of the Iraqis' many military shortcomings in 2003, and how these interacted with particular Coalition strengths. Perhaps the most serious Iraqi shortcoming was their systematic failure to exploit the military potential of urban terrain. Cities offer a natural source of cover and concealment, they canalize attacks, they facilitate barrier construction, they pose difficult problems of intermingling and collateral damage avoidance, and they make effective employment of stand-off precision weapons much harder. The most plausible pre-war scenario for heavy Coalition casualties was the prospect of prolonged urban battles in the streets of Baghdad, Tikrit, Najaf, Nasiriyah, Samawah, Basra, Mosul, or Kirkuk.

Yet the Republican Guard and Iraqi Regular Army systematically avoided major cities, deploying instead in rural areas and suburban outskirts. They appear to have been deliberately denied access to major city centres by the Iraqi high command.

The great majority of the true urban combat in OIF was waged against lightly armed irregular paramilitaries, who fought mostly on the tactical offensive, sallying out into the open to charge Coalition armoured vehicles. Not only did the paramilitaries lack the heavy weapons or armour protection of Iraq's large mechanized formations, they also forfeited the tactical potential of urban terrain by taking the offensive in exposed, unprepared frontal assaults.

More conventional Special Republican Guard (SRG) units deployed some heavy weapons, especially in Baghdad, but these were a tiny fraction of the total available to the Iraqi military. And even the SRG failed systematically to make effective use of urban terrain for their employment. The SRG's prepared positions were almost entirely outdoors, typically in shallow foxholes dug along the roadside or in simple sandbag emplacements on building roofs or at intersections. SRG tanks were often just parked in the open at major intersections, with no effort at cover or concealment. Practically no buildings received the interior preparations that would be normal for urban warfare in Western practice, such as interior barricades, wall reinforcement, loophole construction, or wire entanglements. Outdoor obstacles, barriers, or minefields were almost completely absent.

This systematic failure to exploit urban terrain may be attributable to poor training: the Republican Guard and Iraqi Regular Army had received no instruction whatsoever in urban warfare in the years leading up to the war. In fact, Guard and Army commanders found the entire concept of city fighting unthinkable in 2003. As one Iraqi colonel put it: 'Why would anyone want to fight in a city?' His troops 'couldn't defend themselves in cities.' Only the Special Republican Guard was given any systematic training in conventional urban warfare, and even this was poor quality. The paramilitaries who shouldered much of the burden of actual city fighting in 2003 received no sustained conventional military training of any kind.

Urban warfare and the interaction of Iraqi shortcomings and coalition strengths

The Iraqis' failure to exploit urban terrain's potential enabled the Coalition's close combat technology—together with very skilled employment—to annihilate Iraqi urban defenders at very low cost to the Coalition attackers even without stand-off precision engagement. In particular, the modern armour technology of the US M1 and British Challenger tanks offered extraordinary protection, and their fire suppression, blast localization, and crew escape systems often made it possible to survive even a large-calibre penetration of the armour envelope. The ability of US Bradley Fighting Vehicles as well as Abrams tanks to shoot on the move with both accuracy and tremendous volumes of fire made them extremely lethal even to hostile armoured vehicles, much less paramilitary foot soldiers. For the latter to launch themselves in frontal assaults at such well-protected, highly lethal targets with nothing more than civilian pickup trucks and RPGs was clearly suicidal. Even where the paramilitaries fought on the tactical defence, as in their resistance to 2nd Brigade's

●

'Thunder Runs' in Baghdad, the combination of the paramilitaries' shortcomings and the Americans' lethality meant that tremendous numbers of Iraqis would be mowed down: without adequate cover or concealment once firing had given them away, Iraqi paramilitaries were dangerously exposed. And whereas the Iraqis' fire often missed, Coalition return fire was both voluminous and deadly accurate—exposed paramilitaries thus rarely survived to fire again.

BOX 13.3

Key Events in the Major Combat Phase of the War in Iraq, 2003

The campaign in Iraq began on the night of 19–20 March with an attempt to decapitate the Iraqi regime by bombing locations where Saddam Hussein was believed to be meeting with senior lieutenants. These air strikes failed to eliminate the Iraqi leadership or induce concession, however, and a joint air–ground invasion of Iraq was launched on the night of 20–21 March.

This invasion was conducted on several fronts. In the north, US SOF teamed with air strikes and Kurdish allies on the ground in an economy of force action designed to hold Iraqi forces in place on the 'Green Line' dividing the Kurdish autonomous zone from Iraq proper. In the west, SOF and supporting US conventional forces secured potential Scud missile launching sites and searched for Iraqi WMD.

The main effort was in the south, however, where US and British conventional forces invaded Iraq from bases in Kuwait along three primary axes. On the far right, the British 1st Armoured division cleared the Faw peninsula and advanced on Basra. To their left, the US 1st Marine Expeditionary Force (I MEF) secured the Rumaila oil fields, then moved north toward Baghdad. On the far left was the US Army V Corps, led by the 3rd Infantry Division (3ID). As these forces advanced, Coalition air forces struck Iraqi air defences, command facilities, WMD-capable fire support, and combat manœuvre units in depth.

Iraqi forces were disposed with a combination of regular army and paramilitary forces defending the major approach routes in the south. Behind them, a ring of higher quality Republican Guard divisions defended a 'Red Line' of positions around Baghdad. Within the city itself, a combination of paramilitaries and Special Republican Guards defended prepared positions along key roads and intersections. To the north, a mix of regular army and reinforcing Republican Guard divisions defended the Green Line opposite the Kurds.

The initial advance from Kuwait moved quickly. In the process, many Iraqi units simply melted away, abandoning their arms and disappearing into Iraqi society in civilian clothes. Iraqi defenders of the southern cities of Nasiriyah, Najaf, and Samawah, however, mounted unexpectedly heavy resistance. Sharp battles at these critical river crossing sites cost the Iraqis heavy casualties while delaying the Coalition advance only slightly.

When the ground advance finally struck the Republican Guard, beginning on 31 March, it overran the remaining resistance in battles at Objectives Peach, Murray, and Montgomery, completing the investment of Baghdad on 7 April. In the meantime, an initial probe into the Baghdad metropolitan area proper was conducted by the 2nd Brigade Combat Team (2 BCT) of the 3rd Infantry Division; this 'Thunder Run' consisted of a mounted raid into the city along Highway 8, then back out to a destination at the International Airport. Two days later, a second 'Thunder Run' drove straight into the city centre, reaching and then holding positions on the Tigris River bend. Subsequent advances into Baghdad from the north and east led to the rapid collapse of the city's defences. By 9 April when the statue of Saddam in the city centre was pulled down, Ba'athist rule had effectively ended; though President Bush did not announce the end of 'major combat operations' until 1 May, for all intents and purposes the initial goal of toppling the Ba'athist regime had been accomplished by 9 April, after just twenty-one days of combat operations.

Yet there is every reason to believe that better trained Iraqis could have produced a very different outcome even with exactly the same equipment on both sides. The light weapons wielded by Iraqi irregulars *can* penetrate M1 and Challenger tanks—in fact, at least nine M1s were disabled by RPG fire during the MCO phase of the war in Iraq. If the hundreds of RPGs fired at 2nd Brigade in the two Thunder Runs alone had been fired accurately, the penetration rate could have been dramatically higher. And if the shooters had been firing from covered, concealed positions, they could reasonably have expected to survive their first shot at a much higher rate, enabling them to shoot again and thus increasing the hit rate even further.

Most important, though, a skilled urban defender could not have been broken by an all-mounted assault of the sort waged in Baghdad and Basra. The Iraqis of 2003 were exposed and could thus often be slaughtered in the open even within the city centre without the attacker dismounting from its armoured vehicles. By contrast, a defender who exploited the natural potential of urban terrain by remaining in cover to fire from within buildings, who prepared those buildings for maximum cover and concealment, who used barriers and obstacles to canalize attacks into prepared ambushes, and who used covered retreat routes to slip away for subsequent engagements a couple of blocks away, would have been a much tougher target. Historically, it has been impossible to destroy such urban defenders without coupling armoured advances with dismounted infantry who can enter building interiors to clear rooms, kill concealed defenders, and hold the building interiors to prevent their reoccupation by defenders. Mounted vehicle crews simply cannot find properly concealed defenders in building interiors. And unless such defenders are cleared before the armoured vehicles advance, the vehicles' weaker roof, rear, and flank armour surfaces risk easy penetration from bypassed but unseen defenders. Working together, skilled dismounted infantry and supporting armour can clear urban terrain, but they cannot do so cheaply if the defender makes the most of that terrain: even with skilled attackers, and even with armoured support, dismounted building clearance against skilled defenders has typically been very costly. Urban warfare on the scale of Iraq's in 2003 could easily have produced thousands of Coalition casualties and a fundamentally different outcome for OIF if the Iraqi defenders had been better skilled, even given the technological advantages of the Abrams, the Bradley, and the Challenger, and even given the Coalition's speed, precision, and situation awareness.

KEY POINTS

- Iraqi defenders in 2003 systematically failed to exploit the defensive potential of urban terrain, fighting mostly outdoors and often on the tactical offensive in frontal assaults against heavily armoured Coalition forces.

- Exposure to twenty-first-century firepower can be very costly; OIF's combination of Iraqi exposure and Coalition firepower enabled Coalition forces to destroy ill-prepared urban defences with limited casualties and little need for risky dismounted building clearance.

- If the Iraqis had had the skills needed to exploit urban terrain to reduce their exposure, they could well have inflicted much heavier casualties in spite of the Coalition's technological advantages.

Conclusion

The radically low cost of toppling the Taliban and Saddam thus cannot be explained by reference to Coalition strengths alone. Speed, stand-off precision, and situation awareness all surely contributed to these outcomes, and some combination of these may be sufficient to account for Saddam's or the Taliban's ouster *per se*. But it is not their ouster as such that made these campaigns influential for the subsequent debate—it was the MCO campaigns' radically low cost and apparent ease that has fuelled the case for transformation. And neither the Coalition's speed, its precision, nor its situation awareness were sufficient to prevent Iraq, for example, from waging enough close combat, at point blank range under nominally favourable conditions, to have caused much higher Coalition casualties if Iraq's fighters had been tactically proficient. And these Coalition strengths did not prevent Iraq from carrying out Saddam's threat of scorched earth, which was more a result of Iraqi choices than Coalition capabilities. To explain this outcome thus requires an interaction effect between friendly strengths and enemy weaknesses—and in particular, a synergy between advanced Coalition technology and a major skill imbalance in both Iraq and especially the early stages of the Afghan campaign.

This is not to say that speed is a bad idea, or that either precision or situation awareness are undesirable. Moreover, to say that with hindsight it seems unlikely that the Iraqis would have torched their oilfields or destroyed their ports with more time is not to say this could have been known at the time. A rapid advance made sense given the credible possibility that Saddam might carry out such threats. And both precision and situation awareness were important contributors to the aggregate technological sophistication needed to exploit the enemy's mistakes in both campaigns.

Many factors thus contributed to success. And the analysis above should not be taken as a critique of pre-war planners, who operated with far less than the 20:20 hindsight available to post-war analysts. But not all contributors to these campaigns' outcomes were equally important. And the difference matters, especially in post-war hindsight. Views of past wars always shape future policies, and views on the relative importance of contributing causes can have serious post-war policy implications. It makes a difference which contributors mattered most.

In particular, it would be a serious mistake to overestimate technology or speed's contribution, and to underestimate the skill differential's importance, as many accounts of these campaigns now do. Getting the relative importance of these factors wrong can lead to at least two serious dangers.

First, it could lead to a mistaken assumption that precision and situation awareness can produce similar results against other opponents with better skills than the Iraqis' or the indigenous Afghan Taliban's. Even with skilled US forces, this is a risky proposition. In 2001 and 2003, US technology could operate at near-proving-ground effectiveness against exposed, ill-prepared opponents. Enemies who do a better job of exploiting the natural complexity of the earth's surface for cover and concealment pose much tougher targets—as Al-Qaeda (as opposed to the indigenous Afghan Taliban) showed in Afghanistan. Precision strike technology's performance is strongly affected by the nature of its targets, and the Afghan Taliban and Iraqi military's targets were extremely permissive. To overlook this is to risk exaggerating technology's potential against better skilled enemies.

Second, misunderstanding cause and effect in Afghanistan and Iraq could lead to a mistaken assumption that speed can substitute for mass, and that stand-off precision can substitute for close combat capability. If speed were sufficient to explain these campaigns' outcomes (either alone or in conjunction with precision), and if speed and mass are antithetical, then reducing mass to enable greater speed would make sense. But if speed was *not* sufficient, and if unskilled enemies were necessary to produce the apparent successes of stand-off precision in 2001 and 2003, then to trade speed for mass in US force structure would be a dangerous bargain. Against enemies like Iraq or the indigenous Afghan Taliban, small, fast-moving ground forces with massive stand-off firepower and excellent situation awareness may well succeed again—in fact, against such foes this could well be the optimum solution. But if future warfare involves better skilled opponents, then a small but agile US ground force could find itself unable to cope with concealed, covered enemies in numbers too great to overcome without mass of its own.

And this in turn suggests that the common use of Iraq and Afghanistan as evidence to fuel transformation proposals is often mistaken. The ineptitude of Saddam's and the Taliban's militaries played an important role in the low cost of major combat operations. If one cannot guarantee such inept enemies in the future, then one must be cautious in drawing implications from these conflicts for force planning and defence policy.

? QUESTIONS

1. How do transformation advocates believe the US military must change to meet the challenges of modern warfare?

2. In what ways does the experience of major combat in Afghanistan and Iraq support the transformation argument?

3. Are there inconsistencies between the transformation thesis' expectations and the actual conduct of MCO in Afghanistan and Iraq?

4. In what ways were the Afghan and Iraq campaigns similar? What were the most important differences?

5. Before 2003, some had argued that a war in Iraq should be fought using the 'Afghan Model', that is, replacing large, conventional US ground forces with small numbers of SOF commandos, PGMs, and indigenous allies. Would this have been wise or unwise in light of what we now know of the conduct of the Afghan and Iraqi campaigns?

6. To what degree are the Afghan and Iraq campaigns useful guides to future warfare?

7. What were the most important differences between the campaigns?

8. How far was the ineptitude of the Taliban's and Sadam's strategies and tactics responsible for their defeat?

9. To what degree are the Afghan and Iraq campaigns useful guides to future warfare?

Systematic histories of major combat in Afghanistan and Iraq are only beginning to appear. Probably the best one-volume treatments to date in what is still a very limited literature are:

■ Michael Gordon and Bernard Trainor, *Cobra II: The Inside Story of the Invasion and Occupation of Iraq* (New York: Random House, 2006).

■ Thomas Ricks, *Fiasco: The American Military Adventurt in Iraq* (New York: Penguin, 2006).

■ Gregory Fontenot, E. J. Degen, and David Tohn, *On Point: The United States Army in Operation Iraqi Freedom* (Fort Leavenworth, KS: US Army Training and Doctrine Command, 2004).

■ K. Sepp, R. Kiper, J. Schroder, C. Briscoe, *Weapon of Choice: U.S. Army Special Operations in Afghanistan* (Fort Leavenworth, KS: US Army Command and General Staff College Press, 2004).

■ Anthony Cordesman, *The Iraq War: Strategy, Tactics, and Military Lessons* (Washington, DC: Center for Strategic and International Studies, 2003).

—— *The War After the War: Strategic Lessons of Iraq and Afghanistan* (Washington, DC: Center for Strategic and International Studies, 2004).

■ Norman Friedman, *Terrorism, Afghanistan, and America's New Way of War* (Washington, DC: US Naval Institute Press, 2003).

■ John Keegan, *The Iraq War* (New York: Knopf, 2004).

■ Williamson Murray and Robert Scales, *The Iraq War: A Military History* (Cambridge, Mass.: Harvard University Press, 2003).

■ Jeffrey Record, *Dark Victory: America's Second War Against Iraq* (Washington, DC: US Naval Institute Press, 2004).

■ Stephen Biddle, *Afghanistan and the Future of Warfare: Implications for Army and Defense Policy* (Carlisle, PA: US Army War College Strategic Studies Institute, 2002), presents an extended version of the argument above for Afghanistan; Biddle, 'Operation Iraqi Freedom: Outside Perspectives', testimony before the House Armed Services Committee, 21 October 2003, does the same for Iraq.

By contrast, the literature on military transformation is both voluminous and growing. Good starting points include:

■ Arthur Cebrowski and John Garstka, 'Network-Centric Warfare', *U.S. Naval Institute Proceedings* (January 1998).

■ David A. Deptula, *Effects-Based Operations: Change in the Nature of Warfare* (Arlington, Va.: Aerospace Education Foundation, 2001).

■ US Joint Forces Command, *A Concept for Rapid Decisive Operations* (Norfolk, Va.: Joint Forces Command J9 Joint Futures Lab, 2001).

Older but still essential are:

■ Eliot Cohen, 'A Revolution in Warfare', *Foreign Affairs* (Mar./Apr. 1996), 37–54.

■ Andrew F. Krepinevich, 'Cavalry to Computer: The Pattern of Military Revolution', *The National Interest* (Fall 1994), 30–42.

■ Alvin and Heidi Toffler, *War and Antiwar: Survival at the Dawn of the 21st Century* (Boston: Little, Brown & Co., 1993).

■ Michael Vickers, *Warfare in 2020: A Primer* (Washington, DC: Center for Strategic and Budgetary Assessments, 1996).

For critiques of transformation:

■ Stephen Biddle, *Military Power: Explaining Victory and Defeat in Modern Battle* (Princeton: Princeton University Press, 2004).

■ Colin S. Gray, *Strategy for Chaos: Revolutions in Military Affairs and the Evidence of History* (London: Frank Cass, 2002).

■ James Kievet and Steven Metz, *The Revolution in Military Affairs and Conflict Short of War* (Carlisle, PA: US Army War College Strategic Studies Institute, 1994).

■ Michael E. O'Hanlon, *Technological Change and the Future of Warfare* (Washington, DC: Brookings Institution Press, 2000).

WEB LINKS

- Federation of American Scientists: **www.fas.org**

- US Army War College Strategic Studies Institute: **www.strategicstudiesinstitute. army.mil**

- US Army Training and Doctrine Command Center for Army Lessons Learned: **http://call. army.mil/**

- US Department of Defense: **www.defenselink.mil**

- Center for Strategic and International Studies: **www.csis.org**

- The RAND Corporation: **www.rand.org**

- The Brookings Institution: **www.brookings.edu**

- The Council on Foreign Relations: **www.cfr.org**

- The American Enterprise Institute: **www.aei.org**

- The Project on Defense Alternatives: **www.comw.org/pda/index.html**

 Visit the Online Resource Centre that accompanies this book for lots of interesting additional material http://www.oxfordtextbooks.co.uk/orc/baylis_strategy2e/.

14

Homeland Security: A New Strategic Paradigm

JACOB N. SHAPIRO AND RUDOLPH P. DARKEN

 Chapter Contents

- Introduction
- A New Threat
- Communications and the Frequency of Terror
- What should Preparations Look Like?
- What is the United States Preparing for?
- Conclusions

Reader's Guide

How has the threat of catastrophic terrorism reshaped the strategic environment? We argue that in fact the threat is not dramatically new, what is new is the salience of this threat to the public in some states, particularly the United States. However, the secretive nature of counter-terrorism actions necessarily means that the public is ill-informed about the potential efficacy of government's activities and so cannot assess if their rhetoric matches their actions. Thus public statements can easily be tailored to what decision-makers think the public wants to hear, rather than to what decision-makers genuinely believe. We consequently rely on an examination of how the United States budgets and exercises for the war on terrorism to illuminate what American decision-makers believe to be the links between domestic counter-terror operations and strategy. Along the way we look at the tools states have to prepare for counter-terrorism, and the challenges of doing so. We find strong evidence that the United States remains strategically focused on relationships between states, and argue this is probably an appropriate focus.

Introduction

❝ On September the 11th, 2001, America and the world witnessed a new kind of war. We saw the great harm that a stateless network could inflict upon our country, killers armed with box cutters, mace, and 19 airline tickets. Those attacks also raised the prospect of even worse dangers—of other weapons in the hands of other men. The greatest threat before humanity today is the possibility of secret and sudden attack with chemical or biological or radiological or nuclear weapons.[1] ❞

It has become something of a truism to say that 'the world changed on the morning of September 11th'. Indeed, the introduction to this volume makes that very argument. This chapter is sceptical of that claim, at least with respect to strategy. We believe that in fact the threat of transnational terrorism is neither a new phenomenon, nor is the scale of destruction threatened by transnational Islamist terrorist groups discontinuous with past terrorist campaigns, nor are the goals of the current threat out of line with past experience. In sum, it is not a phenomenon demanding a radically new strategic response. That said, there can be no doubt that the salience of terrorism as a political issue has increased out of proportion to the impact of terrorism on Western societies. But if the salience of terrorism has increased to domestic publics, does that necessarily mean those concerned with the exercise of military power for political objectives need a new paradigm?

This chapter examines the challenges involved in preparing the domestic response to the terrorist threat and compares the actions these suggest to the preparations actually being made by the United States. We find a puzzling disconnect between what must theoretically be done to adequately combat this adversary, and what is being done on a daily basis. One explanation is that the government simply does not know what to do. Rejecting this perspective, we suggest that the United States is behaving as though terrorism after 9/11 does not require a new response. Instead, the United States maintains an artificial distinction between what has been termed homeland security, homeland defence, and counter-terrorism actions overseas. This artificial distinction is a key indicator that American leaders remain focused on traditional concerns about the use of force between nation-states. Our analysis suggests that given the challenges of properly preparing to meet the terrorist threat in contrast to the low expected costs of not doing so optimally, this is an appropriate choice. We begin our analysis by examining claims about how new or different this threat might be.

A New Threat?

Four claims are generally made to support the argument that after 9/11, the world faced a dramatically different strategic environment. The first is that transnational terrorism, groups operating without geographically defined objectives, requires a strategic response that is different from that required by nationalist groups. The second is that modern communications technology and the ready availability of technical know-how have rendered

BOX 14.1

Key Terms

Counter-terrorism. Refers to the practices, strategies, and policies that governments employ to fight terrorism.

Terrorism. Over 120 definitions have been offered. The authors prefer the following: the use of force by non-state actors that: (1) is intended to influence an audience beyond its immediate victims; and (2) violates the standards of discretion and proportionality for the use of force under the customary Law of Armed Conflict.

Transnational terrorism. Following Enders and Sandler (2005), we define an incident as transnational when an incident in one country involves victims, targets, or institutions of at least one other country. Thus, an attack by Iraqis, on Iraqis, intended to influence Americans is transnational terrorism, as is an attack in Spain, by North African immigrants, intended to influence Spain.

Homeland security. The American catch-all term that refers to all non-military actions taken to protect people on American territory from terrorism, industrial disasters, and natural disasters. 'Homeland security' does not include 'Homeland defence', the term for all military actions taken within the United States Northern Command area of responsibility (AOR) to protect the United States from threats by external actors, both state and non-state.

transnational organizations newly capable of achieving strategic impact. The third is that the frequency of attacks around the world has increased to the point where terrorism should be a matter of central strategic concern. The fourth is that the ideology behind the Islamist groups of current concern drives them to seek a fundamentally new scale of destruction. In other words, their goals are sufficiently different to require a different strategic response. We argue that none of these claims can stand up to scrutiny.

A new strategic response?

To evaluate what may be different about today's transnational groups requires a careful parsing of the strategic objectives of transnational terrorist organizations. Al-Qaeda's strategic plan, as espoused by Ayman al-Zawahiri, entails several steps. Step one is to compel Western powers to stop supporting apostate Arab regimes. Step two is to replace these regimes with an Islamic caliphate, something only possible once they no longer have Western support. Step three is to expand the caliphate to spread Islamic rule to the world. This type of plan is nothing new. Left-wing terrorist organizations in Europe have held similar goals since the 1890s. In particular, the Italian Red Brigades are instructive. Their plan also entailed three stages. Stage one was to conduct terrorist attacks both to mobilize industrial workers to communist causes and to weaken the state. Stage two was to lead a revolution within Italy. Stage three was to spread the revolution to other states in Western Europe. The similarities in the ideological plans are striking.

While transnational goals are not new, what may be new is that the proximate targets for the first stage of Al-Qaeda's plan are located in many different states. Yet this too is not fundamentally different. The Palestine cause was moved to the front burner of Israeli–Arab relations by a series of attacks outside of Israel. The most important of these were a series of eight attacks by the Popular Front for the Liberation of Palestine (PFLP) against commercial airliners between July 1968 and September 1970, and the 1972 Black September attacks at the Munich Olympics (Abrahms 2004). In the case of the PFLP attacks, three were against Israeli airlines operating in Europe, five were against American or European airlines. Notice that the targets were neither geographically concentrated, nor were they all of one nationality. Instead, the idea was to sow terror broadly to compel a change in state policy, a similar mode of action to that taken by current Islamist groups.

What was the strategic response to these attacks? What ended this wave of transnational terrorism? Two elements were critical. The first was the installation of additional security precautions in airports including metal detectors. This forced terrorists to move out of hijacking into less efficient methods of sowing terror, such as individual kidnappings. (Enders and Sandler 2004) The second critical element was recognition by the Palestinian leadership that, while terrorism brought political attention, it was not bringing the desired changes. In the case of the PFLP, the goal was to serve as a Marxist revolutionary vanguard, not simply to bring attention to the Palestinian cause. Abrahms (2004: 536–7) The transnational goals of the PFLP in the late 1960s had more in common with Al Qaeda's goals than with those of its nationalist contemporaries. In the case of the PLO, the negative public reaction to the Munich attacks led the group to disavow links to Black September, essentially to retire that organization. Notice that neither critical element involved the use of military power by states to achieve the political goal of ending transnational terrorist attacks. Historically, dealing successfully with transnational terrorism has not required a strategic response. Rather, it has required some combination of political change and effective law enforcement.

A new level of impact?

Now consider the claim that changes in technology have rendered groups newly capable of achieving strategic impact. The concern here is with Thomas Friedman's 'super-empowered individuals' (Friedman 2002). Friedman rests his arguments on an analysis of the immediate destructiveness of attacks. They suggest that the ready availability of information on how to make bombs, or the potential use of contagious biological agents facilitated by advances in biotechnology, make individual attackers orders of magnitude more dangerous then before.[2] This cannot be a satisfactory perspective for strategists who see violence as but a means to an end. From a strategic perspective, the well-placed bullet, or well-timed grenade, can have impact commensurate with the largest of bombs. In June 1914 Gavrillo Princip, a member of the left-wing militant group Narodna Odbrana, triggered a chain of events leading to the First World War by killing Archduke Franz Ferdinand of Austria. That war killed millions and set the stage for the Second World War twenty-one years later. Certainly Princip had strategic impact far beyond that of the 9/11 plotters, even though the immediate destructiveness of his attack paled in comparison.

Note also that questions about destructiveness cannot be considered in isolation from the overall level of activity in a society. Here there is little good empirical evidence. Abadie and Gardeazabal (2004) provide evidence that in a rich country (Spain), terrorist activities (by the Basque separatists) have significant negative macroeconomic consequences.

Blomberg, Hess, and Orphanides (2004) show an inverse relationship between terrorism and investment in poor countries, especially in Africa. However, neither study shows that these negative consequences are increasing over time.

By the United States government's own estimates, the potential economic costs of most major terrorist attack scenarios are small compared to those of natural disasters and even of labour disruptions. According to the draft National Planning Scenarios, the estimated costs of a biological attack using the plague bacterium is millions of dollars, while that of a chemical attack with a blister agent is $500 million. By comparison, cost estimates for the eleven-day closure of twenty-nine West Coast ports due to a 2002 dock-workers' strike range between $140 million and $2 billion per day for a minimum cost of $1.5 billion. Even the 9/11 attacks do not exceed the scale of the worst natural disasters. Insurance payouts related to the 9/11 attacks totalled approximately $20 billion, less than the $20.8 billion paid out for Hurricane Andrew.[3] Preliminary estimates of insured losses from Hurricane Katrina range between $25 and $35 billion.

None of this is meant to argue that terrorism is not a serious problem. We simply seek to point out that, when considered within the context of the massive increases in economic activity over the last fifty years, the relative destructiveness of terrorism has not increased in a way that demands fundamental rethinking of strategy.

Communications and the Frequency of Terror

Perhaps communications technology and new modes of organization have led to a sufficiently large increase in the rate of attacks worldwide that strategists should be more concerned with terrorism then before. The statistical evidence for a secular increase in the rate of terrorism since 1990 is quite ambiguous, with total attacks dropping from 1990 to 2001 and then increasing thereafter.[4] The deadliness of incidents has gone up over that period, but has been rising much more slowly than the total number of incidents. What has increased substantially since 1990 is the use of the most spectacular terrorist tactic, suicide terrorism (Pape 2005). However, if the communications revolution were the cause of this increase, then we should see a steady increase in the use of suicide terrorism by all groups that employ it as communications technology spreads more deeply. This has not been the case, leading us to believe the increase is driven by the strategic dynamics of particular conflicts, and not by a secular change in technology.

Note also that these findings come from data that do not count incidents that are terrorist in nature but are not labelled terrorist (e.g. massacres of civilians in rural Africa). Consequently the data cannot distinguish between an increasing reliance on terrorism as a tactic, or a general secular increase in the number and activity level of rebellions and violent social movements. Nor can the data tell us whether an increase in terrorism reflects an increase in the frequency of terrorist acts, or an increasing tendency for governments to label acts as terrorist because of the new political salience of terrorism.

Furthermore there is scant evidence to confirm that any increase in terrorist activity is due to increased electronic communication capabilities or that the internet and other advances broaden the population of terrorists more then was previously possible. In fact, the most widespread terrorist movement of the last 200 years, the anarchist movement of the 1890s and 1900s, which killed thousands, spread its ideology and inspired attackers throughout the world without the benefit of electronic communications.

New destructiveness demands new strategy?

The evidence is equally ambiguous as to the last claim, that Islamist groups have fundamentally more destructive goals then past groups. Certainly an examination of the strategic writings of jihadi groups reveals the same fundamental task that preoccupies leaders of other terrorist organizations: the controlled use of violence for well-specified political ends (al-Zawahiri 2001; Lia and Hegghammer 2004). Moreover, the organizational manuals and lessons-learned pamphlets of these groups suggest that they struggle with the same organizational dilemma that has plagued covert extremist organizations since the 1890s: how to achieve the appropriate use of violence in an environment in which identification by the government equals operational failure. Even if we accept the proposition that Islamist terrorist groups simply seek to maximize violence, this is nothing new. In the 1970s the Bader-Meinhoff Gang attempted to acquire tactical nuclear weapons from the United States arsenal in Europe, while members of Aum Shinrikyo successfully acquired and used Sarin, a nerve agent (Sagan 2005).

A more problematic point is that those who argue that the new destructiveness of terrorist attacks demands more offensive strategies do not show that such strategies will reduce the risk of catastrophic terrorist attack. There are a number of reasons why taking the offensive may not mitigate the risks of attacks. Chief among these is that offensive actions may create more terrorists than they destroy. United States Secretary of Defence Donald Rumsfeld addressed the uncertainty behind an offensive strategy when he famously asked: 'Are we capturing, killing or deterring and dissuading more terrorists every day than the madrassas and the radical clerics are recruiting, training and deploying against us . . . Is our current situation such that "the harder we work, the behinder we get"?' (Rumsfeld 2003). He is right to be concerned. An interesting finding from the Israeli–Palestinian conflict is that targeted killings can be counterproductive, increasing the stock of terrorists because they serve as a recruiting call (Kaplan *et al.* 2005). Conventional arrests do not have this counterproductive effect. So if the probability of a catastrophic attack increases with the number of active terrorists, an offensive strategy may actually increase the net risk of catastrophic terrorism.

Does the current threat demand a new strategy?

We found little support for the claims that the terrorist threat today is dramatically worse then it has been in the past. We thus argue that a new strategic response is not needed. However, while the mechanics of the threat are not new, the political salience of the threat is, particularly in the United States. As the threat does not merit a new strategic response, but does merit a new political response, we should not be surprised to see a great divergence between what government claims to be doing to prepare for terrorism, and what government actually does. In the next section we will explore what preparations for this threat should look like, in order to better answer the question of what the United States is preparing for.

KEY POINTS

- The transnational goals of the current Islamist terrorist organizations are not a new phenomenon, many terrorist groups have had transnational goals in the past.

- Historically, successful responses to transnational terrorism have not involved a new strategic perspective, but rather a combination of political change and law enforcement.

- Evidence does not support the claim that technology has given terrorists the capability to achieve a fundamentally greater level of destruction.

- Evidence does not support the claim that modern communications have increased the frequency of terrorist actions or that modern communications have increased the number of terrorists.

- Evidence does not support the claim that modern terrorists have more destructive goals than previous terrorist threats.

What Should Preparations Look Like: Dealing with the Small-N Problem

During the cold war, the threat against which Western countries had to prepare was a well-defined adversary: the Soviet bloc. Strategy was made simple by the fact that it could be designed with only one enemy in mind. In dealing with terrorism, the 'adversary' isn't one alliance system with a unified command and control organization, but many smaller, highly varied organizations. Jemaah Islamiyah is organized in a fairly hierarchical fashion, mimicking traditional military structures. The cells involved in the 2004 Madrid bombings were organized around a small core of charismatic leaders who used their connections to draw on a wide variety of individuals for particular resources and expertise. Hamas is somewhere in between. Consequently, any 'model' of the adversary is likely to be misleading. Crafting a serious and strategic response to terrorist operations requires taking into account the great variety of terrorist organizations. This poses tremendous problems for government.

Essentially, building models that can handle the variety of terrorist organizations, and help government craft strategies against them, depends on having a large amount of data. Unfortunately, such data do not exist because the number and frequency of attacks by terrorist organizations is inherently low. This 'small-N' problem means that it is quite difficult, if not impossible, for government to track trends and tendencies in the behaviour of a terrorist adversary. Because the adversary's activities do not follow a strong central tendency, policy adaptation is quite difficult.[5] Changes made in response to one threat may open up a series of new vulnerabilities. To deal with these data problems would require a robust exercise programme with a substantial simulation and experimentation component. As we will show, such elements are noticeably lacking, at least in the United States.

But there is another, more problematic, 'small-N' problem related to what government must prepare for. In designing programmes to deal with large-scale warfare against the Soviet bloc, American military planners could safely prepare the best response to the other side's average operating patterns. Against a terrorist threat, government must get it right for each cell. It is no longer enough to figure out what is the right strategy on average. Thus while government is getting less data than before on how the enemy will behave, government's responses must be more discriminate and carefully calibrated. Simply put, there aren't enough data to model any of the terrorist organizations well, and modelling the 'average' adversary doesn't model any of them at all.

Given the analytical challenges presented by the very nature of the terrorist threat, it is unlikely that a single strategy can be articulated. However, a number of areas for increased attention can be identified. First, the lack of a central tendency to the threat places a significant weight on collecting operational intelligence as a primary prevention mechanism. Second, because an offensive military strategy can be counterproductive—by increasing the total number of terrorists—and because it is impossible to kill all terrorists overseas, local law enforcement must play the major role in prevention. Getting good at filling this role requires that local police officers be able to respond to information generated within the intelligence community. This in turn requires systems to share information and exercises to practise using them. Third, border security takes on an added importance because of the essentially infinite target set found within the United States. Fourth, a greater focus should be placed on securing the most dangerous weapons and materials. Fifth, the small-N problem we've already discussed means that preparing for a highly variable threat is critical. Given the problematic data on terrorism, the best way to prepare is through simulation and exercises that incorporate the variety of adversaries we actually face, rather than using a standardized threat.

If the terrorist threat is truly grave, then preparedness efforts should place significant attention on these five focus areas. As we show in the next section, only border security is receiving that attention.

KEY POINTS

- The number of terrorist events useful for analysis is still so small that it is difficult to statistically determine patterns of behaviour or to predict future trends.

- Current models of the terrorist adversary are generalized across the data. This means they do not match any specific adversary.

- If the threat does merit a new strategy, that strategy should include placing

increased attention on five areas:

(a) intelligence as a prevention mechanism;

(b) the use of intelligence by local law enforcement and the role of law enforcement in intelligence collection;

(c) border security;

(d) securing weapons of mass destruction and dangerous materials;

(e) preparing to respond to a highly variable threat.

What is the United States Preparing for?

Given that no major international attacks have occurred in the United States since 9/11, and given that many strategic actions are largely invisible to analysts, there are two places to look to understand how the United States is preparing for this adversary: budgets and exercises. By investigating both budgeting choices and the US exercise programme we can develop a holistic view of the nation's strategic perspective on counter-terrorism and homeland security; we can develop insight into what American decision-makers feel is most important. In this section we will examine the five focus areas implied by the nature of the terrorist threat: (*a*) collecting operational intelligence for prevention; (*b*) creating an effective link between operational intelligence and law enforcement; (*c*) border security; (*d*) securing the most dangerous weapons and materials; and (*e*) preparing to respond to a highly variable threat.

Operational intelligence collection and the link to law enforcement

In the previous section, collecting operational intelligence and the link to law enforcement were identified as critical focus areas given the nature of the terrorist threat. Because American intelligence budgets are classified, and because efforts to collect operational intelligence against terrorists are among the most highly classified programmes in government, we cannot directly assess how much emphasis is being placed on intelligence for counter-terrorism. We do know from press accounts that significant technical and human intelligence assets were shifted from counter-terrorism targets to prepare for the 2003 invasion of Iraq, but do not know the impact of these shifts (Stone 2003).

What we can observe is how the American intelligence community participates in exercises, especially in the National Exercise Programme. By observing this participation we can answer two questions: (1) does the intelligence community appear to be preparing to collect against an adversary that matches the characteristics of terrorist groups; and (2) are the intelligence and law enforcement communities realistically practising the sharing of information to disrupt and prevent terrorist attacks?

On both counts, the answer is no. The reason is that the exercise programme for homeland security relies on models developed for traditional military engagements. In military simulations, intelligence is highly constrained and predictable, with an emphasis on the use of sensors and digital streams of data where the signal-to-noise ratio—the amount of correct information relative to bad information—is quite high. The key intelligence challenge in these simulations is for the intelligence system to distribute the raw data through systems that are designed for handling classified data to people with clearances. Combat units then act on this information according to well-defined doctrine.

Notice how different this is from the intelligence challenge in counter-terrorism. In counter-terrorism the analyst must first sort through false alarms and ambiguous reporting to find information that is truly about terrorists. He faces an extremely low signal-to-noise ratio, relies much more heavily on human intelligence, and must interpret these data in light of an enemy whose operating patterns are highly variable. The resulting warnings and actionable intelligence must then be scrubbed of information on sources and methods so that they can be passed to law enforcement organizations that lack the classified systems and cleared personnel to receive them in raw form. Finally, these organizations must act on the information without the benefit of standardized doctrine or rules of engagement.

The challenging tasks involved in developing operational intelligence against terrorist organizations and acting on it have only recently been incorporated into exercise play. The National Exercise Programme first included in intelligence play with the third Top Officials Exercise (TOPOFF-3). Here the intelligence play focused on the passing of intelligence injects to relevant homeland security officials in several nations. Two critical elements were not exercised. First, the exercise did not test the ability of intelligence analysts to pick out and integrate relevant information from the stream of reports crossing their desks. This is understandable, given that the press of real-world concerns makes it hard to flood analysts with exercise intelligence, but it still indicates an unwillingness to sacrifice some intelligence in non-terror areas to better prepare intelligence analysts for counter-terrorism. Second, the exercise did not stress the ability of the intelligence community to rapidly pass information received from classified channels down to local law enforcement.

So, while there have been some recent improvements in intelligence community participation in a variety of exercises, the fact remains that intelligence has historically been and remains the 'odd man out'. Intelligence is used for injects that stimulate actions of other players in an exercise, but analysts' ability to recognize the right signals and share this information is not being trained. Having intelligence participate in an exercise and having intelligence analysts benefit from the exercise are not the same thing. As we look beyond the National Exercise Programme into state and local exercises, this problem intensifies. Not only is there little to no intelligence play in state and local exercises, but the role of local law enforcement in using and developing intelligence is almost never addressed. When the authors write about the problem of 'information sharing' and the complications associated with it, they mean intelligence sharing from the Federal level down to the local and vice versa. This is exactly the second focus area we identified. Unfortunately, notwithstanding official statements to the contrary, we could find no evidence that either of the first two focus areas are receiving serious attention.

Border security

In the area of border security, we do see increased spending and exercise activity since 2001. Border security has been the focus of considerable attention in the both national and state exercise programmes. At the Federal level, United States Northern Command (NORTHCOM), the American military command responsible for the continental United States, has participated in a number of exercises that involve border security. These exercises have not focused on the detection of threats crossing the border, but have still focused on important issues. For example, Ardent Sentry included a biological outbreak in Mexico and examined the repercussions to border states. A number of exercises have included mass migration issues. More typically, a terrorist successfully crossing a border into the US is used as the backdrop to an exercise. TOPOFF 2 examined issues related to the Canadian border in the Pacific Northwest. At the state and local level, border states are actively involved in exercises that include border security. Arizona, for example, has participated in several exercises that involve the economic impact of restricting border crossings, checking visas during a mass exodus from Mexico, and shutting down a port of entry in response to a terrorist threat.

Notice, though, that none of these exercises have focused on what matters about border security for counter-terrorism: the ability to catch terrorists trying to cross the border. To our knowledge, there has been no 'red teaming' in which government agents test the effectiveness of border security by trying to cross with false documents or under names that should trigger suspicion.

The picture appears equally mixed when we examine spending priorities. Federal spending on border security increased from $5.5 billion in 2001 to $8.5 billion in 2002, and reached only $8.7 billion in 2005 (Congressional Budget Office 2005: 6). Compared to an overall 300 percent in increase in discretionary spending for homeland security during the four years after 9/11, the increase in border security spending looks paltry. Much of the increase in border security funding has gone towards technical detection equipment that makes the borders more secure against groups trying to smuggle in radiological or chemical weapons. However, as Flynn (2004) effectively points out, the number of detection systems is still woefully inadequate to the task at hand. This suggests to us that the increased budgeting for border security is driven less by a desire to secure the United States against a strategic threat, than by border-state legislators who see spending on border security as an effective way to get more federal spending to their districts.

Securing the most dangerous weapons and materials

The gravest potential threat posed by terrorists is that they might acquire and detonate a nuclear weapon or other weapon of mass destruction (WMD) in a major city. Thus, securing WMD worldwide, and securing targets whose attack through conventional means can lead to WMD-scale destruction, should be a major strategic goal if we believe the threat of terrorism is so grave. Yet, funding for the Nunn-Lugar Cooperative Threat Reduction Programme to help the states of the former Soviet Union secure nuclear weapons and materials has not been dramatically increased since 9/11. United States government funding for Nunn-Lugar was higher in 2000, $458.1 million, than it has been in any year since.[6] Moreover, efforts to secure nuclear stockpiles in the United States have not been treated with great urgency. In late 2003 a Government Accountability Office (GAO) report revealed that security at American nuclear weapons production and storage facilities did not meet the currently required standards, and that even those standards were too low for the threat at hand.

The situation is even starker with respect to targets that can be hit with traditional means to yield WMD-scale destruction. Chemical plants represent the greatest threat in this category, and so are illustrative of the government response. Recent DHS analysis suggests that 'about 600 facilities could potentially threaten between 100,000 and a million people. About 2,000 facilities could potentially threaten between 10,000 and 100,000 people'(US Dept. of Homeland Security 2003).[7] Based on an analysis of all terrorist attacks against chemical facilities since 1900, Kosal (2005) identifies several strategies that would best prevent mass casualties in the aftermath of an attack. These strategies include: (1) enhancing perimeter security; modifying certain processes to reduce the risks of release; (3) switching to less toxic precursors and solvents; (4) minimizing the amount of stored materials by switching to more 'just in time' production; and (5) strengthening the physical structures in chemical plants. None of these steps would enhance profitability, and so require government mandates. Yet the current United States approach to chemical plant security has been to request voluntary increases in perimeter security. No additional security mandates have been issued. This suggests strongly that the United States government does not view securing the most dangerous materials as a strategic imperative.

Preparing for a highly varied threat

The best insight we have on what type of threat the United States is preparing for comes from the National Planning Scenarios. The scenarios include a nuclear detonation, anthrax attacks, biological disease outbreaks, pandemic influenza, chemical or radiological weapons, and natural disasters. The scenarios are meant to be templates or starting points for exercise development, not as a literal exercise design. Even so, it is apparent that the focus of the scenarios is on post-event activities, not pre-event or prevention activities. Further, there is clearly a bias towards WMD focused exercises, eight out of fifteen scenarios involve WMD. This reveals an assumption that the current adversary specifically wants to maximize damage and/or loss of life. Only the cyber attack scenario would deal with a scenario where the adversary seeks to trigger an economic disaster. Yet, we know from al-Zawahiri (2001) and other sources that economic disruption is as strategically important to Al-Qaeda as physical devastation. There are many ways in which an adversary can cause economic devastation without using large-scale physical devastation. In fact most of the scenarios do not closely match historical evidence on the weapons of choice for modern terrorist actions. So who is the threat behind these scenarios?

The most telling piece of the puzzle is the 'Universal Adversary' (UA). The UA is intended to be a generic adversary developed for the purpose of simulation. While many of the details of the UA are classified, we know that the UA is meant to cover a number of categories of conspirators including:

- foreign (Islamic) terrorists;
- domestic radical groups (e.g. anti-war, civil rights, environmentalist, and right-wing groups);
- state-sponsored adversaries (e.g. rogue states);
- disgruntled employees.

Within any one of these subgroups, the variability in behaviour is enormous. Taken over all of these groups, the UA becomes so general as to be meaningless. This generality has pernicious effects. By preparing for a general adversary, we do not prepare for any threat we are likely to face.

Getting around this problem, exercising to meet a highly variable threat, would require exercising our view of the adversary. This means repeatedly conducting similar exercises under different sets of assumptions about the threat. The United States exercises too infrequently to be able to do this. TOPOFF happens every two years, leaving little room for variability in the adversary. Other exercises happen quarterly, but focus on different attack scenarios each time, leaving the threat largely static. In fact, the way homeland security exercises are currently conducted requires such an investment in time and resources, that they cannot occur more frequently without breaking the budget.

Yet, given the small-N problem, raising the frequency of exercising is the only way to explore all the nuances of the terrorist threat, the only way of understanding how different motivations, objectives, and methods should influence our preventive efforts. What is needed is an approach to exercising that raises the frequency and allows a full exploration of this adversary. Figures 14.1 and 14.2 illustrate how such an approach can

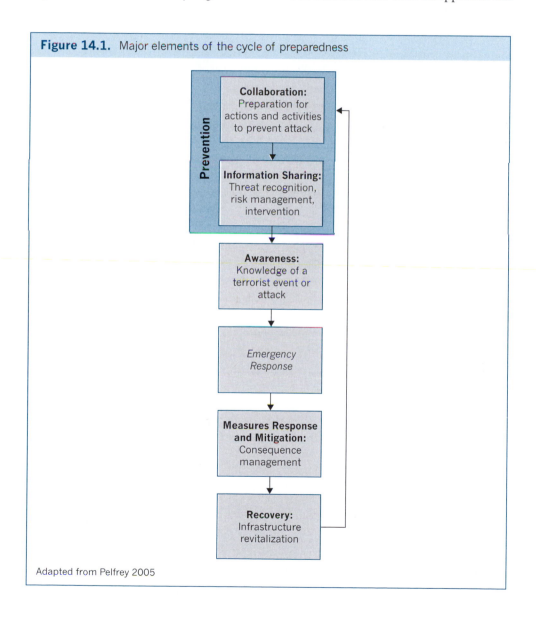

Figure 14.1. Major elements of the cycle of preparedness

Prevention

Collaboration:
Preparation for actions and activities to prevent attack

Information Sharing:
Threat recognition, risk management, intervention

Awareness:
Knowledge of a terrorist event or attack

Emergency Response

Measures Response and Mitigation:
Consequence management

Recovery:
Infrastructure revitalization

Adapted from Pelfrey 2005

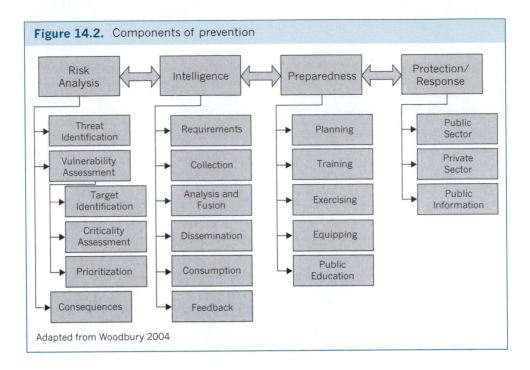

Figure 14.2. Components of prevention

Adapted from Woodbury 2004

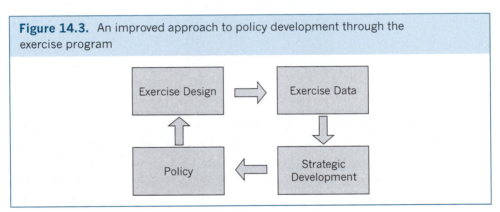

Figure 14.3. An improved approach to policy development through the exercise program

contribute not just to preparedness, but to the production of effective policy. A more extensive understanding of the components of preparedness and prevention will help us to develop exercises that exploit gaps in our capabilities, thus improving our stance while addressing the dynamic nature of this adversary.

Exercise design produces exercise data (measures of performance). These data should be used to develop strategies that result in policy. That policy can then be tested within a simulation environment to determine its projected outcome over a wide variety of scenarios (and adversaries). The process then repeats with the data from those exercises refining the strategy and resulting policies that can again be tested through exercises and experimentation. This is only possible if and when exercising become cost effective and a ubiquitous, routine part of preparedness.

Taking counter-terrorism seriously requires exercising to determine what we need to do differently with respect to each adversary and it requires considering a much wider spectrum of adversarial behaviour than is currently done. We see no evidence that such an approach is being implemented, or even seriously considered.

KEY POINTS

- There is little evidence that government is preparing for the unique intelligence challenges involved in counter-terrorism. These include: interpreting ambiguous signals with a heavy emphasis on human intelligence; passing this information to local law enforcement for action.

- Increased budgets and a robust exercise programme suggest at first glance that border security is receiving increased attention. However, the exercises are not practising what matters for counter-

terrorism, nor are the budget increases as large as they should be if counter-terrorism requires a new strategic response.

- Efforts to secure the most dangerous weapons and materials have not increased.

- Exercises have been directed at a general threat and have not explored how variations in the threat should relate to variations in response. Understanding this relationship is critical against a highly variable adversary.

Conclusions

As the previous pages demonstrate, despite a large exercise programme for counter-terrorism within the United States, there are some curious gaps in how the United States prepares. Specifically, despite rhetoric about the importance of intelligence, the National Exercise Programme gives little attention to the preventive role of intelligence. No work is done to inject signals into the system and ensure they are processed so that timely action is taken. This is despite the fact that many signals that might have prevented the 9/11 attack were missed, not because they were never received, but because they were never passed to people who could/would act upon them[8] (Department of Justice 2004). In like manner, the role of local law enforcement in preventing terrorist attacks has not been exercised to any significant extent in the Top Officials Exercise (TOPOFF) series, the major homeland security exercise involving local agencies. The most important elements of border security have been similarly neglected, as have efforts to secure WMD abroad and the most dangerous materials in the United States.

However, the largest lacuna in the exercise programme has been the lack of attention paid to the war of ideas. There has been an abundance of rhetoric with regard to the 'war of ideas', or 'winning the hearts and minds of the adversary'. It is hard to argue that this is how terrorism will eventually be defeated. But are these just words, or are serious efforts being made to accomplish this? Here is where a better exercise programme can help. With a better understanding of the adversary (particularly the psychological and/or political profile of different groups), developed out of a more robust exercise programme because of the small-N problem, we could begin to experiment with ways to influence the adversary towards peaceful ends. The business world has models of consumer behaviour—why we buy what we buy, how much we buy, when we buy—the same can be done for terrorists. That no serious efforts to build such models are under way suggests strongly that the 'war on ideas' is not being taken seriously.

Finally, there are a number of strategic decisions that should be made with respect to terrorism that have not been made. As Biddle (2005) points out, the United States has not made the fundamental choice between trying to contain the threat of Islamic terrorism and trying to roll-back Islamic extremism worldwide. The United States has not withdrawn from Iraq to try to contain the terrorist threat there, as implied by a containment strategy, nor has it committed the full measure of national power to the stabilization of Iraq, as implied by a rollback strategy. The choice of strategies has huge implications for how government tries to protect the people. Choosing a containment strategy would imply that the choice between placing radiological scanners in every port and funding additional military forces be decided in favour of the radiological scanners. A rollback strategy would suggest a greater focus on offensive counter-terrorism operations, and hence the opposite priority. That the decision has not been made is informative as to how seriously senior American decision-makers take the terrorism issue.

Our analysis leaves us with a question: why isn't the United States exercising to deal with terrorism in a way more suited to the problem at hand? After all, politicians in the United States face strong incentives after 9/11 to be seen as proactively preparing for the terrorist threat. A tentative answer may be that the population at large does not have the time or expertise to evaluate critically government's efforts. As a result, it is enough for politicians to say 'we are exercising.' They do not need to be able to show that they are exercising well or in a way that is likely to succeed, in order to get political credit for their counter-terrorism efforts. Given this disconnect, if senior leaders do not believe a new strategy is required, they will not put the necessary pressure on agencies involved in counter-terrorism to overcome bureaucratic inertia. Since we have not seen a new paradigm in how the United States exercises, we can only conclude that senior leaders do not see a dramatically new strategic environment. Instead, the increased salience of terrorism has led to a domestic emphasis on preparing to deal with an attack, without the concomitant links to a strategy for the conflict.

We have seen that the nature of the terrorist threat has not changed significantly since 9/11. What has changed is that the threat has become more salient to domestic publics. This disconnect between the magnitude of the threat and the public perception has led to a poorly thought-out response in the United States; at least as revealed by the National Exercise Programme. To address this threat seriously would require a wholesale revamping of the use of exercises and budget priorities to prepare for strategic threats. Such changes have not yet occurred.

The bottom line is that United States actions reveal that 'new' security threats take a back-seat to traditional threats of interstate war on the military side and natural disasters domestically. Our assessment is that this is probably an appropriate approach.

KEY POINTS

- The United States' exercises and budget priorities are not consistent with the argument that terrorism requires a new strategic response.

- Hard choices that would have to be made if terrorism did require a new strategic response have not been made.

- This disconnect between action and rhetoric stems from the fact that the political

importance of terrorism has increased, while the threat has not.

- Because counter-terrorism actions are hard for people to see, politicians can say they are attacking the problem without actually doing so.

- Because the threat is not genuinely new, this is an appropriate response.

? QUESTIONS

1. Does terrorism require a new strategy? Are the authors missing important aspects of the problem?

2. If terrorism does require a new strategic approach, what would be some elements of that approach, based on your understanding of terrorist groups?

3. Are there other areas of strategy where political leaders' rhetoric does not match their actions?

4. How are these leaders able get away with such apparent differences in those areas?

5. How would you prepare for a highly variable threat? Could you use computer simulations as an integrated part of the exercise programme? What forms of analysis would it enable that are not possible now? What critical questions could be addressed?

6. How does the small-N problem relate to our understanding of the adversary?

7. Is the Universal Adversary approach sufficient or is there more that can be done?

8. How would you use exercises, simulations, and analysis to evolve or further develop the National Strategy and the policies that we use to attain preparedness?

9. How do the key elements of preparedness identified in Figure 14.1 vary across: (1) threats; and (2) types of attack?

10. How many of these key elements can the average member of the informed public actually observe?

FURTHER READING

■ **Steven D. Biddle, *American Grand Strategy After 9/11: An Assessment* (New York: Harper Collins, 2004).** This very important monograph analyses the costs and benefits of two strategic choices for the war on terror: containment and rollback. Biddle demonstrates that the current American strategy is incoherent and ineffective because it neglects the choice between these strategies.

■ **Stephen Flynn,** *America the Vulnerable* **(Carlisle, PA: Strategic Studies Institute, 2005).** This book identifies a number of serious shortfalls in American Homeland Security efforts. The analysis is strengthened by the author's in depth knowledge of specific vulnerabilities and how they could be remedied.

■ **Robert Pape,** *Dying to Win* **(New York: Random House, 2005).** This very important work outlines one strategic logic behind suicide bombing. Pape very effectively demystifies this tactic, as one among many available to groups seeking political change through violence.

■ **Jeffrey Record,** *Bounding the Global War on Terrorism* **(Carlisle, PA: Army War College, 2003).** Written in late 2003, this outstanding analysis of the limitations of the 'war on terror' is especially relevant as events in Iraq have progressed towards civil war. Record identifies real limitations to American power and works through their implications.

■ **Marc Sageman,** *Understanding Terror Networks* **(Philadelphia: Pennsylvania University Press, 2004).** The best-researched account of why individuals join Al-Qaeda and affiliated organizations. Uses biographical and network data on more then 300 former and present participants.

 WEB LINKS

● **http://www.homelandsecurity.org/** Website of the Homeland Security Institute, a federally funded research center. Provides many useful links to GAO reports, government documents, and the like.

● **http://www.ojp.usdoj.gov/odp/exercises.htm** Describes the National Exercise Program. The site contains details on the major recurring exercises and provides contact information for further research.

● **http://www.hseep.dhs.gov/** Website of the Homeland Security Exercise and Evaluation Program. Provides a series of tools and evaluation criteria for organizations wishing to exercise their homeland security capabilities. Invaluable for gaining insight into what is really being emphasized in homeland security exercises.

 Visit the Online Resource Centre that accompanies this book for lots of interesting additional material http://www.oxfordtextbooks.co.uk/orc/baylis_strategy2e/.

15 Humanitarian Intervention and Peace Operations

THEO FARRELL

Chapter Contents

- Introduction
- From Peacekeeping to Peace Operations
- Intervention Failures
- The Politics of Humanitarian Intervention
- The Military Character of Peace Operations
- Conclusion: Problems and Prospects

Reader's Guide

With the end of the cold war, the international community has found the will and resources to do something about murderous and failed states. Where humanitarian intervention was previously rare and considered illegitimate, the United Nations has sponsored and organized numerous large-scale peace operations since the end of the cold war. This chapter begins by considering the transition from traditional peacekeeping to more ambitious post-cold war peace operations. It focuses on the balance between maintaining consent for peace operations while also being prepared to use force to neutralize those seeking to wreck peace agreements and oppose the humanitarian mission. It draws a basic distinction between intervention optimists and intervention pessimists. A real policy dilemma divides these views—the desire to do much and the risks of mission failure, which is examined in the context of Somalia and Rwanda. In examining the politics of humanitarian intervention, it describes the impact of public opinion and the role of Security Council politics. It explores the military character of peace operations by first considering the applicability of the main principles of war, and then by looking at how, in practice, peace operations are shaped by political imperatives. In conclusion, the prospects for peace operations look hopeful with a return to intervention optimism in the international community, but significant problems remain, especially with regard to underfunding of the United Nations.

Introduction

Humanitarian intervention is directed towards two purposes: providing emergency assistance and protecting fundamental human rights. Strictly speaking, humanitarian intervention often takes non-military forms: emergency aid in the form of money, medicine, food, and expertise, and human rights promotion through diplomacy and sanctions. When reporters and policy-makers speak of humanitarian intervention, however, they mean 'forcible military intervention in humanitarian crises'. Such intervention is necessary in failed states, when ongoing conflict threatens aid operations, and against murderous states to stop massive human rights abuses. To these ends, the intervening forces may undertake a variety of peace operations aimed at creating security and suppressing conflict.

Humanitarian intervention is a post-cold war activity. During the cold war, it was rare for three reasons.[1] First, the cold war dominated international politics. The great powers focused their military efforts on waging the cold war, building up massive deterrent forces for this purpose. The great powers did intervene in Third World conflicts, but this was for the purpose of supporting one's own, or undermining the other side's, client states. Such military intervention served to fuel these proxy wars rather than stop them. The great powers also funded and armed client states engaged in massive human rights atrocities. Second, there was insufficient public pressure for the great powers to do anything to ameliorate Third World conflicts. Eastern and Western publics were indoctrinated into viewing these conflicts and client states as elements of a larger cold war battle, in which human rights could be sacrificed in the interests of national security. Third, cold war politics prevented international collaboration in suppressing Third World conflicts or punishing murderous states, chiefly by paralysing the UN Security Council (UNSC). To be legal, forcible military intervention in a humanitarian crisis must be authorized by a resolution of the Security Council. However, UNSC resolutions can be vetoed by any one of the permanent five members (P5). With the P5 split along the cold war divide—Britain, France, the United States versus the Soviet Union and communist China—each side traded vetoes: 279 in all during the cold war.

The last decade of the twentieth century saw an unprecedented increase in the number and scale of military interventions by United Nations forces: this has been called the new interventionism. Between 1993 and 1998 alone, twenty new peacekeeping missions were established. At the same time, the size of the annual UN peacekeeping budget shot up from $230 million in 1988, to between $800 million and $1.6 billion throughout the 1990s. Behind this increased activity was the end of the cold war, which produced the demand, opportunities, and incentives for UN-sponsored humanitarian intervention. A series of regional peace agreements in Afghanistan, Angola, Namibia, Central America, and Cambodia accompanied the winding down of the cold war, and these demanded peacekeeping forces to supervise ceasefires, military demobilization, and elections. The opportunities to respond to this demand existed with increased great power cooperation in the UNSC and with the freeing up of surplus cold war military capability for peacekeeping duties. Incentives for humanitarian intervention have come from public pressure on Western governments to do something about large-scale civilian suffering in failed and murderous states.

As humanitarian interventions have grown in size and frequency, they also have increased in importance to strategic studies. Traditionally, strategic studies devoted little attention to such low-intensity conflict, focusing instead on war between major regional powers and the nuclear-armed superpowers. With the new interventionism, however, students and scholars have followed soldiers and statesmen in trying to understand the dynamics of humanitarian intervention.

From Peacekeeping to Peace Operations

A few military deployments of limited size and scope were authorized by the UNSC during the cold war in the context of traditional peacekeeping. Commonly referred to as 'Chapter VI and a half' activity, traditional peacekeeping is seen to lie somewhere between Chapter VI of the UN Charter on 'Pacific Settlement of Disputes' and Chapter VII which provides for use of force by the United Nations to uphold international peace and security. Traditional peacekeeping missions were deployed only when a conflict had ceased and with the consent of the belligerents. They typically served to monitor ceasefires and super-vise truces; occasionally, peacekeeping missions were deployed to keep belligerents apart, as in Cyprus in 1964. These missions relied on their impartiality and the goodwill of the parties concerned to fulfil their mandate. Accordingly, they were small in size and lightly armed, typically comprising contingents from neutral and non-aligned states. Between 1948 and 1978, thirteen such missions were established, with none for the decade thereafter. Only once during the cold war did the United Nations authorize a US-led peace enforce-ment mission under Chapter VII; in 1950 against North Korea.[2] On another occasion, the UNSC permitted the peacekeeping mission in the Congo (1960–4) to turn into a peace enforcement operation to restore public order and protect the government.

In contrast, the UN humanitarian interventions of the post-cold war era have been much larger, more complex affairs than predecessor missions. These new interventions have involved a much wider range of tasks, including protecting territory, people, and aid operations, disarming belligerents, policing demilitarized sites and monitoring demo-bilization, monitoring and running elections, and helping to reconstruct governments, police forces, and armies. The British Army initially called these operations 'Wider Peacekeeping'. This term not only reflected the wider range of operational tasks involved. It also recognized that such peacekeeping operations occupied a grey area between tradi-tional peacekeeping and peace enforcement. Not all aspects of these mutli-task missions had the full consent of all the parties on the ground. Whereas consent was central to traditional peacekeeping, it was not to the new breed of wider peacekeeping. Peacekeepers had to be able to threaten and to use force to achieve their mandate; if necessary, to force aid through to the starving, to repulse attacks on civilians, to forcibly disarm troublemakers, and to arrest war criminals.

In fact, the British Army's interim doctrine on *Wider Peacekeeping* (1995) was designed to caution policy-makers and the public about the costs of using force in peacekeeping (unusually for military doctrine, a glossy version was on sale at bookstores). Critical here is the relationship between consent, force, and impartiality. *Wider Peacekeeping* distinguished between the tactical and operational level of consent for peacekeeping missions. It argued that, should consent be withdrawn at the tactical level, where one or more belligerent groups obstruct peacekeepers in the field, small amounts of force may be used to keep the mission on track. However, it warned that excessive use of force could result in a collapse of consent for the mission as a whole (i.e. at the operational level). Under such circumstances, the mission would have crossed the 'consent divide', undermining its credibility as an impartial peacekeeping force and prejudicing mission legitimacy in the eyes of the belligerents. Uncontrolled escalation in violence (including attacks on peacekeepers) was bound to follow.

Wider Peacekeeping deliberately painted a bleak picture of what happens when a modest force is given an ambitious mandate. It came at a time when the British Army was being asked to do much in Bosnia with few resources on the ground. This doctrine also reflected the UN operation in Somalia, which took on one of the warring factions and lost (see next section). It certainly resonated with the first British commander of UN force in Bosnia, General Sir Michael Rose, who referred to the consent divide as the 'Mogadishu Line'. The lesson was clear to General Rose, who later observed: 'In Somalia, it has been well demonstrated that it was the move by the UN Force from peacekeeping to war-fighting which so terminally damaged the prospects of the Mission.' However, this attitude, reflected in *Wider Peacekeeping*, was unhelpful when peacekeeping missions had no choice but to cross the consent divide into peace enforcement. *Wider Peacekeeping* rightly warned that this must be a deliberate act of policy, but gave little advice as to what should happen next. This was because the chief author of *Wider Peacekeeping*, Colonel Charles Dobbie (like General Rose), considered peace enforcement to be synonymous with war, and thus not the business of peacekeepers. In effect, Dobbie saw peacekeepers and peace enforcers as totally different creatures (see Box 15.1).

Dobbie's approach is too passive, however, because it leaves peacekeepers dependent on the cooperation of the warring parties. Under such circumstances, peacekeeping missions can fall prey to 'spoilers—leaders and parties who believe that peace emerging from negotiations threatens their power, worldview, and interests, and use violence to undermine

---

BOX 15.1

Peacekeepers and Peace Enforcers as Pigs and Parrots

[P]eacekeeping and peace-enforcement cannot be guided by a set of *common* principles. The peacekeeper to peace-enforcer is as referee to football player. The objectives of each are different. One is there to win, the other to ensure fair play . . . Like pigs and parrots, the differences between peacekeepers and peace-enforcers outweigh their similarities . . . Peacekeeping is depicted as a scaled-down version of peace-enforcement [in US military thinking]. The pig, in effect, is being regarded as a small species of parrot . . . [This] can lead to peacekeeping being subject to a set of common principles that impose combatant, adversary-orientated attitudes on the impartial third-party activities that constitute peacekeeping. Pigs are, as it were, being encouraged to fly.

(Col. Charles Dobbie 1994)

attempts to achieve it' (Stedman 1997: 5). Where spoilers are identified, peacekeepers must be able to engage in robust and aggressive action to bring them to heel. This option was discouraged by the sharp distinction between peacekeeping and peace enforcement drawn in *Wider Peacekeeping*. In contrast, the US Army grouped peacekeeping and peace enforcement under the category of peace operations. In its doctrine, *Peace Operations* (1994), many of the tasks originally viewed as wider peacekeeping by the British are conceived as peace enforcement by the Americans. These tasks invariably involve coercing belligerents to comply with UNSC resolutions: in short, to use force to induce consent for peace operations. *Peace Operations* advises US commanders as to how combat power can be used to induce consent. The British Army has since moved closer to this position. It now accepts that it must prepare to use force in peace operations, and that impartiality ought to be defined not in relation to the warring parties but to the mission mandate, that is, force will be used equally against all who threaten the mission.

The importance of being prepared to neutralize peace spoilers and thereby induce consent is well illustrated in the UN intervention in Bosnia (see Box 15.2). From 1992 to 1995, a 7,000-strong force deployed in Bosnia as part of the United Nations Operations in Former Yugoslavia (UNPROFOR) attempted to alleviate the suffering of civilians trapped in the midst of a war, waged by Serbia and Croatia (in collusion with their Serb and Croat allies in Bosnia) against the new-born multi-ethnic and democratic Bosnia state. Under General Rose and with the support of the UN Secretariat in New York, UNPROFOR

BOX 15.2

The UN's Failure to Stop Serb Spoilers in Bosnia

With the benefit of hindsight, one can see that many of the errors the United Nations made [in Bosnia] flowed from a single and no doubt well-intentioned effort: we tried to keep the peace and apply the rules of peacekeeping when there was no peace to keep. Knowing that any other course of action would jeopardize the lives of the troops, we tried to create—or imagine—an environment in which the tenets of peacekeeping—agreement between the parties, deployment by consent, and impartiality—could be upheld . . . None of the conditions for the deployment of peacekeepers had been met: there was no peace agreement—not even a functioning ceasefire—there was no clear will to peace and there was no clear consent by the belligerents. . . . Nor was the provision of humanitarian aid a sufficient response to 'ethnic cleansing' and to an attempted genocide. . . . The Bosnia Muslim civilian population thus become the principal victim of brutally aggressive military and paramilitary Serb operations to depopulate coveted territories in order to allow them to be repopulated by Serbs. . . . In the end, these Bosnian Serb war aims were ultimately repulsed on the battlefield, and not at the negotiating table. Yet the [UN] Secretariat had convinced itself early on that broader use of force by the international community was beyond our mandate and anyway undesirable. In a report to the Security Council, the Secretary-General [Boutros Boutros-Ghali] spoke against a 'culture of death', arguing that peace should be pursued only through non-military methods. When, in June 1995, the international community provided UNPROFOR with a heavily armed rapid reaction force, we argued against using it robustly to implement our mandate. When decisive action was finally taken by UNPROFOR in August and September 1995, it helped to bring the war to a conclusion.

(Kofi Annan 1999)

defined its principal mission as helping to deliver aid. Later, it was mandated by the UNSC to watch over six designated 'safe areas' in Bosnia. These were enclaves of Muslim civilians surrounded by the Bosnian Serb military. Under Rose, UNPROFOR was not prepared to use force to push aid through road blockades or to protect civilians (including those in so-called 'safe areas'). During this time, UN policy amounted to a policy of endless appeasement; it relied on the goodwill of Bosnia Serb extremists to let aid through, protect defenceless Muslim civilians, and negotiate a peace. Yet, these same Bosnian Serbs were bent on destroying multi-ethnic Bosnian democracy through a campaign of murder and terror against the Muslim population. There was a dilemma facing UNPROFOR: calling in air strikes to punish Serb transgression would push it across the consent divide, yet it lacked the landpower to defend aid convoys and safe areas against Serb retaliation. UNPROFOR's military weakness was reinforced by a weakness in UN thinking which ruled out a military solution to the Bosnian crisis. For even when UNPROFOR was reinforced by an Anglo-French Rapid Reaction Force of helicopter gunships and artillery, the UN Secretariat was reluctant to get tough with Bosnian Serbs. Thus, even when it was militarily equipped to deal with Serb spoilers, it was conceptually ill-equipped to do so. The final straw was occurred when Bosnian Serb forces overran two safe areas, Srebrenica and Zepa, slaughtering the male civilian inhabitants. Rose's replacement, British General Rupert Smith, decided that it was time to 'escalate to success'. In retaliation for Serbian shelling of Sarajevo (another 'safe area') in August 1995, he called in NATO air strikes. This military pressure in combination with military advances by Bosnian government and Bosnia Croat forces in the Eastern Bosnia persuaded the Bosnian Serbs to sue for peace.

KEY POINTS

- Limited traditional peacekeeping operations have given way in the post-cold war era to larger, more complex, and more ambitious wider peacekeeping operations.

- Critical to wider peacekeeping is the relationship between consent, force, and impartiality. If a peace force uses too much force it risks losing its impartiality and crossing the consent divide into open

conflict. At the same time, a peace force must be prepared to use sufficient force to counter peace spoilers and induce consent for its operation.

- The war dragged on in Bosnia because the United Nations pursued a policy of endless appeasement when it should have used force against Serb spoilers.

Intervention Failures

The consent divide-induce consent debate may be recast in more general terms as a clash of two perspectives: intervention pessimism versus intervention optimism. Intervention pessimism is the belief that little can be done about humanitarian disasters without the consent and cooperation of the major parties concerned; all is lost if the peacekeeping force crosses the consent divide. Intervention optimism is the belief that the international community can forcibly rebuild failed states and reform murderous ones; operational success depends on the ability to induce consent if required. This tension between these opposing perspectives was played out in the cases of the two greatest failures in post-cold war humanitarian intervention: Somalia and Rwanda. Intervention optimism led the United Nations to launch a recklessly ambitious operation aimed at disarming Somalia and reconstructing the government. Intervention pessimism led the United Nations to do nothing to stop genocide in Rwanda. As we shall see, the UN should have done less in Somalia, and could have done much more in Rwanda.

Somalia (1992–1995)

The crisis in Somalia was generated by a combination of civil war and famine. The country descended into a second civil war in mid-1991, which was directly responsible for the deaths of tens of thousands of civilians. Much worse was the deadly famine that gripped Somalia in 1992. War and general lawlessness was making it extremely dangerous and difficult for Western aid agencies to operate in Somalia. The deployment of force of 550 Pakistani peacekeepers in mid-1992, the United Nations Operations in Somalia (UNOSOM I), did little to improve things. UNOSOM I operated with the consent of the main warlords in Somalia. However, since aid was power, the warlords were unprepared to let it flow freely.

Under intense pressure from UN Secretary-General Boutros Boutros-Ghali, and US-based aid agencies, the United States led a 37,000-strong United Task Force (UNITAF) into Somalia (including 28,000 US troops) in early December 1992. Under UNSC Resolution 794, UNITAF was mandated to 'use all necessary means to establish as soon as possible a secure environment for humanitarian relief operations in Somalia'. UNITAF achieved this, setting itself the modest goal for creating demilitarized zones around aid operations (as opposed to the more ambitious goal of disarming the warring factions). It then used overwhelming military superiority to scare off armed groups from its area of operations. By its own measure, UNITAF was a success; aid got to the starving, and the famine receded.

UNITAF handed over to a new 28,000-strong UN force, UNOSOM II, in mid-1993. UNOSOM II had a more much ambitious mandate; nothing less than the forcible disarmament of the warring factions and assisting in the reconstruction of the Somali state (UNSC Res. 814). Boutros-Ghali had wanted to see a general disarmament in order to produce lasting security in Somalia. The new Clinton administration which came into power full of optimism about multinational peacekeeping, was receptive to broadening the UN's role in Somalia. However, the new mandate placed the United Nations on a collision course with the Somali warlords. In June 1993, one Somali faction ambushed a UN patrol, killing twenty-four Pakistani soldiers. The UN responded by effectively declaring war on the warlord responsible, General Aideed: UNOSOM II was mandated to 'take all necessary measures against all those responsible for the attacks' (UNSC Res. 837). It was a war the UN would lose. UNOSOM II spent the summer in pitched battles with Somali gunmen, while an elite US Quick Reaction Force (QRF) buzzed around the Somalia capital (Mogadishu) in helicopters, hunting for Aideed. Any goodwill on the part of the general Somali populace towards the UN melted away as US helicopter gunships blew up buildings.

The mission ended in disaster, when the QRF was ambushed on 3 October during a mission intended to capture top Aideed officials. US helicopters were shot out of the sky, and in the intense fire-fight that followed eighteen US soldiers were killed, seventy-eight were injured, and one was captured. That effectively ended the American involvement in Somalia; within months, US forces had pulled out. UNOSOM II dragged on until 1995, but without much UN heart and US backing, it achieved little.

Somalia is the 'Vietnam' of peacekeeping. Despite pouring money ($1.6 billion), material, and personnel in Somalia, the United Nations failed to restore long-term order and to rebuild the state. UNOSOM II tried to do too much with too little: it lacked the command capabilities and combat power of UNITAF, yet it was tasked to do something UNITAF had deliberately avoided: disarming the warlords. In the wake of the dramatic collapse of UNOSOM II, the modest achievements of UNITAF were forgotten.

Rwanda (1993–1994)

Over about 100 days, between April and July 1994, 800,000 people were massacred in Rwanda. This humanitarian crisis was caused by a power struggle between Hutu extremists and Hutu and Tutsi moderates, which broke out when the Hutu-dominated regime of President Habyarimana bowed in the early 1990s to domestic and international pressure for the introduction of multi-party democracy. The regime sought to increase its base of support by bringing extremist Hutu opposition parties into a transitional government. This occurred in the context of simultaneous military and economic pressure on the government, respectively brought by invasion from neighbouring Uganda by the Tutsi army of Rwandese Patriotic Front (RPF), and a dramatic fall in export revenues combined with severe drought. Once in government, Hutu extremists used their monopoly of mass media to incite attacks against Tutsis and moderate Hutus, and to organize militias to carry out small-scale massacres. In reprisal, the RPF army launched an attack on the capital Kigali in 1993 that was only repulsed with French military support. After such a close call, Habyarimana was forced to sign a peace deal with the RPF that led to Tutsi inclusion in the government and the exclusion of Hutu extremists. This was the trigger for genocide in Rwanda. In order to retain power and avoid judicial accountability for complicity in attacks on Tutsi civilians, Hutu extremists eliminated the President (shooting down his plane on 6 April) and began a systematic campaign of mass slaughter designed to eliminate all opponents and incriminate the entire Hutu population in the process.

There was a UN peacekeeping force on the ground when the genocide started in early April; the 2,500-strong United Nations Assistance Mission for Rwanda (UNAMIR). UNAMIR had been deployed with a very limited mandate (UNSC Res. 872) to monitor the ceasefire between the government and RPF, and to assist in relief operations. Understaffed, under-resourced, and unauthorized to use force to prevent war crimes, UNAMIR was overwhelmed by the horror that unfolded around it. Amidst the massacres, French, Belgian, and Italian troops arrived in force to evacuate Europeans but did not stay to save Rwandese. To make matters worse, the Belgian and Bangladeshi contingents of UNAMIR were withdrawn by their national governments (in Belgium's case, after ten Belgian soldiers were brutally murdered by Hutu extremists). The RPF retaliated by resuming its offensive against the Hutu authorities. The United Nations responded on 21 April by reducing UNAMIR to 270 personnel, and focusing its effects on re-establishing the cease-fire. It was not until 17 May that the UNSC adopted Resolution 918, expanding UNAMIR to 5,500 and authorizing it to protect the populace. However, UN member states were not forthcoming with these forces and, one month later, UNAMIR was still only 500 strong. Eventually, the genocide ran out of steam. The RPF managed to save some civilians by sweeping westwards across the country and pushing back Hutu extremists. On 9 July, the French deployed a force of 2,300 troops ostensibly to create a Humanitarian Protection Zone in the Western corner of Rwanda, but in reality to protect their retreating Hutu allies who eventually fled across the border to (what was then) Zaire.

The current UN Secretary-General, Kofi Annan, has acknowledged the UN's failure in Rwanda. Some suggest that the United Nations could have stopped the genocide in its tracks by rapidly deploying a modest force of 5,000. The counter-argument is that the genocide was so fast paced that the world had no hope of responding in time. Only the United States had the capability to deploy an intervention force quickly enough to stop the bloodshed. But it would have taken at least four weeks for the Clinton administration to realize the scale of massacre and send in even a small force, by which time, the genocide was practically over (Juperman 2000). The international community, however, could have beefed UNAMIR *prior* to the genocide. UNAMIR had reliable intelligence forewarning of the outbreak of violence. This was communicated to the United Nations in New York by UNAMIR Force Commander, Major-General Roméo Dallaire. Furthermore, Dallaire repeatedly sent warnings in February of the worsening security situation. The United Nations could have done a lot more to halt the genocide, according to the independent inquiry set up by Secretary-General Annan to investigate the UN response to the Rwanda crisis. In its report submitted to Annan in 1999, the inquiry found 'an overriding failure [by the United Nations] to create a force with the capacity, resources and mandate to deal with the growing violence and eventual genocide in Rwanda'. Its conclusion is inescapable: 'The Security Council bears a responsibility for its lack of political will to do more to stop the killing.'

The shadow of Somalia

Somalia is partly to blame for the failure of the UN intervention in Rwanda. It explains why Secretary-General Boutros-Ghali and President Clinton started out intervention optimists but ended up intervention pessimists. The Secretary-General's first *Agenda for Peace*, published in 1992, was decidedly upbeat about the prospects for wider peacekeeping, calling on member states to provide more resources for such operations. It defined peacekeeping as 'the deployment of a United Nations presence in the field, *hitherto* with the consent of all the parties concerned', implying that consent may not be required in future. Similarly, President Clinton entered office in 1993 seeking to expand America's commitment to multilateral peace operations. This was reflected in drafts of Presidential Decision Directive 25 (PDD-25), *The Clinton Administration's Policy on Reforming Multilateral Peace Operations*. After disaster in Somalia, Boutros-Ghali and Clinton both changed their tune. Boutros-Ghali's 1995 *Supplement to an Agenda for Peace* reasserts the crucial importance of consent, impartiality, and non-use of force to operational success. Equally, the final version of PDD-25 released in May 1994 stated that 'it is not US policy to seek to expand either the number of UN peace operations or US involvement in such operations'. The lack of political will identified by the independent inquiry on the UN Response to Rwanda was all too evident in Boutros-Ghali's failure to push the case for intervention, matched by US (and UK) obstruction in the Security Council of a rapid UN response.

KEY POINTS

- The debate between those who warn against crossing the consent divide and those who call for use of force to induce consent is essentially a debate between intervention pessimists and intervention optimists.

- The tension between intervention pessimists and intervention optimists was played out in the UN's two greatest intervention failures: Somalia and Rwanda.

- The UN failed in Somalia by trying to do too much; it failed in Rwanda by not doing nearly enough.

- UN Secretary-General Boutros-Ghali and US President Clinton started out as intervention optimists but turned into intervention pessimists following failure in Somalia. This resulting lack of political will prevented effective UN intervention in Rwanda.

The Politics of Humanitarian Intervention

Politics gives meaning to humanitarian crises, defining those that demand international response. It selectively focuses international attention on human suffering and human rights abuses on certain places in space and time. Serbia's brutal repression of Kosovo triggered Western humanitarian intervention; Russia's brutal repression of Chechnya has not. Iraqi attacks on Kurds in 1991 resulted in the creation of a Kurdish 'Safe Haven' in Iraq guarded by thousands of troops and Allied airpower, while even more murderous Iraqi attacks on Kurds several years earlier met with no international response. Politics also shapes the speed and scale of humanitarian intervention. Politics operates to define crises and shape responses, at the level of domestic public opinion, and to shape bargaining within the Security Council itself.

Public opinion

It is commonly believed by policy-makers and commentators alike that Western public opinion can make and break humanitarian interventions. Public opinion can prompt military intervention when the public responds to media images of massive suffering. Thus, 'extensive media coverage of emaciated Somalis ensured a suitable international outcry (the "Do Something" response)' (von Hippel 2000: 59) and later in Bosnia, according to the US Special Envoy Richard Holbrooke, 'the reason the West finally, belatedly intervened was heavily related to media coverage'. This is called 'the CNN effect': coined after the

Cable News Network's total televised coverage of the Gulf War. At the same time, public support for humanitarian interventions are assumed to be conditional on minimal peacekeeper casualties. This is 'the bodybag effect'; referring to the impact of returning bodybags with American war dead on US public support for the Vietnam War. We may expect the public to be particularly sensitive to casualties in humanitarian interventions because these military actions are freely entered into by their government: in this sense, they are 'wars of choice', as opposed to 'wars of necessity' that must be fought to preserve national security. It is also widely believe that the bodybags effect is heightened in the televised age, in that extensive media coverage of dead peacekeepers will lead to a collapse of public support for a mission. The CNN effect is thus a 'double-edged' sword; the off-cited example is Somalia, with the collapse in US support following the deaths of eighteen American soldiers (see Box 15.3).

As a concept, 'the CNN effect' is quite misleading. It underestimates the extent to which governments can frame the media debate, and thereby choose the place and moment of intervention. Generally, governments will be least able to do this when they are uncertain as to the best policy to pursue (whether to intervene or not, and how), and when those lobbying for intervention are able to mobilize opposition politicians behind their cause. Disunity within the politician establishment, be it within the executive or across the executive–legislative divide, not only reduces the executive's ability to influence the media debate but also makes the public more responsive to media calls for intervention. In the case of Somalia, the CNN effect did operate because the Bush administration was uncertain as what to do, and there was a powerful pro-intervention coalition comprised of US aid agencies and sympathetic members of Congress. In the case of Kosovo in 1999, the Clinton administration was able to resist media pressure for a US-led ground force intervention to stop Serbian atrocities against ethnic Albanians. The administration was certain that it did not want to adopt such a policy, and opposition politicians in Congress also were against a ground intervention.

'The bodybag effect' is similarly misleading. Empirical evidence from opinion polling suggests that peacekeeper casualties do not necessarily result in public calls for an immediate withdrawal. In the case of Somalia, most Americans favoured *increased* US military

---

BOX 15.3

The CNN Effect as a Double-Edged Sword

The fact that the USA pulled the plug on its Somali intervention after the loss of 18 US Rangers in a fire-fight in October 1993 indicates how capricious public opinion is. Televised images of starving and dying Somalis had persuaded the out-going Bush administration to launch a humanitarian rescue mission, but once the US public saw the consequences of this in terms of dead Americans being dragged through the streets of Mogadishu, the Clinton administration was forced to announced a timetable for the withdrawal of all US forces from Somalia. What this case demonstrates is that the 'CNN factor' is a double-edged sword: it can pressurize governments into humanitarian intervention, yet with equal rapidity, pictures of casualties arriving home can lead to public disillusionment and calls for withdrawal.

(Wheeler and Bellamy 2005: 564–5).

involvement following the killing of US soldiers. The polls also show that American public support was primarily conditional on evidence of Somali public support for US involvement in the UN mission, and much less so on US casualties. If ordinary Somalis wanted US troops to go home, then ordinary Americans saw little reason for their soldiers to stick around. But if Somalis appreciated what US forces were doing on their behalf, then most Americans were prepared to support the intervention even if there were US fatalities. America pulled out of UNOSOM II following the deaths of its soldiers because of an *anticipated* (rather than actual) collapse of US public support. US policy-makers expected that their public would demand an immediate US withdrawal and acted to head off this public reaction. What the Somali case does reveal is the importance of domestic political unity in sustaining public support interventions. Doubts were expressed in Congress about US involvement in Somali in the summer of 1993 when UNOSOM II drifted into war against Aideed, and this resulted in a drop in public support for the mission; public support actually rallied in the short term following US casualties.

Rather than focusing on public sensitivity to casualties it might be more analytically useful to think in terms of political sensitivity to casualties. Governments will be sensitive to casualties when there is policy uncertainty and political disunity, which, in turn, will have already eroded public support for missions. There also is reason to believe that political sensitivity may vary from country to country. Just as the loss of eighteen US soldiers ended America's involvement in Somalia so the deaths of ten Belgian troops caused Belgian to pulled out of Rwanda. However, Pakistan did not withdraw its contingent from UNOSOM II when it lost twenty-four soldiers, nor was Britain's commitment to its intervention in Sierra Leone in 2000 shaken by battle casualties. This may have something to do with the political structure of countries, with some more likely to encourage and enable political disunity (e.g. sharing of powers and executive–legislative divide in the United States) than others (e.g. executive dominance of Parliament in Britain). Obviously, political sensitivity has operational implications, which are discussed in the next section.

Security Council politics

The fifteen members of the Security Council have the responsibility for authorizing humanitarian interventions. A majority of nine UNSC members are needed to take such a decision. However, real power resides with the P5, and their individual right of veto. As we saw, conflict between the P5 during the cold war made the UNSC moribund as an instrument for managing international security. With the cold war over, cooperation between the P5 has greatly improved. But four political problems still dog UNSC sponsorship of humanitarian interventions.

Even after the cold war, the P5 remain states with great power interests and aspirations. Where a particular humanitarian crisis is associated with a certain P5 member (or members), others may withhold their support or even threaten to veto unless support is promised in exchanged for their interests elsewhere in the world. This is the 'log-rolling problem'. Thus, Russia and later China obstructed UNSC Resolutions on peace operations in Haiti. Russia wanted UN endorsement of its own intervention in Georgia in 1994, while China was seeking a public apology from Haiti for inviting Taiwan's Vice-President to the inauguration of Haiti's new president in 1996. Sometimes, great power differences can produce a veto problem, when one P5 member refuses to contemplate a UN intervention which it considers threatening to its interests and/or aspirations. This was evident in Russia's approach to Kosovo in the late 1990s: Russia refused to recognize the humanitarian dimensions of the evolving crisis and was clearly prepared to veto a UN intervention. This 'veto problem' was solved by independent action by the North Atlantic Treaty Organization (NATO), which argued that force was justified (even in the absence of UNSC resolution) on the grounds of 'overwhealming humanitarian necessity'.

Even when the P5 all agree to authorize the deployment of a UN peace operations force, two problems can still hinder effective UN intervention. The first is the P5 tendency to 'talk the talk' but not 'walk the walk'. The great powers acting through the UNSC often pass grand-sounding resolutions which they fail to back up with force. This is the 'posturing–problem'. The creation of 'safe areas' in Bosnia is a classic example; these areas were not at all safe, because the UNSC was not prepared to deploy additional military forces to protect them. In this case, several UNSC members as well as the UN Secretariat warned at the time that 'without the provision of any credible military threat' these safe areas were meaningless. But the great powers went ahead regardless and set up defenceless 'safe areas'.

Second, even when some of the P5 are prepared to 'walk the walk', they may totally disagree on which direction to take. Great powers may disagree on the nature of the humanitarian crisis as well as the most effective response. This is the 'coordination problem', which again was evident in Bosnia. The United States and its European allies had completely different perceptions of the Bosnian conflict which led them to disagree fundamentally on the appropriate response. The European powers saw an ethnic conflict, the solution to which was some form of partition. However, the United States saw it as a war started by Serbia and consequently were unprepared to support partition because this would reward Serbian aggression. It was only when this coordination problem was resolved in 1995, by the United States accepting that partition was a necessary evil, that the international community were able to take effective action to end the Bosnian war. Militarily speaking, all these political problems have adverse operational implications.

KEY POINTS

- Humanitarian intervention is shaped by politics at the domestic level and in the Security Council, which operates to define crisis and international responses.

- The 'CNN effect', the notion that televised images of humanitarian suffering can produce a public demand for intervention, underestimates the extent to which political elites can frame the media debate to affect the place and timing of intervention.

- The 'bodybag effect', the assumption that casualties can lead to a collapse in public support for intervention, underestimates the public's stomach for casualties.

- However, returning bodybags can induce political elites to withdraw their support for a peace operation.

- UN Security Council cooperation on humanitarian intervention can be hindered by one or more of the P5 seeking to advance their own national interests, either through log-rolling or even vetoing behaviour.

- Even when the P5 agree to act, effective intervention may be hampered by UNSC posturing (where tough talk is not matched by action) and lack of coordination (where states disagree on the best course of action).

The Military Character of Peace Operations

To stop conflict, peace forces must be prepared to engage in combat (not in the least to deal with peace spoilers). Such military forces have been designed, equipped, and trained according to fundamental principles of war. However, these principles rarely apply in practice when it comes to peace operations. In addition, there are a number of specific operational pathologies created by political imperatives to manage public support for peace operations that complicate operations on the ground.

Principles and practicalities

If we look at the four main principles of war—objective, unity, mass, and surprise—we can see that all are problematic when it comes to peace operations. First and foremost is the principle that military operations should be conducted towards clearly defined, decisive, and attainable objectives. This is possible in war, with objectives including seizure of territory and/or destruction of enemy forces. In peace operations, however, objectives are often poorly defined and indecisive. Objectives for peace operations are usually established by UNSC mandate; for non-UN interventions, mission mandates are set by the contributing national governments. Security Council politics often prevent the construction of a clear mission mandate. Mandates may be deliberately vague to reduce the coordinating problem. Imprecise mandates also may emerge as a consequence of the posturing problem; as we saw with the safe areas in Bosnia, UNSC members may want to talk tough without actually committing themselves to tough action. Peace operations are, in themselves, decisive only in the sense of short-term effects; for example, securing aid routes or stopping a massacre. Truly decisive objectives are the long-term provision of societal security, political surety, and economic stability, for which non-military instruments are essential. Unattainable objectives also flow from the posturing problem in the UNSC, which results in grand-sounding mandates being given to under-resourced missions; again the safe areas mandate given to UNPROFOR is a stark example of this. To be sure, military commanders will attempt to translate the mandates they are given into clear and attainable mission objectives. Thus, UNITAF sought to create a secure environment for aid operations by keeping armed bandits at bay rather than disarming them. Equally, UNPROFOR protected humanitarian aid by escorting aid convoys rather than securing aid routes; the latter would have involved using force to clear Serb and Croatian roadblocks, while the former did not. In effect, objectives are rendered clear and attainable by minimizing the mission. Ironically, this makes objectives less decisive: the secure environment in Somalia did not outlive UNITAF, and aid flows in Bosnia depended on the goodwill of the belligerent parties and not on UNPROFOR's power.

Unity of effort, the second principle, is achieved in war through unity of command; that is, having all forces under one commander. Thus, the coalition forces that liberated France in 1944 were led by a single commander (General Dwight Eisenhower) as were those that liberated Kuwait in 1991 (General Norman Schwartzkopf). Unity of command is less assured in peace operations for two reasons. First, peace forces are often drawn from a wider variety of troop-contributing states than in normal coalition warfare. Differences in military culture, lack of prior joint operational experience, and potential political rivalries between contributing states, all inhibit the creation and operation of an effective command structure in peace operations. Sometimes these differences can be so great as to render the chain of command inoperative, as was witnessed in late 2000 by the bitter dispute between the Indian commander and Nigerian and Zambian contingents in the UN force in Sierra Leone. Second, the governments of troop-contributing countries are reluctant to let the UN do as it will with their troops. Thus, national governments frequently bypass the mission command structure and issue instructions directly to their forces in the field. Western powers also have on occasion provided combat forces to support UN missions without actually placing those forces under UN command; the Anglo-French Rapid Reaction Force in Bosnia, the US QRF in Somalia, and British military forces in Sierra Leone all remained under national political and military command. To make matters worse, unity of command is not sufficient in peace operations. Commanders must coordinate their actions with civilian agencies—UN, non-government, and local aid agencies—to achieve unity of effort in peace operations. Here differences in military and civilian organizational cultures are even more pronounced and can place a profound barrier to effective and timely coordination. In Somalia, civil–military cooperation under UNITAF broke down when the military way of doing things—controlling movement and information—infuriated aid agencies that were used to operating independently of such restrictions.

The third principle is for commanders to mass force. This may be achieved through concentration of force at points in space and time that will have greatest impact on the enemy. It also may be achieved through massing the effects of combat power, that is, synchronized use of all the elements of combat power to create decisive effect. When it comes to peace operations, however, forces are more commonly dispersed rather than concentrated in order to maintain high visibility and provide security on the ground. In areas of Somalia, US Marines were parcelled out to villages in the smallest of units (rifle squads). Force dispersal at this level also limits possibilities for massing effects. The smaller the unit, the fewer elements of combat power that will be available to the commander. The problems of under-resourcing and disunity of command that are endemic in peace operations also greatly reduce possibilities for massing force. As Somalia showed, massing force may prove difficult even for the purposes of providing emergency fire support to a unit in trouble; UNOSOM II had trouble pulling together the force of Malaysian and Pakistani tanks and armoured cars that finally bailed out the US QRF from Aideed's ambush.

The principle of surprise, namely, to strike the enemy when and where they least expect it, is difficult to incorporate into peace operations. The critical ingredients for surprise are speed, secrecy, and deception. Speed refers to observing and shaping developments in the area of operations. The unity of command problem in peace operations reduces the ability of peace forces to do this in a timely manner. Secrecy is often compromised by the imperative for unity of effort, which requires peace forces to share operational information with civilian agencies (many of which hire local staff). Aideed, for instance, had excellent intelligence about UNOSOM II operations because some of locally hired aid workers were his spies. Deception is problematic in urban environments, and particularly so in peace operations because the local populace may also act as eyes and ears for belligerent parties.

Public opinion and operational pathologies

In place of traditional principles of war, peace operations are shaped by the political imperative to manage public opinion. As we have seen, this imperative is generated by political sensitivity to casualties, particularly in what are essentially wars of choice. At the level of national policy, this results in a focus on winning the media battle (see Box 15.4). This was clearly illustrated in Kosovo. NATO launched an elaborate public relations campaign directed at countering Serbia's attempt to portray itself as the victim of NATO aggression.

Political concerns with public opinion produce three pathologies in peace operations. First is the strategic compression of the battlefield. In conventional war, strategic outcomes are shaped by military action at the campaign level: such as the British campaign to drive the Argentinean military off the Falklands or the allied campaign in 1990–91 to push the Iraqi Army out of Kuwait. By contrast, tactical military actions can have strategic consequences in peace operations.[3] The loss of eighteen US soldiers in a single fire-fight caused the Somalia mission to collapse. Similarly, the allied bombing of the Chinese embassy shook NATO's strategy in Kosovo. As a consequence, not only must military commanders become effective media managers, they must also anticipate and avoid those military actions likely to result in negative political fallout.

Second is an operational focus on full force protection, that is, with ensuring the peace forces are not vulnerable to attack. This is a peculiarly American obsession that flows from an acute political sensitivity to casualties. Full force protection, as an operational imperative, can hinder effective peace operations in a number of ways. It can result in the concentration of force when security for aid operations would be best promoted through the dispersal of peace forces to provide military presence over a larger area. It can require military commanders to order their forces to wear body armour, visibly demonstrating distrust and insecurity (as US forces did in Somalia), when a more relaxed force posture would make it easier to build relations with the local communities (as British forces did in Sierra Leone). American military opinion appears divided on this issue. Senior officers with memories of Vietnam share the casualty aversion of political leaders. More junior officers with recent experience of peace operations realize that full force protection can be a serious impediment to mission success.

BOX 15.4

Winning the Media Battle

In the propaganda war, the deadlines are set by television schedules and first editions as much as [by] enemy movements and diplomatic engagements. Surprise attack means pre-emption by an enemy press release, reinforced by visits to bomb sites or captured territory by reporters allowed to stay in the enemy capital precisely for this purpose. A poor defence means getting caught by unexplained discrepancies and self-contradictions. The credibility of the commander is determined in the television studio as much as on the battlefield. It is no good being able to motivate servicemen and women to accept the hazards of combat if you cannot motivate an otherwise non-participating public to back them in opinion polls.

(Freedman 2000: 340)

Third is an over-reliance on airpower (see Box 15.5). As the 1990–1 Gulf War demonstrated, airpower is most effective when employed in synergy with landpower: the allied air campaign destroyed the Iraqi military infrastructure and softened up Iraqi land defences, while the land campaign (with air support) smashed the Iraqi army in Kuwait. However, given the aversion to casualties in wars of choice, the Western powers are deeply reluctant to commit ground forces to combat in support of peace operations. In other words, they believe that the best way to achieve full force protection is to ensure that the only forces deployed are in high-flying fast jets. Sometimes Western airpower can be combined with local landpower to achieve mission success. Thus, the NATO bombing of Bosnian Serb bases in 1995, combined with Croatia's successful land offensive against Serb territory in Eastern Bosnia, forced the Bosnia Serbs to sue for peace. Four years later, NATO again relied on airpower to force Serbs to stop committing atrocities, this time in Kosovo. The Clinton administration went so far as to publicly rule out a ground intervention in Kosovo (so as to quell Congressional fears). This gave Serb forces a free hand to terrorize the Albanian populace and drive them out of the province. Unlike the Croatian Army in Bosnia, the Kosovo Liberation Army (KLA) was unable to generate sufficient combat power to act as an effective surrogate ground force for NATO. Accordingly, the Serbs were able to weather NATO bombing for seventy-eight days before finally capitulating. Significantly, Serbian surrender followed NATO finally making a credible threat of a land invasion. Equally significantly, by this stage Kosovo had been emptied of Albanians.

These operational pathologies are not in evidence in coalition military operations in Afghanistan and Iraq. The initial US led invasions of Afghanistan in 2001 and Iraq in 2003 are not examples of humanitarian interventions. Humanitarian outcomes were predicted as by-products of these operations by US policy-makers. But both campaigns were primarily about protecting national security of the United States and its coalition partners and, as such, were portrayed as 'wars of necessity' by coalition leaders. The ongoing post-conflict stabilization operations in both countries, led by the US in Iraq and NATO in Afghanistan, have somewhat the character of peace operations. Coalition forces have taken considerable casualties in both operations—as of November 2005, the coalition had

---

BOX 15.5

Fatal Attraction: America and Air Power

Use of air power can help sustain domestic support or coalition unity [by reducing the risks of own casualties and collateral damage], but it cannot eliminate underlying political constraints. In Eliot Cohen's words, 'Air power is an unusually seductive form of military strength, in part because, like modern courtship, it appears to offer gratification without commitment'. This view poses a challenge for air power. Because policymakers often see air power strikes as a low-risk, low-commitment measure, air power will be called on when U.S. public or allied commitment is weak—a situation that will make successful coercion far harder when casualties do occur or when air strikes fail to break adversary resistance. Air power, like other military instruments, cannot overcome a complete lack of political will.

(Byman and Waxman 2000: 38)

suffered around 1,500 dead since the end of the war in Iraq, and the United States about 150 dead since the end of the war in Afghanistan. These losses have resulted in a marked decline in US public support for operations in Iraq (Afghanistan, which is overshadowed by Iraq, has received little public attention). But, even so, the campaign in Iraq has not collapsed. Moreover, force protection concerns have not prevented patrolling in Afghanistan and Iraq. Nor, given the large coalition ground presence in both countries, can it be said that either campaign has over-relied on airpower. However, it is likely that national security concerns and sunken political costs are bolstering both campaigns and suppressing operational pathologies. The United States cannot afford to walk away from either Afghanistan or Iraq for fear that they could descend into civil war, become havens for terrorists, and make a mockery of American sacrifice in 'liberating' these countries. In short, Iraq and Afghanistan do not demonstrate an end of operational pathologies in peace operations. Indeed, the mounting costs and political fallout from Iraq may serve to reinforce these pathologies in future missions that are properly humanitarian and entirely wars of choice.

KEY POINTS

- In practice, peace operations often breach four of the main principles of war: objective, unity, mass, and surprise.

- The political imperative to manage public support for peace operations can create a number of operational pathologies, specifically, command complications caused by the strategic compression of the battlefield, sacrificing mission success to full force protection, and an over-reliance on airpower.

Conclusion: Problems and Prospects

This chapter described the challenges posed by humanitarian intervention and peace operations. Peace forces must avoid over-use of force so as to maintain consent for their operations while at the same time being prepared to take robust action against peace spoilers. Such careful balancing has dramatically failed in past interventions because the UN tried to do too much (Somalia) or too little (Rwanda). Moreover, contrary to popular belief, Western policy-makers can resist public pressure to intervene and are much more sensitive than public opinion to casualties in their own force. Peace operations also breach many of the principles of war and instead are shaped by adverse political imperatives.

Failure in Somalia had disastrous consequences for Rwanda. More generally, it triggered a return to intervention pessimism. Within the United Nations there were calls for the organization to return to traditional peacekeeping. This 'back to basics' agenda has persisted in new UN doctrine on peace operations. UN *Guidelines for Peacekeeping Operations* (1995) emphasize, much as did the British Army in *Wider Peacekeeping*, the stark divide between consent-based and coercive peace operations. Moreover, the UN *Peacekeeping Training Manual* (1997) is based on Nordic peacekeeping doctrine and so restricts use of force to self-defence only. However, at the political level, we have seen a return to intervention optimism. Leading this development is Secretary-General Annan, who has argued that the UN must 'reconsider some of the most basic [peacekeeping] assumptions about neutrality, the good faith of the parties, and the non-use of force'. Annan also declared in May 2000 that UN peace forces had to be capable of 'countering and isolating those who go against agreed peace processes or commit violations'; in other words, capable of dealing with peace spoilers. Lead states also have a vital role to play in supporting UN efforts in this regard. Thus, the collapse of the UN operation in Sierra Leone in 2000 was prevented by robust British military intervention. Sierra Leone also dramatically showed how coercion can work where consent had failed.

Supporting this new intervention optimism is an emerging norm of humanitarian intervention. Previously, the sovereignty norm codified in the UN Charter has operated to prevent intervention in the internal affairs of sovereign states. At the same time, as noted earlier, Chapter VII of the UN Charter permits the UN to use force to uphold 'international peace and security'. Traditionally, Chapter VII was applied exclusively to interstate war. Over the past decade, however, the UNSC has recognized that internal conflicts of the kind witnessed in Somalia, Bosnia, and Rwanda can threatened international peace and security by spilling (refugees and combatants) over into neighbouring states, and so provide grounds for intervention. Furthermore, in 2000 the UNSC passed Resolution 1296, establishing that 'the targeting of civilians in armed conflict and the denial of humanitarian access to civilian populations affected by war may themselves constitute threats to international peace and security and thus be triggers for Security Council action'. NATO's intervention in Kosovo suggests that states may practise these new norms of humanitarian intervention even when so doing contradicts legal procedure: NATO's war against Serbia was not authorized by the UNSC as required under the UN Charter (although NATO member states argued that they were acting to uphold humanitarian law). Also relevant here is the development of individual criminal responsibility for war crimes. The International Criminal Court, following on from the Criminal Tribunals for the former Yugoslavia and Rwanda, will hold state leaders and officials accountable for breaches of humanitarian law. Sovereignty will no longer be a licence for states to brutalize their own populations. This will further erode the sovereignty norm in favour of a norm of humanitarian intervention.

All the same, this renewed will to act is still not matched by UN capacity. The United Nations remains woefully under-resourced for peace operations. The United States still owes the UN well over a billion dollars, mostly in peacekeeping arrears which it is unlikely to pay for some time yet. The UN Department of Peacekeeping Operations (DPKO) in particular, is under-resourced and understaffed. As of mid-2000, it had fifteen political desk officers running fourteen missions, and thirty-two military officers providing operational support to 27,000 troops in the field. These DPKO staff are so overwhelmed by routine headquarters related tasks in New York that they are unable to provide adequate support to missions in the field. UN missions are also complicated by the need to coordinate the operations of several departments (including, DPKO, Department of Political Affairs and Department of Disarmament Affairs) and agencies (Office for the Coordination of Humanitarian Affairs, Office of United Nations High Commissioner for Refugees, and United Nations Development Program). The UN's bureaucratic procedures make matter worse by making it overly laborious to equip field missions.

These limitations in the UN's capacity have resulted in some regionalization of peace operations. Thus, NATO deployed massive peace forces in Bosnia and Kosovo on behalf of the United Nations. The United States has encouraged African states, in particular, to develop a regional capacity for peace operations. This is an area where there is a high demand for peace forces, which (after Somalia) the United States is not at all keen to fill. Regional coalitions are supposed to enjoy several advantages over UN operations, namely, greater force cohesion, better local knowledge, greater commitment to the mission, and more suitable force structure. However, these advantages were not evident in the case of ECOMOG (Economic Community of West African States Ceasefire Monitoring Group), which attempted to restore order to the failed Liberian state in 1990–6. ECOMOG was divided by subregional rivalries between Francophone and Anglophone West African contributing states, it exhibited poor understanding and judgement of the political scene in Liberia, mission commitment was only maintained through the use of local surrogate forces (who had an interest in continuing the conflict), and it lacked the equipment, training, and logistical support for counter-insurgency operations. In short, regionalization of peace operations is not going to solve the UN's problems.

These problems aside, the United Nations remains very much in the peace operations business. Three new peace operations missions were established in 2004 alone (in Burundi, Cote d'Ivoire, and Haiti). By 2005 the United Nations had over 68,000 troops serving in eighteen missions around the world, and an annual peace operations budget in excess of 3.5 billion dollars. The United Nations also is attempting to improve its institutional capacity for peace operations. Following on from the Report of the Panel on United Nations Peace Operations (August 2000), the DPKO has been given extra staff and sharpened its mission planning practices, and the United Nations has strengthened its logistical capacities (especially in terms of strategic stockpiling and sealift). Training has also been improved for peace forces from developing states. Finally, the UNSC passed UNSC Res. 1327 in November 2000, in which it vowed to give future peace missions clear and achievable mandates, and 'deterrent credibility' where necessary. These are encouraging developments. But UN action falls far short of Annan's aspirations. For two years (2003–4), the UN dithered over intervention in the Sudanese region of Darfur, where government-sponsored atrocities were being committed against the local populace. Finally, in March 2005, the United Nations resolved to send in a peace operations force. But as of September 2006, the force had yet to be deployed. In short, there may be renewed optimism about intervention in the United Nations. But Sudan shows that the international community still lacks the political will, and the United Nations lacks the material resources, to always act when and where action is sorely needed.

? QUESTIONS

1. Why was humanitarian intervention rare during the cold war?
2. How does 'wider peacekeeping' differ from traditional peacekeeping?
3. What is the 'consent divide' and when should it be crossed?
4. What are the lessons of Bosnia for dealing with peace spoilers?

5. Why is Somalia the 'Vietnam' of peacekeeping?

6. Could the UN have done more to stop genocide in Rwanda?

7. To what extent can public opinion 'make and break' humanitarian interventions?

8. What four problems hinder effective action by the UNSC in response to humanitarian crises?

9. How well do the principles of war apply to peace operations?

10. What operational pathologies are created by the imperative to manage public support for peace operations?

11. What are the signs of a return to intervention optimism?

12. Is some regionalization of peace operations to be welcomed?

 FURTHER READING

■ **Annan, Kofi, 'Statement on receiving the report of the Independent Inquiry into the Actions of the United Nations during the 1994 Genocide in Rwanda,' 16 December 1999.** Available at www.un.org/News/ossg/sgsm_rwanda.htm.

■ **Bellamy, Alex J., Paul Williams, and Stuart Griffin, *Understanding Peacekeeping* (Cambridge: Polity, 2004).** An excellent introductory text.

■ **Byman, Daniel A., and Matthew C. Waxman, 'Kosovo and the Great Air Power Debate', *International Security*, 24/4 (Spring 2000).** This article offers a balanced assessment of the role of airpower in Kosovo, and teases out lessons for the future use of coercive airpower.

■ **Department of the Army, *US Army Field Manual 100–23: Peace Operations* (Washington, DC: Dept of the Army, 1994).**

■ **Dobbie, Charles, 'A Concept for Post-Cold War Peacekeeping', *Survival*, 36/3 (1994).**

■ **Findlay, Trevor, *The Use of Force in UN Peace Operations* (Oxford: Oxford University Press, 2002).** Offers detailed and balanced analysis of this topic.

■ **Freedman, Lawrence, 'Victims and Victors: Reflections on the Kosovo War', *Review of International Studies*, 26/3 (July 2000).** Thoughtful analysis of the Kosovo War focusing, in particular, on the battle for public opinion.

■ ***International Peacekeeping*.** This journal is essential reading for scholars and students of peace operations.

■ **Juperman, Alan J., 'Rwanda in retrospect', *Foreign Affairs*, 79/1 (Jan./Feb. 2000).**

■ **Minear, L., and T. G. Weiss, *Mercy Under Fire: War and the Global Humanitarian Community* (Boulder, CO: Westview Press, 1995).** This is a classic text on the application of humanitarian principles to intervention in complex emergencies.

■ **Paris, Roland. *At Wars End: Building Peace After Civil Conflict* (Cambridge: Cambridge University Press, 2004).** Advances a compelling critique of the democratization and marketization agenda that is inherent in many peace operations.

■ **Shawcross, William, *Deliver Us from Evil: Warlords and Peacekeepers in a World of Endless Conflict* (London: Bloomsbury 2000).** A highly readable (and in places damning) account of UN peace operations in Cambodia, Somalia, Rwanda, Bosnia, and Kosovo.

■ **Stedman, Stephen John, 'Spoiler Problems in Peace Processes',** *International Security,* **22/2 (Fall 1997).** Stedman coined the term 'peace spoilers' in this article, which usefully provides a typological theory for identifying and managing spoilers.

■ **Tharoor, Shashi, 'Should United Nations Peacekeeping Go "Back to Basics"',** *Survival,* **37/4 (Winter 1995–6).** Tharoor is a former Special Assistant to the UN Undersecretary-General for Peacekeeping, and he offers an erudite account of the intervention pessimist perspective.

■ **UK Army Field Manual,** *Wider Peacekeeping* **(London: HMSO, 1995).**

■ *United Nations Blue Book Series* **(New York: United Nations).** Has books on Cambodia, Mozambique, Somalia and Rwanda, each one offering a collection of key primary source materials and a lengthy commentary by the Secretary General.

■ **Weiss, Thomas and Cindy Collins.** *Humanitarian Challenges and Intervention: World Politics and the Dilemmas of Help* **(Boulder, CO: Westview Press, 2000).** Thomas Weiss is a leading scholar on humanitarian intervention, and this is a more recent co-authored text on the subject.

■ **Wheeler, Nicholas J.,** *Saving Strangers: Humanitarian Intervention in International Society* **(Oxford: Oxford University Press, 2000).** This book considers the ethical case for forcible humanitarian intervention and analyses cases of interventions during and after the cold war.

—— **and Alex Bellamy, 'Humanitarian Intervention and World Politics', in John Baylis and Steve Smith (eds.),** *The Globalization of World Politics* **(Oxford: Oxford University Press, 2005).** This chapter examines the arguments for and against humanitarian intervention, focusing on the tensions between considerations of power, order, and justice in world politics.

WEB LINKS

● **http://www.un.org/Depts/dpko/dpko/home_bottom.htm** This is the homepage of the UN Department of Peacekeeping Operations. Hit the 'Reports' button for frank and informative official reports on reforming UN Peace Operations, the Rwanda Genocide, and the fall of Srebrenica.

● **http://www.un.org/peace/reports/peace_operations/** This is the website of the Report of the Panel on United Nations Peace Operations (a.k.a. the 'Brahimi Report').

● **http://www.usip.org/library/topics/peacekeeping.html** This is the comprehensive 'Peacekeeping Web Links' page of the United States Institute of Peace Library.

● **http://www.iciss.ca/** This is the homepage of the International Commission on Intervention and State Sovereignty. The commission's two-volume report, offering comprehensive analysis of the ethical, political, and military implications of humanitarian intervention, as well as case study analysis of past interventions, may be downloaded from this site.

 Visit the Online Resource Centre that accompanies this book for lots of interesting additional material http://www.oxfordtextbooks.co.uk/orc/baylis_strategy2e/.

PART III
The Future of Strategy

16

A New Agenda for Security and Strategy?

JAMES J. WIRTZ

Chapter Contents

- Introduction
- The Need for a Conceptual Framework
- Population: The Demographics of Global Politics
- Commons Issues
- Direct Environmental Damage
- Disease
- Sensitivities and Vulnerabilities
- Conclusion

Reader's Guide

This chapter explores a series of issues that have not been traditionally included on national security agendas or considered to be within the purview of strategy. Unlike most assessments of non-traditional security issues, it does not define a specific problem as a threat to national security simply because it creates the possibility of casualties, damage to personal property, or threatens economic prosperity. Rather, it develops a utilitarian assessment of environmental, resource, and population issues to discover if strategy, military force, or existing strategic literature can address these issues and problems in a useful way. If strategy, strategists, or military force can address a specific problem, or if it can be determined that they are a cause of a particular problem, or if they can be forced to change in response to some transnational trend, then the issue should be a subject for strategy and strategists. The chapter also suggests that non-traditional security issues are beginning to influence core national security considerations in ways that were not fully anticipated by proponents of a new agenda for security and strategy.

Introduction

During the cold war, high politics dominated national security agendas. Issues of war and peace, nuclear deterrence and crisis management, summit diplomacy, arms control and alliance politics preoccupied those people with a professional or personal interest in world politics or military strategy. By contrast, low politics—the environment, the management of scarce resources, or efforts to constrain population growth—were often perceived as a source of trouble, but rarely as a threat to national security. Occasionally, issues of low politics managed to reach national security agendas. Fallout from nuclear testing in the atmosphere prompted a growing awareness of the environmental consequences of the nuclear arms race, leading to the Partial Test Ban Treaty (1963). The oil shocks of the 1970s made Americans aware of their dependence on foreign oil and the important role conservation could play in preserving US economic prosperity and diplomatic leverage. But, for the most part, high and low politics were treated as separate issues by policy-makers and scholars alike.

Starting in the late 1980s, some scholars came to believe that the hierarchy between high and low politics had been reversed. They suggested that non-traditional issues should be placed at the top of national security agendas. Several theories of international relations can explain the rise to prominence, so to speak, of low politics. Realists, for example, might suggest that, as the overarching preoccupation with the cold war evaporated, issues once considered 'lesser included threats' could be expected to appear more important. They also would note that with the collapse of the cold war divide, management of these global issues might become increasingly possible, especially if the United States, the lone superpower, used its diplomatic, economic, and military leverage to good effect. Neo-institutionalists would probably add that new forms of transnational management are increasingly important in world affairs. They might point to the prominent role played by international governmental organizations (IGOs, e.g. United Nations), international non-governmental organizations (INGOs, e.g. Carnegie Endowment for International Peace or Greenpeace) or even a plethora of grass-roots movements in tackling tough issues that transcend international boundaries. These local organizations and movements not only push global issues—women's rights, ozone depletion, the AIDs epidemic—onto national agendas, they also help initiate and coordinate international responses to transnational problems. Scholars who focus on the way the communications revolution is changing human interaction often highlight the fact that groups of people scattered across the globe can now orchestrate political or informational campaigns using the internet. Grass-roots organizations now monitor deforestation in the Amazon or search for unauthorized development along the California Coast. Individuals, educated and empowered by new communication technologies, are increasingly aware of the suffering of others in distant lands. There is a growing awareness, especially among people in the developed world, that international boundaries are a weak barrier to the problems that afflict the poorest parts of the planet.

At the dawn of the new century, however, perspectives about the relative importance of low and high politics again changed when the darkest side of the information revolution became apparent. Al-Qaeda and its supporters exploited modern communication and transportation systems to launch terrorist attacks against innocent civilians in New York, London, Madrid, and Bali. The debate about the relative importance of high and low politics seemed to come full circle. The low politics of the information revolution, globalization, and demographics now are the stuff of high politics, influencing national security and homeland defence agendas around the world.

The Need for a Conceptual Framework

To say that low politics are perceived as more important in the aftermath of the cold war is beyond dispute. Major research projects already had been undertaken in the 1990s by Thomas Homer-Dixon and his colleagues at the University of Toronto and by the International Peace Research Institute, Oslo (PRIO), to demonstrate a link between resource scarcity and the outbreak of war or other forms of violence. Other researchers have noted that damage to the environment should be considered as a threat to national security because it can cause casualties or even kill. Marc Levy, for instance, has suggested that damage to the earth's ozone layer should be considered to be a security threat because it causes cancer, blindness, and even death (1995). But to say that environmental damage or resource scarcity should now be considered as national security issues raises a host of problems, especially for those who are concerned with the development of military strategy. It is not exactly clear, for instance, how military forces can help reduce the buildup of greenhouse gases in the atmosphere to prevent global warming. Similarly, it is not clear how military action can help stop the Acquired Immuno-Deficiency Syndrome (AIDS) epidemic that is sweeping Africa and other parts of the world. Non-traditional threats to national security clearly exist, but it is difficult to discern how military formations, strategy, or strategists can respond constructively to these issues. Further complicating the issue is the fact that low and high politics are interacting in complex ways; issues of low politics are not completely divorced from grand strategy. For example, the possibility that Tehran might acquire nuclear weapons does not pose an immediate threat to Middle East energy reserves, but it does have a global economic impact by causing the price of oil to rise in already tight energy markets. Low politics, while not posing direct security threats themselves, are shaping and are in turn being shaped by traditional strategic concerns.

Those who suggest that environmental or global issues are a national security threat often resort to Malthusian scenarios to justify their judgements (Orme 1997). Resource scarcity or the disorder produced by overpopulation or rapid depopulation, for instance, are identified as causes of war. But these Malthusian scenarios are not entirely plausible, and recent studies have found only an extremely modest impact of resource scarcity on the outbreak of violence (Goldstone 2002). Malthusian scenarios seem to suggest that the military should prepare to contain the symptoms of nagging transnational problems before they burst into some sort of cataclysmic fury. One might also hope that educational, technical, or social action could be taken before environmental, resource, or population pressures produce wars that literally involve battles for human survival. No one would disagree that these environmental or global issues are important, it just seems unlikely that

BOX 16.1

Thomas Robert Malthus

Malthus was born on 13 February 1766. He graduated from Jesus College, Cambridge in 1788, worked for a time as a minister and returned to Cambridge as a fellow in 1793, the year Louis XVI was guillotined by revolutionaries. Malthus took a dim view of utopian philosophies advanced by William Godwin and M. Condorcet. In response, in 1798 he published *An Essay on the Principle of Population as It Affects the Future Improvement of Society*. Using data supplied by none other than Benjamin Franklin on the population growth rates of American villages, Matlhus offered a startling observation: populations grow in a geometric fashion while food supplies only increase by merely an arithmetic ratio. In other words, if current trends continued, the human race would inevitably outpace the food supply leading to cataclysmic social collapse. Two factors might hold off this day of reckoning: efforts to reduce birth rates, which Malthus termed 'preventive measures'; and war, disease, and starvation, developments described by the misnomer 'positive measures'. Luckily, Malthus's predictions proved incorrect. He failed to account for the fact that trends rarely continue indefinitely into the future. In fact, the amount of raw materials used per unit of economic output has actually been decreasing over the last century, while available resources have been increasing. Once adjusted for inflation, the *Economist's* index of prices of industrial raw materials has dropped 80 per cent since 1845.

negative trends will continue indefinitely into the future and produce raging resource wars. Already, there are positive signs on the horizon. Population growth rates, which reached a peak of 2 per cent per year in the 1960s, are declining and will continue to do so just as long as people grow healthier, wealthier, and better educated.

Defining some transnational issues as a national security threat can create a new set of problems. Often military forces are the only units available that possess the logistical capabilities or able-bodied and disciplined workforce needed to cope with the aftermath of natural or political disasters. As the effort to provide disaster relief to victims of the 2004 tsunami demonstrated, military and naval forces drawn from nineteen countries and non-governmental organizations worked together to provide food, shelter, and medical supplies, especially to people left isolated by the effects of the tidal wave. Regardless of circumstances or initial intentions, however, the introduction of military forces risks making things worse by turning a public health crisis or police problem into an armed conflict. The UN intervention in Somalia, for instance, quickly deteriorated from an effort to prevent mass starvation into a particularly nasty form of warfare, urban combat. Launching a *war* on drugs inevitably leads to casualties among innocent bystanders, disruption of peasant life, increased rural poverty, and armed resistance. Soldiers also complain that humanitarian operations, peacekeeping duties, or conducting border patrols divert resources and training away from their primary responsibility: preparing to engage in conventional combat and win the nation's wars. Although military forces will continue to play a critical role in responding to natural disasters, simply defining environmental, resource, or population problems as security issues is not without costs or risks.

Instead of becoming mired in the debate about the gravity of today's environmental problems or what constitutes an appropriate mission for military units, it would be better to assess this new security agenda to determine if and how strategy can respond to these issues. This utilitarian assessment would unfold along three dimensions. First, if military units can take some action that addresses a particular problem or issue in a useful way, then the subject is of importance to strategy and strategists. But if the threat of force, the use of force, or even the logistical or technical assistance that can be supplied by military units does little to respond to a given problem, it probably is best not to treat the specific issue as a security threat. Second, if military action somehow produces environmental, resource, or demographic consequences, then these issues are of interest to strategists. The time has arrived to measure the cost of conflict by using more than just the immediate losses of blood and treasure. A global perspective requires strategists to consider the long-term environmental consequences of war and preparations for war. Third, low politics are of strategic interest when they create effects that are likely to shape the way force is used in the future. In other words, will low politics create changes in the international security environment that will force a significant transformation of strategy, military force structure, or doctrine? This utilitarian assessment stands in contrast to typical discussions of environmental or resource issues because it defines security threats in terms of what constitutes an appropriate response (i.e. use of force), rather than the potential of an issue to threaten a nation's or an individual's well-being (i.e. scarcity of portable water).

Is there a new agenda for security and strategy? The answer might in fact be yes: especially if strategy, strategists, or military force can address a specific problem, can be the cause of a specific problem, or can be forced to change in response to some transnational trend. What follows is a brief survey of the relationship of strategy to several transnational issues that are said to make up a new agenda for security and strategy.

KEY POINTS

- Scholars debate whether to include non-traditional issues—pollution, threats to bio-diversity, disease—on national security agendas.

- Malthusian scenarios remain popular as a justification for treating environmental issues as security problems.

- Defining social or environmental issues as a national security problem is not without costs and risks.

- A utilitarian assessment may be useful to determine if there is a new agenda for security and strategy.

Population: The Demographics of Global Politics

Nearly every problem identified in this chapter is rooted in the population explosion that occurred in the twentieth century. Since mid-century, the number of people living on the planet has grown by 3.5 billion; over 6 billion people were alive at the start of the twenty-first century. With luck, total population should stabilize somewhere between 7 and 8 billion and even begin to decrease by the time most of the people reading this book have retired. There is in fact some evidence to suggest that fertility rates are decreasing not just in developed countries, but also in urban areas in the developing world as women gain more access to education, health care, and job opportunities. If people in the developing world do not share in the fruits (wealth, health, and education) promised by globalization, however, global population could reach nearly 11 billion by 2050.

Although the news about the world's population problem is not all bad, three caveats are often raised about these positive trends that paint a somewhat darker picture of both our immediate and medium-term future. First, most of the population growth in the years ahead will occur in the poorest countries that already are strained to the limit when it comes to feeding, housing and educating their existing populations. By contrast, in the developed world, population growth rates in many cases have dipped below 'replacement levels', creating a different sort of crisis. Too few people of working age will be available to contribute to 'pay-as-you-go' pension systems, creating the possibility of a systemic social crisis. Second, most of the population growth is taking place in urban areas. By 2015, the world will have twenty-six megacities with populations exceeding 10 million and at least twenty of them will be located in the developing world. Urban planners, government officials, and military officers are concerned that megacities will tax social and basic services well beyond their limits, leaving millions of people to live in urban squalor and chaos. Megacities also can erupt into spontaneous violence following some local insult or even a sporting event. Even cities in the developed world can burst into violence: thousands of armed gang members can plunge sections of Los Angeles into chaos and looting for days before police and national guard units are able to restore order. Third, most of this additional population will be very young, leading observers to note that, in parts of the developing world, it will be some time before population growth rates peak.

Although strategists find little to dispute in the observation that overpopulation creates enormous social, resource, and environmental strains, they are most interested in exploring the divergent demographic trends at the heart of the population problem. In other words, what are the strategic implications of an ageing and shrinking Western population on the one hand, and an explosion in the number of young people in the developing world on the other? For the developing world, the concern is that the inability to provide basic services to this surging population will produce poverty, chaos, and hopelessness. Some observers believe that young people, concentrated by the millions in megacities, will fall under the sway of a virulent nationalism, messianic leaders, or millenarian movements, leading to waves of local violence or international terrorism. Most major revolutions have been accompanied by so a so-called 'youth bulge', while scholars have also noted that youth bulges are associated with the outbreak of small conflicts (Goldstone 2002). Young men with little prospect of a traditional home, family, or occupation might find an outlet for their ambitions in war. By contrast, the slow or even negative population growth in the West will make it increasingly difficult to fill the ranks of the armed forces, forcing militaries to rely on technology to compensate for an absence of volunteers. The demands for health care and the high pension costs created by an ageing population also will make it difficult for industrialized nations to afford large defence budgets.

These population demographics constitute a strategic issue because they will force changes in defence policies and strategy in the years ahead. Differences in population growth create fundamental trends that influence military strategy and defence policy. But exactly how will demographics transform this strategic setting? Martin van Creveld and Stephen Cimbala offer a pessimistic view of these trends. They believe that nation-states are losing their monopoly on the use of force as urban mobs and transnational movements take matters into their own hands. Violence is becoming less politically organized; the world is descending into chaos and warlordism. By contrast, some observers would predict that these population demographics already are producing different attitudes towards the death and destruction of war. In the West, a rising aversion to casualties already is shaping national strategies. In the developing world, warrior cultures glorify war, swelling the ranks of millenarian, fundamentalist, or anarchist movements with thousands of untrained and lightly armed volunteers. It is probably not a coincidence that most of the terrorists who participate in Al-Qaeda suicide attacks are unmarried males. It probably is wrong, however, to suggest that warrior culture offers a superior approach to the conventional battlefield than the combined arms attack that can be unleashed by military professionals. No amount of elan will save units caught in the open by a well-timed artillery barrage or an air strike using fuel-air explosives, although basic infantry tactics, such as the use of cover, can help mitigate the lethality of modern weaponry (Biddle 2003a). On a more positive note, some observers have suggested that as birth rates decline, people everywhere will be less willing to see what may be their only child sacrificed in some dubious military adventure. And if democracy continues to spread, they would have the means to make these feelings known to their elected officials.

KEY POINTS

- Although population growth rates are slowing, total world population will continue to increase for the next thirty years.

- Future population increases will be centered in the developing world, leading to a concentration of young people in megacities.

- Because they influence the context of diplomatic and military policy, divergent demographic trends will shape strategy and strategic thinking.

Commons Issues

Issues that transcend international boundaries often are referred to as commons problems. Although some countries can contribute more or less to a specific commons problem, efforts to stop the tragedy of the commons, to borrow Garrett Hardin's famous phrase, require some form of collective action on the part of most members of the international community. Most low politics problems could be classified as commons issues, but environmental and resource issues generally come to mind when policy-makers and scholars think about transnational issues.

Air pollution, especially the release of carbon dioxide from automobiles and coal-fired electric plants, destruction of the ozone layer through the release of chlorofluorocarbons,

BOX 16.2

The Tragedy of the Commons

Imagine you lived near the West Coast of the United States and every spring you had the opportunity to go salmon fishing. The fish were plentiful and it was easy for you to catch a couple of dozen fish in a single morning. This makes you very happy because you have many friends and relatives who like salmon. In any event, there are plenty of fish in the sea, and no matter how full you loaded up your boat you could never make much of a dent in the salmon population. There would always be fish willing to take your bait. Now imagine if thousands of your neighbours up and down the coast went fishing too and proceeded to fill their boats with fish. Even though no one wanted it to happen and no one individual would be responsible, it would not be long before salmon became mighty scarce, producing a tragedy of the commons.

   The tragedy of the commons is an example of the tyranny of small decisions, a situation in which unintended and negative consequences are produced by individuals following their reasonable, albeit narrow, self-interest. Each fisher, rationally acting to fulfil their self-interests, gains the extra benefit of their large catch, while the entire community bears the cost of depleting the fishery. Even if individuals refrain from filling their boats, it would only make it safe for others to 'free-ride' on their self-restraint. In other words, collective action is needed to capture the externalities involved in exploiting the fishery (i.e. getting fishers to pay the full cost of their catch) and to prevent free riding. When a commons problem occurs within national boundaries, it is easy for the state to capture these externalities and to corral free riders. When fisheries are open, for example, the State of California limits salmon catches to two fish per day by licensed fishers. Fish have to be longer than 24 inches and it is illegal to take protected salmon species (e.g. Coho salmon). But when the commons crosses international borders, capturing externalities and corralling free riders requires international collaboration.

and global warming produced by greenhouse gases are all quintessential commons problems. In other words, it would be impossible for a single state or a group of states to slow the destruction of the ozone layer, for example, by banning the manufacture of chlorofluorocarbons if other states continued to release these substances into the atmosphere. Water pollution, depletion of underground aquifers, and the protection of migratory species (e.g. fish) are often depicted as commons problems, although their effects often are confined to specific regions. Michael Klare, for instance, sees water scarcity as a source of conflict among countries that share major water systems. The Nile River (shared by Egypt, Ethiopia, and the Sudan); the Jordan River (shared by Israel, Jordan, Lebanon, and Syria) the Tigris and Euphrates Rivers (shared by Turkey, Syria, Iraq, and Iran); and the Indus River (shared by Afghanistan, India, and Pakistan) are identified as likely conflict points by Klare (2001). Sometimes, depletion of aquifers and fish stocks can create local economic catastrophes when farmers lose the water needed to irrigate their crops and fishers are forced to abandon traditional means of earning a living.

   Threats to biodiversity, especially deforestation of tropical rainforests, occur on specific national territories, but they are slowly destroying the 'common heritage of humankind'. Deforestation destroys habitats needed by the planet's non-human inhabitants: tropical rainforests are home to half of the world's known species. Deforestation also can have regional climatic effects because trees are a key link in the evapotranspiration cycle between soil and the atmosphere. Trees also help to protect delicate topsoil by providing erosion control against landslides and flooding. Forests help to slow global warming because trees act as a major sink of carbon dioxide in the atmosphere. Global or regional environmental problems sometimes can have acute local consequences.

By contrast, local environmental damage can produce global environmental consequences. Sometimes commons problems are created when the effects of localized insults to the environment have a global impact and sometimes they are created when millions of small and relatively innocuous events have a cumulative effect that produces global consequences or local disasters. The distinguishing characteristic of all of these issues, however, is the fact that either their causes or their effects are beyond the reach of any one state.

Although commons issues pose an existential threat to all humanity, at times they do shape decisions about war and peace. Concerns about access to oil supplies (one natural resource that remains key to modern industrial economies) was a clear motivation behind the formation of a US–led international coalition to oust Iraq from Kuwait in the early 1990s. By contrast, concern about disrupting tight oil markets has slowed the international response to an apparent Iranian effort to create a nuclear weapons industry. Shots also have been exchanged in fishing disputes as boats and crews are seized for poaching in waters claimed by a specific state. Water wars are possible in the future, especially as rivers and aquifers are drained to make deserts in one state bloom at the expensive of fields in neighbouring countries. Therefore, as a proximate cause of war, commons issues should be a concern to strategists; but, so far at least, with the exception of the Gulf War, shots have been exchanged only in a limited way. A few times, over a limited issues.

By contrast, most commons problems are probably beyond the reach of strategy. It is difficult to imagine how military action might resolve many transnational problems. For instance, the existence of strategists, strategy, and military infrastructure did little to deplete aquifers; it is difficult to see how they can help conserve or replenish these underground water supplies. Moreover, because war is a state activity undertaken to achieve political objectives, there is little political motivation to undertake military action in response to commons issues. In other words, few would suggest that wars should be launched to stop individuals in other states from killing tigers, from practising slash and burn agriculture, or from constructing electric power plants that use coal as an energy source. But even if it were possible to use military force to solve a commons problem, it would be highly unlikely that any single state would launch this type of military endeavour. By definition, the benefits gained from using military force to resolve commons problems are outweighed by the costs of action. Everyone would benefit, but the state taking action would bear all of the costs. This is the very dilemma that lies at the heart of the tragedy of the commons. Collective action is needed to capture the externalities (the unpaid costs that are inevitably involved in all human activity) that lie at the heart of most commons problems. Strategists might contribute to the effort to devise a collective response to commons issues, but it probably would be better if this response were based on enlightened self-interest, not point-of-the-gun environmentalism. Although commons issues might some day force military action or shape military strategies (e.g. military action to protect oil supplies), it is probably best to not treat commons issues as military problems.

Direct Environmental Damage

Military action or the manufacturing of military weapons can result in significant environmental damage, although these insults to the environment probably fall short of constituting a commons problem. Sometimes the impact of military activity is limited or unknown. For example, military aircraft often jettison fuel in an emergency, but it unclear if much environmental damage occurs in peacetime from this practice. As MP Archie Hamilton noted in 1992:

> RN [Royal Navy] and RAF [Royal Air Force] pilots are instructed to jettison fuel under carefully controlled conditions which ensure that the great majority of fuel evaporates before it reaches the ground. There is, therefore minimal environmental impact at ground or sea level. The evaporated fuel is widely dispersed. Most of it is biodegradable and that which remains has no known effects on the atmosphere. There are no products in military aviation jet fuel known to cause greenhouse effects, damage to the ozone layer or air pollution in the lower atmosphere.

Hamilton is probably correct that dumping jet fuel in the atmosphere does not pose much of a problem in peacetime: British flyers were only forced to jettison fuel on average about twice a month in the 1980s. But in wartime, mission requirements might cause enormous amounts of fuel to be jettisoned. If this happened over a relatively small area would it have an environmental impact?

An issue that often bedevils assessments of the environmental impact of military activity is the effort to use 'green' arguments to derail programmes for political purposes. A case in point is the alleged negative environmental and long-term health consequences produced by the use of depleted uranium (DU) in heavy tank armour, anti-tank munitions, and even as counterweights in commercial aircraft. DU is used primarily as a kinetic-kill projectile because it is very heavy and dense: no nuclear reaction occurs when a DU projectile strikes a tank, for example. Depending upon the type of impact, small amounts of DU may be released in the form of tiny, relatively insoluble particles of uranium oxide or even as larger pieces of metallic uranium. There is little scientific data on the health effects on DU, although studies exist about the health effects of uranium, a similar material. Based on studies undertaken on uranium workers, no negative health effects have been established following exposure to radiation through ingestion and inhalation of DU particles or through wounds contaminated by DU. Nevertheless, many media reports and internet campaigns decry the environmental and health impact of the use of DU on the battlefield.

Some military weapons can potentially produce catastrophic damage to the environment and extremely significant health risks, even if they are not used in battle. The cost of dismantling and destroying these weapons is staggering and involves scientific and engineering capabilities that are far more advanced then the original efforts to make the weapons themselves. Successful programmes are possible. For example, in November 2000, after nearly ten years of operation, the Johnston Atoll Chemical Agent Disposal System (JACADS) finally eliminated the remnants of the US chemical weapons stockpile. JCADS was the world's first full-scale facility built to destroy chemical weapons. Johnston Atoll, located 717 nautical miles south-west of Oahu, is one of the most isolated atolls in the world and had been used repeatedly as a US nuclear, biological, and chemical weapons testing and storage facility. Remaining off-limits for the indefinite future, Johnston Atoll will soon serve as a wildlife refuge.

Other facilities, especially those involved in nuclear weapons programmes are neither as isolated nor as easily cleaned up. In the mid-1990s, the US Department of Energy estimated that it would cost at least 160 billion dollars to clean up facilities once involved in the manufacture of nuclear materials at Hanford Reservation, Savannah River, Oak Ridge, Idaho National Engineering and Environmental laboratory, and Rocky Flats. The

Table 16.1 U.S. Stockpile Destroyed by JCADS

AGENT	ITEM	QUANTITY	POUNDS
HD-Blister	155mm projectiles	5,670	66,339.0
HD-Blister	105mm projectiles	46	136.6
HD-Blister	M60 projectiles	45,108	133,970.7
HD-Blister	4.2 mortars	43,600	261,600.0
HD-Blister	Ton containers	68	116,294.0
GB-Nerve	M55 rockets	58,353	624,377.1
GB-Nerve	155mm projectiles	107,197	696,780.5
GB-Nerve	105mm projectiles	49,360	80,456.8
GB-Nerve	8" projectiles	13,020	188,790.0
GB-Nerve	MC-1 bombs	3,047	670,340.0
GB-Nerve	MK 94 bombs	2,570	277,560.0
GB-Nerve	Ton containers	66	101,158.0
VX-Nerve	M55 rockets	13,889	141,769.8
VX-Nerve	155mm projectiles	42,682	256,092.0
VX-Nerve	8" projectiles	14,519	210,525.5
VX-Nerve	Land mines	13,302	139,671.0
VX-Nerve	Ton containers	66	97,360.0

Department of Defense also identified 26,500 other locations at existing or former military bases that have been contaminated by nuclear or industrial pollutants. Only 1,700 of these sites had been cleaned up by 1996.

The environmental problems facing the Russians also are severe. Scores of old nuclear-powered submarines lie rusting at their berths throughout the Russian north and far east and Russian spent fuel storage facilities are nearly full. A lack of resources makes it nearly impossible for the Russians to undertake a complicated clean-up process. The submarine must be retired from active status; its missiles must be removed. Spent nuclear fuel must be extracted; making it safe to disconnect its reactor and reactor circuits. Spent fuel can then be transported for reprocessing and low- and high-level waste collected for storage. The reactor compartment can then be cut away from the rest of the hull so that it can be sealed for long-term storage.

Although the costs of cleaning up after the cold war are only now being assessed, clearly strategists and policy-makers need to take into account the environmental impact of yesterday's and today's defence policies. Of course, at the time, these costs paled in significance when compared to the perceived military threats posed by the cold war, but the lasting legacy of nuclear, chemical, and biological weapons manufacturing and disposal must be considered by strategists and policy-makers. Full disclosure of these 'hidden' costs might cause those who seek to develop a robust nuclear arsenal—here Indian, Pakistani, or Chinese leaders come to mind—to think about the potential consequences of their defence industrial policy.

Disease

Although disease has been a scourge throughout human existence, public health initiatives (providing people with clean water and proper sanitation), vaccination, quarantine and the discovery of antibiotic drugs in the mid-twentieth century helped to reduce the outbreak of communicable disease at least in the industrial world. Today public health officials in the West focus on modifying people's lifestyles to reduce the incidence of cancer (caused by smoking) and cardiovascular disease (accelerated by modern diets and a lack of exercise). The human genome project also holds out the prospect of new treatments for all types of illnesses, especially those linked to genetic disorders. Life expectancies have increased steadily over the last century. More people survived infancy because of prenatal care, public health, and vaccination against childhood diseases and treatments emerged to arrest, if not completely cure, disorders (cardiovascular disease, cancers) that killed previous generations by the time they reached their seventieth birthday. Progress was even achieved on a global scale: ask your parents (grandparents?) to show you their small pox vaccination.

If one takes a global perspective, however, the news is not so encouraging. Public health officials are bracing for a long overdue outbreak of a deadly strain of influenza. They fear the outbreak of new diseases that are resistant to existing treatments and drugs. They worry that unknown bacteria or viruses that have lain dormant deep within tropical rainforests

Table 16.2 Pathogenic Microbes Identified Since 1973 and the Diseases They Cause

Year	Microbe	Type	Disease
1973	Rotavirus	Virus	Infantile diarrhoea
1977	Ebola virus	Virus	Acute haemorrhagic fever
1977	Legionella pneumophila	Bacterium	Legionnaires' disease
1980	Human T-lymphotrophic virus	Virus	T-cell lymphoma
1981	Staphylococcus aureus	Bacterium	Toxic shock syndrome
1982	Escherichia coli 0157:H7	Bacterium	Haemorrhagic colitis
1982	Borrelia burgdorferi	Bacterium	Lyme disease
1983	Human Immunodeficiency Virus	Virus	Acquired Immuno-Deficiency Syndrome (AIDS)
1983	Helicobacter pylori	Bacterium	Peptic ulcer disease
1989	Hepatitis C	Virus	Parentally transmitted non-A, non-B liver infection
1992	Vibrio cholerae 0139	Bacterium	New strain/epidemic cholera
1993	Hantavirus	Virus	Adult respiratory distress syndrome
1994	Cryptosporidium	Protozoa	Enteric disease
1995	Ehrlichiosis	Bacterium	Severe arthritis
1996	NvCJD	Prion	New variant Creutzfeld-Jakob disease
1997	HVN1	Virus	Influenza
1999	Nipah	Virus	Severe encephalitis

will soon be disturbed by encroaching humans, producing new epidemics of dangerous diseases. World Health Organization officials also warn that the seven infectious diseases that caused the highest number of deaths at the turn of the century will remain serious threats for decades to come.

Human immunodeficiency virus/acquired immuno-deficiency syndrome (HIV/AIDS)

At the turn of the century, about forty million people across the globe were living with HIV/AIDS. Infection and death rates have slowed in the West in response to preventive measures and expensive multi-drug treatments. The pandemic continues to spread throughout the developing world and is making inroads in India, Russia, and China. Sub-Saharan Africa is the centre of the AIDS epidemic: already 10 to 20 per cent of the adults in the region are infected with the disease. The social and economic costs of the disease are staggering. Already African economies are experiencing a steady decline in

Gross Domestic Product (GDP) due to the AIDS epidemic and entire generations of children will become AIDS orphans.

Tuberculosis (TB)

Once thought to be controlled in the developing world by public health efforts and drug treatments, TB is increasing in Russia, India, south-east Asia, sub-Saharan Africa, and parts of Latin America. About eight million new cases of TB each year were reported worldwide at the turn of the century. Particularly disturbing is the emergence of a drug-resistant form of TB. Up to 50 per cent of the people infected with drug-resistant TB will die despite treatment. Many TB infections occur in conjunction with HIV/AIDS. By 2020, TB probably will rank second behind HIV/AIDS as a cause of death by infectious disease.

Malaria

Once thought to be coming under control by public health measures and prophylaxis treatments, Malaria is a tropical disease that is on the rise. In sub-Saharan Africa infection rates jumped 40 per cent over the last thirty years and new drug-resistant strains of the disease are emerging. One potential consequence of climatic change could be an increase in malaria's geographic range.

Hepatitis B and C

350 million people worldwide are chronic carriers of these viruses. Up to 25 per cent of the people infected with the virus will develop cirrhosis of the liver or liver cancer. There is no vaccine against hepatitis C.

Influenza and respiratory infections

Airborne viruses pose an increasing threat in an age of air travel. Coronaviruses that can be spread by person-to-person contact (e.g. coughing or sneezing) are difficult to contain. In February 2003, an outbreak of Severe Acute Respiratory Syndrome (SARS) in Asia quickly spread to more than twenty-four countries around the world. Over 8,000 people became infected and about 700 of those infected died. Fears also have emerged about avian influenza, especially the strain H5N1. In humans, the disease has generally been contracted by individuals who have come into close contact with infected birds, but transmission from person to person has been recorded. The virus has not completely jumped the species barrier, but because viruses can change quickly, scientists fear that H5N1 could someday easily infect humans, a species with little natural immunity to this virus. H5N1 might be capable of producing a lethality rate in excess of 50 per cent in humans.

Diarrhoeal diseases

Infection with *Escherichia coli* is the most common cause of this disease, but dysentery and rotaviral diarrhoea occur throughout the developing world and now are beginning to affect parts of the former Soviet Union. Contaminated food and water spread the disease. In 1996, for the first time in a century, there also was a major outbreak of cholera in Latin America. Most of the victims of diarrhoeal diseases are children under the age of 5 in the developing world.

Measles

Because of the relatively low vaccination rates in sub-Saharan Africa, measles kills just under one million people a year and infects about forty million children every year. Measles also is the leading cause of death among refugees and displaced persons, especially during recent humanitarian operations.

Several developments are responsible for the increasing threat of infectious diseases. First, refugee movements caused by political and natural disasters subject millions of refugees to primitive living conditions that breed and spread disease. Ethnic conflict, civil wars, and famine spread disease quickly as refugees move across borders. Second, unprotected sex with multiple partners and intravenous drug use are largely responsible for the spread of AIDS. Third, modern technology and production practices are not foolproof. Imported food produced by non-hygienic practices can spread pathogens and bacteria (*Cyclospora ssp*, *Escherichia coli*, and *Salmonella*) quickly across national borders. Modern food production practices also have created problems in the food supply. Bovine Spongiform Encephalopathy (Mad Cow Disease), for example, was spread by the practice of including mammalian tissues in animal feed intended for cows and other ruminants. Fourth, land use practices, even efforts to restore natural habitats, can breed and spread disease. For example, reforestation in the United States and Europe is responsible for an increase in Lyme disease as deer ticks have more opportunities to find human hosts. Encroachment on rain forests also brings people in close contact with animals carrying malaria, yellow fever, leishmaniasis, or even heretofore unknown and potentially dangerous diseases. Fifth, international travel and commerce can spread viruses, pathogens, and bacteria faster than the incubation period of the diseases they cause. Today's cross-border movement of over two million people per day guarantees that disease outbreaks will be difficult to contain. Sixth, the widespread use of antibiotics in livestock production and the overuse and misuse of antibiotics by people have accelerated the evolution of a variety of strains of drug-resistant microbes. An expanding number of strains of TB, malaria, and influenza are virtually impossible to treat and HIV also displays a high rate of adaptation to drug treatments.

War and civil strife can lead to disease outbreaks by creating refugee disasters and a breakdown in public health care. Throughout history, war has often been accompanied by disease. Soldiers have spread disease in the field and have brought it back with them when they returned home. Today, for instance, the so-called 'Gulf War Syndrome'—a strange mix of debilitating symptoms—is said to occur among US soldiers that returned otherwise unhurt from the 1991 Coalition victory against Iraq. Military forces can be enlisted to help fight the spread of disease through efforts to quarantine affected populations, to move supplies into regions stricken by epidemics, or to use field medical facilities to treat local populations. From a strategic perspective, infectious diseases continue to shape military strategy because disease can create casualties just as easily an enemy fire. In fact, throughout most of history, disease killed far more soldiers than enemy action. Although military forces are at best a third or fourth order defence against the spread of disease (and are just as likely to help spread disease as to contain it), infectious disease shapes the security environment and should be included on the new security agenda.

KEY POINTS

- A variety of factors are causing the spread of infectious diseases, especially in the developing world.

- New strains of drug-resistant diseases are emerging.

- The HIV/AIDS pandemic is likely to spread to India, Russia, and China.

Sensitivity and Vulnerability

Although talk of increasing globalization and interdependence is clichéd, non-traditional security issues have begun to influence strategy and defence priorities in ways that were not fully anticipated by advocates of the new agenda for security in the early 1990s. Malthusian scenarios have not materialized, but low politics are having an impact on real-world conflicts and are shaping national security strategies. Some countries are increasingly sensitive or even vulnerable to developments in the realm of low politics.

Sensitivity and vulnerability are terms drawn from Robert Keohane and Joseph Nye's work on complex interdependence (2001). Sensitivity refers to the ability of developments outside national boundaries to influence domestic events in other countries. An outbreak of H5N1 in Asia, for example, might cause officials in the United States to alert domestic public health officials to monitor hospital admissions for patients who might be exhibiting signs of H5N1 infection. Such a precautionary measure would entail some costs and be a matter of potential public concern, but it would not pose a fundamental disruption to life in the United States. By contrast, vulnerabilities can cause significant disruption to domestic economic, social, or political activity. The emergence and spread of SARS in 2004, for example, crossed the line from sensitivity to vulnerability because it significantly affected international travel and Asian economies.

Since the 1990s, several non-traditional security issues have moved from being best considered as hypothetical scenarios, to creating sensitivities in some countries, to creating significant vulnerabilities in other nations. Commons issues related to environmental degradation, while unlikely to produce Malthusian consequences, are emerging as sensitivities in countries whose policy-makers worry that environmental restrictions could hamper the exploitation of local natural resources. Similarly, the world is in no immediate danger of exhausting its petroleum reserves, but the continued growth in the world economy has tightened world energy markets. Industrial economies around the globe can now see domestic economies threatened by oil markets that are highly sensitive or vulnerable to foreign political or military insults. Resources issues are not sparking wars, but the threat of war or war itself is now poised to have a significant impact on the supply of raw materials and the global economy.

Demographic trends, especially the so-called youth bulge, are also having an impact on strategy and national security. Armies of disaffected youth are not massing in the megacities of the world, but young people are being recruited by terrorist networks to undertake nefarious schemes. Al-Qaeda is a case in point. Osama Bin Laden was able to recruit operatives from disaffected Muslim youth from Western Europe and the Middle East, and young people in the United Kingdom and Spain have organized themselves more or less spontaneously to undertake attacks on urban transit systems. Demographics alone have not created a specific threat, but they have helped to alter the general security environment facing police and military forces. In response to the international terrorist threat, many countries have altered their domestic security and foreign policy strategies and policies. Ideology, disease, politics, economics, and demographics have interacted to produce significant threats to national security.

KEY POINTS

- Although they have not risen to the top of national security agendas, issues of low politics are beginning to interact with local political and military events to produce global consequences.

- Countries are beginning to exhibit sensitivities and vulnerabilities to issues of low politics.

Conclusion

Those who advocate including resource, environmental, or population issues on national security agendas might suggest that this chapter ignores a critical point: many of these global developments threaten the health and welfare of both individuals and states and therefore should be considered as threats to security. They might suggest that the fact that military forces or strategists are ill equipped to deal with emerging problem demonstrates that traditional ways of thinking about security are simply not up to the challenge of dealing with emerging twenth-first-century security issues. A decision not to treat the emergence of a drug-resistant strain of TB as a threat to national security, for example, would thus be viewed as an effort to minimize the importance of the issue. But the fact that something is a threat to health and welfare does not make it a security problem in the sense that strategy or military force can minimize it. Hundreds of thousands of people every year are killed in automobile accidents, but no one would suggest that military force should somehow be used to improve highway safety.

By contrast, the purpose of this chapter was not to dismiss these global trends and transnational issues as threats to national or individual security or to minimize the gravity of the challenges created by environmental damage, disease, or population growth in the developing world. Instead, it offered a mixed assessment of the ability of strategy or military force to respond to global issues. On balance, there was a significant and growing interaction between strategy and many of the items on the new agenda for national security. While not a security issues *per se*, demographics or resource issues (tight energy markets) are interacting with other trends to shape the global security environment and influence strategy. The spread of infectious disease also might play a greater part in the making of strategy and defence policy in the years ahead. Environmental damage caused by the manufacture, maintenance, and disposal of weaponry is also an issue of concern to strategists. Indeed, the issues that appear to be beyond the reach of strategy are the environmental, resource, and commons problems that generated interest in a new concept of security in the first place. Those who see these issues as important should be relieved by the assessment presented in this chapter. Defining these issues as engineering, public health, or educational problems is far more constructive than somehow trying to resolve them by the threat or use of force. But in an increasingly globalized and complex world, issues of low politics appear to be capable not of creating conflict, but of exacerbating the effects of political and military disputes.

QUESTIONS

1. Why are low politics now given priority by policy-makers and scholars?

2. Why would globalization help to slow population growth rates in the developing world?

3. Although other resources are vital, why is it that states have only fought recently over oil?

4. Can you think of a way to threaten or use force to resolve commons issues?

5. What would be the social or political consequences of attempting to use military units to enforce a disease quarantine?

6. Do you think it is realistic to expect that countries currently building a nuclear infrastructure would want to do so in a way that protects the environment?

7. What are the emerging points of interaction between low and high politics today?

8. Will people pay attention to environmental issues if they are not defined as threats to national security?

9. Is the process of globalization increasing the relevance of low politics on national security agendas?

10. Do you think that demographic trends will inevitably lead to decades of violence and instability?

FURTHER READING

■ Stephen J. Cimbala, *The Politics of Warfare: The Great Powers in the Twentieth Century* (University Park, PA: Pennsylvania State University Press, 1997). Discussion of the strategic consequences of the demographic differential between the developed and developing world.

■ Martin van Creveld, *The Transformation of War* (New York: Free Press, 1991). Discussion of the strategic consequences of the demographic differential between the developed and developing world.

■ **Paul F. Diehl and Nils Petter Gleditsch,** *Environmental Conflict: An Anthology* **(Boulder, CO: Westview, 2000).** A recent overview of current research on the relationship between the environment and security.

■ **Thomas F. Homer-Dixon, 'On the Threshold: Environmental Changes as Causes of Acute Conflict',** *International Security,* **16/2 (Fall 1991), 76–116.** An early effort to demonstrate the link between low politics and national security and conflict.

■ **Robert O. Keohane and Joseph S. Nye,** *Power and Interdependence* **(Reading, MA: Addison-Wesley, 1989).** On the theoretical implications of the differences between high and low politics.

■ **Stephen I. Schwartz,** *Atomic Audit: The Costs and Consequences of U.S. Nuclear Weapons since 1940* **(Washington, DC: Brookings Institution, 1998).** On the environmental costs of the cold war.

The Woodrow Wilson Center, which runs the Environmental Change and Security Project (ECSP), publishes an annual report that contains articles, reviews, conference reports and contact information for a host of issues and projects related to the new national security agenda. ECSP can be contacted by email at ecspwwic@wwic.si.edu

WEB LINKS

● **http://www.overpopulation.com/**

● **http://www.cdc.gov**

● **http://www.au.af.mil/au/2025/volume3/chap16/vol3ch16.pdf**

● **http://www.llnl.gov/planetary/**

● **http://www.fda.gov/default.htm**

● Toronto Group Research can be accessed at **http://www.library.utoronto.ca/www/eps/state.htm**

Visit the Online Resource Centre that accompanies this book for lots of interesting additional material http://www.oxfordtextbooks.co.uk/orc/baylis_strategy2e/.

17

The Future of Strategic Studies

LAWRENCE FREEDMAN

Chapter Contents

Reader's Guide

This concluding chapter starts by looking at the development of strategic studies. Strategic studies was largely undertaken outside the universities and was initially influenced by the physical sciences and engineering. Even as traditional military patterns of thought appeared inadequate in the thermonuclear age, academics still found it difficult to impose a scholarly framework for the subject that could survive shifts in policy. By the end of the cold war, strategic studies was essentially a broad enquiry, drawing on a range of expertise. With the end of the cold war, the big issues that had animated the study of military strategy subsided and some questioned the continued relevance of the topic. There was a risk that strategic studies would be caught between the scholarly virtues and disciplinary organization required by the universities and the pressures and urgency of strategic practice, which is inherently interdisciplinary. Realism, the intellectual basis of strategic studies, also has been challenged for being simplistic, for making exaggerated claims for its objectivity, and for disregarding domestic and transnational factors. Furthermore, some view realism as being preoccupied with armed force to the exclusion of peaceful means of exerting influence and resolving disputes, to the point of legitimizing armed force as an acceptable instrument of policy.

A way forward is suggested based on the idea that the course of history can be altered by the choices made by individuals, groups, and governments. These decisions provide the subject matter for strategic studies. They do not need to be choices made only by states nor only about the use of armed force. Armed forces, however, provide the starkest choices that can be confronted and so provide a natural starting point for any attempt to create a general theory of strategy, while organized violence poses a series of challenges that deserves special study.

The Development of Strategic Studies

Strategic studies developed outside the universities. Before the cold war there were military theorists and commentators, such as Boney Fuller and Liddell Hart in Britain, who often had substantial practical experience but who wrote largely for a popular and a professional audience rather than the academy. Their subject matter was similar to strategic studies, and those early theorists who survived into the nuclear age fitted in perfectly well with the new milieu. There was some pioneering activity in the universities after the First World War with moves to establish the scientific study of international affairs as a means to avoid future wars. Many writers in this field had an interest in military matters, although few claimed expertise in how best to fight wars.

The special flavour of post-war strategic studies came from those who had been working in the physical sciences and engineering rather than the social sciences and humanities. Many of the early participants had their consciences stung and their policy interest engaged by the Manhattan Project. (See Chapter 11.) Those who had worked on operational problems from convoy protection to choosing targets for air raids had firm views about how the conduct of war could no longer be left to what they often took to be the rather primitive, intuitive forms of reasoning of the professional military. The conviction that civilians had critical contributions to make to strategic policy grew as traditional military patterns of thought appeared increasingly inadequate in the thermonuclear age. The combination of the arms race and the cold war created the conditions for the growth of a substantial research-led policy community outside the universities—new government agencies, congressional committees, think tanks, and 'beltway bandits'.

This created a market for professionally trained civilian strategists that university departments might attempt to fill. It also meant that academics were never able to impose a scholarly framework for the subject that could survive shifts in the policy framework. Few scholars really tried to do so. From the start it was the salience of the policy issues rather than intellectual curiosity that led to the growth of the strategic studies community. The universities were certainly not hostile to policy-led research. The cold war coincided with the expansion of the universities throughout the Western world—not only in size but also in the range of their activities. They took in practical subjects and moved beyond established disciplinary boundaries. If gender and the media could become appropriate areas of study for university departments, then it would have been surprising if questions of armed force had escaped the net. Those making the case for higher education were pleased to demonstrate to sponsors that their institutions contributed to national strength. When the universities went to the US Congress for more funds after the Soviets had apparently pulled ahead in the technological race with the launch of the world's first artificial satellite (Sputnik), their case was made in the name of national security. (See Chapter 10.) Many academics thrilled to a potential role in a wider public debate, even if this meant enduring policy-makers' snide remarks about their abstract theorizing being removed from real life. They accepted the fact that their weightier tomes would be left unread because their short, snappy, opinion pieces would sometimes reach presidents and prime ministers. Academic exponents of strategic studies might have had extensive training in the use of evidence and sophisticated forms of analysis, but they could still drift easily into advocacy, preferring popular and professional audiences to dustier academic conferences and journals.

Little attempt was made to use cold war opportunities to establish strategic studies as an academic subject. No core curriculum was developed, and there was probably only a brief period in the early 1960s, the end of what was later described as the 'golden age', when there was a serious body of literature that everyone in the field had read. There was not even a consensus on how academic work in this area should be described. The policy influence was always apparent. 'Military studies' appeared too technical and narrow, redolent of map-reading and staff exercises, and contradicted the factors that had shaped the civilian role in strategic policy: the prejudice against professional military thought; the democratic conviction that military officers should be subordinated to civilians; and the Clausewitzian presumption that if, as the master insisted, war is concerned with the pursuit of politics by other means, then military means could only be properly understood by reference to political purposes.

KEY POINTS

- Strategic studies began outside the universities.

- The cold war and the arms race created the conditions for the development of the subject.

- Shifting policy needs made it difficult to establish the academic study of strategy in universities.

In and Out of the Cold War

But what should be the political purposes of strategy? During the cold war, the ends of policy seemed somewhat fixed. The contest between liberal capitalist and totalitarian socialist forms of government was inescapable. The central problem of policy was awesome in its implications but also relatively simple in its formulation. Deterrence was the issue: in what circumstances would nuclear threats work and what would be the consequences if they failed to deter war or were counterproductive in their effects? How could political benefit be extracted from a nuclear arsenal without triggering a cataclysmic riposte? How could credibility be injected into preposterous posturing? The natural inclination of academics was to explore these paradoxes. (See Chapter 7.) This could be done both by developing ways of reinforcing deterrence, thereby avoiding war, but also by creating other policy instruments that might reduce dependence upon this high-risk approach to security. Scholars became interested in particular in arms control. (See Chapter 8.) Over time this had an important consequence. It encouraged a perspective that went beyond the purely national to the systemic. A rational American policy came to be defined as one that coaxed out of Moscow a more rational Soviet policy.

The changes in the character and tempo of the cold war naturally influenced strategic studies. After the Berlin and Cuban crises of the early 1960s further development of the purer theories of deterrence seemed less important. Academics began to find a role in questioning official policy and warning of the limits to deterrence, the distorting effects of domestic and organizational politics on crisis management, and the perils of misperception. The second-order technical studies sought to offer ways out of practical difficulties experienced in arms control negotiations. A further development came when it was recognized that too much of the 'golden age' literature had taken the political context for granted, or had at least failed to appreciate the dynamic consequences of the upheavals in the Third World. After Vietnam, these aspects of strategy were much harder to ignore. To understand the conditions in which armed forces might be used, or at least threatened, it was necessary to delve into a diverse range of regional security issues. It seemed more important to draw attention to the complexities of the Middle East or Central America than to think up fancy but safe ways to threaten Armageddon. Furthermore, as official deterrence policies moved to reduce their nuclear bias by strengthening the conventional forces and doctrine, professional military knowledge and experience appeared much more relevant. So well before the end of the cold war the field of strategic studies (now often referred to as security studies) had become diffuse. There was no recognized academic discipline, only a broad area of study, coming under a variety of headings (peace, war, defence, security, strategy, arms control). The only unifying factor was that the interest lay beyond practical matters, concerned with the actual employment of armed force, to the political purposes for which it might be employed and the political measures that might be adopted either to prevent this employment or to bring it to an end.

In these circumstances it was unavoidable that those working in the universities would have to follow the wider policy debate. Given the sort of upheavals associated with the end of the cold war and its aftermath, this was no small matter. When the policy issues of the day moved from great power confrontation and nuclear arms control to intra-state wars and humanitarian intervention, then quite different skills might be needed. The old agenda demanded scholars with a grasp of traditional statecraft, a knowledge of the political thinking at the highest levels of the world's key capitals, sensitivity to alliance relations, and a technical understanding of the properties of the critical weapons systems and how they might be employed. Add in such questions as the management of defence budgets and the intricacies of arms control negotiations, and it becomes clear that, during the cold war years, strategic studies had to draw on a broad range of expertise.

Then out goes the cold war and in comes ethnic conflict, carrying with it vast quantities of anthropological and sociological literature, combined with the need to follow political developments in small and weak states, whose leading lights are not themselves plugged in to the international policy circuit. Dirty little militia wars and problems of humanitarian intervention have nothing to do with elaborate theories of deterrence. (See Chapter 9.) Some argued for an even more complete shift away from the traditional agenda, insisting that the staples of conflict and violence must give way to the far more important factors of environment and economics. A hypothetical university department set up to address strategic studies during the cold war would find that the original interdisciplinary requirements—polymathic enough—were suddenly expanded to absurd lengths.

Not surprisingly, academics often appeared to be uncertain about the future of the international system and how to handle the new agenda. It became even more difficult to give confident advice in the form of crisp bullet points. Policy-makers became impatient with those qualities that academics believe to be the most valuable: long-term thinking, stretching the bounds of the possible, and taking complexity as a challenge rather than an excuse for not going into too much detail. Academics interested in security could see their funding in decline and their best work crowded out by partisan clamour, parochial agency interest, and more sensationalist fare. While the pull from the policy world was for the simple, snappy, and short-term, the push from the academic world was almost exactly in the opposite direction. The study of international relations, established to address the problem of war, sought to gain respectability by acquiring all the attributes of a proper discipline, including a preoccupation with theory and methodology. Academic advancement has come to depend on 'conspicuous scholarship'—publishing in the right journals, linking relatively innocuous case studies to great theoretical issues and, through extensive footnotes, demonstrating a capacity to reference (though not necessarily to read) all potentially relevant literature. To those for whom language itself has become an ideological battlefield, and all empiricism suspect, policy relevance signifies the antithesis of sound scholarship.

KEY POINTS

- Cold war strategy was relatively simple, focusing particularly on the requirements of deterrence.

- Even before 1991, the field of strategic studies became more diffuse as the political context of international relations changed.

- The opening of a new era of ethnic conflict in the 1990s presented strategists with a more complex international environment that required a wide range of new expertise.

- In the post-cold war period, uncertainty predominated and policy-makers became less interested in what academic strategists had to say. As a result, a number of scholars turned their attention to what was regarded as the academically more respectable pursuit of the study of theory and methodology.

The Academic and Policy Worlds

The relationship between the academic and policy worlds is fraught with ethical and practical difficulties. The need for access and the desire for influence must be balanced against the risk that critical faculties might be blunted and intellectual integrity corrupted by the quest to please policy-makers. The academic may not want to help the practitioner, perhaps disapproving of the objectives being pursued. In terms of defining a field of study, the vantage point of a student of strategy is quite different from that of a practitioner. Efforts by the former to display some superior wisdom may well deserve to be treated with contempt. The most helpful role remains that which can be properly described as 'academic' (even though in the policy world this is all too often synonymous with irrelevant). The task is to conceptualize and contextualize rather than provide specific guidance. If it is done well, then the practitioner should be able to recognize the relevance for whatever may be the problem at hand.

Strategy is rarely atheoretical in practice. The theories may be implicit and undeveloped, following Keynes's famous observation (1947): 'Practical men, who believe themselves to be quite exempt from any intellectual influences, are usually the slaves of some defunct economist. Madmen in authority, who hear voices in the air, are distilling their frenzy from some academic scribbler of a few years back'. Yet is it the case that academic theory, even of the highest quality, can be of great value to the 'practical man'? The complaint might be that academic works rarely address problems in the same form in which policy-makers face them. Officials have little choice but to range far and wide because of the nature of the judgements they are required to make, often in a hurry. It may be necessary to address the efficiency of various forms of coercion as well as inducements, and in so doing to draw on observations about human nature under stress, problems of organization of large groups of people on the move, negotiating techniques, visions of a good society, and standards of ethical conduct.

'Practical men' can expect to be judged by results. They will therefore tend to rely on what works for them. This may be intuition and hunch, or lessons drawn from searing experience or remembered bits of history. Such sources may be relied upon in preference to excellent information sources and exemplary staff work. When matters are finely balanced but a decision has still to be taken, a feeling about the problem may be as good a guide as any. This may strike an academic as being wholly inappropriate or based on disgracefully exaggerated generalizations. Certainly the results from such approaches can be very poor. But whether a proper academic methodology would do any better is moot when there is no time for long projects or tolerance of caveats. Wise strategists may research their decisions as much as possible, but in practice time often precludes extensive deliberation. When a general is wondering whether an enemy formation might break in the face of a sudden attack, he is not going to be impressed if told that more research is needed or that his working hypothesis is inherently untestable. Once a fateful decision has been taken, an open mind becomes a luxury because any reappraisal may result in confused orders and demoralization.

BOX 17.1

What a General Entering into Battle Must Consider

Politics (how best to define the goal of the campaign; the importance of keeping allies happy, what the people back home will stand);

engineering (how well the weapons work or are likely to work in practice; possible modifications to suit local conditions, ensuring that weapons are properly maintained);

sociology (the likely cohesion of the enemy force under fire);

psychology (how to motivate his own soldiers; getting into the mind of the enemy commander);

geography (the possible impact of terrain on particular tactics);

history (what other generals got away with in similar circumstances);

economics (the rate at which he dare expend matériel on specific targets).

All these considerations apply only to getting the best out of one's own side. The need to think about an enemy adds even more issues that must be factored into strategic deliberations.

The 'practical man' offers another observation. Strategic practice, as opposed to theory, demands risk taking on behalf of a wider constituency, normally with the lives of service personnel and possibly with whole societies, and this brings with it awesome responsibilities. It involves mobilizing human and material resources according to a developed plan, against anticipated opposition, and in pursuit of stated objectives. If the objectives are misplaced, the plan misconceived, the resources unavailable or poorly mobilized, then the strategy will fail and this will be the strategist's responsibility. It is this sense of being tested by practice and judged by results that gives strategic reasoning its edge. The unaccountable academic should properly feel a degree of humility when advising on such matters.

This may help explain why the study of strategy is accommodated only with difficulty in academic life. As practice it provides opportunity for chance and irrationality to hold sway. The purist might be appalled at the arbitrary mixture of politics, sociology, economics, psychology, and history that regularly influences decisions in crisis and combat, never mind the great contributions made by intuition and hunch. Yet the fact that reality rarely shows respect for disciplinary boundaries might give the academic pause for thought, as might evidence of the extent to which carefully qualified propositions, excessively crafted formulations, and a reluctance to pronounce until all possible avenues of research have been exhausted can get in the way of clear thinking.

Effective policy outside of academia draws on a range of considerations that within academia are confined to their own disciplinary boxes. Within the universities, intellectual progress is assumed to depend on commonly accepted methodologies being rigorously applied within a known conceptual framework to produce results able to withstand peer review. The process is watched over sternly by professional associations and journal editors—the 'gatekeepers'. They ensure that standards are maintained so that progress can be measured. Without the disciplinary boxes, teaching and research probably would become unmanageable. Nonetheless, disciplinary boundaries are often artificial, and sustained through jargon that excludes the uninitiated. Indeed, academics often develop particular strategies to sustain these disciplinary boundaries and to fight off intellectual intruders. Yet many of the most important academic cleavages cut across these boundaries. Fads and fashions—from rational actor theory to deconstructionism—migrate easily. Often the most innovative and influential figures are those who refuse to be confined by the established boundaries, but are happy to borrow from others. Imaginative academic administrators often ignore them. In universities as in other organizations the closer one gets to particular decisions the more complex and multifaceted they appear. Practical problems can rarely be encapsulated in the terms of a single discipline. Life is interdisciplinary.

KEY POINTS

- Tensions inevitably exist between the academic and policy worlds with their different responsibilities.

- 'Practitioners' often complain about the irrelevance of academic studies to immediate problems they face.

- Strategic reality is wide-ranging and interdisciplinary and does not fit neatly into the narrow focus of most university departments.

The Study of Strategy

Strategic studies poses a further and particular challenge to the social sciences. It tends to adopt the perspective of individual actors within the system, as they try to make sense of their environment and shape it to their needs as best they can. Much social science theorizing necessarily seeks to reduce the importance of human agency by looking for patterns and regularities in areas that we might have thought in our naivety to be governed by choice. Deliberate political change is still inadequately studied in political theory except in a rather cynical way. There is no point in studying strategy unless one believes that the course of history can be altered through the choices made by individuals. Those who believe that the analysis of politics and international relations requires attempts to identify long historical cycles, or universal laws of political life, or invariable patterns of behaviour, or structural determinants of actions that leave little scope for local decision, are unlikely to find strategy particularly interesting or even relevant. Instead of finding anomalous behaviour intriguing, these determinists may find it irritating because it undermines the predictive power of their models.

Strategy is important only if it is believed that individuals, groups, or governments face real choices—to the extent that the reasoning which informs these choices is worthy of careful examination. By focusing on actors within the system and their sense of their own interests and aspirations, strategic studies must be seditious. It encourages the analysis of those situations where order is absent, or else where disorder is encouraged by those who believe that it will be to the advantage of those on whose behalf they are acting.

This appreciation—almost celebration—of choice is essential to the study of strategy. Strategy is undertaken in the conviction that it is possible to manipulate and shape one's environment rather than simply become the victim of forces beyond one's control. For this reason, students of strategy are naturally 'political voyeurs', observing the choices of others with a discerning eye whether or not they have sympathy with the ultimate aims. They assess the efficiency of various forms of coercion as well as inducements. They develop and refine views about human nature under stress, the organization of large groups of people on the move, negotiating techniques, visions of a good society, and standards of ethical conduct.

In light of these broad interests, there is no reason in principle why strategic studies, defined as an intellectual approach to certain types of problems rather than a field of study, could not become more prominent in academic life. Indeed we know this to be the case. There are now far more courses about strategy in management departments than in international relations departments. Unfortunately, this development has encouraged the rather loose view of strategy as being concerned with visionary planning or the management of large organizations in uncertain environments. Nonetheless, the classical military strategists—Sun Tzu more than Clausewitz—loom large in the management literature, far more so than the business strategists loom in the military literature. (See Chapter 1.) Furthermore, many of the more formal methodologies, of which the most famous remains game theory, developed in the late 1950s with nuclear deterrence in mind, have become even more influential in economics and management studies.

Formal methodologies have returned to political science departments as rational choice theory, although in a form that often appears to confirm the old jibe that political science

BOX 17.2

Similarities and Differences between the Ideas of Clausewitz and Sun Tzu

The extent of the cultural and historical gaps separating Sun Tzu's *The Art of War* and Clausewitz's *On War*, not to mention the apparently contradictory nature of their most well-known dicta, has encouraged the a priori assumption that Sun Tzu and Clausewitz espouse essentially antagonistic theories. But closer scrutiny reveals that while a number of differences exist, so do many similarities and complementary ideas . . .

The main points on which Sun Tzu and Clausewitz disagree concern the value of intelligence, the utility of deception, the feasibility of surprise attack, and the possibility of reliably forecasting and controlling the course of events on the battlefield. On the qualities requisite for a military commander, though, they agree in principle but differ in emphasis: Sun Tzu relies chiefly on the master of war's skill in making calculated, rational choices, while Clausewitz considers the military genius's artistic intuition to be the critical factor. Finally they hold similar views on the primacy of politics in war; the need to preserve the professional autonomy of the military in action; the overall importance of numerical superiority; and the folly of not securing victory as rapidly and decisively as possible once war has become inevitable.

(Handel 1996)

is an area of study that in failing to achieve science avoids that dangerous subject politics. It offers undoubted analytical rigour, a shared starting point for numerous lines of enquiry and considerable theoretical promise. The problem is that the methodology can be offputting and restrictive, readily and usefully applied to only a limited number of types of choices. It copes poorly with complexity, as well as requiring bold assumptions about what it means to be rational. This is especially disconcerting when studying armed conflict, famed for its tendency to irrationality and the imperfection of available information (pushed by Clausewitz to the centre of his theory with his stress on friction and the fog of war). Game theory provided an important means of thinking through the alternative options that presented themselves to policy-makers in the nuclear age, and in particular the need to recognize the incentives for cooperation in the midst of antagonism, but it could never capture the range of factors that shaped critical decisions.

KEY POINTS

- Strategic studies, with its focus on individual actors and the importance of deliberate political choice, poses problems for the social sciences, which emphasize wider patterns of behaviour and the limited opportunities for achieving change.

- Strategists are 'voyeurs', scrutinizing the choices made by others concerned with

difficult decisions about the role of armed force.

- Strategic studies can be seen as an intellectual approach to specific problems rather than a distinct field of study.

Realism: Old and New

For a more overtly political view of strategy we might look to the realist tradition. Students of politics and international relations often criticize this tradition as being simplistic and obsolete, bound up with the assumption that the only choices that matter are those that states make about military power. There are three aspects to the critique: an epistemological challenge to what is taken to be an exaggerated claim for objectivity, as if this is the only true reflection of 'reality'; the disregard of domestic and transnational factors; and the preoccupation with armed force to the exclusion of peaceful means of exerting influence and resolving disputes. This latter complaint has developed into a charge that the realists legitimize armed force as an acceptable instrument of policy. This indictment of strategists on moral grounds is directly related to the first, apparently more scholastic, complaint about objectivity. The realists might claim that they do no more than attempt to make sense of the world as they find it, while their critics suggest that the very language and concepts they use encourage a dangerous view of the world. (See Chapter 2.)

A defence of strategic studies does not require a defence of realism. There are, however, elements of the realist tradition that are worth preserving while other aspects need updating. An approach to political analysis that prided itself on coming to terms with the world as it was rather than as idealists would like it to be is now supposed to depend on a dubious claim that key international events can largely be explained by the structurally defined means by which states safeguard their security. There is room for a non-dogmatic realism that would acknowledge the significance of non-state actors, the impact of social, economic, cultural, and local political factors on state behaviour, and the importance of values and mental constructs. Realists also could be more sensitive to the epistemological issues raised by presumptions of objectivity. If practitioners of international politics now talk regularly about issues of identity, norms, and globalization, then they are part of international reality. To be powerful was often described within the realist tradition in terms of possessing substantial assets—so much wealth or military capabilities. Yet poor strategy can see these squandered or trivialized, while good strategy can extract substantial political effects from meagre resources. In this sense strategy is essentially an art, less about applying power and more about creating it in the first place. This requires a more subtle view of power as existing only within political relationships, manifest as actors are able to alter the behaviour of others according to their own preferences.

The constructivist position, a potential safe haven for those troubled by structural realism while leery about following post-modernist theory into a deconstructed, relativist mire, stresses the importance of the interaction between the way we describe the world and how we act within it. This can represent a real advance on the tendency within the realist tradition to think of power as a measurable resource. Such simplistic thinking leads to a view of strategy as no more than a mechanical matter of expending resources in the pursuit of clearly defined objectives. Put this way, it can appear almost as a science, opening up possibilities for prediction. The practical strategist is more likely, however, to be (perhaps unwittingly) something of a constructivist. Effective strategy requires a clear sense of the dynamic relationship between ends and means, knowing that how ends are defined in the first place is critical to whether available means will be adequate. Vital judgements—such as finding the optimum balance among broadening a coalition to maximize the isolation of the opponent, the limited time available for coalition formation, the goals that will have to be dropped to bring in the most reluctant, the extra obligations that might have to be accepted, the otherwise neutral opinions that might be offended—turn on the way we understand the workings of our own and other political systems.

KEY POINTS

- Despite critiques of realism, there are elements of this school of thought that remain very useful in the study of strategy, while there are other elements that can be brought up to date.

- A case can be made for a non-dogmatic realism which provides a more subtle approach to the role of power in international politics than the neo-realist approach, which emphasizes the structural constraints on state behaviour.

- Newer constructivist approaches also help to focus attention on the important dynamic relationship between ends and means, which is crucial in the outcome of any conflict.

The Study of Armed Force

A new realism should therefore have no trouble looking beyond what makes states secure to what makes individuals and particular groups secure. It must also admit that the business of states, once almost completely bound up with security, now involves a range of economic, social, and environmental issues. The course and character of all conflicts, and the role to be played by armed force, must be reappraised. Strong rates of economic growth and forms of interdependence may well reduce tensions between states and create a stake in peaceful coexistence. Environmental disasters can undermine the credibility of the state apparatus so that it becomes vulnerable to other types of challenges. Changes in family structures and social mores may affect attitudes towards violence. Nevertheless, there is a need for more care when it comes to proposals to discard the traditional focus on organized violence, as if this has become, at least in the Western world, unimportant.

Strategy is more ubiquitous than violence. It is present in the politics of all human institutions, evident in any move to mobilize support or sideline opponents. The study of strategy does not depend on incipient aggression in human affairs. Nonetheless, the possibility of violence can have an important impact on attempts to develop general theories of strategy that are capable of addressing all manner of political situations. If strategy is about choice, then armed force provides some of the most perplexing and starkest choices that can be confronted. Opportunities for choice open the door to clashes between conflicting interests and values, to the rough impact of brute force and to the more subtle effects achieved by guile and wiles. Most political objectives can be met without the use or threatened use of violence. There are other sources of power. But physical violence is the ultimate political instrument and, if available, can overwhelm all others. No individual, group, or state can ignore the threat of violence because it challenges their very existence. Threats of force are likely to be made when basic values are at stake. Situations involving the purposive use of violence are likely to stand out from the run-of-the-mill activities at both the national and international levels. By their nature they concentrate minds on fundamentals. Ethically and politically they require exceptional justification. For all these reasons, the potential for violence provides a natural starting point for any attempt to build up a general theory of strategy.

This is not the same, however, as arguing that formulations developed with armed force in mind can serve a variety of purposes. For example, politicians may dramatize the more troublesome social problems by calling for 'wars' against them (on drugs, cancer, etc.) and suggest that strong generalship is needed for them to be defeated. The unreflective application of the war analogy can hinder understanding by attempting to squeeze different types of issues into an inappropriate conceptual framework geared to military threats. In the case of drugs, for example, it may have some relevance to confrontations with Third World drug cartels but less so with attempts to make sense of patterns of consumption. The notion of 'economic security' can encourage a confrontational approach to trade policy. The concept of 'environmental security' can prompt a search for explanations based on hostile actions rather than natural causes or everyday economic activity. Even more difficult is a term such as 'internal security', which might once have referred to the ability of states to deny armed groups, whether criminal or political, the ability to challenge their authority, but which now takes in anything to do with the control of borders, including economic migration or the smuggling of contraband.

A different approach would be to acknowledge that the characters and competencies of states have been subject to many changes, while asserting that an enduring feature remains the aspiration to define and dominate the means of legitimate violence within territorial borders. The challenges can come from other states; or from within states in the form of secessionists, revolutionaries, or elitist conspirators; or from non-state actors in the form of drug cartels and gangsters, religious sects, terrorists, and minority political movements. This continues to provide a relatively sharp focus for strategic studies and provides some compensation for an unavoidably wide context.

There is no reason in principle why the strategic imagination should not be directed towards improving the human condition by finding ways to restrict and marginalize armed force. Much strategic studies activity has been about the peaceful settlement of disputes, arms control, and generally supportive of the work of the United Nations. Major international negotiations require as much of a strategic sensibility as do major wars. Yet, and this may only be a matter of temperament, there does tend to be a dark side to the strategic imagination that picks up intimations of disorder at times of stability, that senses the fragility of human institutions even while striving to reinforce them, that cannot stop thinking of war while promoting peace. This dark side may explain the accusations that strategists allow armed force far more prominence in their deliberations than it deserves. Their response is that constant consideration of the potential for instability and conflict can help prevent it from occurring. Moreover, if the strategic imagination fails to generate scenarios for war, except by combining in an unlikely and tenuous fashion a series of gloomy hypotheses, then that itself is a positive sign.

Conclusion

Karl Marx once observed that people make their own history but not in the circumstances of their own choosing. The study of strategy should help with the understanding of how individuals go about history making and in so doing reshape the circumstances that they face. These circumstances include interacting with others engaged in their own history making. I have argued that this activist view with its stress on choice and power is distinctive and cannot be confined within the boundaries of a specific academic discipline. It is a view that stands in contrast to those of others who are more determinist in their outlook, or transfixed by patterns and cycles in human behaviour, or who see the exercise of power as a failure of social institutions rather than part of their natural condition. I also suggested that the study of strategy can benefit from being pushed to extremes, by looking at those circumstances in which the prospect or actuality of organized violence looms large. Because we have not yet succeeded in banishing armed force from human affairs, we will still have to face many extreme situations.

A striking example of this point was provided by the events of 11 September 2001: an attack inspired in one of the most remote and poor points of the world, directed against one of the wealthiest. The attack was instigated using the most ancient of military technologies—the knife—in order to turn the most modern civilian aviation technologies against the West. Counter-terrorism depends almost entirely on human skills, whether in police detection, intelligence gathering, or the occasional special force operations. This might have raised obvious questions about the relevance of conventional military power to these kinds of threats to national security.

As it happened Al-Qaeda had its headquarters and training grounds in Afghanistan, under the approving eye of the Taliban regime. The case to remove both the regime and its guests was strong and this led to a regular military offensive, although with many irregular elements. The next stage of America's war on terror involved yet another military invasion to accomplish regime change, though in this case the grounds were less strong. Furthermore, the Americans were caught out by their inattention, or indifference, to the requirements of gaining international legitimacy or the impact of the overthrow of Saddam Hussein and the method by which it was achieved on Iraqi society. They were badly caught out by the ferocity of the internal violence triggered by these events. It is also fair to point out that students of regional affairs were less caught out than students of strategy. US policy-makers found themselves within the space of a few years dealing with extreme terrorism and an extreme insurgency.

These extreme situations provide an agenda for policy-makers that students of strategy can address. The future of strategic studies in terms of academic organization will be tested in a number of respects. First, strategists will remain relevant only if they have kept in touch with the range of possible situations that might tend to extremes. This range is expanding, from the many problems of weak states to the unlikely event of major war among the great powers. Second, as the political agenda becomes both more diffuse and in certain respects less pressing, strategic studies may become less coherent. Third, there will remain a need for caution and humility. There is an enormous gulf between offering advice and taking responsibility for decisions with potentially severe consequences, normally taken with insufficient knowledge or time for deliberation. Fourth, it must never be forgotten that strategy is an art and not a science.

QUESTIONS

1. What were the implications of the early development of strategic studies?
2. What role does realism play in strategic studies?
3. What is meant by the term 'the golden age of strategic studies'?
4. How did the cold war affect the development of the study of strategy?
5. To what extent did the end of the cold war alter the agenda of strategic studies?
6. Can the academic study of strategy help the 'practitioner' of strategy?
7. What challenges does strategic studies pose for the social sciences?
8. Does strategic studies have to be bound to the 'realist tradition' in the study of politics?
9. What is the future of strategic studies according to the author?
10. Do you agree with this view?

FURTHER READING

Strategic studies during the 'golden age' of the late 1950s and 1960s

■ B. Brodie, *Strategy in the Missile Age* (Princeton: Princeton University Press, 1959).

■ J. Baylis *et al.*, *Contemporary Strategy*, i–ii (New York: Holmes & Meier, 1987).

■ L. Freedman, *The Evolution of Nuclear Strategy*, 3rd edn (London: Palgrave 2003).

History of strategic thought

■ P. Paret (ed.), *Makers of Modern Strategy: From Machiavelli to the Nuclear Age* (Princeton: Princeton University Press, 1986).

■ Michael I. Handel, *Masters of War: Classical Strategic Thought* (London: Frank Cass, 1996).

Criticisms of strategic studies as an academic subject

■ C. S. Gray, *Strategic Studies: A Critical Assessment* (London: Aldwych Press, 1982). One of the most comprehensive assessments.

■ P. Green, *Deadly Logic: The Theory of Nuclear Deterrence* (Columbus: Ohio State University Press, 1968).

■ A. Rapoport, *Strategy and Conscience* (New York: Schocken Books, 1964).

Post-cold war debates about strategic studies

■ W. Arkin, *The Internet and Strategic Studies* (Washington, DC: SIAS, Center for Strategic Education 1998). Guide to web sources.

■ M. van Creveld, *The Transformation of War* (New York: Free Press, 1991).

■ C. S. Gray, *Modern Strategy* (Oxford: Oxford University Press, 1999).

■ M. Kaldor, *New and Old Wars: Organized Violence in a Global Era* (Cambridge: Polity Press, 1999).

■ L. Freedman, *Deterrence* (Cambridge: Polity Press: 2004).

 Visit the Online Resource Centre that accompanies this book for lots of interesting additional material http://www.oxfordtextbooks.co.uk/orc/baylis_strategy2e/.

Notes

Chapter 1

[1] See e.g. Quester 1984.

[2] For a comprehensive and brilliant account of ethnic conflict up to 1985 see Horowitz 1985.

[3] Quoted by Huntington 1993a: 30.

[4] This comment by Professor Claude Phillips is quoted by Shaw and Wong 1985: 207.

Chapter 4

[1] Colin Gray comments that 'different political and strategic cultures confront distinctive geostrategic problems through the prisms of their individual historical circumstances, and with unique sets of assets and liabilities, will make somewhat individual choices' (1997: 28).

[2] Cruz 2000: 278. For more on the strategic 'use of culture' see Swidler 1986.

[3] Cruz acknowledges that this raises a critical dichotomy between culture as a system of meaning and culture as practice, 2000: 278.

Chapter 7

[1] The JSF is a single-seat fighter with a theoretical radius of 600 nautical miles unrefuelled—its real range is almost surely likely to be less, given the difference between normal combat flying (e.g. flying at varying altitudes, sudden acceleration, and the like) and the more fuel-efficient peacetime variety. For some preliminary data see http://www.jast.mil/html/aboutjsf.htm.

[2] G-5 range: source: http://www-cgsc.army.mil/a302/A302a/Archive/Equipment/155mmG5.htm. Paladin 155 mm range: source: http://www.army-technology.com/projects/paladin/specs.html.

[3] For a short design history of the C-130 see http://www.afrc.af.mil/UNITS/911aw/public/c130.htm.

[4] The author has conducted this experiment with groups of officers perhaps twenty times, always with the same result.

[5] For more on this story see http://www.higginsboat.org.

[6] 'Private Eyes in the Sky', *The Economist*, (6 May 2000), web edition, http://www.economist.com/PrinterFriendly.cfm?Story_ID=333111.

[7] See e.g. the fascinating Shay 1994.

Chapter 10

Portions of this chapter are drawn from C. Dale Walton, 'Navigating the Second Nuclear Age: Proliferation and Deterrance in this Century', *Global Dialogue*, in press.

Chapter 11

[1] This phrase was used in its cold war context by John Lewis Gaddis in 'The Long Peace: Elements of Stability in the Postwar International System', *International Security*, 10/4.

[2] The text of Aspin's speech can be accessed at www.fas.org/irp/offdocs/pdd18.htm.

[3] See the text of the NAC's declaration at http://www.nato.int/docu/handbook/2001/hb0603.htm. The other committees were the Senior Politico-Military Group (SGP) which was given the rather vague task of "consider[ing] a range of factors in the political, security and economic fields that may cause or influence proliferation and discusses political and economic means to prevent or respond to proliferation", and the Joint Committee on Proliferation, which drew together the work of the DGP and SGP.

[4] These principles can be viewed at http://www.state.gov/t/np/rls/fs/23764.htm.

[5] The British Foreign Secretary Jack Straw e.g. told the House of Commons that 'we never, ever said that there was an imminent threat', and claimed that instead he had merely said there was a 'clear and present danger'. See House of Commons, *Official Report*, 22 Oct. 2003, col. 677. In Washington, Defence Secretary Donald Rumsfeld told an interviewer, 'You and a few other critics are the only people I've heard use the phrase immediate threat. I didn't, the president didn't. And it's become kind of folklore that that's what's happened.' http://www.defencelink.mil/transcripts/2004/tr20040314-secdef0542.html

Chapter 14

The authors thank the participants in the Monterey Strategy Seminar at the Center for Contemporary Conflict for their many helpful comments and criticisms.

[1] Taken from remarks by President George W. Bush on Weapons of Mass Destruction Proliferation, Fort Lesley J. McNair, National Defense University, 11 Feb. 2004.

2 Even here it is not clear that modern technology has made possible destruction of a new order of magnitude. After taking into account economic growth and the increased density of commerce over time, we cannot say whether the London bombings of 2005 had a larger impact than IRA attacks in earlier periods, or than attacks with dynamite did during the late 1800s.

3 Note that cost estimated regarding the 9/11 attacks exclude the voluntary and self-imposed costs of invading Iraq, a state opposed to the movement that committed the 9/11 attacks.

4 Based on the RAND/St. Andrews dataset accessed on the website of the Memorial Institute for the Prevention of Terrorism (MIPT), available at http://www.tkb.org/Home.jsp, accessed 12 Dec. 2005.

5 Ironically, Soviet military leaders often stated how difficult it was to predict what the United States would do because they so often violated their own doctrine. Now the tables are turned and it is the United States that finds it difficult, if not impossible, to predict the actions of terrorist organizations that follow no set doctrine.

6 2005 Nunn-Lugar Report, available at the web site of Senator Lugar, at http://lugar.senate.gov/reports/Nunn-Lugar_Report_2005.pdf, accessed 10 January 2006.

Chapter 15

1 The three main humanitarian interventions that did occur during the cold war were unilateral military interventions by one Third World state against another: India's 1971 intervention in East Pakistan, Tanzania's 1978 intervention in Uganda, and Vietnam's 1979 intervention in Cambodia. In all cases, intervention was justified on grounds of self-defence but the effect was to remove murderous regimes from power. Despite this humanitarian outcome, these interventions were condemned as illegal by the great powers.

2 This resolution was not vetoed by the Soviet Union because the Soviets were boycotting the UNSC at the time.

3 The same may be said of battlefield nuclear, chemical, and biological weapons. The political consequences of using such weapons may far outweigh their military effect.

References

Abadie, A., and J. Gardeazabal (2004). *Terrorism and the World Economy*. Cambridge, MA: Center for International Development.

Abrahms, M. (2004). 'Are Terrorists Really Rational? The Palestinian Example', *Orbis*, 48/3: 533–49.

Addington, Larry, H. (1994) *The Patterns of War since the Eighteenth Century*. 2nd edn, Bloomington: Indiana University Press.

Allison, G. (2004). *Nuclear Terrorism: The Ultimate Preventable Catastrophe*. New York: Times Books.

Almond, Gabriel, and Sidney Verba (1965). *The Civic Culture: Political Attitudes and Democracy in Five Nations*. Boston: Little Brown.

al-Zawahiri, Ayman (2001). 'Knights under the Prophet's Banner', in *Al-Sahraq al-Awsat* (London), 2 Dec., tr. Foreign Broadcast Information Service (FBIS), available at http://www.fas.org/irp/world/para/ayman_bk.html, accessed 1 Mar. 2005.

—— (2005). 'Letter from al-Zawahiri to Zarqawi', tr. the Foreign Broadcast Information Service, Oct.

Angell, N. (1914). *The Great Illusion*. London: Heinemann.

Annan, Kofi (1999). 'Statement on receiving the report of the Independent Inquiry into the Actions of the United Nations during the 1994 Genocide in Rwanda', 16 Dec.; available at www.un.org/News/ossg/sgsm_rwanda.htm.

Anthony, I., and A. D. Rotfeld (eds.) (2001). *A Future Arms Control Agenda*. Oxford: Oxford University Press.

Archer, Christon, John Ferris, Holger Herwig, and Tim Travers (2002). *A World History of Warfare*. Lincoln, NE: University of Nebraska Press.

Ardrey, R. (1966). *The Territorial Imperative*. New York: Atheneum.

Arend, A. C., and R. J. Beck (1993), *International Law and the Use of Force: Beyond the Charter Paradigm*. London: Routledge.

Arkin, W. M. (1998). *The Internet and Strategic Studies*. Washington, DC: SAIS, Center for Strategic Education.

Arquilla, J., and D. Ronfeldt (eds.) (2001). *Networks and Netwars*. Santa Monica, Calif.: RAND. http://www.rand.org/publications/MR/MR1382/

Aussaresses, P. (2005). *The Battle of the Casbah: Terrorism and Counter-Terrorism in Algeria, 1955–1957*. New York: Enigma.

Bacevich, A. J. (1986). *The Pentomic Era: The US Army between Korea and Vietnam*. Washington, DC: National Defense University Press.

Ball, Desmond (ed.) (1993). *Strategic Culture in the Asia-Pacific Region (with Some Implications for Regional Security Cooperation)*. Canberra: Strategic and Defence Studies Centre, Australian National University.

Banchoff, Thomas (1999). *The German Problem Transformed: Institutions, Politics and Foreign Policy, 1945–1995*. Ann Arbor, MI: University of Michigan Press.

Banerjee, Sanjoy (1997). 'The Cultural Logic of National Identity Formation: Contending Discourses in Late Colonial India', in Valerie M. Hudson (ed.), *Culture and Foreign Policy*. Boulder, CO: Lynne Rienner.

Baylis, J., and S. Smith (2005). *The Globalization of World Politics: An Introduction to International Relations*, 3rd edn. Oxford: Oxford University Press.

—— et al. (1987). *Contemporary Strategy*, i–ii. New York: Holmes & Meier.

Beam, L. (1992). *Leaderless Resistance*. Available online at http://www.crusader.net/texts/bt/bt04.html.

Beaufre, Andre (1965a). *An Introduction to Strategy*. London: Faber & Faber.

—— (1965b). *Deterrence and Strategy*. London: Faber & Faber.

Bellamy, Alex J., Paul Williams, and Stuart Griffin (2004). *Understanding Peacekeeping*. Cambridge: Polity.

Benjamin, D., and S. Simon (2005). *The Next Attack*. New York: Times Books.

Benedict, Ruth (1946). *The Chrysanthemum and the Sword*. Boston: Houghton Mifflin.

Berdal, M., and M. Serrano (eds.) (2002). *Transnational Organized Crime and International Security*. Boulder, CO: Lynne Rienner.

Bergen, John D. (1986). *Military Communications: A Test for Technology*. Washington, DC: Center of Military History.

Berger, Thomas U. (1998). *Cultures of Antimilitarism: National Security in Germany and Japan*. Baltimore, Md.: Johns Hopkins University Press.

Best, Geoffrey (1982). *War and Society in Revolutionary Europe, 1770–1870*. London: Fontana.

Betts, R. K. (1996). 'Should Strategic Studies Survive?', *World Politics*, 50/1 (Oct.).

—— (1998). 'The New Threat of Mass Destruction', *Foreign Affairs*, 77/1.

Beyerchen, Alan (1996). 'From Radio to Radar: Interwar Military Adaptation to Technological Change in

Germany, the United Kingdom, and the United States', in Williamson Murray and Allan R. Millett (eds.), *Military Innovation in the Interwar Period*. Cambridge: Cambridge University Press.

Biddle, Stephen (2002). *Afghanistan and the Future of Warfare: Implications for Army and Defense Policy*. Carlisle, PA: US Army War College Strategic Studies Institute.

—— (2003*a*). 'Afghanistan and the Future of Warfare', *Foreign Affairs*, 82/2: 31–46.

—— (2003*b*). 'Operation Iraqi Freedom: Outside Perspectives', testimony before the House Armed Services Committee, 21 Oct.

—— (2004). *Military Power: Explaining Victory and Defeat in Modern Battle*. Princeton: Princeton University Press.

—— (2005*a*). *American Grand Strategy After 9/11: An Assessment*. Carlisle, PA: US Army War Studies Strategic Studies Institute.

Black, Jeremy (2001). *War*. London, Continuum.

Blomberg, S., G. Hess, and A. Orphanides (2004). 'The Macroeconomic Consequences of Terrorism', Working Paper No. 1151. CESIFO.

Booth, Ken, and Russell Trood (eds.) (1999). *Strategic Culture in the Asia-Pacific*. New York: Macmillan.

Boulding, K. (1956). *The Image*. Ann Arbor: University of Michigan Press.

Brent, J., and V. P. Naumov (2003). *Stalin's Last Crime: The Plot Against the Jewish Doctors, 1948–1953*. New York: Perennial.

Brodie, B. (1959). *Strategy in the Missile Age*. Princeton: Princeton University Press.

—— (1973). *War and Politics*. London: Cassell; New York: Macmillan.

Brownlie, I. (1963). *International Law and the Use of Force by States*. Oxford: Clarendon Press.

—— (1990). *Principles of Public International Law*. Oxford: Oxford University Press.

Bull, H. (1961). *The Control of the Arms Race*. London: Weidenfeld & Nicolson.

—— (1977). *The Anarchical Society: A Study of Order in World Politics*. London: Macmillan.

Burchill, S., R. Devetak, Andrew Linklater, Matthew Patterson, C. Reus-Smit, and J. True (2005). *Theories of International Relations*, 3rd edn. London: Macmillan.

Butcher, Martin (2003). *What Wrongs Our Arms May Do: The Role of Nuclear Weapons in Counterproliferation*. Washington, DC: Physicians for Social Responsibility; available at http://www.psr.org/documents/psr_doc_0/program_4/PSRwhatwrong03.pdf

Butterfield, H. (1952). *History and Human Relations*. London: Collins.

—— and M. Wight (1966). *Diplomatic Investigations*. London: Allen & Unwin.

Buzan, B., and E. Herring (1998). *The Arms Dynamic in World Politics*. London: Lynne Rienner.

Byers, M. (2000). *The Role of Law in International Politics: Essays in International Relations and International Law*. Oxford: Oxford University Press.

—— (2004). 'Agreeing to Disagree: Security Council Resolution 1441 and International Ambiguity', *Global Governance*, 10/2: 165–86.

Byman, Daniel A., and Matthew C. Waxman (2000). 'Kosovo and the Great Air Power Debate', *International Security*, 24/4 (Spring).

Callwell, C. E. (1899). *Small Wars: Their Principles and Practice*. London: Her Majesty's Stationery Office.

Calvert, John (2004). 'The Mythic Foundations of Radical Islam', *Orbis* (Winter).

Carr, E. H. (1942). *Conditions of Peace*. London: Macmillan & Co.

—— (1946). *The Twenty Years' Crisis 1919–1939*, 2nd edn. London: Macmillan.

Carter, Ashton, and L. Celeste Johnson (2001). 'Beyond the Counterproliferation Initiative', in Henry Sokolski and James Ludes, *Twenty-First Century Weapons Proliferation*. London: Frank Cass.

Cashman, G. (1993). *What Causes War? An Introduction to Conflict*. New York: Lexington Books.

Castells, M. (1998). *The End of Millennium*, iii. *The Information Age, Economy, Society and Culture*. Oxford: Blackwell.

Cebrowski, Arthur, and John Garstka (1998). 'Network-Centric Warfare', *U.S. Naval Institute Proceedings*, 124/1 (Jan.): 29.

Cerny, P. (1986). 'Globalization and the Disarticulation of Political Power: Towards a New Middle Ages', *Civil Wars*, 1/1 (Spring), 65–102.

Churchill, Winston (1926). *The World Crisis, 1911–1914*. New York: Charles Scribner's Sons.

Cha, Victor D. (2000). 'Globalization and the Study of International Security', *Journal of Peace Research*, 37/3: 391–403.

Cimbala, Stephen J. (1997). *The Politics of Warfare: The Great Powers in the Twentieth Century*. University Park, Penn.: Pennsylvania State University Press.

Cirincione, Joseph, Jon B. Wolfsthal, and Miriam Rajkumar (2005). *Deadly Arsenals: Nuclear, Biological and Chemical Threats*, 2nd edn. Washington, DC: Carnegie Endowment for International Peace, 1st edn. 2002.

Clarke, Arthur C. (1970). 'Superiority', in *Expedition to Earth*. New York: Harcourt, Brace & World.

Claude, I. L. (1962) *Power and International Relations*. New York: Random House.

Clausewitz, Carl von (1976). *On War*, tr. and ed. Michael Howard and Peter Paret. Princeton: Princeton University Press.

—— (1982). *On War*, abridged edn. London: Routledge.

—— (1989) *On War*, ed. and tr. Michael Howard and Peter Paret. Princeton: Princeton University Press.

—— (1993). *On War*, ed. and tr. M. Howard and P. Paret. London: Everyman's Library

Cline, L. (2005). *Psuedo Operations and Counterinsurgency: Lessons from Other Countries*. Carlisle, Penn.: Strategic Studies Institute. Available online at http://www.strategic-studiesinstitute.army.mil/pubs/display.cfm?PubID=607.

Clutterbuck, R. (1990). *Terrorism and Guerrilla Warfare: Forecasts and Remedies*. London: Routledge.

Cohen, Eliot (1996). 'A Revolution in Warfare', *Foreign Affairs* (Mar./Apr.), 37–54.

Cohen, Stephen (2002). *India, Emerging Power*. Washington, DC: Brookings Institution Press.

Collins, A. (1998). 'GRIT, Gorbachev and the End of the Cold War', *Review of International Studies*, 24/2 (Apr.).

Congressional Budget Office (2005). *Federal Funding for Homeland Security: An Update;* available at http://www.cbo.gov/ftpdocs/65xx/doc6566/7-20-HomelandSecurity.pdf, accessed 10 Dec. 2005.

Cordesman, Anthony H. (2002). *The Lessons of Afghanistan, Warfighting, Intelligence, Force Transformation, Counterproliferation, and Arms Control*. Washington, DC: Center for Strategic and International Studies, 12 Aug.

—— (2003*a*) *The 'Instant Lessons' of the Iraq War, Main Report, Seventh Working Draft*. Washington, DC: CSIS, 28 Apr.

—— (2003*b*). *The Iraq War: Strategy, Tactics, and Military Lessons*. Washington, DC: Center for Strategic and International Studies.

—— (2004). *The War After the War: Strategic Lesssons of Iraq and Afghanistan*. Washington, DC: Center for Strategic and International Studies.

Cornish, Paul, and Geoffrey Edwards (2001). 'Beyond the EU/NATO Dichotomy: The Beginnings of a European Strategic Culture', *International Affairs*, 77/3: 587.

—— and —— (2005). 'The Strategic Culture of the European Union: A Progress Report', *International Affairs*, 81/4.

Creveld, Martin van (1989). *Technology and War from 2000 B.C. to the Present*. New York: Free Press.

—— (1991). *The Transformation of War*. New York: Free Press.

Croft, S. (1996). *Strategies of Arms Control: A History and Typology*. Manchester: Manchester University Press.

Cronin, Audrey Kurth (2002/3). 'Behind the Curve: Globalization and International Terrorism', *International Security*, 27/3 (Winter), 30–58.

Cruz, Consuelo (2000). 'Identity and Persuasion: How Nations Remember their Pasts and Make their Futures', *World Politics*, 52/3: 278.

Daalder, I., and T. Terry (eds.) (1993). *Rethinking the Unthinkable: New Directions in Nuclear Arms Control*. London: Frank Cass.

Davidson Smith, G. (1990). *Combating Terrorism*. London: Routledge.

Davis, Zachary S. (1994). 'US Counterproliferation Policy: Issues for Congress', *CRS Report for Congress*. Washington, DC: Congressional Research Service.

Dawkins, R. (1976). *The Selfish Gene*. Oxford: Oxford University Press.

Debray, R. (1968). *Revolution in the Revolution? Armed Struggle and Political Struggle in Latin America*. London: Pelican.

Department of Justice (2004). *A Review of the FBI's Handling of Intelligence Information Related to the September 11 Attacks*. Washington, DC: Office of the Inspector General, Nov.; redacted and unclassified: released publicly June 2005.

Department of the Army (1994). *US Army Field Manual 100–23: Peace Operations*. Washington, DC: Department of the Army.

Deptula, David A. (2001). *Effects-Based Operations: Change in the Nature of Warfare*. Arlington, Va.: Aerospace Education Foundation.

Desch, Michael C. (1998). 'Culture Clash: Assessing the Importance of Ideas in Security Studies', *International Security*, 23/1 (Summer).

De Vol, R., and P. Wong (2005). *Economic Impacts of Katrina*. Santa Monica, CA: Milken Institute.

Diehl, Paul F., and Nils Petter Gleditsch (2000). *Environmental Conflict: An Anthology*. Boulder, CO: Westview.

Dixon, C. A., and O. Heilbrunn (1962). *Communist Guerrilla Warfare*. New York: Praeger.

Dobbie, Charles (1994). 'A Concept for Post-Cold War Peacekeeping', *Survival*, 36/3.

Douhet, Giulio (1984). *The Command of the Air*, tr. Dino Ferrari. Washington, DC: New York, Coward-McCann; previously publ. New York, 1942.

Doyle, M. W. (1983). 'Kant, Liberal Legacies and Foreign Affairs', *Philosophy and Public Affairs*, 12.

—— (1986). 'Liberalism and World Politics', *American Political Science Review*, 80.

Dueck, Colin (2004). 'The Grand Strategy of the United States, 2000–2004', *Review of International Studies*, 30/4 (Oct.).

Duffield, John S. (1999). *World Power Forsaken: Political Culture, International Institutions, and German Security Policy after Unification*. Stanford, Calif.: Stanford University Press.

—— (1999). 'Political Culture and State Behavior', *International Organisation*, 53/4: 765–804.

Ebel, Roland H., Raymoind Taras, and James D. Cochran (1991). *Political Culture and Foreign Policy in Latin*

America: Case Studies from the Circum-Caribbean. Albany, NY: State University of New York.

Eckstein, Harry (1998). 'A Culturalist Theory of Political Change', *American Political Science Review*, 82: 790–802.

Eden, Lynn (2004). *Whole World on Fire: Organizations, Knowledge, and Nuclear Weapons Devastation.* Ithaca, NY: Cornell University Press.

Ellis, Jason (2003). 'The Best Defence: Counterproliferation and US National Security', *Washington Quarterly*, 26/2.

Enders, W., and T. Sandler (2004). 'What do we Know about the Substitution Effect in Transnational Terrorism?', in A. Silke and G. Ilardi (eds.), *Terrorism Research*, pp. 119–37. London: Frank Cass.

European Union (2003). *A Secure Europe in a Better World: European Security Strategy,* http://ue.eu.int/uedocs/cmsUpload/78367.pdf.

Fall, B.B. (1998). 'The Theory and Practice of Insurgency and Counter-Insurgency', *Naval War College Review*, 15/1: 46–57.

Farrell, Theo (2001). 'Transnational Norms and Military Development: Constructing Ireland's Professional Army', *European Journal of International Relations*, 7/1: 63–102.

—— and Terry Terrif (eds.) (2001). *The Sources of Military Change: Culture, Politics, Technology.* Boulder, CO: Lynne Rienner.

Feinstein, L., and A.-M. Slaughter (2004) 'A Duty to Prevent', *Foreign Affairs*, 83/1: 136–50.

Feldman, Shai (1982). 'The Bombing of Osiraq: Revisited', *International Security*, 7/2.

Ferris, John (2004a). 'A New American Way of War? C4ISR, Intelligence and IO in Operation Iraqi Freedom, a Preliminary Assessment', *Intelligence and National Security*, 14/1.

—— (2004b). 'Netcentric Warfare and Information Operations: Revolution in the RMA?', *Intelligence and National Security*, 14/3.

Findlay, Trevor (2002). *The Use of Force in UN Peace Operations.* Oxford: Oxford University Press.

Flynn, S. (2004). *America the Vulnerable.* New York: Harper Collins.

Fontenot, Gregory, E. J. Degen, and David Tohn (2004). *On Point: The United States Army in Operation Iraqi Freedom.* Fort Leavenworth, Kan.: US Army Training and Doctrine Command.

Forester, C. S. (1943). *The Ship.* Boston: Little Brown.

Franck, T. M. (1990). *The Power of Legitimacy among Nations.* Oxford: Oxford University Press.

—— (2001) 'Terrorism and the Right to Self-Defense', *American Journal of International Law*, 95/4: 839–43.

—— and N. S. Rodley (1973) 'After Bangladesh: The Law of Humanitarian Intervention by Force', *American Journal of International Law*, 67/2: 275–305.

Freedman, L. (1981). *The Evolution of Nuclear Strategy.* New York: St Martin's Press.

—— (2000). 'Victims and Victors: Reflections on the Kosovo War', *Review of International Studies*, 26/3 (July).

—— (2003). 'Prevention, Not Preemption', *Washington Quarterly*, 26/2.

—— (2004). *Deterrence.* Cambridge: Polity Press.

Friedman, Norman (2000). *Seapower and Space: From the Dawn of the Missile Age to Net-Centric Warfare.* Annapolis, Md.: Naval Institute Press.

—— (2003). *Terrorism, Afghanistan, and America's New Way of War.* Washington, DC: US Naval Institute Press.

Friedman, T. (2002). *Longitudes and Attitudes: Exploring the World After September 11.* New York: Farrar Straus & Giroux.

Freud, S. (1932). 'Why War?', in *The Standard Edition of the Complete Psychological Writings of Sigmund Freud*, xxii. 197–215. London: Hogarth Press.

—— (1968). 'Why War?', in L. Bramson and G. W. Geothals, *War: Studies from Psychology Sociology Anthropology.* New York and London: Basic Books.

Fukuyama, Francis (1999). 'Second Thoughts', *The National Interest*, 56 (Summer), 16–33.

Fuller, J. F. C. (1926). *The Foundations of the Science of War.* London: Hutchinson.

—— (1932). *The Dragon's Teeth; A Study of War and Peace.* London: Constable.

—— (1942). *Machine Warfare; An Enquiry into the Influences of Mechanics on the Art of War.* London: Hutchinson.

—— (1945). *Armament and History; A Study of the Influence of Armament on History from the Dawn of Classical Warfare to the Second World War.* New York: Charles Scribner's Sons.

Gaddis, John Lewis (1986). 'The Long Peace: Elements of Stability in the Postwar International System', *International Security*, 10/4.

Galula, David (1964). *Counter-Insurgency Warfare.* New York: Praeger.

Garnett, J. C. (1975). 'Strategic Studies and its Assumptions', in John Baylis, Ken Booth, John Garnett, and Phil Williams, *Contemporary Strategy: Theories and Policies.* London: Croom Helm.

Gat, A. (1988). *Clausewitz and the Enlightenment: The Origins of Modern Military Thought.* Oxford: Oxford University Press.

—— (1992). *The Development of Military Thought: The Nineteenth Century.* Oxford: Oxford University Press.

Geertz, Clifford (1973). *The Interpretation of Cultures.* New York: Basic Books.

Goldman, Emily O. (2003). 'Introduction: Security in the Information Age', in Goldman (ed.), 'National Security in the Information Age', special issue, *Contemporary Security Policy*, 24/1 (Apr.), 1.

Goldstone, J. (2002). 'Population and Security: How Demographic Change can Lead to Violent Conflict', *Journal of International Affairs*, 56/1: 3–22.

Gordon, M. (1990). 'Generals Favor "No Holds Barred" by U.S. if Iraq Attacks the Saudis', *The New York Times* (25 Aug.).

Gottman, J. (1948). 'Bugeaud, Gallieni, Lyautey: The Development of French Colonial Warfare', in E. M. Earle (ed.), *Makers of Modern Strategy: Military Thought from Machiavelli to Hitler*. Princeton: Princeton University Press.

Government Accountability Office (2003). *Nuclear Security: NNSA Needs to Better Manage its Safeguards and Security Program*, GAO-03–471. Washington, DC: GAO.

—— (2005). *Terrorist Financing: Better Strategic Planning Needed to Coordinate U.S. Efforts to Deliver Counter-Terrorism Financing Training and Technical Assistance Abroad*, GAO-06–19. Washington, DC: GAO, 24 Oct.

Gowans, A. L. (1914). *Selections from Treitschke's Lectures on Politics*. London and Glasgow: Gowans & Gray.

Graeger, Nina, and Halvard Leira (2005). 'Norwegian Strategic Culture after World War II: From a Local to a Global Perspective', *Cooperation and Conflict*, 40/1: 45–66.

Grant, Greg (2005). 'Network Centric: Blind Spot', *Defense News* (12 Sept.), 1.

Gray, C. (2002) 'From Unity to Polarization: International Law and the Use of Force against Iraq', *European Journal of International Law*, 13/1: 1–19.

Gray, C. S. (1981). 'National Style in Strategy: The American Example', *International Security*, 6/2 (Fall), 35–7.

—— (1982). *Strategic Studies: A Critical Assessment*. London: Aldwych Press.

—— (1992). *House of Cards: Why Arms Control Must Fail*. Ithaca, NY: Cornell University Press.

—— (1997). 'The American Revolution in Military Affairs: An Interim Assessment', *The Occasional* (Strategic and Combat Studies Institute, Wiltshire, UK), 28.

—— (1999a). *Modern Strategy*. Oxford: Oxford University Press.

—— (1999b). *The Second Nuclear Age*. Boulder, CO: Lynne Rienner.

—— (2002). *Strategy for Chaos: Revolutions in Military Affairs and the Evidence of History*. London: Frank Cass.

—— (2003). *Strategy for Chaos: Revolutions in Military Affairs and the Evidence of History*. London: Frank Cass.

Gray, John S. (1982). *Strategic Studies: A Critical Assessment*. London: Aldwych Press.

Green, P. (1966). *Deadly Logic*. Columbus, OH: Ohio State University Press.

Griffith, Samuel (1961). *Mao Tse-Tung on Guerrilla Warfare*. New York: Praeger.

Guevara, C. (1997). *Guerrilla Warfare*, 3rd edn. Wilmington, DE: Scholarly Resources.

Gwynn, Charles W. (1934). *Imperial Policing*. London: Macmillan & Co.

Hammes, T. X. (2004). *The Sling and the Stone: On War in the 21st Century* (St Paul, MI: Zenith Press).

Handel, Michael (1994). 'The Evolution of Israeli Strategy: The Psychology of Insecurity and the Quest for Absolute Security', in Williamson Murray, MacGregor Knox, and Alvin Bernstein (eds.), *The Making of Strategy: Rulers, Wars and States*. Cambridge: Cambridge University Press.

—— (1996). *Masters of War: Classical Strategic Thought*. London: Frank Cass.

—— (2001). *Masters of War*, 3rd edn. London: Frank Cass.

Hanson, Victor Davis (2001). *Carnage and Culture: Landmark Battles in the Rise of Western Power*. New York: Doubleday.

Heikka, Henrikki (2005). 'Republican Realism: Finnish Strategic Culture in Historical Perspective', *Cooperation and Conflict*, 40/1: 91–119.

Henkin, L. (1968). *How Nations Behave: Law and Foreign Policy*. New York: Columbia University Press.

Herring, Eric (ed.) (2000). *Preventing the Use of Weapons of Mass Destruction*. London: Frank Cass.

Herzog, A. (1963). *The War–Peace Establishment*. London: Harper & Row.

Hoffer, E. (1952). *The True Believer: Thoughts on the Nature of Mass Movements*. London: Secker & Warburg.

Hoffman, B. (1998). *Inside Terrorism*. New York: Columbia University Press.

Homer-Dixon, Thomas F. (1991). 'On the Threshold: Environmental Changes as Causes of Acute Conflict', *International Security*, 16/2 (Fall), 76–116.

Horowitz, D. L. (1985). *Ethnic Groups in Conflict* (Berkeley, Los Angeles, London: University of California Press).

Howard, Michael (1975). *War in European History*. Oxford: Oxford University Press; pbk edn. 1976.

—— (1991). 'Clausewitz, Man of the Year', *New York Times* (28 Jan.), A17.

Howarth, David. (1974). *Sovereign of the Seas: The Story of British Sea Power*. London: Collins.

Howlett, Darryl, and John Glenn (2005). 'Epilogue: Nordic Strategic Culture', *Cooperation and Conflict*, 40/1.

Hudson, Valerie M. (ed.) (1997). *Culture and Foreign Policy*. Boulder, Colo.: Lynne Rienner.

Hughes, Christopher W. (2004). 'Japan's Re-emergence as a "Normal" Military Power', *Adelphi Paper*, 368.

Hughes, Thomas P. (1998). *Rescuing Prometheus*. New York: Pantheon Books.

Hughes, Wayne (1986). *Fleet Tactics: Theory and Practice*. Annapolis, MD: Naval Institute Press.

Huntington, S. (1993*a*). 'The Clash of Civilizations', *Foreign Affairs*, 72/3.

Huntington, S. (1993*b*). 'Response: If Not Civilizations, What? Paradigms of the Post-Cold War World', *Foreign Affairs*, 72/5.

—— (1996). *The Clash of Civilizations: Remaking of World Order*. New York: Simon & Schuster.

Hurd, I. (1999). 'Legitimacy and Authority in International Politics', *International Organization*, 53/2: 379–408.

Isaacson, W. (1999). 'Madeline's War', *Time* (17 May).

Jackson, R. H. (1993). *Quasi-States: Sovereignty, International Relations and the Third World*. Cambridge: Cambridge University Press.

Jansen, J. (1997). *The Dual Nature of Islamic Fundamentalism*. Ithaca, NY: Cornell University Press.

Jenkins, B. (1987). 'Will Terrorists Go Nuclear?', in W. Laqueur and Y. Alexander (eds.), *The Terrorism Reader: A Historical Anthology*. New York: Meridian.

Jervis, R. (1976). *Perception and Misperception in International Politics*. Princeton: Princeton University Press.

Johnston, Alastair Iain (1995). *Cultural Realism: Strategic Culture and Grand Strategy in Chinese History*. Princeton: Princeton University Press.

Joint Chiefs of Staff (2004). *Joint Doctrine for Combating Weapons of Mass Destruction*. Washington, DC: Dept. of Defense.

Jones, Archer (1987). *The Art of War in the Western World*. Chicago: University of Illinois Press.

Joseph, Robert G., and John F. Reichart (1995). *Deterrence and Defence in a Nuclear, Biological, and Chemical Environment*, Occasional Paper of the Center for Counterproliferation Research. Washington, DC: National Defence University.

Juperman, Alan J. (2000). 'Rwanda in Retrospect', *Foreign Affairs*, 79/1 (Jan/Feb).

Kahn, H. (1960). *On Thermonuclear War*. Princeton: Princeton University Press.

Kaldor, M. (1999). *New and Old Wars: Organized Violence in a Global Era*. Cambridge: Polity Press.

Kaplan, D. E. (2005*a*). 'Hearts, Minds, and Dollars', *US News and World Report* (25 April).

—— (2005*b*). 'The New Business of Terror', *US News and World Report* (5 Dec).

Kaplan, E., *et al.* (2005). 'What Happened to Suicide Bombings in Israel? Insights from a Terror Stock Model', *Studies in Conflict and Terrorism*, 28: 225–35.

Karatzogianni, Athina (2004). 'The Politics of "Cyberconflict"', *Politics: Surveys, Debates and Controversies in Politics*, 24/1 (Feb), 46–55.

Katzenbach, Jr., E. J., and G. Z. Hanrahan (1962). 'The Revolutionary Strategy of Mao Tse-Tung', in F. M. Osanka (ed.), *Modern Guerrilla Warfare: Fighting Communist Guerrilla Movements, 1941–1961*. New York: Free Press.

Keegan, J. (1993). *A History of Warfare*. New York: Knopf.

—— (2004). *The Iraq War*. New York: Knopf.

Kegley, C. W., and E. R. Wittkopf (1997). *World Politics: Trends and Transformation*. New York: St Martins Press.

Keohane, R. O. (1989). *International Institutions and State Power: Essays in International Relations Theory*. San Francisco: Westview Press.

—— (2002). *Power and Governance in a Partially Globalizing World*. New York: Routledge.

—— and S. Nye (1989). *Power and Interdependence*, 3rd edn. New York: Longman; originally Reading, MA: Addison-Wesley.

Kier, Elizabeth. (1995) 'Culture and Military Doctrine: France between the Wars', *International Security*, 19/14: 65–94.

Kissinger, H. A. (1957). *Nuclear Weapons and Foreign Policy*. New York: Harper & Row.

Kievet, James, and Steven Metz (1994). *The Revolution in Military Affairs and Conflict Short of War*. Carlisle, PA: US Army War College Strategic Studies Institute.

Kiras, James D. (2005). 'Terrorism and Globalization', in John Baylis and Steve Smith (eds.), *The Globalization of World Politics: An Introduction to International Relations*, 3rd edn. Oxford: Oxford University Press.

Kitson, Frank (1977). *Bunch of Five*. London: Faber & Faber.

Klare, M. (2001). 'The New Geography of Conflict', *Foreign Affairs*, 80/3: 49–61.

Klein, Yitzak (1991). 'A Theory of Strategic Culture', *Comparative Strategy*, 10/1: 3–23.

Klonis, N. I. (pseud.) (1972). *Guerrilla Warfare*. New York: Robert Speller & Sons.

Kosal, M. (2005). 'Terrorist Incidents Targeting Industrial Chemical Facilities: Strategic Motivations and International Repercussions', Center for International Security and Cooperation, Stanford, Calif., unpublished manuscript.

Krepinevich, Andrew F. (1994). 'Cavalry to Computer: The Pattern of Military Revolution', *The National Interest* (Fall), 30–42.

Kritsiotis, D. (2004). 'Arguments of Mass Confusion', *European Journal of International Law*, 15/2: 233–78.

Kuhn, K. (1987). 'Responsibility for Military Conduct and Respect for International Humanitarian Law', Dissemination, ICRC.

Ladis, Nikolaos (2003). 'Assessing Greek Strategic Thought and Practice: Insights from the Strategic Culture Approach', doctoral dissertation, University of Southampton.

Lantis, Jeffrey S. (2002). *Strategic Dilemmas and the Evolution of German Foreign Policy since Unification*. Westport, Conn.: Praeger.

—— (2005). 'American Strategic Culture and Transatlantic Security Ties', in Kerry Longhurst and Marcin Zaborowski (eds.), *Old Europe, New Europe and the Transatlantic Security Agenda*. London: Routledge.

Laqueur, W. (1996). 'Postmodern Terrorism', *Foreign Affairs*, 75/5: 24–37.

—— (1999). *The New Terrorism: Fanaticism and the Arms of Mass Destruction*. New York: Oxford University Press.

Larsen, Jeffrey (1997). 'NATO Counterproliferation Policy: A Case Study in Alliance Politics', *INSS Occasional Paper 17*. Denver, Colo.: USAF Institute for National Security Studies; available online at www.usafa.af.mil/df/inss/OCP/ocp17.pdf

Lauterpacht, H. (1952). 'The Revision of the Law of War', *British Yearbook of International Law*, 29: 360–82.

Lavoy, Peter, Scott Sagan, and James Wirtz (eds.) (2000). *Planning the Unthinkable: How New Powers Will Use Nuclear, Biological and Chemical Weapons*. Ithaca, NY: Cornell University Press.

Lawrence, T. E. (1920). 'The Evolution of a Revolt', *The Army Quarterly*, 1/1: 55–69.

—— (1935). *Seven Pillars of Wisdom: A Triumph*. London: Jonathan Cape.

Le Bon, G. (1897). *The Crowd: A Study of the Popular Mind*, 2nd edn. London: Fisher Unwin.

Legro, Jeffrey W. (1996). 'Culture and Preferences in the International Co-operation Two-step', *American Political Science Review*, 90/1: 118–137.

Levy, M. (1995). 'Is the Environment a National Security Threat', *International Security*, 20/2: 35–62.

Lia, B., and T. Hegghammer (2004). 'Jihadi Strategic Studies: The Alleged Al Qaida Policy Study Preceding the Madrid Bombings', *Studies in Conflict and Terrorism*, 27: 355–75.

Liddell Hart, B. H. (1967). *Strategy: The Indirect Approach*. London: Faber & Faber.

Lind, Jennifer M. (2004). 'Pacifism or Passing the Buck? Testing Theories of Japan's Security Policy', *International Security*, 29/1 (Summer).

Lindley-French (2002). 'In the Shade of Locarno? Why European Defence is Failing', *International Affairs*, 78/4: 789.

Litwak, Robert (2003). 'The New Calculus of Pre-emption', *Survival*, 44/4.

Lockhart, Charles (1999). 'Cultural Contributions to Explaining Institutional Form, Political Change, and Rational Decisions', *Comparative Political Studies*, 32/7 (Oct), 862–93.

Longhurst, Kerry (2005). *Germany and the Use of Force: The Evolution of German Security Policy 1990–2003*. Manchester: Manchester University Press.

—— and Marcin Zaborowski (eds.) (2005). *Old Europe, New Europe and the Transatlantic Security Agenda*. London: Routledge.

Looney, R. E. (2005). 'The Business of Insurgency: The Expansion of Iraq's Shadow Economy', *The National Interest*, 81 (Fall): 117–21.

Lorenz, K. (1966). *On Aggression*. New York: Harcourt, Brace & World.

—— (1976). *On Aggression*. New York: Bantam.

Lynn, John (2003). *Battle: A History of Combat and Culture*. Boulder, Colo.: Westview.

McCoubrey, H. (1998). *International Humanitarian Law*, 2nd edn. Aldershot: Dartmouth.

McCuen, John (1966). *The Art of Counter-Revolutionary Warfare*. Harrisburg, PA: Stackpole.

McGoldrick, Rowe and Donnelly (eds.) (2004). *The Permanent International Court: Legal and Policy Issues*. Oxford: Hart Publishing.

MacKenzie, Donald (1990). *Inventing Accuracy: An Historical Sociology of Nuclear Missile Guidance*. Cambridge, MA: MIT University Press.

McMillan, Joseph (2005). 'Treating Terrorist Groups as Armed Bands: The Strategic Implications', in Jason S. Purcell and Joshua D. Weintraub (eds.), *Topics in Terrorism: Toward a Transatlantic Consensus on the Nature of the Threat*. Washington, DC: Atlantic Council of the United States, July.

McNeil, William H. (1982). *The Pursuit of Power*. Oxford: Basil Blackwell.

Mahnken, Thomas G. (2001). 'Counterproliferation: A Critical Appraisal', in Henry Sokolski and James M. Ludes (eds.), *Twenty-First Century Weapons Proliferation: Are we Ready?* London: Frank Cass.

Malici, Akan (2006). 'Germans as Venutians: The Culture of German Foreign Policy Behavior', *Foreign Policy Analysis*, 2/1 (Jan.).

Mao Tse-tung (1966). *Selected Military Writings of Mao Tse-Tung*. Peking: Foreign Languages Press.

Marighella, Carlos (1969). *Minimanual of the Urban Guerrilla*: see http://www.baader-meinhof.com/index.htm.

Matthews, K. (1996). *The Gulf Conflict and International Relations*. London: Routledge.

Messenger, Charles (1976). *The Art of Blitzkreig*. London: Ian Allen Ltd.

Meyer, Christoph O. (2004). 'Theorising European Strategic Culture: Between Convergence and the Persistence of National Diversity', Centre for European Policy Studies, Working Document, 204 (June), http://www.ceps.be, accessed 12 Sept. 2004.

Miller, D. (1998). *The Cold War: A Military History*. New York: St Martin's Press.

Minear, L., and T. G. Weiss (1995). *Mercy under Fire: War and the Global Humanitarian Community*. Boulder, Colo.: Westview Press.

Mitra, Subrata Kumar (2002). 'Emerging Major Powers and the International System (An Indian View)', in Alistair Dally and Rosalind Bourke (eds.), *Conflict, the State and Aerospace Power*, pp. 51–80. Canberra: RAAF Aerospace Centre.

Morgan, P. (2003). *Deterrence Now*. Cambridge: Cambridge University Press.

Morris, J. C. (2005). 'Normative Innovation and the Great Powers', in A. Bellamy (ed.), *International Society and its Critics*, pp. 265–82. Oxford: Oxford University Press.

Moskos, Charles C., John Allen Williams, and David R. Segal (eds.) (2000). *The Postmodern Military: Armed Forces after the Cold War*. New York: Oxford University Press.

Müller, Harald, and Mitchell Reiss (1995). 'Counter-proliferation: Putting Old Wine in New Bottles', *Washington Quarterly* (Spring).

—— David Fisher, and Wolfgang Kötter (1994). *Nuclear Non-Proliferation and Global Order*. New York: Oxford University Press.

Munck, R. (2000). 'Deconstructing Terror: Insurgency, Repression and Peace', in R. Munck and P. L. de Silva (eds.), *Postmodern Insurgencies: Political Violence, Identity Formation and Peacemaking in Comparative Perspective*. New York: St Martin's Press.

Murray, Williamson, and Robert Scales (2003). *The Iraq War: A Military History*. Cambridge, MA: Harvard University Press.

—— Macgregor Knox, and Alvin Bernstein (eds.) (1994). *The Making of Strategy: Rulers, States, and War*. Cambridge: Cambridge University Press.

Nadelmann, E. (1993) *Cops across Borders*. State College, PA: Penn State University Press.

Naim, Moises (2005). *Illicit: How Smugglers, Traffickers, and Copycats are Hijacking the Global Economy*. New York: Doubleday.

Nasution, A.H. (1965). *Fundamentals of Guerrilla Warfare*. New York: Praeger

National Intelligence Council (2004). *Mapping the Global Future*. Washington, DC.: Government Printing Office, Dec.

Neibuhr, R. (1932). *Moral Man and Immoral Society: A Study in Ethics and Politics*. New York and London: Charles Scribner's Sons.

Nelson, K. L., and S. C. Olin, Jr. (1979). *Why War: Ideology, Theory, and History*. Berkeley and Los Angeles: University of California Press.

Newmann, Iver B., and Heikka, Hennikki (2005). 'Grand strategy, strategic culture, Practice: The Social Roots of Nordic Defense', *Cooperation and Conflict*, 40: 5–23.

Newman, R. (1961). Review in *Scientific American*, 204/3 (Mar.), 197.

O'Connell, M. E. (2002) 'The Myth of Preemptive Self-Defense', *American Society of International Law*, http://www.asil.org/taskforce/oconnell.pdf.

O'Connell, Robert L. (1989). *Of Arms and Men: A History of War, Weapons and Aggression*. Oxford: Oxford University Press.

O'Hanlon, Michael E. (2000). *Technological Change and the Future of Warfare*. Washington, DC: Brookings Institution Press.

Olson, W. C., D. S. Mclellan, and F. A. Sondermann (1983). *The Theory and Practice of International Relations*, 6th edn. Englewood Cliffs, NJ: Prentice Hall.

O'Neill, Bard (1990). *Insurgency and Terrorism: Inside Modern Revolutionary Warfare*. Washington, DC: Brassey's.

Orme, J. (1997). 'The Utility of Force in a World of Scarcity', *International Security*, 22/3: 136–67.

Osgood, C. E. (1962). *An Alternative to War and Surrender*. Chicago: Chicago University Press.

Osgood, R. E. (1962). *NATO: The Entangling Alliance*. Chicago: University of Chicago Press.

Owens, W. (1995). *High Seas: The Naval Passage to an Uncharted World*. Annapolis, MD: Naval Institute Press.

—— and Edward Offley (2000). *Lifting the Fog of War*. New York: Farrar, Straus, & Giroux.

Paget, Julian (1967). *Counter-Insurgency Fighting*. London: Faber & Faber.

Pape, R. (2005). *Dying to Win: The Strategic Logic of Suicide Terrorism*. New York: Random House.

Paret, P. (ed.) (1986). *Makers of Modern Strategy: From Machiavelli to the Nuclear Age*. Princeton: Princeton University Press.

Paris, Roland (2004). *At Wars End: Building Peace After Civil Conflict*. Cambridge: Cambridge University Press.

Parsons, T. (1951). *The Social System*. London: Routledge and Kegan Paul.

Payne, Keith B. (1996). *Deterrence in the Second Nuclear Age*. Lexington, KY: University Press of Kentucky.

—— (2001). *The Fallacies of Cold War Deterrence and a New Direction*. Lexington, KY: University Press of Kentucky.

Pelfrey, W. (2005). 'The Cycle of Preparedness: Establishing a Framework to Prepare for Terrorist Threats', *Journal of Homeland Security and Emergency Management*, 2/1.

Perkovich, George (2004). 'The Nuclear and Security Balance' in F. R. Frankel and H. Harding (eds.), *The India–China Relationship* (New York: Columbia University Press).

—— Jessica Tuchman Matthews, Joseph Cirincione, Rose Gottemoeller, and Jon B Wolfsthal (2005). *Universal Compliance: A Strategy for Nuclear Security*. Washington, DC: Carnegie Endowment for International Peace.

Peters, R. (1994). 'The New Warrior Class', *Parameters*, 24/2: 16–26.

Petroski, Henry (1982). *To Engineer is Human: The Role of Failure in Successful Design*. New York: Random House.

—— (1992). *The Evolution of Useful Things*. New York: Vintage Books.

Pictet, J. (1985). *Development and Principles of International Humanitarian Law*. The Hague: Martinus Nijhoff.

Pollack, Kenneth M. (2002). *Arabs at War: Military Effectiveness, 1948–1991*. Lincoln, NE: University of Nebraska Press.

Poore, Stuart (2004). 'Strategic Culture', in John Glenn, Darryl Howlett, and Stuart Poore, *Neorealism versus Strategic Culture*. Aldershot: Ashgate.

Porch, Douglas (2000). *Wars of Empire*. London: Cassell.

Preston, Richard A., and Sidney F. Wise, (1970). *Men in Arms: A History of Warfare and its Interrelationship with Western Society*. 2nd edn, New York: Praeger.

Pye, Lucian (1985). *Asian Power and Politics: The Cultural Dimension of Authority*. Cambridge, MA.: Harvard University Press.

Quester, G. (1977). *Offense and Defense in the International System*. New York: John Wiley and Sons.

Quester, G. (1984). 'War and Peace: Necessary and Sufficient Conditions', in R. O. Matthews, A. G. Rubinoff, and J. G. Stein (eds.), *International Conflict and Conflict Management* (Scarborough, Ontario: Prentice-Hall, 1984), pp. 44–54.

Qurashi, A. (2002) 'Al-Qa'ida and the Art of War', *Al-Ansar* www-text in Arabic, FBIS document ID GMP20020220000183[0].

Raine, L. P., and F. J. Cilluffo (eds.) (1994). *Global Organized Crime: The New Empire of Evil*. Washington, DC.: Center for Strategic and International Studies.

Rapoport, A. (1964). *Strategy and Conscience*. New York: Schocken Books.

—— (1965). 'The Sources of Anguish', *Bulletin of Atomic Scientists*, 21/10 (Dec).

Rassmussen, M. (2005). 'What's the use of it?', Danish Strategic Culture and the Utility of Armed Force', *Cooperation and Conflict*, 40: 67–89.

Rattray, Gregory J. (2002). 'The Cyberterrorism Threat', in Russell D. Howard and Reid L. Sawyer (eds.), *Terrorism and Counterterrorism: Understanding the New Security Environment*. Guildford, CT: McGraw-Hill.

Raudzens, George (1990). 'War-Winning Weapons: The Measurement of Technological Determinism in Military History', *Journal of Military History*, 54 (Oct), 403–33.

Rauschning, H. (1939). *Germany's Revolution of Destruction*, tr. E. W. Dickes. London: Heinemann.

Record, Jeffrey (2003). *Bounding the Global War on Terrorism*. Carlisle, PA: Army War College.

—— (2004). *Dark Victory: America's Second War Against Iraq*. Washington, DC: US Naval Institute Press.

Reus-Smit, C. (2004). *The Politics of International Law*. Cambridge: Cambridge University Press.

Rosen, Stephen P. (1995). 'Military Effectiveness: Why Society Matters', *International Security*, 1914: 5–31.

Rosen, Stephen (1996). *Societies and Military Power*. Ithaca: Cornell Studies in Security Affairs.

Rosenau, J. N. (1990). *Turbulence in World Politics*. Princeton: Princeton University Press.

Rousseau, J. J. (1993). 'A Discourse on the Origin of Inequality', in *The Social Contract and Discourses*, ed. G. D. H. Cole. London: J. M. Dent.

Rumsfeld, D. (2003). *Memo on Global War on Terrorism*, available at http://www.usatoday.com/news/washington/executive/rumsfeld-memo.htm, accessed 14 Nov. 2005.

Sagan, S. (2005). 'Learning from Failure or Failure to Learn: Lessons from Past Nuclear Security Events', Paper presented to the IAEA International Conference on Nuclear Security, 16 Mar.

Sageman, M. (2004). *Understanding Terror Networks*. Philadelphia: University of Pennsylvania Press.

Samore, Gary (2003). 'The Korean Nuclear Crisis', *Survival*, 45/1.

Schabas, W. A. (2004). *An Introduction to the International Criminal Court*, 2nd edn. Cambridge: Cambridge University Press.

Schelling, T., and M. Halperin (1985). *Strategy and Arms Control*. Washington, DC: Pergamon-Brassey's.

Schmid, A.P., and A. J. Jongman (1988). *Political Terrorism: A New Guide to Actors, Authors, Concepts, Data Bases, Theories, and Literature*. New Brunswick, NJ: Transaction Books.

Schwartz, Stephen I. (1988). *Atomic Audit: The Costs and Consequences of U.S. Nuclear Weapons since 1940*. Washington, DC: Brookings Institution.

—— (2003). *China's Use of Military Force: Beyond the Great Wall and the Long March*. Cambridge: Cambridge University Press.

Schwartzstein, Stuart J. D. (ed.) (1996). *The Information Revolution and National Security: Dimensions and Directions*. Washington, DC: Center for Strategic and International Studies.

—— (1998). *Cybercrime, Cyberterrorism and Cyberwarfare: Averting an Electronic Waterloo*. Washington, DC: Center for Strategic and International Studies.

Scobell, Andrew (2002). 'China and Strategic Culture', Carlisle, PA: US Army War College, Strategic Studies Institute, May.

Sepp, K., R. Kiper, J. Schroder, and C. Briscoe (2004). *Weapon of Choice: U.S. Army Special Operations in Afghanistan*. Fort Leavenworth, KS: US Army Command and General Staff College Press.

Shaw, R. P., and Y. Wong (1985). *Genetic Seeds of Warfare: Evolution, Nationalism and Patriotism*. London: Unwin Hyman.

Shawcross, William (2000). *Deliver us from Evil: Warlords and Peacekeepers in a World of Endless Conflict*. London: Bloomsbury.

Shay, Jonathan (1994). *Achilles in Vietnam: Combat Trauma and the Undoing of Character*. New York: Simon & Schuster.

Singer, M., and A. Wildavsky (1993). *The Real World Order: Zones of Peace/Zones of Turmoil*. Chatham House NJ: Chatham House Publishers.

382

Sloan, Elinor (2002). *The Revolution in Military Affairs.* Montreal: McGill-Queen's Press.

Smith, H. (2005). *On Clausewitz: A Study of Military and Political Ideas.* New York: Palgrave Macmillan.

Snyder, Jack (1977). *The Soviet Strategic Culture: Implications for Nuclear Options*, R-2154-AF. Santa Monica, Calif.: Rand Corporation.

—— (2002). 'Anarchy and Culture: Insights from the Anthropology of War', *International Organization*, 56/1 (Winter).

Sokolski, Henry (2001). *Best of Intentions: America's Campaign Against Strategic Weapons Proliferation.* London: Praeger.

—— and James Ludes (2001). *Twenty-First Century Weapons Proliferation.* London: Frank Cass.

Spanier, J. W., and J. L. Nogee (1962). *The Politics of Disarmament: A Study of Soviet–American Gamesmanship.* New York: Praeger.

Stedman, Stephen John (1997). 'Spoiler Problems in Peace Processes', *International Security*, 22/2 (Fall).

Stolfi, R. H. S. (1970). 'Equipment for Victory in France in 1940', *History*, 55.

Stone, P. (2003). 'Iraq-al Qaeda Link Weak Say Former Bush Officials', *National Journal* (8 Aug).

Suganami, H. (1996). *On the Causes of War.* Oxford: Clarendon Press.

Sun Tzu (1963). *The Art of War*, tr. Samuel B. Griffith Oxford: Oxford University Press.

—— (1993). *The Art of War*, tr. Roger Ames. New York: Ballentine Books.

Swidler, Ann (1986). 'Culture in Action: Symbols and Strategies', *American Sociological Review*, 51/2 (April 273–286), 73.

Taber, R. (1972). *The War of the Flea: Guerrilla Warfare Theory and Practice.* London: Paladin.

Tannenwald, Nina (1999). 'The Nuclear Taboo: The United States and the Normative Basis of Nuclear Non-Use', *International Organization*, 53/3 (Fall), 83–114.

—— (2005). 'Stigmatizing the Bomb: Origins of the Nuclear Taboo', *International Security*, 29/4 (Spring), 5–49.

Technology Review (2004). ' "We got Nothing until they Slammed into us" ' (Nov), 38.

Terrif, Terry, Aaron Karp, and Regina Karp (eds.) (2006). *The Right War? The Fourth Generation Warfare Debate.* London: Routledge.

Tharoor, Shashi (1995–6). 'Should United Nations Peacekeeping Go "Back to Basics" ', *Survival*, 37/4 (Winter).

Thompson, K. (1960). 'Moral Purpose in Foreign Policy: Realities and Illusions', *Social Research*, 27/3.

Thompson, Michael, Richard Ellis, and Aaron Wildavsky (1990). *Cultural Theory.* Boulder, CO: Westview Press.

Thompson, R. (1966). *Defeating Communist Insurgency: Experiences from Malaya and Vietnam.* London: Chatto & Windus.

Thornton, E. P. (1981). 'A Letter to America', *The Nation*, 232 (24 Jan.).

Toffler, Alvin and Heidi (1993). *War and Antiwar: Survival at the Dawn of the 21st Century.* Boston: Little, Brown & Co.

Transnational Organized Crime (1998). 'Special Issue: The United States International Crime Control Strategy', 4/1.

Trinquier, R. (1964). *Modern Warfare: A French View of Counterinsurgency.* New York: Praeger.

UK Army Field Manual (1995). *Wider Peacekeeping.* London: HMSO.

US Department of Homeland Security (2003). *Characteristics and Common Vulnerabilities Report for Chemical Facilities*, version 1, revision 1. Washington, DC: US Dept. of Homeland Security.

US Joint Forces Command (2001). *A Concept for Rapid Decisive Operations.* Norfolk, VA: Joint Forces Command J9 Joint Futures Lab.

United States White House (2002). *The National Security Strategy of the United States of America*, http://www. white-house.gov/nsc/nss.pdf.

Vickers, Michael (1996). *Warfare in 2020: A Primer.* Washington, DC: Center for Strategic and Budgetary Assessments.

Von Hippel, Karin (2000). *Democracy by Force: US Intervention in the Post-Cold War World.* Cambridge: Cambridge University Press.

Waltz, K. (1959). *Man, the State and War.* New York: Columbia University Press.

Waltzer, Michael (1978). *Just and Unjust Wars.* London: Allen Lane.

Weigley, Russell (1988). 'Political and Strategic Dimensions to Military Effectiveness', in Allan R. Millett and Williamson Murray (eds.), *Military Effectiveness*, iii. *The Second World War.* Boston: Allen & Unwin.

—— (1991). *The Age of Battles: The Quest for Decisive Warfare.* Bloomington, IN: Indiana University Press.

Weiss, Thomas, and Cindy Collins (2000). *Humanitarian Challenges and Intervention: World Politics and the Dilemmas of Help.* Boulder, CO: Westview Press.

Weller, Marc (2000). 'The US, Iraq, and the Use of Force in a Unipolar World', *Survival*, 41/4.

Weltman, John J. (1995). *World Politics and the Evolution of War.* Baltimore and London: John Hopkins University Press.

Wendt, A. (1992). 'Anarchy is what States Make of it: The Social Construction of Power Politics', *International Organization*, 46/2 (Spring), 391–426.

—— (1995). 'Constructing International Politics', *International Security*, 20/1: 73–4.

—— (1999). *Social Theory of International Politics.* Cambridge: Cambridge University Press.

Wheeler, Nicholas J. (1999). 'Humanitarian Intervention in World Politics', in John Baylis and Steve Smith (eds.), *The Globalization of World Politics.* Oxford: Oxford University Press.

—— (2000). *Saving Strangers: Humanitarian Intervention in International Society.* Oxford: Oxford University Press.

—— and Alex Bellamy (2005). 'Humanitarian Intervention and World Politics', in John Baylis and Steve Smith (eds.), *The Globalization of World Politics.* Oxford: Oxford University Press.

White, N. D. (1997). *Keeping the Peace.* Manchester: Manchester University Press.

Wheeler-Bennett, J. (1935). *The Pipe Dream of Peace: The Story of the Collapse of Disarmament.* New York: Morrow.

White House (1993). *Gulf War Air Power Survey.* Washington, DC: Government Printing Office.

—— (2000). *A National Security Strategy for a Global Age.* Washington, DC: White House.

—— (2002) *National Strategy to Combat Weapons of Mass Destruction.* Washington, DC: White House.

—— (2003). *National Strategy for Combating Terrorism.* Washington, DC: Government Printing Office, Feb.

Wilkinson, P. (1986). *Terrorism and the Liberal State.* London: Macmillan.

—— (2001). *Terrorism and Democracy: The Liberal State Response.* London: Frank Cass.

Wilson, E. O. (1978). *On Human Nature.* Cambridge, Mass.: Harvard University Press.

Wilson, H. W. (1928). *The War Guilt.* London: Sampson Low.

Wilson, M. (1978). *On Human Nature.* Cambridge, Mass.: Harvard University Press.

Woodbury, G. L. (2004). 'Recommendations for Homeland Security Organizational Approaches at the State Government Level', Monterey, Naval Postgraduate School, Masters thesis.

Wright, Gordon (1968). *The Ordeal of Total War 1939–1945.* New York: Harper & Row.

Wylie, J. (1989). *Military Strategy: A General Theory of Power Control.* Annapolis, MD: Naval Institute Press.

Index